The Philippines

Priorities and Prospects for Development

A WORLD BANK COUNTRY ECONOMIC REPORT

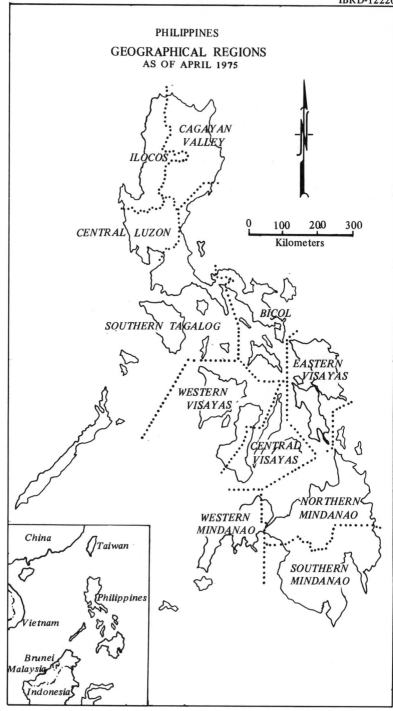

PHILIPPINES

GEOGRAPHICAL REGIONS
AS OF APRIL 1975

IBRD-12220

CAGAYAN
VALLEY

ILOCOS

CENTRAL LUZON

0   100   200   300
Kilometers

BICOL

SOUTHERN TAGALOG

EASTERN
VISAYAS

WESTERN
VISAYAS

CENTRAL
VISAYAS

NORTHERN
MINDANAO

WESTERN
MINDANAO

SOUTHERN
MINDANAO

China

Taiwan

Philippines

Vietnam

Brunei
Malaysia

Indonesia

THE PHILIPPINES

Priorities and Prospects for Development

Report of a mission sent to the Philippines
by the World Bank

Russell J. Cheetham
Chief of Mission

Edward K. Hawkins
Coordinating Author

THE WORLD BANK : *Washington, D.C.*

HC
452
.I58
1976

Manufactured in the United States of America

First Printing, July 1976
Second Printing, March 1977

Library of Congress Cataloging in Publication Data

International Bank for Reconstruction and Development.
  The Philippines: priorities and prospects for development.
  (World Bank country economic report)
  Includes index.
  1. Philippine Islands—Economic conditions—1946–
I. Cheetham, Russell J. II. Hawkins, Edward Kenneth.
III. Title. IV. Series: World Bank country economic reports.
HC452.I58 1976   330.9'599'04   76–17243
ISBN 0–8018–1893–1

Foreword

THIS IS THE THIRTEENTH IN THE CURRENT SERIES OF World Bank country economic reports, all of which are listed on the following page. They are published, in response to a desire expressed by scholars and practitioners in the field of economic and social development, to aid and encourage research and the interchange of knowledge.

Economic reports on borrowing countries are prepared regularly by the Bank in support of its own operations. These surveys provide a basis for discussions with the governments and for decisions on Bank policy and operations. Many of these reports are also used by the governments themselves as an aid to their economic planning and by consortia and consultative groups of governments and institutions providing assistance in development. All Bank country reports are subject to the agreement of—and several have been published by—the governments concerned.

HOLLIS CHENERY
Vice President for Development Policy
The World Bank

Washington, D.C.
June 1976

WORLD BANK COUNTRY ECONOMIC REPORTS

Published for the Bank by The Johns Hopkins University Press

Korea: Problems and Issues in a Rapidly Growing Economy
Kenya: Into the Second Decade
Yugoslavia: Development with Decentralization
Nigeria: Options for Long-Term Development
Economic Growth of Colombia

Published by the World Bank

The Philippines: Priorities and Prospects for Development
Lesotho: A Development Challenge
Turkey: Prospects and Problems of an Expanding Economy
Senegal: Tradition, Diversification, and Economic Development (also published in French)
Chad: Development Potential and Constraints (also published in French as *Le Développement du Tchad: Possibilités et Limites*)
Current Economic Position and Prospects of Peru
Current Economic Position and Prospects of Ecuador
Employment in Trinidad and Tobago

Contents

Maps of the Philippines

List of Tables

Preface

*O*VER THE YEARS THE WORLD BANK HAS PREPARED a series of reports on the Philippines. Most of them are brief documents that provide background for discussions with the government and essential documentation for the executive directors of the bank when they consider loans to the country. This book originated as the first so-called Basic Report on the Philippines. More substantial and more detailed than the earlier World Bank studies on the country, it is now published in the hope that it may prove useful to a wider audience than that for which it was first written.

Although this report was intended to be as comprehensive as possible, it does not deal equally with all aspects of the economy. The objective was to identify areas that are likely to be crucial to the development prospects of the country and in which public policy and action will be particularly important. Attention was therefore given to agriculture, urban and rural development, agrarian reform, industry, and power. With the pervasive influence of population growth on the development prospects of the country, emphasis was also placed on human resources and the potential offered by the dynamic and relatively well-educated population.

The rapid population growth of the 1950s has now been translated into a labor force that will grow by at least 3 percent a year for the next decade. This is a relatively new phenomenon for the Philippines and will call for an increase in the rate of job creation. Because agriculture has a limited capacity to absorb such a growth in the labor force at even moderately higher levels of productivity, the modern nonagricultural sector must play a critical role in the creation of jobs.

In the light of these considerations, the report turns to the financial and resource aspects of the development process and tries to quantify the financial requirements of growth and development. Economic development is inextricably linked to the ability to save, that is, to divert sufficient resources from current consumption to produce an adequate rate of investment. This requires prudent management of domestic resources, as well as special attention to the quality of expenditures, to ensure that both public and private savings are well used. Sound management is also needed in the case of inflows of foreign funds to ensure that the benefits from their use justify the costs of borrowing.

Capital inflows from abroad to supplement domestic savings are projected to be much larger over the next decade than those the Philippine economy has been accustomed to in the recent past, because of an accelerated investment program to help create employment. These inflows must be used wisely to help achieve the structural changes necessary to make the economy relatively less dependent upon such inflows in the future. The report argues that dependence on foreign inflows can be diminished only if sufficient attention is paid to export promotion and prudent management of the balance of payments.

The emphasis on savings, investments, and financial flows is not intended to detract from other aspects of development that have received growing attention in recent years. The mission was able to take note of the valuable work done by the team organized by the International Labour Office (ILO) and now published in *Sharing in Development: A Programme of Employment, Equity and Growth for the Philippines* (Geneva, 1974). Both the ILO and the World Bank reports form part of, and were intended to contribute to, the ongoing discussions of development strategy within the country. There has been a significant shift in government policy toward greater concern for employment creation and income distribution, and both reports agree with the importance of this focus. In other respects the two reports are complementary; the Bank mission did not attempt to cover the historical aspects of development to the same extent as did the ILO, but it placed more emphasis upon the financial implications of the possible pattern of development.

This report is based primarily on the findings of an economic mission that visited the Philippines in April and May 1975. The preliminary findings were further updated after discussions with the Philippine government in December 1975 and January 1976. The present volume, however, does not necessarily reflect the view of the government or any of its officers, and the overall conclusions remain the responsibility of the mission chief and the coordinating author. That is not to ignore the considerable contributions of the individual members of the mission: Vladimir Dragomanovic, industrial economist; Bruce Jones, general economist; Madhusudan S. Joshi, general economist; Carroll Long, editor and urban specialist; Frank Lowenstein, agricultural economist; Peter K. Pollak, commodity specialist; Augustin V. Que, financial economist; Guenter H. Reif, general economist; Ellen Schaengold, research assistant and general economist; and Kevin Young, general economist. Inai Y. Bradfield, Beatriz A. Florendo, and Hajimu Maeda also contributed to the work of the mission. Jane H. Carroll edited the final manuscript; Rachel C. Anderson prepared the index.

RUSSELL J. CHEETHAM and EDWARD K. HAWKINS

Washington, D.C.
June 1976

Acronyms

ADB	Asian Development Bank
AGF	Agricultural Guarantee Fund
AGLF	Agricultural Guarantee and Loan Fund
ALF	Agricultural Loan Fund
ASEAN	Association of South-East Asian Nations
BAECON	Bureau of Agricultural Economics
BBR	Bureau of Barangay Roads
BCS	Bureau of the Census and Statistics
BOI	Board of Investments
COPEs	Coordinating Officers for Program Execution
DBP	Development Bank of the Philippines
DEC	Department of Education and Culture
DLGCD	Department of Local Government and Community Development
DOH	Department of Health
EEC	European Economic Community
EEP	Export Priorities Plan
FACOMAs	Farmers' Cooperative Marketing Associations
FFF	Federation of Free Farmers
FIA	Fertilizer Industry Authority
FIES	*Family Income and Expenditure Surveys*
FNRC	Food and Nutrition Research Center
GATT	General Agreement on Tariffs and Trade
GNP	Gross national product
GSIS	Government Service Insurance System
HYVs	High-yield varieties
IGLF	Industrial Guarantee and Loan Fund
IISI	International Iron and Steel Institute
ILO	International Labour Office
IMF	International Monetary Fund
IPP	Investment Priorities Plan
LWUA	Local Water Utilities Administration
MASICAP	Medium and Small-Scale Industries Coordinated Action Program
MECO	Manila Electric Company

MGC	Manila Gas Corporation
MMA	Manila Metropolitan Area
MWSS	Metropolitan Waterworks and Sewerage System
NCEE	National College Entrance Examination
NCSO	National Census and Statistics Office
NEDA	National Economic and Development Authority
NFAC	National Food and Agriculture Council
NIA	National Irrigation Administration
NIDC	National Investment and Development Corporation
NMYC	National Manpower and Youth Council
NNC	National Nutrition Council
NPC	National Power Corporation
NSCC	National Schistosomiasis Control Commission
OECD	Organisation for Economic Co-operation and Development
OPEC	Organization of Petroleum Exporting Countries
PAASCU	Philippine Accrediting Association of Schools, Colleges, and Universities
PACD	Presidential Arm on Community Development
PCA	Philippine Coconut Authority
PHILEX	Provincial Development Assistance Project
PDAP	Philippine Exchange Company
PHILSUGIN	Philippine Sugar Institute
PMS	Project Monitoring Service
PNB	Philippine National Bank
PNR	Philippine National Railways
POPCOM	Commission on Population
PRODs	Presidential Regional Officers for Development
RDCs	Regional Development Councils
RHUs	Rural Health Units
RMTCs	Regional Manpower Training Centers
SSS	Social Security System
UNCTAD	United Nations Conference on Trade and Development
UNDP	United Nations Development Programme
USAID	United States Agency for International Development
UPPI	University of the Philippines Population Institute
UPSE	University of the Philippines School of Economics
WHO	World Health Organization

The Philippines

Priorities and Prospects for Development

1

The Geographical and Historical Setting

THE PHILIPPINES IS ONE OF THE LARGEST archipelagos in the world with approximately 7,100 islands and a land area of 115,830 square miles (300,000 square kilometers). Surrounded by the South China Sea to the west and north, the Pacific Ocean to the east, and the Celebes Sea to the south, the islands stretch northward to within 65 miles of the island of Taiwan and southward to within 30 miles of Borneo. Only 154 islands have an area of five square miles or more and eleven of the largest islands constitute 95 percent of the total area.[1] The country sits on a series of stress lines along which numerous faulting, folding, and volcanic activities have taken place. As a result of these extensive earth movements mountain ranges divide the islands into small watersheds with short and usually rapid rivers and isolated alluvial plains. About 65 percent of the country is either mountainous or upland.

Climate and Culture

The average annual rainfall is about 120 inches, but it ranges from about 216 inches in Baras, on the island of Catanduanes, to 35 inches in Agunnetan in the Cagayan Valley. Because of typhoons

---

1. The two largest islands are Luzon (40,420 square miles) and Mindanao (36,537 square miles).

Table 1.1. Population, Land Area, and Population Density of Major Geographic Regions

Region	1970 population (millions)	Land area (thousands of square kilometers)	1970 density (persons per square kilometer)
Ilocos	2.99	21.57	138.7
Cagayan Valley	1.69	36.40	46.4
Central Luzon	3.71	18.28	203.1
Southern Tagalog (includes Manila)	8.33	47.51	175.2
Bicol	2.97	17.63	168.2
Western Visayas	3.62	20.22	178.9
Central Visayas	3.03	14.95	202.8
Eastern Visayas	2.38	21.43	111.1
Western Mindanao	1.87	18.69	100.0
Northern Mindanao	3.02	39.84	75.8
Southern Mindanao	3.08	43.47	70.8

Note: The eleven regions listed here are the ones most frequently referred to in these pages, but they have been somewhat modified during the preparation of the report. In 1975 a twelfth region, Southwestern Mindanao, was created out of parts of the other regions of Mindanao, and the Manila Metropolitan Area was made a separate region; in 1976 Western Mindanao was divided into two regions. Before 1972 there were only ten regions in the Philippines: Manila was then separate from Southern Tagalog; the Visayas comprised only two regions, Western and Eastern; and Southern and Western Mindanao constituted one region, Northern and Eastern Mindanao another.

Source: National Economic and Development Authority (NEDA), *Statistical Yearbook, 1975* (Manila: NEDA, 1975).

and local tropical thunderstorms, the rainfall varies regionally from distinct wet and dry seasons to an even monthly distribution. The frequency of typhoons increases generally from south to north; only southern Mindanao is relatively free from their havoc. The predominant north-south alignment of the mountain ranges prevents parts of all the islands from receiving in full force either the northeast or southwest monsoon. One unifying climatic element is temperature, which averages around 26 to 28 degrees centigrade annually and provides the Philippines with a year-round growing season.

Administratively the country was divided into eleven regions in 1975 (see Table 1.1 and frontispiece map).[2] As a result of variations in natural resources and the past concentration of both public and

2. For discussion of the country's administrative structure, see Chapters 4 and 5.

private investment in a few locations, income levels vary considerably among the regions. In 1971 the median income in the city of Manila was three times that in Eastern Visayas, which at the time had four times the population; [3] the income in Central Luzon was twice that in Eastern Visayas and the Cagayan Valley. In 1971 almost 60 percent of the population of Eastern Visayas was in the lowest 40 percent of the national income distribution.

A significant factor in regional development has been the increasing trend toward migration. During the past decade alone perhaps one million people have migrated to greater Manila and about 300,000 to Mindanao, primarily from the Visayas and Bicol. Despite relatively rapid growth in industrial capacity and output, the continued flow of rural migrants into the Manila area has aggravated problems of employment and urban congestion. In Mindanao the movement of large numbers of settlers from the Visayas onto land that was apparently unoccupied but was traditionally Muslim has resulted in competing claims for land and attendant social unrest. Thus solutions to urban poverty and to the peaceful development of Mindanao are heavily dependent on the progress made in dealing with rural poverty, especially in the Visayas and Bicol.

The Philippines has been affected by a unique combination of historical and cultural influences. The original inhabitants of the islands were Negritos who migrated thousands of years ago across land bridges connecting Borneo, Sumatra, and Malaya. The majority of the population, however, is of Malay stock; their ancestors began migrating from the Malay peninsula and the Indonesian islands around 2000 B.C. Although the Philippines has been less influenced by the Islamic and Hindu traditions than much of the rest of Asia, Arab and Indian merchants began trading with the Philippines around the first century B.C., and in the fourteenth century the Arabs brought Islam to the island of Mindanao and the Sulu archipelago. The Chinese, who began trading with the Philippines over a thousand years ago, were another important and early cultural influence.

Superimposed upon this blend of cultures was over four hundred years of Spanish and later American colonial rule, which left the

---

3. In 1971 Eastern Visayas included what is now the separate region of Central Visayas.

strong mark of Christianity on the Philippines. In 1960 over 80 percent of the Filipino people were Roman Catholic, 3 percent Protestant, and about 5 percent Muslim. Another Western legacy was language. In 1960 about 40 percent of the population could speak English, 2 percent Spanish, and about 44 percent Tagalog, a form of Filipino.[4]

Political Trends

Early Spanish exploration in the Philippines began in the mid-sixteenth century followed by gradual expansion of colonial rule. Within forty years Spain controlled almost all the islands with the exception of parts of Mindanao and Sulu.[5] From the outset Spanish rule was highly missionary and committed to the wholesale conversion of the population to Catholicism. The Spanish colonizers were eventually successful in this effort, although Philippine Catholicism was tempered by the underlying traditional religious beliefs. At first Catholic priests acted as the prime administrators in the islands, particularly in the provincial areas outside Manila.[6] During the sixteenth century the papacy transferred the right to administer the church within Spanish colonies to the Spanish crown.

The major political contribution of the Spanish was the integration of the self-contained barangay communities into large muncipalities to facilitate revenue collections, maintain law and order, and focus the local community around the parish church.[7] Because

4. No language in the Philippines is the mother tongue of more than a quarter of the population. Out of about 75 languages in all, 8 are the mother tongues of about 86 percent of the population: Cebuano (24 percent), Tagalog (21 percent), Ilocano (12 percent), Hiligaynon (10 percent), Bicol (8 percent), Samar-Leyte (6 percent), Pampangon (3 percent), and Pangasinan (2 percent). Frederic H. Chaffee and others, *Area Handbook for the Philippines,* DA Pam. no. 550–12 (Washington, D.C.: Government Printing Office, 1969), p. 71.

5. In 1570 the Spanish defeated the sultan of Manila and proceeded to drive the recently arrived Muslims out of the Visayas and Palawan. See *Area Handbook,* p. 52.

6. "The Spanish history of the Philippines begins and ends with the friar." Leon M. Guerrero, *The First Filipino* (Manila: National Historical Commission, 1974), p. xix.

7. *Area Handbook,* p. 27; Onofre D. Corpuz, *The Philippines* (New Jersey: Prentice-Hall, 1965), p. 26. For a discussion of the barangays, see Chapters 4 and 5.

there were few Spaniards in the Philippines, the colonial regime relied upon leading members of the Filipino community (the *principalia*) to assist in governing the country.[8] These local, hereditary aristocrats became "political shock absorbers and cultural middlemen," acting as a kind of bridge between their own people and their colonial rulers.[9] Another important development under the Spanish was the encomienda system, the forerunner of the haciendas which later came to dominate rice and sugar cultivation. The encomienda, originally a tract of land used as the basis for revenue collection, was given to religious orders, charitable groups, and retired government or military officials who had served the crown. Around the late eighteenth century the *encomienderos* became landowners and began leasing the land to Filipino and mestizo families.[10] This system contributed to the unequal distribution of land which has been a problem since that time.[11]

Opposition to Spanish rule broke out sporadically in the eighteenth and nineteenth centuries but did not take on a national character until the latter part of the nineteenth century. At that time a growing number of the more prosperous Filipinos began to educate their sons in Europe, and a small intellectual class developed which held strong ideas about the need for individual rights and freedom. The intellectual leader and one of the great heroes of the Philippine independence movement was Jose Rizal, whose novels of passionate social protest inspired many of the younger intellectuals. Charged with rebellion and sedition in 1896, he was sentenced to death by the Spanish and executed. In 1892 a secret society dedicated to Philippine independence was established, which in 1896 led an armed revolt against the Spanish on the island of Luzon. One of the leaders of the revolt was Emilio Aguinaldo, who went into exile in 1897 but returned the following year after the outbreak of the Spanish-American war. On June 12, 1898, the Filipinos declared their independence and established a provisional republic with Aguinaldo as the first president. With the conclusion of the Spanish-American war, the Philippines along

8. In the first half of the nineteenth century there were only between 2,000 and 5,000 Spaniards in the Philippines. *Encyclopaedia Britannica* (1973), p. 851.

9. Corpuz, *The Philippines*, p. 28.

10. In the Philippines mestizo refers to those of either mixed Spanish-Filipino or Chinese-Filipino parentage.

11. For a discussion of agrarian reform see Appendix A.

with Puerto Rico and Guam were ceded to the United States in the Treaty of Paris (December 1898). The struggle for independence, however, continued until the capture of Aguinaldo in 1901. Under American colonial government the Philippines gradually became self-governing. By 1902 municipal and provincial governments provided limited local autonomy, except in Mindanao, which was under American military authority. In 1916 the United States Congress passed the Jones Act, which declared the intention of recognizing the eventual independence of the Philippines and established an elected Filipino Congress with a Senate and a House of Representatives.[12] In 1935 the Philippines was granted a commonwealth status with independence guaranteed at the end of a ten-year period. One of the first acts undertaken by the newly established commonwealth government was to set up a Philippine army with the assistance of retired U.S. General Douglas MacArthur, whose father had been the last military governor of the Philippines. The Philippines did not become fully independent until 1946 after nearly fifty years of American colonial rule, the devastation of World War II, and Japanese occupation (1942–45).

Although American rule was relatively short compared with that of the Spanish, it had a significant impact on the social, economic, and political life of the country. One of its major contributions was the establishment of an extensive, free, public, and nonsectarian school system, which had far-reaching effects on the values of Filipino society. Although Filipino languages were originally to be used, English eventually became the sole medium of instruction.

On July 4, 1946, the Republic of the Philippines became independent. Its constitution, modeled after that of the United States, provided for presidential government with a strong executive branch balanced by a bicameral congress. Following independence, voter participation in the elections was very high and a two-party system developed with each party frequently holding high elective offices, although elector allegiance often attached more to a particular individual rather than to a political party or an ideology.[13]

During the first three decades as an independent country, the Philippines overcame the challenge of its varied ethnic background and historic traditions to make impressive gains in molding a na-

12. *Area Handbook,* p. 35.
13. Corpuz, *The Philippines,* p. 105.

tional identity. Tagalog has been widely accepted as the national language. Literature, music, and the performing arts in general have flourished as the rich cultural heritage has been reasserted and often blended successfully with Western concepts and artistic values. Educational opportunities have increased greatly and illiteracy has been nearly eliminated. Aided by these factors, progress in scientific areas has earned international recognition. Although significant poverty still exists and income distribution is uneven, the living standard of the population has improved.

In the early years of independence internal stability was challenged by the Huk guerilla movement, mainly in Luzon. Through a combination of military action and social reforms, however, the government was able to subdue the rebellion, which by the mid-1950s had nearly died out. The other major source of dissidence has been the large Muslim minority which has historically resisted integration in the southern islands of the country. An armed revolt broke out in 1973, mainly in response to land pressure as settlers immigrated from other parts of the country. The revolt has hampered development in the affected areas and created a drain on the government's resources, but it has been confined geographically to parts of Mindanao, Palawan, and the Sulu archipelago and involves a relatively small portion of the national population. The government is seeking to deal with the problem through negotiations and by improving economic opportunities, especially for Muslims.

In foreign affairs the country has become an increasingly important member of the international community, active in the United Nations and its affiliated organizations. Manila has been the seat of the Asian Development Bank since its establishment in 1966. Emerging gradually from its traditional ties with the United States, the Philippines has broadened its relations with other major industrialized and developing countries. As a founding member of the Association of South-East Asian Nations (ASEAN), it has more recently put special emphasis on close political and economic ties with other partners in the region. In the last few years the Philippines has also begun to assume a prominent role among the countries of the Third World as one of the leaders of the United Nations Conference on Trade and Development (UNCTAD) Group of 77 and one of the Third World representatives in the Development Committee of the World Bank and International Monetary Fund. While maintaining close economic ties with the United

States and Japan, the Philippines has expanded its relations with socialist countries and in the economic field seeks closer relations with Western Europe.

On September 21, 1972, in response to a sharp increase in domestic unrest, martial law was proclaimed. In accordance with the provisions of the constitution the legislative powers of the Congress were suspended, and in a situation that may be termed "constitutional authoritarianism" the president has assumed legislative power. The government's recent economic, financial, and social reforms are discussed in the following chapters.

2

An Overview of Development Prospects

SINCE INDEPENDENCE IN 1946 THE PHILIPPINES has had an economic growth rate of about 6 percent a year in real terms. After the population growth rate of about 3 percent a year is taken into account, the average annual increase in per capita income has been around 3 percent. In other words, average per capita incomes have increased 1.5 times in thirty years. This would be a satisfactory achievement except that it provided no basis for self-sustained, long-term development; distribution of the benefits of growth has been unequal; and the rate of growth cannot be maintained without changes in the pattern of growth.

Economic Trends Since Independence

In spite of the development of industry, a strong bias toward capital-using industries has generally focused on import-substitution. Because of insufficient industrial exports, the burden of financing the imports of capital goods and raw materials needed by the urban industrial sector has fallen heavily on traditional agricultural exports. But even though agriculture has grown nearly 5 percent since independence, agricultural exports have been unable to earn sufficient foreign exchange to finance the growing import bill. The country has also suffered from poor fiscal administration and a lack of coordination and long-term perspective in financial planning. The pattern of resource allocation and industrialization has not been conducive to providing the broad-based employment opportunities needed in a labor-surplus economy. As a result, the highly skewed pattern of income distribution in the Philippines has changed little if at all.

Toward the end of the 1960s the government became aware of the shortcomings of past development policies, and since the early 1970s it has been introducing economic reforms in an effort to correct the past deficiencies and broaden the base of participation by the population in the development process. More emphasis has been given to agriculture and rural development, to export promotion, to public infrastructure, and to employment creation. There is little question that the Philippines has the physical and human resources required for sustained economic improvement during the next few decades and its more equitable distribution. Moreover, the recent economic and social reforms have contributed to a policy environment more conducive to sustained economic growth. Nevertheless government policies will have to walk a fine line to reconcile the objectives of providing adequate job opportunities and a more equitable distribution of incomes with that of attaining a more viable long-term balance of payments position.

In general the authors of this book agree with the main objectives of the government's development strategy, the principal elements of which are discussed in the following chapters. They concern urbanization, rural development, agricultural production, industry, human resources, the level and allocation of investment, domestic resource mobilization, public finance, and external trade and finance. Although these chapters assess the long-term development prospects of the Philippines, no discussion of strategies and policy reforms can be divorced from the realities of the short-term prospects facing the country. To establish the proper perspective, it is perhaps best to begin by reviewing the events of the recent past and the policy response to those events.

Following a period of acute balance of payments difficulties in 1970–72, the level of economic activity in the Philippines increased sharply in 1973–74. The growth in real gross national product (GNP), which had been about 5 percent a year in 1970–72, doubled to 10 percent in 1973 and then declined to about 6 percent a year in 1974 and 1975. The strong recovery in 1973 was led by the international commodity boom and the resulting increase in export income for the Philippines, by a similar upswing in agricultural and industrial production for the domestic market, and by an expansion in public and private investment. Increased domestic output and a 28 percent improvement in the external terms of trade resulted in a 14 percent increase in gross domestic income in real terms in 1973 compared with an increase of about 2 percent in 1972.

This situation soon reversed itself, however. The abrupt deterioration in the external terms of trade in the second half of 1974 and the recession in the economies of key trading partners posed a different set of issues. In 1975 the balance of payments showed a large external trade deficit. The government responded by trying to maintain the growth momentum that had built up earlier, while reducing domestic inflation. The objective was to prevent as much disruption as possible to the growth in income and employment. The strong balance of payments position that had developed in 1973 was used effectively to ensure the continued flow of imports needed to maintain domestic economic activity. More than a temporary upheaval in the balance of payments, however, the 1973–75 setback brought a distinct change of direction for the economy. The external accounts of the Philippines were roughly in balance in 1970–72, but the sizable current account surplus of 1973 has been followed by large deficits that are expected to continue for some years. In other words, the economy will be relatively more dependent upon foreign inflows in the next decade than it was in the early 1970s.

This dependence, however, can be faced with more confidence than was possible with similar balance of payments deficits in the past. Since the early 1970s the external position has benefited considerably from government policies to improve financial management. The structure of external debt has been transformed by reducing reliance on debt of relatively short-term maturity and carefully controlling new public and private external borrowing. The medium- and long-term debt outstanding has increased by only moderate amounts; at the end of 1974 it was about US$2,000 million compared with US$1,700 million in 1970. The government, supported by members of the Consultative Group,[1] has improved the

---

1. The Consultative Group for the Philippines was formed in 1970. Chaired by the World Bank, it is an informal group that coordinates external aid to the Philippines from major national and international sources. Member countries are: Australia, Belgium, Canada, France, the Federal Republic of Germany, Iran, Italy, Japan, New Zealand, Spain, the United Kingdom, the United

maturity structure of the Philippines debt, bringing the share of long-term maturities from around one-third the public debt at the end of 1969 to over three-fourths by the end of 1974, and from 45 to 60 percent of private debt over the same period.

The burden of medium- and long-term debt has declined dramatically in recent years, in large part because of the very rapid growth of export incomes in 1973 and 1974. The high ratio of debt service payments to export receipts of about 27 percent in 1971 decreased to 15 percent in 1974. Combined with the much improved external reserves, which stood at US$1,200 million at the end of 1974, this decline strengthened the level of the balance of payments and provided a cushion to help absorb the adverse external position that developed in 1975.

In summary, the 1970–75 situation was dominated by fluctuations in the balance of payments which initially benefited economic activity but also generated inflationary pressures. Toward the end of the period a longer term burden emerged in the form of higher prices for imported fuel. Adverse weather conditions affected agriculture and delayed self-sufficiency in rice production, which had seemed in sight in the early 1970s. The authorities took advantage of the boom years to adopt policies that would permit the kinds of structural changes discussed in subsequent chapters.

This analysis of the Philippines' longer term prospects is based on the premise that the country will prepare itself to take full advantage of the opportunities that a worldwide economic recovery will inevitably offer. A policy of accelerated investment should be pursued in the next decade leading to sustained economic growth thereafter.

An Overview of Long-term Prospects

Good short-term economic management is a springboard for a development strategy designed to address the long-term issues. In the Philippines these issues center around the need to maintain the growth rate of the economy in the face of a high population

States, and Yugoslavia. The member institutions include, apart from the World Bank and the International Monetary Fund, the Asian Development Bank, the European Economic Community, the Organisation for Economic Co-operation and Development, and the United Nations Development Programme.

growth rate without endangering the country's internal financial viability or external position. The future depends upon the country's ability to mobilize and deploy domestic resources of all kinds. Although the economy is not and probably should not aim to be self-sufficient, the government has tried to keep down its dependence on outside resources. Nevertheless, given the need for imports of fuel, certain types of capital goods, and food grains, external circumstances must be a major consideration in the formulation of an effective development strategy.

With the expectation of continued current account deficits in the balance of payments, reflecting the foreign inflows required, attention focuses on the projections for external trade. The longer term prospects are therefore best visualized in terms of the country's balance of payments. After a strong balance of payments position in 1973 and 1974, imports of goods and services increased in 1975 by 10 percent while the value of exports fell by 10 percent. The current account deficit therefore increased from 6 percent of imports of goods and services in 1974 to an estimated 21 percent in 1975, largely as a result of the deterioration in the terms of trade, which measure the relation between export and import prices (see Table 2.1).

Projections for the next decade have been made to test the feasibility and consistency of the development policies reviewed in subsequent chapters. The basis for the structural changes that are expected is a substantial increase in investment, both public and private, which would move the economy toward sustained growth of incomes and employment and a more acceptable distribution of wealth. The large investment program needed cannot be financed

Table 2.1. Terms of Trade
(1967–69 = 100)

	Price indexes		Net terms of
Year	*Imports*	*Exports*	*trade*
1960	87	92	105
1970	106	106	101
1973	143	140	98
1974	255	250	98
1975	274	203	74

Source: Central Bank of the Philippines.

out of domestic savings alone; large foreign inflows will be required not only to supplement domestic savings but also to cover the cost of goods and services which cannot be produced in the Philippines.

The expanded investment program will raise investment to 25 percent of GNP by the end of the decade. The program is expected to sustain a growth rate for GDP (gross domestic product) of 7 percent in real terms, provided that imports of goods and services grow at an average annual rate of 13 percent in nominal terms. The balance of payments depends upon the performance of exports, which could grow at an average annual rate of 16 percent in nominal terms. Such export growth is essential to keep the balance of payments deficit manageable in light of the limited availability of external finance. Larger exports are also one direct source of the expected increase in incomes and employment that should emerge from the development strategy.

If these assumptions are realized (and they are considered the most plausible projections for the decade as a whole), the total capital inflows required over the period appear to be reasonable, and the economy's dependence upon such inflows would be much less in 1985 and thereafter than is now the case. The deficit of goods and services (excluding net transfers) in 1975 is estimated at 26 percent of the value of imports and 7.5 percent of GDP. By 1980 these percentages are projected to fall to 18 percent and 5 percent respectively, and by 1985 to 7 percent of imports and 2 percent of GDP.

Any projections depend on the assumptions on which they are built. In the above analysis the projections hinge on the expectation that the volume of Philippine exports can be increased substantially and continuously. Moreover, the external trade projections are particularly sensitive to the future movements of export and import prices. The terms of trade are projected to improve gradually after 1978 and by 1985 to be 19 percent above their 1973 level. The terms of trade are largely outside the control of the authorities, however; if this gradual improvement does not occur, the balance of payments situation is likely to require a reassessment of some policies, particularly those involving ambitious investment expenditures.

It should be possible to finance the required foreign inflow in a way that will not unduly increase the debt service and will still maintain foreign exchange reserves at a level equivalent to only one and a half months of imports. The debt service ratio was 16 percent in 1975; if the above projections materialize, it could rise to 19 percent in 1982 and then fall back to 17 percent by 1985. The assumption here is that the country would be able to finance a significant proportion of its requirements on reasonably favorable terms and would make prudent use of commercial borrowings and short-term debt.

Given the inflexible structure of imports, the buoyancy of exports takes on added importance. Exports accounted for 10 percent of GNP in 1960, 19 percent in 1970, and 22 percent in 1974. The further increases projected are high (an annual growth rate of 16 percent) but should be attainable with structural changes in the economy. Since traditional exports will not earn sufficient foreign exchange to maintain a manageable balance of payments, nontraditional exports, principally manufactures, will have to play a larger part. In earlier years they were insignificant, but since 1970 the total has grown at the rate of 40 percent a year; they now account for 17 percent of total exports by value and by 1985 could account for 33 percent.

The composition of imports into the Philippines is already controlled to conserve foreign exchange and to protect the market for locally produced substitutes. Import substitution has had considerable success in the manufacturing sector that produces consumer goods for the domestic market, but it has not yet made much headway in the intermediate goods and capital goods sectors. The total demand for imports has not been reduced but redirected to new materials, components, and other requirements for the production of formerly imported goods.

Estimates of import requirements must reflect the future evolution of import substitution as the economic structure changes, industrial production expands and becomes more complex, and food production increases to supply a larger proportion of domestic needs. The projections used here (given in Chapter 16) are based on one possible pattern of changing import requirements during the 1975–85 period. The total projected imports of goods and services and the pattern of growth over time would have to be altered if import substitution were to proceed more rapidly than expected.

Assumptions about both imports and exports determine the projections of foreign inflows required to finance balance of payments deficits. Many combinations of assumptions are possible, the most pessimistic being the failure of exports to grow at least as fast as import requirements. Such an outcome would require much larger borrowings, which might not be feasible even at more unfavorable terms at the margin. There would certainly be a consequent rise in the debt service ratio to a range of 25 to 30 percent.

Sound management of external accounts is but one element of a balanced development strategy. Another concern is that the growth of aggregate income and output should be accompanied by an increase in productive employment. New employment opportunities are required, as explained below, for the growing numbers entering the labor force as a result of the high rate of past population growth. Productive employment is also part of the effort to reduce the relative poverty of the 40 percent of the population with the lowest incomes. Improving the lot of the poor will also involve directing more public services to lower income groups in both rural and urban areas. This would be consistent with present plans for a wider regional dispersal of both public and private investments. Such a strategy is possible and is essentially already under way in the Philippines. It has to be translated into sectoral plans and activities, however, and the key elements of such sectoral strategies are outlined below and discussed in detail in later chapters.

The Rapid Growth of Population and the Labor Force

One of the major tasks for the Philippines is to reduce the rate of population growth. For much of the past two decades this rate has been about 3 percent a year, which has created a young age structure with a built-in propensity for future growth. By 1975 about 43 percent of the population was less than 15 years old. Indications are that in recent years fertility has begun to fall, but even the most optimistic projection puts population growth at more than 2 percent a year at least until the 1990s. By the year 2000 the Philippine population could be in the neighborhood of 80 million, approximately double its present size.

The social and economic costs of absorbing these additions to the population are enormous and fall most heavily on the poorest members of society. Some of these costs are borne by the individual household, often by depriving the youngest children in the family of minimal nutritional support and health care. Other costs, such as education, tend to fall as much on society as on the individual.[2]

Rapid population growth also means a rapidly growing labor force, which in turn affects productivity. A major constraint on increasing productivity in the Philippines is the scarcity of capital. At present a large portion of the funds available for fixed capital investment is required merely to hold constant the amount of capital per worker, leaving little for investment to increase the output per worker. The rapid growth of the labor force has also led to high rates of underemployment and downward pressure on wages. In agriculture it has led to the subdivision and fragmentation of land among a growing number of small farmers and possibly an increase in the number of landless laborers.

The need to provide productive employment opportunities for a growing working-age population is so great that it is worthwhile to stress the magnitude of the task. The working-age population (those aged ten years and over) is estimated to have been 29.6 million in 1975. In 1965 it was 21.4 million and in 1955 about 16 million. The average rate of growth over the two decades was therefore slightly more than 3.0 percent, so that the number doubled in 23 years. The labor force participation rate, or the proportion holding or seeking employment, has been falling during this period and is now about 49 percent. This means that the labor force currently numbers about 14.6 million, of whom an estimated 580,000, or 4 percent, were unemployed in 1974. In an economy such as the Philippines where 56 percent are engaged in agriculture and an additional 27 percent in service activities, the distinction between employed and unemployed has to be made with caution. For many, access to productive opportunity is what matters, rather than formal employment for wages. Even those who are employed may not have incomes adequate to raise them above the level of relative poverty.

Nevertheless, employment projections indicate the magnitude of the task of creating productive employment for those entering the labor market. The growth of the labor force, which reflects population growth, is projected in Chapter 10 to fall from a rate of 3.2 percent a year in 1975–80 to 2.8 percent in 1985–90. The result would be an average annual increment to the labor force of 500,000 a

2. Full enrollment of those aged six to fourteen by the year 2000, under a low fertility assumption, would require 47 percent less expenditure on education than if fertility showed no decline.

year for the next decade. If all the annual increment could be accommodated with productive work, the present backlog of the underemployed and unemployed would still remain. To make any inroads on the problem, closer to 600,000 work opportunities will be required each year.

Agricultural Development

To meet the domestic demand for food, agricultural output (excluding fishing) will need to grow at an average annual rate of about 4 percent during the next decade. This growth will have to come primarily from an expansion of acreage or an increase in yields. Although there are still some areas of unused cultivable land in the Philippines, arable and harvested areas combined are unlikely to expand more than 1.5 percent a year over the 1975–85 period. This means that yields will need to grow by about 2.5 percent a year to account for about two-thirds of the increase in production during the coming decade. To achieve significant increases in output from existing cultivated areas, new technologies will be required, irrigation systems will need to be expanded, and supporting services improved.

Investment in irrigation has been expanding rapidly in the last several years and the government's supervised credit programs have been providing production loans to many small farmers. Organization and management, however, remain key constraints, particularly among the extension services, which must reach well over a million farms of less than 4 hectares. Given limited manpower and institutional capability, it may be necessary over the next decade to focus efforts on the more productive small farms, especially those cultivating rice, in order to meet the domestic demand for food. This would mean concentrating the supervised credit programs primarily among small rice farmers in the irrigated areas, which is essentially the tactic the government is following.

The Masagana 99 program for small rice farmers was designed to provide production credit without collateral, to offer improved extension services, and to encourage the use of modern farming practices. Despite the lack of reliable production data and the various difficulties encountered during the first two years, it still appears that this and similar programs will have an important role in the intensification of land use and the provision of much needed production credit to small farmers. Even with this assistance, however, the deficit for cereals will probably be about 10 percent of total net supply in 1980.

Other measures will be needed to spur agricultural production. For at least the next few years emphasis should be placed on up-grading the quality of the existing extension services rather than on expanding them. In addition, prices received by farmers will have to provide sufficient incentives for them to adopt the improved technologies and farming practices that are necessary to raise out-put. The interrelation between product and input prices and the impact of commodity taxation will therefore require closer atten-tion than in the past. The relation between the price of fertilizer and the farm-gate prices for crops—particularly rice and sugar—is likely to be especially relevant for the success of future programs to expand production.

Increased investment in the construction, rehabilitation, and maintenance of irrigation works is also critical to the expansion of agricultural production. The National Irrigation Administration has prepared a very ambitious ten-year program which would irrigate an additional 1.3 million hectares of harvested land by 1985, using large-scale gravity systems on about 700,000 hectares and small-scale pump and communal systems on about 600,000 hectares. In addition, the program calls for the rehabilitation of systems serving some 300,000 hectares, of which about 175,000 are already included in ongoing projects financed by the World Bank and the Asian Development Bank. In view of the present admin-istrative and technical constraints, a more modest but more feasible target for 1985 would be 500,000 hectares of new and rehabilitated large-scale gravity systems and 300,000 hectares of pump and com-munal systems. Under this plan the irrigated harvested area would increase almost 50 percent, and its share of the total harvested area would increase by about 10 to 15 percent by 1985. In the long term this expansion would increase the number of man-days per hectare by 90 percent and would raise production by about 150 percent.

An increase in cereal production is likely to come primarily from concentrating capital investments, purchased inputs, and new tech-nologies on a relatively small percentage of the cultivated area. Such concentration is necessary because of the uneven distribution not only of land and water resources but also of available capital. This focus on areas where increases in marketed output are most readily obtainable is a sound strategy when these increases are needed as quickly as possible.

To balance the support given to the more productive small rice and corn farms, however, programs will also be needed to boost the incomes of families living on farms with less production potential. More widely adaptable varieties of rice and corn need to be developed as well as better marketing arrangements for these farmers. Improved access to social services such as health and education would also raise living standards among families on less productive farms. Exactly how many of these farms are covered by the current land reform is not known, but effective implementation of the program (including the transfer of titles and the leasehold component) would be another way of substantially increasing the earning capacity of tenanted farms. In addition, some of the farms may be able to shift from cultivating rice or corn to raising something of higher value such as sugar or livestock.

The agricultural export sector could be expected to absorb some additions to the labor force, but growth in this sector will be constrained by overseas demand. More favorable opportunities for increasing incomes for many families will probably have to come from nonfarm employment, and the burden of providing this employment will fall on manufacturing and construction as well as the service sector in both rural and urban areas.

Industrialization

The performance of the industrial sector needs major improvement if the Philippines is to be reasonably successful in expanding productive employment and in easing the constraints of foreign exchange. An investment strategy is required that will produce at least 75,000 new jobs a year in industry by the mid-1980s. Also necessary are larger investments to expand the capacity of traditional and nontraditional industrial exports. These are minimum goals, and any shortfall could have dangerous repercussions, such as a rise in open unemployment or more underemployment in both urban and rural areas, with attendant social unrest.

For greater industrial growth the Philippines will need to expand investment in export industries and in a wide range of industries producing intermediate goods with reasonably bright prospects for domestic demand. Processed agricultural products, minerals, and wood products will need larger investments, but these sectors alone will not provide sufficient employment and foreign exchange to meet the objectives. Labor-intensive industrial products for export will also require much more investments. The discussion of how these objectives can be met centers on some of the key industrial sectors: finished consumer goods produced primarily for the domestic market, intermediate and capital goods, and export products.

Industries producing finished consumer goods for the domestic market are in general labor-using, and their accelerated growth would generate employment at a low investment cost. Traditional cottage industries still employ close to one million people, or over two-thirds of the industrial labor force, but their contribution to employment and value added has declined during the past five years. The cost and quality of the goods produced must compete with those of larger scale manufacturers using more efficient production methods. Cottage industries are therefore unlikely to assume a major role in future industrialization but may be expected to maintain their present employment level during the next decade with some help from the government. More favorable prospects for finished consumer goods are found in food processing, wearing apparel, and durable consumer goods industries. A relatively weak domestic demand for these products has so far handicapped their growth. As a result of efforts to improve the living standard in rural areas and in the urban centers other than Manila, however, domestic demand is likely to rise noticeably. The consumer goods sector may thus become increasingly significant in the industrialization effort.

Many intermediate goods industries—basic metals and other metal making, chemicals and chemical products, mineral fuels and lubricants, pulp and paper, cement and other nonoil and non-metallic mineral products—offer room for accelerated growth in the years to come. Relative to the growth of incomes, domestic demand in these areas is likely to rise much faster than in most final demand categories. Until recently relatively generous preferential duties for imports of many of these items and appealing investment opportunities in other highly protected areas have deterred investors from turning to higher manufacturing stages. Current investment plans, however, indicate a significant move toward large import-replacing projects for intermediate and capital goods for the domestic market (steel, fertilizers, other petrochemicals, pulp and paper, and shipbuilding). The high import dependency in many of these industries suggests significant scope for import replacement and foreign exchange savings in the decade ahead. Although these projects do not offer substantial direct employment opportunities, they are nevertheless required at this stage of industrial development in the Philippines to make use of the country's natural resources. To operate efficiently they will need techniques that are necessarily capital intensive, but the further industrialization permitted by the output of these industries is expected to result in many new job opportunities.

Much of the potential for this second stage of import substitution will be realized by the mid-1980s. If this strategy is successful less than 15 percent of aggregate demand for industrial goods (finished and semifinished products) in 1985 will be met from imports, compared with 24 percent in 1974 and 19 percent projected for 1980. Most of these imports will then be goods which cannot be manufactured locally because of the lack of technological capability or the limited size of the domestic market.

In addition to its import-replacing activities the industrial sector will have to embark on an aggressive program to expand export earnings. The Philippines needs to aim for an average increase of about 16 percent a year in the value of exports during the next decade. Since earnings from exports of traditional agricultural products are unlikely to expand at a more rapid rate than in the past, the required growth in foreign exchange receipts will have to come from exports of wood products, minerals, and nontraditional industrial exports. The long-term prospects for substantially larger exports of processed wood and mineral products appear good, and the government is in fact planning for large private investments in these areas. The shorter term, however, is clouded by uncertainty about the pace of recovery from the recession in Japan, the United States, and Europe. (See Table 2.2.)

Commodity export earnings of about US$13,000 million (at current prices and exchange rates) by 1985 would support the required level of imports. If agricultural exports expand by 12 percent a year and exports of processed wood products and mineral products grow at annual rates of 20 and 25 percent respectively, nontraditional industrial exports will also need to grow at an average rate of 27 percent a year (at current prices) if the projected level of ex-

Table 2.2. Past and Projected Export Earnings
(In millions of U.S. dollars at current prices)

Product	Actual			Projected	
	1960	*1970*	*1975*	*1980*	*1985*
Agricultural	384	471	1,363	2,331	4,126
Mineral	61	224	330	1,204	3,035
Nontraditional manufacturing	13	93	392	1,384	4,291
Wood	102	295	226	793	1,423
Total	560	1,083	2,311	5,712	12,875

Source: Central Bank of the Philippines.

port earnings is to be achieved. This rate of growth is less than that experienced by other countries in the region and should be achievable. For most industries which need a large increase in export sales, the main uncertainty about supply is whether entrepreneurs will be willing to undertake and finance the necessary investments. The effective exchange rate apparently continues to favor investments in a broad range of manufactures that serve primarily the domestic market. The relative attractiveness of investments in export industries will have to be increased by changes in the structure of incentives. This will probably entail improving the effective exchange rates for nontraditional industrial exports relative to those for import substitution industries.

Several other constraints hinder the further development of Philippine industry and manufactured exports. First, not enough is known about the factors that currently limit the country's export market. Second, although Filipino entrepreneurs have developed markedly in number, experience, and sophistication, more such skills and experience will be needed rapidly—not only a wider range of technical skills but also international trading skills. Trade institutions and promotional efforts will have to be strengthened and financial constraints overcome if industry is to achieve the large projected expansion of exports, especially nontraditional exports. To a large extent this achievement will of course also depend on whether major industrialized countries abolish or lower their import restrictions on Philippine products.

Expanding Public Services and Infrastructure

Programs to expand production and employment in agriculture and industry will need to be complemented by increased public outlays for infrastructure and manpower training. Considerations of social equity also require expanding access to education and training, and other social services in fields such as health and nutrition need to be more effective, especially among the lower income groups in both urban and rural areas.

Public investment in infrastructure will need to be raised to about US$1,000 million a year by 1980 compared with the present level of about US$400 million (both at 1974 prices). With a GNP growth rate of about 7 percent a year, public investment would need to be raised to at least 5 percent of GNP compared with the present 3 percent. Such an increase would not only provide for future growth but also overcome the existing backlog resulting from years of neglect and low levels of public investment.

Programs to develop power, transportation, and irrigation also require additional public investment in direct support of efforts to expand production. In relative terms the power sector's share of the infrastructure program would probably increase some 10 percentage points, to 35 percent, during the next ten years. This large increase is due to recent policy changes that have given the public sector sole responsibility for new power-generating facilities. Furthermore the government is trying to reduce dependence on imported petroleum by constructing nuclear and geothermal power plants as alternative sources of electrical energy, and there will be a growing demand for power to sustain the rate of industrial growth projected for the 1980s. Because power is thus assigned an increased proportion of the public infrastructure program, the shares of other sectors will decline; transport, for example, will fall from one-half to one-third of the total program. Investment in other sectors will still grow significantly, however, in real terms, and constraints on the absorptive capacity of many of these sectors would make it difficult to achieve a more rapid growth in investment in any case.

The government has also embarked on an ambitious program to remedy deficiencies in the water supply and sewerage in the Manila area and the water supply in a number of provincial cities. The program would increase this sector's share of investment from less than one percent in FY75 to 6 percent in 1980.

The enormous backlog of demand for housing in the urban areas, particularly in Manila, also needs attention. Rough estimates for 1970 show an unmet demand for around 1.1 million dwelling units in the Philippines as a whole, including around 750,000 units in the major urban areas. The large influx into urban areas since then has undoubtedly increased this backlog. Because of the high cost of construction and the shortage of credit available to low-income families, private enterprise cannot be expected to provide adequate housing for the bulk of the population. Nor does the government have the financial and physical capacity to meet the nation's entire housing need. In the past government intervention in housing construction has been inadequate both quantitatively and qualitatively.

A new approach by the public sector is required which will provide realistic housing solutions for low-income families without undue strain on the national budget. This approach should be consistent with government policy on rent control and actions taken to encourage home ownership. Housing designs could take advantage of the ability of low-income families to construct their own housing, and emphasis should be placed on sites-and-services projects and the upgrading of existing dwellings. Minimal building standards should be adopted to give the program the widest possible application.

A program for Metropolitan Manila that would provide sites and services for housing to about 75,000 people and upgraded housing to about 400,000 people annually is estimated to cost about US$350 million over the next ten years and improve the housing conditions of 3.5 million people. If the program were enlarged by about a third and extended to other urban areas, it would equal approximately 0.2 percent of GNP by 1980. This would be substantially larger than the public sector's past provisions for housing but still modest in relation to the private housing market. The key provision of such a program would have to be its self-financing nature. Loans could be extended to the homeowners on terms which would cover the full cost of housing investments. Total housing investment (both public and private) should probably increase from about 2.3 percent of GNP in 1974 to about 2.8 percent in 1980 and 3.0 percent in 1985.

Distributive Impact of the Development Strategy

The growth strategy of the Philippine government for the next decade will focus on: rural development, with emphasis on food production; accelerated industrialization, both in capital-intensive basic industries and in labor-intensive export industries; and substantial expansion of public sector infrastructure investment, particularly in power, to support the growth in the productive sectors. The following summarizes the possible distributive impact of this development strategy.

During the next decade the population and labor force will grow at a rate of 3 percent a year. Unfortunately this growth will occur at a time when agricultural production can no longer be expanded solely by increasing hectarage. As a result, employment in agriculture proper will probably rise at a slightly slower rate than the previous 2 percent a year—maybe around 1.7 percent. It would be accompanied by an annual improvement in agricultural labor productivity of 2.3 percent. Growth in employment (including that in fisheries and forestry) may be around 1.5 percent, with value added per worker rising more sharply in the nonfarming subsectors. (See Table 2.3.)

On the basis of available investment plans, net employment in the manufacturing and construction sectors is estimated to grow at about 5 percent a year during the next ten years, creating almost 160,000 additional jobs a year by 1985. Even though this is the minimum goal that must be achieved, it will be difficult to attain in view of the inadequate growth in manufacturing employment in the last five years. To achieve the estimated labor absorption, value added in manufacturing will have to grow at about 8 percent a year during 1975–80 and at 9 percent thereafter. Equally important will be the successful expansion of the labor-intensive industrial sectors. Here the promotion of the export sector is of crucial importance, because the production of consumer goods for the domestic market is currently limited by the low income levels and the low income elasticity of demand for most of the goods produced. Vigorous efforts will be necessary by both the government and the private sector to increase the exports of manufactured goods.

Labor absorption is such an important target that the government would probably need to rethink its investment program at the margin if industrial production does not provide sufficient jobs. In this case reductions or delays in the large power program or in some of the large capital-intensive industrial investments might have to be considered. At the same time, some of the labor-intensive infrastructure programs such as those for roads, irrigation, and housing would possibly have to be expanded.

Table 2.3. Employment Trends by Sector
(In thousands)

Sector	1960	1965	1970	1975	1980	1985	Annual growth rate		
							1965–75	1975–80	1980–85
Agriculture, forestry, and fisheries	5,777	6,272	6,256	7,661	8,250	8,890	2.0	1.5	1.5
Commerce and services	1,920	2,846	2,813	3,864	5,220	6,170	3.3	6.2	3.4
Construction	254	320	389	428	650	1,050	3.0	8.6	10.0
Manufacturing	1,142	1,205	1,383	1,454	1,690	2,010	1.9	3.0	3.5
Mining	28	22	57	42	50	70	6.7	4.0	7.0
Transport[a] and utilities	320	398	537	534	600	700	3.0	1.7	3.1
Total employed	9,441	11,063	11,437	13,983	16,460	18,890	2.4	3.3	2.8
Total labor force	10,076	11,794	12,378	14,650	17,129	19,802	2.2	3.2	2.9

a. Including communications.
Source: Statistical Appendix and World Bank estimates.

Commerce and other soft services have been the main assimilators of the labor surplus not absorbed by agriculture in the past, but employment in these sectors could rise at only 5 percent a year, compared with over 7 percent during 1970–75, if employment in manufacturing and construction grows at 5 percent a year. This would allow for a growth of labor productivity of about 1.5 percent a year and help reduce underemployment in the service sector.

Projections based on an extrapolation of the growth pattern of the 1975–85 period show that the present development strategy, if vigorously implemented, will considerably improve employment and incomes on a sustained basis in the long run. Under the assumption that the growth of the labor force will decline from 3.0 to 2.8 percent a year beyond 1985 (reflecting the impact of falling fertility), 15 percent of the employed will be working in manufacturing and almost 9 percent in construction by 1995 compared with 10 and 3 percent respectively in 1975. Agricultural employment will have declined from 54 to 40 percent, while employment in commerce and the soft services will rise to around one-third of the total employed by 1980 and stay at roughly this level.

It is difficult to determine precisely the impact that present policies will have on incomes. Past changes in employment and value added suggest that additional measures will be necessary to ensure a more equal distribution of income. Land reform will redistribute assets more equitably, and both rural and urban programs aimed at poverty groups could also make significant contributions to reducing inequalities. A more equal distribution of incomes and assets would increase the size of the domestic market for manufacturers, construction, and services and thus give further impetus to employment creation.

The Role of Government and Administrative Reform

An expansion in the role of the public sector in the Philippines began in the early 1970s with efforts to improve the development orientation of the government. This expansion was a major departure from the policy of the 1950s and 1960s when the private sector had been regarded the principal engine of growth and the public sector had been confined to a limited, largely supporting role. The correction of this imbalance has been gradual and some of the achievements to date may appear modest. Compared with the public sector's poor performance in the past, however, significant progress has been made in virtually all areas of fiscal and financial management. Nevertheless the large public investments proposed for the various economic and social sectors and the substantially higher current outlays needed as public services improve will claim considerably more resources than in the past, place added burdens on administrative capability, and require more government emphasis on training and on administrative and organizational improvements. The increasing importance of the national government will mean that the division of responsibilities among all levels of government will have to be closely reviewed.

Major administrative changes at the national level have already been made under the Integrated Reorganization Plan. Its proposals have been implemented in nearly all government departments except for some units of the Department of Public Works, Transportation, and Communications. The government has now begun to evaluate these administrative reforms and to identify areas for further improvement.

Despite the expanding role of public corporations, the reorganization plan did not deal with that sector nor with its relation to the national government. In the future the Philippine economy will require even more participation by public corporations than in the past, not only by public utilities such as the National Power Corporation, which in the medium term would claim a third of public investment expenditures, but also by public enterprises in such areas as fertilizer production, steel making, and shipbuilding. The effectiveness of the public corporate sector will be critical to the success of the proposed development strategy. Its role must therefore be defined more precisely and action taken to ensure that its implementation capacities are appropriate to its assigned tasks.

Although the reorganization plan advocated decentralization of the national government, it did not deal adequately with the role of local government. In the past the centralized system of government did little to encourage local initiative, and the national government was often insufficiently informed about local needs. In the future the national government should continue to bear the major responsibility for promoting development, but local communities should have a greater role in implementing the programs.

The importance of broadening the base of participation at the local level is recognized by the government, which in the past few years has designed major reforms to expand the role of local authorities in development. Just what this role should be in the immediate future, however, is not yet well defined and is even less clear for the more distant future. The disparate levels of responsibilities among local governments further complicate the situation. Areas in which local authorities might assume responsibility in the near future are: building and maintaining roads, expanding facilities to store and process fish, and participating in national nutrition and health care programs. Care must be taken to ensure that fiscal authority does not devolve more rapidly on local governments than the training of local officials, and conflicts that could arise from overlapping jurisdictions and responsibilities should be minimized.

A series of reforms has recently been introduced in response to the need to upgrade the quality and performance of the civil service. In addition the Development Academy of the Philippines is expanding its activities in training government officials in the Career Executive Service. Important as they are, these reforms in the civil service appear inadequate for the task ahead. Training should be broadened to make a maximum impact on middle-level managers, where the need is greatest, as well as to provide more thorough instruction in the management of development projects. Since the government must be able to compete effectively with the private sector for highly trained manpower, some revisions are also needed in the salary structure and recruiting practices of the civil service.

The priorities for development in the next decade must be translated into sound programs within the various public agencies concerned. This will involve considerably expanding development projects and programs in the pipeline as well as improving the ability to implement them. It is also crucial that the development program be designed within a clear and consistent framework that takes account of the particular circumstances and overall objectives of the Philippines. The government must continue to improve its planning capacity by further strengthening the links between the National Economic and Development Authority (NEDA) and the line agencies and by increasing the capabilities of the various agencies involved. The government has recently prepared a series of plans for the major sectors, an exercise which should be continued in the future, but a longer term perspective of perhaps ten years is needed to integrate the individual sector plans into an overall macroplan.

Tax Reform

Since the late 1960s the Philippine government has initiated policies to raise the level of tax revenues and reform the tax system. Reform began with the introduction of the export stabilization tax in 1970 and an increase in the corporate income tax rates in 1972. More recently a revised tariff and customs code with a simplified and standardized tariff structure, higher rates, and a more rational tariff protection system was enacted. Other measures include the introduction of a permanent system of export duties with differential and generally higher rates, and sharp increases in excise taxes on petroleum products, liquor, and tobacco, as well as in the stamp tax and the sales tax on automobiles. A tax amnesty for previously undisclosed or underreported income and wealth was proclaimed in 1973. Several administrative reforms to improve tax collection and administration as well as to combat corruption were also implemented, resulting in drastic changes in personnel in the entire tax and customs administration. Finally, to strengthen the finances of local governments and reduce their dependence upon the national government, major reforms have increased the efficiency of local revenue collections and improved the system of revenue sharing, both between the national and local levels and among the various local units.

These reform measures and the general increase in economic activity—especially the temporary, dramatic rise in export earnings—boosted tax revenues significantly after 1972. National government tax revenues rose 30 percent in FY73 and 50 percent in FY74, reaching 12.3 percent of GNP compared with 9 to 10 percent a few years earlier. Despite the recession and falling export prices, the tax ratio maintained its same high level in FY75.

Despite the substantial gains in national revenues, tax reforms have not made any significant improvement in the structure of the revenue system, especially in direct taxation. The tax amnesty has not increased the share of direct taxes in total tax revenues apart from possibly one-shot boosts. The complex and time-consuming task of overhauling the corporate and personal income tax system still has to be undertaken. Hence, measures aimed at improving income distribution have so far been limited to increasing excises and import duties on luxury items and taxing windfall gains accruing to the exporters of primary products. Moreover, apart from corporate income taxes virtually the entire increment in tax revenues has come from taxes on international trade. The tax system has thus become highly vulnerable to the fluctuations of the international terms of trade.

The share of revenues in GNP will have to continue to rise if the government is to achieve its development goals. More improvements in tax enforcement and collection under present laws would certainly produce some additional revenue but probably not all the funds required. It is therefore likely that major tax legislation will be needed in the latter half of the 1970s. Moreover, apart from the medium-term need to generate sufficient revenues to finance the budget, the government may in the long term want to correct the inequities of the tax system.

The main thrust of future tax reform should be toward reducing the heavy dependence of revenue on international trade and widening its domestic base, and improving social equity by a sharp rise in direct taxation and by higher indirect taxation of domestic goods and services consumed by the upper income groups. The introduction of a national tax on land and rural property also warrants careful consideration. If reforms were implemented along these lines, it should be possible to raise national government taxes to about 14.5 percent of GNP by FY80 and to 16.5 percent by FY85. If local government tax revenues and social security contributions are added, total taxes could reach 16.6 percent of GNP by FY80 and almost 20 percent by FY85. Such an increase will require determined efforts on the part of the government to formulate concrete legislation and enforce existing tax laws fully. In the short run the government is confronted with recessionary conditions which make immediate increases in the tax rate difficult. But policy decisions will have to be made relatively soon if they are to produce results in the next few years; comprehensive reforms such as those of income taxes usually take a long time to legislate and implement effectively.

Prices and Wages

Historically the Philippines has not had high rates of inflation over long periods of time. Between 1965 and 1970 the average annual increase in the consumer price index was about 2 percent. In the early 1970s, however, this rate accelerated sharply with the index rising 15 percent in 1970 and 22 percent in 1971. The highest increase, 40 percent, was recorded in 1974 following the international rise in oil and commodity prices. The upward trend of consumer prices appears to have leveled off in 1975 to an average of about 8 percent for the year as a whole. Wholesale prices, which reflect international price changes more closely than does the consumer price index, showed similar movements, except that the increase in 1974 (54 percent) was considerably higher. Wholesale prices appear to have almost stabilized in 1975.

Among the various components of the consumer price index, the largest relative increase occurred in 1974 in the category of fuel, light, and water, which rose largely because of the increased price of imported fuel. Prices for food and clothing also showed large increases, however (43 and 44 percent respectively), and domestic production is important for both. The "home goods" component of the wholesale price index rose by 18 percent in 1973 and 52 percent in 1974, demonstrating that domestic inflationary pressures were at work in this period. Again these rapid price increases apparently ended in 1975, when the average increase for home goods during the year as a whole was around 10 percent.

Not only domestic inflationary pressures but also declining terms of trade were at work in 1973–75. The money supply rose by 21 percent in 1973, 25 percent in 1974, and an estimated 4 percent in the first three quarters of 1975 (see Table 2.4). These changes were associated with increases in total domestic credit of 15 percent in 1972, 16 percent in 1973, and 40 percent in 1974. The source of this pressure was external. Although the Philippines suffered marked price increases for key imported goods, the economy also benefited from higher prices for exports. The higher value for exports in turn required an expansion of credit for their financing. The increased domestic incomes raised the liquidity of the banking

Table 2.4. Percentage Change in Prices and Monetary Magnitudes, 1972–75

Item	1972	1973	1974	1975
Total domestic credit	15	16	40	18[a]
Money	26	21	25	4[a]
Net foreign assets	−15	110	49	−48[a]
Consumer price index	8	12	40	8[b]

a. January-September 1975.
b. Preliminary.
Source: Central Bank of the Philippines.

system and thus gave a secondary push to domestic prices.[3] By the end of 1975 the significance of these factors was on the decline and the prospects for a more moderate rate of price increases were good, provided the authorities maintain prudent monetary and fiscal policies and there are no additional large external inflationary shocks.

Throughout the inflationary period of the early 1970s the government intervened to control wages and the price of rice as much as possible. The basic objective of the wage-price policy has been to stimulate employment and investment by, among other things, wage restraints. In recent years, however, inflationary pressures have been such that restraints on money wages would have imposed real hardship on wage earners if the prices of essential consumer goods were determined solely by market forces. Legislation establishing a Price Control Council and authorizing controls on prices of a wide range of goods was passed in 1970 following the floating of the peso. This legislation was renewed in 1971 and extended by presidential decree in 1973.

A resolution of NEDA has restricted the variety of goods subject to price control to "basic commodities that are consumed by low-income groups." At present the commodities under price control are: rice, corn, wheat flour, some basic meat cuts, sugar, condensed milk, cooking oil, ordinary fabrics, some drugs, lumber and plywood, galvanized iron sheets, and infant foods. These price controls on consumption goods have necessitated other controls on some inputs to avoid discouraging the production of fertilizer and animal feed. In principle, the prices set by the Price Control Council reflect the cost of production plus specified markups for the manufacturer, the wholesaler, and the retailer (10 percent, 5 percent, and 10 percent respectively). Price controls generally operate through legal penalties rather than subsidies, although in the cases of rice and fertilizer the government does incur subsidy costs. Price controls, however, have not been able to prevent dramatic increases in the cost of living.

The most recent major piece of wage legislation, enacted in 1970, established a Wage Commission and prescribed minimum wages as follows: ₱8 a day for employees of nonagricultural enterprises

---

3. The increased domestic liquidity was a major factor in the growth of the short-term money market, the rise in deposit substitutes, and the resulting distortions between short- and long-term interest rates.

and the national government; ₱6 a day for employees of small service and retail enterprises; ₱5 a day for local government employees; and ₱4.75 a day for agricultural workers. Members of the Wage Commission represent government, business, and labor (with government predominating) and study wages in various industries and the cost of living in different regions of the country. In industries in which labor and management have failed to reach agreement on wages through collective bargaining and in which the commission finds the national minimum wage insufficient to maintain health and efficiency, it may recommend that the Secretary of Labor order the industry's wages to be higher than the national minimum. To date, wage orders have been issued for four industries with the following minimum daily wages: jeepney transport in Metropolitan Manila, ₱12; copra, ₱9.20; coconut oil products, ₱9.25; and sugar, ₱6.80 for various agricultural tasks and ₱11 for its processing. In 1974 Presidential Decree 525 instituted a cost-of-living allowance of ₱50 a month for national government employees and required medium- and large-scale private firms to give an allowance of ₱30 a month. In December 1975 public sector salaries were raised from 5 to 25 percent and private firms were required to give one month's pay as a bonus each year, effectively raising wages by aboot 8 percent. These measdres, however, have stored only a part of the real income lost to inflation by wage earners since 1969.

The effective minimum legal wage is therefore now about ₱11 a day (or ₱264 a month and ₱3,170 a year) for the industrial worker and the national government employee. A survey made by the Wage Commission estimates that in January 1975 the daily cost of food and other basic requirements in Manila was ₱29.90 a day for a family of five. For the household to meet the Wage Commission's basic requirements it would have to include at least three breadwinners, each of whom received the minimum wage. The fact that only 33 percent of the population are employed suggests that this would be extremely unlikely.

The question of how many workers receive the minimum wage bears on the relevance of the statutory minimum wage for promoting or protecting wage incomes. A lengthy survey by the Wage Commission in 1971–73 of 2,699 firms found that 7 percent of the wage earners were paid less than ₱8 daily; 53 percent received between ₱8.00 and ₱8.99; 17 percent received between ₱9.00 and ₱9.99; and 23 percent received ₱10.00 or more. Similarly, labor force surveys conducted by the Bureau of the Census and Statistics (BCS) found that in 1973 the average weekly earnings of craftsmen, production-process workers, and those in related jobs was ₱48, while the weekly earnings of manual workers and laborers amounted to ₱38. With a work week of five and a half days, these earnings translate into daily wages of ₱8.70 and ₱6.90 respectively. Clearly the majority of Philippine wage earners receive little more than the minimum wage and a considerable proportion earns less.

Future prospects for price stability also depend upon balance of payments developments, fiscal policy, and prudent monetary management. The shifts in the structure of economic activity detailed in the following chapters, particularly the increase in public investment and the rise in government expenditures, could have inflationary consequences. As set forth here, however, they represent a coordinated program that will permit investments to be carried out with adequate financing and without adding to inflation. The balance of payments projections include the external financing requirements. Given a reasonably favorable external environment, it should be possible to hold price changes to within a 7 percent annual increase in 1975–78. Price changes beyond that period are more difficult to project, although price stability will depend very much on the achievement of policy objectives for exports and employment.

A Decade of Change

The focus of this book is on the forthcoming decade, 1975–85, and what might be achieved in that period. Many of the projects and policies now under way will be fully effective only in the early 1980s; others now being considered will not materialize until then. What is proposed would restructure the economy to permit a relatively modest rate of economic growth—about 4 percent per capita GNP growth, which is not much higher than that achieved in the recent past. It is recognized, however, that it will not be possible to maintain this economic growth in the face of the continued high rate of population growth without some changes in the policies followed in the past. The changes proposed would strengthen the ability of the economy to earn foreign exchange and reach toward a more viable balance of payments position while simultaneously providing additional work opportunities for the growing labor force.

These policies have to be such that the dynamics of growth in the private sector—in both industry and agriculture—are not adversely affected. At the same time, the public sector has to be strengthened in order to play a larger and more effective role than in the past. This will necessitate an increase in investment to 25 percent of GNP by 1985 instead of the average 20 percent achieved in 1970–74. There will have to be both a larger public share to reflect the increased investments in infrastructure and a more effective and productive pattern of private investment, particularly in agriculture and manufacturing.

The changes foreseen in the public sector undoubtedly represent the maximum that could be achieved by 1985 and will be difficult to implement. To strengthen and broaden public sector capability will require an increase in public revenues to a permanently higher percentage of the national income. In addition, the tax system will need reforms to make it less dependent upon international economic conditions and to reduce the present inequities of the tax structure. Higher public revenues are necessary for the increased investment in infrastructure to meet both public and private needs and for maintaining the public sector's ability to implement and manage larger programs. In practice, these large investments in human resources and in upgrading public services would be deployed in such a way as to support regional development and the decentralization of economic activity.

Decentralization of economic growth opportunities is closely linked with possible changes in the private sector. Because of the high rate of growth of the population and labor force, agricultural productivity will have to increase during the decade. Agriculture's contribution to food supply, exports, and employment opportunities should draw a significant share of policy attention and public resources to the sector. A good deal can be achieved by continuing the present direction of policy, which lays the basis for new activities in rural development to redistribute wealth through land reform and attack the problems of rural poverty.

Agricultural products, which have in the past been the main source of export earnings, will still account for 32 percent of exports in 1985, but they will no longer provide sufficient earnings to cover the economy's import needs. A fundamental change during the next decade should therefore be the emergence of manufacturing exports as a significant contributor to foreign exchange earnings. Included in this category would be agricultural products in more highly processed forms than were previously exported. Of all the goals outlined here, this expansion of manufacturing exports may be the most difficult to achieve. Nevertheless it is fundamental to the development program in several respects. In the first place it represents the most basic structural change of the economy—industrialization—and it is doubtful if the domestic market alone could carry the process very far. Second, industrialization, if properly pursued in a labor-using rather than a labor-saving form, will be the main vehicle for creating jobs. Third, the type of industrialization followed will have a close bearing on the attainment of other objectives, particularly the expansion of nonfarm employment in rural areas, the decentralization of economic activity, and the attack on rural and urban poverty.

The detailed impact of the development strategy on the Philippine economy over the next decade cannot be projected with any certainty. It is possible, however, to estimate the order of magnitude of certain economic indicators (see Table 2.5). The population will be 30 percent larger in 1985 than in 1975, but the rate of growth will be lower during the decade as the impact of reduced fertility begins to be felt. Employment will be higher by about 35 percent, with job opportunities for new entrants to the labor

Table 2.5. The Philippine Economy, 1975–85

Item	1975	1985
Population (millions)	42.5	55.3
Population growth rate (percent)	2.8	2.4
Employment (millions)	14.0	18.9
Unemployment rate (percent)	4.6	4.6
GDP (millions of U.S. dollars)	15.4	63.1
GDP per capita (U.S. dollars at 1975 prices)	363	550
Exports of goods and nonfactor services (millions of U.S. dollars)	3.1	15.9
Imports of goods and nonfactor services (millions of U.S. dollars)	4.2	16.7
Total government revenues as a percentage of GNP	16.2	21.7
Investment as a percentage of GNP	22.9	25.0
Public investment as a percentage of GNP	3.0	6.0

Source: Statistical Appendix and World Bank estimates.

force but no reduction in the incidence of unemployment. The GDP could increase by a factor of 4 at current prices, although real per capita GDP would rise 1.5 times, from US$363 to US$550, after allowance is made for price changes. If this achievement is accompanied by a more equitable distribution of incomes and wealth, it would be a creditable performance.

The key to these changes lies in an improved balance of payments position and an increase in investment. Exports could increase by a factor of 5, while imports are projected to grow 4 times, a relative decline in inflows from abroad; by 1985 the current account deficit would be less than 2 percent of GDP, compared with 6 percent in 1975. Investment will increase from 23 percent of GNP in 1975 (itself an increase over the recent past) to 25 percent in 1985. Within that proportion, public investment will rise from 3 to almost 6 percent, reflecting the marked increase in total government revenues, which are projected to increase from 16 percent of GNP to almost 22 percent.

These selected indicators outline the possible quantitative impact of the development strategy discussed in the following chapters. The strategy represents a distinct departure from the policies of the 1960s, and its objectives appear modest. Looking back from 1985 observers may not regard it as more than a change in direction. More than that, however, it lays an indispensable foundation for the economic growth that the Philippines can and must achieve in the rest of this century if it is to provide better opportunities for its growing population. The policies discussed here are aimed at improving the welfare of this growing population, which is itself the main obstacle to achieving those policy objectives quickly. The high rate of population growth remains, for the moment, the largest single impediment to raising the standard of living of the average Filipino. Although economic development will bring about the conditions under which human fertility will fall and the rate of population growth decline, the present high rate of growth makes economic development more difficult. Without a firm foundation no building is secure, and the economy of the Philippines cannot be built to serve the interests of the people unless the foundations for future growth are properly laid as outlined in this report.

3

Patterns of Urban Growth

*A*LTHOUGH THE PHILIPPINES IS STILL a predominantly rural economy, in 1974 almost 30 percent of the population lived in chartered cities and other urban areas.[1] This is a higher percentage than in many other southeast Asian countries[2] and represents a steady increase over the 25 percent of the Philippine population in urban areas in 1960 (Table 3.1). The Manila Metropolitan Area (MMA) accounts for over a third of the urban population, but there are a number of rapidly growing secondary cities.

Much of the population growth of these urban centers may be attributed to migration from rural areas to search for more productive employment. Rapid expansion of the service sector, especially the informal subsector, has provided more than three-fourths of the new jobs in the cities, well over half of the total urban employment, and prevented the population growth from being trans-

---

1. The definitions of urban concepts used in this chapter are discussed in the technical note to this chapter.

2. The proportion of the population in urban areas of some other Asian countries in 1970 was: 10 percent in Laos, 15 percent in Thailand, 18 percent in Indonesia, and 28 percent in Malaysia. Figures are based on Population Division, Department of Economics and Social Affairs of the United Nations Secretariat, "Trends and Prospects in Urban and Rural Population, 1950–2000," ESA/P/WP54 (New York, April 25, 1975).

Table 3.1. Urban Population, 1960 and 1970

Area	Population (thousands)		Percent of urban population		Average annual growth rate
	1960	*1970*	*1960*	*1970*	*1960–70*
Manila Metropolitan Area (MMA)[a]					
Manila City	1,139	1,331	13.9	11.0	1.6
Quezon City	398	754	4.9	6.2	6.6
Caloocan	146	274	1.8	2.3	6.5
Pasay	133	206	1.6	1.7	4.5
Other	906	1,839	11.1	15.2	7.3
Total MMA	2,722	4,404	33.3	36.5	5.0
Major chartered cities[b]					
Davao	226	392	2.8	3.2	5.6
Cebu	251	347	3.1	2.9	3.3
Iloilo	151	200	1.8	1.7	3.4
Zamboanga	131	200	1.6	1.7	4.3
Bacolod	119	187	1.5	1.5	4.6
Basilan	156	144	1.9	1.2	−0.8
Angeles	76	135	1.0	1.1	5.9
Butuan	80	131	1.0	1.0	3.3
Cagayan de Oro	69	124	1.0	1.1	6.0
Cadiz	89	124	1.1	1.0	3.4
Batangas	83	109	1.0	1.0	2.8
Olongapo	45	108	1.0	1.0	9.2
San Pablo	71	106	1.0	1.0	4.1
Iligan	58	104	1.0	1.0	6.0
Other urban areas	3,841	5,246	47.0	43.5	3.2
Total urban	8,168	12,071[d]	100.0	100.0	4.0
Adjusted urban[c]	6,861	10,140			4.0
Total Philippines	27,088	36,684			3.0

a. As defined by the Bureau of the Census and Statistics (BCS) in 1970.

b. Chartered cities with populations over 100,000 in 1970, excluding cities in the MMA.

c. For adjustment rationale and methodology, see Table 5.1.

d. Based on the 1960 definition of urban by the BCS. According to the 1970 census definition the urban population was 11,668,000.

Note: Figures may not add up because of rounding.

Sources: BCS, *The Growth of the Urban Population of the Philippines and Its Perspective* (Manila, 1973), p. 23; Mercedes B. Concepcion, "110 Million by the Year 2001," *Philippine Sociological Review,* vol. 18 (July-October 1970), p. 216; and Ernesto M. Pernia, "The Philippine Urban Structure," Research Note no. 25 (Manila: University of the Philippines Population Institute, 1974; processed), table 3.

lated into open unemployment.[3] Despite the fact that average incomes in urban areas—especially in the MMA—are significantly higher than in rural areas, disparities are greater. A substantial proportion of the urban population lives in absolute poverty with inadequate housing and limited or no access to water supplies and sanitation facilities, electricity, and urban transportation.

Size and Distribution of Urban Centers

The urban population of the Philippines increased from approximately 6.9 million in 1960 to about 10.0 million in 1970, at an average annual growth rate of 4.0 percent (Table 3.1). During the same period the overall population of the country increased from 27 to 37 million at an average rate of 3.0 percent a year. This urban growth has not, however, spread evenly across all cities, but appears to have been greatest in a few of the largest urban centers. The MMA, for example, which has 12 percent of the national population, also has one of the highest growth rates of the country.

Natural increase accounts for approximately two-thirds of the growth rates in most urban areas, and rural-urban migration is estimated to account for about one-third. Many of those who migrate are able to earn higher incomes in the urban areas than in their places of origin; few therefore return to their rural homes in spite of the squatter and sum conditions in which many of them live when they arrive in the largest cities.[4] Although the mortality rate is lower in urban than in rural areas, the urban natural rate of increase (2.6 percent in 1970) is less than that in the countryside (3.2 percent) because of the rising age of marriage and the more rapid spread of family planning methods.

The centers of concentration of the urban population are distributed across the major islands (map p. 45). Apart from the MMA

---

3. The service sector includes: commerce; electricity, gas, water, and sanitation; transport, storage, and communications; government, community, business, and recreation; domestic services; and personal services other than domestic. Although the reliability of data for the various subsectors varies widely, this broad definition is normally used in the Philippines for the collection of employment information.

4. K. L. Zachariah, "Migration in the Philippines with Particular Reference to Less Developed Regions," restricted-circulation memorandum of the Development Economics Department, World Bank, July 2, 1975.

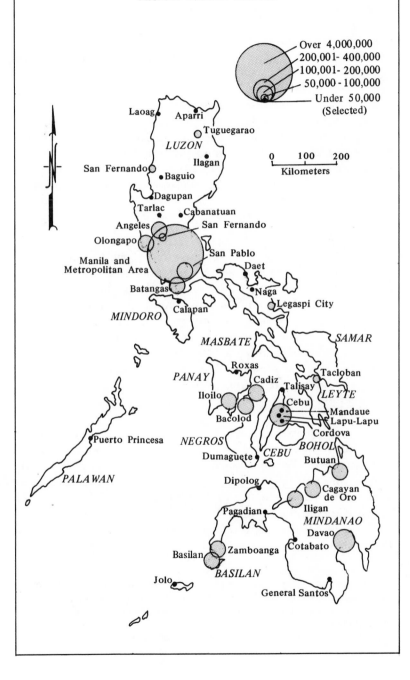

PHILIPPINES
MAJOR URBAN AREAS

Over 4,000,000
200,001- 400,000
100,001- 200,000
50,000 - 100,000
Under 50,000
(Selected)

many of these urban areas with substantial growth rates are on Mindanao where the availability of hydroelectric power, particularly in the Iligan Bay area, has produced significant industrial activity and opportunities for employment. The availability of land on Mindanao has also caused new farmlands to be cultivated and agricultural processing and marketing centers to grow, but agricultural opportunities have recently begun to decline as immigration has placed population pressures on the land.

The location of the urban centers appears to reflect the significant economic and social disparities among the eleven regions. The less developed regions (Ilocos, Cagayan Valley, Bicol, Eastern Visayas, and Central Visayas) are generally less urbanized than the more developed ones, and the rate of urbanization has been slower.

MANILA METROPOLITAN AREA

The MMA dominates the urban sector with 37 percent of the total urban population.[5] It contains over 4.5 million inhabitants and has been growing at a rate of 5 percent a year. The MMA comprises five cities and twenty-three municipalities which form part of four provinces. These jurisdictions, with a total land area of 870 square kilometers, include the core city of Manila, an inner ring of nine urbanized communities, and an outer ring of eighteen communities which have only recently begun to urbanize (map p. 64). The inner ring has grown rapidly and now contains over half the MMA population. In contrast, Manila City has declined steadily as the population center of the MMA and now accounts for only a third.

It is estimated that in the largest urban centers, including the MMA, migration accounted for about half the total population gain in recent years. Because the largest proportion of migrants to the MMA in the past settled in the core city, Manila City became the most densely populated area in the Philippines, with 34,750 persons a square kilometer. Overcrowding is reflected in the average household size of 6.9 persons, the largest among the urban areas of the Philippines.[6]

5. In only nine other developing countries does the principal city hold a larger percentage of the total national population than does Manila, and in only two (Thailand and Peru) is there a greater dominance of the principal city over the next three largest cities within the nation.

6. The number of households in the Philippines increased by 43 percent from

Until very recently no one administrative or political entity had jurisdiction over the entire area generally known as the MMA. This lack of a central authority may be traced to the rapid growth of the area and the resulting blurring of boundaries, as well as to the strong commitment to the autonomy of local government among some of the units. Only in November 1975 were four cities [7] and thirteen municipalities [8] placed under the authority of a governor and a Metropolitan Manila Commission to coordinate the integrated development of the area.

OTHER URBAN AREAS

The structure of and relationships among the urban areas of the Philippines are rapidly changing. The population of cities with 100,000 or more people grew at 4.2 percent a year during the 1960s, compared with 5.0 percent for the MMA and 4.0 percent for all urban centers (Table 3.1). Although the number of cities over 100,000 doubled during the decade, in 1970 they continued to represent about 20 percent of the total urban population. In contrast, urban areas with less than 100,000 grew much more slowly, increasing on average by 3.2 percent a year during the 1960s. While it is possible that there were significant gross population flows to and from these centers, on a net basis migration accounted for only a small proportion of their growth.

A detailed discussion of the growth of small- and medium-size urban centers is hampered by a lack not only of information but also of a clear and consistent definition of an urban place in the Philippines over successive census periods. The current definition includes places with certain urban characteristics even though a large part of the labor force and land may be in agriculture. In addition, some of the places listed in the census as cities have popu-

---

1961 to 1971, whereas in urban areas the number increased by only 26 percent. The average size of urban households grew, however, largely because of migration and the high cost of land and other amenities. In Manila and its surburbs the average household increased from 6.1 members in 1960 to 6.9 members in 1970. In other urban areas household size increased from 4.7 in 1960 to 6.1 in 1970. See Bureau of the Census and Statistics (BCS), *Population Census of the Philippines, 1960* and *1970.*

7. Manila, Quezon, Pasay, and Caloocan.

8. Makati, Mandaluyong, Parañaque, San Juan, Pasig, Navotas, Malabon, Valenzuela, Marikina, Las Piñas, Muntinlupa, Pateros, and Taguig.

lations of less than 5,000, while others with populations in excess of 5,000 are not defined as urban.

Production and Employment in Urban Areas

The functional characteristics of the major urban centers are indicated by the distribution of employment. In 1973 almost 30 percent of employed persons were in urban areas. Since 1965, when relevant data first became available from the Bureau of the Census and Statistics (BCS), urban employment has expanded at approximately the same rate as the labor force (about 3.5 percent a year), with no apparent consistent trend in urban unemployment, which ranged from 8 to 12 percent during 1965–73. This growth in employment went almost wholly into the service sector, which accounted for over 80 percent of new jobs and increased its already large share of employment in urban areas from 60 percent in 1965 to 67 percent in 1973. Industry provided about a quarter of employment in 1973, while the remainder was in agriculture.[9] In the MMA alone, which accounts for approximately one-tenth of the national employment, two-thirds of employment in 1970 was in services and slightly less than one-third in manufacturing and construction (Table 3.2).[10]

A large portion of the growth in service sector employment has apparently been in the informal subsector, which is estimated to account for over 60 percent of total service employment in both urban and rural areas combined. Low-wage employment in informal services provides an important "safety valve," especially for migrants to the rapidly growing cities.

The unemployment rate in Metropolitan Manila has tended to be significantly higher than the national rate.[11] The BCS data on the labor force, employment, and unemployment show that between

9. Because of the way in which the census defines urban areas, much of the "urban" population lives in areas that are predominantly rural in character, and much of the employment is in agriculture. See the technical note to this chapter.

10. There are, however, a large number of people in the informal services sector whose earnings and savings potential is not substantially greater than that of the mass of people in rural areas.

11. Much of the unemployment in the MMA and other urban areas, however, is of a temporary nature; migrants often spend their initial weeks or months in the area searching for employment.

Table 3.2. Resident Employment in Metropolitan Manila by Sector

Sector	Metropolitan Manila		Philippines	
	Number	Percent	Number	Percent
Agriculture[a]	46,515	3.1	6,440,000	51.2
Commerce	207,237	13.8	1,531,000	12.2
Construction	98,665	6.6	467,000	3.7
Manufacturing	332,750	22.1	1,472,000	11.7
Mining and quarrying	5,495	0.4	56,000	0.5
Services	595,554	39.6	1,132,000	9.0
Transport and communications	145,178	9.7	518,000	4.1
Utilities	11,484	0.8	58,000	0.4
Total[b]	1,503,350	100.0	12,584,000	100.0

a. The BCS definition of the MMA reflects a larger share of the population engaged in agricultural activity than indicated elsewhere in this report.
b. Because sectors with relatively little employment are excluded, columns do not add to totals.
Source: BCS, *Population Census of the Philippines, 1970,* and *Survey of Households, 1971.*

1965 and 1971 measured unemployment remained at approximately 6 to 7 percent for the Philippines as a whole and declined within the MMA from 16 to 11 percent. In general the highest unemployment rates were found among males.

Metropolitan Manila has traditionally been dominant not only as the population center of the country but also as a source of growth within the national economy. The MMA's economic dominance is vividly demonstrated by its contribution to gross national product (GNP), which has been increasing and is now over 26 percent.[12] It is significant in nearly all nonagricultural sectors in terms of gross value added: 63 percent in manufacturing, 71 percent in utilities, 64 percent in commerce, 77 percent in transport, 69 percent in communications and storage, and 54 percent in services.[13] The MMA accounts for a very high proportion of sectoral value added in all secondary and tertiary fields, with a relatively low percentage of the national labor force working in these sectors. This indicates

12. National Economic and Development Authority (NEDA), "Regional Accounts" (Manila, 1967; processed).
13. The MMA's contribution was, as would be expected, much less significant in agriculture, fisheries, and forestry (18 percent) and in mining and quarrying (7 percent).

that average labor productivity is substantially greater in the Manila area than in the rest of the Philippines.

Level of Urban Incomes

It is estimated that total family income in the Philippines grew by about 4.7 percent a year in real terms during 1961–71, and that urban incomes probably increased at about 5.5 percent a year during that period. By 1971 the average family income in urban areas was about ₱9,500 (US$1,500), more than twice that in rural areas.[14]

According to the income and expenditures surveys the distribution of incomes in urban areas improved between 1965 and 1971; the Gini coefficient decreased from 0.53 in 1965 to 0.45 in 1971 (Table 3.3). The share of reported income going to the 40 percent of urban families with the lowest incomes increased from 11.3 percent in 1963 to 14.0 percent in 1971. The share of the top 20 percent decreased from 57.2 percent in 1965 to 50.7 percent in 1971. In view of the problems of understatement of income, however, it is not clear that these were in fact actual trends.

A more accurate assessment of household incomes can probably be obtained by analyzing changes in the pattern of family expenditures over the same period. The share of consumption among the lowest 40 percent in urban areas remained approximately the same from 1961 to 1965—around 15 percent—but grew to approximately 17 percent in 1971 (Table 3.3). Among the upper 20 percent consumption declined slightly in the same period, from 48 to 45 percent of the total. Any such improvement in the distribution of wealth probably reflects the greater access to educational opportunities in urban areas and the upward mobility associated with higher educational levels, as well as the expansion of the informal service sub-

14. The main source of information about urban and rural incomes and expenditures are the *Family Income and Expenditure Surveys* conducted by the BCS in 1957, 1961, 1965, and 1971. Their usefulness in studying trends in income and expenditure growth and distribution, however, is limited by the apparently extensive underreporting of income and, to a lesser extent, expenditures and population. It is believed that incomes were underestimated by about 25 percent in 1957, 1961, and 1965, and about 35 percent in 1971; private consumption expenditures were probably underestimated by about 19 percent in 1961 and 17 percent in 1971, but roughly matched the national accounts in 1965.

**Table 3.3. Distribution of Family Income and Household Expenditure
in All Philippines and Urban Areas**
(In percent)

Family income group	1957 Total	1957 Urban	1961 Total	1961 Urban	1965 Total	1965 Urban	1971 Total	1971 Urban
Distribution of total family income								
Lowest 20 percent	4.5	4.5	4.2	3.8	3.5	3.8	3.7	4.6
Second 20 percent	8.1	8.0	7.9	7.5	8.0	8.0	8.2	9.4
Third 20 percent	12.4	12.2	12.1	12.5	12.8	12.0	13.2	13.4
Fourth 20 percent	19.8	20.0	19.3	19.5	20.2	18.7	21.0	21.9
Top 20 percent	55.1	55.3	56.4	57.1	55.4	57.5	53.9	50.7
Top 10 percent	39.4	39.6	41.0	40.9	40.0	41.7	36.9	33.4
Distribution of total household expenditure								
Lowest 20 percent	5.04	n.a.	5.98	5.09	5.65	5.24	5.92	6.20
Second 20 percent	9.03	n.a.	10.32	9.78	10.25	9.67	10.18	10.52
Third 20 percent	13.02	n.a.	14.68	14.56	14.57	14.41	14.76	15.68
Fourth 20 percent	20.03	n.a.	21.03	22.36	21.10	21.37	21.98	24.59
Top 20 percent	52.88	n.a.	47.98	48.22	48.43	49.31	47.16	45.23
Top 10 percent	35.42	n.a.	31.66	31.09	32.49	32.73	30.81	26.79
Top 5 percent	23.38	n.a.	21.00	18.73	21.43	18.80	19.37	16.50
Gini coefficient	0.48	0.49	0.50	0.52	0.51	0.53	0.49	0.45

n.a.: Not available.
Source: BCS, *Family Income and Expenditure Survey* for 1957, 1961, 1965, and 1971.

sector, which provides income-earning opportunities for those with
even relatively little education.

There is considerable evidence that urban incomes are substantially higher than rural incomes and that significant disparities exist
both among and within cities. After the average minimum income
of ₱650 per capita [15] was adjusted for higher living costs of urban
areas, 30 percent of the urban population was found to be below
the minimum income level in 1971 (Table 3.4). Urban poverty,
however defined, appears to be concentrated in Metropolitan Manila
and in the key urban centers of the Visayas which have absorbed
some of the spillover of the rural poor. Although the incidence of
urban poverty is higher in the Visayas than in Metropolitan Manila,
the absolute number of poor is significantly less in the Visayas.

Living conditions of the urban poor are best illustrated by refer-

15. See Chapter 11.

Table 3.4. Urban Poverty, 1971

Category	Metropolitan Manila	Other urban areas	All urban areas
Threshold income per capita[a]	₱ 870	₱ 700	n.a.
Population (in thousands)[b]	4,648	7,907	12,555
Population below threshold income (in thousands)	1,525	2,230	3,755
Percentage of population below threshold income	32.8	28.2	30.0

n.a. Not available.
a. Pesos per capita in 1971 prices.
b. Unadjusted urban population; see Table 3.1.
Note: In Chapter 11, ₱650 per capita is given as the average threshold income for the Philippines, that is, the minimum amount needed to provide an adequate diet and other essential needs. This income level, however, is not an adequate measure of minimum needs in urban areas, where living costs are significantly higher. Different threshold incomes were therefore estimated for Metropolitan Manila and other urban areas. This was done by using the Philippine-wide estimate of ₱650 as a base and applying to it the cost of living factors for Manila and other urban areas implicitly derived by Lucinda Abrera, "Philippine Poverty Thresholds," in Development Academy of the Philippines, *Measuring Philippine Welfare: Social Indicators Project* (Manila, 1975), ch. 5.
Source: BCS, *Family Income and Expenditure Survey, 1971,* and World Bank estimates.

ence to those in the Metropolitan Manila area. Low-income households in the MMA have tended to concentrate in Manila City, where 45 percent of the total slum and squatter population reside. Six municipalities in the inner ring also have heavy concentrations of the poor, while the outer ring has a relatively low percentage who are poor. Available data suggest marked similarities in the characteristics of the poor within Metropolitan Manila, regardless of their location.

Poor families are distinguished from the rest of the metropolitan population by a lack of regular employment, poor housing, and a relatively low level of publicly provided services. There is a greater concentration of employment in marginal sectors (for example, informal services), more sporadic employment, and a higher percentage of unemployed. According to a 1968 survey of a slum settlement in Tondo, the common complaints of the respondents were the lack of water, roads, and toilets.[16] The level of education

16. Aprodicio L. Laquian, "Slums and Squatters in Six Philippine Cities," final report on a research grant from the Southeast Asia Development Advisory

among poor families in Metropolitan Manila is surprisingly high, however. Between 5 and 15 percent have some postsecondary-school training, although the average level is lower than that of the overall metropolitan area.

In general, despite the economic and social disadvantages, squatters and slum dwellers consider their present lives better than their former situations. Those making such a positive assessment include 86 percent of respondents in a survey in Baguio, 90 percent in Cebu, 82 percent in Davao, 81 percent in Iligan, and 68 percent in Iloilo. The smallest proportion of positive responses (51 percent) is found in Manila.[17]

Patterns of Urban Expenditures

Future patterns of both urban and rural production and employment will be increasingly influenced by the consumption preferences of urban households. Urban areas account for about 30 percent of the total population and approximately 40 percent of total private expenditures in the Philippines and are expected to account for an increasingly larger proportion of both.

Food accounts for nearly half the household budget of all income groups in urban areas (Table 3.5). There is a high level of malnutrition, however, and a correlation between income level and nutritional status. Large, low-income families receive fewer calories per capita and less adequate nutrition than higher income groups, although the same percentage of the household budget is spent on food. Housing expenditures represent 12 to 13 percent of total family expenditures and have fluctuated around that level since 1961. Expenditures for most other items have remained nearly the same percentage of the household budget for the same period.

Expenditure elasticities appear to be highest for consumer durables, housing, medical care, education, and transport, all of which are greater than unity. Estimates suggest that elasticities for expenditures on services within urban areas are less at higher levels of income, following the same pattern as in rural areas.

Group (SEADAG) of the Asia Society (New York: SEADAG, March 23, 1972; processed), p. 70, and Zachariah, "Migration in the Philippines," p. 34.

17. Laquian, "Slums and Squatters," p. 70.

Table 3.5. Distribution of Expenditures and Expenditure Elasticities for Urban Families

Expenditure	Percentage distribution of family expenditures[a]			Expenditure elasticities		
	1961	1965	1971	I[b]	II[c]	III[d]
Food	50.3	48.2	48.9	0.95	0.80	0.77
Alcohol and tobacco	5.7	4.6	4.7	0.62	0.63	1.08
Clothing	6.4	6.0	6.3	0.97	1.02	1.63
Consumer durables	2.1	2.0	2.6	1.39	1.19	} 1.63
Housing	10.9	13.7	12.5	1.26	1.27	
Utilities	3.9	3.6	3.6	0.84	0.84	
Medical care	1.9	1.7	2.0	1.10	1.02	2.20
Education	4.0	4.4	4.4	1.18	1.20	} 2.77
Transport	2.9	3.6	4.0	1.59	1.42	
Other services	10.2	10.1	9.8	0.92	1.32	} 1.90
Taxes and gifts	1.7	2.1	1.2	0.32	n.a.	
Total	100.0	100.0	100.0			

a. Data from BCS, *Family Income and Expenditure Survey* for the relevant years.

b. World Bank calculation of aggregate expenditure elasticity using ratio of percentage change during 1961–71 of specific items to that of total expenditure, at 1965 constant prices, after first adjusting the expenditure survey data to correct for underestimation of population and expenditures.

c. Unpublished per capita expenditure elasticities estimated by A. Kelly, Duke University, and J. Williamson, University of Wisconsin, from BCS, *Family Income and Expenditure Survey, 1965.* Elasticities are derived from a log-linear expenditure function for each commodity group.

d. Data from Edita A. Tan and Gwendolyn R. Tecson, "Patterns of Consumption in the Philippines," Institute of Economic Development and Research, University of the Philippines, Discussion Paper no. 74-9, July 15, 1974; processed. Estimates used a double log expenditure function.

The Shortage of Housing in Urban Areas

The large and growing housing shortage in the urban areas of the Philippines has been caused by a number of interrelated factors, including the low level of household incomes, high and rising costs of land and construction, a shortage of credit, and relatively inactive public sector involvement in construction and financing. Although the housing shortage appears to exist in all major urban areas, it is particularly acute in the Manila area because of the inflow of migrants.[18] A large proportion of low-income households in rapidly

18. In a 1972 study the Presidential Assistance on Housing and Resettlement Agency concluded that about 50 percent of the national housing shortage was concentrated in the MMA.

growing urban areas is squatting or living in dwelling units without adequate access to services or credit to improve their housing conditions. Although the housing problems of the Philippines are not unique, they appear to be more serious than in at least some other developing countries in the region where the rate of urbanization has not been as high (Malaysia, for example), or where the government has played a more active role in the housing sector (as in Singapore).

STOCK AND QUALITY OF DWELLINGS

In 1970 the total stock of housing in the Philippines was estimated at 5,573,000 units, of which 1,350,000 (or 24 percent) were in urban areas. It is difficult to analyze changes in the housing stock with any degree of accuracy because of the lack of annual construction statistics and the differentiation in classifications used in the 1960 and 1970 censuses. Roughly speaking, the annual growth rate of housing construction between 1960 and 1970 was about 3.0 percent, with urban areas averaging 4.5 percent a year and rural areas only 1.9 percent.[19] These figures indicate that housing in urban areas has just kept pace with population growth and has not allowed for the replacement of physically inadequate dwellings.[20] The urban housing shortage, with the consequent overcrowding, poor quality of construction, and inadequate services, appears to be growing particularly rapidly as population pressures increase. According to information from the 1967 survey of households, only about 20 percent of existing dwellings had piped water, and flush toilets were available in only about 10 percent of the units. Electricity was used for lighting in between 15 and 20 percent of the dwellings and for cooking in only about 10 percent.

A variety of housing units are currently available in the urban areas of the Philippines. Eighty-five percent in 1970 were single family dwellings, while 5 percent were apartments, and 6 percent

19. International Labour Office, *Sharing in Development* (Geneva: ILO, 1974), p. 212.

20. Of the total dwelling units classified as physically inadequate in 1970, 64 percent were in urban areas. See Jacob S. De Vera, "Housing Need up to the Year 2000 and Its Financing Implications," NEDA, National Conference on Housing, Development Academy of the Philippines (Tagaytay City, October 19–21, 1973), p. 6.

Table 3.6 Quality Indicators of Dwelling Units, 1967
(In percent)

Indicator	All Philippines	Urban	Rural
Lighting used			
Electricity	22.9	62.8	5.8
Kerosene pressure lamp	14.2	10.7	15.8
Other kerosene lamp	57.7	24.1	72.1
Other	5.2	2.3	6.4
Not reported	0.1	0.1	
Total	100.0	100.0	100.0
Source of drinking water			
Water works	22.9	56.2	8.6
Communal drilled wells	15.9	13.7	16.8
Private drilled wells	11.4	13.5	10.5
Closed well with pump	11.5	6.7	13.5
Open well	21.3	6.9	27.4
Spring	11.5	0.8	16.1
Creek, stream, river irrigation	4.4	0.6	6.0
Rainwater	1.3	1.5	1.2
Total	100.0	100.0	100.0
Toilet facilities			
Water sealed[a]	12.8	34.0	3.7
Cement bowl[b]	7.2	14.1	4.2
Closed pit	26.9	21.4	29.3
Open pit	17.6	9.4	21.2
Public toilet	1.7	3.8	0.8
Pail system	0.3	1.1	
None	33.2	16.0	40.7
Not reported	0.2	0.1	0.2
Total	100.0	100.0	100.0
Type of tenancy			
Both house or building and lot owned	49.3	37.9	54.2
House or building owned; lot free or squatted on	28.9	17.4	33.8
House or building owned; lot rented	11.1	18.6	7.9
Both house or building and lot free of charge	4.6	6.7	3.6
Both house or building and lot rented	6.0	19.3	0.3
Not reported	0.1	0.1	0.2
Total	100.0	100.0	100.0

a. Enamel or cement bowl with seat.
b. Set level with the floor, without a seat.
Source: "Living Quarters in the Philippines," *Journal of Philippines Statistics*, vol. 19, no. 3 (July–September 1968), pp. ix–xxiii.

Table 3.7. Value of Housing Construction in the Philippines
(In millions of pesos at current prices)

| Year | Housing construction investment | | | Share in GNP (percent) |
	Public[a]	Private[b]	Total	
1968	1	771	772	2.7
1969	2	829	831	2.6
1970	1	895	896	2.4
1971	1	1,021	1,022	2.3
1972	2	1,214	1,216	2.3
1973	1	1,538	1,539	2.5

a. Investment in public-sponsored housing by the private sector.
b. Includes housing constructed by the private sector and financed by public institutions such as Government Service Insurance System and Social Security System.
Source: National Education and Development Authority (NEDA).

were makeshift dwellings.[21] In urban areas 38 percent of the households are estimated to own both their houses and lots, compared with 54 percent in rural areas; 19 percent of those in urban areas rent both their houses and lots, compared with 0.3 percent in rural areas. The type of tenancy of the remaining population is described in Table 3.6.

CONSTRUCTION AND ACCESS TO FINANCE

Expenditures on housing construction during 1968–73 averaged about 2.5 percent of GNP (Table 3.7). The traditional heavier construction is gradually being joined by more self-constructed, lighter dwellings as migrants move to the urban centers and build makeshift homes. Virtually all housing has been constructed by the private sector. Government construction of low-income housing is numerically negligible, with only 13,500 units built from 1948 to 1972. Neither the government nor private industry has related housing construction to overall urban development plans, with the result that services as well as employment opportunities are inadequately provided near residential areas, particularly low-income districts.

The major portion of housing financing has also been carried

21. BCS, *Census of the Philippine Population and Housing: Summary,* vol. 2, 1960; and BCS, "Metropolitan Manila" (Manila, January 1973; processed).

out by the private sector. Though there are public programs aimed at financing low-cost dwellings, in practice they have nearly always excluded the low-income populations. The major formal sources of credit have been the Government Service Insurance System (GSIS) and the Social Security System (SSS). Their loans are available only to members, however, and usually benefit the highest paid employees in urban areas, particularly Metropolitan Manila.

Since the average loans of both GSIS and SSS (about ₱28,609 and ₱21,767 respectively in 1970) amount to 8 to 9 times the median Philippine family income, it is evident that both institutions finance housing for families in the top 10 to 20 percent of the income distribution scale. Thus the relatively low-earning GSIS member has, through his mandatory contribution, subsidized the housing of a few high-income employees. A less important source of housing has been the Development Bank of the Philippines (DBP). Together the GSIS, SSS, and DBP provided about 20 percent of the ₱1,100 million estimated to have been invested during 1971. As far as the private sector goes, savings banks, commercial banks, and savings and loan associations have become increasingly important sources of housing finance and currently account for another 20 to 30 percent of investment in housing.[22]

Level and Quality of Other Urban Services

Directly related to housing and overall land use is the provision of public services, including social and physical infrastructure as well as transport facilities. In the Philippines urban growth appears to have outpaced these services, and there is no set pattern for administering them in the MMA or elsewhere. Some services are the responsibility of the central government, city, or province, while others are shared among various levels of government or provided privately. Many variations in the provision of services exist among jurisdictions, depending on the financial and technical resources available, historical precedent, and political factors.

The range of services provided by the chartered cities generally depends upon their income. Manila City and Quezon City are more autonomous than many because of their relatively high incomes; they can administer and even expand their services without de-

22. ILO, *Sharing in Development,* pp. 214–15.

pending on national aid. Manila City, for instance, provides free education from first grade to high school, while other local units of Metropolitan Manila rely much more on the central government. Disparities in the level of public service exist not only among jurisdictions but also among neighborhoods within local jurisdictions.[23]

In addition, some services are unevenly distributed throughout the country, with the poorer regions less adequately served. This tends to hold back development there and promote migration to the richer regions. The unequal pattern of investment in public services within jurisdictions and among regions is apparent not only for public utilities such as water supply and sewerage but also for health and education, the location of government offices and financial institutions, and transport facilities. The lack of government intervention in the provision of some services has tended to exacerbate the situation. In the privately controlled telecommunication system, for example, cutthroat competition in the high-density areas has led to underutilization of channel capacity and parallel services; but there is a complete absence of service in about two-thirds of the country where profitability seems low.

WATER SUPPLY

The present infrastructure for water supply, sewerage, and drainage is inadequate throughout the Philippines (Table 3.8).[24] The most recent National Health Plan (1975–78) cited poor environmental sanitation as a major factor in the high incidence of communicable diseases in the country. Potable water is currently available to less than half the population in the Philippines. Only about 16.9 million people are estimated to have had an adequate supply of water in FY70; 3 million of these were in the MMA. More than 1,000 barrios, 800 municipalities, and 6 cities are currently estimated to

23. The ratio of 1.26 hospital beds per 1,000 population in Tondo, the largest squatter area within the MMA, is far below the Manila City average of 6.48, and bus and jeepney capacity is below the city average in 80 percent of the below-average income districts, including Tondo.

24. In the Manila area water is provided by the Metropolitan Waterworks and Sewerage System (MWSS), while in the provinces the Local Water Utilities Administration (LWUA) aids in developing facilities in districts with populations of 30,000 or more. Water supply facilities for rural areas and populations of less than 30,000 are under the Department of Local Government and Community Development.

Table 3.8. Percentage of Urban Population Served by Water Supply and Sewage Disposal Facilities in Selected Countries, 1970

Urban connections	Philippines	Thailand	Korea	India
Water supply				
House connections	55	52	84	39
Public standpipe	10	8	4	17
Total population served	65	60	88	56
Sewage disposal				
Public sewer system	4	n.a.	31	34
Treated	28	n.a.	. . .	12
Untreated	72	n.a.	100	88
Household systems[a]	84	66	31	46
Total population served	88	66	61	80

. . . Zero or negligible.
n.a.: Not available.
a. Pit, privy, septic tank, and buckets.
Source: World Health Statistics Report (Geneva: World Health Organization, 1973), vol. 26, pt. 2, tables 3 and 5.

be without water supply systems. Moreover, existing systems require improvement and rehabilitation to meet the needs of a fast-growing population. The carrying capacity of the transmission and distribution mains has, in many instances, decreased and leakage has increased because of fractures in pipes as they settle, corrosion, and heavier traffic and loadings.

In the past springs or wells located in or adjacent to urban centers provided water with little or no treatment. Although the growth in the urban population has now greatly increased the demand for a safe water supply, distribution systems have not expanded. The growing demand, the age of the systems, and the high leakage rates have gradually reduced water main pressure throughout the distribution systems; consequently the majority of those served receive an inadequate supply. Many systems supply water for only a few hours at night; others suffer negative pressures for at least part of the day and risk siphoning foul water back into the mains.

There are few public faucets in many urban areas; their use is discouraged by many water districts because of excessive wastage. Frequently, however, one or two adjacent households will share a connection. Those not served by the public supply obtain water from springs, wells, streams, and rivers, or from vendors who sell water in cans or trucks. Preliminary census data show no substantial changes in the distribution of households by type of water supply used from 1967 to 1970; in addition, the absolute number of households with and without "adequate" [25] service has grown at about the same rate as the total number of households. The inadequacy and unreliability of existing water supply systems may even affect the location of industries, forcing them to sites near a watercourse to supply their own needs.

SEWERAGE AND DRAINAGE

Sewerage and drainage facilities in the Philippines also need improvement and expansion. In 1975 not a single municipality in the country was completely sewered. Many districts rely principally on individual septic tanks, pits, and the direct discharge of untreated sewage into nearby watercourses. Well-planned and maintained drainage systems are nonexistent, and low-lying parts of many urban areas are subject to flooding each year. Because of population growth and the larger quantity of sewage, the already high risk of contaminating private wells and boreholes is increasing every year, especially during flood periods.

The prevailing method of solid waste disposal in the Philippines is open dumping, coupled with burning and scavenging, which introduces health hazards such as rats and vermin and the pollution of air and water. Because of inadequate sewage disposal facilities in the MMA, raw sewage is discharged into Manila Bay. With no other way to dispose of industrial waste, companies are obliged to locate their plants near waterways, thus contributing to the incidence of disease and pollution.

Technical Note. Definitions of Urban Areas

The degree of urbanization of a nation is usually defined as the proportion of the population resident in urban places. The

---

25. Adequate service for urban dwellings refers to piped water. See Development Academy of the Philippines, "Measuring Philippine Welfare," Social Indicators Project, pt. 2 (Tagaytay City, January 1975; processed), pp. 6–18.

definition of what is urban in the Philippines, however, has changed over time. In the 1948 census the urban population included all persons living in poblaciones, or central districts, of chartered cities and provincial capitals, plus the population living in all poblaciones in all municipalities and municipal districts. This census definition embraced only a small portion of the population of certain cities but included the entire population in poblaciones, many of which were nearly as rural as the outlying barrios. In 1948 more than half of these poblaciones had fewer than 2,500 inhabitants.[26]

The definition of urban areas was expanded in 1956 to take in the entire areas of chartered cities and municipalities, including the provincial capitals and Metropolitan Manila. Metropolitan Manila included Manila City and its suburbs, that is, the cities of Quezon, Pasay, and Caloocan, and the municipalities of San Juan, Mandaluyong, Makati, and Parañaque. To overcome the limitations of the earlier definitions, which still classified as urban many populations living in quite rural conditions, the following criteria were established in 1963:

a. All municipal jurisdictions (whether or not designated chartered cities or provincial capitals) were urban that had a density of at least 1,000 persons per square kilometer, but the whole of Quezon, Baguio, and Cebu cities were included regardless of their density.
b. For all other cities and municipalities with a density of at least 500 persons per square kilometer, only the poblacion (regardless of population size) plus any barrio with at least 2,500 inhabitants and any barrio contiguous to the poblacion with at least 1,000 inhabitants were regarded as urban.
c. For all other cities and municipalities with a population of at least 20,000 persons, only the poblacion (regardless of population size) and all barrios contiguous to the poblacion and having at least 2,500 inhabitants were urban.
d. All other poblaciones having a population of at least 2,500 inhabitants were urban.

---

26. Much of the information for this technical note is taken from Tito A. Mijares and Francisco V. Nazaret, *The Growth of Urban Population in the Philippines and Its Perspectives,* BCS Technical Paper no. 5 (Manila: Bureau of the Census and Statistics, n.d.).

According to the above criteria 1,599 places were classified as urban in 1960. Of these, 38 percent had populations of less than 2,500. Doubts were raised as to the suitability of minimum population and density criteria because many places classified as urban were still small and primarily rural and the density ratio was not employed for the barrios inasmuch as barrio boundaries were not known.

In 1970 the census definition of urban areas was again changed to include criteria related to the functions of urban centers, particularly their economic and social activities. It established the following criteria:

a. In their entirety, all cities and municipalities that had a population density of at least 1,000 persons per square kilometer

b. Poblaciones or central districts of municipalities and cities that had a population density of at least 500 persons per square kilometer

c. Poblaciones or central districts not included in *a* and *b* (regardless of population size) that had the following:

   i. a street pattern with either a parallel or right-angle orientation

   ii. at least six establishments (commercial, manufacturing, recreational, or personal services)

   iii. at least three of the following:

      (a) a town hall or chapel where religious services were held at least once a month

      (b) a public park, plaza, or cemetery

      (c) a marketplace or building where trading activities were carried on at least once a week

      (d) a public building such as a school, hospital, or health center.

d. Barrios having at least 1,000 inhabitants which met the conditions set forth in *c* above and in which the occupation of the inhabitants was predominantly neither farming nor fishing.

The essential difference between the various definitions of urban areas is that the criteria of density, minimum size, and administrative center were used in the earlier two censuses, while in 1970 the density rule was combined with urban characteristics. There were

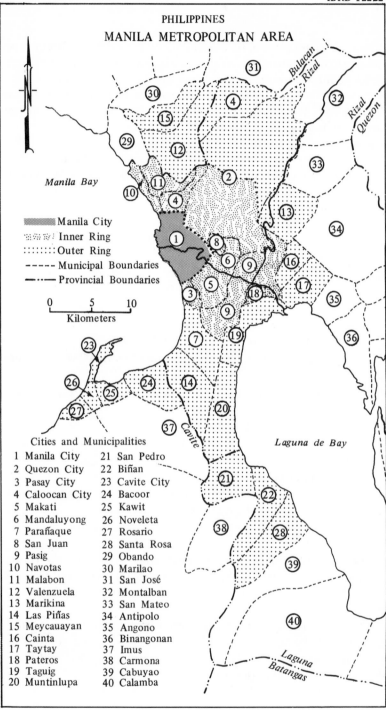

IBRD-12222

PHILIPPINES
MANILA METROPOLITAN AREA

Manila Bay

▨ Manila City
▧ Inner Ring
⋯ Outer Ring
- - - - Municipal Boundaries
—·— Provincial Boundaries

0   5   10
Kilometers

Cities and Municipalities

1 Manila City	21 San Pedro
2 Quezon City	22 Biñan
3 Pasay City	23 Cavite City
4 Caloocan City	24 Bacoor
5 Makati	25 Kawit
6 Mandaluyong	26 Noveleta
7 Parañaque	27 Rosario
8 San Juan	28 Santa Rosa
9 Pasig	29 Obando
10 Navotas	30 Marilao
11 Malabon	31 San José
12 Valenzuela	32 Montalban
13 Marikina	33 San Mateo
14 Las Piñas	34 Antipolo
15 Meycauayan	35 Angono
16 Cainta	36 Binangonan
17 Taytay	37 Imus
18 Pateros	38 Carmona
19 Taguig	39 Cabuyao
20 Muntinlupa	40 Calamba

Laguna de Bay

2,406 areas classified as urban in 1970; [27] if the 1960 definition were applied to the 1970 population, 2,349 areas would be included. The new definition covered 246 more poblaciones and city districts than the old because it included those living in places with urban characteristics irrespective of population size. The old definition took in 189 more barrios than the new, however.

The definitions that have been used over time to delimit the MMA have also varied greatly. National agencies, such as those dealing with transport, water supply, sewerage, and drainage, have each defined the metropolitan area to suit their own needs.[28] As a result at least eight definitions of Metropolitan Manila are in use (Table 3.9 and map p. 64), which differ in terms of population, land area, and number of overlapping jurisdictions. The one used most frequently in this report is that of the Bureau of the Census and Statistics, which is the most rigorously defined of the concepts. It includes five chartered cities (Manila, Quezon, Caloocan, Pasay, and Cavite) and twenty-three municipalities [29] selected according to the following criteria:

a. The city or municipality must be contiguous to "Manila and suburbs" [30] or adjoining an intermediate city or municipality of qualifying population density (that is, greater than 1,000 persons per square kilometer), and must show evidence of "strong integration," economically and socially, with Manila and suburbs.

b. The city or municipality must be "urban in its entirety," in accordance with the BCS definition of urban areas.

c. At least 75 percent of the labor force of the city or municipality must be engaged in nonagricultural occupations.

---

27. Among these places, 1,164 had populations of less than 2,500.

28. See, for example, Manila Bay Metropolitan Region Strategic Plan, *Various Definitions of Metropolitan Manila Area*, Planning and Project Development Office, Department of Public Works, Transportation, and Communications (Manila, April 6, 1973), p. 1.

29. Makati, Mandaluyong, Navotas, San Juan, Malabon, Pasig, Marikina, Parañaque, Pateros, Cainta, Las Piñas, Muntinlupa, Taguig, Taytay, Bacoor, Kawit, Noveleta, Rosario, Meycauayan, Valenzuela, Biñan, San Pedro, and Santa Rosa.

30. See Table 3.9.

Table 3.9. Definitions of Metropolitan Manila

Definition	Total population 1970 (thousands)	Number of local governments	Area (square kilometers)	Population density	Description
1. Manila City[a]	1,331	1	38	34,765	Definition 1, plus Quezon City, Pasay City, Caloocan City, and the municipalities of Makati, Mandaluyong, Parañaque, and San Juan in Rizal
2. Manila and suburbs	3,168	8	343	9,236	Definition 1, plus Quezon City, Pasay City, Caloocan City, and the municipalities of Makati, Mandaluyong, Parañaque, and San Juan in Rizal
3. Manila Metropolitan Area (MMA) as defined by the Metropolitan Mayors' Coordination Council	3,821	14	545	7,008	Definition 2, plus the municipalities of Pasig, Navotas, Las Piñas, Marikina and Malabon in Rizal, and Valenzuela in Bulacan
4. MMA as defined in MMA transportation study	3,996	19	699	5,717	Definition 3, plus the municipalities of Pateros and Taguig in Rizal, and Meycauayan, Marilao, and Obando in Bulacan
5. MMA as defined by Metropolitan Waterworks and Sewerage System	4,019	20	1,016	3,956	Definition 3, plus the municipalities of Pateros, Taguig, Taytay, Cainta, and San Mateo, and Montalban in Rizal

6. MMA as defined by the Board of Investments	4,340	26	828	5,242	Definition 3, plus Cavite City and the municipalities of Pateros, Taguig, Taytay, Cainta, and Muntinlupa in Rizal; Biñan and San Pedro in Laguna; Bacoor, Noveleta, and Kawit in Cavite; and Meycauayan in Bulacan
7. MMA as defined in 1970 by the Bureau of Census and Statistics and as used in this report	4,404	28	871	5,056	Definition 6, plus Rosario in Cavite and Santa Rosa in Laguna
8. MMA as defined by the Manila Bay Metropolitan Region Strategic Plan (MBMRSP)	4,786	40	2,328	2,056	Definition 6, plus Angono, Antipolo, Binangonan, San Mateo, and Montalban in Rizal; Cabuyao and Calamba in Laguna; Carmona and Imus in Cavite; and Obando, Marilao, and San José in Bulacan
9. Manila Bay Metropolitan Region as defined by MBMRSP	8,625	188	18,051	478	Definition 1, plus all the cities (11) and municipalities (176) in the provinces of Bataan, Batangas, Cavite, Laguna, Bulacan, Zambales, Rizal, and Pampanga

a. This is, strictly speaking, not a definition of Metropolitan Manila but the starting point from which all other definitions are derived.
Note: A Metropolitan Manila Commission was recently created which includes the cities and municipalities listed in Definition 3, plus the municipalities of Pateros, Taguig, and Muntinlupa. See map p. 64.

4

Altering Urban Development

AN INCREASING PROPORTION OF THE PHILIPPINES population will become urban in the future. Although the natural rate of urban growth may decrease, the limited employment opportunities in rural areas will probably cause the rate of rural-urban migration to accelerate, at least during the next decade. The net effect of these two trends is likely to be a continuation of the present urban growth rate of 4 percent a year, which would result in an urban population in 1985 of approximately 18 million, one-third of the total compared with one-fourth in 1960.

Urbanization patterns in the Philippines have been influenced more by general economic conditions than by any specific policies for altering the distribution of activities and population among regions, rural and urban areas, or urban centers of different sizes. In the past much urban growth was spontaneous, but indications are that it will be increasingly directed in the future. More attention will have to be given to the geographical distribution of the population across the national territory and to the decentralization of urban development away from the MMA to a number of other urban centers. There will also need to be an intensification of efforts to absorb the growing population in individual urban areas. Because of Metropolitan Manila's large size and the inadequate living conditions of much of the population, particular attention should be given to improving the level of services there and making them more accessible to low-income families.

Decentralization

Despite the predominance of the MMA, a network of urban areas already exists across the major islands—centers of trading, agricultural processing and marketing, and industrial activity. The growth of these centers has brought people from rural areas to form large slum and squatter communities. The heaviest flow of migrants has traditionally been to Metropolitan Manila, and there is a strong case for trying to slow population growth there by an active policy of decentralization. To date the intermediate-size cities have been neglected in the Philippines as a focus of policy. The national government and even municipal officials have in most instances given only scant attention to local development planning because of limited fiscal resources.

Increased attention to the development of small and medium-size cities and the creation of urban growth centers appear desirable. Such a policy should relieve population pressures both in the MMA and in rural areas, while at the same time increasing the modernizing spin-off from urban centers to the surrounding rural areas, particularly to those such as Cagayan Valley and the Visayas which have been neglected in the past. The recently issued Presidential Decree 752, which grants local governments the power to borrow from lending institutions, could significantly spur the growth and development of urban centers outside the MMA. Clear and detailed guidelines will still be required, however, to implement a policy of decentralization.

One regional center where significant growth may be expected is Cebu City in the Visayas, which in 1970 was the third largest city in the Philippines, with about 350,000 people. Cebu, with the contiguous cities of Mandaue, Lapu-Lapu, Talisay, and Cordova, is already becoming rapidly urbanized because of its mining and industrial potential. It has the second most varied manufacturing base in the Philippines, and its strategic location and accessibility make it the trading center for the central part of the Philippine archipelago. The Visayas currently contribute heavily to migration to both the MMA and Mindanao; the development of infrastructure and services in Cebu could promote private investment in the region and alter that pattern of migration.

On the island of Mindanao, two possible regional centers—Davao City in the south and the Iligan Bay area in the north—should probably be encouraged. Davao, the largest city in Mindanao and the second largest in the country, had a population of 392,000 in 1970 and is basically oriented toward agriculture. The Iligan Bay area includes two closely linked cities, Iligan and Cagayan de Oro, with populations of 104,000 and 128,000 respectively in 1970. This region has significant industrial growth potential. Separated by only 60 kilometers, the twin cities should provide flexibility in planning the growth of the region and complementary opportunities. Cagayan de Oro presently has Xavier University and several good secondary schools, which offer an educational base to build on. Iligan City, with its growing industrial base, could develop specialized facilities for technical and machine-trade skills.

Where there are several urban centers to be built up within a single region, as in the Cagayan de Oro–Iligan area, a persuasive case can be made for not confining development plans to individual cities. In some regions (for example, Southern Mindanao) where better transportation and communication systems are needed, regional measures, perhaps introduced through the Regional Development Councils,[1] could aid in improving linkages among urban centers. A broader planning approach should also consider the competing demands made on the land by urban-industrial needs and agricultural activity and protect prime agricultural land from urban encroachments so that it can provide food for the growing urban complexes. Particular attention will have to be given to this problem in the Manila area and in Western Visayas.

Decentralization can be promoted by the government through policies which encourage the regional dispersal of industry [2] and which improve the physical and social infrastructure. Subsequent sections discuss in detail some closely interrelated measures dealing with water supply, housing, and transport. Another important measure for the development of growth centers is the government's program to improve the electric power base outside the Central Luzon region. It proposes a relatively rapid annual growth in capacity and production in Mindanao (15 percent) and the Visayas (13 percent) compared with Luzon (8 percent).[3]

1. See Chapter 5.
2. See Chapter 9 for a more detailed discussion of this issue.
3. This effort is discussed in detail in Appendix C.

Distribution of Urban Services

The need to improve the distribution of services within cities is particularly urgent for Metropolitan Manila. Manila dominates the urban sector, and even with successful decentralization of urban growth it will remain by far the Philippines' largest city in the foreseeable future. It accounts for a large share of the urban poor and has not been able to cope with its rapid population growth. As a result a large and growing number of families do not have access to essential urban infrastructure and services, notably water supply, sewage disposal, and transport. In addition, housing has not been provided at standards that low-income families can afford, with the inevitable development of a large slum and squatter population. For these reasons, an intensive effort must be made to improve the living conditions of low-income households in Metropolitan Manila. To assure the maximum impact of these improvements, trade-offs between the quality of service and the number of persons covered should be made in favor of the latter.

Administration is an important element of any attempt to improve the level of public services. The newly created Metropolitan Manila Commission under the overall supervision of a governor should help coordinate the activities of seventeen local governments. An attempt is also being made to coordinate certain metropolitan services, notably fire control and police activities.

A National Housing Authority was established recently which is expected to have a separate division related to Metropolitan Manila, and the government is considering a Metropolitan Manila Transportation Council which would be responsible for the planning and budgeting of all transport projects. Each of these agencies is expected to be transferred eventually to the new metropolitan government. They should make it significantly easier for the government to formulate and implement coherent strategies for the individual sectors and to focus available resources on disparities of service among jurisdictions.

Sector Strategies

Strategies for three sectors—housing, water supply and sewerage, and transport—that are particularly pertinent for urban develop-

Table 4.1. Family Expenditure, 1971
(In percent)

Expenditure item	Total family expenditure	₱500 to ₱2,999	₱3,000 to ₱5,999	₱6,000 and over
Clothing	6.2	5.4	6.4	6.6
Education, transport, and communications	6.6	3.6	6.5	9.6
Food	53.7	63.6	54.7	42.5
Housing and furnishings	17.7	14.1	16.6	22.6
Recreation and personal care	5.2	3.9	5.2	6.8
Miscellaneous	10.6	9.5	10.6	11.9
Total	100.0	100.0	100.0	100.0

Source: BCS and Jacob S. De Vera, "Housing Need up to the Year 2000 and Its Financing Implications," NEDA, National Conference on Housing, Development Academy of the Philippines (Tagaytay City, October 19–21, 1973).

ment are set out below. Other significant sectors—electric power, industry, health, and education—are discussed elsewhere in the report.[4] In general the strategies proposed here aim at a more equitable distribution of public and private resources among and within urban areas.

HOUSING

The ILO mission estimated the future growth of demand for housing in the Philippines as a function of the growth rate of household formation, the growth rate of real income per household, and the income elasticity of housing demand.[5] Under the assumption of 5 percent real income growth per household, the ILO model indicates the growth of housing construction will be about 9 percent a year during the 1970s. If this rate is applied to the estimated investment in housing in 1974, it results in a housing investment of ₱3,800 million (at 1974 prices) by 1980 or about 2.6 percent of GNP (Table 4.1). This forecast, however, does not include public housing, because the analysis is based on effective demand, which is negligible for low-income groups under existing supply conditions.

The combination of very low average incomes, high natural rates

4. See Appendix C and Chapters 9, 11, and 12.

5. International Labour Office, *Sharing in Development* (Geneva: ILO, 1974), pp. 218–19.

of population growth, rapid urbanization, and public sector in-
activity in the field of low-cost housing has accentuated the housing
problem in the Philippines. The shortage of adequate housing is
particularly acute in the larger and faster growing urban centers,
as evidenced by the high concentrations of squatters. A number of
estimates, although rough, indicate that housing construction needs
of the Philippine population will be enormous over the next two
decades. One forecast, for instance, suggests that the present annual
pace of two dwelling units constructed per 1,000 population will
satisfy only a third of the future needs.[6]

The large variance between estimated housing requirements and
production reflects a fundamental discrepancy between the current
conditions of supply and demand in the housing market. Though
this discrepancy cannot be measured precisely, its magnitude can
be illustrated. It has been estimated that only 14 percent of urban
families—those with annual incomes of at least ₱10,000—can afford
current market prices for housing provided by the private sector.
On the basis of family expenditure data in Table 4.1, an example
of an "average" family would be one with an annual income equal
to the national average (₱3,746 or US$564),[7] no savings, and 55
percent of total income spent on food. After food expenses, the
family has ₱1,690 (US$254) left to meet other living needs. It seems
reasonable to assume that a "low-priced" house of ₱28,000
(US$4,217) [8] is beyond such families' means, since even under moder-
ately concessional terms (10 percent down payment and 10 percent
interest over 20 years), this would involve an annual outlay of
₱2,800, which is almost 80 percent of total income and one and

6. For instance, Jacob S. De Vera, "Housing Need up to the Year 2000 and
Its Financing Implications" (NEDA, National Conference on Housing, Development Academy of the Philippines, Tagaytay City, October 19–21, 1973, p. 6),
estimates the additional housing requirement as 3.2 million units during
1970–80 and as 1.6 million during 1980–85, increasing the total stock by 51
percent during 1970–80. K. V. Ramachandran, and others, in "Housing Projections for the Philippines, 1960–80," *Economic Research Journal,* vol. 19, no. 1
(June 1972), pp. 20–33, estimate the housing need as 10 million additional units
during 1960–80, more than two and a half times the housing stock in 1960.

7. Approximately a third of MMA families and 45 percent of those in Tondo
Foreshore—a slum area within the MMA—earn less than this amount.

8. A World Bank urban survey mission in 1973 estimated this to be about
the lowest priced house currently being brought to the market in Manila.

two-thirds times the available income.[9] If the situation is difficult for a person with an average income, it is hopeless for the poor.

The income constraint to increases in the housing stock is becoming more severe because the costs of land, building materials, and construction have been rising faster than the average level of family income. The cost of dwellings has also been affected by the gradual adoption (and often imposition) of higher construction standards. This, together with the shortage of credit available to low-income families, makes it improbable that the private market will be able to provide adequate housing for the bulk of the population. The need for government intervention is clear; its exact role less so. Because there appears to be a great deal of undeveloped and underdeveloped land within the presently urbanized area of the MMA, one step the government should probably consider is the formulation of a policy to locate, acquire, and develop vacant land for housing and general urban expansion.

As noted above, the government's past involvement in constructing housing has been negligible. The largest government effort to date to aid the lower income groups has been the relocation of squatter families in the MMA. By 1973 over 16,000 families, or about 20 percent of that portion of the MMA squatter population believed to be indigent, had been resettled; more than half of them went to three project areas—Carmona, San Pedro, and Sapang Palay. An additional 9,000 families were relocated in their province of origin or elsewhere. The program has suffered serious setbacks, however, with families abandoning the resettlement sites and returning to the MMA.[10]

Although the public efforts have been small and less than successful, fully meeting the housing need is beyond the financial and

9. This is a crude calculation based on rough estimates of cost of house, income, and percentage of income which might be available to purchase housing.

10. Nearly 80 percent of those relocated to Sapang Palay returned by 1973, and 45 percent of those in Carmona abandoned their allocated lots. The main reason for this failure seems to have been the distant location of sites and the lack of employment opportunities nearby. With the time and money costs of transportation high in relation to their low incomes, heads of families found it necessary to stay in Manila during weekdays and were forced to maintain two households. As a result, many appear to have relocated their families to more central locations. In addition these specific projects appear to have been poorly sited and planned, and there were other drawbacks such as inadequate basic services.

physical capacities of the government alone. To triple the rate of housing investment, which some projections indicate is necessary, would require the government to invest annually some 4 to 5 percent of GNP in housing—substantially more than the current rate of total public investment—and would involve a considerable subsidy. A more realistic goal for the government at this time would be to allocate public funds equal to about 0.2 percent of GNP by 1980. These funds could provide inexpensive home improvements for existing dwellings and the low-cost construction of new dwellings. Standards could be tailored to the income level of the population so that there would be full cost recovery. Designs could attempt to take advantage of the obvious capability of lower income groups to construct their own housing, and emphasis could be put on sites-and-services projects and the upgrading of existing dwellings. Squatter upgrading, the process of extending minimum urban services to the poorest areas, could significantly improve the living conditions of Manila's poor if done comprehensively, area by area, and accompanied by measures to regularize land tenure.[11]

If housing investment of this type and magnitude is to occur, however, the costs of construction materials and land will need to be stabilized. In addition, housing legislation will be needed to provide more benefits to low-income groups.

An indicative program of sites-and-services housing and squatter upgrading has been roughly sketched for Metropolitan Manila by the World Bank's Urban Projects Department. Because the program would be self-financing, it aims at those between the fifteenth and seventieth income percentile. The group below the fifteenth percentile is assumed to lack an effective demand for permanent housing, while the top 30 percent can be provided for by the private market. The target population is divided into those in existing squatter dwellings, which would be upgraded, and those which would require new housing. For each group three different housing packages are envisioned to reflect the range of income levels and hence the ability to pay. The cost (in 1974 prices) for a single new unit ranges from US$1,070 to US$1,675 and for upgrad-

11. Sites-and-services programs provide plots of land, basic infrastructure, and credit for building materials to enable the recipient to construct his own dwelling. Squatter-upgrading programs usually involve improvement of existing housing units and the simultaneous rather than phased provision of water supply, sewerage, surface water drainage, roads, and footpaths.

ing from US$470 to US$600 a unit.[12] By 1980 the program could be providing sites and services for new dwellings to about 75,000 people and upgraded housing to about 400,000 people annually. The annual costs of this program would reach about US$33 million (1975 prices) by 1980. Over the ten-year period, 1976–85, the program would cost about US$350 million and improve the housing conditions of almost 3.5 million people. If extended by about a third to cover other urban areas, the overall program would be approximately the equivalent of 0.2 percent of GNP by 1980. This would be a substantial improvement over the past provision of public housing, yet it would be modest in relation to the private housing market.

Self-financing is the key element of this program. Loans would be extended to the homeowner at 12 percent for twenty years to cover the full cost of the housing investment. Financing could be provided by the National Housing Authority (NHA), which would also implement the construction and upgrading. In this case the NHA would need considerable financing to bridge the gap between annual construction costs and annual loan repayments. If the plan for Manila were extended to other urban areas, the bridging finance required in 1980 would be about US$45 million. NHA financing could be provided from a number of sources: equity contributions by the national government, local market borrowing, and foreign assistance. If shared equally among these sources, the burden would be manageable. Although these figures are crude, they do indicate that the government could make a sizable impact on the housing plight of lower income groups without putting undue strain on the national budget.

The projections given above imply that housing as a share of GNP would increase from about 2.3 percent in 1974 to about 2.8 percent in 1980 and, if continued at these rates, to 3.0 percent by 1985. The private market would still account for the bulk of housing construction, although there would be a considerable increase in public expenditures in housing from less than ₱5 million at present to about ₱300 million by 1980 in 1974 constant prices. (See Table 4.2.)

Owing to deficiencies in housing data, the number of dwellings that this investment would create can be only roughly estimated. If the average unit price of private housing remains at about the

12. These costs are based on estimates in the Manila Urban Development Project proposed to the World Bank for financing.

Table 4.2. Housing Forecast

Year	Housing stock (millions of units)	Investment (millions of constant 1974 pesos) Public	Private	Total	Share in GNP Public	Private	Total
1960	4,791	n.a.	n.a.	n.a.	n.a.	n.a.	n.a.
1970	5,573	1	1,720	1,721	n.a.	2.2	2.2
1980	6,630	300	3,780	4,080	0.2	2.6	2.8
1985	7,570	635	5,820	6,455	0.3	2.7	3.0

n.a.: Not available.
Source: World Bank estimates.

same level in real terms as is estimated for 1970, this investment would provide about 830,000 new units and 160,000 upgraded units during 1976–80. With allowance for some replacement of existing units, the housing stock at the end of the decade would be about 6.6 million units compared with 5.6 million in 1970. On a per capita basis this would mean an increase in the number of persons per dwelling unit from 6.6 in 1960 to 7.5 in 1980; however, if construction continues at this pace, by 1985 this ratio should not deteriorate further but remain at about the 1980 level.

WATER SUPPLY

Although the proportion of dwelling units with adequate water supply increased from 43 percent in 1956 to 51 percent in 1970, the absolute number of dwelling units without adequate water increased by almost 40 percent (Table 4.3).[13] In addition lower income urban families frequently have less adequate access to water and pay significantly higher proportions of their incomes for it than do upper income households.

The government has embarked on an ambitious water supply program to remedy its past neglect. Water supply requirements to be met by the Metropolitan Waterworks and Sewerage System (MWSS) are expected to increase from about 395 million gallons daily (mgd) at present to 830 mgd by 1985. To meet this demand the MWSS has embarked on a long-range Manila Water Supply Project.

13. Development Academy of the Philippines, *Measuring the Quality of Life: Philippine Social Indicators* (Manila, 1975).

Table 4.3. Dwellings with Adequate Source of Water

Year	Number of units with adequate service[a]		Number of units with inadequate service	
	Thousands	Percent	Thousands	Percent
1956	1,631	42.8	2,181	57.2
1967	2,688	51.3	2,439	48.7
1970[b]	3,112	50.7	3,027	49.3

a. Adequate service is defined by BCS as piped water for urban units and piped water or drilled and closed wells for rural units.
b. Number of households with adequate and inadequate service.
Source: BCS, Philippines Statistical Survey of Households, May 1956; Survey on Housing, May 1967; Census of the Population, 1970.

The first phase aims at increasing the total water supply to the Manila Metropolitan Area by an average of about 120 mgd, which the Asian Development Bank estimates will meet demand up to 1982. The implementation of this project would substantially increase the level of investment by MWSS; expenditures could increase from about ₱30 million in 1975 to an average of over ₱270 million annually during 1976–80.

An ambitious development program for provincial waterworks has also been proposed. Approximately 300 communities of 30,000 population and more now need safe and reliable water supply systems. These communities represent approximately 50 percent of the total Philippine population outside the MMA; many are areas of rapid population increase, where traditional water sources such as shallow wells, springs, and streams have become inadequate.

In 1973 the government initiated a major program to provide potable water to the provinces.[14] The Local Water Utilities Administration (LWUA) was created in that year to provide standards and regulations related to the design, construction, operation, and fiscal practices of local utilities as well as technical assistance and training programs. It was also given the power to monitor and evaluate local water utilities, provide loans for developing them, and undertake systems integration. Staff have been appointed and foreign consultants obtained to provide technical assistance in institution building and engineering. There is no doubt, however, that it will take several years before LWUA can provide the

14. See Presidential Decree 198, the Provincial Water Utility Act of 1973.

technical assistance needed without relying on outside consulting services.

Using funds provided by the governments of Denmark and the United States, a series of feasibility studies has been initiated and construction of a number of municipal water supply systems has begun. During 1975–79 the LWUA plans to improve and expand the waterworks system in sixteen major areas, including Bacolod, San Pablo, Davao, Cagayan de Oro, Tacloban, Baguio, Batangas, and Mandaue. Information is still needed on the facilities available outside the urban centers as well as in the rural areas of the Philippines. Studies will have to be undertaken to provide that information, to investigate the possibilities of cost recovery from the potential beneficiaries of the systems, to review the financial aspects, and to identify projects for possible financing by lending agencies.

Sewerage and drainage

In the MMA and other urban areas adequate sewage and drainage facilities are essential if stagnant water is not to increase the already formidable health hazards. The provision of solid waste disposal facilities is equally important. At present solid waste collection and disposal is left entirely to the individual community, and the only sewerage development program proposed—the review of an earlier study of the situation—is concentrated entirely within the MMA. Since open dumping is the prevailing method of disposal, the inspection and spraying of dumping sites is a critical first step in inhibiting pollution; draining the poblacion in each city may be the beginning of a solution to the problem of waste water disposal.

Flood control

Intense and prolonged rainfall during the monsoon and typhoon seasons frequently floods large areas of the Philippines, both urban and agricultural. In the Manila area alone more than 20 kilometers of *esteros*, channels which were originally natural drains for storm water, have disappeared. In the delta area of the Pampanga River, riparian property owners have caused the silting up of river beds and banks in order to claim more land under the doctrine of ownership by natural accretion. Extensive squatting on existing floodways and the haphazard construction of embankments and bridges without adequate waterways cause backwaters to innundate the up-stream areas. Largely as a result of the considerable damage done by the 1972 floods, expenditures on flood control increased from an average of ₱6 million a year in FY67–72 to ₱280 million in FY75, and it should be possible for the government to maintain its momentum in this area.

One of the main objectives of the future is to solve the flood problems in the MMA. The government program would include construction of the Mangahan floodway to divert the excess flow of the Marikina River into the Laguna de Bay; construction of river banks on both sides of the Pasig River; pumping stations to drain flooded areas which cannot be drained by gravity; deepening and widening natural drainage streams; and renovating and improving existing drainage facilities. Other major flood control work is also planned or proposed for the Central Luzon, Mindanao, and Bicol regions.

URBAN TRANSPORT SERVICES

The major urban transport problems of the Philippines are concentrated in Metropolitan Manila, where congestion is chronic.[15] Excessive crowding of population and activity into a small land area [16] and the disorderly arrangement of land uses are placing ever greater demands on transport facilities. The high density of urban buildings and the concentration of employment in downtown Manila have created a volume of passenger and freight traffic that has become increasingly difficult to accommodate effectively. The lines of automobiles, jeepneys, buses, taxis, and other vehicles inching their way through Manila's numerous intersections are obvious manifestations of a continuing and growing imbalance between transport demand and available capacity.

The situation has been exacerbated by the fact that population growth and transport demand have been accompanied by a large

15. Other Philippine cities do not have transport problems of the dimension and magnitude that require outside assistance. Their major task is to assure a development pattern that avoids the problems of overconcentration and dispersion. They have a unique opportunity to circumvent the need for expanded transport facilities by eliminating long-distance commutes between residences and employment.

16. The MMA comprises 870 square kilometers out of the total land area of 300,000 square kilometers.

growth in private passenger vehicles. With only about 10 percent of the total population, Metropolitan Manila now has over 40 percent of the total registered motor vehicles in the country. In 1975 the nation as a whole had one motor vehicle for every 60 inhabitants, while Manila had one for every 12. The available data show that in 1975 about 69 percent of the total registered vehicles in Metropolitan Manila were cars. Trucks accounted for 26 percent, buses for a mere 1.0 percent, and jeepneys for 4.6 percent. Between 1971 and 1975 the number of registered motor vehicles in Metropolitan Manila increased 36 percent, from 242,200 to 325,500. Trucks registered the largest growth, amounting to 46.6 percent, while the number of cars grew 34 percent, jeepneys 12 percent, and buses 7 percent. Clearly the growth rate of buses and jeepneys has been substantially less than that of private cars as well as that of the population. (See Table 4.4.)

The transport system in Metropolitan Manila is almost entirely road-based, with commuter traffic less than one percent of daily passenger trips by rail. The major network consists of four semi-circumferential roads around the central business district, none of which is complete, plus nine radial roads, most of which are complete, extending from the business district to outlying areas. Most of these roads have either four or six lanes.

The rest of Manila's roads wind through densely settled areas and have been built to standards that are inadequate for today's traffic. The rights-of-way and lanes are narrow, drainage poor, and the grid pattern for the most part antiquated. Laid out long before

Table 4.4. Growth in Number of Registered Motor Vehicles in
Metropolitan Manila, 1971–75

Motor vehicle[a]	1971		1975		Percent growth 1971–75
	Number	Percent	Number	Percent	
Cars[b]	167,300	69.3	224,100	68.5	34.0
Trucks	58,000	24.0	85,000	26.0	46.6
Jeepneys	13,400	5.6	15,000	4.6	11.9
Buses	2,700	1.1	2,900	0.9	7.4
Total	241,400	100.0	327,000	100.0	35.5

a. The table does not include motorcycles, which registered the largest increase—70 percent—from 20,806 in 1971 to 35,400 in 1975.
b. Includes automobiles and jeeps for private use.
Source: The Land Transport Commission and the Board of Transport.

the automobile age and designed principally to give access to property for the convenience of real estate developers, these obsolete rights-of-way are now crowded on both sides with commercial activities and dwellings. Most important, the concentration of traffic on narrow streets with many crossings makes it impossible to realize the speed and service potentials of the motor vehicle. Moreover, because of poor drainage and maintenance road surfaces are cracked and pocked with potholes. There are only a few grade-separated intersections on major corridors and about 65 intersections that have signals—many of which are poorly placed and frequently out of operation.

Metropolitan Manila surface transport is further complicated by the Pasig River, which divides the city into north and south and is spanned by nine bridges of different capacities. Numerous esteros, waterways, and creeks also stand as natural barriers, producing discontinuities in the road system and constraining traffic flows.

The major transport works in Metropolitan Manila since the 1960s include the construction of circumferential road C–4 and the two intercity expressways emanating from C–4 to the north and south. The construction cost of C–4 cannot readily be estimated, because the road was constructed in stages and by sections over several years with federal, local, and provincial funds. Except for C–4 and the northern and southern expressways, which were built primarily to give better access to other economic centers in the country, there was only a minor upgrading of a few radial roads inside C–4 until the early 1970s. At present some of the missing links, notably C–1 and C–2, are being completed, but road construction in the urban center moves slowly.

In 1974 it was estimated that about 4.3 million inhabitants of Metropolitan Manila made 7.8 million trips in a typical work day, a rate of 1.8 trips per inhabitant. Jeepneys and buses, the major forms of mass transportation, account for three-quarters of the total trips. About half the total trips are by jeepney, by far the most dominant mode; buses account for 25 percent, and the remaining 25 percent is distributed among cars, taxis, and others.

Jeepneys and buses in Metropolitan Manila provide a variety and frequency of services seldom found in other cities and at no direct capital or recurrent cost to the government. The system has been largely developed through private investment and operated with the vitality of private entrepreneurship. These two modes carry a one-directional hourly flow of 15,000 to 20,000 persons on the main roads during peak hours. In contrast, only about 1,500 to 2,000 passengers are moved by cars, although private cars are numerically predominant, often 50 percent or more of vehicular traffic. On the Guadalupe Bridge, where 92,000 vehicles were recorded daily in a 1971 survey, private cars accounted for 64 to 70 percent of the total traffic and buses only 4.5 percent; buses, however, carried almost as many passengers as private cars.[17]

Despite the importance of public transport, service has not kept pace with the increased travel demands generated by the pattern of metropolitan employment and residential locations. The antiquated system of roads has been strained for many years. Minor additions to the network have offered only temporary relief, and the strains are increasing rapidly in what is already a highly motorized city. It is estimated that the volume of daily trips will rise to 14 million by 1987 or almost double the present level.[18] On this basis peak hourly movements might reach as high as three times present levels, and the capacity of the road and mass transport facilities would be overwhelmed.

In recognition of the urgent need to relieve existing congestion, the first major transport study in Metropolitan Manila was initiated in 1971 and completed in 1973 by a team of Japanese experts working with the Department of Public Works, Transportation, and Communications as counterpart agency. This study recommended an intermodal transport plan and an investment program based on the projected land uses and employment and residential densities.[19] The plan contained a network of six circumferential roads, ten radial roads, six elevated expressways, north-south commuter rail lines, and five subway lines. From this scheme initial transport investment proposals have evolved which are estimated

17. This analysis assumed a vehicle occupancy ratio of 3 for private cars and 40 for buses, as found in Japan's Overseas Technical Cooperation Agency, *Urban Transport Study in Manila Metropolitan Area* (n.p.: Government of Japan, 1973).

18. Estimate based on data supplied by the Department of Public Works and Telecommunications.

19. Government of Japan, Overseas Technical Cooperation Agency, *Urban Transport Study in Manila Metropolitan Area*. These projections were related to neither past and existing development patterns nor to the present travel movements in Metropolitan Manila. They were based on assumptions which are highly questionable.

to cost upward of ₱7,900 million (US$1,200 million).[20] To imple-
ment the complete system proposed by the study would require at
least ₱17,300 million (US$2,600 million), an amount far beyond that
proposed for any other sector in the MMA.

The capacity of the existing transport system can be greatly expanded through more effective traffic management, geometric improvements at key intersections, and regulatory procedures that can
be implemented quickly with relatively little or no public funds.
They include:

a. More efficient traffic signals and a better use of existing facilities
   through improved measures of traffic control such as bans on
   parking and turning in the central area, one-way and reversible
   flows, and bus and jeepney lanes. These improvements would
   greatly increase effective road capacity and facilitate vehicular
   movement. Other improvements include clear markings, strip-
   ing, traffic signs, and better regulation of pedestrian crossings
   at specified intersections by appropriate signals. Better driver
   education and enforcement of the traffic code should not be
   overlooked.

b. Improved geometric designs and signalization at selected intersections where major traffic bottlenecks occur to balance the
   performance of the street junctions with that of the links in the
   network.

c. Abandoning the present policy of restricted entries for buses and
   jeepneys in favor of encouraging new capacity, within the limits
   of profitable competition, and new routes commensurate with
   population growth and the number of trips generated. Currently there is a shortage of 480 buses to accommodate the
   present level of traffic.[21] For the next five years projected population increases for the MMA would require a 5 percent annual
   expansion of the transport fleet, or about 150 new buses and
   750 new jeepneys a year. If private bus and jeepney operators
   are provided with easier entry, credit facilities, and financial concessions accorded to the Metropolitan Transit Corporation (such
   as exemptions from Board of Transport fees and import duties
   and foreign exchange restrictions on imported spare parts),

20. At the exchange rate of US$1.00=₱7.00.

21. Estimates based on data supplied by the Project Planning and Development Office of the Department of Public Works and Telecommunications.

they will be encouraged to expand and rehabilitate the fleet to provide a higher level of service.

Certain streets in Manila (Avenida Rizal and Taft Avenue, for example) have substantially more daily traffic than do similar streets in Western countries (Canada and Germany) where light rapid transit systems are being built at substantial public cost. Of course fiscal constraints are more acute in Metropolitan Manila. Nevertheless, a minimum program of road expansion is necessary to supplement the improved traffic management and expanded bus and jeepney operations and accommodate growing traffic volumes. An estimated ₱131 million (US$22.3 million) will be required to construct three grade-separated interchanges on C–4 with Japanese assistance and to complete circumferential roads C–2 and C–3.[22] In addition highest priority should be given to minor intersection improvements throughout the metropolitan area where major bottlenecks exist. Given the difficulty of acquiring rights-of-way in the city, the time required for detailed engineering, and limited financial resources, it will not be feasible to implement more than this minimum program in the next five years.

Any hope of coping with existing and future transport problems lies in a twofold approach. On the one hand a concerted effort should be made to increase the capacity of the existing facilities and build a viable public transport system through effective management and regulatory procedures as discussed above. On the other hand it is equally important that investment decisions and programs to reduce congestion be accompanied by a plan to deal with the underlying factors that generate growing volumes of traffic. Experience elsewhere suggests that excessive population density in a rapidly expanding urban area where housing is separated from employment centers will result in severe congestion no matter how large the supply of transit facilities (Tokyo and Madrid) or how efficient the street systems (large cities in the United States and Caracas).

Given the difficulty, if not impossibility, of obtaining sufficient funds to finance the needed transport infrastructure in Metropolitan Manila as well as secondary cities in the coming years, a substantial

22. The exchange rate of US$1.00=₱7.00 is used as cost estimates were made prior to the July 1975 devaluation of the peso. For the construction of three grade-separated interchanges the local cost is ₱70.9 million and foreign exchange US$3.62 million; the total cost of R–10, C–2, and C–3 is ₱60 million.

effort appears to be needed to combine transport with other urban programs. Spatial arrangements should be designed to minimize transport requirements and to support new residential-industrial centers outside the concentrated areas. The location, design, and redesign of streets and other transport infrastructure can help bring about new uses of land, create new sites for housing, shopping, and industry, and enhance the appearance of the city. Such spatial strategies are needed not only for Metropolitan Manila but for secondary cities as well, where there are more possibilities of shaping the demand for transport. Once such strategies are formulated, a host of fiscal and regulatory policy measures and implementing mechanisms must be instituted to carry out the programs. This will take a relatively long time and should be started now to assure a rational transport framework for the future.

Technical Note. The System of Local Government in the Philippines

For administrative purposes the Philippines is divided into 72 provinces, 61 chartered cities, and approximately 1,440 municipalities and municipal districts; [23] the latter include some 34,000 barrios or barangays.[24] The chartered city, unlike the municipality, is administratively independent from the province in which it is located and linked directly to the national government, as shown below:

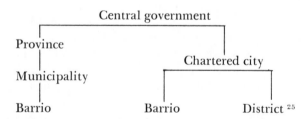

23. As of 1973.
24. A barrio or barangay is a group of dwellings that may constitute a hamlet, village, suburb, or even an urban district. Although there is some disagreement over the precise geographical definitions of each, the terms will be used interchangeably here.
25. Unlike the barrio, the district is purely an administrative unit with no government or budget.

Each province has jurisdiction over an average of twenty munici-palities, and each municipality is composed of the poblacion (the town proper) and about twenty or more barrios surrounding the town. In matters of local administration, services, and the like the poblacion completely dominates the municipality.

UNITS OF LOCAL GOVERNMENT

The office of the provincial governor was established under the Spanish and is probably one of the oldest political institutions in the Philippines.[26] Under Spanish colonial rule the provincial governor was appointed from Madrid to act as an agent for the governor-general. With the American colonial administration the provincial governor became an elective position,[27] and a provincial board was created which established a form of Filipino government with lim-ited powers at the local level. Until 1975 positions in local govern-ment—such as the provincial governor, provincial board, the munic-ipal mayor, and the municipal council—were elected offices. In February 1975 a referendum was passed which gave the president the authority to appoint all local officials after their terms expired in December 1975.

Provinces. The provincial governments have responsibility for the collection of taxes, the construction of highways, bridges, and public buildings, and the supervision of the municipal governments. Administratively the provinces have a governor, vice-governor, provincial board, treasurer, assessor, district auditor, registrar of deeds, Court of First Instance, superintendent of schools, district engineer, and health officer. Except for the provincial board, however, most of these officials are not under the executive authority of the governor but are representatives of departments and bureaus of the national government.

Municipalities. The municipal government is much smaller than the provincial. It has only a mayor, vice-mayor, council, treasurer,

---

26. J. M. Arguego, *Philippine Government in Action* (Manila: University Publishing Co., 1954), p. 618.

27. Suffrage was limited, however, to males who were 23 years or older; owned property valued at ₱500 or more; could read, write, and speak English or Spanish; and who had held local office prior to August 13, 1898. Arguego, *Philippine Government in Action*, p. 595.

secretary, justice of the peace, and police force. Before the development of the barrios, or barangays, as functioning governmental units,
the municipality was considered the core of local government in the
Philippines. With control over the local police force, local markets,
public morality, and public works, the municipal government came
into closer personal contact with the Filipino people than any other
level of government. The provincial government has traditionally
been considered the intermediary between the national and municipal governments with supervisory authority over the municipalities.
The municipality stands in a similar relationship to the barangays
but appears to have more direct control over local affairs, for each
municipal councilor has been traditionally responsible for the
supervision of a barangay. Recently attempts have been made to
give the barangays, through their captains, more influence in the
municipal councils.

Chartered cities.   Cities have usually been created from municipalities which were relatively heavily populated and had compara-
tively high incomes, although there are no fixed standards for
granting city charters. Makati, for instance, recently requested independence from Rizal province and city status, but was denied.
The new constitution (January 1973) states that only highly
urbanized cities will be allowed to become independent of their
provinces. The new local government code establishes detailed
criteria for defining highly urbanized cities and for creating, abolishing, merging, or altering boundaries.

Cities are governed by their charters, while provinces and municipalities are governed by the provincial and municipal codes as
amended by several acts and decrees: the Revised Administrative
Code (1917), the Local Autonomy Act (1959), and the Decentralization Act (1967). These acts increased the functions and powers,
especially taxing powers, of all local government units, including
cities. Because of the highly centralized government structure,
however, national officials, particularly the president, exercise considerable power at all levels.

The provisions regarding city departments or offices are generally the same in all city charters. They cover the city mayor; vice-
mayor; municipal board or city council; and different city departments, including those of finance, engineering and public works,

law, health, police, fire, and assessments.[28] The main difference
among cities relates to the number of departments. For example,
only Manila has a Department of Public Service specifically established in the charter. Other offices and agencies rendering services
in the cities are extensions of national government bureaus and
offices (for example, the city auditor and the city superintendent
of schools).[29]

Barangays. Initially the barangays or barrios were settlements of
30 to 100 families located primarily along the coast and rivers. They
are believed to have been independent, similar to the ancient Greek
city-states. With Spanish colonial rule the barangays were con-
federated and placed under a revenue official, the cabeza de barangay. The colonial administration gradually became centered in
towns or pueblos, and the barangays subsequently declined in importance. Under the American colonial administration the barangays began to emerge as a recognized—though still nominal—
form of local government. The Revised Administrative Code set
up barrio councils headed by a barrio lieutenant, the members
of which were appointed by the municipal council but had
virtually no power. In 1955 the code was amended to provide for
an elected barrio council consisting of a barrio lieutenant, one or
more vice-lieutenants, and three councilmen. The council was
given the powers of assembly, representation in the municipal level
of government, and authority to pass resolutions affecting the expenditure of barrio funds.[30]

Four years later, in 1959, the Barrio Autonomy Act recognized
the barrio as a legal entity and expanded its power to include
limited taxation for the development of the barrio and the enactment of local ordinances. In 1963 this act was revised, and assemblies were organized which could elect a barrio captain and six
councilmen for a four-year term. With the development of elected
councils and limited local autonomy, the potential for strengthening

---

28. The mayor and vice-mayor are both elected at large by qualified voters of
the city for a term of four years. Councilors are elected either at large or by
the district. City department heads are appointed by either the city mayor or
national officials.

29. See National Tax Research Center, *Delivery and Financing of Services in
Metro Manila* (Manila, 1974), pp. 26–30.

30. ILO, *Sharing in Development,* pp. 514–15.

the barangays was increased. In 1973 the Barangay or Citizens Assemblies were created under Presidential Decree 86 with the idea of further increasing local participation in the affairs of government.[31] A barangay secretariat was established under the Department of Local Government and Community Development (DLGCD) in February 1973 to handle matters concerning the barangays.[32]

POWERS OF LOCAL GOVERNMENTS

A distinctive feature of the Philippine government's administrative structure is the local governments' lack of power in the area of taxation and financing. Local governments are unduly dependent on national financial aid, though the larger units, particularly the cities, are less so.[33] The lack of financial independence has been one of the main stumbling blocks to more effective involvement in development on the part of local governments. Only a few services are undertaken locally; most are administered by the national government through its field agencies. The bulk of the resources that local governments do expend come from the national government. Although the Decentralization Act was intended to promote the autonomy of local units by increasing their powers and resources, during 1967–74 local revenues declined from 17 to 11 percent of combined government revenues, and expenditures declined from 20 to 15 percent of combined expenditures.[34]

The major reforms in local government taxation that were introduced in 1973 do not appear to have provided local governments with significantly more autonomy.[35] Presidential Decree 752, however, authorizes local governments to borrow from public financial institutions for priority development projects such as power plants, public markets, waterworks, irrigation, communications, and

---

31. F. E. Marcos, *Notes on the New Society of the Philippines* (n.p., 1973), p. 72.

32. The responsibilities of the barangay secretariat include settling barangay disputes, holding local referendums, overseeing the rice distribution system in August and September when supplies are low, organizing barangay medical councils, and implementating the rationing programs for DLGCD.

33. For a discussion of the barrios' access to resources, see Chapter 5.

34. R. M. Bird, D. Shimori, and R. S. Smith, "Taxes and Tax Reform in the Philippines," restricted-circulation draft of the International Monetary Fund (Washington, 1974), pp. 248–50.

35. These reforms are discussed in Chapter 15.

housing, as well as for budgetary needs. This represents an important step in the direction of increased financial responsibility for local governments and may strengthen local autonomy. Moreover the decree provides a mechanism whereby the national government can obtain external resources and lend them to local governments, a method of supporting local projects that foreign donors should consider. Of course the flow of resources to local governments must not be allowed to outstrip their capacity to use them prudently and to repay them. This will mean closer attention to proper accounting procedures among local governments than has been the case in the past.

The shortage of trained personnel in local and municipal government, their lack of financial resources, and their limited expenditure powers have been important constraints to development. One of the more important programs designed to help overcome these difficulties is the Provincial Development Assistance Project (PDAP), which was begun in the late 1960s. This project is supported by the United States Agency for International Development and is now being implemented in cooperation with the DLGCD. The program has been focusing on infrastructure (primarily roads and small irrigation systems), development planning, fiscal management, and tax administration. At the end of 1974 it covered 23 out of a total of 72 provinces. The PDAP program is being extended to five more provinces each year and to the municipal level.

5

Profile of the Rural Sector

ALMOST THREE-QUARTERS OF THE POPULATION in the Philippines lives in the rural areas, where social services are poor, economic activities limited, agricultural productivity low, and underemployment high. Characteristic of Philippine agriculture are the dominance of small farms and the pervasiveness of tenancy, particularly among rice and corn farmers. To remedy its past neglect, the national government is giving high priority to the economic development of rural areas. It will undoubtedly continue to play a dominant role in rural development, but efforts should be made to enlarge local responsibility for formulating and administering projects and programs.

Characteristics of the Rural Population

The proportion of the population in rural areas of the Philippines has declined from about 78 percent in the late 1940s to about 71 percent in 1975 (Table 5.1). During this period the rural population increased at an average rate of 2.7 percent a year, from 15 million in 1948 to 30 million in 1975. As in other developing countries, the natural rate of population growth in the Philippines is higher in rural than in urban areas; in 1970, for example, the rate of natural increase among the rural population was about 3.2 percent. Since the rural population has been growing at about 2.7 per-

Table 5.1. Distribution of Population between Urban and Rural Areas, 1948–75

(In thousands)

Year	Total population	Total urban	Total rural	Farming	Fishing and forestry	Other rural
			Rural population			
1948	19,234	4,298	14,936	11,436	850	2,650
1949	19,790	4,468	15,322	11,678	875	2,769
1950	20,362	4,644	15,718	11,922	902	2,894
1951	20,950	4,828	16,122	12,168	930	3,024
1952	21,555	5,018	16,537	12,419	958	3,160
1953	22,179	5,217	16,962	12,674	986	3,302
1954	22,820	5,423	17,397	12,932	1,015	3,450
1955	23,479	5,637	17,842	13,192	1,045	3,605
1956	24,158	5,860	18,298	13,454	1,076	3,768
1957	24,855	6,091	18,764	13,718	1,108	3,938
1958	25,574	6,332	19,242	13,985	1,141	4,116
1959	26,313	6,585	19,728	14,253	1,175	4,300
1960	27,088	6,861	20,227	14,522	1,210	4,495
1961	27,920	7,134	20,786	14,871	1,220	4,695
1962	28,777	7,418	21,359	15,224	1,230	4,905
1963	29,660	7,713	21,947	15,587	1,235	5,125
1964	30,570	8,020	22,550	15,955	1,240	5,355
1965	31,510	8,339	23,171	16,326	1,250	5,595
1966	32,476	8,671	23,805	16,648	1,307	5,850
1967	33,473	9,016	24,457	16,977	1,367	6,113
1968	34,501	9,375	25,126	17,310	1,429	6,387
1969	35,560	9,749	25,811	17,645	1,494	6,672
1970	36,684	10,140	26,544	18,009	1,565	6,970
1971	37,901	10,546	27,355	18,440	1,635	7,280
1972	38,991	10,967	28,024	18,709	1,710	7,605
1973	40,122	11,406	28,716	18,985	1,787	7,944
1974	41,297	11,862	29,435	19,270	1,867	8,298
1975	42,495	12,335	30,160	19,560	1,950	8,650

Note: Total urban population is that reported by the Bureau of the Census and Statistics (BCS), reduced by 16 percent to eliminate the portion classified as urban but engaged in agriculture (as revealed by BCS labor force surveys). Total rural population is the difference between total population and total urban. Benchmark years are 1948, 1960, and 1970; other years are by interpolation or extrapolation, except 1971–74 national totals which are from the medium projection of the National Census and Statistics Office (NCSO).

Sources: National Economic and Development Authority (NEDA), *Statistical Yearbook, 1975* Manila, 1975), p. 40; BCS, *The Growth of the Urban Population of the Philippines and Its Perspective* (Manila, 1973), p. 23; Mercedes B. Concepcion, "110 Million by the Year 2001," *Philippine Sociological Review*, vol. 18 (July–October 1970), p. 216; Ernesto M. Pernia, "The Philippine Urban Structure," Research Note no. 25 (Manila: University of the Philippines Population Institute, 1974; processed), table 3; Development Economics Department, World Bank, "Manila Urban Sector Survey," restricted-circulation memorandum, 1974, ch. 2, p. 7; NCSO, *Age and Sex Population Projections for the Philippines* (Manila, 1974), p. 34.

cent a year, this would indicate an annual rural-urban migration rate of about 0.5 percent. It is estimated that the growth rate of the rural population will decline to about 1.6 percent by 1985, reflecting a decline in the natural rate of increase to about 2.7 percent and an increase in the rural-urban migration rate to about 1.1 percent a year.[1]

INCOME DISTRIBUTION

During 1961–71 rural incomes probably increased by about 4.5 percent a year, and by 1971 the average family income in rural areas was about ₱4,400 (US$680) or about 75 percent of the national average. Since 1956, however, there has been a deterioration in the distribution of incomes among the rural population as measured by the Gini coefficient, which increased by 21 percent between 1957 and 1971 (Table 5.2). The share of reported income going to families with the lowest incomes (the bottom 40 percent) fell sharply, from 18 percent in 1957 to only 13 percent in 1971, while the share of families with the highest incomes (the top 20 percent) increased from 46 to 51 percent. These figures suggest that the incomes of the families in the lowest 40 percentile were growing very slowly—by less than one percent a year in real terms. Because incomes are frequently understated, however, it is not clear that these were the actual trends.[2]

A somewhat more balanced picture can be obtained from an analysis of changes in the distribution of family expenditures. There was only a slight deterioration in the share of expenditures for the lowest 40 percent over the 1961–71 period; thus consumption among the lowest 40 percent of the families probably increased by more than 2 percent a year in real terms. Levels of living probably improved somewhat for the lowest income groups in rural areas, but not as fast as for groups higher in the income distribution scale. Although the income and expenditure data indicate the number of rural families in the lowest 40 percentile, they do not reflect satisfactorily the extent of rural poverty. Using the concept of a "minimum needs" budget as set out in Chapter 11 [3] and

1. See Chapter 10 for a discussion of population growth.
2. See Chapter 3, note 14.
3. In Chapter 11, ₱650 per capita is given as the average threshold income for the Philippines, that is, the minimum amount needed to provide an ade-

Table 5.2. **Percentage Distribution of Total Family Income and Household Expenditure in All Philippines and Rural Areas**
(In percent)

Family income group	1957 Total	1957 Rural	1961 Total	1961 Rural	1965 Total	1965 Rural	1971 Total	1971 Rural
Distribution of total family income								
Lowest 20 percent	4.5	7.0	4.2	5.9	3.5	5.0	3.7	4.4
Second 20 percent	8.1	11.1	7.9	11.8	8.0	9.5	8.2	8.9
Third 20 percent	12.4	14.7	12.1	13.5	12.8	15.3	13.2	13.9
Fourth 20 percent	19.8	21.1	19.3	21.9	20.2	23.0	21.0	21.8
Top 20 percent	55.1	46.1	56.4	46.9	55.4	47.2	53.9	51.0
Top 10 percent	39.4	30.1	41.0	31.1	40.0	30.0	36.9	34.4
Distribution of total household expenditure								
Lowest 20 percent	5.05	n.a.	5.98	7.52	5.65	6.79	5.92	6.92
Second 20 percent	9.03	n.a.	10.32	12.65	10.25	12.23	10.18	12.08
Third 20 percent	13.02	n.a.	14.68	16.93	14.57	16.87	14.76	13.66
Fourth 20 percent	20.03	n.a.	21.03	22.97	21.10	23.20	21.98	22.45
Top 20 percent	52.88	n.a.	47.98	39.94	48.43	40.91	47.16	43.00
Top 10 percent	35.42	n.a.	31.66	24.30	32.49	24.29	30.81	26.71
Top 5 percent	23.38	n.a.	21.00	15.29	21.43	15.06	19.37	16.74
Gini coefficient	0.48	0.38	0.50	0.40	0.51	0.42	0.49	0.46

n.a.: Not available.
Source: BCS, *Family Income and Expenditure Survey* for various years.

adjusting this budget for cost of living differences between urban and rural areas, it is estimated that in 1971 about half of all rural families had incomes below that required to provide adequate nutrition and other essentials of life. On the same basis it is estimated that of all the families in the Philippines with less than the minimum needs budget over 80 percent are in rural areas.

Although existing income and expenditure data on the Philippines do not reveal a precise link between poverty, income, and

---

quate diet and other essential needs. To compare minimum needs in areas where living costs differ significantly, however, it was necessary to estimate different threshold incomes for Metropolitan Manila, other urban areas, and rural areas. This was done by using the Philippine-wide estimate of ₱650 as a base and applying it to the cost of living factors implicitly derived by Lucinda Abrera, "Philippine Poverty Thresholds," in Development Academy of the Philippines, *Measuring Philippine Welfare: Social Indicator Project* (Manila, 1975), ch. 5.

access to services, some of the characteristics of those in the bottom 40 percent of the national income profile can be established. Approximately 90 percent of this group, or 14 million people, reside in rural areas (Table 5.3). Put another way, the bottom 40 percent includes about half the total rural population but only 15 percent of those in urban areas. Most of these people are engaged in farming, but a substantial minority have important secondary earnings from nonagricultural sources. Very few families are either totally dependent on agriculture or, alternatively, receive no income at all from agriculture. For very poor rural families (those reporting annual incomes of ₱1,000 or less), who accounted for 22 percent of the total in 1971, fishing activities are a more important source of income than either agricultural or nonagricultural wages. Geographically, the rural population in the bottom 40 percent is concentrated in Eastern Visayas, Southwest Mindanao, and Bicol.

There are no specific data on the relationship between income

Table 5.3. Rural Families Classified by Level and Main Source of Income, 1971

Main source of income	Families in lower 40 percent		Families in upper 60 percent		Total families	
	Thousands	Percent	Thousands	Percent	Thousands	Percent
Farming	1,756	64.8	1,208	31.2	2,964	45.1
Self-employed	1,409	52.0	852	22.1	2,261	34.4
Wage labor	347	12.8	356	9.1	703	10.7
Forestry and fishing	165	6.1	117	3.0	282	4.3
Other occupations	388	14.3	900	23.4	1,288	19.6
Self-employed	190	7.0	231	5.9	421	6.4
Wage labor	198	7.3	669	17.5	867	13.2
Other sources	130	4.8	107	2.9	237	3.6
Agricultural rents	54	2.0	31	0.9	85	1.3
Other	76	2.8	76	2.0	152	2.3
Total rural families	2,439	90.0	2,332	60.5	4,771	72.6
Total urban and rural families	2,710	100.0	3,862	100.0	6,572	100.0

Note: The data presented here and in Table 5.4 were adjusted in two ways. First, all urban households reporting their main earnings from agriculture, forestry, and fishing were shifted into the rural category. Second, to allow for the fact that the surveys underestimate the national population, the number of families in each group was increased using the following ratios: for 1961, 1.0879; for 1965, 1.0403; and for 1971, 1.0355.

Source: Based on BCS, *Survey of Households Bulletin*, no. 34 (1971) and no. 22 (1965), and on *Philippine Statistical Survey of Households Bulletin*, no. 14 (1961).

levels and type of farming activities. In 1971–72, however, there were about one million rice farmers harvesting an average of 0.88 hectares of rice per farm. Even if their yields were as high as the national average for farms growing high-yield varieties under irrigation, their average gross income would have been only about ₱1,000 (US$150) per farm at 1972 prices. After allowing for a substantial amount of income from other crops (with the possible exception of sugar) and nonfarm sources, it would seem that a majority of these farm families would still be among the poorest. Lack of current data precludes any further breakdown of farming activities, but most of the other 400,000 self-employed farm families (Table 5.3) probably operate corn and coconut farms, with roughly equal numbers of each. At the same time, many small rice (and some corn) farms grow sugar as a second crop on part of their land, which gives a high gross income per hectare and supplements the income of farmers who are near sugar mills. This is perhaps the main explanation for the fact that, in 1960 at least, sugar was grown on a large number of farms not classified as sugar farms.

EMPLOYMENT

Production in the rural sector is dominated by agriculture, forestry, and fishing; other economic activities include mining, small-scale manufacturing (mainly for local markets), and a range of service industries. Farming is of course the main rural activity, and in 1975 almost 20 million people depended directly on it for their main source of income, the majority of them self-employed. As Table 5.4 indicates, almost 3 million families depended primarily on farming for their livelihood in 1971, and of these 2.3 million were self-employed.

Data indicating the size of the rural population dependent primarily on agricultural wages appear contradictory. According to the labor force survey conducted by the Bureau of the Census and Statistics (BCS), wage and salary employment in agriculture has remained relatively stable over the past decade and a half. In 1961, for example, there were about 920,000 laborers, in 1971 about 840,000, and in 1974 about 1 million.[4] The *Family Income and Expenditure Surveys* (Table 5.4) suggest that the number of families

4. Wage employment in sugarcane farming, currently estimated at about 400,000 workers, accounts for a major part of this group.

Table 5.4. Rural Families Classified by Main Source of Income, 1961, 1965, and 1971

Main source of income	1961		1965		1971	
	Thou-sands	Percent	Thou-sands	Percent	Thou-sands	Percent
Farming	2,500	51.9	2,663	49.1	2,964	45.1
Self-employed	2,056	42.7	2,118	39.5	2,261	34.4
Wage labor	444	9.2	515	9.6	703	10.7
Forestry and fishing	217	4.5	215	4.0	282	4.3
Other occupations	664	13.8	998	18.6	1,288	19.6
Self-employed	221	4.6	391	7.3	421	6.4
Wage labor	443	9.2	607	11.3	867	13.2
Other sources	169	3.5	154	2.9	237	3.6
Agricultural rents	49	1.0	85	1.6	85	1.3
Other	120	2.5	69	1.3	152	2.3
Total rural families	3,550	73.7	4,000	74.6	4,771	72.6
Total urban and rural families	4,815	100.0	5,363	100.0	6,572	100.0

Source: See Table 5.3.

primarily dependent on agricultural wages increased about 60 percent from roughly 440,000 in 1961 to 700,000 in 1971. These data are at variance with the labor force figures unless of course the average number of laborers per family had decreased to about 1.5 by 1971. At this stage it is impossible to say whether the number of "landless" laborers employed in agriculture has significantly increased, because the extent to which these families also operate farms is not known. The problem, however, does not appear to be as acute as in some other countries such as India and Indonesia.

Perhaps surprising is the growing importance of nonagricultural economic activities in rural areas. Between 1961 and 1971 the number of farm families with nonagricultural income grew about 5.6 percent a year, while the number dependent on agriculture grew only 1.7 percent a year. Agricultural employment (excluding fishing and forestry), which has historically grown at about 2.0 percent, is expected to expand about 1.7 percent a year for the next decade. This would mean that about 7.5 million people, or 38 percent of the total labor force, would be employed in agriculture by 1985. With the farm population growing at about 1.4 percent, about 22.5 million may then depend primarily on farming for a livelihood. Nonfarm employment is expected to increase about 4.5 percent a year, which would imply a total nonfarm population of about 15.0 million people in 1985. Thus the proportion of the total rural population depending primarily on incomes from nonfarm employment would rise from about 35 percent in 1975 to 40 percent in 1985.

AGRICULTURE AND THE STRUCTURE OF FARMING

In the Philippines rice, corn, and coconuts are the dominant crops and in 1960 accounted for almost 80 percent of all farms, 86 percent of the farm population, and 77 percent of the physical farm area. Their relative importance has not changed significantly since then, and about 16 million people probably still depend on these crops for their main source of income. Moreover it is on these types of farms that the majority of the low-income households are to be found. Other farming activities, including sugar, abaca, and livestock production, account for the remaining farm population. The nonfarm population directly dependent on fishing and forestry amounts to another 2 million people.

The 1960 census provides information on the characteristics of farming in the Philippines, but since then rapid population growth and the decreasing potential for expanding the area of land under cultivation have caused important structural changes. Because comprehensive data are not yet available from the 1970 census, the World Bank has estimated these changes from a variety of sources. Although some of the specific details reported below may be modified when more accurate information becomes available, the broad outline of trends over the past decade is probably accurate. One further word of caution is needed. References to rice farms, corn farms, coconut farms, and so on, are customary, but more than one crop is often cultivated, and quite a few rice, sugar, or coconut farms would probably be more aptly described as mixed farming enterprises. As an illustration, there were only 18,000 so-called sugar farms in the Philippines in 1960, but sugar was grown on 53,000 farms.[5]

5. According to the 1960 census of agriculture, a farm consisted of one or more parcels of land, irrespective of ownership, which could be located in different barrios or even in different municipalities. The farms were enumerated in the districts where the farm operators resided. When a parcel of land with one owner was divided among and operated separately by several tenants, the

From the standpoint of the contribution to value added and to employment, rice cultivation has been the single most important economic activity in the Philippines. According to the 1960 census there were 1.46 million farms growing rice, which accounted for 68 percent of all farms in the Philippines and covered 2.7 million hectares of paddy. Of these, 1.04 million or 71 percent were exclusively rice farms, accounting for about 80 percent of the total rice area and 84 percent of total rice production in 1960. The rest of the rice output came from coconut, corn, and other farms. The degree of specialization was especially noticeable among rice farms in the major river basins of the Philippines, which accounted for 86 percent of the total lowland production. Upland farming, in contrast, was more diversified; a third of upland rice production in 1960 was accounted for by other than rice farms.

Another important characteristic of Philippine agriculture has been the dominance of small farms. In 1960, 74 percent of all farms were less than four hectares in size and 41 percent were under two hectares. Many small farms of less than one hectare engaged in such specialties as poultry, hogs, and fruit. On farms of one to four hectares, the three major crops—rice, corn, and coconuts—accounted for 65 to 70 percent of the total value of output. But farms below four hectares accounted for only 35 percent of the total farm area in 1960, and those under two hectares for only 12 percent. Although less than one percent of the farms were more than 24 hectares in size, they accounted for 16 percent of the area in 1960 (Table 5.5).

There have been some important changes in the size distribution of farms since 1960, and to a considerable extent these changes reflect the growing population pressure on the arable land available. Perhaps the nature of the change is best illustrated in rice farming. The Bureau of Agricultural Economics estimates that in 1972 there were 1.69 million rice farms cultivating about 2.63 mil-

---

farms operated by different members of a household were reported together land actually cultivated by each tenant was enumerated as one farm. Separate as one farm. A crop farm was typed according to the crop occupying 50 percent or more of the cultivated area; between two temporary crops usually covering 50 percent or more of the tilled area, priority was given to the one that contributed most to total farm production and the value of output. See Bureau of the Census and Statistics, *Census of the Philippines, 1960: Agriculture* (Manila, May 1965), vol. 2.

lion hectares.[6] This suggests that the number of rice farms increased a little more than 4 percent a year during 1960–72, but the area cultivated grew only 1.7 percent a year. Average farm size must have declined about 2.4 percent a year, indicating that many have been subdivided into smaller units since 1960. It is probably not just coincidence that the decline in the average cultivated area per rice farm is about the same as the growth rate of the farm population during the period (about 2.2 percent). This decline has, however, been almost exactly offset by an annual increase of about 2.7 percent in average rice yields per hectare since 1960.

The predominance of small farmers in rice growing is dramatically illustrated by the fact that in 1960 about 77 percent of all rice farms were less than four hectares, and by 1972 according to data from the Bureau of Agricultural Economics 94 percent were less than four hectares and almost 70 percent were less than two hectares (Table 5.6). Moreover the area planted with rice on rice farms larger than seven hectares was only about 3 percent of the total cultivated rice area. In other words, large rice farms were not a significant feature of the rice industry by 1972. Their virtual disappearance, especially in densely populated regions like Central Luzon, appears to have been the result of the subdivision of farmland in the face of a rapidly expanding farm population, although some of the larger farms may have switched to more profitable sugar growing. This process of subdivision has potentially important implications for farm incomes and for the design of programs to raise land productivity.

Not much information is available about the current structure of corn farming, but there were probably about 500,000 corn farms in 1972. Some subdivision of farms may have taken place in the more densely populated, major corn-growing regions such as the Visayas and Southern Tagalog. In Mindanao, however, where the area planted with corn has expanded, the average size of corn farms has probably not changed as much. In the case of coconuts, the area planted has doubled from 1.1 million hectares in 1960 to 2.2 million hectares in 1974. Some of this growth undoubtedly comes from the expansion of existing coconut farms, but a large

6. No data were available for nonrice farms growing rice, but the total area harvested in 1971–72 was about 3,250,000 hectares, suggesting that these farms cultivated about 600,000 hectares.

Table 5.5. Distribution of Farms by Major Crop, Size, and Tenancy, 1960

Category	Rice Number[a]	Rice Area[b]	Corn Number[a]	Corn Area[b]
Hectares				
Less than 2.0	426.0	463.0	206.8	200.7
2.0–3.9	382.0	963.0	104.4	255.4
4.0–6.9	122.6	609.5	33.0	166.3
7.0–9.9	72.6	454.9	21.7	135.4
10.0–23.9	35.6	436.6	12.1	147.9
24.0 and above	3.1	185.1	0.8	43.6
Total	1,041.9	3,112.1	378.8	949.3
Tenancy				
Owner	385.2	1,399.6	136.6	481.7
Part owner	164.6	528.2	47.8	144.6
Tenant	479.1	1,089.3	191.7	303.2
Other	13.1	95.0	2.7	19.8
Total	1,041.9	3,112.1	378.8	949.3
Percentage composition				
Hectares				
Less than 2.0	40.9	14.9	54.6	21.1
2.0–3.9	36.7	30.9	27.6	26.9
4.0–6.9	11.7	19.6	8.7	17.5
7.0–9.9	7.0	14.6	5.7	14.3
10.0–23.9	3.4	14.0	3.2	15.6
24.0 and above	0.3	6.0	0.2	4.6
Total	100.0	100.0	100.0	100.0
Tenancy				
Owner	37.0	44.9	36.1	50.8
Part owner	15.8	17.0	12.6	15.2
Tenant	46.0	35.0	50.6	31.9
Other	1.3	3.1	0.7	2.1
Total	100.0	100.0	100.0	100.0

a. In thousands.
b. In thousands of hectares.
Source: BCS, *Census of the Philippines, 1960: Agriculture* (Manila, 1965), vol. 2.

number of new farms have been established since 1960, especially in Mindanao. By 1972 there were probably about 520,000 coconut farms with a dependent population of perhaps 3 million people.

Unlike the rice, corn, and coconut sectors the sugar industry is dominated by large estates. In 1960, for example, farms larger than 100 hectares accounted for 50 percent of the total sugar area cultivated and 56 percent of the industry's output. Yet only about one

Coconut		Other		Total	
Number[a]	*Area*[b]	*Number*[a]	*Area*[b]	*Number*[a]	*Area*[b]
138.9	147.7	120.2	108.6	891.9	920.0
140.2	358.8	84.8	220.3	711.4	1,797.5
71.2	371.7	41.4	220.1	268.2	1,367.6
49.0	318.5	30.5	198.4	173.8	1,107.2
36.0	470.8	23.6	299.5	107.3	1,354.8
4.9	271.1	4.8	725.6	13.6	1,255.4
233.1	1,938.6	354.8	1,772.5	2,166.2	7,772.5
266.6	1,222.7	179.3	1,029.3	967.7	4,133.3
55.9	268.7	42.5	198.5	310.9	1,140.0
115.4	388.6	78.3	219.1	864.5	2,000.0
2.3	58.6	5.1	325.6	23.1	499.0
440.2	1,938.6	305.2	1,772.5	2,166.2	7,772.5
31.6	7.6	39.4	6.1	41.2	11.8
31.8	18.5	27.8	12.4	32.8	23.1
16.2	19.2	13.5	12.4	12.4	17.6
11.1	16.4	10.0	11.2	8.0	14.3
8.2	24.3	7.7	16.9	5.0	17.4
1.1	14.0	1.6	41.0	0.6	15.8
100.0	100.0	100.0	100.0	100.0	100.0
60.6	63.1	58.7	58.1	44.7	53.2
12.7	13.9	14.0	11.2	14.3	14.7
26.2	20.0	25.6	12.4	39.9	25.7
0.5	3.0	1.7	18.3	1.1	6.4
100.0	100.0	100.0	100.0	100.0	100.0

percent of the farms were in this category. Conversely, 78 percent of all farms growing sugar were less than four hectares in size but accounted for only 19 percent of the cultivated area and 15 percent of the output. As these data suggest, yields on large sugar farms were almost 40 percent higher than those on small farms in 1960, contrary to rice yields which were higher on smaller farms. The only recent data about the size distribution of sugar farms are for

Table 5.6. Distribution by Size and Tenancy of Farms Cultivating Rice, 1960 and 1972

| | All farms growing rice, 1960 | | | Farms with rice as a major crop | | | | | |
| | | | | 1960 | | | 1972 | | |
Category	Number[a]	Area planted with rice[b]	Average area[c]	Number[a]	Area planted with rice[b]	Average area[c]	Number[a]	Area planted with rice[b]	Average area[c]
Hectares									
0–1.9	526.7	496.8	0.94	425.9	397.7	0.93	1,161.8	1,024.4	0.88
2.0–3.9	524.0	966.6	1.84	382.0	800.5	2.10	422.0	1,019.4	2.42
4.0–6.9	201.6	519.4	2.58	122.6	415.1	3.39	92.1	436.8	4.74
7.0–9.9	130.3	350.8	2.69	72.6	279.7	3.85	10.1	78.8	7.80
10.0–23.9	75.9	270.0	3.56	35.3	216.3	6.13	4.2	53.8	12.81
24.0 and above	9.9	126.8	12.86	3.5	100.5	29.05	0.4	19.5	48.75
Total	1,468.4	2,730.4	1.86	1,041.9	2,209.9	2.12	1,690.6	2,632.7	1.56
Tenancy									
Owner	614.4	1,077.7	1.75	385.2	772.9	2.01	665.1	988.8	1.49
Part owner	240.1	463.4	1.93	164.6	359.8	2.19	299.1	490.9	1.64
Tenant	596.9	1,123.8	1.88	479.1	1,023.7	2.14	726.4	1,143.3	1.57
Other	17.0	65.6	3.86	13.0	53.4	4.11	n.a.	n.a.	n.a.
Total	1,468.4	2,730.4	1.86	1,041.9	2,209.9	2.12	1,690.6	2,632.7	1.56

n.a.: Not available.
a. In thousands.
b. In thousands of hectares, based on World Bank calculations and 1960 agricultural census.
c. In hectares.
Source: 1960 data from BCS; 1972 data from the Bureau of Agricultural Economics.

crop year 1972–73. The available information suggests some dramatic changes since 1960, with a substantial increase in the number of sugar farms of 10.0 to 99.9 hectares. In 1960 this group accounted for about 8 percent of the sugar farms and 19 percent of the cultivated area; by 1973 they accounted for about 28 percent of the farms and probably for most of the 260,000 hectare growth in the cultivated area that occurred since 1960. At the same time there has been a sharp drop in the relative importance of sugar farms of less than 5 hectares. This increase in medium-size sugar farms may have stemmed from the conversion of medium-size rice farms (and perhaps corn farms) in the 1960s, when the Philippine quota in the United States market increased and the relative profitability of sugar cultivation grew as a result of the 1960–62 exchange rate adjustments.

Another important characteristic of Philippine agriculture is the pervasiveness of farm tenancy. In 1960, for example, about 865,000 farms, or 40 percent of all farms in the Philippines, were operated by tenants—one of the highest rates in Asia. But tenant farms accounted for only 26 percent of the total farm area, their average size being relatively low. Rice and corn farms accounted for about 77 percent of all tenant farms in 1960 (Table 5.5), and the highest incidence of tenancy was found in Central Luzon and Southern Tagalog, which are both important rice-growing areas. Despite the apparently rapid subdivision of rice farms the rate of tenancy did not increase in rice-farming areas. By 1972 the number of tenant-operated rice and corn farms had increased to about one million, but the rate of tenancy—about 45 percent of all rice and corn farms—stayed about the same as in 1960. Because of the dominant position of the large sugar estates, about half the sugar production in 1960 came from owner-operated farms. Tenant-operated sugar farms (as distinct from tenant-operated farms growing sugar) accounted for almost 70 percent of the sugar farms in 1960 but probably accounted for only about 20 percent of the cultivated area and output. There are no current data about the extent of tenancy in the sugar industry, but the number of tenants is probably small in comparison with rice, corn, and coconut farms.

RURAL INDUSTRIES AND SERVICES

Data from the BCS labor force surveys, which provide the best indication of employment, suggest that the rural population engaged in nonfarm work depends on a variety of industrial, commercial, and service occupations for a livelihood. Industrial activity employed about 40 percent of the rural labor force not in agriculture, forestry, or fishing in 1973. The next most important source of employment was commerce (about 26 percent in 1973) and then government (about 13 percent). The remaining 21 percent of the labor force in 1973 was employed in a variety of occupations, including transportation, domestic, personal, and other services. In other words, the nonfarm rural population is primarily engaged in service occupations.

Rural employment in industry and services is closely linked with, and in fact arises in response to, the needs of farm households. There are probably few backward or forward linkages among these local activities. They typically produce for final household demand, using raw materials and inputs of nonlocal origin. The manufacture of producer goods is not common because it usually requires a larger market than the local one. Of course this type of production may exist in some locations, but nonagricultural activity among the rural population is essentially dependent on the level of agricultural incomes in the area rather than on the demand from a nonlocal market. Moreover the average income of nonfarm families appears to be closely linked to that of farm families in each region.

The relatively rapid growth in service occupations stems partly from the strong demand and relatively large outlays for services—especially transportation and medical care—among rural households as opposed to their relatively weak demand for industrial consumer goods. This pattern of demand, which is expected to continue, is the guiding force in an increasingly important structural transformation in rural areas in the Philippines.[7] The quick growth of service employment has clearly eased the pressures of migration in major urban areas. As indicated earlier, rapid expansion of the rural nonfarm population will probably continue, thus raising the policy issue of employment prospects for this group.

7. There is relatively little information available about the occupational mobility of the rural population. One study is by C. M. G. Cuento, "Occupational Mobility in the Rural Setting," *Journal of Agricultural Economics and Development*, vol. 2, no. 2 (July 1972), pp. 352–76.

PATTERNS OF RURAL EXPENDITURES

Because future patterns of rural production and employment will be strongly influenced by the demand of rural households, an understanding of their consumption preferences is important for the subsequent discussion of rural development strategies. Total household expenditures in rural areas probably increased by about 5 percent a year in real terms during 1961–71, and rural households may have accounted for almost 60 percent of total private consumption in the Philippines in 1971.[8] Since the rural population was growing at about 2.7 percent a year in that period, per capita expenditures were probably rising at close to 1.5 percent a year.

As Table 5.7 indicates, food, particularly cereals, is by far the most important item in the rural household budget, accounting for about 61 percent of total expenditures. Alcohol, tobacco, clothing, and consumer durables account for another 14 percent; housing and utilities for 10 percent; and other services for most of the remaining 15 percent. There appears to be a strong demand among rural households for meat and dairy products, miscellaneous food preparations, housing, medical services, education, transportation, and other services. These items all have expenditure elasticities greater than unity.[9]

A noteworthy trend is the decline in the share of the household budget allocated to clothing and the relatively stable share devoted to consumer durables. Only about 8 percent of total rural outlays are allocated to these items, but rural demand accounts for more than half the total Philippine expenditures on these products. The very slow growth in this rural demand during the past decade may explain in part the sluggish growth of these industries during the 1960s. The reasons for the slow growth are not clear, but in the case of consumer durables, the lack of electricity in most areas has probably limited the demand for appliances. The present rural

8. BCS, *Survey of Households Bulletin* no. 34 (1971), and *Philippine Statistical Survey of Households Bulletin*, no. 14 (1961).

9. That is, a one percent increase in total expenditure results in an increase of more than one percent for these items, because outlays for other items increase by less than one percent (for example, alcohol and tobacco, utilities, and some food items).

Table 5.7. Distribution of Expenditures and Expenditure Elasticities for Rural Families

| Expenditure | Percentage distribution of family expenditures[a] | | | Expenditure elasticities | | |
	1961	1965	1971	I[b]	II[c]	III[d]
Food	61.3	62.8	61.5	1.02	0.96	0.54
Alcohol and tobacco	6.8	5.9	5.9	0.70	0.85	0.84
Clothing	7.6	7.0	6.3	0.61	1.14	1.44
Consumer durables	2.2	1.9	2.1	0.91	1.20	
Housing	5.6	5.0	6.8	1.39	1.01	1.28
Utilities	4.1	3.7	3.6	0.73	0.73	
Transport	1.6	1.8	2.0	1.44	1.35	2.58
Medical care	1.6	1.7	1.7	1.13	1.14	1.71
Education	2.2	2.7	3.1	1.68	1.81	
Other services	6.1	6.7	6.3	1.06	1.30	1.70
Taxes and gifts	0.9	0.8	0.7	0.47	n.a.	
Total	100.0	100.0	100.0			

a. Data from BCS, *Family Income and Expenditure Survey* for the relevant years.

b. World Bank calculation of aggregate expenditure elasticity using ratio of percentage change during 1961–71 of specific items to that of total expenditure, at 1965 constant prices, after first adjusting the expenditure survey data to correct for underestimation of population and expenditures.

c. Unpublished per capita expenditure elasticities estimated by A. Kelly, Duke University, and J. Williamson, University of Wisconsin, from BCS, *Family Income and Expenditure Survey, 1965*. Elasticities are derived from a log-linear expenditure function for all commodity groups except alcohol and tobacco and education, which were from linear expenditure functions.

d. Data from Edita A. Tan and Gwendolyn R. Tecson, "Patterns of Consumption in the Philippines," Institute of Economic Development and Research, University of the Philippines, Discussion Paper no. 74-9, July 15, 1974; processed. Estimates used a double log expenditure function.

electrification program could stimulate demand for these products in the years ahead.

Policies Affecting Rural Development

The potential impact of the government's present rural development strategy on the distribution of incomes in the rural sector needs to be considered.[10] As suggested in Chapter 2, average output per laborer in agriculture will probably grow more slowly than the

10. See Chapters 6 and 7.

national average. Changes in the relative position of average farm incomes will depend on the behavior of the terms of trade in agriculture and on the government's fiscal policies, particularly on the taxation of agricultural commodities. The future direction of the internal terms of trade is difficult to project. The task of increasing food production in line with domestic demand will not be easy, however; and to the extent that there are shortfalls, the terms of trade could be expected to continue moving in favor of agriculture, particularly the food sector. This could partly offset the projected relative decline in output per laborer in agriculture. The outcome will also be influenced by the continued rapid growth in nonfarm employment in rural areas, as well as by the success of public programs to expand services to the rural population.

Within the rural sector itself there appear to be opposing forces at work that will influence the distribution of growth benefits. On the one hand, the intensification that is needed to increase agricultural production will probably benefit only a limited number of farmers. On the other, the government's program of agrarian reform is redistributing some assets in the rural sector, and the plan is to convert all tenant rice and corn farmers into leaseholders or amortizing owners. This program will significantly affect the incomes of many tenant farmers, but at present levels of productivity the amount of the income transfer from landlords to tenants is very small in relation to total rural income. Thus the impact of the program on distribution within the rural sector will be negligible for some years to come. In the longer term, the redistribution effect could be significant if land reform is rigorously implemented and supported by major efforts to increase production on small farms. More effective taxation of agricultural land could also have a redistributive impact. As discussed below, however, the present heavy reliance on agricultural export taxation will need to be gradually reduced by more effective taxation on agricultural land or incomes.

For the rest of the 1970s and perhaps for a period in the 1980s, it is unlikely that there will be any improvement in the distribution of incomes in the rural sector. This does not suggest that the situation will necessarily deteriorate any further, but without stronger measures than are presently contemplated, the currently uneven distribution of incomes both within rural areas and between rural and urban areas will probably persist.

AGRARIAN REFORM

Because of the history of peasant unrest in the Philippines and the high incidence of tenancy, especially in Central Luzon, there has been a long-standing government commitment to land reform programs.[11] Prior to 1972 the government's efforts focused primarily on rent reductions and the conversion of sharecroppers to leaseholders. Little progress was made in the implementation of the reforms, primarily because of landlord opposition, insufficient financing, and poor administration. In 1972 the entire country was declared a land reform area, and tenants on rice and corn land were deemed owners of the land they cultivated.[12] An ambitious program, the reform will potentially cover about 956,000 tenants, 431,000 landlords, and about 1.5 million hectares.[13]

The rationale for land reform is that it would help raise productivity by providing the incentive of ownership to former tenants, and that it would have a beneficial impact on the distribution of incomes in rural areas. The implications of a change in tenure for farm productivity are not clear, but there is some evidence to suggest that by itself such change may have little, if any, effect on output. For example, surveys conducted in Central Luzon indicate that there is little or no difference in productivity between a tenanted and an owner-cultivated farm.[14] The real constraint on productivity is the inadequacy of supporting services and access to irrigation. Significant changes in yields will depend on improving these production inputs. Recognizing that a change from tenant to owner status would mean the loss of landlord support (in obtaining credit, seeds, and other inputs), the government has been making

11. A more complete discussion of agrarian reform is given in Appendix A.

12. Although Presidential Decree 2 declared the entire country a land reform area, the 1963 Agrarian Reform Code remains the basic land reform law. The 1963 code technically applies to all crops except tree crops, such as coconuts, and sugar, which are covered by Republic Act 1199 (1954), amended in 1959.

13. In the Republic of China, which is often cited as an example of a successful land reform, the program covered an area (144,000 hectares) only one-tenth the size of that in the Philippines, with about one-fifth the number of tenants (195,000) and about one-fourth the number of landlords (106,000). The entire program was carried out over a five-year period, from 1949 to 1954.

14. See Mahar Mangahas, Virginia A. Miralao, and Romana P. de los Reyes, *Tenants, Lessees, Owners: Welfare Implications of Tenure Changes* (Manila: Institute of Philippine Culture, 1974).

a vigorous effort to provide the necessary services through a newly organized cooperative movement and programs of supervised credit —Masagana 99 for rice farmers and Masaganang Maisan for corn farmers. A prerequisite for transferring land titles to tenants is membership in a recognized farmers' cooperative, which will provide marketing facilities, credit, and other production inputs. The cooperative movement appears to be making progress, but much more needs to be done to ensure that the tenant farmers receive the necessary supporting services.[15]

Although a change in tenure would probably not affect farm productivity, it could have a significant impact on individual incomes. If there is no difference in productivity and if incomes are affected only by changes in annual payments for the land, the income of a sharecropper who had become an amortizing owner could increase by as much as 80 percent in terms of present value over a thirty-year period (see Table 5.8). In other words, an amortizing owner's income in real terms could be double that of a sharecropper's after fifteen years.[16]

Implementation of the present land reform could benefit 6 to 7 million people, or almost a quarter of the entire rural population. Inasmuch as two-thirds of all tenant family incomes probably fall into the bottom 40 percent of the national income scale, land reform's potential for increasing tenant income makes a strong case for pressing forward with the present program. But these calculations do not take productivity into account. Little detailed

15. Kenneth Parsons writes that: "Land reform, which provides only land to the tiller, is of minor significance without access to markets and adequate credit." See "Land Reform and Agricultural Development," in *Land Tenure*, Kenneth H. Parsons and others, eds. (Madison: University of Wisconsin Press, 1956), p. 10. Philip M. Raup notes: "The Egyptian experience also illustrates the crucial importance of supporting land reform by programs of government assistance through cooperatives, community development programs and supervised agricultural credit. It is one of the few instances in which a distribution of land was followed by a vigorous attempt to provide guidance to new land owners on the scale needed." See "Land Reform and Agricultural Development," in *Agricultural Development and Economic Growth*, Herman M. Southworth and Bruce F. Johnston, eds. (Ithaca: Cornell University Press, 1967), p. 286.

16. See technical note to this chapter. For a discussion of how the redistribution of income might affect consumption, see M. R. Laforteza and T. M. Reyes, "How Some Rice Farmers Used Their Increased Incomes" (National Food and Agriculture Council, Special Studies Division Paper no. 74-28, September 1974; processed).

Table 5.8. Estimated Net Incomes of Land Reform Beneficiaries
(In pesos)

Year	1.0 Hectare farms (rain-fed)			2.5 Hectare farms (rain-fed)			2.5 Hectare farms (irrigated)		
	Sharecropper	Leaseholder	Amortizing owner	Sharecropper	Leaseholder	Amortizing owner	Sharecropper	Leaseholder	Amortizing owner
Current prices									
1975	560	840	708	1,750	2,625	2,213	2,585	3,877	3,076
1980	884	1,325	1,355	2,778	4,167	4,269	4,138	6,207	6,183
1985	1,406	2,108	2,399	4,402	6,602	7,516	6,617	9,926	11,141
1990	2,226	3,338	4,451	6,967	10,451	13,934	10,548	15,821	21,095
2004	8,018	12,026	16,035	25,341	38,011	50,681	39,096	58,643	78,191
Constant 1975 prices[a]									
1975	560	840	708	1,750	2,625	2,213	2,585	3,877	3,076
1980	616	923	944	1,935	2,903	2,974	2,882	4,324	4,307
1985	682	1,023	1,164	2,136	3,203	3,647	3,211	4,816	5,406
1990	752	1,128	1,504	2,355	3,532	4,709	3,565	5,347	7,129
2004	916	1,374	1,832	2,894	4,342	5,789	4,466	6,698	8,931
Present value over thirty-year period[b]	14,536	21,803	25,941	45,613	68,419	81,433	68,960	103,439	121,996

a. Deflation rate of 7.5 percent.
b. Discount rate of 10 percent.
Source: See technical note to this chapter.

information is available on the agricultural conditions of tenanted rice and corn farms—that is, the extent of supporting services, average yields, and the irrigated area (though the World Bank estimates the latter to be about 40 percent of the 1.5 million hectares under the program). If the productivity of the farms could be raised by improving services, the long-term impact of the reform would be even more significant.

TERMS OF TRADE BETWEEN URBAN AND RURAL AREAS

It is important for rural development that the overall relationship between input and output prices within agriculture, and the terms of trade between agriculture and other sectors of the economy, should be such as to stimulate growth in production. The government has from time to time pursued specific policies with respect to individual agricultural commodities,[17] but it has not adopted any overall policy with respect to agricultural prices and the terms of trade.

Nevertheless there have been rather distinctive movements in the prices of agricultural products relative to those of other sectors (Table 5.9). Prior to 1960 there was a tendency toward slight improvement in the terms of trade for the nonagricultural sector (or urban sector, as it will be loosely referred to below). Since about 1960 this trend has been reversed in a rather dramatic way. Owing partly to shortfalls of food supply as a consequence of the relative stagnation in agriculture, and partly to increased demand because of rapid urban population growth, the urban sector's terms of trade have steadily worsened. During 1960–74 the terms of trade for the food-producing sector in agriculture improved by a massive 70 percent, or at an average rate of 3.7 percent a year.[18] That is to say, since the early 1970s the urban sector has had to pay more for the goods that it has acquired from the agricultural sector. The resulting redistribution of income from urban to rural areas has helped prevent the disparity in incomes from becoming even larger.

This form of redistribution has been somewhat regressive, however. The burden has probably fallen most heavily on the lower

---

17. These are discussed in Chapter 6.

18. For the agricultural sector as a whole (that is, including nonfood production), the improvement has been almost equally dramatic, with the terms of trade improving by about 2.8 percent a year since 1960.

Table 5.9. Terms of Trade of the Agricultural and Food Sectors
(1965 = 100.0)

Year	Agricultural terms of trade			Food terms of trade		
	Agricultural prices	Nonagricultural prices	Terms of trade	Food prices	Nonfood prices	Terms of trade
1950	78.7	68.2	1.157	72.4	86.5	0.837
1951	76.7	69.1	1.110	81.8	88.5	0.924
1952	72.3	68.8	1.051	78.5	85.5	0.918
1953	68.2	68.3	0.999	72.8	83.7	0.870
1954	64.3	67.2	0.957	70.0	82.3	0.851
1955	67.2	65.7	1.023	69.4	81.1	0.856
1956	67.9	67.2	1.010	69.9	83.5	0.837
1957	69.8	70.0	0.997	74.2	84.7	0.876
1958	69.3	72.5	0.956	76.2	85.7	0.890
1959	70.8	73.6	0.962	70.5	87.2	0.808
1960	73.9	77.4	0.955	75.2	89.0	0.845
1961	75.3	80.4	0.937	80.5	90.5	0.890
1962	82.2	85.6	0.960	79.5	93.1	0.854
1963	90.7	92.2	0.984	88.7	95.4	0.930
1964	96.0	95.9	1.001	97.6	97.7	0.999
1965	100.0	100.0	100.0	100.0	100.0	1.000
1966	106.4	105.9	1.005	111.0	103.5	1.072
1967	116.4	110.6	1.052	113.2	106.4	1.064
1968	126.8	114.8	1.105	113.2	108.6	1.042
1969	140.3	119.1	1.178	114.5	110.9	1.032
1970	161.7	135.7	1.192	138.2	127.1	1.087
1971	199.0	150.3	1.324	175.7	142.3	1.235
1972	222.7	163.3	1.364	203.0	151.1	1.343
1973	250.3	188.1	1.331	228.5	168.2	1.359
1974	344.4	245.4	1.403	322.4	227.8	1.415

Note: The agricultural price index is the implicit price deflator for net domestic value added by agriculture, forestry, and fishing. The price index for nonagricultural products is the implicit price deflator for net domestic value added by all sectors except agriculture, forestry, and fishing. The food price index is the wholesale price index of locally produced food for home consumption in Manila. The nonfood price index is the weighted average of consumer price indexes for areas outside Manila for clothing, housing, and miscellaneous items, weighted as they enter the combined consumer price index. (Prior to 1957 corresponding items from the Manila consumer price index are used.)

Sources: Agricultural sector terms of trade are based on national accounts data supplied by NEDA. Food sector terms of trade are based on data supplied by the Central Bank of the Philippines.

income groups in urban areas, since they account for a large share of total outlays on food and typically spend a much larger proportion of their budget on food than do higher income groups. Since the average income of the lower income households in urban areas is not very different from that of many farm families, the redistribution has tended to be from one low-income group to another. The equivalent of about 0.5 percent of gross national product is currently being transferred to the food-producing sector as a result of this improvement in the terms of trade.

While it may not be necessary or practical for the government to adopt an overall policy with respect to the terms of trade between the rural and urban sectors, close attention to some particular aspects will probably be needed. The government has tried to control increases in the prices of basic foods in order to stabilize the cost of living in urban areas; at the same time it has recognized that a gradual increase in food prices is necessary to provide production incentives to farmers and to adjust to world market conditions. The recent food shortages, however, have made it difficult for the government to control price increases, and limited public resources have ruled out the possibility of providing subsidies for food production on anything more than an intermittent basis.

As long as chronic food shortages persist in the Philippines, food prices will tend to rise more rapidly than prices of other products. This problem is probably best dealt with by placing the main emphasis on expanding food production. It is therefore essential that the prices received by farmers provide sufficient incentives for them to adopt the improved technologies and farming practices needed to raise output. This will require continuing close attention to the interrelationships between product and input prices and to the impact of commodity taxation. A unit should be set up within one of the government's departments to undertake a comprehensive analysis of agricultural price policies. The establishment of agribusiness desks in the office of the Secretary of Agriculture, with representatives of the private sector, may help provide the government with the information necessary to implement effective agricultural price policies.

IMPACT OF FISCAL POLICIES ON THE RURAL SECTOR

Fiscal policies offer one means of influencing the distribution of growth benefits between urban and rural areas and within the rural sector itself. The government has not as yet had any consistent approach to fiscal policy in relation to its rural development strategies, and in fact little information is available about the past redistributive impact of government taxation and expenditure policies on the rural sector.[19] The incidence of taxation in the Philippines as a whole is relatively low and regressive. This is probably as true for rural as for urban areas; unfortunately no data are available about the extent of direct and indirect taxation of rural incomes and wealth. Perhaps the most important forms have been the taxes on exports of agricultural, forestry, and mineral products that have been in effect since 1970. In fiscal 1974, for example, these amounted to almost ₱1,100 million, or about 4 percent of the net value added for these sectors.

Because of the absence of a national system of land taxation and low effective income tax rates, the export tax represents the only significant means of taxing agriculture. In the short run it has contributed to a more equitable application of the tax system by taxing hitherto untaxed or undertaxed incomes. Its impact has been uneven, however, because it is imposed on only a few agricultural activities, particularly sugar and coconut production. Although the export tax on sugar seems to fall primarily on the return earned by sugar exporters and producers who are frequently in the upper income groups, the export tax on coconut products, the most important smallholder export crop in the Philippines, has distinct regressive features. In view of the stiff competition of copra with other oils and fats in international markets, it is safe to assume that the tax has been borne mainly by the domestic economy and, given the structure of coconut production, primarily by the smallholders growing coconut. This may hamper the government's efforts to revitalize this long-neglected agricultural subsector.

One area of fiscal policy that may have a potential impact is the effective taxation of agricultural land. Even if the agrarian reform program is fully implemented, the distribution of agricultural landholdings will continue to be heavily skewed in favor of a relatively small number of owners. Like many other developing countries, the Philippines does not have an effective system of taxing agricultural land; there has been widespread evasion by nominal transfers of landholdings to relatives, by misclassification of land

19. See Chapter 15 for a discussion of these issues.

potential, and by lax collection procedures. A more effective system of agricultural land taxation would offer one means of obtaining a reasonable contribution from the richer members of the rural community without destroying incentives related to agricultural output.

Another issue of fiscal policy affecting the rural sector is that of cost recovery. In the past those benefiting from publicly financed investment projects or services have not been adequately charged. Because the amount and quality of many public services provided in rural areas has been low, revenue losses have not been too great and the beneficiaries have not received excessive subsidies. This situation is likely to change dramatically in the future, however, with such projects as the government's ambitious irrigation program. Farmers with irrigation facilities are likely to be one group in the rural community whose incomes could rise relatively rapidly, and it will be important to ensure that they pay a reasonable share of the costs of providing this service. The government is aware of this issue, and in recent years the charges for irrigation water have been increased in order to recover part of the investment cost. The government has also been attempting to improve the collection record.[20]

Administration and Institutional Development in Rural Areas

The national government will continue to carry the major responsibility for promoting rural development programs, but local governments could play a greater role. Unfortunately, until recently the system of public administration in the Philippines did little if anything to foster local initiative. All too often higher levels of government were insufficiently informed about local needs, in part the result of overcentralization. The government is cognizant of this problem and has been attempting to decentralize some of its authority. Administrative reforms should aim at enlarging local responsibility for formulating and administering projects and programs and at increasing financial and technical assistance at the local level. With the increased emphasis on training local officials and with the gradual expansion of their financial powers, the need

20. See Chapter 7 for a more detailed discussion of water charges.

for a clearer statement of local responsibility will become more urgent. The agency providing technical assistance to local officials is the Department of Local Government and Community Development (DLGCD), which was created in 1972.

The reorganization and decentralization of the national government which began in 1972 has encountered some resistance from vested interest groups that are reluctant to relinquish control over resources and some areas of decisionmaking. In addition there is the danger that the devolution of fiscal authority may proceed more rapidly than the training of local officials, or that overlapping jurisdictions and responsibilities will cause conflicts among agencies and levels of government. All these problems are inevitable in any real attempt by the government to broaden the base of participation, but they will need close attention.

THE ROLE OF PROVINCIAL AND MUNICIPAL GOVERNMENT

Although the national government has indicated an interest in expanding the role of local authorities in development, there do not appear to be any guidelines on precisely what this role should be in the immediate future; even less clear is what their role should be in the more distant future. The situation is further complicated by the uneven levels of responsibilities exercised by local governments.[21] In the near future one responsibility that could be given to local authorities is the building and maintenance of local roads. Providing services such as those to support fishing could also be a legitimate activity for local governments.

EXPANDING LOCAL PARTICIPATION: THE ROLE OF THE BARANGAYS

More than 99 percent of the almost 34,000 barangays or barrios in the Philippines in 1972 were in rural areas; their average population is about 700 to 800 people.[22] Programs to increase participation by the rural population in the development process, and to improve their incomes and access to services, must clearly involve

21. See the technical note to Chapter 4 for a more complete discussion of local government.

22. A barangay or barrio is a group of dwellings that may constitute a hamlet, village, suburb, or even an urban district. Although there is some disagreement over the precise geographical definition of a barangay and a barrio, the terms are used interchangeably here.

these local units. Their past success with self-help projects indicates that there is scope for expanding their participation in development. Since the 1963 Revised Barrio Charter the barrios have had the power to tax stores, signboards, and cockfights and to impose a small tax on property within the barrio. To date these powers have been exercised to only a limited extent. A government survey of 215 barrios conducted in 1970 indicates that less than 10 percent of the barrio councils attempted to collect revenues. The main reasons given were that the residents of the barrio were too poor or the councils unaware they had the power.[23]

Since 1963 the barrios are also entitled to 10 percent of all taxes levied by the provincial and municipal governments on real property located within the barrio. This tax has been a meager source of funds for at least two reasons. First, in rural areas a large amount of the land does not belong to residents of the barrios; and second, effective real estate taxes have traditionally been very low, especially in rural areas, so that the 10 percent share has often been insignificant.[24] More recently Presidential Decree 144 provided for annual contributions to the barrios from each province, city, and municipality, not to exceed ₱500 a barrio. These allocations are at the discretion of the upper levels of local governments, however; there is nothing automatic or definite about them, and the barrios cannot really count on them.

Until 1972 when the DLGCD was created, the traditional source of funds was the Presidential Arm on Community Development (PACD). Although the PACD allocations were distributed primarily at election time, the program did support almost 50,000 self-help projects for the barrios through grants-in-aid. As a result the barrios have shown that, given financial and administrative support, they can organize and carry out small-scale development projects. In 1971–72 the barrios undertook a wide range of self-help projects in addition to those of the PACD, financing some 85 percent through the provision of voluntary labor, locally available materials, project sites, and cash.[25]

In January 1972 the PACD was dissolved and the Bureau of Com-

---

23. International Labour Office, *Sharing in Development* (Geneva, 1974), p. 515.
24. In 1971, for example, the actual collection of real property taxes was only 55 percent of the collectable amount, and the assessed value of provincial agricultural land was only 39 percent of the fair market value in 1967.
25. ILO, *Sharing in Development*, pp. 517–18.

munity Development was formed under the DLGCD. The bureau funds projects primarily through grants-in-aid and interest-free loans. Grants-in-aid are provided in the form of processed material for self-help projects under the direction of the barrio councils. The barrio is required to supply 50 percent or more of the project costs in the form of manpower, material, and project sites. Interest-free loans are made for such concerns as communal irrigation, cottage industries, fisheries, and livestock. In-service training and seminars are also carried out by the bureau to support the self-help projects. In 1973–74 the DLGCD provided ₱5 million for 829 grant-in-aid projects and ₱4 million for 2,373 projects under Rural Improvement and Community Development Funds released from the Office of the President; the barrios provided ₱22 million or 85 percent of the total cost for about 157,000 purely self-help projects in the form of materials and labor.

There are no data on the total amount of financial resources allocated to the barrios, but it is almost certainly a relatively small amount and irregular in supply. Ways could be found to make available more financial resources and technical expertise to the barrios for development projects such as local roads, water supply, public buildings, and communal irrigation. Before any significant expansion of barrio participation in rural development, however, a careful assessment is needed of the role of the barrios in relation to the cooperative and farmer organizations that the government is vigorously promoting. Because most members of these groups are also barrio residents, barrio responsibilities may overlap with those of the other organizations and cause conflict in the future. A clearer definition of roles is therefore required.

COOPERATIVE DEVELOPMENT AND FARMER ORGANIZATIONS

In recent years government emphasis on the rural cooperative movement and on developing farmer organizations has included: the requirement that tenant farmers in the agrarian reform program be members of a cooperative; the use of small joint liability groups (seldas) for supervised credit programs; and the organization of various other pilot projects in different parts of the country. As a result some kind of farmer organization has now been established in almost every province, municipality, and barrio in the country. Some are profit making while others are not; some are registered with government agencies while others are independent. All, however, exhibit a similarity of purpose, which is to promote the social and economic welfare of small farmers, and all reflect the serious effort of the government to involve the farmer more closely in the country's political system and economic development.

Organizations and membership. Among the large number of different cooperative and farmer organizations the most important in terms of geographical coverage and size of membership is the Samahang Nayon movement which began in 1973. Others have been in operation for many years. With the suppression of the Huk movement in the early 1950s, numerous attempts were made by both the government and private institutions to establish farmer organizations which would provide supporting services to the rural areas. In 1953 the government set up the Agricultural Credit and Cooperative Financing Administration (the Agricultural Credit Administration after 1963), which was followed by the rapid expansion of cooperatives throughout the country. During the first three years 400 Farmers' Cooperative Marketing Associations (FACOMAS) were established. After an initial period of success the FACOMAS ran into serious difficulties. Management was weak and sometimes dishonest; government supervision was inadequate; delinquencies on loans rose to two-thirds; and four-fifths of the cooperatives lost money.[26]

Since the agrarian reform program was revitalized in 1972, the cooperative movement has been receiving much greater attention. In response to the requirement that former rice and corn tenants be members of a recognized farmers' cooperative to receive title to their land, the newly formed DLGCD began organizing the Samahang Nayons, or barrio associations, which have provisional status as cooperatives. Upon the formation of a Samahang Nayon, the members have two years in which to qualify for registration as part of a full-fledged cooperative at the provincial level. During this time the members are required to take 65 weeks of educational courses in cooperative principles, agricultural practices, and man-

26. Although the following is not an exhaustive list, other farmer organizations include: Farmers' Barrio Cooperatives, compact farms, seldas, Irrigator Groups, General Ricarte Agricultural Cooperative, Nueva Ecija Integrated Livestock Cooperative Program, Federation of Free Farmers' Association, and Philippine Federation of Farmers Association. For a detailed discussion, see Mark A. Van Stenwyk, *A Study of Philippine Farmer Organizations* (Manila: United States Agency for International Development, 1975).

agement. The Samahang Nayons conform roughly to the geographic limits of a barrio and must have a minimum of 25 members. They have a registered corporate status with the right to own or dispose of property and enter into contracts.

The Samahang Nayons began in August 1973, and by December 1974 about 16,000 had been organized with a membership of 707,000 or 44 percent of the target membership of 1.6 million. Despite the requirement that recipients of Certificates of Land Transfer be members of a cooperative, there are indications that less than 40 percent of those affected have complied. It is too soon to evaluate the effectiveness of the Samahang Nayons, and the organization of a nationwide cooperative system is clearly in its infant stage. As of March 1975 only one cooperative bank was registered in the whole country, and it has encountered stiff opposition from the established rural banks.

Among private institutions the largest farmer-based organization is the Federation of Free Farmers (FFF), which was created in 1953 by a group of Catholic laymen. The FFF had only minimal success in expanding its organization during the 1950s and early 1960s, but membership began to increase during the latter half of the 1960s. In 1974 the FFF had organizations in 60 provinces with a membership of about 200,000. Its main functions are to provide legal services to farmers and develop local leadership through education and training.

Almost all farmer organizations receive some extension assistance from external sources, but the nature and degree of this support varies and often is not adequate to meet the specific needs of the organization. To cite an example, Farmers' Barrio Cooperatives in the province of Nueva Ecija received technical assistance from the Department of Agrarian Reform. Although the technicians were well schooled in land reform policies, they lacked education and experience in the technical aspects of agriculture, and consequently their extension services proved ineffective.

Because the government's extension service is often distant and at times undependable, groups such as the Samahang Nayons, Farmers' Barrio Cooperatives, and many compact farms have found it advantageous to organize their own internal extension support. Some have already designated members and committees to serve as intraorganizational extension agents, but they will need education and training before they become functional. Thus it is important to determine priorities in providing the nation's farmers with more effective extension services.

Functions performed by organizations. For the most part the various farmer organizations provide one or both of the following services: the supply and distribution of production inputs and the processing and marketing of members' products. Some such as the Farmers' Barrio Cooperatives have developed elaborate cooperative structures to procure and funnel production inputs to their members; other organizations such as the seldas maintain only a loosely knit distribution channel, relying heavily on outside sources (rural banks or private dealers) for input procurement. On occasion conflict has occurred when members of a selda or compact farm who are also members of a Farmers' Barrio Cooperative or Samahang Nayon have been required by a credit source (a rural bank, for example) to purchase from an outside supplier as a precondition for credit assistance. In the same way, credit sources may insist that farmers market their produce through designated outlets such as the National Grains Authority or private buyers. Again this may weaken an organization which seeks to offer its members the advantages of economies of scale. Credit institutions should therefore coordinate more closely with seldas and become more familiar with the production and marketing needs and services of larger organizations such as the Samahang Nayons. The result should be greater economic returns for the farmer and a reduction in unnecessary duplication of effort and unwarranted competition.

The degree to which a farmer organization may become involved with marketing activities varies. Farmers' Barrio Cooperatives in Nueva Ecija, for example, process and market portions of members' produce through their jointly federated Area Marketing Cooperative. This system is similar to the federated grain-processing and marketing facilities being developed by the Samahang Nayons in limited target areas. Smaller farmer organizations such as seldas and compact farms generally serve only as assembly or collection points for marketing. Actual marketing may be done either through larger organizational structures, such as Farmers' Barrio Cooperatives or Samahang Nayons when they are present, or through private marketing channels.

Unnecessary conflicts and duplication of services exist among farmer organizations to a degree which could be considered detrimental. Although there may not be an immediate solution to the problem, the need to coordinate the activities of farmer organizations seems clear. In planning some kind of regulatory system consideration should be given to regional differences which could have an important bearing on the type of organization likely to be most effective locally. The apparent lack of cooperation among government agencies responsible for rural and agricultural development serves only to exacerbate the competitive spirit which appears to dominate much of the organizations' activities and which to some degree causes the duplication of services.

Access to financial resources. Many farmer organizations charge membership fees or annual dues; in some cases the members are also required to purchase shares of stock or contribute to special funds. The Samahang Nayons, for example, have a small entrance fee, and the members are expected to contribute one cavan per hectare toward the Barrio Guarantee Fund, which guarantees amortization payments for members affected by Presidential Decree 27. They must also contribute 5 percent of the value of each production loan received from an institutional source; this contribution is then credited to their individual accounts in the Barrio Savings Fund and is used for investment purposes in the barrio. Members in areas serviced by more than one farmer organization complain that their combined obligations often become excessive. If allowed to go unchecked, this problem could undermine the very purpose for which the organizations were originally created.

ROLE OF THE NATIONAL GOVERNMENT

Although efforts are being made to decentralize development planning and implementation, the national government and its line agencies will undoubtedly continue to play a dominant role in the economic development of rural areas. No attempt is made here to provide a comprehensive overview of the many-faceted role the national government is expected to have. The full extent of its involvement becomes apparent from the discussion of individual programs in subsequent chapters. In brief, however, it should continue to have primary responsibility for public investment in rural areas and for major public services such as education, health, family planning, and nutrition.

The government has been formulating a number of programs that call for the combined efforts of more than one agency. Since no one agency is responsible for coordinating all rural development programs, however, there is a tendency for these activities to be fragmented and dispersed. At times the situation is further complicated by insufficient knowledge about the location and characteristics of specific rural groups or about the development potential of key areas. Efforts are being made to promote better planning and coordination at the regional level with the recently established Regional Development Councils (RDCs).

One of the objectives of the reorganization plan that was implemented in 1972 (Presidential Decree 1) was to decentralize the national government by dividing the country into eleven administrative regions with an RDC for each. Each department of the national government was then asked to reorganize by appointing a director to oversee its operations in each region. It is still too early to tell whether this attempt to strengthen planning and administration at the regional level will be more successful than previous efforts. If local participation in development is to expand, however, a less centralized national government bureaucracy will be necessary. The national government is likely to control most of the public sector resources allocated for development programs even at the local level. If all decisions about the disposition of these resources have to be referred to Manila, local participation will probably be severely circumscribed. Regional representatives of the national government will therefore have to be given a greater voice in the allocation of resources within their regions if increased local autonomy is to become a reality.

The RDCs consist of some of the regional directors of the national government departments and bureaus, the mayors of the chartered cities, and the provincial governors in each region. The chairman is chosen from among the local representatives, with the National Economic and Development Authority (NEDA) director automatically named as deputy chairman. The council is solely a planning group with technical support provided by regional NEDA staff. The major task of the RDCs is to coordinate and integrate all the planning and program implementation activities in their respective regions. This is supposed to be done in close collaboration with the regional offices of different national government implementing agencies and with the provincial development councils of each region. One of the weaknesses of the present RDCs is that not all the pertinent agencies are represented. For example, there are no representatives of agencies dealing with fisheries, agricultural credit, forestry, agrarian reform, and tourism. But if all were included the RDCs would comprise up to fifty people, which is far too unwieldy a group to be effective. This situation is of course symptomatic of the excessive fragmentation of administration in the Philippines.

As a body, the RDCs have no financial resources available to implement any development plans that they may conceive. All budgetary appropriations must come through the line agencies of the national government or from the provinces or cities. Budgeting by the line agencies is not done on a regional basis, and since the regional directors generally have little influence on their departmental budgets, the regions must largely accept the resources (including manpower) available to them. In effect the RDCs must plan by persuasion, and their role is severely limited by the absence of regional budgets for the line agencies and by the lack of any effective mechanism to deal with conflicts in resource allocation at the regional level.

It appears that the RDCs will not become effective vehicles for regional development unless they are provided with more legal and budgetary authority than at present. These difficulties are recognized by the national government, and there has been some discussion of the possibility of a presidential appointment of the RDC chairman as a regional coordinator. Some consideration has also been given to establishing a system of regional budgets among the national government line agencies.

Technical Note. Estimating Net Incomes of Land Reform Beneficiaries

Estimates of the impact of land reform on tenant incomes were based on typical farm budgets prepared for a 1.0 hectare rain-fed farm with an initial yield of 1.6 metric tons a hectare, a 2.5 hectare rain-fed farm with an initial yield of 2.0 metric tons a hectare, and a 2.5 hectare irrigated farm with an initial yield of 2.5 metric tons a hectare. Seven assumptions were used to calculate the net farm income for sharecroppers, leaseholders, and amortizing owners over a thirty-year period:

a. Yields were assumed to be the same for sharecroppers, lease-holders, and amortizing owners. Production was increased by 2 percent a year. Cropping intensity was assumed to be 100 percent for rain-fed farms and 130 percent for irrigated farms.

b. The inflation rates used were 8 percent in 1976 and 7.5 percent from 1977 to 2004.

c. The farm-gate price of rice for 1975 was assumed to be ₱1,000 a ton.

d. Production costs were assumed to be 30 percent of the gross value of production.

e. The cost of hired labor was based on the maximum of 40 man-days a month and a total of 480 man-days a year of family labor. Water charges were assumed to be ₱25 for the wet season and ₱35 for the dry season in 1974.

f. Annual payments in rentals and amortization were deducted to give net income. For the sharecropper, rental payments were assumed equal to 50 percent of net production; for the lease-holder, 25 percent of net production; and for the amortizing owners, payments were based on 2.5 times the gross production in 1975, valued at ₱1,000 a ton of paddy, and paid in fifteen equal annual installments at 6 percent interest.

g. A discount rate of 10 percent was used to calculate the present value of the loss of income to landlords. The model farm budget for the 1.0 hectare rain-fed farm was used and the land was valued at ₱4,000. The initial cash payment was assumed to be 30 percent of the land value and the remaining 70 percent was paid in Land Bank bonds with a 6 percent interest rate and a twenty-five-year maturity. It was also assumed that a loan with a 10 percent interest charge was made to the landlords, equivalent to 80 percent of the value of the bonds, and that there was a 15 percent return on the investment made with this loan.

6

Strategies for Rural Development: Expansion of Agricultural and Fishery Production

THE RAPID GROWTH OF THE POPULATION during the past two and a half decades, combined with the gradual decline in the amount of new land available for cultivation, has created serious problems for the Philippines. Income distribution among the rural population has been deteriorating, and the average farm size and value added per laborer have been declining. Despite the overwhelmingly rural character of the Philippine economy, most efforts at modernization have been concentrated in urban areas. Government development policies, coupled with the influential role of a small but effective entrepreneurial class, have tended to emphasize capital-intensive and geographically concentrated industrialization at the expense of agricultural and rural improvement. Recently the government has recognized the limitations of this approach and has been giving priority to development in the countryside in an effort to correct the past urban bias and its tendency to increase income disparities between urban and rural areas. The government has focused on the following objectives: self-sufficiency in food-grain production, improved income distribution and nutrition, employment opportunities, and increased agricultural exports to improve the balance of payments.

Until about 1960 agricultural growth was based primarily on an increase in the physical area of land under cultivation,[1] with relatively little change in technology and total factor productivity.[2] The harvested area grew by about 4.4 percent a year in the 1950s, in large part as a result of a rapid increase in the area devoted to food crops, particularly rice and corn. This expansion was concentrated on the readily accessible land of major river basins and lowlands.

By the end of the 1950s most of the lowlands had been brought under cultivation. As a result the overall rate of land expansion slowed down to 1.5 percent a year in the 1960s,[3] and the ratio of harvested area to population declined steadily from 0.29 hectares in 1960 to about 0.24 hectares by the beginning of the 1970s. Expansion onto previously uncultivated land will probably continue to slow down in the future, but the harvested area is expected to maintain its growth rate as a result of irrigation and the intensification of land use. It seems likely that the cropped area could grow by about 1.5 percent a year during the next ten years, reaching about 11 million hectares by 1985; even so, this would mean only about 0.20 hectares a person (Table 6.1).

It is clear that increases in farm production and incomes must come from higher yields per hectare and the cultivation of higher value crops.[4] The intensification of land use will depend primarily

1. The following definitions are used in this chapter: "Physical area" refers to the maximum number of hectares which can be cultivated at any one time. "Cropping intensity" is the percentage of the physical area cultivated within a twelve-month period (that is, a one-hectare farm which is cultivated for only one season a year has a cropping intensity of 100 percent; a one-hectare farm which has one hectare cultivated during the wet season and one-half hectare in the dry season has a cropping intensity of 150 percent). "Cropped (or planted) area" is the physical area multiplied by the cropping intensity and covers a twelve-month period. "Harvested area" is the amount of the cropped area which is not lost during the growing season as a result of such factors as weather or disease.

2. For a detailed analysis of the sources of past growth of agricultural output, see C. Crisostomo and R. Barker, "Growth Rates of Philippine Agriculture: 1948–1969," *The Philippine Economic Journal,* First Semester, vol. 11, no. 1 (1972), pp. 88–148.

3. The harvested area of food crops rose by only 0.4 percent a year during the 1960s, but that of export crops grew by almost 5 percent a year, primarily as a result of increased coconut plantings in upland regions.

4. An agricultural sector survey undertaken by the World Bank in 1972 concluded that as many as 2.5 million hectares could still be available for cultivation, including about one million hectares of cogon grasslands that are

Table 6.1. Actual and Projected Harvested Area of Crops
(In thousands of hectares)

Crop	Actual[a]			World Bank projection	
	1950	1960	1970	1980	1985
Food crops					
Rice	2,210	3,278	3,186	3,500	3,700
Corn	909	2,000	2,350	3,000	3,100
Other	485	882	855	850	850
Subtotal	3,604	6,160	6,397	7,350	7,650
Export and other crops					
Coconuts	979	1,088	1,926	2,400	2,600
Sugarcane	143	242	384	530	550
Other	353	291	280	270	250
Subtotal	1,475	1,621	2,590	3,200	3,400
Total	5,079	7,791	8,987	10,550	11,050
Ratio of area harvested to Philippine population (hectares)	0.25	0.29	0.25	0.22	0.20

a. Based on three-year averages of 1949–51, 1959–61, and 1969–71 respectively.
Sources: Bureau of Agricultural Economics (BAECON) and World Bank estimates.

on expansion of the irrigated area to permit multiple cropping and the introduction of new technology such as high-yield varieties of seeds (HYVs). To achieve the best results from HYVs there must be adequate water control, careful attention to the timing of operations, and improved farming practices including the control of weeds, pests, and disease and the application of the appropriate type and quantity of fertilizer. Adoption of these practices on a large scale will depend in turn on the development of an effective, well-managed extension program.

Meeting Domestic Food Requirements

In general, food production in the Philippines has kept pace with the rapidly growing population during the past three decades.

difficult to rehabilitate. World Bank, "Agricultural Sector Survey: Philippines" (May 2, 1973), restricted-circulation internal document no 39a–PH. More recent calculations by the International Labour Office, *Sharing in Development* (Geneva: ILO, 1974), p. 457, indicate higher figures. Most of the remaining large tracts of cultivable land appear to be in the Cagayan Valley, the Agusan Valley, and other parts of Mindanao.

Domestic production provided most of the food consumed in 1974. During the next decade it is estimated (Table 6.2) that demand for food will grow at about 4.0 percent a year.

INCREASING CEREAL PRODUCTION

Cereals provide most of the calories consumed by the population. In 1974, for example, they accounted for about 72 percent of the total; of the cereals consumed, rice provided a little more than half the calories. Total cereal production expanded by about 3.0 percent a year during the 1950s and 1960s (Table 6.3), but in the early 1970s adverse weather and plant diseases caused production to decline sharply. Imports of cereals increased in 1971–73, with the ratio of imports to total supply rising as in the mid-1960s to about 16 percent. In 1974–75, however, both rice and corn production increased, and because of favorable weather conditions in the latter part of 1975 food-grain production is expected to reach record

Table 6.2. Actual and Projected Demand for Selected Food Items
(In thousands of metric tons)

Item	Actual 1973	World Bank projection 1980	World Bank projection 1985	Average annual increase (percent)
Cereals				
Rice	3,568[a]	4,509	5,329	3.4
Corn[b]	1,262	1,573	1,842	3.2
Wheat	412	542	660	4.0
Total	5,242	6,624	7,831	3.4
Dairy products	568	799	1,020	5.0
Fish and other marine products	1,609	2,089	2,517	3.8
Meat and poultry				
Pork	359	540	722	6.0
Beef	87	131	175	6.0
Poultry	117	172	226	5.7
Total	563	843	1,123	5.9
Sugar	738	958	1,155	3.8
Vegetable oil	169	233	293	4.7

a. Adjusted downward for a milling rate of 64 percent from the Food Balance Sheet figure of 3,681,000 metric tons, which is based on a milling rate of 66.2 percent.
b. Corn grits for human consumption only.
Sources: National Economic and Development Authority (NEDA), *The Philippine Food Balance Sheet, 1973* (Manila, 1975) and World Bank estimates.

Table 6.3. Domestic Production and Imports of Cereals, Calendar Years 1953–75
(In thousands of metric tons)

Calendar year	Milled rice Domestic production	Milled rice Net imports	Milled rice Import dependence[a]	Shelled corn Domestic production	Shelled corn Net imports	Shelled corn Import dependence[a]	Wheat Net imports	All cereals Domestic production	All cereals Net imports	All cereals Import dependence[a]
1953	2,093	−5	...	745	...	...	171	2,838	166	5.5
1954	2,113	35	1.6	775	...	...	201	2,888	236	7.6
1955	2,143	105	4.7	830	...	...	257	2,981	362	10.8
1956	2,190	43	1.9	901	...	...	225	3,091	268	8.0
1957	2,167	78	3.5	874	11	...	300	3,041	389	11.3
1958	2,279	231	9.2	934	21	...	332	3,213	584	15.4
1959	2,457	−6	...	1,091	−77	−7.6	232	3,548	149	4.3
1960	2,463	−2	...	1,187	−14	−1.2	293	3,650	277	7.0
1961	2,570	188	6.9	1,238	−6	...	347	3,721	529	12.4
1962	2,627	...	...	1,269	...	...	365	3,896	365	8.6
1963	2,605	256	8.9	1,283	7	...	433	3,888	696	15.2
1964	2,613	299	10.3	1,303	7	...	414	3,916	720	15.5
1965	2,690	569	17.5	1,346	6	...	506	4,036	1,081	21.1
1966	2,747	108	3.8	1,407	2	...	495	4,154	605	12.7
1967	2,844	237	7.7	1,481	50	3.3	476	4,325	763	15.0
1968	3,289	−41	1.3	1,537	3	...	525	4,826	487	9.2
1969	3,264	...	...	1,870	29	1.5	505	5,134	534	9.4
1970	3,582	...	...	2,007	...	...	449	5,589	449	7.4
1971	3,496	370	9.6	2,002	83	4.0	485	5,518	936	14.5
1972	3,149	451	12.5	1,920	168	8.0	490	5,069	1,109	18.0
1973	2,870	310	9.7	1,830	100	5.2	504	4,700	914	19.4
1974	3,279	168	4.9	2,289	110	4.8	...	5,568	278	4.8
1975	3,861[b]	152[b]	3.8	2,568	121[b]	4.5	557	6,429	830	12.9

... Zero or negligible.

a. Import dependence is the ratio of imports to total supply.

b. Projected as of November 1, 1975.

Sources: Data for 1953–69 are from the Food Balance Sheets of the Philippines as published in various issues of *The Statistical Reporter.* Data for 1970–72 are from NEDA, *The Philippine Food Balance Sheet, 1971* (Manila, 1974) and *1972* (Manila, 1973) and *1972* (Manila, 1974). Data for rice and corn in 1973 are from BAECON, *Commodity Profiles* (Quezon City, 1974). Wheat imports for 1973 are from NEDA, *Foreign Trade Sector Study* (Manila, 1975). Data for 1974 and 1975 are from the Department of Agriculture.

levels in crop year 1975–76. As a result of the decline in production during the early 1970s, the government intensified its efforts to achieve self-sufficiency in rice and corn production, primarily through supervised credit programs aimed at small farms. These programs and others are examined below.

Rice. Until the 1960s rice production was increased primarily by expanding the physical area under cultivation from an average of about 2.0 million hectares in the late 1940s to about 3.3 million in 1960. This expansion was strongly promoted by the government and kept pace with population growth. Since 1960, however, the harvested area of rice has leveled off to an average of about 3.2 million hectares. National paddy yields were virtually stagnant at about 1.2 metric tons a hectare until the mid-1960s. With about 60 percent of the irrigated area planted with HYVs, yields increased to about 1.6 metric tons a hectare but tended to level off after 1970. The difficulties in realizing significant yield increases have led to a more cautious assessment of the prospects for attaining sustained self-sufficiency in rice.

In the wake of disastrous flood and typhoon damage to the main rice crop in 1972–73, the government launched the Masagana 99 program to provide institutional credit, inputs, and technical advice to the many small farmers who dominate the industry.[5] The program enjoyed considerable success in its first year and covered about 36 percent of the total lowland rice area. But its second year, 1974–75, revealed difficulties such as not enough well-trained production technicians and a low rate of loan repayment. In addition, the high farm-gate price of fertilizer relative to the price of rice discouraged farmers from applying sufficient quantities.[6] Officials are well aware of the present weaknesses of the program and are taking steps to correct them. Despite these difficulties, supervised credit programs such as Masagana 99 have a valuable role in providing greatly needed supporting services to small farmers.[7]

It appears possible to meet domestic demand and eliminate

---

5. "Masagana" is a Tagalog word meaning "abundant"; "99" refers to the target yield of 99 cavans (4.4 metric tons) per hectare. See the section on agricultural credit (Chapter 7) for a more detailed discussion of the program.

6. See the section on price policies for rice and fertilizer.

7. This need is more urgent since the agrarian reform removed landlords as a source of production credit.

Table 6.4. Average Annual Yields of Paddy Rice in Selected Countries
(In kilograms per hectare)

Country	1961–65	1966–70	1971–73
Philippines	1,257	1,510	1,532
Asia	2,048	2,172	2,322
Burma	1,641	1,642	1,695
China, People's Republic of	2,780	2,928	3,145
Indonesia	1,761	1,910	2,300
Korea, Republic of	4,111	4,311	4,681
Thailand	1,775	1,818	1,898

Source: Food and Agriculture Organization, Production Yearbook, 1972 and 1973 (Rome: FAO).

imports by 1985 if total rice production expands by about 4.0 percent a year. Because new arable land is severely limited, however, efforts to raise production will have to be concentrated on increasing the irrigated area and on improving yields. Average yields in the Philippines continue to be among the lowest in Asia (Table 6.4), primarily because of an inadequate extension service, a lack of inputs and credit, and inefficient irrigation systems. Although about 40 percent of the harvested area is presently irrigated, since 1970 yields on irrigated areas have averaged only about 2.0 metric tons a hectare.[8]

The potential for raising yields is greatest on irrigated areas planted with HYVs (Table 6.5). With better water control, improved extension efforts, and adequate supplies of inputs at prices acceptable to farmers, average yields on these areas could be increased from the present level of about 2.0 metric tons a hectare to about 2.6 metric tons in 1980 and 3.0 metric tons in 1985, a growth rate of about 3 percent a year. The potential for increasing yields on irrigated areas planted with traditional varieties, while less than that for the irrigated HYV areas, could also be substantial. With the same level of improved services, average yields for irrigated areas planted with traditional varieties could be increased from their present level of about 1.7 metric tons per hectare to about 2.2 metric tons in 1980. But for top yields the extension service should

8. If the average yield on irrigated areas had been 4.0 metric tons a hectare instead of 2.0 metric tons in 1974–75, rice production that year would have increased about 50 percent.

aim to have 100 percent of the irrigated area planted with HYVs by 1980.

For lowland rain-fed areas, significant increases in yields are less likely because of the dependence on weather, the reluctance of farmers to use inputs in such a high-risk situation, and technical limitations to the optimum use of available water. With an improved extension service in the lowland rain-fed areas, however, it should be possible to raise the growth rate of yields from the historical level of a little more than one percent a year to about 2 percent a year by 1980. For upland areas the potential for increasing yields is much more limited.

High priority is already being given by the government to expanding and improving the irrigation systems. As discussed in Chapter 7, it seems likely that the total irrigated harvested area could be expanded by about 650,000 hectares to reach a total of 2.0 million hectares by 1985. Thus there would be almost a 50 percent increase by 1985 compared with 1971–72. As a proportion of the total harvested area, however, the irrigated area would rise only from about 43 percent in 1971–72 to 53 percent in 1985; about 1.4 million hectares of lowland rice would still be grown under rain-fed conditions in 1985. Moreover the full incremental increase in yields anticipated from the expansion and improvement of irrigation systems is usually not attained until several years after the work is completed.

The government is also increasing its efforts to improve the extension service, but upgrading and expanding the training facilities and improving the quality of management will necessarily be a gradual process. At least for the next five years efforts to improve available organizational and managerial resources should probably be concentrated in areas where the potential yields are greatest: first, the irrigated HYV areas and, second, the irrigated areas planted with traditional varieties.[9] Nonirrigated areas would continue receiving the same level of services as in the past, but based on the experience gained in the irrigated areas it should be possible to broaden the extension program eventually to include the rain-fed areas. If these ambitious targets could be achieved, the Philippines

---

9. Problems of income distribution that might result from such concentration could be partly offset by more aggressive policies on water charges and land taxes. See the section on irrigation and water management in Chapter 7 for a more detailed discussion.

**Table 6.5. Actual and Projected Rice (Paddy) Production,
Yields, and Area Harvested**

	Actual			
	1968–69[a]		1971–72[a]	
Item	Amount	Percent	Amount	Percent
Area harvested (thousands of hectares)				
Area with HYVS	1,140	35.1	1,604	51.0
Irrigated	731	22.5	912	29.0
Rainfed	409	12.6	692	22.0
Area without HYVS	2,110	64.9	1,542	49.0
Irrigated	650	20.0	434	13.8
Rainfed	1,017	31.3	714	22.7
Upland	443	13.6	394	12.5
Total	3,250	100.0	3,146	100.0
Yield (kilograms of paddy per hectare)				
Area with HYVS				
Irrigated	1,711	117.2	2,046	128.2
Rainfed	1,298	88.9	1,455	91.2
Area without HYVS				
Irrigated	1,701	116.5	1,743	109.2
Rainfed	1,278	87.5	1,392	87.2
Upland	880	60.3	923	57.8
Average national yield	1,460	100.0	1,596	100.0
Production (thousands of metric tons of paddy)				
Area with HYVS	1,950	41.1	2,893	57.6
Irrigated	1,419	29.9	1,743	34.7
Rainfed	531	11.2	1,150	22.9
Area without HYVS	2,796	58.9	2,130	42.4
Irrigated	1,106	23.3	753	15.0
Rainfed	1,300	27.4	1,015	20.2
Upland	390	8.2	362	7.2
Total	4,746	100.0	5,023	100.0

— Not applicable.
HYV: High-yield varieties of rice.
a. Based on a three-year average.
Sources: Actual data from BAECON; World Bank projections.

would probably be able to meet, on a sustained basis, the demand
for rice from domestic production by 1985 (Table 6.6).

Corn. Corn production has increased at an average rate of about
5.5 percent a year since the early 1960s. Most of the increase
occurred in the latter part of the 1960s when output rose by almost
9 percent a year; since 1970 expansion has slowed to about 5 percent

Projected				
1979–80		*1984–85*		
Amount	*Percent*	*Amount*	*Percent*	*Item*
				Area harvested (thousands of hectares)
2,700	75.0	3,100	83.8	Area with HYVS
1,600	44.4	2,000	54.1	Irrigated
1,100	30.6	1,100	29.7	Rainfed
900	25.0	600	16.2	Area without HYVS
100	2.8	—	—	Irrigated
500	13.9	400	10.8	Rainfed
300	8.3	200	5.4	Upland
3,600	100.0	3,700	100.0	Total
				Yield (kilograms of paddy per hectare)
				Area with HYVS
2,600	129.5	3,000	125.8	Irrigated
1,600	79.7	1,750	73.4	Rainfed
				Area without HYVS
2,200	109.6	—	—	Irrigated
1,600	79.7	1,750	73.4	Rainfed
950	47.3	1,000	41.4	Upland
2,007	100.0	2,385	100.0	Average national yield
				Production (thousands of metric tons of paddy)
5,920	82.0	7,925	89.8	Area with HYVS
4,160	57.6	6,000	68.0	Irrigated
1,760	24.4	1,925	21.8	Rainfed
1,305	18.0	900	10.2	Area without HYVS
220	3.0	—	—	Irrigated
800	11.1	700	7.9	Rainfed
285	3.9	200	2.3	Upland
7,225	100.0	8,825	100.0	Total

a year. Increases in area cultivated and in yields contributed equally to output growth until 1970, but yields have stagnated since that time. During the 1960s and early 1970s the harvested area of corn increased by an average of about 3 percent a year.[10] The physical

10. In many cases three crops of corn a year are obtained. According to the 1960 census the first corn crop accounts for about 40 percent of the harvested area, and the second and third crops each account for another 30 percent.

Table 6.6. Actual and Projected Production and Consumption of Rice
(In thousands of metric tons)

Crop year	Paddy production	Paddy to be milled[a]	Milled rice output[b]	Net imports	Domestic consumption[c]	Change in commercial stocks[d]	Per capita consumption (kilograms)
Actual							
1965	3,992	3,848	2,374	482	2,802	54	89.5
1966	4,073	3,926	2,423	327	2,767	−17	85.8
1967	4,094	3,947	2,435	215	2,575	−75	76.0
1968	4,561	4,397	2,713	119	2,596	236	75.9
1969	4,445	4,285	2,644	...	2,704	−87	76.7
1970	5,233	5,045	3,113	...	3,227	−115	87.7
1971	5,343	5,151	3,178	18	3,272	−76	86.4
1972	5,100	4,916	3,033	620	3,660	−7	93.9
1973	4,415	4,256	2,626	239	2,839	26	70.8
1974	5,594	5,393	3,327	317	3,527	117	85.4
Projected							
1980	7,225	6,965	4,458	...	4,509	−51	93.0
1985	8,825	8,507	5,444	...	5,329	115	96.9

... Zero or negligible.
a. Assumed to be 96.4 percent of production.
b. Assumed to have a recovery rate of 61.7 percent for 1965–74 and 64 percent for 1980 and 1985.
c. Includes changes in household stocks.
d. Stocks held for sale on the commercial market.
Sources: Data on paddy production and commercial stocks are from BAECON; imports are from National Grain Authority; other data are World Bank estimates.

area of land cropped with corn grew from about 740,000 hectares in 1959–60 to about 1.1 million hectares in 1973–74. Since 1960 there has been a dramatic change in the regional distribution of corn production. More than 60 percent of the increase in output has come from Mindanao, which accounts for about 44 percent of the total harvested area and about 54 percent of total corn production.

Corn yields in the Philippines, like those for rice, are very low by international standards (Table 6.7) owing to such factors as the unavailability of disease-resistant HYVs, the lack of drying facilities, inadequate seed control, the low level of fertilizer and pesticide use, and the resulting heavy losses from pests and diseases. Another problem is that corn farms are often not easily accessible and geographically scattered, which makes extension work difficult. In some areas weather conditions are unfavorable, and consequently losses during the growing season are often high.

In recent years the government has been developing the Masaganang Maisan program of supervised credit for small corn farmers, modeled on the Masagana 99. The first phase began in March 1974 but failed to have any significant impact on production. There were several reasons for this failure, including the dispersal of effort over all regions, which diluted the effects, the use of traditional seeds, the poor quality of the available HYV seeds, the misuse of fertilizer, and inadequate storage and drying facilities. In the second year of the program the government attempted to overcome these problems, for example by reducing the target area by 30 percent to about 350,000 hectares, largely concentrated in Mindanao. A significant increase in yields and production is expected during the next few years.

Table 6.7. International Comparison of Average Annual Yields of Corn
(In kilograms of shelled corn per hectare)

Country	1961–65	1966–70	1971–73
Philippines	660	798	824
Asia	1,652	1,990	1,833
China, People's Republic of	2,479	2,688	2,798
India	992	1,066	1,039
Indonesia	997	952	1,012
Thailand	1,932	2,094	1,801

Source: FAO, *Production Yearbook, 1972* and *1973.*

Table 6.8. Actual and Projected Supply and Consumption of Corn
(In thousands of metric tons of shelled corn)

Year	Supply			Consumption			
	Production	Imports	Total	Food	Feed	Other	Total
Actual							
1969–70	2,008	. . .	2,008	1,600	300	108	2,008
1970–71	2,005	. . .	2,005	1,650	305	50	1,005
1971–72	2,013	. . .	2,013	1,700	290	23	2,013
1972–73	1,831	90	1,921	1,730	250	−59	1,921
1973–74	2,289	91	2,380	1,800	300	280	2,380
Projected							
1979–80	2,850	. . .	2,850	2,174	450	226	2,850
1984–85	3,200	. . .	3,200	2,545	600	255	3,200

. . . Zero or negligible.
Sources: Actual production and import data from BAECON and National Grain Authority respectively. The estimates of actual consumption are World Bank calculations based on NEDA, The Philippine Food Balance Sheets. The projections are World Bank calculations as explained in the text.

By 1980 total domestic demand for corn will probably be in the neighborhood of 2.8 million metric tons of shelled corn (Table 6.8). In considering the prospects for expanding output to meet this demand, a plausible assumption is that the rate at which new land is brought under corn cultivation during the second half of the 1970s will decrease to an average of perhaps 2 percent a year. The cultivated area should then stabilize in the 1980s, implying a harvested area of about 3.1 million hectares from 1979–80 on. The rate at which yields rise is obviously a matter of conjecture at this stage, because it depends largely on the successful development of new corn varieties and government efforts to provide the necessary supporting services. But an average increase in yields of 2 percent a year during 1975–80 and 4 percent in 1980–85 should be possible.[11]

Even if yields reach 1,174 kilograms a hectare by 1985, however, they would only equal present yields in Indonesia and India, and be only 65 percent of those in Thailand (Table 6.7). The new varieties obviously offer the potential for much more rapid increases

11. Even with a 4 percent increase between 1980 and 1985, corn yields would be only about one-fourth of those obtainable under experimental conditions.

in yields, and with a more concerted effort the Philippines could possibly have an exportable surplus of corn in the 1980s. If attractive export markets could be found, consideration might be given to expanding small-farm output specifically for export, which should help increase income opportunities.

EXPANDING THE OUTPUT OF OTHER FOODS

Because of the relatively high elasticities of products such as meat, poultry, and fish, and the projected increases in the proportion of the total population living in urban centers, a more rapid rise in the marketable surplus of such products will be needed over the next decade. Although expanding output will place additional burdens on the institutions responsible for providing the supporting services, it should increase the incomes of many of the small farmers who may not benefit from the program to expand rice production.

Meat and poultry. The per capita intake of meat and poultry products has not grown significantly over the past decade, and in recent years may even have decreased as a result of their relatively high prices. Although demand has shifted in part to cheaper fish products, these have also increased substantially in price so that the total consumption of meat, poultry, and fish has decreased since 1970. With the projected recovery in the growth of urban incomes in real terms, however, demand for meat and poultry products could grow at about 6 percent a year in the future (Table 6.2). Most of the demand during the next decade will probably continue to be for pork, although the relative importance of beef and poultry will also increase.

To limit dependence on imports the government has been placing special emphasis on livestock development, particularly swine production, concentrating on improving extension services, animal health, artificial insemination services, and research activities. An increase in the supply of credit has been an important factor in helping farmers expand livestock production, and government support has also been given to food-grain and fish-meal production. Although conflicting data make it difficult to assess these programs, in general the demand for hogs and poultry has been met fairly successfully, while beef production has lagged behind requirements, causing beef imports and domestic prices for beef to rise.

Opportunities appear good for promoting pork production

among small farmers in order to diversify output and increase incomes. Raising pigs is a well-developed, traditional occupation in rural areas, and although most enterprises are small (around 5 to 10 sows) farmers have considerable experience. At present there are about 9.7 million pigs spread over all the islands, some 80 to 90 percent of them raised and slaughtered in the backyard for home consumption or sale in local markets. Commercial piggeries have expanded very fast in the last few years, however, particularly in Central Luzon and South Cotabato. Consumption of pork is projected to be about 700,000 metric tons by 1985, which means that nearly 20 million hogs will be needed for slaughter. To support this level of production the national herd will have to be expanded by about 7 percent annually during the next decade.

About 3 million households raise poultry, but 1.2 million are nonfarm units which raise birds primarily for home consumption or sale in local markets. It is estimated that noncommercial units produce about 15 percent of the eggs and 60 percent of the poultry meat consumed in the country. A small number of totally integrated farms, with 30,000 to 100,000 broilers or layers, produce about 10 percent of all the eggs and broilers. Most commercial farms, however, have flocks ranging from a few hundred to several thousand birds.

The trend in commercial poultry production in the Philippines, as elsewhere, is toward larger production units, contract production, and integration of services under centralized management. The motivating force is the feed industry. At present an estimated 60 to 80 percent of commercial broilers are produced under contract to feed mills or by the mills themselves. Similar developments in other countries show that integrated firms can rapidly gain control of the poultry, meat, and egg market, and independent growers generally have to secure contractual arrangements with a firm in order to market their output.

Beef production offers another opportunity to improve incomes of small farmers, particularly in coconut-growing areas where the land can also be used as pasture. At present more than 80 percent of the 5 million buffalo (or carabao) and 2.2 million beef cattle are found on Luzon and Mindanao. Carabaos are used by small farmers for draft in rice paddies and are killed when they become too old to work or breed. Meat from these animals accounts for 60 to 70 percent of the total beef production. Beef cattle (not including carabaos) are raised mainly by smallholders in one of four ways.

Hill beef farming is a traditional source of feeder cattle but usually involves low-quality natural pastures. It is practiced most often in Masbate, Mindoro, Northern Mindanao, and the Cagayan Valley and accounts for about 12 percent of the national beef herd. Feeder cattle, fattened in backyards by families as a sideline activity, are produced mainly in Central Luzon and Southern Tagalog. This method is numerically the most important, accounting for more than 75 percent of all beef cattle. It has considerable potential for using underutilized feed resources and providing additional income for small farmers. The third method is the small but expanding feedlot operation using by-products of the banana and sugar industries. The fourth method—and the one with the greatest potential for raising beef output among small farmers—grazes cattle under coconut trees on improved pastures. Only about 800,000 hectares of the coconut area are now grazed, and by only 13 percent of the cattle. The main cattle-coconut areas are in northern and eastern Mindanao.

The key to success in cattle-coconut farming is the establishment and maintenance of high-quality pasture. With the application of fertilizers and other improvements to the land, copra production could more than double on the average farm within seven years and the cattle-carrying capacity of two animals a hectare could be achieved within two years. The government's proposed development program for smallholders would establish strategic livestock markets supported by provincial trading posts connected with distribution facilities in the Manila area (the country's largest meat-consuming center); provide livestock extension services through the Samahang Nayons (barrio associations); and lease purebred bulls to the farmers. The Bureau of Animal Husbandry, in collaboration with the Department of Local Government and Community Development, would be responsible for assisting small farmers in backyard projects to breed and fatten cattle.

Fish and fishery products. The main types of fishing in the Philippines are commercial marine operations, municipal or coastal fisheries, and inland fishponds. Only rough estimates of employment are possible because many small fishermen also engage in other activities such as farming and logging, but roughly 700,000 persons are probably employed in fisheries and about 80 percent are small-scale, traditional fishermen. Since 1965 fisheries production has more than doubled and per capita consumption has increased by almost 50 percent. Retail prices of fish have risen faster since 1960 than any other component of the retail price index of foodstuffs in Manila, although they remain about half those of meat. Most of the recent increases in production have come from traditional fisheries in coastal waters, where only a small proportion of the catch enters commercial trade. To meet the demand over the next decade, which is expected to grow at about 4 percent a year (Table 6.2), commercial marine and inland fisheries will need to expand.

Commercial fisheries production has been increasing at about 10 percent a year since the early 1950s and was estimated at about 465,000 tons in 1973, almost 40 percent of the total. The commercial fishing fleet comprised an estimated 2,500 vessels in 1973, operated by about 1,500 owners with about 47,000 licensed fishermen. Activities are restricted to water 12.6 miles beyond the coast or 7 fathoms deep, and the fleet is based primarily near the Manila area and around the Visayan Sea. The Food and Agriculture Organization (FAO) estimates that the potential annual catch from territorial waters is about 1.65 million metric tons, more than triple the present catch.

Municipal or coastal fishing is highly labor intensive; it employs almost 575,000 persons and currently accounts for about 640,000 metric tons of fish a year, 53 percent of the total production. These fishermen generally use traditional craft, 80 percent of which are not motorized and must operate near the shore and only during good weather. Productivity is low, largely at subsistence level, with the catch consumed locally. The FAO estimates that the annual municipal catch represents about 80 percent of the potential in coastal waters. But the limitations of their vessels prevent many small fishermen from tapping the large resources in deep-sea waters.

Municipal fisheries lack modern equipment, credit at reasonable interest rates, and infrastructure and marketing facilities. Large boats are needed to increase catching efficiency and allow fishermen to bring the catch to more attractive markets. This in turn requires that medium- and long-term credit be made available to finance the purchase of modern equipment. The lack of adequate means for handling and distributing the fish adversely affects the quality of fresh fish for sale, and there is also a need for public facilities such as municipal wharves, piers, and shipways.

Inland fishponds currently produce only about 10 percent of the total output, but between 1965 and 1970 fishpond production increased by over 50 percent as a result of the extension of fishpond area and higher yields. Production has been estimated at about 100,000 metric tons a year and has involved primarily milkfish (bangus) for domestic consumption. Annual average yields of 570 kilograms a hectare compare with 300 in Indonesia and 1,700 in the Republic of China. Research results show that average yields could reach about 1,500 kilograms a hectare annually with improved pond design, appropriate fertilization, pest control, and intensive management of fish populations.

In 1971 the registered fishpond area was about 175,000 hectares. About half this area is leased from the government under long-term arrangements (up to twenty-five years and renewable for another twenty-five), and the remainder is privately owned. Freshwater pond cultivation is not yet common in the Philippines, nor is the technical base for management as well developed as for brackish water ponds. Shrimp cultivation is under consideration by several research stations, but its large-scale commercial development is not expected for at least another five years.

The government has four on-going programs to increase fishery production and marketing: The Fishpond Development Program includes stocking inland waters with milkfish, oysters, and carp; technical assistance to help improve yields; research in pond fertilization; pest and disease control; and the leasing of swampland. The Commercial Fishing Development Program for promoting deep-water fishing provides technical assistance to fishing boat operators, conducts biological and oceanographic research, and constructs fishing ports and harbors. The Municipal Fishing Program provides extension services, credit, and marketing facilities to subsistence farmers. The Fish and Fishery Products Utilization Program includes research, extension services for processing and marketing, and the construction of ice plants and cold storage facilities.

Included in the government's program is the development of "family-size" fishponds for long-term leasing to qualified participants in the land reform areas. The objective is to establish modern fishpond villages run on a cooperative basis with government supervision and financial assistance. Greater attention, however, should be given to providing assistance to the majority of small municipal fishermen. Although helping them would require a substantial investment by the government, it would benefit a significant number of families with incomes that are now in the lowest 40 percent of the national income distribution.

Prospects for Agricultural Exports

Agricultural export production is dominated by the coconut and sugar industries; a wide range of other crops such as abaca, tobacco, bananas, and pineapples are produced on a much smaller scale. The sector is organized in a variety of forms, ranging from the large plantations that grow sugar, bananas, and pineapples to the smallholders raising coconuts. Agricultural exports account for an overwhelming share of foreign exchange earnings. Their share has been declining, however, and at present accounts for half of all export receipts, compared with about 85 percent in 1950 and 70 percent in 1960. This downward trend will probably continue, even though by 1985 agricultural exports could still account for a third of total export earnings. In addition to their importance in the balance of payments, agricultural exports currently represent 11 percent of GNP and are the main source of income and employment for about 20 percent of the total farm population. Moreover about 2.9 million hectares, or 30 percent of the total harvested area in the Philippines, are devoted to agricultural exports. Production for export markets has been growing at about 3.5 percent a year since the early 1960s; the increase in output has come almost entirely from an expansion of the cultivated area.

THE COCONUT INDUSTRY

The Philippines is the world's leading producer and exporter of copra. Coconut growing is one of the country's most important economic activities, yet it has been one of the most neglected in many respects. Traditionally, coconut growing has been a smallholder activity. The 1960 census showed that 65 percent of the 440,252 coconut farms were less than 4 hectares and 98 percent less than 20 hectares. According to the same census 25 percent of the farm operators were tenants, 56 percent were owners, and 18 percent were part owners.[12] It is estimated that there are now more than 500,000 exclusively coconut farms in the Philippines, although coconuts are grown on many other kinds of farms as well. Probably about 3 million people depend directly on coconut growing for their main source of income.

12. Estimates of tenancy on coconut farms is complicated by the fact that many of those classified as tenants are believed to be wage laborers employed as watchmen.

Production. Coconut production was relatively stable throughout the 1950s at a little above a million metric tons of copra equivalents (Table 6.9), but it has risen in recent years to about 1.8 million metric tons (the 1972–74 average), representing an increase of about 3 percent a year since 1960. This growth reflects a steady expansion in the area cultivated, from about 1.1 million hectares in 1960 to 2.2 million hectares in 1974. There has been no discernible trend in copra yields in the past two decades, which have averaged about 1,200 kilograms a hectare. Although it is widely believed that copra yields in the Philippines are low, they compare favorably with those in other major coconut-producing countries such as Indonesia, Mozambique, and Sri Lanka.[13] Six regions in the Philippines account for about 83 percent of the coconut production: Southern Tagalog, Bicol, Eastern Visayas, and Northern, Southern, and Western Mindanao. A most striking geographical change has been the emergence of Mindanao as the major coconut-producing area— accounting for half the total produced in 1974 compared with 26 percent in 1960—and the decline in the relative importance of Southern Tagalog and Bicol.

The government is aware of the need for improving farm productivity. Indeed, a number of plans to revitalize the industry have been drawn up during the past decade. Until recently, however, government programs have fallen far short of their original objectives, largely because of a lack of funds and staff. They have also been hampered by a proliferation of quasi-government agencies and other organizations concerned in various ways with the industry. To achieve a greater degree of coordination among these agencies, the Philippine Coconut Authority (PCA) was created in 1972, replacing several other organizations that were previously responsible for developing the industry.

The PCA recently formulated a program for production, marketing, and processing. A major component is the Coconut Seedling Nursery Project, which will provide free of charge to farmers each year some 300,000 coconut seedlings of improved varieties, developed locally and abroad. Emphasis is being placed on replanting high-yielding varieties from West Africa, but this will not begin until 1981 because of the limited supply and the time required to generate new planting material. Authorities hope that about 60,000

---

13. World Bank, "Agricultural Sector Survey: Philippines," vol. 4, annex 12, p. 3.

Table 6.9. Actual and Projected Trends in Cultivated Area, Yields, Production, and Disposition of Coconuts

| | Area planted (thousands of hectares) | | Copra production (thousands of metric tons) | Yield of bearing area (metric tons per hectare) | Disposition of copra (thousands of metric tons of copra) | | | | | | |
| | | | | | Export market | | | | Domestic market | | |
Year	Bearing[a]	Total			Copra	Coconut oil	Desiccated coconut	Total	Coconut oil	Other	Total
Actual											
1960	892	1,059	1,235	1,385	834	95	74	1,003	183	49	232
1961	993	1,200	1,198	1,206	705	119	72	896	194	108	302
1962	1,114	1,284	1,533	1,376	880	244	77	1,201	219	113	332
1963	1,222	1,392	1,752	1,433	956	343	86	1,385	241	126	367
1964	1,276	1,483	1,638	1,283	852	376	83	1,311	235	92	327
1965	1,235	1,605	1,593	1,290	859	389	89	1,337	232	24	256
1966	1,234	1,611	1,795	1,455	909	505	83	1,496	272	27	299
1967	1,261	1,821	1,508	1,196	763	379	74	1,216	261	31	292
1968	1,240	1,800	1,468	1,184	681	436	89	1,206	227	35	262
1969	1,367	1,846	1,260	922	554	345	63	961	272	27	299
1970	1,434	1,884	1,356	946	424	539	74	1,038	269	51	320
1971	1,555	2,049	1,756	1,129	711	654	92	1,456	262	38	300
1972	1,591	2,126	2,174	1,366	969	757	95	1,820	313	41	354
1973	1,633	2,133	1,871	1,146	728	691	95	1,514	319	38	357
1974	1,750	2,200	1,504	859	323	754	81	1,158	316	30	346
Projected											
1980	2,100	2,400	2,500	1,200	310	1,600	140	2,050	400	40	450
1985	2,500	2,600	3,000	1,200	140	2,150	160	2,450	500	50	550

a. The data on bearing area for 1960–74 were computed by dividing the number of bearing trees (as reported by the United Coconut Association of the Philippines, UCAP) by 150, which is the approximate planting density per hectare.

Sources: 1960–74 data are from UCAP; 1980 and 1985 are World Bank projections.

hectares a year will be replanted during the 1980s. Such a medium-term replanting program is worth implementing, but the present Coconut Seedling Nursery Project could be accelerated by relying on locally developed, high-yielding varieties and by giving PCA more direct control over the supply of seedlings. Inasmuch as supplies are limited, the initial replanting should probably be concentrated in areas where there is a high proportion of overaged trees.[14]

Because the benefits of the replanting program will take some time to emerge, increased efforts are being made to improve farm management by giving farmers access to credit and increasing their participation in processing and marketing. The existing extension service for coconut farmers is being strengthened by the PCA, and an integrated model farm program is being started in order to test the feasibility of developing cooperatively managed farms. Money from the Coconut Investment Fund, established in 1971, will be used to help establish more rural banks, credit unions, and cooperatives in coconut-growing areas, and to provide loans for coconut production and farmer training. The fund, which is financed through a levy on copra, collects only about ₱10 million a year, however, and can benefit only a small proportion of the estimated half million coconut farms. If yields are to improve significantly during the next five to ten years (before the replanting program has an impact), a more ambitious program to improve farm practices and intensify land use with intercropping and coordinated livestock development, backed by larger allocations of resources and extension staff, will probably be needed.

Because of the long gestation period for new plantings, production over the next decade will be determined largely by the changes in cultivated area that occurred during 1965–75. By 1980 there will be about 2.1 million hectares of bearing trees. If yields remain at their historic level of about 1,200 kilograms a hectare, production would be about 2.5 million metric tons of copra equivalents, an average increase of about 4 percent a year (Table 6.9). Production by 1985 will obviously depend on future plantings, but the rate of planting will probably slow down in the latter part of the 1970s because of the increasing difficulty in finding new cultivable areas.

14. About 24 percent of all coconut trees in the Philippines, excluding Bicol and Eastern Visayas, were older than 60 years in 1970. World Bank, "Agricultural Sector Survey: Philippines," vol. 4, annex 12, p. 6.

The bearing area could be about 2.5 million hectares by 1985, in which case production would probably be about 3 million metric tons.

Processing and export marketing. Approximately 90 percent of the coconuts produced in the Philippines is processed into copra. The remaining 10 percent is consumed either directly as food nuts or used to manufacture desiccated coconut. About 20,000 middlemen are involved in marketing copra. End users, which number about fifty, include copra exporters, oil millers and refiners, desiccators, soap and detergent makers, coir fiber manufacturers, and charcoal producers. The Philippines accounts for about two-thirds of the world's copra exports and about 70 percent of coconut oil exports. There are nine active copra exporters, of which three export about 95 percent of the total produced. Of the nineteen active coconut oil exporters, the three largest firms account for about 60 percent of oil exports.

Important changes have been taking place in the processing and disposal of copra in the Philippines. During the 1950s and early 1960s about 40 percent of the total production was absorbed by the domestic oilseed-processing industry; the remaining 60 percent was exported as copra. Since 1965 there has been a steady increase in the share of copra that is crushed domestically into coconut oil; by 1974–75 it had reached 70 percent. As a result of private initiative and government efforts to expand the coconut oil industry, this trend is expected to continue, and additional crushing capacity, equivalent to about 450,000 metric tons of copra a year, is due to be installed in the next two or three years. By 1980 domestic production of oil will probably be about 2 million metric tons of copra equivalents, and by 1985, with no further increase in crushing capacity, domestic oilseed production could be about 2.6 million metric tons in copra equivalent, absorbing almost 90 percent of the projected production of copra.

Domestic consumption of coconut products, primarily in the form of coconut oil, has been growing at slightly more than 4.5 percent a year since the early 1960s (Table 6.9). If this trend continues, domestic consumption of coconut oil would be about 400,000 metric tons in copra equivalents in 1980 and 500,000 metric tons in 1985. Total domestic consumption of coconut products would probably be about 550,000 metric tons by 1985. Exports of coconut products are expected to rise from 1.6 million metric tons in copra equivalents in 1975 to about 2.5 million in 1985. More than 80 percent of exports by the 1980s would be in the form of coconut oil if the present plans to expand the oilseed-processing industry materialize. The expected shift to exporting coconut oil will not be without difficulties. The traditional markets for coconut oil are being threatened by cheaper oils, such as palm and soybean, and by the petrochemical industry's development of less expensive synthetic detergents and laundry soaps. Another problem is the termination of the Laurel-Langley trade agreement in 1974, which ended the preferential treatment of Philippine copra and coconut oil in the U.S. market.[15] In the world market copra now enters most importing countries duty free, but coconut oil exports face a number of trade barriers. For example, members of the European Common Market impose a duty on coconut oil to protect their domestic crushing and refining plants. If almost its entire export crop is crushed, the Philippines will have to increase its share of the oil market in Europe or develop new markets.

THE SUGAR INDUSTRY

In 1960 sugar was grown on 53,000 farms; only about 18,000 were exclusively sugar farms that cultivated more than 80 percent of the total area and accounted for almost 90 percent of the total production. Since the beginning of the 1960s sugar production has expanded steadily at about 4 percent a year, reaching 2.45 million metric tons in 1973–74, of which 63 percent was exported to the United States. This growth was primarily in response to increased demand from the United States after it stopped importing sugar from Cuba in 1961 and because of the Laurel-Langley agreement of 1965 which increased the U.S. annual sugar quota for the Philippines from 980,000 metric tons to 1.3–1.5 million metric tons.

Production. Practically all the increase in sugar production has come from expanding the harvested area, which amounted to almost 470,000 hectares in 1974. During the 1960s much of the expansion

15. Copra imports from the Philippines were exempt from a 2 percent additional processing tax collected on all copra imports to the United States. Consequently the Philippines supplied almost the total United States' requirement of copra.

Table 6.10. Actual and Projected Trends in Cultivated Area, Yields, Production, and Disposition of Sugar

Crop year	Area planted (thousands of hectares)	Yield (metric tons per hectare)		Ratio of sugar to cane (percent)	Sugar production (thousands of metric tons)	Sugar disposition (thousands of metric tons)	
		Cane	Sugar			Export market	Domestic market
Actual							
1959–60	204	61.78	6.80	11.0	1,369	1,090	279
1960–61	n.a.	n.a.	n.a.	n.a.	1,317	1,071	246
1961–62	n.a.	n.a.	n.a.	n.a.	1,468	961	507
1962–63	n.a.	n.a.	n.a.	n.a.	1,555	1,027	528
1963–64	n.a.	n.a.	n.a.	n.a.	1,684	1,027	657
1964–65	343	46.76	4.54	9.7	1,558	1,094	464
1965–66	310	42.61	4.52	10.6	1,402	980	422
1966–67	286	53.38	5.45	10.2	1,560	974	586
1967–68	297	51.71	5.38	10.4	1,595	964	631
1968–69	321	51.34	4.78	9.7	1,597	980	617
1969–70	377	56.82	5.11	9.0	1,927	1,228	699
1970–71	473	49.93	4.34	8.7	2,056	1,345	711
1971–72	420	46.45	4.32	9.3	1,816	1,210	606
1972–73	435	52.17	5.19	9.9	2,258	1,474	784
1973–74	468	55.55	5.22	9.4	2,442	1,542	900
Projected							
1979–80	530	55.00	5.50	10.0	2,900	1,850	1,050
1984–85	550	60.00	6.30	10.5	3,400	2,150	1,250

n.a.: Not available.
Sources: 1959–74 are from the Philippine Sugar Institute; 1979–80 and 1984–85 are World Bank projections.

occurred in the Eastern Visayas and Mindanao. At the same time sugar yields were declining from an average of about 6.5 metric tons a hectare in the early 1960s to an average of 4.9 metric tons in the mid-1960s (Table 6.10). This decline was caused by the spread of sugarcane production onto rolling land and hillsides without adequate soil conservation, a deterioration in cane varieties, increased delays between harvesting and milling, and the failure to control pests and diseases.

The potential for expanding sugar production is considerable, but much will depend on the future growth of export demand and on whether exports will be controlled by international marketing agreements. As the subsequent discussion of market prospects suggests, future production may increase by about 3.5 percent a year, which is somewhat less than the past rate. Continued growth in the area planted would almost certainly be at the expense of other crops, particularly rice and corn. The extent to which this occurs will depend on the relative profitability of the competing crops and on government policies regarding the location of additional milling capacity. Locating mills in rain-fed lowland areas where there is little prospect of introducing irrigation could encourage sugar production and provide opportunities for increasing the incomes of many small rice and corn farmers. Of course consideration will also have to be given to the milling capacity in established sugar-producing areas, particularly if yields increase substantially over the long term.

Concerted efforts should be made to meet the growing demand for sugar by raising yields in established areas. Perhaps the most important step is to reduce the shrinkage in sugar content that occurs between harvesting and milling of the cane. The recovery of sugar from cane in the 1970s was about 20 percent less than in the 1950s (Table 6.10). With the rapid expansion of the cane area and the limited number of mills in the 1960s, the once strict scheduling of harvest and delivery of cane to mills deteriorated. It is conservatively estimated that the Philippines loses at least 10 percent of its sugar production through delayed milling. This means the loss of 250,000 metric tons of sugar.

In addition to reestablishing strict schedules for harvesting and delivery, other measures needed to raise yields include better management, closer attention to the problem of erosion where sugar has been planted on hillsides, and increased use of fertilizer.[16] Most of the growth in output in the remainder of the 1970s will probably come from an increase in area cultivated, which may reach 530,000 hectares, and possibly some improvement in sugar yields. In the 1980s, however, the area planted may level off at perhaps 550,000 hectares, so that increased production will depend primarily on higher cane yields and continued improvements in the rate of sugar recovery. Cane yields will probably have to be raised about 15 percent from their present levels, and the cultivated area would be about 20 percent higher than at present.

Processing and export marketing. In 1974 the government assumed control over marketing the entire sugar crop. The Philippine Exchange Company (PHILEX) became the sole exporter of sugar in that year, and the Philippine National Bank already controlled the domestic marketing.[17] Sugar milling capacity has doubled since the early 1960s and reached 160,000 metric tons a day in 1973–74, with a crushing season of 250 days. Of the 38 mills in operation in 1973–74, 14 were new ones with a total daily capacity of 58,000 metric tons. The remaining 23 mills had a combined capacity of somewhat over 100,000 metric tons a day. There are plans to expand the milling capacity by 20,000 metric tons with the addition of five more mills. Actual expansion will, however, depend on the growth of demand for sugar.

PHILEX determines the price received by the miller; in 1974 this was ₱139 a picul,[18] but in May 1975, following the decline in the international price, it was reduced to ₱106 a picul. If the customary milling contract is assumed, specifying 65 percent of sales to the grower and 35 percent to the miller, the price received by the farmer would be ₱1.14 a kilogram, which in real terms is almost the same as in the early 1970s before the sharp rise in sugar prices. PHILEX allocates 30 percent of the crop to domestic use and 70 per-

16. Through the efforts of the Philippine Sugar Institute (PHILSUGIN), a government-sponsored corporation responsible for research and development planning in the sugar industry, farmers are already using improved varieties, fertilizers, and pesticides. PHILSUGIN carries out research on plant breeding, agronomy, pest control, fertilizer application, weed control, and sugar cane physiology.

17. PHILEX is a subsidiary of the National Investment Development Corporation (NIDC), which is owned by the government's Philippine National Bank.

18. One picul is equivalent to 63.5 kilograms.

cent to exports. Since 1974 high export prices have generated large profits for PHILEX. Retail prices are controlled to keep the price of household sugar below that of industrial sugar and both substantially below export prices. Thus the domestic consumer is subsidized, partly at the expense of the producer. Under this system the government must obviously watch the international market and adjust producer and retail prices appropriately.

Domestic consumption of sugar was about 20 kilograms per capita in 1973; during the past decade it has grown by about 7 percent a year [19] but is unlikely to continue at the same rate. Recent estimates of income elasticities for the Philippines suggest that, all things being equal, domestic disappearance will grow by only about 4 percent a year in the decade ahead. By 1985 it is projected to reach about 1.3 million metric tons, or 22 kilograms a person; at present levels of production this would leave about 1.2 million metric tons available for export.

The Philippines is currently the twelfth largest exporter of sugar in the world. Since world demand is projected to grow at about 3 percent a year over the next decade, it is plausible to assume that exports of sugar from the Philippines could approach 2.2 million metric tons by 1985 (Table 6.10). The precise outcome could be affected by marketing strategies, however. Until 1974 when both the Laurel-Langley trade agreement and the U.S. Sugar Act expired, the United States was the sole export market for Philippine sugar. Since July 1974 Philippine sugar exports to the United States have been subject to full U.S. duty and since December 1974 have lost their preferential treatment among U.S. importers.

In view of the supply potential and lower transport costs of Caribbean and Latin American sugar-exporting countries, the Philippines may be at a competitive disadvantage and find it difficult to maintain its previously preeminent position in the U.S. market. A major source of uncertainty is the extent to which the sugar trade with Cuba will be resumed now that the Organization of American States has agreed to remove its trade embargo. A decline in U.S. imports of Philippine sugar would require a substantial change from the traditional pattern of sugar marketing. Under these

---

19. This is unusually high, but since domestic disappearance is computed as a residual from available production and export figures, it represents not only actual sugar consumption but also changes in sugar stocks as well as possible illegal exports of sugar.

circumstances the Philippines would have to strengthen its position in the free market as well as in the centrally planned economies. The free market is the largest among the four major international markets for sugar, and more than half of world trade is channeled through it. It is "free" only in the sense that prices are not controlled, but the supply of sugar to the market has been regulated during several periods in the past by multilateral agreements. Following the example of Australia, the Philippines may find long-term contracts advantageous in reducing the uncertainty that could accompany a loss of its preferential position in the U.S. market.

7

Strategies for Rural Development: Supporting Services and Infrastructure

Because of the limited potential for extending cultivation onto new land, programs to increase agricultural production and productivity will require more intensive use of the established farmland, particularly in the major river basins. Increased land productivity will, in turn, depend primarily on the quality of supporting services, particularly those to small farmers.

Supporting Services for Agriculture

Among the agricultural services that will be needed are continued expansion of rural infrastructure (including irrigation and a better network of farm-to-market roads), stronger financial services and increased allocations of credit, improved marketing facilities, and a more dependable supply of nonfarm inputs. A more effective, but not necessarily larger, extension force will be needed, and there will have to be continued close attention to input and product prices to ensure that there is sufficient incentive for farmers to adopt more productive technologies.

FERTILIZER USE

The application of fertilizer has increased considerably in the last decade, largely because of the introduction of HYVS. Traditionally fertilizers have been used primarily for sugar and rice.[1] In 1964 these two crops absorbed 76 percent of the total amount of fertilizer; in 1973 their share dropped to 70 percent. The government's supervised credit programs for rice and corn have been encouraging the use of fertilizer. Consequently there was a 40 percent increase in the amount of nitrogen applied to rice in 1973. Anticipating a severe worldwide shortage of fertilizer in 1975 and an enlarged demand as a result of the supervised credit programs, the Philippines imported 900,000 metric tons of fertilizer in 1974, more than twice the level of previous imports. The anticipated increase in demand, however, did not materialize; in fact, it seems likely that there was a sharp drop in the use of fertilizer in rice areas in 1974–75, although detailed data are not yet available. This decline was apparently due to a much less favorable fertilizer-rice price relationship.

Despite the government's efforts to expand the use of fertilizer, the rate of application remains low (in 1973 only about 400,000 metric tons were consumed) primarily because of inadequate institutional credit to finance fertilizer purchases and an uneven distribution network which does not adequately serve the more remote areas. If the rice production program discussed earlier is to be realized, demand for fertilizer will need to grow at about 15 percent a year during the next decade. Substantial improvements will be needed in the channels for distributing fertilizer, and the relation between the farm-gate prices for fertilizer and rice will need to be adjusted to provide sufficient incentive for farmers to adopt this technology.

Fertilizer is distributed in the Philippines by private dealers. Each manufacturing company has its own outlets with local or national coverage. Of about 2,700 fertilizer and chemical dealers in the country, almost half are either in Central Luzon (25 percent) or Southern Tagalog (17 percent). The Fertilizer Industry Authority (FIA) was created in 1973 to coordinate the supply and distribution of fertilizer. It is empowered to regulate, control, and develop the industry to ensure an adequate supply. The FIA also has authority over all aspects of manufacturing and marketing, including

---

1. A survey of coconut farms in 1968 indicated that out of 1,230 farms only 5 percent used fertilizer, and those were mostly the large farms. Gil R. Rodriguez, Jr., "Fertilizer Supply and Demand, 1952–1980" (M.B.A. thesis, Ateneo University, 1974), p. 22.

price control, the allocation of fertilizer by crop, and imports and exports.

Although there has been a gradual expansion in the production capacity of its fertilizer industry, the Philippines remains largely dependent on imports to meet domestic demand. Since the early 1960s imports have been increasing at about 7 percent a year (Table 7.1). The value of manufactured fertilizer imports averaged about US$12 million for 1970–73 but then jumped to US$84 million in 1974, the result of substantial increases in both quantity and price. Domestic production has increased by about 15 percent a year since 1960, more than doubling with the opening of a new plant in 1966.

Fertilizer production is in the hands of three private companies with a total rated capacity in nitrogen equivalents of 90,000 metric tons. At present, however, they are producing only 65,000 metric tons a year, or 72 percent of capacity, because of such problems as lack of feedstock, inefficient plant design, poor maintenance, power failures, and competition from imports. The government is actively examining the possibility of building an ammonia-urea complex which would have a production capacity of 900–1,000 metric tons

Table 7.1. Estimates of Total Supply of Fertilizer Nutrients
(In thousands of metric tons)

	Nitrogen			Phosphorus			Potassium		
Year	Imports	Domestic production	Total	Imports	Domestic production	Total	Imports	Domestic production	Total
1960	24	7	31	9	5	14	9	1	10
1961	33	10	43	9	6	15	14	4	18
1962	57	14	71	14	8	22	22	6	28
1963	14	14	28	3	8	11	7	5	12
1964	42	15	57	15	8	23	7	6	13
1965	33	16	49	16	8	24	16	5	21
1966	17	18	35	1	10	11	57	7	54
1967	45	39	84	4	13	17	10	12	22
1968	30	37	67	17	27	44	19	19	38
1969	40	54	94	7	25	32	29	17	46
1970	48	48	96	10	23	33	16	16	32
1971	76	52	128	3	25	28	27	17	44
1972	54	52	106	3	25	28	42	17	59

Sources: Gil R. Rodriguez, Jr., "Fertilizer Supply and Demand, 1952–1980" (M.B.A. thesis, Ateneo University, 1974); Fertilizer Industry Authority; and International Potash Institute.

a day of ammonia and 1,500–1,700 metric tons a day of urea. The total cost would be about US$300 million, and the complex would probably be owned by the government. Although no decision has been made, it is likely that fuel oil would serve as feedstock.

Plans for expanding domestic fertilizer production in the next ten years include two possible phosphate plants with a combined capacity of 150,000 metric tons a year. They would import phosphate rock from Australia or the United States and utilize the sulfuric acid that will be a by-product from the proposed copper smelters. The first smelter is due to become operational in 1978. It is expected to produce 33,550 metric tons a year of commercial grade sulfuric acid and 8,000 metric tons a year of crude arsenic acid. Depending on the availability of sulfuric acid, the Philippines could eventually be in a position to export part of its phosphoric acid to other countries in the region, such as Indonesia.

PRICE POLICIES FOR RICE AND FERTILIZER

While pursuing a policy of self-sufficiency in rice, the government has at the same time been concerned about the retail price in urban areas. In 1970 the government imposed a ceiling on the retail price of rice, which in 1975 was ₱1.90 a kilogram. To maintain the ceiling price in the face of much higher world market prices from late 1973 to mid-1975, the government supplied imported rice below cost, thereby depressing the domestic price structure for rice. The public cost of this subsidy was about US$20 million in both FY74 and FY75.

The policy of maintaining an artificially low domestic price structure for rice may have been understandable in 1973–75 when the international price was high. It is expected, however, that the world market terms of trade will turn against primary agricultural commodities during the next ten years, and that the price of rice will fall by 20 percent from 1976 to 1985 in terms of 1973 constant dollars.[2] Moreover, if in years of surplus production the domestic price of rice falls substantially, the government's policy of maintaining a floor price will place severe demands on its procurement capacity. In 1975–76 the government is expected to encounter storage problems because of record production levels. In evaluat-

2. World Bank, "Price Forecasts for Major Primary Commodities" (July 1975), restricted-circulation internal document no. 814.

ing the overall cost of the present subsidy program, consideration should be given to the need for more storage capacity to provide the cushion necessary for periods of production shortfalls. In order not to discourage domestic rice production, the government should carefully review its policy of subsidizing urban rice consumers and consider gradually reducing the subsidy if the real price of rice falls.

The other side of the coin for agricultural incentives concerns the price of inputs. During 1973–75 the world price of fertilizers and other chemical inputs rose even faster than the price of food grains. To maintain production incentives in the face of artifically low domestic grain prices, the government, through the FIA, adopted a two-tier price system for fertilizers, charging essentially the world market price for fertilizers used to grow export crops and a lower, subsidized price to producers of food grains. Despite this effort the ratio of the price of fertilizer to that of both food grains and export crops increased substantially from its historic level (see the case of rice and sugar in Table 7.2), and there is evidence that the use of fertilizers declined. There are also indications that, as a result of the two-tier price system, fertilizer was diverted from food crops to export crops, particularly in areas where both are grown side by side, such as rice and sugarcane in parts of Central Luzon.[3]

The specific effect of relative input and output prices on the use of inputs in the Philippines has not been analyzed, and hence their effect on yields and production is not known. Historical information indicates that farmers increased their use of fertilizers when price ratios were in the 1.0 to 1.5 range (Table 7.2). Rough projections on the basis of the World Bank's commodity price forecasts through 1985 make it appear that the ratios of the farm-gate price of fertilizer to the prices of rice and sugar would be in the lower part of their historical range if all price controls were removed. While a more detailed analysis is obviously needed, these projections are at least indicative of the future price situation. The government should gradually reduce the subsidy on consumption and inputs as world market prices for these commodities fall in real terms, so that domestic prices would correspond to world market prices by 1980. In any case there is good reason to eliminate the two-

3. In addition to real production problems, this diversion created data problems insofar as the official statistics overstate the amount of fertilizer used for food crops and understate the amount used for export crops.

Table 7.2. Relation between Fertilizer Prices and the Farm-Gate Prices of Paddy Rice and Sugarcane, 1965–75, at Current Prices

Year	Farm price (pesos per 100 kilograms)		Urea fertilizer price (pesos per 100 kilograms)		Ratio of urea price to price of:	
	Paddy rice	Sugarcane	To rice farmers	To sugar farmers	Paddy rice	Sugarcane
Actual						
1965	33.85	28.65	53.97	53.97	1.59	1.88
1966	37.50	32.83	52.91	52.91	1.41	1.61
1967	37.95	35.32	51.81	51.81	1.37	1.47
1968	35.30	37.57	48.50	48.50	1.37	1.29
1969	36.05	37.08	44.09	44.09	1.22	1.19
1970	39.73	46.75	61.90	61.90	1.56	1.32
1971	55.37	58.01	65.40	65.40	1.18	1.13
1972	59.66	66.55	67.70	67.70	1.13	1.02
1973	79.00	73.28				
May			55.40	70.70	0.89	0.96
November			55.40	96.20	0.70	1.31
1974	100.00	142.78				
April			139.30	231.40	1.39	1.62
November			223.40	334.80	2.23	2.34
1975						
May	100.00	108.42	181.40	281.40	1.81	2.60
Projected						
1980	200.00	210	230		1.15	1.10
1985	290.00	290	350		1.21	1.21

Source: Actual data are from the World Bank, "Agricultural Sector Survey: Philippines" (May 2, 1973), restricted-circulation internal document no. 39a-PH, annex 15, and the Fertilizer Industry Authority. Projections are based on the World Bank, "Price Forecasts for Major Primary Commodities" (July 1975), restricted-circulation internal document no. 814.

tier price structure for fertilizers as soon as possible in order to reduce the incentive for diverting fertilizer from food grains to export crops, and to encourage rice farmers to use their fertilizer supplies effectively.

To the extent that the government finds it desirable to continue subsidizing the retail price of rice, it should consider alternatives to the present policy of buying rice abroad and selling it below cost to consumers. The government could buy rice from domestic producers at the domestic world market price and sell it below cost to consumers, or it could subsidize domestic traders who perform the same function. The result would be to keep the subsidy element in the country rather than to pay it abroad as at present.

This alternative policy would not depress the internal producer price and hence would encourage domestic production and promote self-sufficiency. But such subsidization would have to be kept in line with prudent government budget management which calls for strict constraints on the growth of current expenditures.[4]

AGRICULTURAL EXTENSION AND RESEARCH

The experience of countries like the Republic of China and Japan indicates that success in raising agricultural productivity depends in part on the rate of adoption of innovations among farmers. This in turn is influenced by the quality of the agricultural extension services and the role of farmer organizations. In the Philippines this potential for promoting more rapid adoption of innovations has not been adequately exploited. As discussed in Chapter 5, the government has recently begun to give more attention to the role of farmer organizations, but much remains to be done; these programs are being adversely affected by the duplication of effort and overlapping responsibilities among government agencies. The role of the extension services, their relations with farmers and farmer organizations, and the interrelations among the latter all deserve close attention in the future.[5]

At present the inadequacies of the extension services are essentially those of organization and quality rather than a shortage of personnel. Some twenty-one different government agencies and institutions provide advisory services to farmers; seven of these have a total of about 20,000 technicians and the remaining fourteen another 3,000 technicians.[6] Just how many are regarded as field staff is uncertain, but even if it were only half (one technician for every 200 farmers) to two-thirds (1:150), the ratio would not be an unfavorable one.[7]

Although each agency has a specialized function, the large number of technicians spread among so many different agencies in-

4. See Chapter 15.
5. For a discussion of farmer training, see Chapter 12.
6. The seven important agencies and the number of their technicians are: the Bureau of Agricultural Extension (4,000), the Department of Agrarian Reform (4,000), the Department of Local Government and Community Development (3,500), the Bureau of Plant Industry (3,000), the Bureau of Animal Industries (2,200), the National Irrigation Administration (1,700), and the Bureau of Soils (1,200).
7. In Korea, for example, the ratio in 1970 was one technician for every 385 farmers.

evitably gives rise to duplication of efforts, if not conflicting advice to farmers. To cite only one example, field teams of the Department of Agrarian Reform which are carrying out the country's agrarian reform program are becoming unnecessarily involved in agricultural extension work. In many cases technical training of extension workers is poor, but even when it is adequate, coordination with research laboratories, which should provide technical support, is lacking.

For the next few years at least, emphasis should be placed upon upgrading the quality of the existing extension services rather than on expanding them. The relative roles of the many agencies should be carefully reviewed with an eye toward closer cooperation and supervision. In addition to incentives to personnel such as salaries and promotions, an intensive four-year program to retrain the existing field staff should probably also be given high priority. In developing a comprehensive training program, consideration should be given to the long-term approach the government wishes to take toward extension work. In the immediate future the training program will of course be limited by the facilities available, but in the long term flexibility exists to upgrade the quality of education provided by agricultural schools and colleges.

On the whole, the Philippines is building a competent research establishment. The Bureau of Agricultural Economics (BAECON) is developing increasing competence to provide data and analyses for agricultural policymakers. The research institutions are well advanced in work on HYV rice and have developed varieties of corn which are resistant to downy mildew. Research on sugarcane has had a long and generally fruitful history, but varieties resistant to the ratoon-stunting disease have not yet been developed. Other research is less impressive, particularly for coconuts, which are infested with the cadang-cadang disease. Research on sorghum and soybeans has not yet had time to make a large contribution to the development of a feed base.

The Philippine Council for Agricultural Research, established in 1972, is carrying out a seven-year program to expand research capabilities, which will include investments in infrastructure, laboratory and farm equipment, and the training of manpower. As part of this program the United States Agency for International Development is providing financial support to strengthen four research centers in Negros Occidental, Southern Mindanao, Bicol, and Central Luzon. For agricultural research to be relevant, it must not only focus on the current needs of the farmer but also anticipate future problems. For example, disease resistent HYVS take several years to develop; a researcher must identify the characteristics of a desirable variety and if possible develop the seed for it. Moreover the capacity of a strain to resist a given disease does not remain constant. Thus a good research program must constantly be not only in touch with the farmer but also developing new technology which can be made available when the need arises.

IRRIGATION AND WATER MANAGEMENT

Increased investment in the construction, rehabilitation, and maintenance of irrigation works will be essential during the next decade to intensify land utilization. Estimates vary as to the harvested area that is now irrigated. In the lowlands less than half the total rice area is irrigated, and virtually no facilities have been established in the uplands. According to BAECON there were 1.33 million hectares of irrigated harvested rice land in 1972.[8] The National Irrigation Administration (NIA) estimated the total irrigated harvested area at 1.11 million hectares in 1972, and the World Bank, after taking into account the past deterioration of the irrigation systems and the inaccuracy of reporting, estimated it at 833,000 hectares (Table 7.3).

Rehabilitation and maintenance of existing systems. In 1972 the geographic area actually served by existing irrigation systems was substantially less than their design capacity (Table 7.3).[9] Al-

8. In 1975 the BAECON estimate was 1.41 million hectares.
9. There are three main types of irrigation systems in the Philippines:

a. National irrigation systems are gravity fed, constructed, operated, and maintained by the NIA. In general each system covers an area of over 1,000 hectares. The total physical area served was estimated at 407,000 hectares in 1972, although the actual area was probably closer to 300,000 hectares.
b. Communal irrigation systems are for the most part also planned, designed, and constructed by the NIA but are turned over to an irrigation association for operation and maintenance. The normal size of these projects is 50 to 500 hectares. The total physical area served was estimated at about 130,000 hectares in 1972.
c. Pump irrigation systems utilize shallow wells, rivers, and irrigation canals as sources of water. The service area of the individual pump units is small, with the majority serving less than 20 hectares. According to the NIA there were about 10,300 pumps operating in 1972, covering an area of about 240,000 hectares.

Table 7.3. Estimates of Geographic and Harvested Area of Irrigated Land, 1972
(In thousands of hectares)

Type of system	Potential irrigated area	Actual irrigated area		Harvested area of irrigated land		Intensity of irrigation (percent)	
		NIA estimate	World Bank estimate	NIA estimate	World Bank estimate	NIA estimate	World Bank estimate
Gravity systems	719	577	519	861	735	119.7	102.2
NIA	407	314	305	470	441	115.5	108.4
Communal (NIA)	222	133	133	211	186	95.0	83.8
Communal (private)	90	130	81	180	108	200.0	120.0
Pump systems	239	165	110	248	148	103.8	61.9
Total	958	742	629	1,109	883	115.8	92.2

NIA: National Irrigation Administration.

Note: The potential area is the geographic area the systems were designed to serve. The harvested area includes two cropping seasons. The intensity of irrigation is the ratio of harvested area to potential geographic area that could be irrigated, expressed as a percentage.

Source: World Bank, "Agricultural Sector Survey: Philippines," vol. 2, annex 3, p. 9.

though the NIA and World Bank estimates differ somewhat, they both suggest that only about 70 percent of capacity was being utilized. To a large extent this reflects inadequate maintenance and operation of the systems. As a result, cropping intensity was as low as 116 percent in 1972 according to NIA estimates, but with proper maintenance, it should reach 140 percent relatively easily. The high returns from rehabilitation and improvement of the present systems are demonstrated in Table 7.4. The government recognizes that much more attention should be given to making better use of existing systems. The ten-year program drawn up by the NIA calls for the rehabilitation of about 340,000 hectares during FY75–84, which is about half of NIA's existing gravity systems. About 50 percent of this proposed area, or about 175,000 hectares, is already included in the ongoing projects being financed by the World Bank and the Asian Development Bank. The remainder, which accounts for most of the area proposed for rehabilitation in FY80–85, has yet to be identified, but it should be possible to rehabilitate a total of about 300,000 hectares during the FY75–84 period.

New irrigation facilities. The total amount of new land that is potentially suitable for irrigation is not known with any degree of

Table 7.4. Investment and Operating Costs per Harvested Hectare for NIA Gravity Systems and Pump Systems
(In 1974 U.S. dollars)

	NIA *gravity systems*		*Pump systems*	
Cost item	*Rehabilitation*	*New*	*Electric*	*Diesel*
Installation[a]	270	540–810	210	230
Operations and maintenance[b]	13	13	32	34
Recovery of capital[c]	27	68	21	22
Total costs (excluding installation)	40	81	53	56

a. Based on costs per hectare of physical area of US$400 for rehabilitation, US$800–1,200 for new gravity systems, US$290 for electric pump systems, and US$300 for diesel pump systems. The ratio of harvested area to geographic area was assumed to be 1.48 for NIA gravity systems and 1.40 for pump systems.

b. Based on information supplied by the NIA, these costs are in line with those reported for similar systems in other countries.

c. Assuming that for the NIA gravity systems the capital cost is recovered over fifty years; for pump systems, over ten years. Interest is charged at 10 percent a year for both systems.

Source: World Bank estimates.

certainty. A 1973 World Bank agricultural study conservatively estimated that about 1.4 million hectares of land could be irrigated. Since the potential area of existing systems accounted for close to one million of the 1.4 million hectares, the report suggested that only an additional 400,000 hectares could be irrigated. The NIA, however, has estimated that a much larger potential area of 1.7 million hectares remains to be developed, particularly in the Cagayan Valley, Central Luzon, and northern and eastern Mindanao.[10] Obviously the amount that can be developed is a matter of cost, but even with the more conservative World Bank estimate the irrigation potential is large.

The NIA prepared an ambitious program for 1975–84 that calls for an accelerated pace and would irrigate an additional 1.3 million hectares by 1985. About 700,000 hectares would be irrigated with large-scale gravity systems operated by the NIA, and the remaining 600,000 hectares would use smaller communal and pump systems. A program of this magnitude raises two important questions: Do the agencies concerned have the capacity to undertake the program? And is the balance between large-scale gravity projects and the smaller communal and pump projects appropriate? Obviously both kinds of projects are needed, but just what the proportions should be is less clear.

Small-scale projects have low investment costs per hectare but high operating costs (Table 7.4). The reverse situation exists for large-scale projects when allowance is made for recovering capital costs, but their current costs are about 50 percent higher than for the small-scale projects. One reason why pump systems are cheaper to install is that they are built to lower standards. Individual farmers are responsible for tapping the main canal (which is provided by the pump system) to deliver water to their own fields. Furthermore no drainage is provided. In the NIA gravity systems each ten-hectare block of land is served by canals which deliver water, by drainage systems, and by roads which allow the delivery of inputs and products. As a result the NIA systems tend to have more water control and to provide for a better distribution of inputs, and yields are therefore usually 30 to 50 percent higher than with pump systems. When this difference is taken into account, the cost of irrigation per unit of output in the large and small schemes is roughly comparable. Nonetheless the small-scale projects do have

10. International Labour Office, *Sharing in Development* (Geneva: ILO, 1974), p. 460.

shorter gestation periods and thus produce quicker results. For this reason, efforts should be made to accelerate the pump irrigation development program.

The proposed NIA ten-year program calls for the development of about 800,000 hectares with new large-scale gravity and communal systems and about 500,000 hectares with pumps. In view of administrative and technical constraints, a more reasonable target for 1985 would be about 200,000 hectares with new large-scale gravity systems and 100,000 hectares with communal systems. For the pump systems, in addition to the administrative problems, there is a lack of detailed information about the availability of groundwater or the power needed to operate the pumps. Although the potential for expansion is difficult to assess accurately, it may be possible to develop 200,000 hectares with pumps by 1985.

In the past year the government has begun to emphasize small-scale irrigation projects. The Farm Systems Development Corporation was recently set up to develop additional irrigation by tapping groundwater sources and pumping from streams. It has authorized capital of ₱800 million to be funded over an eight-year period and has sole responsibility for developing small-scale irrigation systems, leaving NIA to concentrate on developing the national gravity systems. A successful small-scale irrigation development program will require more knowledge about groundwater availability and stream flows, better operation and maintenance, and clarification of water rights. Groundwater development still remains at a tentative and investigative stage. The Bureau of Mines is undertaking groundwater and hydrological surveys in the Agusan River basin, northwestern Luzon, eastern Misamis, Pangasinan, Samar, and southern and western Mindanao.

Water charges. Until 1975 irrigation fees on the national systems were fixed at ₱25 a hectare for wet season rice and ₱35 a hectare for dry season rice.[11] Over the years these amounts were eroded by inflation so that they failed to cover even operating and maintenance costs, let alone the recovery of any capital cost.[12] In 1975 the government developed a new rate formula which repre-

11. Since virtually all national irrigation systems are in rice-producing areas, this discussion is limited to water charges for irrigated rice.

12. Under Republic Act 3601 the NIA has the power to "collect from the users of each irrigation system constructed by it such fees as may be necessary to finance the continuous operation of the system and reimburse within a period of not less than 25 years the cost of construction thereof."

sents a major improvement over the old system. Irrigation fees on the national systems are now the equivalent of 100 kilograms of paddy rice a hectare in the wet season and 150 kilograms a hectare in the dry season. At the 1975 government support price for paddy, the new fees equal ₱100 and ₱150 a hectare in the wet and dry seasons respectively, or about four times the previous rates. By specifying the rates in terms of rice equivalents, the government has built in a hedge against inflation. For a typical new or rehabilitated national system, these rates would cover annual operating and maintenance costs but would contribute little toward capital cost recovery.

As an exception to the uniform rate policy, the government has agreed to gradually raise water rates on irrigation systems in Central and Northern Luzon and the island of Mindoro to the equivalent of 175 kilograms of paddy a hectare in the wet season and 225 kilograms in the dry season. These rates are expected to recover from 30 to 40 percent of the full cost of constructing, operating, and maintaining these systems over the lives of the projects when both costs and water charges are discounted at a rate of 10 percent. They would also recover from the beneficiaries of the systems from 10 to 20 percent of the incremental net farm incomes expected to result from the investments; in fact, after allowances for the value of farm family labor, return to farm capital, farm management, and the uncertainty of future income streams, they actually represent a much higher contribution. But there may still be room to increase water charges in the future, and the government might consider doing this after it has had time to evaluate the impact of the new 1975 rates.

Of primary importance to the question of water charges is the issue of collections. NIA's record of irrigation fee collection has improved steadily during the last few years. Total collections rose from ₱4.8 million in FY69 to ₱9.2 million in FY74; as a percentage of fees charged the collection rate improved from 50 to 66 percent over the same period, although it is still low. Improved collection will become even more important with the new water charges and increases in the level of investment. Unfortunately, sufficient information is not now available to relate actual collections to prior cost and the availability of services or benefits. It is possible, for example, that some farmers are charged for water they do not actually receive. Collection rates appear to be better wherever NIA provides reasonable service; the ambitious program to improve and expand irrigation should therefore also improve collections. NIA is currently studying the level of service provided by the national system and the relationship between service and collections. Results should be available in 1976 and will be used to determine ways of improving collection. Even less is known about water charges and collection rates in areas which use small, communal gravity systems and where NIA is not responsible for operation and maintenance.

One result of the proposed strategy for rice is that farmers in irrigated areas would probably be better off than their counterparts in rain-fed and upland areas, particularly in the early years when improved agricultural supporting services would be concentrated on the irrigated areas. The strategy would also have regional implications since most of the existing and potential irrigated rice land is in central and northern Luzon. This imbalance could be offset by increasing water charges (as discussed above) or levying other improvement-specific taxes on beneficiaries of irrigation systems. It is strongly recommended that the government review the overall implications of its policy toward agricultural taxation and water charges. Increasing these charges or taxes would: (a) help equate the private and public benefits of public investment in irrigation; (b) reduce the net public cost of a given level of investment or, alternatively, permit a larger investment for the same outlay of public funds; and (c) minimize the income disparities between those with and without irrigation.

The appropriate level of water charges or benefit taxes must be carefully determined so that charges do not discourage farmers from participating in the irrigation schemes. Benefit taxes should also be simple to administer and collect and difficult for farmers to evade. The government should explore ways to discourage the conspicuous waste of water through more effective taxation of irrigated land in conjunction with water charges. Different tax rates for irrigated and rain-fed land would make it easy to identify taxpayers in either category and would not deter the use of water because land in the service area would be taxed at the higher rate whether the water is used or not. Similar reasoning would apply to other public investments. For example, differential land tax rates could be applied where proximity to public roads or other amenities leads to private benefits in terms of increased land values as a result of public investment. The land tax could also be made progressive by assessing higher rates for larger holdings, although too much progressivity would probably cause farmers to evade taxes by subdividing larger holdings among family members.

AGRICULTURAL CREDIT

Little is known about the amount of agricultural credit available for financing production inputs and farm development. It is generally believed, however, that the amount has been inadequate and that the lack of credit on reasonable terms has constrained growth in agricultural production. Institutional sources probably provide somewhere around one-third of the total credit for agriculture, but for almost a decade there has been no growth in real terms in the amount granted. The one exception to this alarming trend has been the supervised credit programs for rice and corn introduced in 1973 and 1974 respectively. Credit granted to agriculture by institutions will probably have to grow at 6 to 8 percent a year in real terms over the next decade if the production programs discussed earlier are to be realized. Before reviewing the role of these institutions, it may be useful to examine briefly the contribution of noninstitutional sources of credit in agriculture.

Noninstitutional sources of credit. A considerable amount of the short-term credit available—more than half the production credit and about 95 percent of the nonproduction credit—has come from traditional sources. In the Philippines as elsewhere in the world, these sources include landlords, relatives, merchants, and moneylenders. A survey by the BAECON in 1968–69 reported that about 20 percent of the loans from noninstitutional sources came from landlords and 30 percent from merchants and moneylenders.[13] The advantages of these sources for small farmers are that collateral is not necessary, loans do not encounter administrative delays, and repayment schedules are flexible. A major disadvantage is the exorbitant interest rates that reach up to 300 percent a year. One early study in 1957–58 indicated that half the loans made by relatives had no interest charge (though 17 percent charged interest rates equivalent to 200 to 300 percent a year), while 43 percent of the loans made by landlords and 33 percent of those made by merchants

13. BAECON, "Integrated Agricultural Surveys, 1968–69" (n.p.).

had an interest rate of 100 to 200 percent a year.[14] A more recent study indicates somewhat lower interest rates, averaging between 10 and 50 percent on an annual basis.[15] It is not clear whether private rates may have declined in response to competition from financial institutions.

Access to institutional credit. One of the major issues in credit policy is the extent to which the supply of institutional credit for agriculture can be expanded. What is most striking about the pattern of credit allocation in the Philippines is that the share of total credit going to agriculture has declined steadily from 40 percent in the early 1950s to less than 10 percent in 1973. Although the productive sectors do not necessarily require credit in proportion to their contribution to overall production, it appears that agriculture has tended to receive a smaller share of institutional credit than factor intensities would warrant. The most important reason for this state of affairs has been the government's policy of encouraging the growth of import-substitution industries through a variety of policy instruments, including preferential access to substantial amounts of financial resources.[16]

Part of the explanation also lies within the agricultural sector itself. Until recently, at least, there has been little attempt to expand the network of financial institutions serving rural areas; as a result it has become a bottleneck to increased lending. Moreover the institutions' requirement of collateral for their loans has excluded a large number of small farmers, particularly tenants. Expanding institutional credit to agriculture by 6 to 8 percent a year in real terms over the next decade will require a much stronger network of financial institutions serving the agricultural sector in general and small farmers in particular.

The government is aware of this problem and in recent years it has been vigorously promoting the rural banking system. These banks have now become one of the main sources of institutional credit for agriculture. At the end of 1973 there were 628 rural

---

14. Jose P. Gapud, "Financing Lowland Rice Farming in Selected Barrios of Munos, Nueva Ecija, 1957–58" (undergraduate thesis, University of the Philippines College of Agriculture), p. 79.

15. J. M. Manto and R. D. Jones, "Sources and Cost of Credit of Rice Farms in Central Luzon," Report no. 74–15 (Quezon City: National Food and Agriculture Council, June 1974; processed), p. 10.

16. These policies are discussed further in Chapters 8 and 14.

Table 7.5. Loans Outstanding for Agriculture by Financial Institution
(In millions of pesos)

Year	Agricultural Guarantee and Loan Fund	Agricultural Credit Association	Rural banks	Philippine National Bank	Development banks	Commercial banks	Total	Deflated total (at 1967 prices)
1965	...	87	167	569	293	458	1,574	1,760
1966	...	88	199	630	317	448	1,682	1,777
1967	n.a.	96	259	751	380	450	1,936	1,933
1968	15	106	302	857	438	612	2,330	2,208
1969	16	106	325	923	485	687	2,542	2,273
1970	17	119	391	973	500	741	2,741	2,139
1971	24	127	261	902	498	877	2,689	1,835
1972	65	127	508	855	740	919	3,214	2,010
1973	58	109	825	1,283	820	961	4,056	2,225
1974	80	110	1,334	1,429[a]	877	1,278[a]	5,108	2,098

... Zero or negligible.
n.a. Not available.
a. As of June 30, 1974.
Source: Central Bank of the Philippines.

174

banks in the Philippines; 415 were in Luzon, 131 in the Visayas, and 88 in Mindanao. The rural banks lend seasonal production credit almost exclusively. They are locally owned, usually by families with interests in landholdings and the rice trade. Their borrowers have traditionally been the larger farmers who have had access to other sources of credit. In 1973, however, the rural banks became a major source of production credit for the Masagana 99 and Masaganang Maisan programs and widened the scope of their lending to include small farmers with holdings averaging about 2.5 hectares. Subsidized by the Central Bank through preferential rediscounting rates, the rural banks' share of total agricultural credit has increased steadily in the past decade. Since 1965 they have accounted for 75 percent of the total increase in agricultural credit provided from institutional sources.

The government plans to continue expanding the rural banking system as a means of improving the financial infrastructure in rural areas. Since 1970, 305 new banks have been established toward the goal of about 1,000 by 1977. This expansion will require an intensified savings mobilization campaign in rural areas and a broadening of the equity base of existing rural banks. Currently the system depends heavily on the government's willingness to channel subsidized resources to the banks. The profits of the rural banking system are low by Philippine standards; higher profitability could be achieved by an increase in loan volume, which in many banks could be handled without proportionately increasing operating expenses.

The other major source of funds for agriculture has been the Philippine National Bank (PNB). In the mid-1960s, for example, it accounted for about 40 percent of the total loaned to agriculture, but since 1969 the amount of the PNB's loans has declined in real terms and by 1974 accounted for only 28 percent of loans outstanding to agriculture (Table 7.5). More than any other commercial bank the PNB, with 161 branches and 121 mobile banks, has the size and geographic coverage to play an important part in filling the country's agricultural credit needs. The PNB has historically extended short-term credit to the sugar industry.[17] Its lending to the food-grain sector has been limited to large farms (twenty-five

17. In 1971, for example, 93 percent of all agricultural loans went to sugar production. Manuel Soliven, "The Philippine National Bank," *Agricultural Credit Report* (April 15, 1972), app. D and E.

hectares or more) and financing the deficit of the now defunct Rice and Corn Administration. In 1973 and 1974 the PNB expanded its lending by providing more than half the loans for Masagana 99 and Masaganang Maisan, a dramatic increase of some 700 percent over its previous loans to the rice industry. Recently the Central Bank directed that at least 25 percent of all loanable funds from commercial banks should be for agricultural credit; not less than 10 percent should be available for agrarian reform, and the other 15 percent for agricultural credit in general.

Special credit programs for small farmers. In the past an important shortcoming of financial institutions has been their bias toward the larger and more affluent farmers, especially those in the sugar industry, which left small farmers to rely on moneylenders and other sources of credit. In one study conducted several years ago it was estimated that farmers with less than three hectares received less than 2 percent of their production credit from institutional sources. Yet this group constituted about three-fourths of the total farm population and accounted for about 40 percent of the cultivated area.[18] One reason for this pattern has been the insistence of financial institutions on collateral to secure a loan. To broaden access to institutional credit, the government has been promoting a series of supervised credit programs which do not require farmers to pledge collateral.

To overcome the hesitation of rural bankers to lend to small farmers, the Agricultural Guarantee and Loan Fund (AGLF) was established in 1966. Channeled through rural banks in the form of special time deposits, the fund was administered by the Central Bank. Minimal supervision by government extension workers created difficulties, however, and after five years of operation the AGLF accounted for only about 2 percent of the volume of agricultural loans. The Agricultural Guarantee Fund (AGF), which was established in 1971, originally guaranteed 70 percent of the losses of the rural banks on unsecured production loans to support the agrarian reform program. The guarantee was recently raised to 85 percent to encourage the rural banks to participate more actively in the supervised credit programs. Although the AGF guarantee

---

18. Study cited by Orlando Sacay in *Small Farmer Credit in the Philippines,* United States Agency for International Development, Country Paper no. SR 113 (February 1973).

overlapped with that of the AGLF, it nonetheless provided a more liberal guarantee scheme.

In 1972 the Agricultural Loan Fund (ALF) was established to finance an accelerated rice production program, largely in response to the severe floods that affected Central Luzon in that year. Administered by the Central Bank, the ALF took over the functions of the AGLF. The Land Bank of the Philippines administers all these agricultural guarantee funds, including those used in the Masagana 99 and Masaganang Maisan programs.

By far the most important special credit program to date is the Masagana 99, which was initially undertaken in May 1973 to aid recovery from damages to the rice crop in 1972–73. It is designed to increase production by providing credit without collateral, improving extension services, and encouraging modern farming practices. Rice farmers cultivating seven hectares or less are encouraged to join an informal liability group called a selda, with each member cosigning for the others as a substitute for collateral. At the beginning of the Masagana 99 program the government took steps to strengthen the agricultural credit system. First, as mentioned above, the AGF raised its guarantee on losses from 70 to 85 percent. Second, additional funds were channeled to the ALF as special time deposits in rural banks. Third, the whole rediscounting system was overhauled. Rural banks were allowed to rediscount up to 100 percent of their unsecured loans, and the rediscount rate for supervised credit was lowered from 3 to 1 percent, compared with 5 percent for collateralized loans. Fourth, regional departments were established within the Central Bank which administered the ALF to expedite rediscounting.

During the two years the Masagana program has been in operation about ₱950 million of production credit a year has been granted (Table 7.6). About 1.3 million hectares have been covered each crop year, or about a third of the total harvested area of rice. About two-thirds of the area covered by the program has been irrigated land, which suggests that about half the irrigated area in the Philippines is covered by the Masagana program. In the main season of the 1974–75 crop year the program reached about 734,000 farmers, compared with about 638,000 the previous year. These data suggest that about 45 percent of the rice farms are benefiting from the program. The few studies which have been undertaken indicate that the average farm size for participating

Table 7.6. Progress of the Masagana 99 Program

Category	Crop year 1973–74		Crop year 1974–75	
	May–October 1973	*November 1973– April 1974*	*May–October 1974*	*November 1974– April 1975*
Area financed (thousands of hectares)	622	353	865	. . .
Farmers supervised (thousands)	402	236	429	305
Total credit (millions of pesos)	369	231	717	572
Average loan per hectare	595	654	829	. . .

. . . Zero or negligible.

Sources: Philippine National Bank, "Progress Report," February 6, 1975; PNB, "Fact Sheet on Selected Industries," May 1975; and Department of Agriculture, "Management Information Systems Progress Reports," various numbers.

farmers is about 2.5 hectares, whereas the national average for rice farms is about 1.7 hectares.[19] Most of the government's extension agents are concentrated in the Masagana program, and though the ratio of production technicians to farmers varies with the season the average is about 1:200. The expanded coverage of the program in crop year 1974–75 created considerable strains and led to a deterioration in the quality of supervision. It is generally believed that this partly explains why the repayment record faltered in the second year of the program.

In the early phases of the program it was clear to borrowers that the rural banks, the Central Bank, and the government were determined to collect loans. As a result, repayment records were very good, with a collection rate of about 90 percent for loans granted from May 1973 to April 1974. In the third phase, however, the repayment rate declined, and by mid-1975 about ₱237 million were overdue and demandable. This was about 18 percent of the total amount loaned in the first three phases.[20]

19. See, for example, the study of S. P. Mariano, *Masagana 99* (Manila: National Food and Agriculture Council, October 1974; processed).

20. The details of the repayment record as of September 30, 1975, were (in millions of pesos):

The government has undertaken a program to improve the credit system; the most significant measures are:

a. The basic pay of the field technicians was increased and their salary incentives adjusted. Every technician now receives an incentive allowance of ₱0.50 for every farmer supervised plus ₱6.00 upon full payment of the loan.

b. Rural bank managers were given administrative control over the production technicians. This authority will be exercised jointly with the technicians' provincial supervisors. In addition, rural banks were instructed to hire additional collectors funded out of the service charges collected from borrowers.

c. Additional production technicians have been bonded so that they are now authorized by the banks to make collections for them.

d. The technicians' work load has been lightened by concentrating only on farmers who are having difficulty adopting the new technology or have an unsatisfactory loan repayment record.

e. A barangay chairman is now also entitled to an incentive allowance if he accompanies a farmer to the rural bank in the payment of the Masagana loan. In addition, Barangay Action Teams have been formed, composed of the barangay leader, the production technician, a representative of the rural bank, and two exemplary farmers, to encourage delinquent farmers to settle their loan obligations.

f. Before production technicians are transferred or allowed to resign they are required to familiarize their replacement with the farmer-borrowers in their area for two months to assure continuity of adequate supervision.

g. The Land Bank of the Philippines has revised the rules of the guarantee fund to lessen the administrative delays involved in approving guarantee claims.

The Masagana 99 approach was extended to corn, sorghum, and

	Loaned	Repaid	Delinquent (percentage of amount loaned)
May–October 1973	369	337	9
November 1973–April 1974	230	206	10
May–October 1974	716	535	25
Total	1,315	1,078	18

soybeans in 1974 with a program called Masaganang Maisan. Results to date are generally acknowledged to be disappointing without enough staff, improved seeds, or market outlets. Steps have been taken to improve the program, but it is still too early to determine the results.

In view of the dominant position of small farmers in agriculture today, it is clear that institutional credit programs for these farmers need to be developed. Despite the recent difficulties, the Masagana program or some variant of it will need strengthening. Close attention will have to be given to the training and supervision of field technicians and the continued expansion of the network of financial institutions in key agricultural areas. But success in the long term will also require a good record of loan repayments among small farmers. The frequent crop failures in the Philippines that stem from typhoons and floods may make it difficult to achieve a high average repayment record in all major agricultural regions.[21] Perhaps a collection rate of 80 to 90 percent is the best that can be accomplished.

Other Infrastructure Programs

In addition to improving supporting services and irrigation facilities, it will be necessary to expand access to electricity and transport services and improve water resource management in rural areas. The government has already given high priority to rural electrification and transportation, although access to rural markets and feeder roads remains a serious problem.

EXPANDING ACCESS TO ELECTRICITY

The low-cost electricity needed to upgrade irrigation services and to promote small industry or other production is not currently available in most rural areas. An integral component of the government's strategy for rural development, and one to which a high priority is attached, is the electrification of the entire country during the next twenty years—for household use as well as agricultural

---

21. In the past quarter century the Philippines has been struck by an average of twenty typhoons a year. They occur most often in July through November in Ilocos and the Cagayan Valley, Batanes Islands, the southern part of the Visayas, and Bicol; less frequently in Central Luzon.

and industrial activities. The first stage of the program is the establishment of an electric cooperative system in each of the seventy-two provinces of the country by 1977; the second stage is the provision of electricity to 75 percent of the population by 1984; and the final goal is the provision of electricity for the entire population by 1994. By the end of 1974, twenty-nine electric cooperatives had systems in operation. Over 160,000 cooperative members, representing a population of over one million, were receiving electrical service.

Although some electricity will be used for farm mechanization, its main productive use in agriculture is for small electric pump irrigation. Companion programs either in operation or in the planning stage are expected to fund the necessary equipment, technical assistance, and training to expand the use of pump irrigation in the electric cooperative areas. The introduction of electricity in rural areas is stimulating nonagricultural activities as well. In one area lumber mills, feed mills, a fish research unit, and some small-scale industry have been developed, and three small municipal water systems have been installed using local funding. Small-scale industrial cooperatives are being promoted in areas served by the rural electrification program, and the World Bank has provided US$2.5 million to the government to support and expand this program as part of a US$30 million loan for small- and medium-scale industrial development.

The government estimates that between 80 and 95 percent of the population will be able to afford electrical service when it is made available by a cooperative. Even though the incomes in many rural areas are low, Filipinos are willing to allocate a large portion of their cash income to electrical service, which is used in the home primarily for lighting, irons and hotplates, food preservation, and entertainment. This strong demand among rural households is encouraged by the low rates being charged by the cooperatives.

IMPROVING TRANSPORT SERVICES

Increased agricultural production is possible only if fertilizers, seeds, sprays, and other inputs can be delivered where and when they are needed, and if surplus produce can be transported to markets. The present inadequacies of transport service in the Philippines increase the cost of agricultural production, worsen the competitive position of exports, and further isolate rural areas from the orbit of development activities. But transportation networks are particularly difficult to establish because of the insular character of the country. Domestic trade requires, in addition to infrastructure for land transport, many ports and ferries and complex networks of shipping and air services. Although the government has made considerable progress in improving the major highway systems, particularly on the islands of Luzon and Mindanao, access to markets in rural areas is severely hampered by poor interisland transportation, inadequate farm-to-market and feeder roads capable of accommodating motorized traffic, and the lack of all-weather facilities.

Roads. It is estimated that half of all rural barrios have poor farm-to-market roads which may be impassable during the rainy season, and another 20 percent have little more than footpaths. These inadequacies contribute to local surpluses and shortages and act as a deterrent to increased production. A major task in rural areas is therefore to upgrade footpaths and maintain existing gravel roads to prevent their deterioration during rainy periods.

The poor quality of roads frequently drives up the price of transport, and freight rates, although set by the Board of Transport, are not followed closely in practice. In readily accessible areas such as the Cagayan Valley, competition produces rates somewhat lower than those prescribed by the board, but elsewhere they are frequently higher. In relatively inaccessible areas inputs such as fertilizers, insecticides, and seeds are not economical to purchase because of high transport costs, and marketing of output is difficult.

The government has begun to stress improvement of farm-to-market and feeder roads to aid food-production programs. The long-term goal is to establish one kilometer of effective feeder road for every 100 hectares of cultivated land; this would require about 75,000 kilometers of feeder roads for the presently cultivated area. The government intended to maintain and upgrade some 7,500 kilometers of feeder roads at a cost of about ₱130 million in 1974–75 and to sustain improvements at this level in future years. In the past several years the United States Agency for International Development (USAID) has helped finance the construction and rehabilitation of low-standard, low-cost feeder roads under the Provincial Development Assistance Project with outlays of US$750,000 a year. The World Bank is helping to finance the upgrading of 700 kilometers of minor roads, and the Asian Development Bank is considering including the upgrading of 800 kilometers of minor roads in Mindanao in a possible highway loan.

At present the main responsibility for planning and allocating the resources for the improvement of local roads rests with two national agencies, the Department of Public Highways and the Department of Local Government and Community Development. Consideration should be given to expanding local government responsibility for the construction and maintenance of local roads as a concrete step toward increasing local participation in rural development programs. The Bureau of Barangay Roads (BBR) could play a particularly important role in this regard. The various local road improvement programs operated by the national government agencies could possibly be consolidated and incorporated into local programs administered by the provincial governments and supported by the BBR. The central authority could make an annual allocation to the provincial governments for local road improvement. The local governments would be responsible for choosing which roads to improve or maintain and for using funds efficiently in accordance with national norms. Such an approach would provide all local governments with a regular flow of funds for improving and maintaining minor roads; it would also help strengthen local capabilities to plan, select, design, and implement projects on the basis of the local leaders' and technicians' intimate knowledge of the region's economy and needs.

Ports and shipping. With increasing regional specialization in production patterns and rural development, hitherto neglected aspects of interisland shipping need to be improved, including ferry connections, port and storage facilities, and land access in the hinterland to ports. Small watercraft (bancas, batels, and kumpits) provide low-cost, short-haul transport of agricultural products for local as well as interisland markets, and barges are used extensively to move raw and refined sugar, rice, and other produce. Coastal transport is frequently a logical alternative where cross-island road construction is made difficult by mountainous terrain, and numerous roadsteads and shallow water ports have been developed where land access is severely limited.

Despite their importance, the potential of interisland and coastal shipping has not yet been fully realized, partly because of inadequate port facilities for local shipping. In the past few years the government, with assistance from the World Bank and the Asian

Development Bank, has improved the port facilities of Cagayan de Oro, General Santos, Davao, and Cotabato. The majority of ports, however, still suffer from inadequate work areas and transit sheds, antiquated cargo-handling facilities, disorganized port operations, and poor maintenance. A major task in outlying areas is to consolidate ports of various sizes and functions where improved overland mobility makes possible economies of scale and efficiency. The port location must be selected in the context of the total transport network—traffic patterns, the development potential of the hinterlands, the natural conditions of the harbors, and the existence of over 500 private ports which handle about two-thirds of the loaded and unloaded cargo tonnage.

Interisland shipping will play a major role in the government's plans for increased food production and regional specialization. The growing need for food in deficit areas has to be met by increased production in surplus areas such as Mindanao. This in turn requires efficient marine transport of both agricultural inputs and outputs. But the local shipping fleet is in poor condition: An estimated 40 percent of interisland vessels are over 24 years old, a high proportion of the smaller ships are converted naval or military vessels, and overloading and prolonged journeys are characteristic. The cumulative effects of these deficiencies are congestion and confusion, which unduly restrict the movement of cargo and slow stevedoring and ship turnaround time. This is particularly true at ports where offshore loading and unloading are frequent. A modernized and expanded interisland shipping fleet, operating on a reliable, regular schedule, could make a major contribution to the Philippines' rural and regional development. Much could be accomplished by developing domestic facilities for the construction of barges and small river crafts.

Development of water resources

Although the Philippines is generally regarded as having abundant water resources, efforts to develop and regulate them have lagged. Lack of public funds and inadequate programs have impeded the development of irrigation facilities, water supply systems for household and industrial use, and flood control for agricultural basins. The development of an adequate rural water supply system should be given high priority in the government's program to improve the level of services in the rural areas. The importance of irrigation has already been stressed and is well recognized by the government.

Intensive and prolonged rainfall brought on by typhoons and the southwest monsoons between July and January causes extensive flooding in some of the major river basins, with heavy losses of agricultural crops, livestock, and property. Largely as a result of the severe damage caused by the 1972 floods in Luzon, the government has accelerated its program for flood protection and river control. Expenditures on flood control increased from an average of ₱6 million a year in FY67–72 to ₱280 million in FY75; the share of public investment for flood control increased from one percent during FY67–72 to 8 percent in FY74. USAID has assisted with flood disaster relief, and existing flood control facilities have been reconstructed and improved. The program includes projects in Central Luzon, Mindanao (Cotabato and Agusan), and Bicol.

Drainage is a prerequisite to increased agricultural production in many river basins. Given the high intensity of rainfall and the large watershed area relative to the plains, the natural drainage system is frequently not sufficient to dispose of the large amounts of water that accumulate during the wet season. Crops may be totally destroyed or yields lowered. No information is available on the costs of crop damage by flooding or waterlogging, but they have undoubtedly been considerable. To improve both health and land productivity, drainage and land reclamation are being used to attack schistosomiasis in the government's Mindoro development project. On the islands of Leyte and Samar as well, schistosomiasis is believed to be endemic. A special development project being prepared at the provincial level will focus on Leyte and include drainage, other land improvements, and credit for farm production. Many of these drainage projects are appropriate for labor-intensive methods, and many other infrastructure requirements of the rural areas can probably be met by economically justifiable small-scale projects using local development funds.

8

Industrial Growth, Employment, and Investment

INDUSTRIALIZATION HAS ALWAYS BEEN a prime objective of Philippine economic policy since independence. In pursuing this goal the country has had the advantages of vast agricultural, forest, and mineral resources; abundant, literate, and relatively cheap labor; rapid urban population growth, including an aggressive entrepreneurial class; proximity to the Japanese market and relatively free access to that of the United States; and a rather unrestricted inflow of foreign direct investment. Yet the pace of industrialization over the past quarter of a century has been fairly moderate by any standard. With an industrial growth rate of 7.7 percent a year it took 24 years (1950–74) to raise the share of mining and manufacturing industries in total net domestic product from 14 to 23 percent.[1]

Industrial growth has obviously been affected by other, less favorable factors. Established industries in the region have offered strong competition; the country has depended on a small number of foreign markets for the bulk of its external trade; much of the gain from foreign investment has accrued to the countries of origin; and there have been difficulties in meeting the requirements for transportation and other infrastructure so vital for industrializa-

---

1. At constant 1967 prices.

tion, especially in a multi-island country with a rapidly growing population.

Past Industrial Growth

Historically the highest and most stable growth rates were recorded in the initial phase of Philippine industrial development: 40 to 50 percent a year in 1946–49 and around 10 percent in 1950–60. Even taking into account the low starting point and the circumstances of early postwar reconstruction, it is evident that highly sheltered import substitution made a major contribution to that growth. A protective system was built up which strongly favored the domestic production of light consumer goods. Policy tools included quantitative import controls, an overvalued exchange rate, low long-term interest rates, and specialized incentives to attract foreign investment. In this early postwar period industrial policy focused on large-scale, capital- and import-intensive enterprise located in or around Manila and catering to domestic urban markets. Visible by-products of that strategy were a sharp fall in the share of consumer goods in total imports and a movement in the internal terms of trade which favored the nonagricultural sectors.[2]

Import-replacing production of nondurable and, later, durable consumer goods set off progressive changes in the traditional economic structure and was a necessary stage in the development process. The strategy resulted in the productive employment of surplus labor and capital, the creation and education of a new entrepreneurial class, and the setting of new national and social goals. At the same time, however, the inherent weaknesses of this strategy were not sufficiently appreciated by policymakers. The emphasis on finished consumer goods, for example, provided little stimulus for the domestic production of raw materials and intermediate goods and implied an increasing dependence on imports for manufacturing. This import dependence contributed to a heavy concentration of manufacturing activity in the area of the main port, Manila. The built-in preference for the domestic market and the absence of any systematic export orientation put the Philippines at a disadvantage at a time when several other countries in the region had success-

2. The ratio of nonagricultural to agricultural prices if 1950 is taken as a base year amounted to 1.21 in 1960.

fully launched extensive export drives. The emphasis on large-scale, capital-intensive enterprises tended to put small-scale producers in an inferior economic position and to reduce the labor-absorptive capacity of manufacturing and extractive industries.

The early economic momentum halted when the primary exporting sector was no longer able to supply all the foreign exchange needed to keep industry growing. A severe balance of payments crisis developed as gross international reserves fell to a low of less than US$100 million, and the industrial growth rate dropped sharply to 2.1 percent in 1960 compared with an average 10 percent a year during the early 1950s. The government devalued the peso and relaxed exchange controls in 1960–62. Although quantitative import controls were replaced by relatively high import tariffs, the basic structure of incentives, subsidies, and other price-distorting factors remained largely untouched. Import substitution began in the field of intermediate goods, and some new exports were induced by the devaluation, but there was no major change in the rate and pattern of growth. With an industrial growth rate of 4 percent, the relative contribution of the industrial sector to GNP remained almost unchanged at around 19 percent during 1960–65.

To revitalize industrial production, the government undertook a series of measures to attract investment into the industrial sector, redirect import-replacing production, and give an impetus to export industries. The Investment Incentives and Export Incentives Acts were passed in 1967 and 1970 respectively; the Board of Investment (BOI) was established; the peso was devalued by 40 percent in 1970; and tariffs were realigned in 1972.

These policies, which are discussed below in some detail, brought little improvement in overall growth except in the export sector. During 1968–73 the industrial growth slowed further, industrial employment virtually stagnated, and total manufacturing investment remained at around ₱2,000 million (in 1967 prices). Moreover, no adquate strategy has yet been found to deal with the low employment-generating capacity of the industrial sector, undoubtedly the most difficult problem inherited from the past development pattern.

OUTPUT AND EMPLOYMENT TRENDS

In order to analyze past industrial growth, three periods have been defined on the basis of major policy characteristics and the availability of data: 1956–62 demonstrated the accumulated effects of foreign exchange and import controls; 1962–68 illustrated partial decontrol along with devaluation; and 1968–73 witnessed a further devaluation in conjunction with steps to improve the structure of investment. Except for employment, the analysis has been confined to "organized" industry (firms with five or more workers), because information is generally lacking on the number of units and value added for cottage industries (those employing less than five persons).[3] The aggregate trends in manufacturing appear to be strongly influenced by the large-scale sector because of its increasing share of total output and employment. Table 8.1 summarizes these trends.[4]

The overall growth rate in the organized sector was 7.8 percent a year in real terms during 1956–73, with a distinct declining trend. Small-scale industries performed most poorly: Those with 5 to 19 employees stagnated in that period, with only a 0.3 percent growth rate (compared with 8.3 percent for larger firms), and small- to medium-scale industries with 20 to 99 employees had a negative growth rate in 1968–71. Information on cottage industry is lacking, but declining employment figures point to a parallel decline in output in recent years.[5]

During 1956–73 industry showed an annual growth rate of 1.4 percent, but its share in total employment dropped from 12.9 to 10.5 percent. While the modern manufacturing sector (industries

3. For official administrative purposes, small-scale industries are defined as those with total fixed assets (including land) of between ₱100,000 and ₱1,000,000; medium-scale industries are those in the ₱1 to 4 million range, and large-scale are those over ₱4 million. At current price levels this definition of small scale probably comprises establishments with 10 to 50 employees. A fourth group is composed of "unorganized" industries with 1 to 4 employees. Reference here to the small-scale sector is in the broad sense of industries with 1 to 50 workers; those with 1 to 4 workers will be referred to as cottage industries, and the rest as modern small-scale industries.

4. In spite of some improvement in recent years, the year-to-year comparability of the manufacturing census data used in Table 8.1 is somewhat affected by inconsistent methodology and coverage. The *Annual Survey of Manufactures* data on value added are not quite comparable with the national accounts figures and are inflated by interindustry resales. The use of the GNP deflator in manufacturing value added computations (instead of the manufacturing price index) is another weak point. Basic output and employment trends can nevertheless be used as approximations.

5. Cottage industry's contribution to total industrial value added has been estimated by the National Economic and Development Authority (NEDA) at 4 percent (*Strategy for Action: The Industry Sector* [Manila, n.d.]) and by the International Labour Office (ILO) at around 6 percent (*Sharing in Development* [Geneva: ILO, 1974]).

Table 8.1. Growth of Manufacturing Industries, 1956–73

Category	1956	1962	1968	1973	Annual growth rate (percent)			
					1956–62	1962–68	1968–73	1956–73
Number of firms								
20 or more workers	1,833	2,180	2,385	2,912	2.9	1.5	4.1	2.8
5-19 workers	5,375	6,289	7,673	9,469	2.7	3.4	4.3	3.4
Total	7,208	8,469	10,058	12,381	2.7	2.9	4.2	3.2
Employment (thousands)								
20 or more workers	150.9	230.5	325.1	454.4	7.3	5.9	6.9	6.7
5-19 workers	54.9	48.0	69.2	72.4	-2.2	6.3	0.9	1.6
1-4 workers	829.2	845.5	912.7	788.2	0.4	1.3	-3.0	-0.3
Total	1,035.0	1,124.0	1,307.0	1,315.0	1.4	2.5	0.1	1.4
Value added (millions of pesos at 1967 prices)								
20 or more workers	1,532.8	2,769.9	4,457.1	5,948.0	10.3	8.2	5.9	8.3
5-19 workers	181.8	132.3	266.9	191.3	-5.4	13.8	-7.0	0.3
Total	1,714.6	2,902.2	4,724.0	6,139.3	9.2	8.5	5.4	7.8
Value added per worker (thousands of pesos at 1967 prices)								
20 or more workers	10.2	12.0	13.7	13.1	2.8	2.2	-1.0	1.5
5-19 workers	3.3	2.8	3.9	2.6	-3.0	5.8	-7.3	-1.4
Average	8.3	10.4	12.0	11.7	3.8	2.4	-0.5	2.0

Note: The implicit GDP deflator from the national accounts (revised April 23, 1975) was used in value added computations.
Sources: Bureau of the Census and Statistics (BCS), *Annual Survey of Manufactures, 1969*; preliminary results of the *Annual Survey of Manufactures, 1973*; and national accounts.

employing over 20 employees) was able to maintain a fairly high and stable rate of new labor absorption (6 to 7 percent a year throughout 1956–73), employment in firms of 5 to 19 workers showed an erratic trend, with a modest average growth rate of 1.6 percent. The relative shares of industrial groups with 5 to 19 and 1 to 4 workers decreased from 0.7 to 0.6 percent and from 10 to 6 percent respectively, while that of the modern manufacturing sector increased from 1.8 to 3.5 percent.

Employment trends deteriorated in the most recent period (1968–73). The gain in modern sector employment (from 325,000 in 1968 to 454,000 in 1973) was offset by an absolute fall of employment in the cottage sector (from 913,000 to 788,000) and a basically stagnating employment level in mining and industries with 5 to 19 workers. Total industrial employment reached 1,411,000 in 1974, compared with 1,068,000 in 1956; the annual increment amounted to 19,000, of which 18,000 were absorbed by the modern manufacturing sector.

CHANGES IN INDUSTRIAL STRUCTURE

Changes in the relative importance of individual industries in total manufacturing value added and employment are shown in Table 8.2. The present structure of industry is not substantially different from that of the mid-1950s. The five fastest growing industries—chemicals, basic metals, electrical machinery, rubber, and tobacco—increased their combined share in total value added from 17 percent in 1956 to 29 percent in 1974. The five slowest growing industries—food, metal products, machinery, transport equipment, and miscellaneous industries—decreased from 46 to 36 percent during the same period. Similar trends were registered in the distribution of employment, although with a somewhat different industrial composition.

Table 8.3 links changes in the composition of manufacturing value added with trends in the relative factor use and market orientation.[6] Somewhat surprisingly, after a long period of relative

6. The classification of industries according to their products' end-use corresponds with that in NEDA publications, except that miscellaneous industries are included here under consumer goods. Industries are classified by factor intensity and capital productivity on the basis of capital–value added and capital-per-worker ratios taken from the Bureau of the Census and Statistics (BCS), *Annual Survey of Manufactures* for 1969 and 1970. Industries with export potential are defined as those producing largely for export or having substantial export potential.

Table 8.2. Distribution of Value Added and Employment in Organized Manufacturing
(In percent)

Industry	Value added (constant 1967 prices)							Employment				
	1956	1960	1964	1968	1972	1973	1974	1960	1964	1968	1971	1973
Apparel	6.5	3.7	2.6	2.4	5.3	5.0	4.8	13.1	9.8	9.6	7.8	7.4
Beverages	9.2	7.6	8.4	8.2	8.9	8.1	8.1	4.0	3.9	3.3	3.8	3.4
Chemicals	8.9	9.8	10.1	11.9	13.6	14.3	11.9	5.5	5.8	5.9	6.1	8.9
Food processing	30.1	27.6	28.5	23.5	27.8	26.2	27.8	18.1	20.8	21.1	20.8	21.5
Furniture	1.1	0.9	0.9	0.6	1.1	1.0	1.0	2.5	2.4	2.0	1.5	2.0
Leather products	0.4	0.5	0.3	0.3	0.1	0.1	0.1	0.7	0.7	0.6	0.5	0.4
Machinery	1.6	1.9	0.7	0.9	1.1	1.2	1.2	1.7	1.4	1.5	1.6	2.1
Electrical machinery	1.0	3.1	4.6	3.3	3.8	3.8	4.7	3.3	4.4	3.3	3.5	3.2
Metal products	3.9	5.5	4.1	4.4	3.0	2.9	2.8	6.3	5.3	5.9	4.3	4.0
Metals, basic	0.9	1.5	1.6	2.6	1.6	2.0	2.2	1.5	1.5	2.1	2.8	3.0
Nonmetallic mineral products	3.6	3.7	4.8	5.1	3.1	3.4	2.8	3.5	3.8	4.1	5.1	3.5
Petroleum	3.0[a]	3.0[a]	3.8	4.9	4.8	4.4	4.2	0.3[a]	0.4	0.3	0.4	0.2
Printing and publishing	3.4	3.5	3.2	2.9	2.9	2.7	3.0	5.3	4.5	3.8	3.4	2.9
Pulp and paper	1.5	2.6	1.9	2.7	1.8	1.7	1.8	2.0	2.2	2.0	2.5	2.3
Rubber products	0.9	3.2	3.2	2.8	1.9	1.8	2.7	2.2	2.1	2.3	2.2	2.4
Textiles	3.8	5.7	5.9	7.0	5.4	5.5	4.9	10.7	11.1	11.8	13.0	15.9
Tobacco	5.4	4.8	3.9	6.4	5.6	7.0	7.2	5.8	4.4	4.8	5.0	4.3
Transport equipment	5.1	3.0	5.0	3.6	2.1	2.0	2.4	3.2	3.9	3.8	3.5	2.6
Wood products	4.6	4.3	5.4	5.5	4.5	5.3	4.9	8.5	9.5	9.9	9.9	8.9
Miscellaneous	5.1	4.1	1.1	1.0	1.6	1.6	1.5	1.8	2.1	1.9	2.3	1.1
Total	100.0	100.0	100.0	100.0	100.0	100.0	100.0	100.0	100.0	100.0	100.0	100.0

a. World Bank estimate.

Sources: BCS, *Annual Survey of Manufactures, 1969, 1971* and *1973;* national accounts data; and, for 1956, R. M. Bautista, "Industrial Capital Utilization in the Philippines," Discussion Paper no. 74-13 (Manila: University of the Philippines, September 30, 1974).

decline the share of consumer goods in total manufacturing output increased from 52 percent in 1968 to around 58 percent in 1972–74. Several important consumer goods industries—particularly the export-oriented ones such as food processing, garments, footwear, and furniture—have been able to maintain relatively high growth rates. The share of intermediate goods declined from 40 percent in 1968 to 34 percent in 1972–74, primarily because of a sharp fall in the growth rate of intermediate industries such as pulp and paper, other wood products, cement, and metal products from 15 percent in 1960–68 to 4 percent in 1968–74. The third industrial group of durable consumer and capital goods maintained its share at a fairly constant level of around 8 percent.

These developments coincided with an enormous increase in the import of industrial raw materials and intermediate inputs in 1968–74, while domestic production of finished consumer goods enjoyed almost absolute protection. There has apparently been little import substitution in some intermediate and capital goods with a ready domestic market (for example, metal products and simple industrial and agricultural machinery), largely because imports of these items are virtually tax free under the existing incentives schemes, and investment opportunities in more sheltered areas have greater appeal. Intermediate goods produced for export (particularly wood, cement, minerals, and rubber products) have proved more vulnerable to market fluctuations than most other products. A high degree of underutilized capacity developed in these industries, further eroding their cost competitiveness. Until recently both import-replacing and export-oriented industries were insufficiently encouraged to turn to higher processing stages, create new industrial linkages, and thus increase the demand for inputs made domestically.

In the 1968–74 period industries having an export potential grew at 8 percent a year whereas those geared only to domestic markets grew at only 6 percent (Table 8.3). This indicates how important it may be for industries facing limited domestic demand to have an additional outlet for their products.

Factor use and productivity

As shown in Table 8.3, industries characterized by high capital-output and capital-labor ratios have experienced a sharper fall in their growth rates in recent years than have those with low capital-output and capital-labor ratios. Industries with generally high pro-

Table 8.3. Structural Changes in Manufacturing Industry, 1956–74
(At constant 1967 prices)

Industrial characteristics	Percentage shares in value added							Annual rate of change in value added (percent)		
	1956	1960	1964	1968	1972	1973	1974	1960–68	1968–74	1960–74
End use										
Consumer goods[a]	65	58	55	52	59	57	58	10.8	9.0	10.0
Intermediate goods[b]	27	34	35	40	34	36	34	14.9	3.9	10.0
Durable and capital goods[c]	8	8	10	8	7	7	8	12.3	8.0	10.5
Factor intensity										
Capital intensive[d]	49	51	54	54	55	54	53	13.0	7.0	10.4
Labor intensive[e]	51	49	46	46	45	46	47	11.7	7.1	9.7
Capital productivity										
High capital-output ratio[f]	37	43	43	47	41	42	39	13.8	3.9	9.5
Low capital-output ratio[g]	63	57	57	53	59	58	61	11.3	9.5	10.5
Import substitution and export orientation										
Domestic-market oriented[h]	41	41	42	47	45	46	44	14.1	5.9	10.5
With export potential[i]	59	59	58	53	55	54	56	10.6	8.0	9.7
Total	100	100	100	100	100	100	100	12.4	7.0	10.0

a. Food, beverages, tobacco, textiles, apparel, furniture, printing, leather, miscellaneous.
b. Wood, paper, rubber, chemicals, petroleum, nonmetallic mineral products, basic metals, metal products.
c. Machinery, electrical machinery, transport equipment.
d. Food, paper, rubber, chemicals, petroleum, nonmetallic mineral products, basic metals.
e. Beverages, tobacco, textiles, apparel, wood, furniture, printing, leather, metal products, machinery, electrical machinery, transport equipment, miscellaneous.
f. Textiles, paper, leather, chemicals, petroleum, nonmetallic mineral products, basic metals, metal products, electrical machinery, transport equipment, miscellaneous.
g. Food, beverages, tobacco, apparel, wood, furniture, printing, rubber, machinery.
h. Beverages, tobacco, printing, chemicals, petroleum, basic metals, metal products, machinery, transport equipment.
i. Food, textiles, apparel, wood, furniture, paper, leather, rubber, nonmetallic mineral products, electrical machinery, miscellaneous.
Source: Table 8.2.

ductivity of capital (a low capital-output ratio) grew at a rate of 9.5 percent a year in 1968–74 compared with only 3.9 percent for those with a high capital-output ratio. This trend coincided with the revival of consumer goods industries and the slower growth in intermediate sectors at least in part because investment was diverted from intermediate sectors.

The relationship between the factor use and market orientation of manufacturing industries and their utilization of capacity is shown in Table 8.4. It was compiled from two recent surveys based on representative samples of 400 large- and medium-scale firms (those with over 20 employees) and 91 export-oriented, BOI-registered firms. Labor-intensive industries generally operate at

Table 8.4. Average Capital Utilization Rates

Item	General industry survey (1972)	Export industry survey (1973–74)
Number of firms surveyed		
One shift	180	16
Two shifts	73	17
Three shifts	147	36
Total	400	91
Capital utilization rate (percent)		
Capital-intensive industries	43.4	55.7
Labor-intensive industries	40.5	50.4
Consumer goods industries	39.2	48.3
Intermediate goods industries	49.4	61.6
Capital goods industries	27.0	35.6
Import-dependent industries	41.9	51.8
Industries depending on local inputs	41.2	53.2
Export-oriented industries	50.8	52.7
Nonexport-oriented industries	38.6	—
Average rate	41.6	52.7

— Not applicable.

Note: Capital utilization rates in this table are based on the proportion of time the plants are in operation and on the intensity of use of the equipment installed. These rates represent simple averages for the firms in the sample; the capital-weighted mean of capital utilization rates would be considerably higher (by 19 percent in the case of the 1972 survey), reflecting better capital utilization by larger plants.

Sources: R. M. Bautista, "Industrial Capital Utilization in the Philippines" and B. Diokno, "Capital Utilization in Government 'Favored' Export-oriented Firms," Report no. 74-8 (Manila: University of the Philippines, July 10, 1974).

lower rates of capacity utilization, a fact which limited their employment generation during the 1968–73 period; capital and consumer goods industries, both predominantly labor intensive, have fewer shifts and use their capacity less efficiently than intermediate goods industries, which are largely capital intensive. Firms using local raw materials do not utilize their capacity any better than those depending on imports, but export-oriented industries are more efficient in utilizing their capacity than those geared to the domestic market, as are larger firms.

Import Substitution and the Role of the Domestic Market

Philippine industrialization during the 1950s and 1960s was clearly directed toward traditional import substitution in final consumption goods as well as extractive and agricultural export industries. More recently the authorities have been endeavoring to shift the emphasis toward import substitution of intermediate and capital goods and the export of nontraditional manufactures. They have also sought to promote labor-intensive and small- and medium-scale production. Real change in the pace and direction of industrial growth in the Philippines will depend upon the existing investment programs and the relative importance they give to the major growth factors—further import substitution, increased nontraditional manufactured exports, and the expansion of industrial production into new areas of demand in the domestic market.

THE BOARD OF INVESTMENTS

The BOI investment program set out in the eighth Investment Priorities Plan (IPP) and the sixth Export Priorities Plan (EPP) combines intended investment by the private sector with government designations of preferred growth areas, which include most of the industrial sector. The BOI program is not firm, however; some of the listed projects may never materialize, and new ones may be added later. Inasmuch as BOI-registered projects are likely to make up over half (perhaps even two-thirds) the total industrial investment in the next few years, the program is fairly representative of the main features of the planned growth in large-scale industry.

The eighth IPP and the sixth EPP list 130 and 61 priority areas, respectively, for investment. Cost and employment requirements

Table 8.5. The Board of Investments Expansion Program, 1976–79
(At 1974 prices)

| | | | Investment cost | |
Item	Number of projects	Employment (thousands)	Total (millions of pesos)	Per worker (thousands of pesos)
Eighth Investment Priorities Plan				
Agroprocessing	30	4.8	3,174.5	655.7
Chemicals and chemical products	59	4.0	3,461.7	865.4
Engineering	27	3.5	729.8	208.5
Mining and mineral processing	14	8.8	6,456.9	733.7
Total	130	21.1	13,795.9	653.8
Sixth Export Priorities Plan				
Agroprocessing	18	3.9	477.5	122.4
Chemicals and chemical products	21	3.2	947.1	296.0
Engineering	15	2.7	324.4	120.1
Mining and mineral processing	7	1.4	605.4	432.4
Total	61	11.2	2,354.4	210.2
Total				
Agroprocessing	48	8.7	3,625.0	416.7
Chemicals and chemical products	80	7.2	4,408.8	612.3
Engineering	42	6.2	1,054.2	170.0
Mining and mineral processing	21	10.2	7,062.3	692.4
Total	191	32.3	16,150.3	500.0

Source: Board of Investments (BOI).

implied by these plans are broken down by sector in Table 8.5. The most striking feature of this program is undoubtedly its heavy bias toward capital-intensive projects. The capital-labor ratio of ₱500,000 (US$71,000) per worker for the program as a whole is one rarely found in countries at a similar stage of development. Even if the cost estimates turn out to be overstated and the anticipated employment understated (employment is frequently registered in terms of one shift though additional shifts may be introduced

Table 8.6. Major Industrial Projects (Approved or under Consideration)

Sector	Project status	Location	Assumed construction period	Annual capacity (thousand metric tons)	Estimated cost (millions of pesos)
Mining export					
Rio Tuba Nickel (mining)	Planned	Palawan	1976–77	500.0	148
Atlas (copper smelting, refining)	Approved by BOI	Toledo, Cebu, or Bataan	1976–78	131.0	1,673
Marinduque Mining Industrial Corporation–Lepanto (copper smelting, refining)	Approved by BOI	Negros Occidental	1976–78	84.0	1,218
Apex (magnetite iron sand mining)	Feasibility study completed	Cagayan and Zambales	n.a.	300.0	n.a.
Mindanao Alloy Corporation (ferrosilicon plant)	Under study	Iligan	1976–77	28.0	130
Commonwealth Aluminum Company	Under study	Samal	1976–80	1,300.0	4,648
Agro-based export					
Wood-processing program	Under study	Many sites	1975–80	1,800[a]	2,435
Sugar mills (4)	Under study	Many sites	1975–79	n.a.	1,120
Import substitution					
Integrated steel plant	Under study	Cagayan de Oro	1976–79	2,000.0	7,700
Aluminum Corporation of the Philippines	Under study	Ormoc, Leyte	1976–78	20.0	208
Atlas Fertilizer (expansion of complex fertilizer production)	Approved by BOI	Toledo, Cebu, or Bataan	1976–78	n.a.	350
Urea fertilizer	Under study	Central Philippines	1976–78	1.5 a day	1,400
Philippine National Oil Company	Under study	Many sites	1976–?	n.a.	7,000
Agusan Pulp and Paper Corporation	Under study		1976–78	0.5	609
Shipbuilding program	Under study	Mindanao, Cebu, Luzon	1975–80	71 units	779

n.a.: Not available.

a. Cubic meters of logs.

Sources: BOI and National Economic and Development Authority (NEDA).

later), this capital-worker ratio is much higher than in previous years.[7]

The increase in capital-intensity of the BOI program is largely owing to a drastic shift in the distribution of industries. Agro-processing and engineering industries, which are generally more labor-intensive than those in mining and chemicals, account for 47 percent of all projects in the eighth IPP and sixth EPP combined, whereas they made up about 70 percent of all projects registered with the BOI in 1968–72. Resource requirements for engineering industries—the least capital intensive of the four sectors—accounted for only 6.5 percent of the total. The more export-oriented projects in Table 8.5 (those under the EPP) are also generally less capital intensive, but the 1975 additions to the IPP and EPP show a different picture. Twelve projects added to the IPP in 1975 will cost ₱182.6 million and provide 1,418 new jobs (at ₱129,000 per worker), while ten projects included in the EPP in the same year appear to be more capital intensive with 3,237 new jobs costing ₱516.9 million (at ₱160,000 per worker).

The program shown in Table 8.5, however, does not give a complete picture of the investments in large capital-intensive projects that are likely to arise in the next five years or so. Such projects are listed in Table 8.6. The total cost approximates ₱30,000 million (US$4,300 million) during the 1975–80 period, although a few of the largest projects may extend well into the 1980s. The three largest projects (an integrated steel plant, a petrochemical complex, and the Commonwealth Aluminum Company) account for ₱20,000 million (US$2,900 million) or two-thirds of the total program.

By a rough calculation the aggregate direct employment effect of the investments listed might be approximately 65,000 new jobs, of which 20,000 would be in wood processing. This implies a cost of ₱462,000 per job for the program as a whole (₱613,000 per job without wood processing), which are ratios similar to those for the BOI-registered projects in Table 8.5. The projects under active consideration complement those already registered with the BOI or specifically designated for promotion by the BOI; all the projects can therefore be analyzed as a group.

Approximately ₱24,500 million, or 53 percent of the total estimated investment requirement of ₱46,300 million (US$6,600

7. It averaged ₱200,000 in 1968–72 at 1974 prices.

Table 8.7. Sectoral Origin and End Use of Industrial Output, 1974–80
(In millions of pesos, at 1974 prices)

	1974				1974–80		1980			
Sector	Gross output[a]	Imports[b]	Exports[c]	Domestic demand (1+2−3)	Demand coefficients[d]	Demand growth rate[e] (percent)	Gross output	Imports[b]	Exports[f]	Domestic demand (7+8−9)
	(1)	(2)	(3)	(4)	(5)	(6)	(7)	(8)	(9)	(10)
Basic metals industries	1,448	1,596	. . .	3,044	1.50	10.50	4,168	1,373	. . .	5,541
Chemicals and oil products	8,508	2,856	224	11,140	1.20	8.40	16,194	2,580	700	18,074
Engineering	6,625	5,985	70	12,540	1.28	9.00	11,523	9,979	490	21,012
Food, beverages, and tobacco	24,095	1,162	8,967	16,290	0.83	5.80	35,047	1,250	13,450	22,847
Nonmetallic mineral products	1,152	140	154	1,138	1.30	9.10	2,188	151	420	1,919
Pulp and paper	1,158	399	49	1,508	1.20	8.40	2,447	280	280	2,447
Textiles and apparel	5,086	483	245	5,324	0.97	6.80	8,550	540	1,190	7,900
Wood processing	2,779	. . .	847	1,932	1.15	8.05	6,924	. . .	3,850	3,074
Other light industries[g]	3,691	1,099	238	4,552	1.10	7.70	6,770	1,314	980	7,104
Total	54,542	13,720	10,794	57,468	1.10	7.70	93,811	17,467	21,360	89,918

. . . Zero or negligible.

a. Computed from gross value added data supplied by NEDA, by using value added coefficients implied in BCS's preliminary *Annual Survey of Manufacturers, 1973.*

b. Includes finished and semifinished manufactures, but not raw materials used by industry.

c. Estimate based on incomplete data.

d. World Bank estimates based on past consumption patterns, future development programs, and experience from other countries.

e. Assuming a GDP growth rate of 7 percent a year.

f. Projection based on existing and suggested programs (see the section on industrial exports).

g. Printing and publishing, leather and rubber products, footwear, plastic products, and miscellaneous industries.

Source: World Bank estimates.

million), relates to projects catering to the domestic market, the majority of it consisting of large import-replacing projects (steel plants, fertilizers, other petrochemicals, pulp and paper, and shipbuilding). The remaining ₱21,800 million is divided between mining exporting industries (₱14,900 million)—with aluminum, nickel, and copper as the main items—and other exporting industries (₱6,900 million), mainly wood processing, sugar, coconut oil, and other agro-based products.

The new investments under consideration are likely to include a larger number of smaller and less costly projects than those in Table 8.5, and many of them will not seek to register with the BOI. The above analysis of the combined programs nevertheless gives some indication of the main directions industrial growth is expected to take in the near future. Policy changes are necessary if more investments are to be directed to labor-intensive industries and if manufacturing exports are to be diversified. Any such changes should consider carefully the relevant growth potential in both the domestic and foreign markets.

GROWTH IN THE DOMESTIC MARKET

About three-fourths of total domestic demand for manufactured goods in 1974 was met by local production, while one-fourth was imported (Table 8.7). The highest import ratios [8] are for basic metals (53 percent), largely steel, and for engineering industries (48 percent); the lowest are for food and wood processing (well below 10 percent).[9]

To estimate the growth potential in the domestic market for manufactured goods, a set of income coefficients of demand was worked out and applied to an assumed annual GDP growth rate of 7 percent (Table 8.7).[10] This calculation shows domestic demand growing at 6 to 7 percent a year for products of such traditional industries as food processing and textiles, 10.5 percent a year for products of basic metals industries, and roughly 8 to 9 percent a year for all other industries. In the aggregate the domestic market

---

8. The ratio of imports to total consumption.

9. Industrial raw materials are not included in these imports.

10. World Bank projections assumed these growth rates to be 5 percent in 1975, 6.5 percent in 1976, and 7.5 percent thereafter. For 1975–80 this comes close to an average of 7 percent.

for manufactured goods would grow at a rate of 7.7 percent with a 7 percent GDP growth. Incremental consumption of those goods would thus amount to ₱32,400 million at 1974 prices.

Once it is determined how much of the projected demand for manufactured goods in 1974–80 can be met by domestic production, the amount that will have to come from imports will be obvious. In Table 8.7 an attempt was made to answer this question on the basis of BOI-sponsored investment plans (Table 8.5), other major projects under consideration (Table 8.6), and various programs or estimates in such industries as sugar and coconut, basic metals, engineering, mining, wood processing, and other export-oriented sectors. In the absence of input-output data, however, and because of various other statistical weaknesses such as double counting,[11] there is no reliable basis for the projection of growth in domestic demand, gross output, and import requirements for the manufacturing sector as a whole. The totals in Table 8.7 are therefore not exact quantifications, but they do indicate the general direction the manufacturing sector is likely to follow.

The indications are that the proportion of domestic demand for manufactured products met by imports will noticeably decline. In all major industrial groups except engineering, the estimated increase in domestic demand during 1974–80 will be met almost if not entirely by domestic production. In engineering, despite an estimated annual growth in gross output of nearly 10 percent, imports will rise from around ₱6,000 million to ₱10,000 million in 1980 because of the time needed to develop domestic capability to supply capital goods for the large investment programs in industry, construction, power, and other infrastructure. The import dependency of engineering products is projected to remain unchanged, however, with the ratio of imports to domestic demand remaining at 47 percent. The import–domestic demand ratio for chemicals and oil products and for basic metals would be halved (from 52 to 25 percent and from 26 to around 14 percent respectively) and reduced significantly in the case of light consumer goods, processed food, and beverages.

---

11. Gross output figures in Table 8.7 include interindustrial transactions and some overlapping between import and export value.

Employment Creation and Investment Needs

The export component of total manufacturing growth (column 9 of Table 8.7) is used to project the aggregate growth of manufacturing value added, employment creation, and investment requirements. The main results and the underlying methodology of these projections for 1974–80 are presented in Table 8.8. The table shows not only what is likely on the basis of existing development programs but also World Bank estimates of what could be achieved through intensified efforts under an improved policy framework. The organized manufacturing sector is assumed to grow at 9.1 percent a year during the 1974–80 period,[12] which would represent a marked acceleration in comparison with past trends. With an incremental capital-output ratio of 3.3, total investment requirements would amount to ₱44,000 million (US$5,900 million). The employment gain is estimated at 251,000, a 48 percent increase over the 1974 level. Implied are an employment-income elasticity of 0.74, an investment per worker of ₱176,000 (US$25,000), and a growth in labor productivity of 2 percent a year.

Although no time lag was assumed between investments and the generation of value added, in the case of the large steel project indications are that full production will be realized only after 1980. The capital-output ratio for the manufacturing sector as a whole is therefore 3.3 instead of approximately 3.1. This variation has been slightly offset by the assumption that in some of the subsectors (particularly in the wood processing and cement industries) there is room to increase production by better utilization of capacity.

In reality there will of course be many more offsetting effects of this kind. The average investment-output time lag must be well over two years, and there are high-cost projects with long gestation periods. The spillover of output from investments made in previous periods will thus be much more pronounced at the end of the period than at the beginning.

The food-processing sector, which employs almost 30 percent of total labor in manufacturing, will grow more slowly than other industrial groups. Its rate of growth is to a large extent determined by limitations on the potential supply (a growth rate of 4 percent has been estimated for agriculture) and by less than bright prospects

12. A growth rate of 6 percent is assumed for 1975 and 9.7 percent in subsequent years.

Table 8.8. Manufacturing Growth Projections, 1974–80
(At 1974 prices)

Sector	Value added (millions of pesos) 1974	1980	Employment (thousands) 1974	1980	Growth rate, 1974–80 (percent) Value added	Employment	Value added per worker (thousands of pesos) 1974	1980	Investment, 1975–80 Total (millions of pesos)	Per worker (thousands of pesos)	Incremental capital-output ratio
Basic metals industries	434	1,492	16	35	23.0	13.9	28	43	9,400	490	8.9
Chemicals and oil products	3,148	5,344	48	58	9.2	3.2	60	92	9,882	1,000	4.5
Engineering	2,169	3,687	63	96	9.3	6.2	34	38	4,099	124	2.7
Food, beverages, and tobacco	8,433	12,266	153	217	6.4	6.0	55	57	8,433	132	2.2
Nonmetallic mineral products	542	963	18	27	10.0	7.0	30	36	1,600	180	3.8
Pulp and paper	348	734	12	16	13.2	4.9	29	46	1,698	420	4.4
Textiles and apparel	1,882	3,164	123	174	9.0	6.0	15	18	3,461	68	2.7
Wood processing	1,167	2,700	58	98	15.0	9.1	20	28	3,066	77	2.0
Other light industries	1,439	2,572	36	57	10.2	8.0	40	45	2,606	125	2.3
Total	19,562	32,922	527	778	9.1	6.7	37	45	44,245	176	3.4

Note: Two methods, or their combination, were used in value added projections: (a) where the magnitude of investment was known or could easily be approximated, the growth rate was derived by applying an incremental capital–value added ratio (in metals, pulp and paper, chemicals, wood processing); and (b) a growth rate was first assumed on the basis of demand projections, improvised income elasticity coefficients, and, as an orientation point in some cases, NEDA's targets for 1974–78; the investment requirements were then computed, again using assumed capital-output ratios. No time lag between investment and value added generation was assumed except for basic metals and, in part, petrochemicals.

Project information, historical labor coefficients, and assumed capital-labor ratios were used to derive employment projections. The employment figure for the organized manufacturing sector in 1974 was assumed to be the same as given by preliminary census results for 1973 because of an unusually high increase in employment in 1973 (the employment figure given was 526,000, 25 percent higher than in 1971 and too high to be credible) and the very sluggish growth of industry in 1974.

Sources: National accounts statistics for 1973 and 1974, producers' associations, and World Bank estimates.

for sugar, the Philippines' principal export crop, in the world markets (a 4 percent long-term real growth rate has been projected). Much of the sector's growth will depend on meat and fish processing, export-oriented fruit and vegetable canning, and the phasing out of unprocessed copra exports in favor of coconut oil and other processed coconut products.

Textile and chemical industries, metal products, machinery and equipment, and other light industries are all envisaged to grow at a rate of 9 to 10 percent a year. Almost a third of the increment in textile output will be generated through exports, and another third will originate in import substitution, particularly in the production of yarns and synthetic materials. A certain revival of the rubber-based industry and a considerable expansion in footwear, furniture, plastic products, and some other light industries are projected for the latter half of the 1970s.

In the engineering sector the expansion effort will be spread over a wide range of industries, notably agricultural machinery and irrigation equipment, shipbuilding, car assembling and manufacturing, construction equipment, goods related to rural electrification, machine tools, electronics, and household durables. By far the fastest growing subsectors will be basic metals and wood processing, with compound growth rates of 23 and 15 percent respectively.

The chemical sector

The development program for the chemical sector includes a major new oil refinery, expansion of the existing refineries, two or three large fertilizer plants, and several downstream projects in petrochemicals. The Philippines currently meets about two-thirds of its fertilizer requirements from imports. The government would like to cover at least 70 percent of its needs through local production and the rest through joint ventures with neighboring countries, notably Indonesia, Malaysia, or Brunei. For this reason the government is undertaking a major nitrogenous fertilizer project. Consumption of nitrogenous fertilizer rose by an average of 20 percent a year in the 1969–74 period, and recent projections show that it will increase from 53 percent of total fertilizer consumption in 1974 to 60 percent in 1980 and 65 percent in 1985. Demand estimates and expansion plans for the existing plants indicate that the urea supply gap will be as follows (in thousands of metric tons):

	Actual	Projected	
	1974	1980	1985
Demand	212	440–520	610–750
Production	53	100	120
Gap	159	340–420	490–630

The proposed fertilizer project would have a capacity of 1,550 metric tons a day of urea and 1,200 tons a day of ammonia, 300 tons of which would supply the existing urea plants. There would therefore be little need for imports of urea in the early 1980s when the new plant is to start operation. According to preliminary calculations the project would cost some US$260 million if based on naphtha; this amount will probably have to be raised somewhat if the plant has its own power-generating unit. It is generally agreed that naphtha from local refineries should be used as feedstock for urea production. At full production the plant will require 8,500 barrels per day (BPD) of naphtha and 2,500 BPD of fuel oil for steam and power generation. The present operating capacity of Philippine oil refineries is 245,000 BPD, while actual production amounted to 199,500 BPD in 1975. Irrespective of the naphtha requirements of the fertilizer project, a further expansion of the refining capacity will be necessary after 1980 to keep up with the growing demand; naphtha requirements for urea represent only a small fraction of that expansion.

BASIC METALS

The planned expansion in the basic metals sector consists primarily of the integrated steel plant, which came under active consideration after the highly regarded International Iron and Steel Institute (IISI) in late 1974 forecast a worldwide shortage of steel in 1978–85.[13] The Philippines currently consumes around 1.5 million metric tons of steel products in terms of crude steel equivalents, of which 80 to 85 percent is imported. Consumption is generally expected to reach 2.5 million metric tons in 1980 and 4.1 million metric tons in 1985.[14] When the existing capacity and specialty steel

13. The IISI estimates that the world demand for steel in 1985 will exceed the supply by 49 million metric tons.

14. Center for Research and Communication, *A Projection of Philippine Steel Demand up to Year 2000* (Manila, October 1974).

requirements (to be met from imports) are taken into account, it is believed that there is room for a plant of economic size producing 2 million metric tons.

Preliminary studies by British and Japanese consultants indicate that the proposed integrated steel mill would utilize the blast furnace–basic oxygen process and continuous casting and would have rolling facilities for flat and nonflat products (billets, slabs, hot and cold rolled steel, and long products). Iron ore and coking coal would be largely imported; only about 5 percent of the iron ore requirements could be obtained through local iron sand mining. Several ferroalloy ingredients could be supplied domestically, but the use of domestic limestone may be problematic.

The mill would be adjacent to the iron ore sinter plant of Kawasaki Steel Corporation in Northern Mindanao and could use the same deep-water harbor.[15] The total cost of the project has been estimated at US$1,200 million at 1974 prices, of which US$160 million would be for infrastructure; the government would own the majority of equity shares. After 1981 another facility could be added to expand capacity by 2 million metric tons. Taking account of the enlarged market opportunities presented by the Association of South-East Asian Nations (ASEAN),[16] a modified project proposal envisages a plant with a capacity of 2.4 to 3 million metric tons of crude steel to be completed by 1982 at a cost of US$1,700 million.

There is little doubt that an integrated steel plant could benefit the economy. The uncertainties arising from an erratic steel supply would be eliminated, and the rapidly growing domestic demand for diverse steel products could be met locally when Japan—hitherto the main source of Philippine steel imports—faces severe restrictions on further expansion of its steel capacity. There would be some foreign exchange savings, preliminarily estimated at about US$200 million a year at 1974 prices. Through backward and forward linkages the new industrial complex could spur the development of secondary and tertiary industries and thus lead to employment generation. Much more study will be needed, however, before the feasibility of the project can be clearly established. The main con-

15. Under a long-term agreement with the Kawasaki Steel Corporation, the Larap iron ore mine will continue to produce for export until its depletion and cannot be counted on as a source of ore for the steel mill.

16. This proposal was submitted by the Philippines at a high-level ASEAN conference in Kuala Lumpur in March 1976.

cern is whether, and to what extent, a developing country lacking its own natural resources can establish a viable steel industry. The experience of Japan and more recently of the Republic of Korea suggests that under certain circumstances this is possible. In comparison with these two countries, the Philippines has a certain edge in terms of transportation costs and the possession of some important ferro-alloy elements.

Two copper smelters–refineries (sponsored by Atlas Consolidated Mining Company, Marinduque Mining and Industrial Company, and Lepanto Consolidated Mining Company) are in a more advanced stage of planning and project preparation. The two projects combined would produce 215,000 metric tons of electrolytic copper, 90 to 95 percent of which would be for export. The total cost has been estimated at US$400 million (or around US$470 million without BOI incentives). Most of the copper concentrates needed for smelting and refining would come from expanded mining operations and the rest from the existing output.

Although these projects make only a negligible contribution to direct employment creation, they do offer several advantages:

a. Domestic value added and foreign exchange would be increased and transportation costs reduced by processing the ore and exporting the high copper-content blister or refined products instead of the bulky concentrate.

b. The Philippines would gain an additional competitive margin insofar as smelting charges continue to rise worldwide in response to more stringent controls on environmental pollution in industrialized countries.

c. The country would benefit from a greater diversification of markets.

d. The development of domestic industries producing copper and copper alloys would be encouraged.

e. About 734,000 metric tons of sulfuric acid, a by-product of copper smelting, would be produced annually that could be used to make superphosphate fertilizers (by acidulation of imported phosphate rock) and exchanged for nitrogenous fertilizers under the ASEAN schemes.

LABOR-INTENSIVE AND CAPITAL-INTENSIVE INDUSTRIES

Some of the more important implications of growth in individual subsectors are presented in Tables 8.9 and 8.10, which group the subsectors according to factor-intensity and product type. Mining, cottage industry, and manufacturing industries having more than five workers are analyzed to derive global trends and evaluate relative costs and benefits. The analysis is extended beyond 1980 in an attempt to determine the longer term pattern of industrial growth.

Industry as a whole (including mining) is projected to grow at a rate of slightly over 9 percent during 1974–85. Capital-intensive activities (the mining and manufacturing industries as defined in Table 8.9) would have a growth rate of 11.6 percent, labor-intensive industries 8.5 percent, and cottage industry 1.0 percent. Under another classification, intermediate goods industries (the capital-intensive group plus wood processing) would grow at a rate of about 12 percent, capital goods industries at 9.6 percent, and consumer goods industries at 7.4 percent. As a result, the share of consumer goods and labor-intensive industries in total output would sharply decrease in favor of intermediate and capital-intensive industries. Analogous shifts would occur in employment.

The contribution of these industrial groups to the growth in value added and employment must, of course, be weighed against its cost. The contribution of the cottage industry sector is assumed to be negligible and is therefore omitted. The pattern that emerges for the decade from 1975 to 1985 is shown in Table 8.11. With 43 percent of all investment, the capital-intensive manufacturing industries would contribute 27 percent of incremental value added and 15 percent of new employment. On the other end of the scale are the labor-intensive industries, whose shares in incremental value added and employment in particular are substantially higher than that in investment. Mining lies between these extremes. For a country short in capital and abundant in labor, such a growth pattern would seem inappropriate were it not for other considerations.

The cottage industry cannot assume a major role in future industrialization.[17] Although the sector would provide significant employment and require primarily low-cost investment, many cottage production lines are ill suited to provide goods and services at a cost and of a quality competitive with larger scale manufacturers using more efficient production methods. The model adopted in Tables 8.9 and 8.10 assumes that, while some further displacements

17. See the section on small-scale industry.

Table 8.9. Growth Projections by Broad Industrial Groups
(At 1974 prices)

Item	Value added (millions of pesos) 1974	1980	1985
Amount			
Type of activity			
Mining[a]	2,154	4,483	7,554
Capital-intensive manufacturing[b]	4,472	8,533	14,705
Labor-intensive manufacturing[c]	15,090	24,389	36,842
Cottage industry[d]	1,350	1,433	1,506
Total	23,066	38,838	60,607
Type of product (excluding cottage industry)			
Final demand goods[e]	11,754	18,002	25,713
Intermediate goods[f]	7,793	15,716	27,450
Capital goods[g]	2,169	3,687	5,938
Total	21,716	37,405	59,101
Percentage shares			
Type of activity			
Mining	9	11	12.5
Capital-intensive manufacturing	19	22	24
Labor-intensive manufacturing	66	63	61
Cottage industry	6	4	2.5
Total	100	100	100
Type of product			
Final demand goods	54	48	44
Intermediate goods	36	42	46
Capital goods	10	10	10
Total	100	100	100

a. Includes metal making other than basic metals.
b. Pulp and paper, chemicals, oil products, cement and other nonmetallic mineral products, and basic metals.
c. Food, beverages, and tobacco; textiles and wearing apparel; wood processing; engineering; and other light industries.

in the cottage sector are inevitable, they would be counterbalanced by government support for the more viable production units. On balance, cottage industry may be able to maintain its present employment level over the next ten years. This is an optimistic outlook, however, in view of its recent declining trend, and of course implies a sharp drop in the sector's relative share in total industrial employment from 60 percent in 1974 to 42 percent in 1985.

Employment (thousands)			Investment (millions of pesos)	
1974	*1980*	*1985*	*1975–80*	*1981–85*
40	69	99	5,822	8,292
94	136	186	22,580	27,774
433	642	880	21,665	31,133
844	844	844	125	117
1,411	1,691	2,009	50,192	67,316
312	448	600	14,500	16,964
192	303	433	31,468	44,157
63	96	132	4,099	6,078
567	847	1,165	50,067	67,199
3	4	5	12	13
6	8	9	45	41
31	38	44	43	46
60	50	42	0	0
100	100	100	100	100
55	53	52	29	25
34	36	37	63	66
11	11	11	8	9
100	100	100	100	100

d. Establishments with less than five workers.
e. Food, beverages, and tobacco; textiles and wearing apparel; and other light industries.
f. Mining, pulp and paper, chemicals, oil products, cement and other nonmetallic mineral products, basic metals, and wood processing.
g. Engineering industries.
Source: Table 8.8.

The growth potential of the other labor-intensive industrial group has limitations of its own, despite relatively more favorable cost-benefit relationships. As already stressed, some major final demand industries such as food processing and wearing apparel are handicapped by the relatively weak potential growth of domestic demand (Table 8.7). Another limitation is the unfavorable export prospects for some labor-intensive traditional agroprocessing sectors such as sugar. What remain as major sources of industrial growth in the

Table 8.10. Economic Indicators

	1974–80					1980–85				
	Annual growth rate (percent)		Value added per worker (thousands of pesos)	Incremental capital-output ratio	Investment per worker (thousands of pesos)	Annual growth rate (percent)		Value added per worker (thousands of pesos)	Incremental capital-output ratio	Investment per worker (thousands of pesos)
Category	Value Added	Employment				Value added	Employment			
Type of activity										
Mining	13.0	9.5	80	2.5	200	11.0	7.5	102	2.7	276
Capital-intensive manufacturing	11.4	6.4	97	5.6	538	11.5	6.5	123	4.5	555
Labor-intensive manufacturing	8.3	6.8	44	2.3	104	8.6	6.5	52	2.5	131
Cottage industry	1.0	...	...	1.5	...	1.0	...	...	1.6	...
Total	9.1	3.1	56	3.2	179	9.3	3.5	68	3.1	212
Type of product										
Final demand goods	7.4	6.2	53	2.3	107	7.4	6.0	51	2.2	112
Intermediate goods	12.4	7.9	71	4.0	283	11.8	7.4	90	3.8	340
Capital goods	9.3	6.2	46	2.7	124	10.0	6.6	63	2.7	169
Total	9.5	6.9	56	3.2	·179	9.6	6.6	68	3.1	211

... Zero or negligible.

Note: For 1974–80 the basic assumptions are as in Table 8.7. For 1980–85 these assumptions were modified to reflect the partially applied investment–value added time lag and a further (policy-induced) shift in investments in favor of labor-intensive exports.

Individual industries are classified into broad groups on the basis of their predominant characteristics. The textile sector, for example, is placed under labor-intensive and final demand industrial groups, even though a part of it can be described as capital intensive and belonging to the intermediate group. It is believed that this has not significantly affected the projection of basic trends.

The following assumptions were used in the projections of growth in the cottage sector: (a) the 1974 value added figure is established by multiplying the number of persons employed (which is known) by a certain value added per worker ratio (assumed to be equal to the minimum wage level in the organized sector); (b) employment is taken to remain unchanged during 1974–85; and (c) a growth rate of 1.0 percent a year is assumed in this sector's value added over 1974–85.

Source: See Table 8.8.

Table 8.11. Growth Pattern by Industrial Group

Sector	Investment	Value added increment	New employment
		Percent share	
Mining	12	15	10
Capital intensive	43	27	15
Labor intensive	45	58	75

labor-intensive group are wood processing and a wide range of non-traditional manufacturing industries. This group of industries is estimated to increase exports at an annual rate of well over 30 percent in 1974–80 and consequently to raise their contribution to total industrial exports from 12 percent in 1974–75 to 26 percent in 1980. This is a formidable task, implying an average increment in these exports of close to US$150 million annually. A more rapid growth of these exports would be difficult to imagine, although quite a few countries have scored even higher rates of export growth in recent years.

For a variety of reasons considerable scope for accelerated growth is found in a large group of intermediate goods industries (mining, basic metals and other metal making, chemicals and chemical products, mineral fuels and lubricants, pulp and paper, cement and other nonoil and nonmetallic mineral products, and wood processing). Relative to the growth of incomes, domestic demand for these products is likely to rise much faster than for those in most final demand categories. Prospects for foreign markets for several Philippine mining products and their processed derivatives are also likely to be favorable. Except for some basic metals, oil, and many chemical products, intermediate goods industries rely on domestic natural resources, which will continue to give them a comparative advantage. Because of the high import dependency in intermediate goods industries other than mining, wood processing, and cement and because of substantial imports of many items that could be produced domestically, there is considerable room for further import substitution and foreign exchange savings.

Philippine industrial growth, at least for the next ten years, should therefore be based on a two-pronged strategy: Labor-intensive activities should be promoted as much as possible to generate employment, and the intermediate sector should be permitted to expand further in order to reduce import dependency and utilize external market opportunities. Although capital-intensive and intermediate goods industries should under no circumstances expand at the expense of labor-intensive activities (for both economic and social reasons), they will have to grow rapidly if industry is to develop faster than the economy as a whole.

This dual emphasis on labor-intensive activities and import substitution in intermediate sectors suggests what should have happened during the 1960s, after import substitution in finished consumer goods was virtually achieved. Much of the potential for this second-stage import substitution will be exhausted by the mid-1980s. Less than 15 percent of aggregate demand for industrial goods (finished and semifinished products) in 1985 will come from imports, compared with 24 percent in 1974 and 19 percent projected for 1980. Most of these imports will be goods which cannot be manufactured locally because of the lack of technological capability or the limited size of the domestic market. Additional sources of growth will therefore have to be developed during the next decade.

There will still be a serious employment problem in the 1980s. According to the above projections, about 600,000 new jobs will be created in manufacturing during 1975–85, and the sector will be able to absorb nearly 80,000 new workers a year by the end of this period. This would represent 13 to 14 percent of the incremental labor force in 1985, a fairly low labor-absorption capacity in view of the amount of financial resources expected to be drawn into this sector over the period. The major alternative source of growth is to be found in labor-intensive exports. Employment will also need to be created by rural industrialization and small-scale industry.

GROWTH-ORIENTED POLICIES

Traditionally industrial growth in the Philippines has been generated and influenced by protectionist policies, changes in exchange rates and regimes, interest rates and other monetary policies, and investment incentives. These policies successfully diverted domestic resources from nonproductive sectors into industry, attracted foreign capital, and provided a shelter from foreign competition in the initial stages of development. In retrospect, however, they were less successful in channeling investments into socially desirable sectors and in encouraging exports. Moreover they failed to provide for necessary changes in the structure of protection once import substitution in finished consumer goods was achieved. There is little chance that the recommended growth program can be implemented without major changes in the policy framework to restructure protection, resource allocation, and, most importantly, the relative position of manufactured exports.

THE ISSUE OF PROTECTION

The basic structure of protection was shaped during the 1950s and has been altered very little since then in spite of two major devaluations and other policy changes. Table 8.12 shows the effective protection rates for major categories of imported and exported goods. Nonessential consumer and producer goods are strongly favored. This helps explain the pattern of import substitution that emerged in the early period of Philippine industrialization and the incentives gap that has diverted resources from manufactured exports and nonconsumer goods industries. The relatively low effective protection rates for semiessential and essential producer goods, especially in the early stage of development, explains at least partly why a number of capital and intermediate goods are still not produced locally.

Since 1971 the basic features of the protection system have changed little, although there has been an increasing awareness of the need for change. Lowering the general level of protection and changing the order of priorities within the system will be a formidable task, however, because of conflicting interests and active resistance.

Philippine industry currently receives a high degree of protection through quantitative restrictions, tariffs, sales taxes, preferential interest rates, and fiscal incentives. This report concludes that quantitative restrictions should be gradually removed, tariff levels restructured and lowered, and the protective element removed from all other fiscal and monetary policies. It is difficult to concur with the recommendation in the ILO report [18] to abolish all quantitative restrictions immediately. A more realistic approach would be to relax the import-licensing system gradually by removing an increasing number of commodities. This would of course have to be coordinated with other liberalization measures and with steps

18. ILO, *Sharing in Development.*

Table 8.12. Effective Protection Rates, 1949-71
(In percent)

Year	Consumer goods			Imported producer goods			Traditional exports	New exports
	Non-essential	Semi-essential	Essential	Non-essential	Semi-essential	Essential		
1949-50	5	4	...	5	...	...	...	23
1951-52	114	23	-7	24	19	19	-15	23
1953	114	23	-7	24	19	19	-15	31
1954	110	19	-7	17	19	19	-15	31
1955	141	19	-8	19	21	20	-16	31
1956	154	34	-5	28	22	23	-19	31
1957	179	18	-6	26	24	24	-19	31
1958	178	37	-7	25	24	24	-20	27
1959	183	31	-18	5	51	52	-43	25
1960	349	149	-15	173	52	50	-27	40
1961	230	61	-9	56	40	39	-45	2
1962	337	54	-2	169	21	28	-37	-4
1963	332	53	...	174	14	25	-38	-9
1964	326	50	...	171	12	25	-38	-9
1965	365	56	...	198	12	28	-22	12
1966	354	50	1	191	12	26	-20	12
1967	357	52	1	193	13	26	-21	13
1968	363	54	1	195	15	27	-22	13
1969	365	55	1	197	15	27	-21	13
1970	354	51	2	193	14	26	-43	21
1971	362	57	5	203	14	19	-33	26

... Zero or negligible.

Note: Effective protective rates are defined as follows: for imported items, the effective protection is taken to be the percentage by which the effective exchange rate in any given year exceeds the effective exchange rate for producer goods used by "new and necessary" industries in that year. The nominal subsidy on new exports is taken to be equal to the percentage by which the effective exchange rate for this category exceeds the effective exchange rate for traditional exports.

The effective exchange rate is defined as the number or units of local currency actually paid or received per dollar of a given international transaction. It also includes the difference made in these transactions by tariffs, discriminatory sales or compensating taxes, special foreign exchange taxes, exemption from domestic taxes, subsidized borrowing rates, and marginal deposit requirement on imports.

Source: R. E. Baldwin, *Foreign Trade Regimes and Economic Development: The Philippines* (New York: Columbia University Press, 1975), table 5-10.

to promote the operational efficiency of domestic production and to ease the adjustment process.

The last major reform of the tariff system was undertaken in January 1973 (Presidential Decree 34). At that time 271 specific tariff rates were reduced to 2, and all the ad valorem rates were grouped into six levels ranging from 10 to 100 percent depending on the degree of product completeness and the existence of local production. Rates of 10 to 20 percent are in principle imposed on basic necessities such as food products and medicines, raw materials not available in the country (such as cotton, basic iron and steel products, chemical substances), and industrial equipment not manufactured within the country. Rates of 30 to 60 percent are levied on a vast range of intermediate and capital goods such as tubes, synthetic fibers, machine parts, cigarette paper, chemicals, tools, trucks, barges, motors, and some easily smuggled consumer goods like watches and cameras. Rates of 70 to 100 percent are applied to luxury goods and products available within the country, mostly finished consumer goods such as confectionary, varnishes, rubber tires, leather and wood products, garments, home appliances, toys, and jewelry. Although very successful in generating revenue, this reform has not reduced the protective element. It has actually raised more tariff rates than it has reduced, and in terms of the average nominal tariff rates it appears to have slightly increased protection.

Although little time has elapsed since that reform, a careful reexamination of the levels and structure of tariffs is urgent. There is a definite need for the readjustment of tariffs on certain products —and product classifications should be modified as well—in accordance with important changes in the structure of production. In fact, tariff rates should be monitored in such a way as to anticipate and influence changes in the production structure. At present decisions are made case by case at the instigation of individual producers, but they should be incorporated in a more systematic effort on the part of the government and producers' associations. Industries producing finished consumer goods currently enjoy the highest rate of protection. As the industrial structure diversifies, new industries, many of them in intermediate and capital goods, will be added to the list of the highly sheltered, further raising the average level of protection. The system should evolve in such a way that well-established industries are gradually shifted into lower rate tariff groups while some essential nonconsumer goods receive timely and effective protection.

The Philippines should formulate and pursue a program to reduce the average tariff level. Industrial growth will be increasingly constrained by high production costs that built up under the inward-looking industrialization strategy, and it will be progressively more difficult to expand if these cost disadvantages are maintained. A substantial proportion of total industrial growth envisaged for

1975–85 under the recommended strategy should be generated by exporting industries.[19] Since these industries will require a significant increase in the domestic production of their inputs and are also indispensable for reasons of the balance of payments, the role of exports can be enlarged only if the production costs of supplying and participating industries can be brought down to competitive levels.

Any program to reduce tariffs will take time to implement and will have to be done gradually, but its concrete forms are difficult to visualize without further study.[20] A substantial decrease of the average tariff level seems possible within the next ten years, and the distortion of the exchange rate in favor of final demand goods could therefore be reduced considerably. The role of the tariff system in generating fiscal revenues should also be diminished, despite the increasing importance of import duties in government revenues in recent years.[21] A first step should be to reconsider the decision to impose a general 10 percent duty on all imports with the possibility of an additional 10 to 90 percent for some commodities.

19. See Chapter 16.

20. The ILO report recommends a uniform tariff level of 20 or 30 percent after eight or ten years. This would raise the cost of many imported inputs that now have only a 10 percent duty, however, and even after eight or ten years the country may temporarily need higher protection for certain new industries.

21. The average custom rate (that is, the revenue as a percentage of the value of imports) declined during the 1960s and then rose from 9.2 percent in 1970 and 10.7 percent in 1971 to 12.3 percent in 1972 and 13.3 percent in 1973, the first year with the revised tariff code. (Data are from the Central Bank of the Philippines and the Bureau of the Census and Statistics.)

9

The Changing Role of Industry

*B*ECAUSE EMPLOYMENT CREATION and export expansion are crucial
to Philippine development, the rapid growth of labor-intensive
manufacturing exports will probably be the most important goal of
the future industrial strategy of the country. Efforts will be needed
to revive and sustain the growth in modern small-scale industries
and to keep employment in the traditional cottage sector from
declining further. Artificial disadvantages affecting small-scale
industries must be reduced, those firms within the traditional
small-scale industrial subsector that have favorable prospects for
growth must be actively promoted, and industrial development
must be directed toward a regional balance.

Expanding Industrial Exports

Historically Philippine industrialization has been geared largely
to the domestic market and import substitution; traditional exports
have provided foreign exchange to pay for the intermediate inputs
and machinery needed for the growing production of consumer
goods. For a long time exporters were in fact penalized; they had to
pay more for their inputs because of the overvalued exchange rate
and because highly protectionist policies raised the costs of both
imports and local production. Two major postwar devaluations
(in 1960–62 and 1970–73) provided only temporary relief because

the economic system continued to favor import substitution and capital-intensive production. Built-in incentives worked to shift resources from the production of exports and essential goods into the production of consumer goods particularly oriented to the domestic urban markets. Between 1950 and 1971 the effective exchange rates for imported nonessential consumer and producer goods increased 9.4 and 6.2 times respectively, while in the case of essential consumer and producer goods they increased 3.5 and 3.2 times, and in the case of traditional and new exports they increased only 2.9 and 3.2 times respectively.[1]

In spite of some countervailing measures such as import duty rebates, special export incentives, and the switch to a floating exchange rate, the gap has persisted between the increasing real cost of importing commodities with import substitution potential and the domestic purchasing power of traditional—and even new—exports. The situation has changed little since 1971; export incentives have been increased but so has the average degree of protection—3 to 4 percentage points according to the International Labour Office. The new tariff code that went in effect at the beginning of 1973 raised the duty rates of 796 items and reduced them for 451 others; in 392 cases the rates were unchanged. Even more important, however, has been the administrative imposition of many import restrictions in recent years.

Some positive trends began to develop with regard to Philippine exports in the late 1960s. The government made a special effort to counter the mounting balance of payments crisis and, more recently, to deal with structural imbalances that emerged under the past inward-looking industrialization strategy. The Investment Incentives Act of 1967 and the Export Incentives Act of 1970 provided stronger fiscal incentives to exporting industries; multiple and later floating exchange rates were adopted; several development programs were introduced in sectors geared to exports; and an Export Processing Zone was established in Bataan.

With an average growth rate of 5.0 percent, Philippine exports took twelve years (1960–72) to double at current prices (see Table 9.1). The export price index did not change significantly during that time, however, and in real terms the situation remained the

1. R. E. Baldwin, *Foreign Trade Regimes and Economic Development: The Philippines* (New York: Columbia University Press, 1975).

Table 9.1. Structure of Philippine Exports, 1960–74

Category	1960	1968	1972	1973	1974
Value of exports (in millions of U.S. *dollars at current prices)*					
Nonindustrial[a]	276	360	332	548	466
Traditional industrial[b]	271	454	674	1,093	1,917
Nontraditional manufacturing[c]	7	29	67	133	171
Re-exports and undefined exports	6	15	33	112	171
Total	560	858	1,106	1,886	2,725
Percentage share					
Nonindustrial	49.3	42.0	30.0	29.0	17.0
Traditional industrial	48.4	52.9	60.9	57.9	70.3
Nontraditional manufacturing	1.2	3.4	6.1	7.1	6.3
Re-exports and undefined exports	1.1	1.7	3.0	5.9	6.3
Total	100.0	100.0	100.0	100.0	100.0

a. Logs, copra, bananas, abaca, and tobacco.
b. Sugar, coconut and other food products, lumber and other wood products except furniture, copper concentrates, gold, and other mining products.
c. Manufactures other than food and wood products, and base metals.
Source: Central Bank of the Philippines.

same. Most of the growth occurred during the years immediately following the peso devaluations in 1960–62 and 1970–73. Because of an unprecedented rise in the price of several export commodities, export earnings showed a dramatic increase in 1973 and 1974. In real terms, however, the growth of exports in 1973 was in line with that of the preceding years and in 1974 even declined 24 percent.

These general trends conceal significant changes in the relative position of broad export categories. Industrial exports (consisting largely of traditional semiprocessed and processed products of agriculture, forestry, and minerals) increased their share in total exports from 50 percent in 1960 to 77 percent in 1974 at the expense of unprocessed products of the same origin. Among these industrial exports a wide range of new manufactured products also became increasingly important.

EXTRACTIVE AND AGRO-PROCESSING INDUSTRIES

Traditional industrial exports reached a record US$1,917 million in 1974 primarily as the result of favorable price movements in the

Table 9.2. Traditional Industrial Exports, 1960–74
(In millions of U.S. dollars at current prices)

Sector	1960	1968	1972	1973	1974
Coconut oil and products	40	113	118	206	469
Sugar and products	143	151	218	295	766
Other food products	10	22	28	30	46
Wood products (excluding furniture)	17	54	71	140	117
Copper concentrates	30	89	191	275	397
Other mining products	31	25	48	147	122
Total	271	454	674	1,093	1,197

Source: Central Bank of the Philippines.

first part of the year.[2] During the entire year the export price index jumped 87 percent, which meant the volume of traditional industrial exports declined by a sizable margin.

Table 9.2 reveals several significant changes in the composition of traditional industrial exports. Sugar, coconut, and other food products declined from 71 percent of the total in 1960 to 49 percent in 1973, although they rose to 67 percent in 1974 because of the unusual price trends in that year. The share of mining exports increased from 22 percent to 39 percent, decreasing to 27 percent in 1974, while that of forest-based products doubled from 6 to 13 percent between 1960 and 1973 and returned to 6 percent in 1974. These figures reflect not only cyclical movement in the prices of raw materials in the world markets but also changes in the commodity composition of Philippine exports. For some time there has been a tendency to phase out exports of raw materials in favor of processed materials. In 1960 the Philippines earned 4.5 times more from copra than from coconut products, but in 1974 sales of processed coconut products were 3 times higher than those of unprocessed products. For timber, the relation between sales of logs and processed wood products changed from 5:1 in 1960 to 2:1 in 1974. A similar shift is beginning to be apparent from copper concentrates to refined metal and, more slowly, from centrifugal to refined sugar.[3]

2. According to Central Bank data the price of coconut oil, desiccated coconut, and sugar was 2.5 times higher in 1974 than in 1973; that of lumber, sugar, copper concentrates and some other mineral products, and canned pineapple was 12 to 37 percent higher in 1974.

3. The prospects for sugar and coconut exports are discussed in Chapter 6.

NONTRADITIONAL MANUFACTURES

With nominal average growth rates of 20 percent a year in 1960–68 and over 34 percent in 1968–74, new industrial products make up the most dynamic export group. Real growth, however, was well below 20 percent a year for the entire 1960–74 period even though the starting base was only US$7 million. By 1973 the value of these exports reached US$133 million, or 7 percent of total exports, and in 1974 it increased to US$171 million despite the worldwide recession, although the share in total exports declined to 6 percent. Since 1970 Philippine exports of nontraditional manufactures have diversified significantly. Consisting of little more than woven materials and light chemical products in 1960, today they include a wide variety of products: garments, cement, paper, mineral fuels and lubricants, metal products, car and machinery components, footwear, furniture and fixtures, travel and sporting goods (Table 9.3).

At present only a little over 3 percent of total manufacturing

Table 9.3. Exports of Nontraditional Manufactures, 1960–74
(In millions of U.S. dollars at current prices)

Item	1960	1964	1968	1972	1973	1974
Building elements and fixtures	. . .	. . .	0.1	1.6	0.5	1.3
Cement and other nonmetallic mineral products	. . .	. . .	0.9	7.9	24.9	36.5
Chemicals and products	2.0	3.0	3.7	6.2	10.0	15.2
Clothing	0.1	0.3	0.4	2.4	11.4	23.7
Electrical machinery and appliances	. . .	. . .	. . .	1.8	0.9	2.1
Footwear	. . .	0.1	0.4	1.2	2.1	3.7
Furniture and fixtures	0.4	0.4	0.8	1.7	3.3	6.1
Machinery and parts (excluding electrical)	. . .	0.1	0.2	3.0	2.3	4.2
Metal products	. . .	0.1	0.1	1.4	2.4	3.2
Oil products	. . .	3.6	15. 2	19.3	16.0	17.3
Paper and products	. . .	. . .	0.4	1.9	9.1	5.0
Textile products (excluding clothing)	3.4	4.0	4.1	8.5	24.3	20.1
Transport equipment	. . .	. . .	. . .	0.2	1.4	1.3
Travel goods, handbags, and similar products	. . .	0.1	0.5	1.7	4.5	7.6
Miscellaneous	0.9	1.1	1.8	8.4	20.0	23.3
Total	6.8	12.8	28.6	67.3	133.1	170.6

. . . Zero or negligible.
Source: Central Bank of the Philippines.

output is marketed abroad. The important questions are: To what extent can export activities generate industrial growth and in which fields can new manufacturing exports achieve a breakthrough? Although specialized studies of individual industries would be needed to assess the future growth of export demand as well as the potential supply to meet that growth, a desirable pattern of development can be drawn on the basis of existing knowledge. For this purpose nontraditional manufacturing industries may be grouped into four categories: cement, pulp and paper, chemicals and oil products; textiles and garments; engineering goods; and other light industries.

Growth prospects

On the basis of past trends in industrial exports and the export potential of major industrial groups, Tables 9.4 and 9.5 project the growth in industrial exports for 1975–80 and include investment and employment projections. Major changes in the pattern and dynamics of industrial exports could take place by 1980. Traditional agroprocessing exports (sugar and coconut products), although hampered by a sluggish growth in demand, would grow at a rate of 6 percent a year, reaching US$1,736 million in 1980 at 1974 prices, largely because copra exports would be phased out completely in favor of coconut oil and other processed products. The primary export items in the mining sector—refined nickel, copper, and gold—would grow at 14 percent a year. Four capital-intensive export groups[4] would achieve a significant relative gain with an 18 percent growth rate, partly as a by-product of the intensive growth in production necessary to supply the domestic market. Because of a low starting point (US$73 million in exports in 1974), however, the absolute level of these exports would not exceed US$200 million. The greatest change is expected in labor-intensive exports, which would have an average growth rate of 26 percent and amount to US$1,050 million in 1980 compared with US$260 million in 1974. The wood-processing sector alone would contribute 60 percent of the increase in labor-intensive and light industrial exports.

Because of the dominant share of sugar and coconut products (almost 60 percent of total industrial exports in 1974), total indus-

---

4. Pulp and paper, cement and other nonmetallic mineral products, chemicals, and petroleum products.

trial exports would grow at about 12 percent a year, or 3 percentage points above the rate of growth of aggregate industrial value added. Export activities would thus account for some 28 percent of total industrial growth in 1974–80.

Aggregate employment to be created through industrial export activities has been roughly estimated at 94,000 persons. The largest single contributor is again expected to be the wood-processing industry with 28,000 new jobs. Export-oriented employment would represent some 34 percent of total projected additions to industrial employment during that period (Table 8.9), demonstrating that export activities are considerably more labor intensive than is the industry as a whole. These export projections imply investments of ₱12,000 million during 1975–80, with a third earmarked for labor-intensive industries and another third for mining.

Table 9.5 shows that the four major industrial groups differ significantly in their relative export performance and factor intensity. The cost of export growth is highest in capital-intensive industries and mining, where investment per unit of net foreign exchange earned is 1.5 and 1.1 respectively; but these sectors also have the largest foreign exchange yields per laborer. In contrast, labor-intensive exports incur little cost per dollar earned and provide much employment, although they rank low in productivity with a foreign exchange–labor ratio of ₱98,000.

This analysis suggests that none of the four industrial groups is at an explicit disadvantage when their respective costs and benefits are compared. In view of the importance of employment creation at this stage of Philippine development, however, labor-intensive exports deserve the highest priority in the industrialization program.

EXPORT PROMOTION POLICIES

Without well-designed promotional policies, manufactured exports cannot figure prominently in Philippine economic growth. An expansionary export policy would involve policies regarding the exchange rate, investment incentives, and financing, as well as promotional measures such as free trade zones.

The major issue for future government strategy is how to reduce the incentives gap between exports and import-substituting manufacturing effectively without disrupting industrial growth. This can be achieved only by tackling the problem from both sides, that is, by reducing the amount of protection enjoyed by import-replac-

Table 9.4. Projection of Industrial Exports, Implied Investment, and New Employment, 1975–80
(At 1974 prices)

Industry	Exports (millions of U.S. dollars[a]) 1974 (1)	1980 (2)	Annual growth rates, 1974–80 (percent) (3)	Increment in export earnings (millions of pesos) Gross (2-1) (4)	Net[b] (5)	Value added component of incremental exports (millions of pesos)[c] (6)	Investment 1975–80[d] (millions of pesos) (7)	New employment (thousands) (8)	Capital–foreign exchange ratio (7/5) (9)	Foreign exchange–labor ratio (thousands of pesos) (5/8) (10,)
Mining and metal making	519	1,140	14	4,347	3,825	1,454	4,217	23	1.1	166
Traditional agroindustrial exports	1,235	1,736	6	3,507	3,156	1,263	3,158	24	1.0	132
Coconut products	469	790	9	2,247	2,022	809	2,023	15	1.0	132
Sugar	766	946	4	1,260	1,134	454	1,135	9	1.0	132
Labor-intensive manufacturing	259	1,055	26	5,572	4,401	1,653	3,892	45	0.9	98
Food processing other than sugar and coconut	50	125	17	525	446	147	353	4	0.8	112
Textiles and garments	44	170	25	882	529	190	532	7	1.0	76
Wood products, except furniture	112	550	30	3,066	2,698	1,052	2,314	28	0.9	96
Engineering	11	70	36	413	248	82	238	2	1.0	124
Other light industries[e]	42	140	22	686	480	182	455	4	0.9	120

Capital-intensive manufacturing	73	200	18	889	571	192	844	2.2	1.5	260
Pulp and paper	5	40	41	245	208	62	273	0.7	1.3	297
Cement and other nonmetallic mineral products	36	60	9	168	101	44	176	1.0	1.7	101
Chemicals and products	15	50	22	245	147	54	248 }	0.5	1.7 }	524
Oil products	17	50	20	231	115	32	147 }		1.3 }	

a. The exchange rate of US$1.00 = ₱7.0 is used.

b. The following import dependency coefficients (imported inputs/exports) were used in the computation: 0.10 for coconut and sugar products; 0.12 for mining and wood products; 0.15 for other food products and pulp and paper; 0.30 for other light industries; 0.40 for chemicals, cement, and other nonmetallic mineral products, textiles and garments, and engineering industries; and 0.50 for oil products.

c. The following value added coefficients are used: 0.38 for mining and other light industries; 0.36 for textiles; 0.39 for wood products; 0.33 for food products and engineering; 0.30 for pulp and paper; 0.44 for cement and other nonmetallic mineral products; 0.37 for chemicals; 0.28 for oil products; 0.40 for coconut and sugar industries.

d. Slightly modified capital-output and capital-labor ratios from Table 8.8 are used in these computations. For mining, the respective ratios are assumed to be 2.9 and 180.

e. Footwear, travel and sports goods, furniture and fixtures, building elements and fixtures, plastic products, and miscellaneous.

Source: Central Bank of the Philippines and World Bank estimates.

227

Table 9.5. Summary of Projections for Industrial Exports and Related Indicators, 1975–80
(At 1974 prices)

Category	Mining	Traditional agroindustries[a]	Capital-intensive manufacturing	Labor-intensive manufacturing	All industry
Annual growth rate, 1974–80 (percent)	14	6	18	26	12
Investment, 1975–80 (millions of pesos)	4,217	3,158	844	3,892	12,111
New employment (thousands)	23	24	2.2	45	94
Incremental capital-output ratio	2.9	2.5	4.4	2.4	2.7
Investment per laborer (thousands of pesos)	183	132	384	86	129
Investment per unit of incremental net export earnings	1.1	1.0	1.5	0.9	1.0
Net export earnings per laborer (thousands of pesos)	166	132	260	98	127

a. Sugar and coconuts.
Source: Table 9.4.

ing sectors and increasing the effective subsidy given to export activities. To prevent excessive disruptions this process will have to be stretched over a reasonable period and supplemented by compensatory measures.

Import liberalization is a vital element of a long-term industrialization strategy in the Philippines, and action should be taken to reduce quantitative restrictions and tariffs on imports.[5] In addition, investment incentives should gradually be reduced for import substitution and ultimately confined to labor-intensive and export activities.[6] The relative position of exports must be improved soon, and one important strategy will be to strengthen investment incentives in favor of export industries.

The emerging industrial cooperation schemes of the Association of South-East Asian Nations (ASEAN) represent a potentially important element in the future export growth strategy that should not be overlooked. An agreement was announced in March 1976 to develop five projects as ASEAN industries: urea in Indonesia and Malaysia, superphosphates in the Philippines, soda ash in Thailand, and diesel engines in Singapore. A decision was also made to study the feasibility of establishing additional regional industries in newsprint, potash, metalworking, machine tools, electrolytic tin plating, heavy-duty tires, and electronic components. Future negotiations will determine the related preferential trade arrangements. In the meantime the Philippine government has announced its plan to finance imports from other members of ASEAN and thus strengthen regional industrial cooperation. The scheme will enable Philippine importers to purchase goods from other ASEAN countries at preferential rates and to use low-interest loans from government institutions for that purpose.

EXPORT INCENTIVES

The Investment Incentives Act of 1967 gave a noticeable boost to new industrial exports since most of its benefits accrued to export producers as well. The act accorded export producers an additional tax credit on taxes and duties paid on the supplies, raw materials, and semimanufactured products used in export production, as well

5. See section on the issue of protection in Chapter 8.
6. See section on investment incentives and Table 13.8 in Chapter 13.

as a double deduction of promotional expenses for exports. These export incentives were granted for all activities listed in the Investment Priorities Plan (IPP), but in the case of nontraditional exports they could be granted even if the activity was not specifically listed in the IPP. The Export Incentives Act, introduced in 1970, added to the package of incentives by exempting industrial exports from export taxes and providing additional tax credits on export sales and excise taxes on inputs. An important innovation extended incentives to export traders and service exporters. A 1973 decree made the total cost of direct labor and local raw materials used in export production deductible from income before taxes. The ceiling for income tax deductions is now 25 percent of total export revenues for export producers, 10 percent for export traders, and 50 percent for service exporters.

Incentives under the Export Incentives Act are in principle available to firms that export at least 50 percent of their output and whose activities are listed in the Export Priorities Plan (EPP). The EPP lists two types of exportable products: those produced in existing facilities, which may, however, undergo an export-oriented expansion (List A); and those in preferred areas of investment, whose export potential warrants the establishment of new production facilities (List B). To prevent abuses, the Export Incentives Act stipulates that any firm which imports capital equipment using the incentives must earn foreign exchange equivalent to the cost of that equipment within five years. Any firm that fails to export within the period imposed by the Board of Investments (BOI) or whose exports fall below 70 percent of the projected export sales can have its registration canceled or be subject to other prescribed penalties.

The relative preference accorded to export activities under the existing tax laws is thus only marginal. Exporting enterprises in preferred areas enjoy substantial fiscal benefits, but these benefits are only slightly greater than those enjoyed by all enterprises in the preferred areas. Enterprises ae now making more applications under the Export Incentives Act, however, than under the Investment Incentives Act. They do this to strengthen their case for receiving government loans, allocations of foreign exchange, and fiscal incentives. In this way they also circumvent the limitations that the Investment Incentives Act imposes on new projects by provisions relating to "measured capacity" and "overcrowded industries." Since the incentives given to exporting activities are not very different from those given to all preferred activities, it is clear that more effective encouragement is required. Import liberalization would benefit manufactured exports greatly by allowing cheaper inputs, and, more important, by weakening the relative attractiveness of import-competing sectors it would make more resources available for the export sector. Because many export incentives are related to imported inputs, fewer import restrictions would in turn make export incentives less important and tax preferences redundant.

Lowering the effective subsidy to nonexporting sectors is only one essential, however; equally important are direct export incentives. They should be tied directly to export performance rather than to the level of investment cost or the quantity of imported inputs. Just as general investment incentives should not merely increase output but also raise its domestically generated value added, export incentives should seek to raise not only the level of exports but also net export earnings. Furthermore, incentives should not be restricted to firms which export more than half their total sales; all export sales above a certain point, and within prescribed limitations, should be encouraged.

Promoting Small-scale Industries

In 1973–74 the small-scale sector employed close to a million people, or 68 percent of the total industrial labor force, and represented 12 to 13 percent of total industrial value added. Small-scale industry has been decreasing in relative importance over the past two decades, however, and during the last 5 or 6 years it seems to have been declining even in terms of absolute employment and value added. Moreover, the sector is relatively smaller in the Philippines than in many other countries with comparable per capita incomes.

PAST TRENDS AND STRUCTURE

Roughly 6 percent of the industrial value added in the small-scale sector is accounted for by firms employing less than 5 workers,[7] 3 percent by those with 5 to 19 workers, and 3 to 4 percent by those

---

7. See the explanation in the note to Table 8.10.

with 20 to 49 workers. The respective shares of the same groups of firms in total industrial employment can be estimated at 60, 5.5, and 2.5 percent.

In the 1956–74 period the relative importance of the cottage sector (1 to 4 workers) declined steadily in terms of industrial value added and employment, while that of the modern small-scale sector (above 5 workers) stagnated. These long-term trends were reversed during 1962–68, however, with an upsurge in modern small-scale industry, unparalleled before and after this period.[8] Industries of 5 to 19 workers scored better than the larger-scale industrial group in gross value added, productivity of labor, the number of establishments, and employment. Similar trends can be detected among small-scale firms employing over 20 workers. Even industries employing 1 to 4 workers grew at 1.3 percent a year in terms of employment during those years, in contrast with both the preceding and following periods.

Although the reasons for these trends are not clear, it is possible that the relaxation of foreign exchange controls during 1962–68 had much to do with the upswing. In the Philippine setting small enterprises seem to have been more responsive to liberalization measures as well as more affected by controls than their larger counterparts. And access to foreign exchange and imports is apparently more important for these small firms than is usually thought. Cottage industries, however, seem to have also benefited from specialized incentive laws promulgated at that time.[9]

FACTOR USE AND SIZE OF OPERATIONS

Table 8.1 shows that during 1968–73, despite the stagnation in output and the decline in employment, the number of establishments with 5 to 19 workers rose sharply at a rate of 4.2 percent a year, compared with 3.4 percent in 1962–68 and 2.7 percent in 1956–62. Between 1956 and 1973, however, the average size of firms employing 20 or more workers doubled in terms of employment (from 82 to 156 workers) and grew 2.5 times in terms of gross value added (from

8. See Table 8.1.

9. Particularly Republic Acts 3470 and 5326 and Presidential Decrees 34 and 62 (cottage industry); Republic Act 4086 (textile industry); Republic Act 4155 (tobacco industry); and a number of laws and decrees regulating the activities of rural banks and nonagricultural cooperatives.

Table 9.6. **Factor Intensity and Productivity in Manufacturing, 1971**

Number of workers per firm	Capital per worker (thousands of pesos)	Value added per worker (thousands of pesos)	Capital–value added ratio[a]
9–19	5.1	5.9	0.85
20–99	11.4	12.3	0.9
100–199	14.0	19.6	0.7
200 and above	22.3	22.3	1.0

a. Book value of fixed assets.
Source: Central Statistical Office.

₱836,000 to ₱2,043,000 at constant 1967 prices). During the same period the average size of small-scale firms (5 to 19 workers) declined in both respects (from 10.2 to 7.6 workers, and from ₱34,000 to ₱20,000 gross value added). Taken together, the increasing number of small-scale firms, their diminishing size, and the absolute decrease in cottage industry employment seem to reflect both favorable and unfavorable conditions: a continuous effort to improve the investment climate and the emergence of a vigorous Philippine entrepreneurial group on the one hand, and on the other a policy-induced proliferation of inefficient units as well as the lack of a normal process of consolidation and growth from smaller into larger units.

In the Philippines as elsewhere an industry's use of productive factors is in proportion to the size of the firm. The larger a firm, the more capital intensive it tends to be (that is, the higher its fixed capital per worker) and the higher its level of labor productivity (value added per worker; see Table 9.6). The extent to which the size of the enterprise affects its capital productivity is less clear.[10] If fixed assets are expressed in terms of replacement rather than book value, however, small-scale firms definitely tend to need less capital for the same amount of output.[11]

These generalizations apply to the aggregate, but a more detailed classification of industries would reveal a less clear pattern in the efficiency of factor use in firms of different sizes. The only rational policy therefore appears to be one that encourages the development

10. In terms of fixed capital needed to produce one unit of value added.
11. See International Labour Office, *Sharing in Development* (Geneva: ILO, 1974), table 25, p. 144.

of the most efficient industries, irrespective of their size. There is ample room for the successful development of all sizes of industry if artificially induced distortions in factor use can be eliminated.

PROBLEMS OF FUTURE GROWTH

If small-scale industry as a whole is to reach a labor absorption target of 75,000 to 80,000 a year by 1985, the modern small-scale and cottage sectors will need to reverse their trends drastically. The value of their contribution lies in their low capital use, favorable capital productivity, and above all their role in maintaining the level of employment and generating new jobs. To revive and sustain the growth in modern small-scale industries and to maintain the present employment level in the cottage sector, policies will have to be developed to remove artificial disadvantages and to promote actively firms within the cottage sector that have propitious prospects. For the kind of growth described in Tables 8.9 and 8.10, small producers need an accessible market for their increased output; the cottage and small-scale sectors have to be made attractive for potential investors and be able to absorb productively the increased investment; an adequate supply of producer goods and financing on favorable terms are needed for expanded production; and the growth of small industries will have to be dispersed throughout the country.

Despite the government's recent efforts in some of these areas, much more needs to be done, especially in financing. Several major development banking institutions have set up special funds for small- and medium-scale industries. The Development Bank of the Philippines (DBP) has earmarked ₱500 million for this purpose, out of which 626 loans amounting to ₱76 million were granted in 1973–74; ₱121 million was invested in small- and medium-scale industries outside greater Manila, half of it in 1973–74. In the second half of 1974 the DBP approved 497 new loans for small- and medium-scale industries amounting to ₱33 million,[12] with an additional 285 loan applications for ₱65 million in the pipeline. A number of rural, commercial, and development banks are also engaged in financing small-scale projects under the Industrial Guarantee and Loan Fund (IGLF), whose total assets amounted to

12. One half of these loans are for ₱10,000 and below.

₱56 million in 1974. Much of the lending to small industries now originates from field branches of development institutions; the DBP, for example, has about 60 branches and agencies and is still expanding the network.

The Medium and Small-Scale Industries Coordinated Action Program (MASICAP) is another instrument for the promotion of small-scale investments. From its inception in November 1973 until March 1975, MASICAP had generated 479 projects (261 for DBP, 155 for IGLF, and 63 for other financial institutions), with a total project cost of ₱330 million and a loan requirement of ₱132 million. The number of projects increased sharply in 1975: 276 out of 479 projects were completed in the first quarter and about 150 additional projects were in preparation in March. One-third of the total cost of all MASICAP-assisted projects was less than ₱50,000.

The financial position and requirements of small-scale industries, however, have to be compared with those of their large-scale counterparts. The large-scale sector benefits fully from the BOI incentives. It has access to easy-term credit for expansion and working capital, its voice is heard in the formulation of policy, and it can tap a pool of skills both within the country and abroad. Small-scale producers do not enjoy these advantages, however, and additional efforts will be needed to facilitate their access to institutional finance, particularly for working capital. One necessary innovation would be for banking institutions to relax their collateral requirements, a step that would not endanger the viability of their operations. Technical assistance schemes now being implemented in the provinces should improve the selection of both projects and sponsors, help overcome procedural difficulties, and broaden the basis for further expansion of small-scale industries.

Ways must be found to remedy the neglect of both the traditional sector and the smallest units of the modern sector. Special funds might be earmarked for them either under existing financing programs or independently; larger loans could be provided on concessionary terms (at 9 percent interest) to modernize very small units; and a fair share of the fiscal benefits provided to the large-scale sector could be given to their small-scale subcontractors.

Other improvements are necessary in technical services and expertise. This vast and critical area comprises improved technical information and extension services, technological adaptation and product design, the availability of material inputs and spare parts, marketing information and organization, assistance in project preparation, and above all the acquisition of entrepreneurial and managerial skills. The basic organizational framework to deal with these specific fields already exists,[13] but two questions deserve further consideration. First, the institutional machinery seems to be geared primarily to modern small-scale industries, particularly the larger firms in that group; except for the National Cottage Industries Development Authority, the cottage sector is only marginally affected by it. What are needed are not new institutions but modifications of existing institutions to serve the needs of both the traditional cottage sector and the modern small-scale industries. The second question concerns the relation of coordinating councils for small and medium industries at provincial and city levels with regional technical centers and the Central Commission on Small and Medium Industries.

The following problems can therefore be identified:

a. Even with an improved organization, it will be difficult to ameliorate the position of cottage-industry entrepreneurs. They are individually hard to reach and ill equipped to make use of any technical services offered. Separate cottage-industry organizations, such as producers' and traders' cooperatives, if well organized, could perform many useful functions on their behalf—mediating loans, bulk purchasing, joint marketing (and perhaps even joint production), disseminating technical advice, and training.

13. It includes: the Department of Industry's Commission on Small and Medium Industries created by Presidential Decree 488 of June 1974, whose task is to "promote, assist and develop small and medium-scale industries, particularly in the rural areas" and which is composed of the representatives of various government agencies involved with small industries in one way or another; the DBP, IGLF, and other development institutions, together with their regional networks; the University of the Philippines Institute for Small-Scale Industries, the Development Academy of the Philippines, the Design Center of the Philippines, and the National Manpower and Youth Council, which are all involved in various technical assistance and training schemes; and the Trade Assistance Center, Food Terminal, Philippine International Trading Corporation, and National Cottage Industries Development Authority, which are all concerned primarily with marketing. By early 1975 some 150 industrial specialists or small-industry coordinators had been trained by the Development Academy of the Philippines for posting to local governments to help in the selection of projects and their proponents.

b. More needs to be done to multiply the linkages between small- and large-scale industries, especially under specific development schemes sponsored by the BOI. A system for exchanging information on supply and demand and technological matters should be established and given some fiscal encouragement.

c. Any serious drive to enhance and revitalize small-scale industries in the Philippines must also improve infrastructure and services in rural areas: electricity and water, roads and interisland coastal shipping, improved health, education, and housing.

d. The government has set up various organizations and mechanisms to promote small industries, but these agencies know very little about existing cottage and other small-scale industries or where the true potential for sound growth lies. A comprehensive survey of the small-scale sector, as well as subsectoral and regional studies are needed, and with some financial support the Institute for Small-Scale Industries could conduct them.

e. A fresh look into new opportunities for small producers is called for as a result of the planned programs of rural electrification and agricultural mechanization, the growth in rural incomes, the labor-intensive exports drive, and the policy of industrial decentralization. Planning authorities might consider establishing a separate unit to study these issues on a permanent basis.

Regional Dispersal of Industries

Manufacturing activity has remained heavily concentrated in greater Manila and the adjoining provinces of central and southern Luzon since the 1950s. Data for industrial establishments employing five or more workers indicate that the Manila area alone accounted in 1969 for 39 percent of their number, 45 percent of their employment, 44 percent of their value added, and 31 percent of their fixed assets. If the adjoining Luzon provinces were included, these percentages would rise by 20 or 30 points. More detailed information on the regional distribution of establishments employing twenty or more workers indicates that of about 332,000 industrial workers in 1969, 156,000 were employed in Metropolitan Manila, an additional 100,000 in other parts of Luzon, and only 76,000 in the rest of the country, chiefly in Negros, Cebu, and three industrial centers in Mindanao.

Regional imbalances in the distribution of industry in the

Table 9.7. Log Supply and Processing Capacity, 1972–73
(In thousands of cubic meters)

Region	Supply	Processing capacity	Excess capacity	Excess supply
Luzon	1,721	3,819	3,098	—
Greater Manila[a]	508	1,917	1,409	—
Visayas	714	579	—	135
Mindanao	8,022	4,885	—	3,137
Palawan	59	38	—	21

— Not applicable.
a. Bulacan, Manila, Laguna, Nueva Ecija, Pampanga, Quezon, Quezon City, and Rizal.
Source: Department of Agriculture.

Philippines are now likely to encumber future growth. For example, the wood-processing industry has developed a large excess capacity in Luzon, much of it in greater Manila (see Table 9.7). Wood processing is therefore made costlier by capacity underutilization and the need to import logs from Mindanao. Similar examples can be found in other resource-based industries.

The government is well aware of the consequences of increasing regional imbalances and has taken several steps to check expansion in the Manila area and create conditions for more balanced growth. These steps include: fiscal incentives to encourage projects to locate in less developed areas (which have, however, had little impact); [14] promotional measures by the BOI such as regional seminars and an experimental regional development pilot program in Northern Mindanao; negotiation of the project location before BOI approval; a ban on new plants within a 50 kilometer radius of Manila, except for export industries; and the requirement that financing institutions in the provinces allocate 75 percent of their accumulated deposits for loans to projects in their respective areas.

These measures may have had a positive impact, but, as Table 9.8 shows, they did not significantly change the regional distribution of investments. Out of 590 projects approved by the BOI in 1968–74, 363 are located in Southern Tagalog. This region, which comprises greater Manila and its adjoining areas, accounts for 23 percent of the total population and 61 percent of BOI-approved projects. Central Luzon, Central Visayas, Northern Mindanao, and Southern

14. See section on investment incentives in Chapter 13.

Table 9.8. Regional Distribution of Projects Approved by the Board of Investments, 1968–74

Region	Number of projects approved under		Total
	Republic Act 5186 (1968–74)	Republic Act 6135 (1971–74)	
Ilocos	8	3	11
Cagayan Valley	2	. . .	2
Central Luzon	23	30	53
Southern Tagalog	144	218	363
Bicol	7	4	11
Western Visayas	9	4	13
Central Visayas	19	14	33
Eastern Visayas	8	. . .	8
Western Mindanao	9	1	10
Northern Mindanao	39	6	45
Southern Mindanao	30	10	40
Total	300	290	590

. . . Zero or negligible.
Source: Board of Investments, statistical appendix to the eighth Investment Priorities Plan and sixth Export Priorities Plan.

Mindanao, where other major industrial centers are located (Bataan, Cebu, Cagayan de Oro, Iligan, Davao), account for 35 percent of the total population and 29 percent of the BOI projects. The rest of the country, with 42 percent of the total population, accounts for only 10 percent of BOI projects. Many of the large-scale projects in Manila are export oriented; 218 out of 290 projects approved under the Export Incentives Act in 1971–74 are in Southern Tagalog, as are a number of export-oriented projects approved under the Investment Incentives Act. The predominance of Manila as a location for BOI projects did not decrease in 1973 and 1974; on the contrary, Southern Tagalog accounted for 65 percent of all projects approved in those years, compared with 58 percent in 1968–72.

Obviously new and stronger efforts are needed to shift the balance of industrial investment in favor of other regions. The value of investment is likely to become more dispersed in years to come in any case because of a small number of very large projects in mining, basic metals, petrochemicals, and pulp and paper. This dispersal, however, will effect little change in the geographical distribution of industrial employment. A real shift in the regional balance of industry will occur only with a shift in the labor-intensive sectors, such as in wood processing, textiles, and the production of other goods for mass consumption and export.

To direct investments into desired locations it is absolutely essential to provide adequate supporting infrastructure such as electricity, water, transportation, and communications as well as financial and technical services and a supply of qualified labor. Fiscal incentives without these provisions are unlikely to stimulate much new investment in the outer provinces, and with such infrastructure incentives are probably not needed. The government has launched several programs outside Manila to improve the basic infrastructure, such as substantial electricity-generating projects in Mindanao and the Visayas, road construction, and a ten-year shipping and shipbuilding program. These efforts should be continued and extended to other infrastructure as well as to other regions.

Both large- and small-scale industries need not only substantial infrastructure facilities but also the support of other industries. Government policy must therefore be directed not only to dispersal away from Manila but toward the creation of other areas of industrial concentration. Emphasis should be placed initially on establishing industrial estates and export processing zones in a few selected growth centers, and possibly later in other suitable areas.

The Export Processing Zone in Bataan is already functioning, and there are several preinvestment studies and proposals for establishing industrial estates in Bicol, Batangas, Manila, Cagayan de Oro, and Bulacan. The long-term objective seems to be to establish one or more industrial estates in each of the regions, but the government intends to concentrate first on a few highly promising projects. A study for a nationwide industrial estate program is now in preparation by various government agencies—undoubtedly the most appropriate way to proceed with the planning and programming.[15]

Another policy that might be changed now permits an almost indiscriminate proliferation of industrial units in the Manila area

15. This work is being coordinated by the National Economic and Development Authority; the main implementing agency is the Planning and Project Development Office in the Department of Public Works, Transportation, and Communications.

if they are producing for exports. Many of these export-oriented projects would possibly have been established even if the Manila area had been closed to them. Modification of this policy, together with the establishment of more free trade zones and bonded factories and warehouses in the outer regions, could greatly contribute to an effective decentralization of industry.

10

Population Growth and Family Planning

RAPID POPULATION GROWTH IS ONE of the most serious problems facing the Philippines. It restrains the growth of incomes; exacerbates unemployment, income distribution, and nutritional problems; and overburdens schools and other facilities. Because of this population growth, the incomes of many people will not rise rapidly even with good aggregate economic performance. Publicly provided services for human resource development can therefore make an important contribution to raising the level of individual and collective welfare, and in recent years the government has increased the availability of such services.[1]

Demographic Facts and Trends

The postwar censuses of 1948 and 1960 enumerated populations of 19,234,182 and 27,087,685. The most recent census in the Philip-

---

1. In addition to the family planning, nutrition, health, and education activities discussed in this and the two succeeding chapters, the government has programs, within the framework of its limited resources, specifically oriented to disadvantaged groups. These programs, administered through the Department of Social Welfare, include self-employment assistance for unemployed adults, day care for needy preschool children, skill training for out-of-school youths, assistance to victims of natural disasters such as typhoons, and rehabilitation for those such as the aged, ex-prisoners, and persons recovering from drug dependency or mental illness. Although these programs are not examined here, they undoubtedly make a useful contribution to human resource development.

pines, held May 6, 1970, showed a population of 36,684,486. The intercensal annual average growth rates for 1948–60 and 1960–70 were 3.06 and 3.01 percent respectively, which represent a considerable acceleration over the prewar period. Since 1948 the growth rate has been high enough to double the population every 23 years. Such rapid growth is caused by the persistence of traditionally high birth rates and by falling death rates.

Because vital statistics are incomplete, the current population level and growth rate are not accurately known; the evidence that is available points to a slight decrease in the growth rate. The Commission on Population, on the basis of the 1973 National Demographic Survey and reported family planning acceptance rates, estimates the population growth rate in 1975 to be in the range of 2.80 to 2.85 percent. This would indicate that the population is following the middle of three projections prepared by the National Census and Statistics Office (NCSO),[2] which estimates the 1975 population of the Philippines at 42.5 million. This would mean that the population has increased by about 5.8 million since the 1970 census and is currently growing by about 1.2 million a year.

Filipinos traditionally have large families. The total fertility rate, which is the average number of children born to a woman who survives throughout the reproductive years, was found to have been 6.3 for 1963–67 by the 1968 National Demographic Survey and is estimated by the NCSO to have also been 6.3 for 1965–70. Since the base on which the total fertility rate is calculated includes single as well as married women, the marital fertility rate must have been even greater.

The problem of high fertility is particularly acute in rural areas, which had a total fertility rate of 6.7 in 1968–72, as against only 4.1 for Metropolitan Manila and 4.5 for other urban areas. Urban women have a lower fertility rate because they marry at a higher age and, once married, have fewer children. The national crude birth rate of 42 per 1,000 in 1970 was thus composed of a rural birth rate of 45 per 1,000 and an urban birth rate of 35 per 1,000.[3]

2. See the technical note to this chapter.

3. Peter C. Smith, "Fertility in Metropolitan, Other Urban and Rural Areas: A Decomposition into Sources of Variation, 1968–72," Research Note no. 40 (Manila: University of the Philippines Population Institute, 1975; processed). Total fertility rates and crude birth rates are not correlated perfectly because the latter is influenced by the age-sex composition of the population.

That Filipino parents want large families is evidenced by knowl-edge-attitude-practice surveys on fertility and family planning.[4] The 1968 National Demographic Survey found the preferred family size to be 5.2 children. In summarizing the results of four com-munity surveys in the mid-1960s, University of the Philippines demographers at the Population Institute wrote that "The most important fact about ideal family size in the Philippines is that Filipino women favor large families . . . For the Philippine low-lands, nearly one-half of the younger women said that the ideal family has at least five children." [5]

It is also clear that the marital fertility rate is higher than the ideal family size. This may be partly because parents wish to insure themselves against the possibility of infant and child mortality (which is quite high in the Philippines) and, on balance, over-insure. But undoubtedly some fertility is unwanted but caused by a lack of knowledge as to how to control it. A program to reduce fertility must therefore bring realized family size down to desired size as well as change attitudes about the size of families, which is the more difficult task.

Mortality has been falling due to public health measures and improved standards of living. The death rate, which is estimated to have been 12 per 1,000 in the late 1960s, is projected by the NCSO to decrease to 10 per 1,000 in 1975 and 8 per 1,000 by 1985. This means that the population growth rate would increase by 0.4 per-cent (from 3.0 to 3.4 percent) in the absence of any offsetting decline in fertility.

Consequences of Rapid Population Growth

Although there is no aspect of the economy that is unaffected by rapid population growth, this discussion will consider, for the sake of illustration, four areas of concern: income, jobs, food, and schools. Current family planning efforts will have their most sig-

---

4. Some demographers have argued that responses to survey questions on desired family size may be meaningless on the grounds that traditionally minded people in developing countries do not make conscious decisions on family size. This problem is discussed in Mercedes B. Concepcion and William Flieger, "Studies of Fertility and Family Planning in the Philippines," *Demography* (1968), p. 718.

5. Concepcion and Flieger, "Studies of Fertility," p. 719.

nificant effects sometime in the future. In order to indicate the benefits of success (or the costs of failure), two alternative scenarios for 1990 will be presented, based on the medium and low projections of the NCSO.[6] The medium projection assumes that the family planning program will be only moderately successful and that fertility will drop slowly, resulting in a population of 65.0 million in 1990. The low projection assumes that the family planning program will be highly successful and that fertility will drop relatively quickly, leading to a population of 59.6 million in 1990.

INCOME

Population growth has two opposing effects on gross national product (GNP). On the one hand, it adds to the labor factor of production; on the other hand, it diverts resources toward consumption and away from investment, thus reducing the growth of another factor of production, capital. This is because high fertility results in a large proportion of dependents. In the Philippines the dependency ratio (the ratio of persons under fifteen or over sixty-five to persons of working age) is 0.94 compared with 0.5 which is typical in low-fertility countries. The combination of a high proportion of dependents and low incomes makes it difficult for families to save. Rapid population growth also forces up current expenditures by the public sector.

Whether the increased growth of labor or the reduced growth of capital has the greater effect in a particular economy is a question that must be answered on the basis of empirical research. An economic-demographic model of the Philippines developed at the University of the Philippines School of Economics (UPSE) indicates that here the second factor outweighs the first and that the net effect of population growth is to retard the growth of GNP. This would be expected in an economy generally believed to have a shortage of capital and a surplus of labor. In particular the model predicts that, with moderate assumptions about the impact of family planning, GNP at the end of the century would be 10 percent higher with family planning than without it.[7]

6. These projections are shown in the technical note attached to this chapter.

7. Agustin Kintanar and others, *Studies in Philippine Economic-Demographic Relationships* (Quezon City: University of the Philippines, School of Economics, 1974), p. 188.

If population growth has a negative effect on aggregate product, its effect on per capita product is even more strongly negative. The World Bank projects GNP to be about ₱87,000 million in 1985. If GNP were to grow at 7 percent a year in the following five years, it would be ₱122,000 million in 1990. With the medium projection, this would indicate a per capita GNP of ₱1,877 in 1990, or 9 percent less than the ₱2,047 indicated with the low projection. If fertility were to remain constant (as the high projection of the NCSO assumes), the figure would be only ₱1,730. These calculations assume that GNP is independent of population growth—a more conservative assumption for assessing the benefits of fertility reduction than that suggested by the UPSE model. Clearly, fertility reduction is an extremely effective way of raising per capita income.

Fertility reduction would further benefit Philippine development because of the effect of population growth on the distribution of income. With population growth the capital-labor ratio rises more slowly than it otherwise would, and the ratio of land and natural resources to labor falls. The decrease in the average size of farms discussed in Chapter 4 is evidence of the latter. The result is that wages fall relatively, and perhaps absolutely, aggravating the skewed distribution of income. Indeed, real wages in the Philippines have fallen considerably in recent years. According to the family economic survey in 1971 the per capita income of large families (seven persons or more) was only ₱534 as against ₱744 for small families (three to six persons), which again indicates that high fertility is one cause of the highly skewed distribution of incomes in the Philippines.

JOBS

The labor force of the Philippines is currently growing by 500,000 workers a year. Most have been able to find jobs, but industrial and agricultural employment opportunities have not kept pace with labor force growth in recent years. Many workers are therefore forced into the service sector, where jobs are of inferior quality, adding little to the national product and bringing little income to the worker. The prospects are not bright for agriculture and industry to absorb all the increments to the labor force projected for the next decade; it is therefore likely that the service sector will continue to grow and provide jobs that actually represent underemployment.

Current efforts to reduce fertility will not significantly affect the size of the labor force until the 1990s. At that time, however, the impact would be considerable. If the medium projection is realized, and if the labor force participation rate remains at the recently observed level, the labor force will be 23.0 million in 1990 and 30.5 million in 2000. But if family planning efforts are more successful and the low projection is achieved, the labor force will be only 22.4 million in 1990 and 27.8 million in 2000. With the medium projection, the average annual increment to the labor force during that decade would be 750,000 as against only 540,000 with the low projection. These figures probably exaggerate somewhat the effect on the labor supply because with lower fertility more women would probably participate in the labor force. The demand side of the labor market should also be considered, however. With lower fertility there would be higher incomes, more capital and land available for each unit of labor, and thus a greater demand for labor. Although the effect is difficult to quantify precisely, it is clear that reduced fertility would substantially improve the prospects for absorbing the labor force in the Philippines in future decades.

FOOD

Rapid population growth in the Philippines has frustrated efforts to achieve self-sufficiency in rice and corn and to make adequate nutrition available to all. In the bumper year of 1970 the Philippines imported neither rice nor corn. Adverse circumstances, including bad weather and high fertilizer prices, caused food-grain production to drop in subsequent years, but in 1975 it may once again attain the 1970 level. But this level no longer implies self-sufficiency because population has grown about 15 percent in the meantime. In recent years substantial amounts of foreign exchange, which otherwise could have been utilized for development purposes, have necessarily been diverted to food-grain imports to feed the growing population. At the same time, nutritional standards have deteriorated.

The pattern of the future may be illustrated by the example of rice. In a normal year rice consumption in the Philippines is about 90 kilograms per capita. Therefore rice requirements in 1990 would be 5,364,500 metric tons with the low projection but 5,950,000 metric tons with the medium projection, if the possibility of increased consumption due to higher incomes or improved nutritional standards is disregarded. The difference between these two figures is 486,000 metric tons. One of the principal means of raising rice yields in the Philippines is to irrigate previously rain-fed areas. If it is assumed that irrigation increases yields by two metric tons per hectare, new irrigation is needed for 243,000 hectares. This would represent a major burden on resources and implementation capacity. Similar constraints can be expected in raising the production of other foodstuffs. Without a substantial reduction in fertility it is difficult to see how the Philippines can achieve its objectives of rice and corn self-sufficiency and adequate nutrition for all.

SCHOOLS

As discussed later in Chapter 12, school facilities in the Philippines are seriously overburdened, mainly because of the rapid growth of the school-age population. The National Economic and Development Authority (NEDA) estimates that there is a national shortage of about 40,000 classrooms. Textbooks are in such short supply that there is only one for every eight students. The need to cope with large yearly increases in the quantity of students has made it impossible to improve the quality of the educational system. Depending on whether the medium or the low projection is realized, elementary and secondary school enrollment in 1990 could be as much as 15,052,000 or as little as 13,219,000. With a standard of forty students to a class, the medium projection would indicate a need for 45,825 more classrooms than the low one. At the current cost this would mean an incremental ₱815 million for school construction. Continued rapid expansion of enrollment would also force up operating costs, and prospects for improving quality would probably be forestalled.

The Family Planning Program

In the Philippines, government concern about the population problem came relatively late. Family planning was pioneered in the early 1960s by two private organizations, the Institute for Maternal and Child Health and the Family Planning Organization of the Philippines. In 1964 the University of the Philippines Population Institute (UPPI) was established to train demographers and carry out research. Two UPPI-sponsored conferences on population in 1965 and 1967 drew attention to the adverse consequences of rapid population growth for Philippine development. Indirect government involvement in family planning began in 1967 with the signing of an agreement with the United States Agency for International Development (USAID) for channeling assistance to private agencies. A few municipal and provincial health departments also began to offer family planning services.

In 1969, in response to increasing concern, the Commission on Population (POPCOM) was established. Initially POPCOM's responsibility was limited to studying the situation and making recommendations. In 1970, however, the government decided for the first time to adopt an active population policy. POPCOM was given additional duties, namely "to organize and implement programs that will promote a broad understanding of the adverse effects on family life and national welfare of unlimited population growth" and "to make available all acceptable methods of contraception . . . to Filipino citizens desirous of spacing, limiting or preventing pregnancies." [8] The budget of the population and family planning program has increased rapidly in recent years, reaching ₱108 million in FY74 compared with ₱12 million in FY70.

PROGRAM ACTIVITIES

Although charged with carrying out the government's population and family planning program, POPCOM does not directly provide family planning services or engage in other operational activities. Rather, it is principally a planning, policymaking, coordinating, fund-channeling, and reporting agency, although it intends to become directly involved to a limited extent in communications and training. Operational activities are carried out by a wide spectrum of public and private organizations, the great majority of which predate POPCOM. The activities of the family planning program under POPCOM's guidance are divided into four areas: clinical services; information, education, and communications; training; and research and evaluation.

At the end of FY74 there were 2,192 clinics offering family

8. Presidential Decree 79, as cited in Commission on Population, *Four-Year Population Program* (Manila, 1974), p. 16.

planning services, compared with only about 300 in 1969. Most of these are multipurpose clinics and are not confined to family planning. About two-thirds are government clinics, mainly Rural Health Units (RHUS) of the Department of Health. The other third are private clinics, located primarily in urban areas. Clinics are typically staffed by a physician, a nurse or midwife, and sometimes a motivator (a person without medical training who engages in communication work). Following the rapid expansion of recent years, the number of clinics is now considered to be adequate. Many of the RHUS are in unsatisfactory physical condition, however, and the network is being upgraded as part of a World Bank–funded population project. Clinics reported 763,000 new family planning acceptors in FY74, only a modest increase over the 692,000 reported for FY73.[9] Of the new acceptors, 56 percent chose to use oral contraceptives, 23 percent chose condoms, 12 percent chose intrauterine devices (IUDS), and 9 percent chose rhythm and other methods.

The purposes of the information, education, and communication (IEC) component of the program are to educate the public about population issues and create a demand for family planning services. Several channels are used for this purpose, one of which is the school system. The Department of Education and Culture has initiated a program to integrate the subject of population into mathematics, social studies, and natural science curricula. About 14,000 teachers were trained briefly in population education in FY74, and the subject is now a required course in teacher-training institutions. Another channel is the mass media. The Population Information Education Office of the National Media Production Center and the University of the Philippines Institute of Mass Communication are engaged in the development, production, and dissemination of mass media materials on population and family planning. The media used include radio, dramatic presentations, comic books, and films shown by mobile vans. Finally, there is direct interpersonal communication by lay persons trained to give information about family planning and encourage use of the services available. Some of these persons are clinic-based motivators; others are social workers or local government employees for whom family planning activities are only a part of their work.

9. Because of reporting errors, these figures are believed to overstate somewhat the true number of new acceptors.

The training component of the program supports clinical and IEC services by providing them with the trained personnel required. The clinical personnel receiving training include physicians, nurses, and midwives; nonclinical personnel include motivators, social workers, volunteer couple workers, and opinion leaders. Training is conducted by twelve agencies, including the Institute for Maternal and Child Health and the Family Planning Organization of the Philippines in the private sector, and the Departments of Health, Social Welfare, Local Government and Community Development, and the University of the Philippines in the public sector. In FY74, 21,322 persons received training, bringing the total number of trainees since 1970 to more than 50,000.

Research and evaluation consist of both basic research—in such areas as demography, biomedicine, behavioral sciences, and law reform—and applied program research, which attempts to evaluate various activities and has included studies of clinic effectiveness, motivator performance, and the results of training. Research work is contracted out to a wide variety of institutions; the Family Planning Evaluation Office of UPPI has done much of the applied program research.

PROGRAM PERFORMANCE

One criterion against which performance of family planning programs is sometimes assessed is the population growth rate. POPCOM had set a target of 2.43 percent by the end of its four-year program, 1974–77; the target has recently been reset to 2.4 percent by 1980. Accurate measurement is one problem with such targets. NCSO is attempting to develop a system of virtually complete registration of vital statistics in sample enumeration districts in order to estimate rates for the country as a whole. Pending the successful outcome of this effort, the current rate of population growth in the Philippines is known only with a considerable margin of error and is not precise enough to use as a "success indicator" for the family planning program. Another problem concerns outside factors, such as falling mortality and increasing urbanization and education, that also affect fertility.

Another and probably more reasonable criterion for assessing program performance is family planning practice. When family planning continuation rates are applied to new acceptor statistics (Table 10.1), the proportion of women practicing family planning

Table 10.1. Family Planning Acceptors, 1970–74
(In thousands)

Fiscal year	New acceptors (reported)[a]	New acceptors (adjusted)[a]	Practicing acceptors[b]	Eligible population[c]	Coverage of eligible population (percent)
1970	120	89	89	4,704	2
1971	302	204	262	4,907	5
1972	520	344	520	5,095	10
1973	686	349	794	5,288	15
1974	701	491	1,039	5,501	19

a. New acceptors (reported and adjusted) for 1970–73 from the Commission on Population (POPCOM), *Four-Year Population Program*, p. 13. Reported figures are adjusted for over-reporting and transfers from one clinic to another; the adjusted figures are therefore the best estimates of new acceptors in a given year. New acceptors (reported) for 1974 from POPCOM, *Annual Report, 1973–74*, p. 20. New acceptors (adjusted) for 1974 is the difference between the corrected cumulative number of acceptors as of the end of FY74 (1,567,000 in *Annual Report*, p. 24) and the cumulative total for previous years.

b. The estimated number of women currently practicing contraception. It is calculated as the sum of new acceptors for the current year and continuing acceptors from previous years on the basis of the following continuation rates: first year, 65 percent; second year, 48 percent; third year, 37 percent; fourth year, 26 percent (1974 National Acceptor Survey).

c. Eligible population for 1973 and 1974 from POPCOM, *Annual Report*, estimated as 60.5 percent of the women aged 15–45, according to the medium projection of the National Census and Statistics Office (NCSO). Eligible population figures for 1970–72 are derived by applying this factor to NCSO projections for those years.

can be calculated.[10]   It can be seen from Table 10.1 that family planning practice has increased from 2 percent of the eligible population in 1970 to 10 percent in 1972 and 19 percent in 1974. These results are in accordance with the 1973 National Demographic Survey (NDS) that found 18 percent of married women of reproductive age practicing contraception at that time (but only 15 percent if ineffective folk methods not recommended by the program are excluded).[11]   Further, the NDS found that the total fertility rate had fallen to 5.9 from the level of 6.3 observed five years earlier— a slight but nonetheless significant decline. Clearly the clinical component of the program has made substantial progress.

The 1973 NDS also surveyed attitudes toward family planning and

10. Some women accept family planning because they wish to space their children, and they discontinue contraception to complete their families; others will discontinue because they are not sufficiently motivated or because they believe, rightly or wrongly, that they are no longer fertile.

11. John E. Laing and James F. Phillips, "Survey Findings on Family Planning Program Effects in the Philippines" (Manila: University of the Philippines Population Institute, 1974; processed).

compared them with 1968 findings, giving an indication of the success of another aspect of the family planning program, the IEC component. The median number of children preferred decreased to 4.1 from 5.2 found five years earlier.[12] The proportion of women wanting to have five children or more decreased from 61 percent in 1968 to 36 percent by one measure and to 42 percent by another measure.[13] The proportion who were aware of at least one method of family planning increased from 63 percent to 87 percent. The proportion of respondents disapproving of contraception decreased from 37 to 14 percent. These findings are encouraging in that they suggest that the IEC component of the program has had an impact. At the same time they demonstrate the need for continued strong emphasis on IEC activity, because the desired number of children remains far above the replacement level (about 2.3) required for population equilibrium, and the proportion of women favoring large families remains disturbingly high.

Despite the Philippine program's very creditable accomplishments, it is falling somewhat short of the rather ambitious targets it has set for itself. POPCOM's four-year population program sought 39 percent coverage of the eligible population in 1975 and 50 percent in 1976.[14] These targets are unlikely to be met. This may reflect unrealistic target-setting as much as inadequate program performance, but it remains true that the level of family planning practice in the Philippines is far below the 40 to 50 percent level found in some neighboring Asian countries such as Korea and Taiwan. Further, the number of new acceptors has leveled off and was only 2 percent more in FY74 than in FY73.

The problems facing the program at this time have been analyzed in some detail in recent UPPI evaluation studies.[15] The main findings are as follows:

---

12. Laing and Phillips, "Survey Findings," p. 4.

13. Respondents were asked essentially the same question two different times using different languages in order to validate the responses.

14. It is not clear whether these targets refer to cumulative new acceptors or to currently practicing acceptors. The manner in which the number of acceptors is calculated suggests the former, whereas the manner in which averted births are calculated suggests the latter. POPCOM indicates that the four-year plan is obsolete in some respects and no longer governs all aspects of the program.

15. Laing and Phillips, "Survey Findings," and James F. Phillips, "The Philippine Family Planning Programs: Strategies for Program Improvement" (Manila: University of the Philippines Population Institute, 1975; processed).

a. The aggregate number of new acceptors has stabilized following rapid growth in the earlier years of the program.
b. Urban women are more than twice as likely to practice family planning as rural women—28 percent as against 12 percent.
c. The number of new acceptors per clinic has declined from 41 a month in 1972 to 31 a month in 1974, partly as a consequence of the expansion of the number of clinics.
d. Continuation rates are slightly lower for women who accepted family planning in recent years of the program than for those who were reached in the earlier years. This is attributable partly to the fact that early acceptors were predominantly women who had completed their families, whereas recent acceptors include many women who are spacing their families.

If 50 percent coverage is taken as a target, 81 percent of the women remaining to be reached by the program are rural residents and only 19 percent are urban. Increasing rural acceptors from 12 to 21 pecent would enlist as many into the program as would raising urban coverage to its probable maximum of 50 percent. This means that the future of the program lies in reaching the rural areas. There is also a need, however, to improve the low rate of family planning among urban low-income groups.

One factor influencing rural acceptance rates is cultural values. As POPCOM put its, "The program has now begun to confront target sectors with increasingly resistant attitudes and cultural environments less receptive to new acceptor recruitment." [16] Another factor is the accessibility of family planning services. The 1973 National Demographic Survey found that of the women practicing family planning 26 percent live less than one kilometer from town, 15 percent live four to five kilometers from town, and only 10 percent live nine or more kilometers from town.[17] There is no conclusive evidence as to which of these two factors is more important in holding down rural acceptance rates, but an inference may be made from the 1973 NDS finding that 73 percent of married women approve of contraception. If the proportion of urban women approving is assumed to be no more than 90 percent, the proportion of rural women approving must be at least 66 percent, given the urban-rural distribution of the population (and assuming a random

---

16. *Annual Reports, 1973–74*, p. 2.
17. Phillips, "The Philippine Family Planning Programs," p. 18.

sample). At any given time some of these women will not practice contraception, although they approve of it, because they have not completed their families. But these figures do suggest a potential for much higher coverage of the rural population through improved accessibility of services.

Future Demographic Prospects

The number of women in the reproductive age bracket is expected to increase by 56 percent over the next fifteen years, and mortality will continue to fall. This built-in momentum makes it difficult to slow down the rate of population growth quickly. In some countries urbanization has been a significant factor in reducing population growth. In the Philippines, however, although cities are growing rapidly in absolute terms, the rural population is large enough and its rate of natural increase high enough that the urban-rural distribution of population is changing relatively slowly. If World Bank projections of rural-urban migration are realized, the proportion of the Philippine population that is urban will increase from 29 percent in 1975 to about 33 percent in 1985.[18] This factor alone would slow down the rate of population growth by less than 0.1 percent. Therefore primary reliance will have to be placed on the family planning program to reduce the burdens imposed by the current demographic situation.

The government is keenly aware of the obstacles to expanding family planning practice in the Philippines. POPCOM has recently shifted the emphasis of its program and developed a strategy for future development that contains the following key elements:

a. A further increase in the number of clinics is seen as uneconomic and likely to simply reduce the acceptor load at existing clinics. Instead there will be increased emphasis on effective use of existing clinics and their number will be increased only marginally.
b. Barrio resupply points will be established in rural areas for family planning acceptors who initially enrolled at a town clinic. These will be operated by barrio councils, health clubs, stores, or other appropriate local institutions.
c. The commercial distribution of contraceptives will be promoted;

18. See Chapter 4.

for example, oral contraceptives and condoms will be made available in ordinary shops.

d. Paramedics (nurses and midwives) will be allowed to prescribe contraceptives, and lay motivators (nonmedically trained personnel) will be permitted to resupply users who are not experiencing problems. Midwives will be trained for family planning work at regional training centers, which are being constructed as part of a World Bank–financed population project.

e. Mobile vans will be used to reach remote barrios.

f. Local governments will become increasingly involved in the planning, implementation, and monitoring of population activities.

These commendable efforts to increase the accessibility of family planning services to the rural population should substantially enlarge family planning practice; the extent to which they succeed should be revealed by the program's reporting system in 1976. Because the proportion of women favoring large families still remains excessive, it will also be necessary to make the motivational aspects of the program more effective, in order to lay the foundation for expanding family planning practice in future years.

The prospects for influencing demographic rates through the family planning program are illustrated in Table 10.2. The figures show that if family planning practice remains at its current level, population growth will accelerate. On the basis of the improved program and POPCOM's demonstrated capacity to react flexibly to an evolving situation, family planning practice rates should improve considerably over the next decade. Improvements in the accessibility of services should bring family planning practice up to about 30 percent of eligible couples by 1980. Further progress will depend on a continuation of the recent changes in attitudes toward childbearing and family planning. If attitudinal change continues during the second half of the 1970s at the same rate as during 1968–73, it should be possible to raise family planning rates among eligible couples to 40 percent by 1980. But of course such change is difficult to forecast, and in encouraging family planning among rural people the government has relatively little experience to draw on as it does in implementing rural roads or electrification.

As mentioned earlier, the population to date appears to have followed the medium projection of the NCSO. But with a 40 percent rate of family planning, which is a reasonable objective, the future course of the population will probably lie between the medium

Table 10.2. Possible Demographic Rates, 1980

Family planning practice (percent)	Births (thousands)	Crude birth rate	Crude death rate	Population growth rate (percent)
20	1,996	41	9	3.2
30	1,855	38	9	2.9
40	1,715	35	9	2.6
50	1,574	32	9	2.3

Note: NCSO projects that there will be 11,073,000 women aged 15–45 in 1980. If the eligibility factor of .605 (Table 10.1) is applied, there will be 6,699,000 eligible women in that year. POPCOM statistics indicate that the natural annual fertility rate among eligible women is .34; that is, in the absence of contraception there will typically be 34 births per year among 100 eligible women. Survey findings on the family planning program indicate that the average annual fertility rate among women practicing family planning is .13 (greater than zero because some methods such as the use of condoms and rhythm are relatively unreliable). Where x is the proportion of women practicing family planning, the number of births is calculated as (6,699) (x) (.13) plus (6,699) $(1-x)$ (.34). The number of births is divided by the projected population in 1980 to derive the crude birth rate. The crude death rate is as projected by NCSO; population growth rate is the difference between the two.

Sources: NCSO, *Age and Sex Population Projections for the Philippines by Province, 1970–2000* (Manila, 1974), pp. 22, 40: POPCOM, *Four-Year Population Program* (Manila, 1974), p. 22; John E. Laing and James F. Phillips, "Survey Findings on Family Planning Program Effects in the Philippines" (Manila: University of the Philippines Population Institute, 1974; processed), p. 14.

and low projections. (The medium, low, and medium-low projections are discussed in the technical note appended to this chapter.) This would mean a growth rate of more than 2 percent a year for the remainder of this century. It would also mean a population of about 55 million in 1985 and about 77 million by the year 2000.

Technical Note. Population and Labor Force Projections

On the basis of the 1970 census and the 1973 National Demographic Survey, the National Census and Statistics Office (NCSO) has constructed three projections of the Philippine population to the year 2000—high, medium, and low—based on different assumptions about fertility and mortality rates (Table 10.3).

POPULATION PROJECTIONS

The enumerated population of 36,684,486 on May 6, 1970, is estimated to be 36,851,955 on July 1, 1970; this midyear figure is used as the base.

Table 10.3. Population Projections and Implicit Growth Rates to the Year 2000

Year	Population projections (millions)			Implicit growth rates (percent)		
	Medium	Medium-low	Low	Medium	Medium-low	Low
1970	36.9	36.9	36.9			
				2.9	2.8	2.7
1975	42.5	42.4	42.2			
				2.9	2.7	2.5
1980	49.1	48.5	47.9			
				2.9	2.6	2.3
1985	56.7	55.3	53.8			
				2.8	2.4	2.1
1990	65.0	62.3	59.6			
				2.6	2.2	1.8
1995	73.9	69.4	64.9			
				2.4	2.0	1.6
2000	83.4	76.7	70.0			

Source: Medium and low projections are from NCSO, *Age and Sex Population Projections for the Philippines by Province, 1970–2000*. Medium-low projection is the average of these two.

Fertility. The three population projections differ chiefly with respect to their assumptions about fertility. Fertility may be summarized in the single statistic of the total fertility rate (TFR), which is the number of children born to an average woman who survives throughout the childbearing years. The high projection assumes that the TFR remains constant at the 5.8 births per woman estimated for the early 1970s. The medium projection assumes that the TFR falls at a moderate rate to 5.2 in the late 1970s, 4.6 in the late 1980s, and 4.2 in the late 1990s. The low projection assumes that the TFR falls rapidly to 4.5 in the late 1970s, 3.3 in the late 1980s, and 2.6 in the late 1990s, bringing the Philippines close to replacement level (the fertility rate at which the population just replaces itself) in the year 2000. The evidence on fertility decline discussed in this chapter indicates that the high projection assuming constant fertility can be dismissed as a possible outcome. A combination of the medium and low projections is the most likely future course of fertility rates.

Mortality. The crude death rate of a population is a function of age-specific death rates and the age structure of the population. The NCSO assumes the same pattern of decline of age-specific death rates for all three projections, with the rate of decline decreasing as the normal biological life span is approached. It is projected that during 1970–75 mortality will decline at the same rate as in the 1960s; during 1975–85 it will decline at half that rate; and during 1985–2000 it will decline in such a way that life expectancy increases one year in each five-year period. The NCSO regards the future trend of mortality as relatively certain and predictable, which appears to be reasonable. Because of differing age structures resulting from varying fertility rates under the three projections, the resulting crude death rates diverge, being highest under the high-fertility assumption because of infant mortality. The population growth rate could thus be expected to decline to about 2.5 percent a year by 1985 and to be about 2.0 percent a year by the year 2000. At this time the population would approach 80 million people.

Labor force projections

The statistics of the NCSO (formerly the Bureau of the Census and Statistics, BCS) for labor force and employment understate the time values by substantial amounts in some years.[19] The published statistics are based on rates of labor force participation and employment of the working-age population, as measured by periodic surveys, and on the assumed size of the working-age population. The labor force is underestimated because the data have not been revised to reflect the growth of the working-age population as indicated by the censuses of 1960 and 1970.

Table 10.4 therefore presents a net set of labor force statistics. The working-age population figures for 1960 and 1970 come from the censuses of those years. The figures for the intervening years are derived by interpolation; for 1956–59 by extrapolation backwards, and for 1971–74 from the projections of the NCSO. Labor force participation and employment rates are from BCS labor force surveys.[20]

With these revised series it was possible to make a projection of the labor force based on the projected population ten years of age or older and the expected labor force participation rate (LFPR).

19. For example, the published labor statistics for 1960 imply a working-age population (defined as persons aged ten years or older) of 16,944,000, only 92 percent of the actual working-age population in 1960 as revealed by the census—18,354,000.

20. As published in various issues of BCS, *Survey of Households Bulletin*, and NEDA, *Statistical Yearbook, 1975*. The October series was used because May is affected by students working during their summer vacation. For 1964 and 1969, when no October survey was conducted, the May figures were used instead, reduced by 3 percent to offset the summer vacation factor.

Table 10.4. Labor Force, Employment, and Unemployment, 1956–74
(In thousands)

Year	Working-age population[a]	Participation rate[b] (percent)	Labor force	Employed	Unemployed	Unemployment rate (percent)
1956	16,206	56.8	9,205	8,285	921	10.0
1957	16,719	56.6	9,463	8,791	672	7.1
1958	17,247	56.1	9,676	8,979	697	7.2
1959	17,791	55.1	9,803	9,225	578	5.9
1960	18,354	54.9	10,076	9,441	635	6.3
1961	18,934	55.5	10,508	9,835	673	6.4
1962	19,532	56.0	10,938	10,227	711	6.5
1963	20,149	56.4	11,364	10,841	523	4.6
1964	20,786	55.1	11,453	10,720	733	6.4
1965	21,443	55.0	11,794	11,063	731	6.2
1966	22,121	54.3	12,012	11,171	841	7.0
1967	22,820	53.1	12,117	11,184	933	7.7
1968	23,541	51.1	12,029	11,079	950	7.9
1969	24,285	49.2	11,948	11,147	801	6.7
1970	25,057	49.4	12,378	11,437	941	7.6
1971	25,901	49.2	12,743	12,068	675	5.3
1972	26,782	49.8	13,337	12,617	720	5.4
1973	27,700	49.4	13,683	13,026	657	4.8
1974	28,656	49.4	14,156	13,576	580	4.1

a. Ten years of age or older.
b. The labor force participation rate is defined as the proportion of the working-age population holding or seeking employment; three-year moving average.
Source: World Bank estimates.

The population projection used is the medium-low one. The choice of the medium or low projection would have altered the resulting series somewhat, but not greatly, because of the lag of ten to twenty years between fertility change and its effect on labor force size. For example, medium and low projections for the population ten years of age or older in 1980 coincide exactly, because all such persons were already living and presumably were counted in 1970; for 1985 they differ by only 280,000.

From Table 10.4 it can be seen that the three-year moving average of observed LFPRs has hovered in the range of 49.2 to 49.8 percent within the last six years, with an average of 49.4 percent; 49.4 percent was also the figure actually observed for 1974. In the absence of any detectable trend upward or downward, and with no reason to expect the emergence of a strong factor influencing participation

Table 10.5. Labor Force Projections
(In thousands)

Year	Labor force	Annual growth rate	Average annual increment
1975	14,650		
1980	17,129	3.2	496
1985	19,802	3.0	535
1990	22,736	2.8	587

Source: World Bank estimates.

rates (such as increasing school enrollment rates during the 1960s), it is assumed that this rate will prevail in the future.

The use of an aggregate LFPR for the entire working-age population, rather than disaggregated LFPRs for various age-sex groups, is justified only if there are: (a) no marked trends in age- and sex-specific LFPRs, and (b) no marked changes over time in the age and sex composition of the working-age population. As to the former, an inspection of age- and sex-specific LFPRs reported in the quarterly labor force surveys from 1971 through 1974 reveals no discernible trends. Regarding the latter, the sex composition of the population remains essentially constant. As projected, the age composition changes slightly: The proportion of teenagers, who have a low participation rate, goes down because of decreased fertility; and the proportion of older people, who also have a low participation rate, increases slightly, because of decreased mortality. The projections would be changed so slightly by using age-specific rates, however, that in view of the other uncertainties involved it was decided to use simply the aggregate rate.

The assumed participation rate was applied to the working-age population figures for 1975, 1980, 1985, and 1990 (the years for which figures are available). The results are given in Table 10.5. The series shows that, although the annual rate of growth of the labor force will decrease slowly from 3.2 percent in 1975–80 to 3.0 percent in 1980–85 and 2.8 percent in 1985–90, the absolute magnitude of the increment to the labor force will increase year by year. For the foreseeable future, the Philippine economy will have to generate 500,000 new jobs annually in order to keep unemployment from growing, and it will have to generate 600,000 jobs annually if any tightening up of the labor market is to be achieved.

11

Nutritional Status and Health Standards

A ROUND 1950 THE NUTRITIONAL STATUS of the Philippine population was comparable to that found in neighboring Asian countries such as Malaysia, Taiwan, and Japan. In most of these other countries nutrition has improved so much over the past twenty-five years that it is no longer a major problem. In the Philippines there has also been considerable improvement, but the nutritional status of much of the population remains unsatisfactory because of a more highly skewed distribution of income, more rapid population growth, and relatively disappointing production of food in comparison with some neighboring countries.

Current Nutritional Status

There are three major nutritional problems in the Philippines today. One is the inadequate caloric intake of much of the population, caused by insufficient incomes in relation to food prices, that is, a problem of nutritional poverty. The second is the special problem of infant and child malnutrition in which poverty is only one element of an etiology that also includes excessive childbearing and poor child spacing, the high cost of available weaning foods and faulty weaning practices, false beliefs and ignorance of proper nutrition, and inadequate food distribution within the family. The third is the problem of dietary imbalance leading to vitamin and

Table 11.1. Daily Nutritional Requirements for the Philippine Population

Category	Persons (thousands)	Caloric requirements		Protein requirements	
		Per person (calories)	Total (millions of calories)	Grams per person	Total grams (millions)
0–4 years	6,212	1,100	6,833	12	75
5–9 years	5,529	1,700	9,399	17	94
10–14 years	5,030	2,300	11,569	29	146
Adult males	9,732	2,900	28,223	39	380
Adult females NPNL[a]	8,715	2,050	17,866	35	305
Adult females PL[b]	1,467[c]	2,250	3,301	39	57
Total or average	36,684	2,104	77,191	29	1,057

a. NPNL: Nonpregnant, nonlactating.
b. PL: Pregnant or lactating.
c. Assumed equal to estimated annual number of births.
Sources: Population figures are for 1970 and are from National Census and Statistics Office, *Age and Sex Population Projections for the Philippines by Province, 1970–2000,* p. 12. Caloric and protein requirements per person from World Health Organization, Western Pacific Regional Office, *The Health Aspects of Food and Nutrition* (Manila, 1960), p. 245.

mineral deficiencies, caused by poverty, ignorance of good nutritional practices, and cultural preferences that interfere with an adequate diet. The nutrition of much of the population is also adversely affected by intestinal parasitism.

THE PROBLEM OF NUTRITIONAL POVERTY

The nutritional requirements of a population are determined by the body size, which is influenced by genetic factors and past nutritional levels; climate; the age-structure of the population; and the proportion of physical work that is done by human labor rather than by animals or machines. The World Health Organization (WHO) has published interim standards for developing western Pacific countries, which are the ones adopted here.[1] When applied to the Philippine population, these standards indicate an average daily requirement of approximately 2,100 calories and 30 grams of protein (Table 11.1). This compares with the "tentative" require-

1. World Health Organization, Western Pacific Regional Office, *The Health Aspects of Food and Nutrition* (Manila, 1969), p. 245. The WHO requirements are called "interim" because they refer to existing average body size, rather than to greater body size believed to be attainable if adequate nutrition were available to all groups in the population.

ment of about 2,190 calories and 54 grams of protein used by the National Economic and Development Authority in its food balance sheets. The latter evidently does not reflect the current thinking of nutritionists which holds that the protein requirement of adults is less than previously believed but which continues to emphasize the vital importance of adequate protein intake for infants and children.

Cereals currently provide the major portion (about 66 percent) of the calories consumed by the population, followed by meat, poultry, and seafood (8 percent); sugar (9 percent); root crops, fruits, and vegetables (8 percent); and others (9 percent).[2] The portion of the diet coming from meat, poultry, and seafood is sufficient to provide enough protein if an average quantity of food is eaten. The portions of dairy products and vegetables are grossly inadequate, however. In 1972 the consumption of dairy products was only 28 percent of the allowance recommended by the Food and Nutrition Research Center, and consumption of leafy green and yellow vegetables was only 27 percent of the recommended allowance.

Long-term trends in food availability over the past twenty years are illustrated in Table 11.2. The availability of cereals has increased only modestly. It has been offset particularly by the decline in root crops, an important secondary source of calories, as land has been diverted to more valuable crops. The availability of meat and poultry has merely kept pace with population growth. In contrast, the per capita availability of fish and dairy products has approximately doubled, although that of dairy products remains very low by international standards.

The per capita availability of calories improved substantially during the 1950s and early 1960s, but since 1963 has stagnated at an unsatisfactory level. In recent years the Philippine economy has fallen somewhat short of providing enough food to meet the minimum caloric requirements of the population. In 1972, the most recent year in which a Food Balance Sheet has been published, an average of 2,048 calories a day was available to the population from domestic production and imports. Food consumption survey data indicate a decline in the per capita availability of calories

---

2. NEDA Food Balance Series, nos. 1 and 2, *The Philippine Food Balance Sheet, 1971* (Manila, 1973) and *The Philippine Food Balance Sheet, 1972* (Manila, 1974). Figures in the text are three-year averages for 1970–72.

Table 11.2. Daily per Capita Availability of Major Food Groups, 1953–72

	Grams available				Calories available[b]	
Year	Cereals	Roots and tubers	Meat and poultry	Fish and shellfish	Dairy products[a]	Calories (all foods)	Three-year moving average
1953	308	121	40	46	20	1,691	
1954	310	120	42	48	22	1,725	1,727
1955	321	119	43	52	27	1,766	1,733
1956	307	121	44	53	31	1,709	1,744
1957	305	119	45	52	37	1,756	1,760
1958	330	115	44	56	38	1,814	1,768
1959	308	114	44	53	33	1,735	1,777
1960	312	117	43	57	34	1,782	1,793
1961	331	110	40	55	35	1,862	1,827
1962	318	108	40	53	32	1,836	1,925
1963	353	119	38	82	31	2,077	1,990
1964	347	122	38	84	41	2,057	2,098
1965	375	121	37	88	41	2,161	2,090
1966	332	110	47	90	42	2,053	2,124
1967	354	99	50	95	41	2,159	2,093
1968	359	93	45	107	50	2,068	2,125
1969	365	89	45	103	54	2,148	2,104
1970	376	81	43	103	43	2,097	2,123
1971	392	58	42	103	43	2,123	2,089
1972	363	66	43	107	47	2,047	

a. Whole milk equivalents.
b. Refers to calories available for all foods, not just the five categories shown in this table.
Source: National Economic and Development Authority (NEDA), *Statistical Yearbook, 1975* (Manila, 1975), p. 488. Figures for 1962–69 have been adjusted to compensate for the fact that the population figures used in the Food Balance Sheets in the 1960s must be considered, in the light of the 1970 census, to have been overestimated by as much as 3 to 4 percent.

in 1973 and 1974 and a deterioration in the quality of diet, as measured by the proportion of calories coming from foods other than cereals and root crops (Table 11.3). This deterioration was caused by the food-price inflation in recent years, which was set off by the failure of food production to keep pace with population growth.

Although the Philippine economy has come close to providing sufficient food to meet minimum nutritional requirements, there has always been a substantial portion of the population suffering from malnutrition because of the uneven distribution of food among

Table 11.3. Daily Nutritional Intake per Capita by Annual Income

Survey data	Group 1 (less than ₱400)				Group 2 (₱400–799)				Group 3 (₱800–1,499)				Group 4 (₱1,500 or more)				Undernourished group[a]
	Calories	Caloric adequacy (percent)	Protein (grams)	Percentage of group in sample	Calories	Caloric adequacy (percent)	Protein (grams)	Percentage of group in sample	Calories	Caloric adequacy (percent)	Protein (grams)	Percentage of group in sample	Calories	Caloric adequacy (percent)	Protein (grams)	Percentage of group in sample	Percentage of group in sample
October-November 1970	1,843	87.5	46	30.3	2,127	101.1	57	31.0	2,293	109.0	63	19.2	2,615	124.3	73	19.4	30.3
May-June 1971	1,955	92.9	48	34.7	2,235	106.2	62	26.0	2,637	125.3	72	22.4	2,809	133.5	82	16.8	34.7
August-September 1972	1,770	84.1	42	31.9	2,169	103.1	53	31.4	2,353	111.8	62	21.3	2,765	131.4	75	15.5	31.9
February-March 1973	1,974	93.8	48	32.1	2,098	99.7	54	28.4	2,291	108.9	58	21.5	2,790	132.6	73	18.0	32.1
June 1973	1,868	88.8	40	34.7	2,144	101.9	48	28.8	2,696	128.1	58	21.4	2,618	124.4	68	15.2	34.7
September 1973	1,828	86.7	45	35.8	1,971	93.7	49	29.4	2,275	108.1	60	21.1	2,501	118.9	67	13.7	35.8
December 1973	1,869	88.8	44	33.9	1,978	94.0	46	28.6	2,233	106.1	53	21.4	2,460	116.9	65	16.1	33.9
February-March 1974	1,867	88.7	42	31.6	2,072	98.5	47	28.1	2,199	104.5	53	23.1	2,551	121.2	64	17.2	31.6
May-June 1974	1,673	79.5	37	23.7	1,901	90.4	39	31.3	2,027	96.3	47	28.2	2,674	127.1	65	16.8	39.3
Average	1,850	87.9	44	32.1	2,077	98.2	51	29.2	2,334	110.9	58	22.2	2,642	125.6	70	16.5	33.8

a. Includes Group 1 in all surveys except the last; Group 1 plus half of Group 2 in the last survey.
Note: Caloric adequacy is intake divided by requirement.
Source: Physical quantities, in kilograms, of food consumption were taken from E. D. Dosayla, *Income and Food Consumption: Summary of Nine Economic Surveys* (Quezon City: Office of the Secretary of Agriculture, Special Studies Division, 1975). These were converted into calories and grams of protein by means of factors from *Food Composition Table for Use in East Asia (1972)*, prepared by Food and Agriculture Organization (FAO), Food Policy and Nutrition Division, and United States Department of Health, Education, and Welfare, Nutrition Program.

Table 11.4. Caloric Intake and Diet Quality by Region

	Caloric intake		Diet quality[c]
Region	FNRC[a] data (year)	NFAC[b] data (1970–72)	NFAC[b] data (percent)
Greater Manila	1,730 (1958)	n.a.[d]	n.a.[d]
Ilocos–Mt. Province	1,970 (1960)	} 2,190	} 70
Cagayan Valley	1,790 (1962)		
Central Luzon	n.a.	2,300	70
Southern Luzon	1,700 (1962)	2,010	66
Bicol	n.a.	2,080	70
Western Visayas	1,640 (1964)	2,120	71
Central Visayas	n.a.	2,055	72
Eastern Visayas	1,500 (1965)	2,170	74
Northeastern Mindanao	} 1,750 (1967)	2,240	69
Southeastern Mindanao		2,240	68
Southwestern Mindanao	1,600 (1966)	2,190	69

n.a.: Not available.
a. Food and Nutrition Research Center.
b. National Food and Agricultural Council.
c. Diet quality is indicated by the percentage of total calories coming from cereals and root crops; the higher the percentage, the lower the quality.
d. Greater Manila is included in Southern Luzon.
Sources: E. W. Quiogue, G. M. Villavieja, and V. Ramos, "Summary Results of the Eight Regional Nutritional Surveys Conducted in the Philippines by the Food and Nutrition Research Center," *Philippine Journal of Nutrition,* vol. 22 (April–June 1969), pp. 61–101. M. Z. V. de los Angeles and others, *Regional Consumption Patterns for Major Foods* (Quezon City: National Food and Agricultural Council, Department of Agriculture and Natural Resources, 1973).

regions and income groups. The evidence on the regional distribution of food comes from nutrition surveys conducted by the Food and Nutrition Research Center (FNRC) during the early and middle 1960s and food consumption surveys conducted by the National Food and Agriculture Council (NFAC) in 1970–72 (Table 11.4).[3] The earlier surveys show that the regions with the greatest nutritional deficit were the Visayas and Southwestern Mindanao, with

3. The FNRC and NFAC surveys are better suited for interprovincial than for intertemporal comparisons, since the two series were done by different agencies and possibly employed different measurement techniques. Whereas Food Balance Sheet and NFAC figures for caloric availability and consumption agree very closely, the average intake of 1,674 calories recorded in the FNRC surveys was only 85 percent of the average availability indicated by the Food Balance Sheets for the same years. Since the Food Balance Sheets were prepared on a consistent basis over the period in question, this is a clear indication that the two series are not readily comparable.

Southern Luzon, including Manila, also faring poorly. The more recent surveys also reveal the Visayas and Southern Luzon as lowest in food consumption, in addition to Bicol which was not included earlier. The relatively high caloric intake of Eastern Visayas, perhaps surprising in view of the region's reputation as one of the poorer ones, is offset by its diet quality rating, which was the lowest. Southern Luzon's rating is probably explained by the low caloric intake among the urban poor and the good diet quality among the middle classes in the Manila area. In general, therefore, the poorer regions are the most nutritionally deficient, but the correlation is not perfect. Northern Luzon, for example, is among the poorer regions but has approximately average food consumption.

More severe than the uneven regional distribution of food is the maldistribution among income groups; as a result, inadequate nutrition appears to be commonplace among low-income groups in the Philippines. There are two kinds of evidence: direct observation from food consumption surveys, and inference from data on income distribution and food prices. Direct evidence from the NFAC surveys conducted since 1970 is shown in Table 7.5. The regularity with which caloric intake increases from the poorest to the richest income group strongly supports the validity of the data. The poorest group is consistently deficient in caloric intake, averaging only 88 percent adequacy, while the richest group achieves 125 percent adequacy. Protein intake is, by WHO standards, adequate for all groups, which confirms the prevailing view that the Filipino diet provides enough protein if it provides enough calories and that there is no separable problem of protein deficiency. Within all income groups caloric adequacy deteriorates quite dramatically over time, largely because the groups are defined by their money income rather than real income, which has deteriorated with inflation. Families have apparently adjusted consumption habits to cope with the erosion of real income, and as a result diet quality has been impaired.

The data in Table 11.3 also provide a basis for calculating the proportion of families that is inadequately nourished. Those in Group 1 were certainly undernourished throughout the period in question. By the time of the last survey food-price inflation had brought the caloric adequacy of Group 2 down to 90 percent, and it is reasonable to regard half the families in this group as not receiving sufficient nutrition. The undernourished group thus defined ranges from 32 to 36 percent of the total, with an average of 34 percent. If the distribution before the last survey is assumed to be normal, this figure should be regarded as a lower limit and a probable underestimate.

Another method for arriving at the proportion of families receiving inadequate nutrition is to calculate the minimum cost of an adequate diet and then compare this cost with income distribution data. The year 1971 is convenient for this purpose, since one of the NFAC food consumption surveys, which included food prices, was conducted in May 1971, and the Bureau of the Census and Statistics published a *Family Income and Expenditure Survey* (FIES) for May 1971. The representative weekly diet of the poorest group in the NFAC surveys is shown in Table 11.5. An austere diet, it draws the greatest proportion of its calories from cereals, roots, and tubers and allows little consumption of meat, eggs, or dairy products. This diet provides only 1,913 calories daily and needs to

Table 11.5. Weekly Diet of Low-income Group, 1971

Food	Kilograms (1)	Calories (2)	Price (pesos per kilogram) (3)	Cost (pesos) (3 × 1)
Rice	2.00	7,320	1.16	2.32
Beef	0.05	109	5.17	0.26
Corn	0.50	1,745	0.91	0.46
Dairy products	0.10	325	2.61	0.26
Eggs	0.05	73	4.12	0.21
Fish	0.50	435	2.76	1.38
Fruit	0.70	378	0.65	0.46
Pork	0.10	406	4.58	0.46
Poultry	0.08	194	5.30	0.42
Roots and tubers	0.40	400	0.39	0.16
Sugar	0.20	702	1.11[a]	0.22
Vegetable oil	0.05	442	1.32[a]	0.07
Vegetables	0.70	133	0.70	0.49
Wheat products	0.20	728	1.93	0.39
Total		13,390		7.56

a. These prices are from Bureau of Agricultural Economics, *Prices Paid by Farmers, 1971 and 1972* (Quezon City, 1973), since no prices were published for these commodities in the NFAC study reported by de los Angeles.

Source: E. D. Dosayla, *Income and Food Consumption.*

be increased by 10 percent to achieve caloric adequacy. A minimum adequate diet of such a composition cost ₱432 a person in 1971. The FIES found that the poorest groups devoted 66.5 percent of their expenditures to food. If this proportion of the family budget is allocated to food and the remainder to nonfood necessities, a budget of ₱650 would have been needed for each family member in 1971 to meet minimum needs.

With an appropriate adjustment to reconcile the FIES data with the national accounts, the World Bank has estimated that about 44 percent of the families could not afford a minimum adequate diet in 1971. This result compares with the finding of the Development Academy of the Philippines (DAP), which used similar methodology, that "Due to the extremely unequal distribution of income and consumption, perhaps two-thirds of the people are below the minimum [daily allowances]." This conclusion was based on assumptions slightly different from those used by the World Bank and does not appear to agree with the results of food consumption surveys, but it helps make the point that a large fraction of the Philippine population has difficulty in obtaining an adequate diet.[4]

The results of the food consumption surveys and the family economic survey make it reasonable to conclude that about 40 to 45 percent of Philippine families are undernourished as a consequence of low income. Their effective economic demand for food is less than their biological need.

THE SPECIAL PROBLEM OF INFANT AND CHILD MALNUTRITION

Because incomes that are inadequate for nutritional needs are concentrated among larger families, the proportion of the Philippine population that is undernourished must be even larger than

---

4. Development Academy of the Philippines, *Measuring the Quality of Life: Philippine Social Indicators* (Manila, 1975), p. 8. The DAP assumptions differ from those of the World Bank in three ways: (a) an FNRC-recommended model diet was used rather than the empirically observed diet of low-income groups; (b) it was assumed that families would spend no more than 60 percent of their income on food, whereas empirical observation shows that the very poorest group spends 69 percent of its income on food; (c) no effort was made to correct the FIES data for the probable underestimation indicated by comparison with the national accounts.

the 40 to 45 percent of families estimated as undernourished. More worrisome still, undernutrition is concentrated among those susceptible to the greatest permanent damage from it: infants and children. This generalization is supported by the following kinds of evidence. In four community nutrition surveys carried out between 1965 and 1971, two in rural areas and two in low-income urban areas, the FNRC measured the adequacy of caloric intake by age group.[5] It found that, although the caloric intake of adults was 81 percent of adequacy, the intake of toddlers (aged one to three) was only 64 percent of adequacy and of older children (aged four to nine) only 69 percent of adequacy. Another finding with disturbing implications for fetal and infant nutrition is that pregnant women attained only 64 percent caloric adequacy and lactating women only 46 percent. A recent survey of the Tondo area of Manila found that 87 percent of the children had some clinical sign of malnutrition. The FNRC regional surveys mentioned earlier did not disaggregate caloric intake by age group, but they included blood chemistry studies which indicate that, at least with respect to some nutrients, infants and children were in a worse position than adults.[6] Hemoglobin, the iron-containing compound which carries oxygen to body tissues, was found to be low or deficient in 43 percent of the adults but 73 percent of the young children. Serum vitamin A was found to be low or deficient in 26 percent of the adults but 77 percent of the young children.

In order to identify the children with the greatest nutritional need, the National Nutrition Council[7] inaugurated Operation Timbang in 1974, a program to weigh every preschool child in the country.[8] The weight-for-age and weight-for-height measurements are compared with standards based on well-nourished, middle-class Filipino children. Weighed children are classified as severely undernourished, moderately undernourished, mildly undernourished, or

---

5. Carmen L. Intengan, "What Is Protein Gap?" *Philippine Journal of Nutrition*, vol. 25 (January-March 1972), p. 10.

6. E. W. Quiogue, G. M. Villavieja, and V. Ramos, "Summary Results of the Eight Regional Nutritional Surveys Conducted in the Philippines by the Food and Nutrition Research Center," *Philippine Journal of Nutrition*, vol. 22 (April-June 1969), pp. 79–89.

7. The National Nutrition Council is the agency charged with coordinating the government's nutrition programs and preparing a national nutrition plan.

8. *Timbang* means "weighing."

normal, depending upon whether their weight is less than 60 percent, 60 to 75 percent, 75 to 80 percent, or greater than 90 percent of the standard. Of the 1.5 million preschool children weighed by September 1975, 23 percent were found to have normal weights; 48 percent were mildly undernourished; 24 percent were moderately malnourished; and 5 percent were severely malnourished.

The above results suggest that the majority of Filipino children do not get an adequate diet. Of the 6.8 million Filipino children aged four and under it may reasonably be assumed that at least half, approximately 3.4 million, are in need of nutritional intervention. But how can the estimate that about 40 to 45 percent of Philippine families are undernourished be reconciled with this indication of much more extensive undernutrition among infants and children? It is clear that a complete description of the nutritional status of the Philippine population must consider distribution of food *within* as well as *among* families. Within the family the father has priority at mealtime because he is the breadwinner and may be in an occupation, such as farming, which requires heavy physical labor. The mother also has priority because she may be pregnant, lactating, or also a breadwinner. Of the food available for the children, the larger share goes to the older children who can give voice to their needs and are better equipped physically to reach for it. It is therefore the younger children who suffer the greatest deficit.

The hypothetical situation described above can be aggravated by poor methods of weaning and poor spacing of children. A 1972 survey of body weights of children in Bulacan province, Central Luzon, as part of the Integrated Family Planning and Nutrition Program demonstrates the influence of these factors. Weighed infants were found to be 93 percent of standard weight at six months of age, but only 86 percent of standard weight at nine months, and 80 percent of standard weight at twelve months. According to the authors the data suggest that "growth progresses satisfactorily while the child is breastfeeding and the supply of mother's milk is adequate; but, after the sixth month, mother's milk alone is not sufficient to support the rapidly growing infant . . . the poor performance of one-year-olds is probably due to the complete loss of breast milk to supplement the meager weaning food." [9] Tradi-

9. M. Minda Caldo, Victoria Santiago, and P. W. Engel, "Report of the

tional weaning foods used in the Philippines, such as rice gruel, are not nutritionally sufficient.

The same survey found malnourishment among 55 percent of the children who were no longer nursed because the next baby had been born in 18 months or less; in 35 percent of the cases when the interval between children was 19 to 30 months; and in only 29 percent of the cases where the interval was 31 months or more. Undernutrition was found among 49 percent of the children in families with three preschool children; 39 percent of those in families with two preschool children; and 36 percent of those in families with one preschool child. These facts indicate the close linkage between child nutrition and family planning.

THE PROBLEM OF DIETARY IMBALANCE—VITAMIN AND MINERAL DEFICIENCIES

The only systematic evidence on vitamin and mineral adequacy in the Philippines comes from the FNRC surveys. The dietary phase of the survey found calcium and riboflavin consumption to be a third of the recommended allowances, vitamin A a half, and thiamine two-thirds. The average intake of niacin and iron was found to be adequate. In spite of this, the biochemical phase of the survey found hemoglobin to be low or deficient in 51 percent of the subjects. The authors attributed this inadequacy to deficient intake by some individuals and to intestinal parasitism, which was found in 88 percent of the subjects. Serum vitamin A was found by the biochemical study to be deficient in 47 percent of the subjects, and clinical examination revealed signs of vitamin A deficiency in 45 percent and riboflavin deficiency in 36 percent of the subjects.

The above results are readily understandable in view of the finding that consumption of leafy green and yellow vegetables was only 26.5 percent of FNRC recommended allowances. According to an FNRC nutritionist these are "protective" food, "separated from other vegetables because they are better sources of vitamins and minerals." [10]

Bulacan Province Nutrition and Family Planning Program" (Manila: USAID, 1972), p. 4.

10. Carmen L. Intengan, "Changes in Food Habits in Relation to Increased Productivity," *Philippine Journal of Nutrition*, vol. 25 (October-December 1972), p. 255.

Programs to Improve Nutrition

Several departments of the government have had small-scale nutrition activities for many years. These were coordinated by the NFAC, which had many other responsibilities as well. In 1974, however, with mounting concern about malnutrition, the government established the National Nutrition Council (NNC) to be responsible for nutrition policy. At the same time a private foundation, the Nutrition Center of the Philippines, was established to involve the private sector in nutrition programs. Since then there has been rapid progress in formulating a wide-ranging effort to deal with nutritional problems, particularly infant and child malnutrition.

NNC is broadly analogous to POPCOM in that it is a planning, coordinating, and reporting body, while operational activities are carried out by government departments. NNC encourages greater involvement of local governments in nutrition programs. A Municipal Nutrition Committee, composed of the mayor and representatives of government departments, is to be organized in each municipality, and a Barangay Nutrition Committee in each barangay.[11] These committees are responsible for developing programs to assist the malnourished children identified by Operation Timbang and for monitoring their progress.

GENERAL CALORIC INADEQUACY

As described earlier, there is a widespread problem of caloric inadequacy due to nutritional poverty. NNC has no programs specifically oriented toward this problem, but the government has general programs, discussed elsewhere in this report, to raise incomes and increase food production. While not usually labeled nutrition programs,[12] they will have a significant influence on the

11. A barangay, or barrio, is the smallest administrative unit in the Philippines.

12. The boundaries of nutrition policy are difficult to define precisely. Since nutritional status is determined primarily by income and food supply, any program that affects either one will have nutritional consequences although not ordinarily regarded as a nutrition program. Rather, nutrition programs as such usually take the major features of income distribution and food supply as given and from that starting point attempt to improve nutrition. They may involve minor modifications to the distribution of real incomes or food supply as, for example, in child feeding or the promotion of vegetable growing for local use.

nutritional status of the population through their effect on the relationship between incomes and food prices. As indicated in Chapter 5, the demand for food is expected to grow at about 4.0 percent a year, or about 1.2 percent per capita a year. But since the nutritionally deficient groups undoubtedly have a higher than average income-elasticity of demand for food, it is reasonable to suppose that their per capita demand will grow at a greater rate, perhaps 1.5 to 2.0 percent a year, provided the distribution of income does not deteriorate. Reasonable success with the food production programs discussed in Chapter 6 would mean that this demand could be met. In this case the problem of caloric inadequacy would be largely eliminated by 1985, but the question for nutrition policy remains what, if anything, should be done in the meantime.

The National Nutrition Council states that deaths, absenteeism, accident proneness, and work inefficiency caused by malnutrition may cost the country as much as ₱2,000 million a year. Hence a program to import larger amounts of food and supply it to needy families might be justified on cost-benefit grounds,[13] but the implications for public finance and the balance of payments would probably render such a program infeasible. There is also the question of whether such resources would be better invested in food production rather than spent for food itself. Finally, such a program would not deal effectively with all of the nutritional problems in the Philippines. On balance, the expansion of subsidized imports would not appear to be desirable. But other things could be done to make food relatively cheaper. One would be to improve the low recovery rates in rice milling. These are caused by outdated equipment in many mills and by the cultural preference for highly polished white rice over brown rice, which is less heavily milled. A statutory requirement that brown rice make up the greater part of mill output would increase the supply of calories, because of higher recovery rates, and leave more vitamins and

---

13. From Table 11.3, it can be seen that in 1973 and 1974 the daily caloric deficit of the approximately 14 million people in Group 1 was 250 calories per person, while the average daily deficit of the approximately 12 million people in Group 2 was 70 calories per person. To fill such a deficit would require the importation of an additional 430,000 metric tons of food grain annually. At current grain prices and exchange rates such a program would cost about ₱1,300 million a year.

minerals in the portion of the grain that is otherwise milled away in the polishing. Another possibility is the development of flours based on local foods, as an extender or replacement for imported wheat flour. Banana, defatted coconut, and cassava are some of the foods being investigated in laboratories with financial support from the government and USAID. Technological development is, of course, difficult to predict, but this work might eventually lead to a cheaper flour.

INFANT AND CHILD NUTRITION

NNC has declared that the government's nutrition policy will focus primarily on the cure and prevention of malnutrition among infants, preschool children, and pregnant and lactating women. This is a logical priority because these people stand to suffer the greatest permanent damage from malnutrition, and the costs of treating or preventing malnutrition among them appear to be much less than the costs of failure to do so. A study was conducted recently in Cebu on the costs and benefits of preventing vitamin A deficiency, which reduces resistance to illness and may eventually cause blindness in children. It found that the benefits of prevention (increased lifetime earnings and reduced costs of medical treatment) outweighed the costs of the most expensive intervention (public health measures, including the promotion of home gardening and nutrition education) 15:1, and outweighed the costs of the least expensive intervention (vitamin A capsules) 640:1.[14] Although no studies on the economics of protein-calorie malnutrition appear to have been done in the Philippines, a study in Santiago, Chile, estimated the rate of return to a program of infant feeding to be at least 20 percent.[15] The programs that are particularly oriented to infant

14. Florentino S. Solon, *Report of the Research to Determine the Cost and Effectiveness of Alternate Means of Controlling Vitamin A Deficiency* (n.p., 1974); and Barry M. Popkin, "An Application of Benefit-Cost Analysis to Nutrition Program Planning" (Ithaca, N.Y.: Cornell University, Department of Agricultural Economics, 1974; processed).

15. Marcelo Selowsky and Lance Taylor, "The Economics of Malnourished Children: An Example of Disinvestment in Human Capital," *Economic Development and Cultural Change*, vol. 22 (October 1973), pp. 17–30. The authors conclude that "The most practical remedy for infant malnutrition is a redistribution of income toward the infant and his family; the cost of not undertaking this redistribution now is massive disinvestment in early human capital formation and, perhaps, greatly increased distributional problems with a low-income, low-productivity segment of the population in the future."

and child malnutrition include nutrition education, supplementary feeding, curative treatment for severe cases, and the development of low-cost weaning foods. Because of the close connection between malnutrition and poor child spacing, the government's family planning program also has a significant impact on child nutrition.

Nutrition education takes place both within and outside the school setting. Major progress has been made in recent years in training teachers in nutrition education and making it part of the public school curriculum. Many schools outside cities now have garden plots whose produce, chiefly vegetables, roots, and tubers, is consumed at school as a practical complement to classroom instruction. The Mothercraft Centers of the Department of Health's National Nutrition Service are the chief out-of-school settings for nutrition education. These centers teach mothers about the nutritional needs of infants and children and the preparation of an appropriate diet from local foods. They also provide supplemental feeding to pregnant and lactating women and to infants and children from needy families. Only 252 of the country's municipalities have such centers, which indicates that many more are needed. In addition, workers of the Department of Social Welfare, the Bureau of Agricultural Extension, and other agencies are being trained in nutrition education and communication, and use is made of mass media.

Supplementary feeding takes place primarily in schools but also in other settings. Most of the food is channeled through USAID; the rest is locally donated. About 630,000 schoolchildren and 330,000 preschoolers are being reached by this program. The latter figure suggests that only a small minority of the preschoolers in nutritional need are being reached and that the program should be expanded. NNC has decided to phase out school feeding over the next few years so that more food can be directed to preschoolers. Since donations of foreign food commodities have been decreasing, current NNC policy recognizes that reaching most of the preschoolers in need will require greater mobilization of domestic food resources and more involvement of local communities.

Educational programs to teach mothers how to prepare weaning foods for infants cannot reach all of the target group, and in urban areas the required ingredients may be expensive or unavailable. Presently available commercial products are based on imported foods and are also too expensive. The government and USAID are therefore supporting efforts by the local food industry to develop a low-cost weaning food.

VITAMIN AND MINERAL DEFICIENCIES

The government has two programs which are aimed in part at vitamin and mineral deficiencies. One, nutrition education, informs the population about the need for vitamins and minerals and the foods in which they can be found. The other promotes growing vegetables and other nutritious foods on school, home, and community plots. These foods are expensive to transport and market because of their perishability and bulk but are relatively easy to grow for local consumption. A vegetable nursery is planned for each municipality, and technical assistance for the program is provided by the Bureau of Agricultural Extension.

One possibility to which the government may be giving insufficient attention is the fortification of cereals with vitamins and minerals. Technology already exists to fortify cereals with vitamin A and iron, the two micronutrients least available in the Philippines. Such fortification is relatively inexpensive and can easily reach most of the population. The Department of Health does distribute iodized salt in areas where goiter is a major problem, and this program has had encouraging results.

Health Standards

The major health problems of the Philippines are communicable diseases and malnutrition. The prevalence of the former is due to a lack of sanitary water and sewerage in the case of water-borne diseases, to crowded and unsanitary housing in the case of air-borne diseases, and to a lack of immunization. The promotion of better health in the Philippines will require better nutrition, as discussed in the previous section, expanded health services, particularly in rural areas, and improved environmental sanitation.

MAJOR HEALTH PROBLEMS

The leading causes of death in the Philippines are pneumonia, tuberculosis, and gastrointestinal infections (Table 11.6). The leading illnesses are influenza, bronchitis, gastrointestinal infections, tuberculosis, and pneumonia. The seriousness of these diseases is aggravated by a lack of medical services; about 22 percent of registered deaths, which are believed to be only about three-fourths of all deaths, are not medically attended. This figure is as high as

Table 11.6. Leading Causes of Death and Illness, 1972

Cause	Percentage of deaths	Recorded cases of illness (thousands)
Pneumonia	17.1	96
Tuberculosis	10.4	137
Gastroenteritis and colitis	6.0	258
Heart disease	5.9	—[b]
Diseases peculiar to infancy	5.5	—[b]
Accidents	5.1	—[b]
Vascular disease	4.5	—[b]
Avitaminosis and other nutritional deficiency states	4.3	—[b]
Bronchitis	3.2	335
Influenza	—[a]	395
Malaria	—[a]	27

a. Not a leading cause of death.
b. Not defined as a notifiable disease in the reporting system of the Department of Health.
Source: Department of Health, *Philippine Health Statistics, 1972* (Manila, 1974), pp. 41, 178.

32 percent for less well-served regions such as Eastern Visayas and Mindanao. Resistance to disease is greatly diminished by vitamin and mineral deficiencies, particularly vitamins A and C and iron. Malnutrition and gastrointestinal infections often act synergistically in children, with the infection causing diarrhea which leads to further malnutrition.

A particular problem in the Philippines is the high rate of infant and child mortality. The recorded infant mortality rate is 68 per 1,000, and demographic life tables suggest that the true rate is about 80 per 1,000. Leading causes of infant mortality are pneumonia and bronchitis (34 percent of the total), diseases peculiar to infancy (24 percent), gastrointestinal infection (9 percent), and avitaminosis and other deficiency diseases (5 percent). Of the total deaths in the Philippines, 23 percent are infants, 17 percent are children aged one to four, and 4 percent aged five to nine. The infant mortality rate in the Philippines is about average for a country at its level of income. The high child mortality rate, however, is characteristic of a much poorer country and believed to be due to the prevalence of malnutrition.

Some diseases are not found nationwide but are prevalent in certain regions because of local environmental conditions. Notable are malaria in Mindanao and parts of Luzon and schistosomiasis, a parasitic disease transmitted by an aquatic snail, in Eastern Visayas and Mindanao. Although not major causes of death, both diseases result in serious debilitation and economic loss.

HEALTH SERVICES

On average, health care is more available in the Philippines than in many developing countries but is considerably less so than in developed countries. The ratios of physicians and hospital beds to population, for example, are, respectively, about one-third and one-fifth of those typically found in developed countries. The low average availability of services is seriously aggravated by their uneven distribution (Table 11.7). In the Manila area services appear to be as much as four times more available than in outlying areas such as Cagayan Valley, Bicol, Eastern Visayas, and Mindanao. The regional problem is largely one of urban-rural distribution, as can be seen from the fact that the predominantly rural regions are less well served.

Most of the population cannot afford private medical care, which is available primarily to the urban middle classes. The task of providing health services to the majority has therefore fallen upon the Department of Health. At the base of the public health system are the Rural Health Units (RHUS) and city health department

Table 11.7. **Regional Distribution of Physicians and Hospital Beds, 1973**

Region	Population per physician	Population per hospital bed
Ilocos	2,094	750
Cagayan Valley	4,769	1,538
Central Luzon	3,861	1,403
Southern Luzon	1,889	337
Bicol	5,713	1,722
Western Visayas	3,776	1,187
Central Visayas	3,056	1,072
Eastern Visayas	6,250	1,678
Western Mindanao	7,165	2,377
Northern Mindanao	4,228	1,413
Southern Mindanao	4,776	1,688
Philippines	3,222	797

Source: Department of Health, *National Health Plan, 1975–78*, vol. 2, tables 23 and 42.

clinics. Cases requiring hospitalization are referred to city or provincial hospitals. If more specialized care is needed the case is referred to a regional hospital in one of the country's eleven health regions. At the apex of the referral system are specialized hospitals in Manila affiliated with university medical schools.

In principle, therefore, every Filipino has access to comprehensive public health care. In practice there are serious deficiencies, stemming basically from inadequate funding. Urban clinics are usually overburdened, and drugs and other supplies are sometimes scarce. Deficiencies in rural areas appear to be more serious. Only about 500 of the approximately 1,500 RHUs occupy buildings designed for them, with the remainder in all-purpose municipal buildings or rented quarters. A survey of RHUs done in preparation for a World Bank population loan found that many lack electricity and a potable water supply, and more than 90 percent had inadequate clinical equipment.

Accompanying the deficiencies of infrastructure and supplies in rural health care has been a long-standing shortage of personnel. At the end of 1972 posts were vacant for 23 percent of the physicians and 46 percent of the nurses needed to staff the RHU system. This situation is due to a number of factors. First, working conditions are unsatisfactory because of supply shortages, and physicians need to devote much time to subprofessional tasks that ought to be delegated to paramedical workers but are not because of the lack of support staff. A WHO-financed team of consultants studying rural health services in Rizal province found that the greater part of the physicians' time was devoted to subprofessional tasks.[16] Second, the salaries are low; physicians, for example, earn about half as much as they could in urban private practice. Third, the lack of amenities in the rural as compared with urban areas is unattractive to some medical personnel. Fourth, Philippine medical education appears to be unconducive to rural practice.[17]

All of the country's seven medical schools are located in urban areas, with five in Manila and two in Cebu. These institutions emphasize high-technology, hospital-centered, curative medicine. Clin-

16. M. Subramanian, "Report on Study to Increase Efficiency of Health Services in Rizal" (Manila: WHO Regional Office for the Western Pacific, 1974; processed).

17. This problem is discussed in Paulo C. Compos, "Reversing the Brain Drain," *Far East Medical Journal,* vol. 9 (September 1971), pp. 294–96.

ical medicine is taught almost entirely by faculty who received specialized training in North America, and the emphasis is on the pattern of diseases found in urban areas. The great majority of Filipino medical graduates go abroad for advanced training, and it is estimated that only about half return. This is because there is only a limited demand for specialized services in the urban areas, and physicians with such training find the relatively simple tasks of rural health care professionally less interesting as well as unremunerative. Proposals to remedy this situation include: locating facilities for undergraduate medical training in predominantly rural areas, such as Mindanao and Bicol, and granting preferential fiscal treatment to medical schools according to how many of their graduates practice in the Philippines.[18]

Deficiencies at the basic level of the health care system, although caused by shortages of funds, are very uneconomical. They have meant the relative neglect of simple and economical preventive treatments such as immunizations or vitamin capsules and placed greater burdens on curative services at the hospital level and on society at large.

The Department of Health (DOH) is cognizant of these problems and will direct the major thrust of its 1975–78 national health plan toward providing adequate health services to the rural population along with family planning and better nutrition. Programs for expanding and upgrading rural health infrastructure include:

a. Establishment of health stations in barrios or districts remote from the local RHU, which is usually located in the town proper.
b. Construction of 150 new RHUs and repair and renovation of 150 existing RHUs each year during 1975–79.
c. Provision of 200 jeeps a year for RHUs to transport both health personnel and patients.

The DOH has also recently taken two important steps relating to personnel for the rural health services. One is the redistribution of tasks among different levels of health workers, largely along the lines recommended by the WHO-financed Rizal study. This system was tested in two rural municipalities in Rizal and found to show "superiority in terms of community acceptance, performance, and

18. Paulo C. Compos, "Medical Education and National Development," address before the Philippine Academy of General Practice (Manila, n.d.; processed).

efficiency." [19] Implementation will require retraining some workers at DOH Regional Training Centers. The new system should make service in the rural health care system more attractive to health professionals.

The second measure, the Rural Practice Program, requires all newly graduated physicians and nurses to serve for six months in the rural health care system. This program has two objectives: to fill the manpower gap and encourage young health professionals to consider a career in rural health care. Initial experience with the program indicates that the second objective will not be achieved unless working conditions are improved.[20] The Rural Practice Program can be a logical complement to other measures dealing with the personnel problem, but it cannot substitute for the development of a career service based on good working conditions and more competitive salaries.

Implementation of DOH's plan for expanded rural services will require a substantial increase in funding. According to DOH projections the operating budget for rural health services may have to increase from ₱95 million in 1974–75 to as much as ₱280 million in 1977–78. This would enable DOH to fill existing vacancies as well as the new posts created and to provide adequate operating supplies. DOH's share of the national budget decreased from 4.5 percent in 1970 to 3.4 percent in 1973 and an estimated 2.6 percent in 1975, and public spending on health as a proportion of GNP has decreased from 0.45 percent in 1970 to 0.40 percent in 1974. In view of the small portion of the budget going to health, it should be possible to accommodate an expanded program.

IMPROVING ENVIRONMENTAL HEALTH

The DOH estimates that only 39 percent of the population has access to potable water and only 32 percent has access to sanitary toilet facilities, with the rural areas less well served than the urban.

---

19. M. Subramanian, "Report on Study to Increase Efficiency," p. 13.

20. In April 1975 the annual convention of the Philippine Medical Association was addressed by a recently graduated physician who had participated in the program. Among the discouraging problems he described were supply shortages, absenteeism of regular personnel, and records incorrectly altered to show progress. "Rural Health Criticisms Aired," *Manila Bulletin*, April 25, 1975.

Responsibility for constructing water supply and sewerage systems of course lies not with DOH but with the Metropolitan Waterworks and Sewerage System in Manila and the local government or Local Water Utilities Administration in other cities. These agencies have programs for the expansion of municipal systems, but it will be many years before they reach the majority of the population. In the meantime most of the population will have to rely on water supplies and toilet facilities not connected with such systems. The Environmental Sanitation Service of the DOH is responsible for inspecting such facilities and educating the public about environmental health. DOH plans to increase the budget of this agency and to give more emphasis to environmental health in its overall program.

Two environmentally related diseases of local importance, schistosomiasis and malaria, are the objects of special programs. Schistosomiasis is believed to affect almost 500,000 people, principally in Leyte and Mindanao. There is no completely effective clinical treatment. Responsibility for controlling the disease lies with the National Schistosomiasis Control Commission (NSCC) of DOH. NSCC engages in epidemiological studies, testing of drugs and molluscicides, and education related to schistosomiasis. The only effective method of controlling schistosomiasis, however, is drainage of the vector's habitat followed by terminal mollusciciding. NSCC can therefore accomplish little unless the Department of Public Works or the National Irrigation Administration undertakes agroengineering works in the affected areas.

Malaria, which was found throughout the Philippines thirty years ago, is found today only in the Cagayan Valley, Palawan, the Sulu Archipelago, and parts of Mindanao. About 4.6 million people live where eradication measures are required, and surveillance is necessary in some other areas. Responsibility for eliminating malaria lies with the Malaria Eradication Service, which devotes most of its resources to spraying but also engages in case detection and referral. Eradication has been hampered by difficult transport in the affected areas, population movements between malarious and nonmalarious areas, and the resistance of the parasite to some drugs.

12

The Education System

THE PHILIPPINES ENJOYS A REPUTATION for having a relatively highly educated population, but this generalization is subject to important qualifications. There appear to be considerable urban-rural and income-class disparities in education. Furthermore, funding has not matched the unusually large enrollments, which has meant lower quality than in countries with more restricted educational opportunities (Table 12.1). Enrollments grew particularly rapidly during the 1960s,[1] and widespread concern about quality and the relevance of the education system to national needs led to the appointment of a Presidential Commission to Survey Philippine Education in 1969. In 1970 the commission issued its landmark report, *Education for National Development,* which contained a number of major proposals for reform. In general the pace of reform and improvement has not been rapid, which is understandable in view of the magnitude of the task, but it should accelerate now that the reorganization plan for the Department of Education and Culture (DEC) has been implemented. Improved education will have important effects not only on labor productivity by imparting

1. In the 1970–71 school year elementary enrollment was 66 percent greater than a decade earlier; secondary enrollment, 177 percent greater; and enrollment in higher education, 116 percent greater. See Department of Education and Culture (DEC), "Annual Report, 1973–74" (processed).

Table 12.1. Comparison of Educational Indicators for Selected Countries

Indicator	Philippines	Korea	Thailand	Malaysia
Public education expenditure per capita (in U.S. dollars)	6	11	7	32
Percentage of GNP devoted to public education	2.5[a,b]	2.9	3.0	6.4
Percentage of government budget devoted to education	14.9[b]	17.9	18.7	20.9
Ratio of primary enrollment to relevant age group (in percent)	104	97	87	90
Ratio of secondary enrollment to relevant age group (in percent)	46	51	21	33
Ratio of tertiary enrollment to population (in percent)	1.7	0.5	0.2	0.2

a. If it is assumed that spending per student is the same in private as in public education, the proportion of GNP going to *all* education would be 2.9 percent; this would most likely be an underestimate. One source suggests that this figure "approaches 4 percent"; 3.5 percent is probably not far from the true value. See International Labour Office, *Sharing in Development* (Geneva: ILO, 1974), p. 305.

b. Department of Education and Culture (DEC) budget, plus estimated ₱130 million for school buildings from the Department of Public Works, as indicated by Budget Commission, *Fiscal Year 1975 National Budget*, p. 24.

Source: Figures for Philippines are estimates based on DEC data. Philippine financial statistics refer to 1973–74; enrollment statistics refer to 1970–71. Figures for other countries are from recent World Bank appraisal reports of education projects.

attitudes and skills but also on welfare in such areas as nutrition and family planning.[2]

The Quality of Elementary and Secondary Education

Formal education is divided into a six-year elementary cycle, a four-year secondary cycle, and higher education, with the role of the public sector decreasing from the elementary to the tertiary level. Free elementary education is supported entirely by the national government, mandated by the constitution, and 95 percent of the

2. There is a substantial negative relationship between education and fertility. Furthermore all the fertility decline of recent years has been among women with at least some secondary schooling; fertility among women with no schooling or only elementary schooling is as high as ever. See Peter C. Smith, "Educational Differentials in Overall and Marital Fertility, 1968–1972," Research Note no. 48 (Manila: University of the Philippines Population Institute, 1975; processed).

elementary students are enrolled in the public school system. Since 1960 elementary enrollment has been expanding at the rapid rate of 4 percent a year owing to increases not only in the number of children but also in the enrollment ratio. Elementary enrollment can now be considered almost universal in the Philippines, with the exception of some tribal groups.

The rapid growth of enrollment has outpaced the availability of all educational inputs except for teaching staff, which has grown proportionately. The shortages of classrooms and textbooks are particularly severe. The nationwide classroom shortage is estimated to be about 40,000, and the DEC operates two shifts in many schools. The government has an active school-building program, but at current rates of construction the classroom shortage will not end until the early 1980s.

The textbook problem is even more serious. A survey done in preparation for a World Bank education loan found that the pupil-textbook ratio in the public elementary schools is 10:1 and 79 percent of the textbooks are more than five years old. This situation has persisted for a number of years. Textbooks produced under the World Bank project will not become available in large quantities until 1977. Other teaching tools, such as simple science materials and audiovisual aids, are also in short supply. This situation has arisen because the majority of operating expenditures in the education sector (more than 90 percent of DEC's budget) has gone to salaries and other personnel expenses. The school-building program has accounted for the second largest portion of expenditures in the education sector, and textbooks and supplies have been a poor third. The shortage of textbooks and other educational materials handicaps the teaching staff in its work. Reliance on learning by rote results in low-quality education, and high drop-out and repeater rates occur at the upper grades of elementary education.

To upgrade the low quality of education the growth of enrollment must be reduced by decreasing the number of repeating students, more educational materials must be made available, and teachers retrained to use the materials effectively. In 1971 an important enrollment reform was instituted, namely a continuous progression scheme under which all students will be passed on to the next grade. Although implementation of this scheme calls for improved curricula and teaching, it is possible that some children completing the elementary cycle may be unprepared for the secondary level. This may seem unattractive, but it is probably preferable to the alternative of continuing to burden the elementary system with excessive enrollments. The World Bank projections (see the technical note to this chapter) show that if continuous progression were completely enforced, enrollment growth would be greatly reduced. This policy would make it possible to improve the quality of elementary education over the next few years, which in turn should reduce the incidence of student failure. In addition, incremental resources allocated to elementary education should be devoted primarily to educational materials. Large classes and double shifts may be undesirable, but a minimally adequate supply of textbooks and other materials is by far the more critical need.

At the secondary level the education system is characterized by greater diversity than at the elementary level. Youths of secondary school age are enrolled approximately as follows: 24 percent in public secondary schools; 28 percent in private secondary schools, many of which have religious affiliations; perhaps 5 percent in elementary schools; and about 43 percent out of school. In recent years the ratio of public to private enrollment has increased, and in the 1980s a majority of secondary students will probably be in public schools. Parents who can afford to send their children to a private school usually do so, a fact that has contributed to a lack of public pressure for good public secondary schools. Most of the public school students are enrolled in general secondary schools supported by provincial or city governments and typically located in provincial capitals. A smaller number is enrolled in barrio high schools which have been started as self-help projects in rural communities without other access to secondary education. About one-tenth of public secondary students are enrolled in vocational schools, which concentrate on agriculture or technical training for industry.

Responsibility for support of the vocational schools lies with the national government, while the other public schools are supported primarily by local governments with some assistance from the national government. Tuition fees are charged and provide a substantial source of revenue for the public secondary schools and the great bulk of funds for private schools.

At the secondary as at the elementary level, the chief problem is the poor quality of education. In 1970 the Presidential Commission to Survey Philippine Education observed that "secondary education is widely believed to be the weak link in the educational ladder" and that studies had found college freshmen poorly prepared in language skills, mathematics, and science.[3] The low quality of education was attributed to the relatively short secondary cycle (four years as compared with six in most countries, including neighboring Thailand and Korea), an inappropriate curriculum, and inadequate financing.

The commission recommended that secondary schooling be lengthened to five years, consisting of a three-year common track followed by two years of preparation for higher education or technical training for employment. The commission felt that such an extension would remedy weaknesses in college preparation and the problem of enrolling students in vocational education before they were sufficiently mature to make occupational choices. The proposal was not accepted, however, owing to a lack of funds.

The commission's principal finding about the curriculum was that the traditional distinction between general and vocational secondary schools had not worked well. Students in the academic track who did not go on to higher education found themselves unprepared for the world of work, and the vocational schools suffered from inadequate equipment and competition from industry for the most qualified personnel. For many students vocational schooling was a second choice, and relatively few students actually took jobs in the fields for which they supposedly had trained. The commission accordingly recommended that the distinction between general and vocational schools be abolished.

This recommendation was adopted in DEC's secondary curriculum reform of 1973. In the new curriculum all secondary students will study language, mathematics, science, and social studies. In addition they will take one practical arts course each year, with the possibility of additional electives during the third and fourth years. The precise nature of the practical arts (agriculture, fishing, industrial skills) will depend on the demands of the local community and the facilities available. The academic subjects have also been revised so as to make them more relevant to the Philippine situation.[4] The curriculum reform should now proceed rapidly, following the

3. Presidential Commission to Survey Philippine Education, *Education for National Development: New Patterns, New Directions* (Manila, 1970), pp. 71, 73.

4. For example, the new third-year social studies course, Development and Progress, deals with economic and other aspects of development. The subject of population and nutrition has been integrated into the content of several courses.

implementation of the DEC reorganization plan (discussed later in this chapter) in July 1975. Among other things, the reorganization abolished the Bureau of Vocational Education and established a new Bureau of Secondary Education to oversee all secondary education, private as well as public.

This admirable curriculum reform will have to be accompanied by an increased allocation of resources to secondary education if the objective of improving quality is to be achieved. Some commentators regard curriculum reform as a costless way of upgrading quality, but it is one thing to design a curriculum and another thing to teach it. In general the public secondary schools suffer from the same shortages and deficiencies as the elementary schools; the pupil-textbook ratio, for example, is 8.5:1. Until a special national appropriation ended the anomalous situation last year, secondary teachers were actually paid less than elementary teachers because of secondary schools' dependence on local governments for financial support. Another consequence of local financing of secondary schools is the much greater variation of quality compared with the relatively homogenous elementary system.

To the extent that tuition fees do not cover marginal costs, the problem of adequate financial support for the secondary system will be magnified by an enrollment boom in years ahead. As shown in the technical note to this chapter, secondary enrollment will probably increase from about 2.2 million in 1975 to about 3.2 million in 1985, owing in part to demographic trends but primarily to an increased enrollment ratio. Most of the recent increase in secondary enrollment has been in the public sector, which has grown about 8 percent a year as against 4 percent for private secondary enrollment. In 1972–73 there were about 850,000 students in public secondary schools and 1,029,000 in private schools. By 1985 there could be about 1.8 million in public schools and 1.4 million in private schools.[5]

This prospect has significant implications for the government's education budget. One option would be to permit expansion in enrollment but increase allocations for secondary education at a slower rate, which would lead to a decline in quality. This would be undesirable because low-cost education becomes inefficient when

5. Although the World Bank agrees with DEC's low projection of total enrollment in secondary schools, the DEC has assumed that only 40 percent will be in public schools, which seems too low on the basis of recent trends.

it fails to accomplish its objectives and merely shifts the problem of quality to the next level or out of the system. A second option would be to restrict the growth of enrollment, as recommended in a report by the International Labour Office (ILO), which concluded that, "in our view, it is difficult really to justify the expansion of any level of education in the Philippines at the present time." [6] One way to restrict enrollment could be to increase tuition fees, which would deter students whose parents are poor or not highly motivated to provide education for their children. The exclusion of poor but able students could be offset to some extent by a loan scheme. Another means could be academic testing. A third means could be to retrench on the school-building program and fail to provide secondary schools in areas not now served; this would maintain existing urban-rural disparities.

Yet another option, which is recommended here, would be to permit the prospective increase in enrollment and to maintain or slightly increase the allocation per student in secondary education so as to provide a minimally adequate supply of textbooks and other educational materials. This would probably necessitate increasing the share of education in the national budget from the current 17 percent to perhaps 19 percent by 1980.

Rationalizing Higher Education

In 1971–72 there were about 648,000 students enrolled in higher education in the Philippines, including about 43,000 (7 percent of the total) in the public sector and 605,000 (93 percent) in the private sector. Higher educational enrollment in the Philippines is about four times that of Korea and ten times that of Thailand, countries of roughly comparable populations and development levels (Table 12.1).

Public institutions of higher education are either state universities or state colleges. The secretary of education is the chairman of their governing boards, but they are not under the effective control of DEC. The public institutions include the University of the Philippines, which is the leading institution of the country in

6. International Labour Office, *Sharing in Development* (Geneva: ILO, 1974), p. 317. The authors indicate that this judgment is formed on strictly economic (as opposed to social or political) grounds.

many academic fields, and other institutions designed to meet regional needs, such as Central Mindanao University which offers
agriculture and forestry. Also included are low-qality institutions
(in some cases high schools reclassified as colleges), the existence of
some of which can be understood more as a consequence of con-
gressional politics than the result of any rational planning. The
presidential commission found that "with few exceptions, state
institutions are inadequately financed, staffed, and equipped." [7]

The private education sector is characterized by similar diversity.
Many private colleges are church affiliated; others are profitmaking
enterprises. A few have competitive admissions standards and
charge tuition fees high enough to permit the operation of a sound
academic program, but most are open to any student willing and
able to pay a relatively low tuition. Private institutions have inadequate facilities and underqualified and overburdened faculty; only
28 out of about 600 are accredited by the Philippine Accrediting
Association of Schools, Colleges, and Universities (PAASCU).

The combination of inadequate budgets and relatively unrestricted admissions results in a low cost per student in most private
institutions. The presidential commission found that the average
cost per student in private colleges and universities was only half
that of PAASCU institutions and one-fourth that of the University of
the Philippines and a few elite private colleges.[8] This means that
private institutions necessarily concentrate on low-cost fields of
study (liberal arts, commerce, business administration, and teacher
training, as shown in Table 12.2), and that quality is unsatisfactory
in fields requiring relatively high costs per student (for example,
engineering, a field in which many graduates fail the professional
examination).

The poor quality of education and rapidly expanding enrollments in the 1960s, particularly in fields not in short supply in
relation to development needs, led the presidential commission to
forecast widespread unemployment among the educated in the 1970s
and to recommend a cutback in enrollment. Similarly, the ILO
report found that, on the basis of rates of return, most fields of
higher education were overexpanded, and it also recommended
restraining enrollment. Before a discussion of the mechanisms suggested by the presidential commission and endorsed by the ILO

7. *Education for National Development,* p. 99.
8. *Education for National Development,* p. 48.

Table 12.2. Enrollment in Private Colleges, by Field of Study, 1971–72

Field of study	Enrollment (thousands)
Commerce and business administration	245
Liberal arts and sciences[a]	147
Teacher training	84
Engineering	70
Medical sciences	33
Nautical sciences	6
Food, nutrition, and dietetics	5
Agriculture	4
Total	594

a. Includes law and foreign service and music and fine arts.

Note: Data were collected by Bureau of Private Schools. No data were available for public institutions because the responsibility of Bureau of Public Schools extends only to the secondary level. There were about 43,000 students enrolled in public institutions in 1971–72. Agriculture is offered primarily in the public sector.

Source: NEDA, *Statistical Yearbook, 1975*, p. 462.

report for accomplishing this objective, several points should be made.

First, the enrollment boom in higher education seems to have tapered off of its own accord. The most recent data available show that enrollment in higher education increased at a rate of 10 percent a year from 1960–61 to 1967–68 (from 300,000 to 590,000), but at a rate of only 2.5 percent a year from 1967–68 to 1971–72 (from 590,000 to 648,000). This means that the enrollment ratio has remained constant or even declined slightly in recent years, and on this basis future enrollment growth is expected to be slower than in the 1960s (see the technical note to this chapter). It is not clear whether these figures represent a genuine trend or a temporary fluctuation. One possible reason for the slower growth is the modest improvement in the employment situation in recent years, which has increased the very low opportunity cost of higher education (that is, the wages that would be earned if the student were employed instead of in school).

Second, the expected unemployment among the educated has not materialized. Instead, the overexpansion of higher education has put college graduates in many office jobs in government and business that would be filled by secondary school graduates in countries such as Thailand or Malaysia with a more elitist philosophy about higher education. In making such a comparison, it should be remembered that the secondary school graduate in most countries has had as many years of schooling as the Filipino with two years of college.

Third, it is undoubtedly correct to argue, as do the presidential commission and the ILO report, that much of the large-volume, low-cost private education in the Philippines is economically inefficient. But the value of such education as consumption and the alternative uses of these private resources should be considered in formulating public policy. If the alternative is merely some other form of private consumption, the grounds for public policy interference with consumers' sovereignty would appear to be weak. But if the alternative would be to tax these resources for the public sector or somehow channel them into selected quality improvement of private education, the rationale for public policy intervention would be strong.

The mechanisms proposed by the presidential commission and endorsed by the ILO report for the improvement and rationalization of higher education include: the establishment of a State College and Universities Board to administer public higher education and a Bureau of Higher Education to oversee all of higher education; admissions examinations; accreditation; and scholarships to enable poor but able students to pursue the more expensive programs such as engineering and medicine. The State Colleges and Universities Board has not, unfortunately, been created. The Bureau of Higher Education was established only in July 1975. A National College Entrance Examination (NCEE) was developed by the Fund for Assistance to Private Education, a private, nonprofit foundation, and was given for the first time in the school year 1973–74. The examination has already been used to restrict college admissions, and guidance counselors are supposed to take NCEE scores into consideration when advising students. Responsibility for administering the NCEE is being transferred to DEC following its reorganization. Relatively little has been done to implement suggestions for promoting accreditation and quality in private higher education through fiscal measures such as taxes and subsidies. A small scholarship fund has been established, but its resources will have to be expanded if it is to make an impact on equalizing access to higher education.

Administration of the Formal Education System

The making and implementation of education policy in the Philippines has long been handicapped by organizational problems.

A major advance toward remedying this situation was the reorganization of the Department of Education and Culture in July 1975. The chief units, which previously functioned largely independently,[9] have now been reorganized into bureaus of elementary, secondary, and higher education. Staff functions have been brought into line with the common scheme for all government departments developed by the Integrated Reorganization Plan. Regional offices intended to orient the school more closely to regional needs have also been established.

A significant feature of the reorganization is the establishment of an Office of Planning Services, which is intended to be a high-level, well-staffed unit engaged in ongoing policy analysis and planning. The presidential commission in 1970 identified planning as an area that needed strengthening. In the DEC, however, planning has been hindered by the dispersal of authority, since the operating bureaus have largely continued to do their own planning,[10] and also by tardy and incomplete statistical information.[11] The reorganization should deal with the former problem, and the latter problem should be dealt with by the installation of a computerized management information system.

There is also a need to bring more people with high-level managerial ability into DEC. In 1970 the presidential commission found a problem of "administrative in-breeding with otherwise qualified persons whose academic backgrounds are not in education excluded from the upper executive levels. . . . In view of the need for professional management in education, the policies of promotion

9. The Bureau of Public Schools, with responsibility for the public elementary system and for aiding and supervising the public secondary schools operated by local governments; the Bureau of Private Schools, with responsibility for supervising private schools from the elementary level through college; and the Bureau of Vocational Education, with responsibility for vocational schools.

10. A recent study by NEDA found that "Plans and programs are short-range and fragmented by sectors. There seems to be no articulation of the projects developed and implemented by these educational bureaus." NEDA, *Education Sector Study* (Manila, 1974), p. 13.

11. The presidential commission pointed out that "there is a need for an efficient statistical and research service that will generate adequate, reliable, and timely baseline data for planning purposes" (*Education for National Development*, p. 61), but statistics have remained seriously out of date. In DEC's "Annual Report, 1973–74," released in October 1974, the most recent year for which actual (as opposed to projected) public school enrollment statistics were available was 1970–71. Similarly, 1970–71 statistics were used in 1974 as the base of DEC's enrollment projections for 1975–85.

Table 12.3 Public Education Operating Expenditures, 1965/66–1974/75

Fiscal year	Total outlay (millions of pesos)	Public school enrollment (thousands)	Index of expenditures at constant prices (1965 = 100) Total outlays[a]	Index of expenditures at constant prices (1965 = 100) Outlays per pupil	Expenditures as percentage of budget
1965/66	656	5,972	100	100	29
1966/67	709	6,396	102	95	28
1967/68	762	6,652	104	94	26
1968/69	878	6,902	114	99	24
1969/70	993	7,421	122	98	24
1970/71	1,108	7,627	118	93	25
1971/72	1,255	8,044	117	87	22
1972/73	1,321	8,477	113	80	17
1973/74	1,496	n.a.	112	75[b]	17
1974/75	1,642	n.a.	92	59[b]	15

n.a.: Not available.

a. Nominal expenditure reduced from current prices to constant prices by GNP deflator. A price index for the goods and services purchased by the education system would be ideal for this purpose but of course does not exist. The price of the major item, namely teachers' services, has risen less rapidly than prices in general because teachers' salaries have decreased in real terms. The extent to which real education spending has been eroded by inflation is therefore exaggerated somewhat by the above figures.

b. Assumes enrollment growth at rate observed in previous years.

Source: NEDA, Statistical Yearbook, 1975, pp. 460–68; DEC, "Annual Report, 1973–74," p. 17.

by merit and recruitment of competent staff from the outside are proposed." [12] Executives with broad experience could play a useful role in managing a large enterprise such as the Philippine education system, and with the reorganization of DEC it would be timely to consider the implementation of the commission's proposal.

Financing the Educational System

In the mid-1960s the DEC budget was almost 30 percent of the national budget and the school-building program (outside DEC) took a small amount more. Since then public expenditures on education have increased substantially in nominal terms, but when inflation is taken into account the real level of spending has decreased since 1969 (Table 12.3). The real level of spending per

12. Education for National Development, p. 184.

student has decreased even more, and today is perhaps 80 percent of what it was ten years ago. At the same time, the portion of the national budget going to DEC has decreased to 17 percent in recent years. The result has been the quality problems previously discussed.

The principal recommendation of the presidential commission, which was not adopted, was to decentralize financial responsibility for elementary and secondary schools to local governments. In view of the fact that the lack of local government support is the principal reason for the relative weakness of secondary schools, this recommendation may seem curious. Its stated rationale was to free a larger amount of the national budget for higher education and for innovation and quality improvement in the whole system. The commission was also undoubtedly influenced by the general feeling at the time that education's share of the budget should be reduced in order to increase the share for infrastructure investment and economic services. However, the large share of education in the national budget was due less to an overgrown education system than to the small share of the public sector in the national economy, which in turn was a consequence of low rates of tax collection.

In recent years the substantial boost to government spending on economic infrastructure has implicitly entailed sharp restraint on other sectors, including education. A further reduction in education's share of the national budget would only compound problems of quality and increase educational inefficiency. Also, with the increase in tax collections in recent years, much of the force goes out of the proposition that spending in sectors such as education must be held back if infrastructure development is to be stepped up. In order to accommodate enrollment increases and provide for urgently needed quality improvements, real spending on operating the educational system should probably increase by about 10 percent a year over the next few years. This would bring the share of education to 19 percent of the budget by 1980, which would be a satisfactory level.

Training Manpower for Industry and Agriculture

Manpower is trained for industry in the Philippines through: the vocational schools of the DEC; training courses for out-of-school youths and unemployed adults sponsored by the National Manpower and Youth Council (NMYC), a unit of the Department of Labor;

recognized apprenticeship programs; and informal training programs in industry. NMYC, which has primary responsibility for manpower development, states that at the present time "The absence of an adequate and efficient reporting system prevents an intelligent assessment of the type, nature, and exact magnitude of training programs conducted by public and private agencies . . ." [13] A Coordinating Committee on Manpower Development has recently been established to perform this function.

Approximate figures currently available for some types of training indicate that in 1973–74 the vocational schools of the DEC enrolled 111,000 students in the four-year secondary cycle and an additional 16,000 in postsecondary courses, generally lasting two years. The dropout rate from the secondary cycle is substantial, however, and a considerable number of those who graduate go on to college rather than obtain employment in a trade. NMYC therefore projects that the vocational schools will graduate between 13,000 and 15,000 each year in the 1970s. During 1970–72 NMYC, using for the most part existing vocational schools and state colleges, provided courses in industrial skills lasting from one to three months to 85,000 persons. Only 58,000 graduated from the courses, 99 percent of them semiskilled and only one percent skilled craftsmen, technicians, or foremen. A survey of the graduates of one year's courses found that fewer than half were employed in the occupations for which they had received training.[14]

In recent years about 6,000 persons have been enrolled in apprenticeship programs recognized by the Department of Labor, with about 3,000 apprentices graduating annually. Thus the vocational schools and the apprenticeship programs together may have been supplying between 16,000 and 18,000 skilled workers annually, while the briefer NMYC courses have been supplying perhaps 20,000 semiskilled workers each year. There are no statistics available on training by private industry other than recognized apprenticeship programs, but such training is believed to be quite substantial. The

13. National Manpower and Youth Council, *Interim Manpower Plan* (Quezon City, 1974), p. 137.

14. Rony Diaz, "The Role of Vocational and Accelerated Training Programs," in University of the Philippines School of Economics and National Economic Council, *Papers and Proceedings of the Workshop on Manpower and Human Resources* (Manila, 1972). Typical rates were: machine trades, 42 percent; electricity, 39 percent; welding, 41 percent; garment trades, 30 percent.

government encourages it by permitting firms to deduct half the cost of the programs from their taxable income.

There has been some disagreement as to whether there is a shortage of vocational and technical training in the Philippines. The Presidential Commission to Survey Philippine Education found that the education system has produced a predominantly literate population and a large professional class, but that vocational and technical training has been neglected in relation to the need for skills. The commission apparently reached this conclusion on the basis of two surveys. One showed that for each engineer, Philippine industry employed 1.8 technicians, 11 skilled workers, and 12 unskilled workers, compared with an international average of 5 technicians and 25 skilled workers for one engineer. The commission concluded that more technical education was needed. Another survey revealed that industrial firms found it necessary to train new workers because their schooling had not prepared them for industrial work, and that the firms planned to increase their employment of technicians and skilled workers.[15]

The government, following the commission's report, has moved to expand industrial training by establishing ten Regional Manpower Training Centers (RMTCS) and three technical institutes as part of a World Bank–financed education project which also receives support from the United Nations Development Programme and the ILO. The RMTCS will provide suitable facilities for NMYC's training programs, which will include both full-time and part-time courses lasting two to six months. An important feature of these centers is that they will carry out local manpower studies to ensure that the courses offered are relevant to local needs. Mechanics, industrial electricity, sheet metalwork, welding, and boatbuilding will be among the courses offered. When in full operation, the output of the centers will be 7,200 craftsmen a year. The three technical institutes will provide three-year postsecondary courses that will graduate 800 technicians annually in such fields as electronics, mechanics, civil construction, and chemical technology.[16]

15. These surveys are discussed in Manuel Alba and Thelma Magno, "Manpower Development Strategy and Investment in Education," in *Papers and Proceedings of the Workshop on Manpower and Human Resources.*

16. A technician is considered to be at an intermediate level between the engineer and the skilled worker or craftsman, with more theoretical training than the latter. The technician may use complex equipment or do work such as process control, costing and estimating, and product testing. Jesus P. Gotidoc,

The view that there are critical shortages of technicians and skilled workers was, however, recently challenged in the ILO report. The report characterized the evidence underlying the commission's view as generally unconvincing and observed that the poor employment experience of vocational school graduates and NMYC trainees suggests that "not a single skill is in short supply." [17] This is not the only possible explanation for the low employment rates; another possibility may be that inadequate training has produced unqualified graduates. Industrial firms have been dissatisfied with trade school graduates and attribute their insufficient preparation to poor methods of instruction and lack of equipment.[18] But there is other evidence that supports the ILO's view. In 1973 unemployment rates among experienced workers were as follows: professional and technical workers, 2.0 percent; craftsmen and production-process workers, 5.0 percent; manual workers and laborers, 9.7 percent; all experienced workers, 2.4 percent.[19]

Although the unemployment rate for skilled workers was lower than that for unskilled workers, it was greater than that for the experienced labor force as a whole. Furthermore, the real wages of skilled labor have declined steadily during recent years, and the margin separating the wages of skilled and unskilled labor has decreased. The proposition that middle-level manpower is in seriously short supply would thus appear to need substantial qualification. One possibility may be that skilled workers are not in short supply, but the more highly trained technicians are.

A related issue is the relative role of industry and other institutions in providing industrial training. The presidential commission asserted that "Skills that require basic scientific knowledge and familiarity with modern machines may best be provided in schools," whereas the ILO report suggested that "schools are inappropriate

---

"An Assessment of Industry Demand for Technicians and Skilled Workers," *Philippine Review of Business and Economics*, vol. 8 (June 1971), p. 68.

17. ILO, *Sharing in Development*, p. 646.

18. Jesus P. Gotidoc, "An Assessment of Industry Demand," pp. 65-67.

19. Bureau of the Census and Statistics (BCS), *Survey of Households Bulletin: Labor Force, May 1973*, no. 38 (Manila, 1974), p. 16. In interpreting the 2.4 percent unemployment rate for all experienced workers, it should be remembered that a large proportion of the unemployed in the Philippines are new entrants to the labor force. Also, the rate is affected by the large number of agricultural workers, who had an unemployment rate of only 1.2 percent.

institutions for the preparation of *specific* skills." [20] Since basic scientific knowledge has always been a part of the secondary curriculum, the real issue is that of more specific skills. Little work appears to have been done in the Philippines on the relative costs and effectiveness of training in schools as against industry. Schools apparently have not done this job very well in the past, but that does not mean that they could not do a much better job in the future with increased financing and greater attention to the needs of industry. The promotion of more training within industry might be a less expensive proposition, however. NMYC assists private industry by such means as training in-plant instructors and has stated that it will encourage private industry to take a greater share of the responsibility for training the country's manpower.

Employment statistics indicate that employment in manufacturing and construction, which are the major sectors absorbing skilled labor, has been growing by only 20,000 workers a year in recent years. It is projected, however, that manufacturing and construction could absorb about 100,000 new workers annually by 1980. This would create a major demand for trained manpower, much of which could be taught within industry. There probably will not be a general need for new training facilities beyond the Regional Manpower Training Centers and the technical institutes now being developed. But specialized facilities may be needed to serve the scientifically complex and faster growing industries such as metals which are likely to need manpower more at the level of technicians than skilled workers.

Although the leading center of rice research is in the Philippines, rice yields there are low by international standards, which suggests a need for better agricultural training. There is in fact wide agreement in the Philippines that agricultural extension work needs substantial strengthening. At present the work is fragmented among a number of different agencies whose activities are not generally coordinated, and extension workers are inadequately trained. They are required to have a B.S. degree in agriculture, but many agricultural colleges are of low quality, and the better graduates are usually hired by the private sector. Some extension workers have been well trained in the natural sciences but not in farm

20. *Education for National Development*, p. 85, and ILO, *Sharing in Development*, p. 320.

economics and extension methodology. A recent study found that extension workers remain at the hiring level without promotion for many years, and there is little in the way of career development or advancement.[21] There seems to be a need to retrain much of the staff through in-service programs as well as to improve the organization of the extension services.

Short courses in training centers for farmers have been relatively neglected in the Philippines, but the recently established Bulacan Farmers Training Center has demonstrated its effectiveness in disseminating modern rice technology. Such courses, properly designed, could teach better methods to progressive farmers and thereby supplement the work of the extension services.

In higher agricultural education there are 46 colleges and universities, most of which are in the public sector. The University of the Philippines at Los Baños has developed into a national center of recognized quality in agricultural education and research. Most of the agricultural colleges, however, suffer from a lack of qualified faculty, library, equipment, and practical instruction. Some are agricultural high schools which have been promoted to college status without sufficient upgrading of their facilities and curricula. There are more than enough agricultural graduates, but not enough with the necessary expertise.

As a start on improving the system the government will develop regional centers of quality agricultural education in each of the country's three major geographical areas. The institutions selected for development are the Central Luzon State University, the Visayas State College of Agriculture, and the Central Mindanao University. The government has not yet formulated a coherent policy to strengthen the remainder of the agricultural colleges, some of which need upgrading and others reconversion to high school status. There is also a strong case for improving the coordination of the colleges through the establishment of a National Board of Agricultural Education.

21. L. V. Carino and O. F. Sison, "Agricultural Extension: Problems of Organization and the Profession," First Agricultural Policy Conference (Los Baños: University of the Philippines, 1973).

Technical Note. Enrollment Projections

The DEC has prepared high and low enrollment projections for all three levels of education up to 1985.[22] The World Bank has prepared its own enrollment projections, using recent population projections of the NCSO. Both are shown in Table 12.4 and are based on the methodologies discussed below.

ELEMENTARY ENROLLMENTS

The DEC's high projection for elementary enrollments comes from a second degree equation derived by least squares. Since quantities such as school enrollments are generally believed to grow linearly or exponentially, this projection lacks intuitive appeal; furthermore, it leads to an enrollment ratio of 133 percent in 1980, which runs counter to the announced and highly desirable policy of reducing the enrollment ratio. Nonetheless the high projection appears to be the one being used for planning purposes.[23] The low projection is based on population projections of the BCS (the predecessor of NCSO) together with the assumption that compulsory education at the first-grade level is strictly enforced and that at each grade level enrollment will be normalized by age and therefore reduced. Clearly, the low projection is the more reasonable one.

The World Bank's projection is based on the assumption that the enrollment ratio will be brought down to 100 percent by 1980. For 1980 and 1985 the World Bank projection is lower than the DEC low projection, but it shows almost identical growth during the 1980–85 period. Depending on the vigor with which continuous progression is instituted, elementary enrollment will probably run somewhere between these two projections.

SECONDARY ENROLLMENTS

The DEC high projection for secondary enrollment is derived using the same method as that for the high elementary projection. The

22. Republic of the Philippines, Department of Education and Culture, Division of Educational Planning, "Projections for the Ten-Year Development Plan for Education" (Manila, 1975).

23. The high projection was given by NEDA in response to an item concerning future enrollments on a World Bank questionnaire.

Table 12.4. School-age Population and Enrollment, Actual and Projected, 1965–85
(In thousands)

Category	Actual 1965	Actual 1970	Actual 1974	Projected 1980	Projected 1985
Population by educational level and age group[a]					
Elementary (7-12)	5,557	6,364	6,795	7,576	8,275
Secondary (13-16)	2,945	3,661	4,113	4,584	5,023
Higher (17-20)	2,412	3,075	n.a.	4,103	4,466
Enrollment, actual and projected[b]					
Elementary	5,816	6,969	7,257		
DEC high projection				10,099	11,252
DEC low projection				8,375	9,013
World Bank projection				7,576	8,275
Secondary	1,169	1,715	1,637		
DEC high projection				3,117	4,050
DEC low projection				2,705	3,246
World Bank projection				2,659	3,215
Higher	509	638	n.a.		
DEC high projection				1,238	1,626
DEC low projection				1,137	1,364
World Bank projection				861	938
Ratio of enrollment, actual and projected, to relevant age group (in percent)[b]					
Elementary	105	110	107[c]		
DEC high projection				133	129
DEC low projection				110	109
World Bank projection				100	100
Secondary	39	47	40[c]		
DEC high projection				68	81
DEC low projection				59	65
World Bank projection				58	64
Higher	21	21	n.a.		
DEC high projection				30	36
DEC low projection				28	31
World Bank projection				21	21

n.a.: Not available.

Note: Population figures refer to calendar years. Enrollment figures refer to school year beginning in that calendar year; for example, enrollment figures for school year June 1970–March 1971 are shown under 1970.

a. The basic source of data on population is NCSO, *Age and Sex Population Projection for the Philippines by Province, 1970–2000.* The NCSO data are disaggregated by five-year age groups (0-4, 5-9, 10-14, and so on). The figures calculated here assume that the elementary group is

rate of increase in the secondary enrollment ratio that is implied is contrary to past experience and seems unreasonably high. The DEC low projection is based on the assumption that an enrollment ratio of 65 percent will be achieved by 1985, which seems reasonable.

HIGHER EDUCATION ENROLLMENTS

The DEC's projections for higher education enrollments are based upon its secondary enrollment projections, together with the assumption that past ratios of enrollment in college and past continuation rates will persist. Since secondary enrollment ratios are expected to rise, higher education enrollment ratios are projected to rise as well. The World Bank forecast assumes that the higher education enrollment ratio will remain at the constant level maintained during 1965–70. This is in accordance with stated policy, which aims to restrain the growth of higher academic education by means of the National College Entrance Examination and to promote postsecondary technical training.

---

60 percent of the 5-9 and 10-14 NCSO age group; the secondary group is 40 percent of the 10-14 and 15-19 age groups; and the higher group is 75 percent of the 15-19 age group. For 1972, for which there was no NCSO projection, the figures are by interpolation. For 1965 the figures were derived by applying five-year survival probabilities for 1965–70 (NCSO, p. 5) to 1970 age groups.

b. Actual figures for 1965 and 1970 from NEDA, *Statistical Yearbook, 1975*, p. 458. Figures for 1974–75 are unpublished preliminary estimates by NEDA; the estimate for secondary enrollment would appear to be on the low side. DEC projections are from DEC, Division of Educational Planning, "Projections for the Ten-Year Development Plan for Education" (Manila, 1975). World Bank projections are based on the following assumptions about enrollment ratios: Elementary ratio in 1975 is the same as the 1970–72 average, but is reduced to 100 percent by 1980 as a result of government policy. Secondary ratio increases by 6 percent every five years. Higher education ratio remains constant as a result of government policy.

c. NEDA estimates that the school participation rate, which is the proportion of children in the relevant age group who are enrolled in school, was 98 percent for children of elementary school age and 40 percent for children of secondary school age in 1974–75. This rate differs from the enrollment ratio because many students of secondary school age are enrolled in elementary school.

13

The Level and Allocation of Investment

THE UNEQUAL DISTRIBUTION OF BENEFITS among the population and the unbalanced pattern of sectoral development that characterized Philippine growth for much of the past three decades was closely linked to resource management policies and to the pattern of resource allocation. Although the aggregate level of resources available for investment was relatively high, output and employment growth were disappointing. Limited access to the investable resources and the concentration of investment in large-scale enterprises reinforced rather than changed the concentrated pattern of asset ownership and income distribution that existed at the time of independence.

The strategies outlined in preceding chapters for developing rural and urban areas, as well as agriculture, industry, and human resources, should help to broaden the distribution of benefits in the Philippines. If these programs are moderately successful they should, over a period of years, help speed the growth in employment opportunities and improve the level of services. But successful implementation of these programs will call for a substantial increase in the level of investment in the Philippines and for important changes in the sectoral allocation of that investment. Aggregate investment would probably have to grow by about 12 percent a year in real terms during the second half of the 1970s. The ratio of investment to gross domestic product (GDP) would have to rise from about 20 percent (the average of recent years) to no less than

25 percent by the early 1980s and thereafter remain at about that level. Within this total, the share of public investment would need to double to at least 5 percent of GDP.

An investment program of this magnitude raises three main issues regarding resource management: (a) How can the required sectoral allocation of investable resources be accomplished? (b) Can sufficient domestic resources be mobilized to carry out the program without excessive dependence on foreign financing? (c) If the needed domestic and foreign resources are not forthcoming, what are the main elements of flexibility in the investment program; that is, to what extent should the investment program be reduced, and to what extent can dependence on external foreign financing be increased? Issues dealing with resource mobilization are discussed in Chapters 14, 15, and 16, while those related to the size and allocation of investment are dealt with below.

Overview of Investment Needs

In aggregate terms the level of fixed investment in the Philippines rose from about 13 percent of GDP in the early 1950s to about 16 percent during the late 1950s and early 1960s (Table 13.1). In the latter half of the 1960s, a period of heavy investment in steel, chemicals, cement, and other intermediate goods industries, the investment rate rose to about 20 percent of GDP. Since 1970 the rate has dropped back to average about 18 percent as a result of the sluggish growth in domestic demand, the excess industrial capacity stemming from the heavy investment in the late 1960s, and the sharp increase in the cost of imported capital goods after the 1970 devaluation. Following the boom in incomes in 1973, the investment rate recovered to about 20 percent of GDP in 1974. The yearly increase in stocks has climbed steadily from a little more than 1.0 percent of GDP in the early 1950s to about 2.5 percent in the 1970s.

PAST TRENDS IN INVESTMENT

A striking feature of past development has been the high level of investment relative to output—the average incremental capital-

Table 13.1. Share of Gross Domestic Capital Formation in GDP and Incremental Capital-Output Ratios, 1950–74
(*At 1967 constant prices*)

Year	Fixed capital formation			Increase in stocks	Gross domestic capital formation	Incremental capital-output ratio[a]
	Private	Public	Total			
1950	n.a.	n.a.	14.7	1.4	16.1	2.01
1951	n.a.	n.a.	13.1	1.0	14.1	1.66
1952	n.a.	n.a.	11.9	0.9	12.8	1.57
1953	n.a.	n.a	13.8	1.3	15.1	1.73
1954	n.a.	n.a.	13.6	1.8	15.4	1.88
1955	n.a.	n.a.	13.8	1.9	15.7	2.12
1956	n.a.	n.a.	15.6	1.3	16.7	2.70
1957	n.a.	n.a.	17.6	1.5	19.1	3.55
1958	n.a.	n.a.	16.7	1.7	18.4	3.72
1959	n.a.	n.a.	18.1	1.8	19.9	5.33
1960	n.a.	n.a.	15.7	1.6	17.3	4.85
1961	n.a.	n.a.	16.5	2.0	18.5	4.98
1962	n.a.	n.a.	15.5	2.2	17.7	3.06
1963	n.a.	n.a.	16.8	2.4	19.2	4.15
1964	n.a.	n.a.	19.1	2.2	21.3	4.32
1965	n.a.	n.a.	19.0	2.2	21.2	4.73
1966	n.a.	n.a.	18.3	2.2	20.5	3.77
1967	18.9	2.2	21.1	1.9	23.0	3.79
1968	18.4	2.2	20.6	1.9	22.5	3.80
1969	17.4	2.2	19.6	1.8	21.4	3.61
1970	15.6	1.9	17.5	2.4	19.9	3.49
1971	15.9	1.6	17.5	2.1	19.6	3.55
1972	15.1	2.0	17.1	2.2	19.3	3.21
1973	15.1	2.2	17.3	2.6	19.9	3.43
1974	17.9	2.4	20.3	3.1	23.4	

n.a.: Not available.
a. Three-year moving average. The incremental capital-output ratio is defined as the ratio of fixed capital formation in the current period to the current increase in GDP over the previous period.
Source: Based on data supplied by the National Accounts Staff, Statistical Office, National Economic and Development Authority (NEDA), and Auditor General's reports.

output ratio in the 1960s was 3.9.[1] Unfortunately there are no data available on the sectoral allocation of investment during this period, so it is not possible to pinpoint the reasons for what appears

1. The incremental capital-output ratio is defined as the ratio of fixed capital formation in the current period to the increase in gross domestic product over the previous period.

to be a relatively inefficient use of resources. It is generally agreed, however, that a large share of fixed investment was concentrated in manufacturing, particularly in projects whose impact on output and employment was relatively small.

Table 13.2 presents a rough picture of the sectoral allocation of investment for the first half of the 1970s. Although the data are only estimates, they highlight several characteristics of investment in the Philippines: (a) industry (manufacturing and mining) has probably accounted for about 40 percent of total fixed investment in recent years; (b) the transport sector has had a rather significant share of investment, most of it private, primarily in transport equipment (including private automobiles) rather than public investment in infrastructure; (c) the agricultural sector has had a relatively small share of investment, no more than 10 percent of the total; and (d) only a small amount of investment has been undertaken by the public sector, about 2 percent of GDP.[2] Only in recent years has the share of public investment increased; in 1975 it had risen to about 3 percent of GDP. Previously the private sector in the Philippines undertook a large share of investment in areas that many other countries consider the responsibility of the public sector. There has thus been substantial private investment in power generation and transmission and in roads, ports, and communications facilities, although not all these have been for public use.

FUTURE LEVEL AND ALLOCATION OF INVESTMENT

There is no up-to-date government statement of the planned level and sectoral allocation of future investment.[3] This report has therefore attempted to formulate a statement of investment priori-

2. Public investment is defined here as capital expenditures by the national and local governments and by public corporations in such areas as transport, power, and public irrigation works. Specifically excluded are equity investments and loans from the public sector in industrial activities and the banking system. Also excluded, but discussed separately, is public investment in housing projects. Unfortunately there is no one series of data that adequately measures public investments in infrastructure. The data used here are a composite of infrastructure expenditures of the national government as reported by the National Economic and Development Authority (NEDA) and capital expenditures by local governments as reported in Auditor General Reports.

3. The most recent statement was in the *Four Year Development Plan, FY74–77*, which is now out of date in many respects.

Table 13.2. Sectoral Allocation of Fixed Investment Estimated for 1970-74 and Projected for 1980
(In millions of pesos at 1974 prices)

	Annual average, 1970–74						Projected, 1980					
	Amount			Percentage of GDP			Amount			Percentage of GDP		
Sector	Public	Private	Total	Public	Private	Total	Public	Private	Total	Public	Private	Total
Agriculture	170	1,400	1,570	0.2	1.6	1.8	600	3,100	3,700	0.4	2.1	2.5
Housing	... a	2,100	2,100	...	2.4	2.4	300	3,800	4,100	0.2	2.6	2.8
Mining and manufacturing	...	6,570	6,570	...	7.5	7.5	...	13,400	13,400	...	9.1	9.1
Power	180	700	880	0.2	0.8	1.0	3,350	150	3,500	2.3	0.1	2.4
Other utilities	180	80	260	0.2	0.1	0.3	450	150	600	0.3	0.1	0.4
Transport	880	2,620	3,500	1.0	3.0	4.0	1,800	4,400	6,200	1.2	3.0	4.2
Other	350	530	880	0.4	0.6	1.0	1,150	1,150	2,300	0.8	0.8	1.6
Total	1,760	14,000	15,760	2.0	16.0	18.0	7,650	26,150	33,800	5.2	17.8	23.0

... Zero or negligible.
a. Refers to housing construction by the public sector and excludes government financing through the Government Service Insurance System (GSIS) and the Social Security System (SSS) of houses built by the private sector.
Source: Data for 1970–74 are World Bank estimates; data for 1980 are World Bank projections.

ties that are considered necessary to support the sectoral development strategies outlined earlier.

Because of the need for relatively larger investment in utilities, especially in power generation and transmission, and the initiation of a number of large, capital-intensive projects in the industrial sector, a sharp rise in the investment rate will be necessary. The rate of fixed investment to GDP, which has been about 18 percent in recent years, would have to rise by about 12 percent a year and reach 23 percent of GDP in 1980; it will need to be maintained at least at that level in the first half of the 1980s. As Table 8.2 indicates, this would mean fixed public and private investment of about ₱34,000 million by 1980 at 1974 constant prices. As a result of the probable composition of investment, the incremental capital-output ratio is not expected to change significantly from the current level of about 3.4 during the next five years. Better utilization of capacity in industries such as steel, wood products, pulp and paper, and cement will tend to bring down the ratio, while capital-intensive projects with long gestation periods, such as nuclear power plants, will tend to raise it.

Successful implementation of the development strategy would result in significant increases in the rate of investment in agriculture, industry, transportation, and power. Because of the size of their current share, industry and mining would account for about a third of the total increase in investment. Nevertheless the share going to industry would decline somewhat, and successful implementation of the development strategy would increase the share going to power, agriculture, and other services.[4] At the same time public investment would become relatively more important, rising sharply from about 11 percent of the fixed total in the first half of the 1970s to about 23 percent by 1980 if the proposed programs were implemented. Similarly the share of public investment in GDP would go from an average of 2 percent in the first half of the 1970s to about 5 percent by 1980. After taking into account increases in stocks, gross capital formation in the Philippines would probably have to rise from an average of 20 percent of GDP in the first half of the 1970s to about 25 percent by 1980, and then remain there during the first half of the 1980s.

---

4. This category includes educational facilities, flood control and drainage canals, medical facilities, and commercial buildings.

Raising aggregate investment to this level will require vigorous efforts to mobilize more domestic resources. It should be possible to raise domestic savings to about 22 percent of GDP by 1980.[5] The remainder of the program would have to be financed with foreign savings, but the ratio of foreign savings to GDP would still decline from the present high level of about 4.5 percent to about 3 percent by 1980. The decline would continue in the 1980s, and by 1985 foreign savings would probably be only about 1.0 percent of GDP. Provided these external resources are available on suitable terms,[6] the task of maintaining internal and external financial stability should be manageable.

The present relatively strong dependence on foreign savings is primarily the result of the recent large increases in the price of petroleum. It will be a number of years before the Philippine economy can fully absorb these higher energy costs. Increased investment in the export sector, in import-replacing industries, and in alternate sources of energy will be required to reach that point. Some of these investments are necessarily capital intensive with large foreign exchange requirements. But a smooth transition is desirable, and attempting a sharp reduction in foreign savings in the next couple of years would have unduly disruptive effects on income and employment growth. Since finished consumer goods are now only a small proportion of total imports, and cutbacks in raw materials would have an immediate and unacceptable impact on production and employment, rapid cutbacks would have to be concentrated on imported capital goods. Such a decrease would not only hamper the Philippines' adjustment to higher energy prices but also adversely affect programs aimed at expanding productive employment opportunities.

The projected rise in the share of investment in GDP and the decline in the relative importance of foreign savings will undoubtedly not progress entirely smoothly. The actual outcome in any one year will be influenced by the world prices of capital goods, short-term changes in domestic incomes and savings, and the timing of major investment projects. The mobilization of foreign and domestic resources is discussed in subsequent chapters, but it may be helpful at this stage to give some indication of the extent to which investment may deviate from the projected trends.

5. See Chapters 14 and 15.
6. See Chapter 16.

There are several reasons why investment expenditures in any one year could be somewhat different from those projected. Of course physical investment programs may not turn out exactly as expected. Final decisions on a number of major industrial projects have not yet been made,[7] and it is therefore difficult to be precise about their timing and investment requirements. In addition, although this report argues for a major increase in investment in so-called nontraditional industrial exports by 1980, it is by no means certain that, even with the promotional policies of the government, individual Filipino entrepreneurs will feel that the potential profits outweigh the risks inherent in greater exposure in export markets. A more cautious approach among private investors may therefore result in smaller investments in industry.

For the agricultural sector, gross investment is projected to grow at about 12 percent a year, compared with an almost negligible rate of increase in the past few years. Whether this will materialize will depend on incentives for private investment and on the availability of credit. With the relaxation of credit restrictions (for example, collateral requirements) under new agricultural credit programs, effective private demand in agriculture for capital from institutional sources is probably far in excess of supply. Moreover the provision of private incentives will depend in part on the rate of progress in the public agricultural program. Hence, shortfalls in public programs may not be entirely offset by an increased demand for private investment. These and other uncertainties in the agricultural program may preclude an investment as large as planned.[8]

The total investment program of the public sector could fall short of projected levels if difficulties are encountered in project preparation and implementation. This is perhaps most likely in the power sector which requires a large buildup of projects. Such a setback could, however, be offset by programs larger than projected in other sectors, especially transport and public housing.

Any reduction in investment expenditures caused by delays in project preparation and implementation might be partially offset by substantial cost overruns, particularly for equipment in the steel, chemical, and mining industries and in the power sector. Because of long gestation periods, several large capital-intensive

7. See Chapter 6.
8. See Chapter 5.

projects in these sectors have not yet been fully developed, and no accurate estimate of their cost is established. In transportation, too, cost overruns may be an important factor that tends to raise investment needs.

These possibilities suggest that the costs of investment could vary from the projection in any one year by about 10 percent. Such a variation is of course not substantially different. If, however, investment needs exceed the projected level by 10 percent and the difference has to be met by an increased dependence on external financing, foreign borrowing requirements would be considerably above the estimated amount. In such an event, the alternative to heavy reliance on foreign capital is some combination of a reduced investment program and a higher level of domestic savings. Fortunately the Philippines appears able to adjust without seriously affecting the targets for economic growth and employment.

The kinds of adjustments that could be made in the face of excessive investment demand will depend to some extent on how the demand is manifested. Excess demand for investment in construction may have largely internal inflationary effects, and adjustments could be made, for example, by delaying some construction starts. In contrast, excess demand for machinery and equipment is apt to have much more important consequences for the balance of payments. In this case imports could be reduced by tax measures and other controls.

The Expansion of Public Sector Infrastructure Expenditures

In the Philippines public investment has historically been very low and sector accomplishments very uneven. Even though the government has in recent years been making vigorous efforts to improve the public infrastructure, facilities are still grossly inadequate. If the sectoral strategies outlined earlier are to succeed, it will be necessary to continue giving a high priority to public investment and raise it from the present level of about 3 percent of GDP to at least 5 percent by the end of the decade.

This increase is required in part because relatively larger amounts must be spent in such areas as irrigation and transport to directly support efforts to expand production. In addition, recent policy changes have given the public sector sole responsibility for developing power-generation facilities and the national power grid. This new policy, together with the government's efforts to reduce dependence on imported petroleum by developing alternative sources of electric energy, will require an increase in the share of expenditures on power from about 10 percent in recent years to about 35 percent in the future. The share allocated to transport would decline from 50 to 33 percent. Despite these changes in the composition of the public investment program, there would still be substantial growth in real terms in public investment in all sectors.

Another major change in the pattern of public investment would be to improve the regional distribution of the benefits of development. The government is already making noteworthy progress in this area, and there is likely to be a substantial shift in the geographical concentration of public investment away from Metropolitan Manila and Central Luzon to other regions such as Mindanao, Bicol, the Visayas, and the Cagayan Valley.

During the next ten years public investment outlays of about ₱76,000 million (at 1974 constant prices) would be needed, 45 percent of it in foreign exchange for imported goods and services. In the past, public investment was constrained both by insufficient funds and by the government's inadequate capacity for planning and implementation. In recent years there has been substantial progress in overcoming the problems created by the lack of funds, but, even so, a program of the above magnitude will require additional fiscal reforms in the latter part of the 1970s.[9] Moreover continued efforts are needed to improve the capacity of government agencies to plan, prepare, and implement projects, especially in such sectors as power and irrigation.

THE PAST RECORD

Public investment in the Philippines during the 1960s and early 1970s averaged about 2 percent of GNP. About 75 percent of the public investment was undertaken by the national government, 15 percent by public corporations, and 10 percent by local governments. Compared with many other developing countries, public investment in the Philippines is relatively low. Intercountry comparisons, however, are complicated by variations in

9. See Chapter 10.

the extent of government responsibility for providing infrastructure and services. As noted above, for example, the private sector undertook much of the past investment in power and telecommunications in the Philippines, but infrastructure facilities that serve the needs of the public at large have been relatively neglected. As Table 13.3 indicates, public investment outlays of 4 to 7 percent of GDP are not uncommon among countries at roughly the same per capita income level.

The low level of investment by the national and local governments and by public corporations during the 1960s resulted from a shortage of public funds from domestic sources, the public sector's weakness in preparing and implementing projects, and a concomitant lack of external financial support. During the past three or four years, however, a considerable effort has been made to overcome these bottlenecks. Government revenues have increased substantially, external assistance has burgeoned since the Consultative Group for the Philippines was formed in 1970, and the project pipeline has expanded. Public investment has therefore grown considerably during the past few years, and the ratio of public investment to GDP is now about 3 percent (Table 13.4). There has also been a dramatic increase in the official external assistance available for investment projects, which rose from US$125 million in 1970 to over US$700 million at the end of 1974.

Table 13.3. Public Capital Formation in Selected Countries

Country	Per capita GNP, 1972 (U.S. dollars)	Public capital formation[a] as percentage of GDP	Period
Philippines	220	2.2	1969
Jamaica	810	4.1	1968–70
Kenya	170	4.0	1969–71
Korea	310	7.0	1969–71
Malaysia	430	5.1	1963, 1966, and 1967
Mexico	750	3.8	1963, 1966, and 1967
Zambia	380	6.9	1968–70

a. Public capital formation is defined for Jamaica, Kenya, and Mexico as gross fixed capital formation by producers of government services; for Malaysia, Zambia, Korea, and the Philippines as gross capital formation by general government. These countries were selected on the basis of availability of data and level of economic development.

Source: Data on public capital formation is from United Nations, *Yearbook of National Income Statistics, 1972*, ST/STAT/Sec. 012, Add. 1 (1974), vols. 1 and 2. Data on GNP per capita is from the *World Bank Atlas, 1974*.

Table 13.4. Public Investment Expenditures in the Philippines

Item	1960	1965	1970	1975	Average annual increase (percent) 1960–70	1970–75	1960–75
Total public investment (millions of pesos at 1974 prices)	1,000	1,186	1,579	2,936	4.5	13.2	7.3
National government	n.a.	n.a.	1,164	2,449	n.a.	16.0	n.a.
Local governments	n.a.	n.a.	183	125	n.a.	−7.2	n.a.
Public corporations	n.a.	n.a.	232	362	n.a.	9.4	n.a.
Share of public investment in GNP (percent)	2.2	2.0	2.1	2.9	—	—	—
National government	n.a.	n.a.	1.6	2.4	—	—	—
Local governments	n.a.	n.a.	0.2	0.1	—	—	—
Public corporations	n.a.	n.a.	0.3	0.4	—	—	—

n.a.: Not available.
— Not applicable.
Source: World Bank estimates based on government construction figures in the national accounts, infrastructure expenditures reported by NEDA, and capital expenditures of local governments listed in Auditor General's reports.

Only since 1967 has reliable information been available on the allocation of public investment among sectors. More than half the total outlays went to the transport sector during FY67–75, 11 percent to irrigation, 9 percent to power and rural electrification, and 5 percent to water and sewerage. The remaining 18 percent was allocated for flood control, school construction, and other programs. The dominance of transport reflects both the government's priorities during that period and the sector's relative superiority in implementing projects. The allocation may at first glance appear unbalanced, but spending in all sectors was still insufficient.

Outlays have been unevenly distributed among the various geographic regions in the Philippines, with infrastructure investments heavily concentrated in Manila and Central Luzon. The International Labour Office (ILO) reported that "between 1965 and 1972 almost half (47.5 percent) of the total infrastructural investment took place in only two regions: Rizal (which includes Manila) and Central Luzon." [10] Perhaps even more revealing is a recent analysis

10. International Labour Office, *Sharing in Development* (Geneva: ILO, 1974), p. 196.

Table 13.5. Regional Allocations of Public Investment Expenditures per Capita on Projects During FY74–FY77
(In pesos per capita at current prices)

Region	Ongoing projects (December 1974)	Projects to be implemented in FY74	Projects to be implemented after FY74
Metropolitan Manila	754	24	167
Ilocos	174	85	145
Cagayan Valley	138	85	972
Central Luzon	375	93	107
Southern Luzon[a]	83	58	367
Bicol	146	27	282
Western Visayas	74	27	196
Central Visayas	54	31	162
Eastern Visayas	131	30	173
Western Mindanao	69	55	179
Northern Mindanao	215	99	442
Southern Mindanao	225	62	227
Philippines	243	55	255

a. Excluding Metropolitan Manila.
Source: NEDA, "Regional Distribution of Public Investment" (n.p., 1975; processed).

done by the National Economic and Development Authority (NEDA).[11] For ongoing projects in December 1974, per capita investment in Metropolitan Manila was three times higher than the national average. Central Luzon was second with a per capita investment about 50 percent higher than the national average (Table 13.5).

There is evidence that the government is attempting to redress this imbalance in its current infrastructure program. In its analysis of the FY74–77 infrastructure program, NEDA indicated a substantial shift away from Metropolitan Manila and Central Luzon to Mindanao and the Cagayan Valley. While the Visayas continue to receive less than the national average, their share per capita has improved from less than a third to over two-thirds of the national average. The short-term horizon of the analysis, together with the lumpy nature of public investment projects, caution against attaching too much significance to the particular numbers presented in Table 13.5. The overall indications are, however, that the govern-

11. "Regional Distribution of Public Investment," NEDA *Development Digest*, vols. 2–22 (April 1975).

ment is moving in the direction of a more balanced regional allocation of funds than in the past.

PUBLIC INVESTMENT NEEDS FOR THE NEXT DECADE

If the Philippines is to expand output and employment opportunities, a relatively larger share of investable resources will have to be channeled into public programs to upgrade and expand existing facilities. Particularly large investments will be needed in direct support of power and irrigation. Public investment in infrastructure will need to rise from the current level of 3 percent of GDP to 5 percent by the end of the decade and to remain at about that level during the 1980s. This would require more than a fourfold increase in real terms compared with the level of FY67–75. The average rate of increase would be about 13 percent a year in real terms during 1975–85 as against an annual average of 7 percent during 1967–75. In 1974 prices the program would require outlays of over US$10,000 million for the next ten years.

Sectoral allocation. More than just an increase in the overall level of public investment, however, the particular circumstances of the Philippines warrant a major change in the sectoral distribution of funds during the next ten years (Table 13.6). If output in the Philippine economy is to grow at about 7 percent, there must be a major increase in investment in power-generation and distribution facilities. Previously a private company, the Manila Electric Company (MECO), provided much of the power in the country, but now the government has made the National Power Corporation (NPC) responsible for all new generation facilities and decided on a substantial increase in the supply of power in Mindanao and the Visayas, which have been largely neglected by private utilities.

A detailed review of the proposed program is given in Appendix C. Briefly, however, the demand for power is expected to grow at about 11 percent a year during the next decade, so that additional generating capacity of about 5,000 megawatts (MW) will be needed during 1975–85. The government is actively engaged in a program to reduce dependence on oil-fired power plants which presently account for almost 80 percent of generating capacity. The program includes development of additional hydroelectric projects, exploitation of geothermal resources, and construction of two nuclear power plants with a combined capacity of 1,200 MW. After

Table 13.6. Investment Outlays by the Public Sector

Sector	Average annual expenditure (millions of pesos at 1974 prices)		Composition (percent)		Share in GNP (percent)	
	FY67–75[a]	FY76–85[b]	FY67–75[a]	FY76–85[b]	FY67–75[a]	FY76–85[b]
Flood control	64	460	3.7	6.1	0.1	0.3
Irrigation	186	590	10.8	7.8	0.2	0.4
Power[c]	117	2,680	6.8	35.3	0.1	1.8
Rural electrification	38	330	2.2	4.3	—	0.2
Transport	977	2,410	56.9	31.7	1.2	1.6
Water and sewerage	88	400	5.2	5.3	0.1	0.3
Other	248	730	14.4	9.6	0.4	0.4
Total	1,718	7,600	100.0	100.0	2.1	5.0

— Not applicable.
a. Actual expenditures.
b. World Bank projections.
c. Excluding rural electrification.
Sources: Actual data are derived from the infrastructure expenditures of the national government and public corporations reported by NEDA, and capital expenditures of local governments reported by the Auditor General's reports. The projections are World Bank estimates based on analysis of the individual sector programs that are reviewed in the present work.

allowance for additional transmission and distribution facilities, it is estimated that investment outlays in the power sector will have to amount to about ₱29,000 million during 1976–85 at 1974 prices (equivalent to US$3,900 million at the present exchange rate). The program would absorb about a third of public investment during the period, compared with the 7 percent allocated to the power sector during the past decade. The government recognizes that a program of this magnitude presents a major challenge. It has therefore begun to upgrade the capacity of NPC, which is mainly responsible for implementing the program.[12] These expenditures do not include the requirements of the government's ambitious rural electrification program discussed in Chapter 4.

The other major component of the proposed investment program is transportation. Transport infrastructure will have to be expanded significantly during the next decade if the amount and quality of service are to continue to rise. Public transport in Metropolitan

12. The steps being taken are discussed in more detail in Appendix C.

Manila should be improved as well as interisland shipping and farm-to-market roads to support rural development in other parts of the country. A substantial part of the current government transport program is essentially only a project list, however, with little supporting data and justification. In the absence of a meaningful review of this program,[13] a reasonable target would be to increase capital expenditures on transport by about 10 to 12 percent a year. This would total about ₱24,000 million (at 1974 prices) during FY76–85, equivalent to about 1.6 percent of GNP during the period and about one-third of the public investment program.

As discussed in Chapters 5, 6, and 7, continued expansion of irrigation facilities should receive a high priority. At this stage it seems likely that about 500,000 additional harvested hectares could be brought under irrigation with new gravity schemes operated by the National Irrigation Administration and another 250,000 hectares could be rehabilitated. In addition, some public investment expenditures would be required in the companion program to expand pump irrigation, adding about 300,000 hectares during the next ten years. Total public investment in new irrigation facilities would probably amount to about ₱5,900 million at 1974 prices during FY76–85. Although the share of public investment in irrigation would decline to about 8 percent, there would still be a threefold increase in the level of outlays over FY67–75. Although this program does not meet the entire need for additional facilities, the present constraints on constructing and operating irrigation systems make even this target optimistic.

Other sectors would continue to account for about a quarter of the overall program but would nevertheless require a more than threefold increase in the average level of investment. Because of past neglect, flood control warrants a larger share of the total, and the government has recently increased investment in this sector considerably. If this momentum is maintained, flood control would account for about 7 percent of investment during the next ten years. Similarly, the government has embarked on a large water supply and sewerage program in Metropolitan Manila and will improve the water supply in a number of provincial cities as well. That sector's

---

13. The World Bank is considering providing technical assistance to the government to review the immediate four-year infrastructure program (FY76–79) and to assist in updating the "Philippine Transport Survey" prepared in 1970 by Metra International and Sauti Consulting Engineers.

share would thus increase from less than 1 percent in FY75 to 6 percent by FY80. No substantial changes are proposed in other sectors; telecommunications will probably continue to account for less than 1 percent of public investment, schools 3 to 4 percent, and miscellaneous public works and projects 4 to 6 percent.

Financial implications. The financial implications of the proposed public investment program are considerable. In 1974 prices the program will require ₱76,000 million during FY76–85, more than four times the actual outlays during the previous ten years. Along with this substantially larger overall requirement, there would also be a significant change in the pattern of expenditure (Table 13.7). Primarily because of the increase in expenditures on power, the public corporate sector would account for almost half the program compared with its current share of about 12 percent. Local governments would maintain their share of about 4 to 5 percent of public investment, and the national government's share would decline to about 48 percent. The foreign exchange component of this program is roughly estimated to be ₱34,000 million (at 1974 prices) or US$4,500 million.

PLANNING AND IMPLEMENTING THE PROGRAM

The proposed public investment program is ambitious and, in view of the past record, there is a question as to whether the program can be fully implemented. It can succeed only if close attention is paid to project formulation and planning among the various agencies of the government and if concerted efforts are made to build up the capabilities of these agencies and of the domestic construction industry.

Table 13.7. Projected Public Investment Expenditures by Source, 1976–85
(In thousand millions of pesos at 1974 prices)

Public sector	Amount	Percent
National government	36.5	48.0
Public corporations[a]	36.5	48.0
Local governments	3.0	4.0
Total	76.0	100.0
Foreign exchange component	34.2	45.0

a. Includes the Philippine National Railways, National Power Corporation, National Electrification Administration, Metropolitan Manila Waterworks and Sewerage System.
Source: World Bank estimates.

Sector and project planning. Public sector investment planning in the Philippines has in the past suffered from poor coordination of the macro- and project-planning units within the central planning agency and a lack of adequate planning units in the various operating agencies. As a result, projects have not been grouped into sound sector programs, and the central planning authority has not had a significant influence on the individual sector programs or the intersectoral investment mix. The government has recognized this shortcoming, and NEDA has begun sectoral planning exercises in education, industry, tourism, infrastructure and utilities, agriculture, housing, health, social welfare, and foreign trade.

Because this is the first effort of its type in the Philippines, there is considerable room for improvement of the sector plans. The treatment of the individual subsectors is sketchy and overall financial planning is largely neglected, but NEDA is aware of these deficiencies and intends to remedy them in the future. Despite these weaknesses, however, NEDA's basic approach is commendable. It makes an effort to include the implementing agencies in the planning so that the final plans will have their backing, although the amount of involvement has varied considerably among agencies. The first drafts of the sector plans were reviewed in workshops including representatives from the Budget Commission and the Central Bank to translate the sector plans into budget allocations. In the future NEDA intends to emphasize longer term planning in the various sectors and to add a regional dimension to the sector plans. The eventual goal is to have the operating agencies define the sector plans and to limit NEDA's role to general guidance, coordination, and determination of intersectoral priorities.

In the past, the approved infrastructure program has usually been too large to be undertaken with available funds and implementation capacity. Priorities have thus been determined by another agency or by an agency's own capability to implement its program. Actual expenditures have usually not matched planned priorities, and the highway sector has received the major portion of the funds available for public investment. The capacities of the various agencies need to be evaluated to determine whether they can implement the proposed programs and, if not, what action should be taken to build up their capacities.

Project selection. Many considerations enter into the choice of the specific projects to be undertaken in any one year. In the past, political influence probably played an unduly large role; projects were concentrated in a few regions and, on occasion, not economically justified.

Efforts are now being made to improve the methods of selection. With the assistance of the United States Agency for International Development (USAID), an interagency team (including NEDA, the Development Academy of the Philippines, the Project and Planning Development Office, and the Presidential Economic Staff) has been developing a methodology for project ranking.[14] Using a large number of specific indicators, which are related to particular development objectives, the team ranks proposed projects according to their potential for achieving the various goals set out in the Philippines' development strategy. These indicators are weighted to give an overall performance rating, which can then be used to select projects. The goals against which projects are rated are much broader than economic efficiency as measured by traditional cost-benefit analysis; they include such objectives as job creation and a more equitable distribution of income. To determine weights for the various goals, opinion surveys asked Filipinos to rank social objectives.[15] The approach is still being developed with only experimental application, but the model could improve the process of project selection and bring the investment program in better alignment with the nation's overall development goals.

In a separate exercise, Deepak Lal has developed accounting ratios for a large number of tradable goods and the major non-traded goods for the Philippine economy.[16] These ratios, when divided into the market price of a good, yield the accounting price, which is an estimate of the social value as distinct from the market value of the commodity or service. The two prices often diverge due

14. The following discussion is based on a summary of the preliminary report of the "Methodology for Project Ranking," prepared by the Project Economic Staff of NEDA.

15. The weights worked out from these surveys are as follows: promotion of social development, 28 percent; more equitable distribution of income and wealth, 26 percent; maximum feasible economic growth, 19 percent; maximum use of labor force, 19 percent; preservation of environmental stability, 8 percent. Of course such ranking is arbitrary since an individual's evaluation of a social goal may well differ from its value to society at large.

16. Deepak, Lal, *Men or Machines: A Philippine Case Study of Labor/Capital Substitution in Road Construction* (Geneva: ILO; forthcoming).

to market distortions.[17] Although Lal's study made use of these shadow prices to evaluate alternative production techniques for a road project, they could be used to evaluate other investment projects in the Philippines.

Project implementation and monitoring. Project implementation was frequently poor in the past, with long delays in initiating projects and in construction schedules that in turn led to cost overruns. Reasons for this rather poor record include a shortage of financial resources, delays in release of budgeted funds, the release of funds for nonapproved projects, poor maintenance and organization of government-owned equipment, and weak project management and implementation capacity.

The poor fiscal position of the national government has been largely overcome, but delays in releasing funds when needed have persisted. Because of administrative delays and the weakness of the link between approved programs and the budget, planned priorities were not always those that were funded. In the most recent report of the Project Monitoring Service of NEDA, however, the funding problem, including inadequate and delayed releases, was estimated to account for only 7 percent of the delays encountered in ongoing projects and thus seems to have dwindled as a serious source of project delay. Nevertheless some implementing agencies continue to identify budget releases as a problem.

In an effort to further streamline the budgetary process, the government has recently implemented a system of automatic cash releases. This empowers the Budget Commission to release funds for approved programs without approval from the Office of the President for quarterly releases as was the previous practice. It is too early to see what effect this modification might have, but obtaining releases for the approved annual program and the budget should now be easier. In general, it should strengthen the relationship between the approved program and the budget.

The government is attempting to strengthen other areas of project implementation as well. It has established a system of

17. The accounting prices were derived along the lines of the Organisation for Economic Co-operation and Development (OECD) manual, *Social Cost-Benefit Analysis,* except that a somewhat different means of measurement was used. See I. M. D. Little and J. A. Mirrlees, *Manual of Industrial Project Analysis in Developing Countries,* vol. 2, *Social Cost-Benefit Analysis* (Paris: Development Center of the OECD, 1969).

sector and regional specialists to monitor and identify problems in ongoing projects. This system includes Presidential Regional Officers for Development (PRODs) and Coordinating Officers for Program Execution (COPEs) under the Office of the President. A PROD in every region is responsible for seeing that projects are operating on time, within the budget, and according to standard. The line agency project officers call problems to the PROD's attention, and the PROD attempts to resolve the problem himself, if possible, or report it to the Office of the President. The PRODs operate without any official budget and do not receive any additional remuneration for carrying out this responsibility. The COPEs monitor at the national level, with a senior official to see that programs or projects are implemented on schedule and that interdepartmental programs escape the normal bureaucratic hazards.

More structured and formalized monitoring is undertaken by the line agencies providing data to the National Computer Center, which maintains a standard and efficient project-monitoring format. Actual target and variance data are recorded for the key projects and programs on a monthly basis. In addition, NEDA recently created the Project Monitoring Service (PMS) to monitor the implementation of ongoing projects. It functions similarly to the defunct Infrastructure Operations Center in that it relies on reports from the line agencies on the status of its projects. The PMS issues quarterly reports on national development programs, identifies major problem areas, and makes recommendations to the NEDA board for improving the process of implementation. The Department of Public Works, Transportation, and Communication is now starting its own data bank, apparently to provide the basis for both planning and implementing the infrastructure projects under its Planning and Project Development Office.

These monitoring systems usually operate independently of each other, and there is both a duplication of effort and a failure to take advantage of each other's efforts. It is not clear at present what the government's intentions are regarding the long-term role of the monitoring agencies, but there is a strong case for improving communication and coordination among them. The PMS, for instance, could make use of the data generated by the National Computer Center's monitoring service as well as of the reports of PRODs on the problems they encounter in the field.

The administrative capacity of the line agencies responsible for implementing major parts of the public investment program is crucial for the proposed development program. In areas such as power and irrigation, the proposed increases in investment will undoubtedly strain this capacity. To keep the programs on schedule the government will have to give close attention to the needs of the technical and managerial staff and to the planning and administrative procedures of the line agencies.

Influencing the Pattern of Private Investment

Even though the relative importance of public investment should rise in the future, the major portion of total investment will continue to be provided by the private sector. The creation of new public infrastructure and the improvement of existing facilities will have an important indirect effect on the pattern of private investment. Nonetheless the government will have to depend primarily on indirect methods of influencing investment decisions. Credit and interest rate policies will of course have considerable bearing, and these as well as the level and allocation of private investment are discussed in the next chapter. The fiscal incentives and administrative controls over domestic and foreign private investment that are operated by the Board of Investments (BOI) will also have an important influence.

INVESTMENT INCENTIVES

Investment incentives have been used in the Philippines since the early 1950s as a major tool to mobilize domestic and foreign resources and channel them into socially desirable directions. The present incentives were established by the Investment Incentives Act of 1967 and the Export Incentives Act of 1970 and amended by presidential decrees. They are administered by the BOI, which also prepares annual investment and export priority plans. Apart from nonmeasurable rights and guarantees, investment incentives consist of a number of tax exemptions and deductions summarized in Table 13.8. These incentives are used to encourage investment in manufacturing, mining, some agricultural activities, fisheries, exports, tourism, and public utilities.

In all these areas "preferred" activities to which incentives apply are those included in the current Investment Priorities Plan (IPP)

Table 13.8. Summary of Incentives under the Investment Incentives Act and Export Incentives Act as Amended by Presidential Decree Nos. 92 and 485

Rights and guarantees to registered enterprises	Export Incentives Act			Investment Incentives Act		
				Filipino-owned		Foreign-owned pioneer
	Export producer	Export trader	Service exporter	Pioneer	Nonpioneer	
Basic rights and guarantees under the constitution	X	X	X	X	X	X
Right to repatriate investments and remit earnings*	X	X	X	X	X	X
Right to remit foreign exchange to service foreign loans and obligations arising from technological assistance contracts*	X	X	X	X	X	X
Freedom from expropriation of investment	X	X	X	X	X	X
Freedom from requisition of investment, except in event of war or national emergency and only for the duration thereof	X		X	X	X	X
Deduction of organizational and preoperational expenses from taxable income over a period of not more than ten years from start of operation				X	X	X
Deduction of labor-training expenses from taxable income equivalent to half of expenses but not more than 10 percent of direct labor wage				X	X	X
Accelerated depreciation	X[a]			X	X	X
Carry-over as deduction from taxable income of net operating losses incurred in any of the first ten years immediately following the year of such loss	X[b]	X[b]		X	X	X
Exemption from tariff duties and compensating tax on importations of machinery, equipment, and spare parts	X[a,c,d]		X[e]	X[d]	X[c]	X[d]
Tax credit equivalent to 100 percent of the value of compensating tax and customs duties that would have been paid on machinery, equipment, and spare parts (purchased from a domestic manufacturer) had these items been imported	X[a]		X[e]	X[d]	X[c]	
Tax credit for tax withheld on interest payments on foreign loans provided such credit is not enjoyed by lender-remittee in his country and registered enterprise has assumed liability for tax payment	X[a]			X	X	X

Incentive						
Right to employ foreign nationals in supervisory technical or advisory positions within five years from registration	X			X	X	X
Deduction from taxable income in the year reinvestment was made of a certain percentage of the amount of undistributed profits or surplus transferred to capital stock for procurement of machinery and equipment and other expansion				X	X	X
Antidumping protection	X[a]			X	X	X
Protection from government competition	X[a]			X	X	X
Exemption from all taxes under the National Internal Revenue Code, except income tax on a gradually diminishing percentage	X[f]			X	X	
Postoperative tariff protection	X[f]			X	X	
Tax credits equivalent to sales, compensating and specific taxes and duties on supplies, raw materials, and semimanufactured products used in the manufacture, processing, or production of export products	X		X[g]	X	X	X
Additional deduction from taxable income of direct labor cost and local raw materials used in the manufacture of export products but not exceeding 25 percent of total export revenues for producers, 10 percent for traders, and 50 percent for service exporters	X[h]	X	X	X	X[l]	X[l]
Preference in grant of government loans	X[a,j]	X[l]	X[l]	X	X[l]	X
Employment of foreign nationals within five years from operation or even after said period in exceptional cases	X[f]	X		X		X
Exemption from export and stabilization taxes	X	X				
Additional deduction from taxable income of 10 percent of incremental export sales	X[b,k]	X[b,k]				
Additional incentives whenever processing or manufacturing plant is located in an area designated by BOI as necessary for proper dispersal of industry or which is deficient in infrastructures, public utilities, and other facilities.	X[l]					

(Table continued next page)

Table 13.8 (continued)

Incentives to investors	Export Incentives Act						Investment Incentives Act			
	Filipino			Foreign			Filipino		Foreign	
	Export producer	Export trader	Service exporter	Export producer	Export trader	Service exporter	Pioneer	Nonpioneer	Pioneer	Nonpioneer
Basic rights and guarantees	X	X	X	X	X	X	X	X	X	X
Right to repatriate investments and remit earnings*	X	X	X	X	X	X	X	X	X	X
Freedom from expropriation of investments	X	X	X	X	X	X	X	X	X	X
Freedom from requisition of investments	X	X	X	X	X	X	X	X	X	X
Protection of patents and other proprietary rights	X	X	X	X	X	X	X	X	X	X
Exemption from capital gains tax on disposition of capital assets provided proceeds of sales are invested in new issues of capital stock of a registered enterprise within six months from the date gains were realized	X[m]	X	X	X	X	X	X	X	X[m]	X
Tax allowance to the extent of actual investment but not to exceed 10 percent of taxable income	X[f]						X			

Tax exemption on sale of stock dividends provided sale occurs within seven years from date of registration	X^t	X
Preference in grant of GSIS and SSS loans for purchase of shares (for members only)	X^a	X X

* Subject to Central Bank regulations.

a. Applicable only to all projects for expansion and to both pioneer and nonpioneer projects listed in the Export Priorities Plan.

b. Applicable whenever a registered export producer or export trader shall use a brand name for an export product that distinguishes it from products produced outside the Philippines.

c. Applicable to new and expanding nonpioneer projects with total assets not exceeding ₱500,000 for the first two years of commercial operation. Nonpioneer projects with assets exceeding said amount and expanding nonpioneer projects with less than 20 percent return on equity are entitled only to reduced tariff and compensating tax, on a deferred payment basis for a period not exceeding ten years. Expanding nonpioneer projects with 20 percent or greater return on equity shall be entitled to mere deferment of taxes and duties without any reduction thereof.

d. Applicable to new or expanding pioneer projects with less than 20 percent return on equity. Expanding pioneer projects with 20 percent or greater return on equity and existing pioneer projects desiring to replace and modernize their facilities are entitled to mere deferment of taxes and duties without any reduction thereof.

e. Same as note g below but limited to expansion projects only and to service exporters catering primarily to foreign tourists.

f. Provided registered export producer is engaged in a pioneer area.

g. Applicable to service exporters producing and exporting television and motion pictures or musical recordings.

h. Applicable to all registered export producers except foreign firms exporting 70 percent of their productions.

i. In the case of traditional export, local raw material component is not included in the computation of said deduction.

j. Applicable to enterprises at least 60 percent Filipino-owned.

k. Applicable whenever financial assistance is extended by export trader to export producers in an amount equivalent to not less than 20 percent of export trader's export sales during the year.

l. Additional incentives consist of using an amount equivalent to double the export producer's direct labor cost in applying the reduced income tax formula and/or tax credit on infrastructure.

m. Exemption under sec. 6(b) of Republic Act 5186 is applicable only to Filipino investors in pioneer projects.

Source: Board of Investments (BOI), *Philippine Progress,* vol. 8, 2d quarter, 1974.

331

and the Export Priorities Plan (EPP). All industrial activities that are not included in the list of "overcrowded industries" are potentially preferred.[18] They must be included in the IPP or EPP, however, in order to be registered with BOI and thus eligible for incentives. Since about one-fourth the industrial sector (in terms or value of output) falls in the category of overcrowded industries, it is clear that by far the greater part is either explicitly (through priorities plans) or potentially eligible for incentives. At present about 130 subsectors under the IPP and 280 under the EPP are listed as investment priority areas, as against 40 overcrowded industries.[19]

Size and cost of investment incentives. It is difficult to assess with any degree of accuracy the real cost of tax reliefs granted by the government, since the data are simply nonexistent. According to one estimate, the total tax forgiveness on industrial investment as a result of general and special sectoral incentives amounted in 1965–68 to ₱430 million, or ₱108 million per year, which was about 20 percent of gross investment in those years. The same ratio for BOI-registered projects in 1969–72 was estimated at 15 percent.[20] This decline is attributed partly to the fact that the textile industry—the greatest beneficiary of incentives during 1965–68—enjoyed no benefits during 1970–72 after it was classified as overcrowded.

The relative incidence of fiscal incentives has probably risen

18. Overcrowded industries are those with a capacity deemed sufficient to cover domestic and external demand: processed meat, coffee and cocoa, milled flour and sugar, soft drinks, beer, alcoholic drinks, cordage, tanned leather, rubber tires, matches, paints and varnishes, ammonium sulphate (excluding urea), complex and mixed fertilizers, superphosphate (with qualifications), paper (nonintegrated plants), cement, soap and detergents, cold-rolled metal, iron sheets, pipes, steel wires, plated tin, bar mills, copper wires, nails, liquefied petroleum gas cylinders, room air conditioners; the assembly of automobiles, trucks, and tractors; electric and gas stoves, refrigerators, sewing machines, fluorescent ballasts, light bulbs, pencils, soybean oil and meal, radios, phonographs, and storage batteries.

19. Actual projects under the sixth EPP number 61.

20. See World Bank, "Industrial Development Problems and Prospects in the Philippines," restricted-circulation internal report no. 280-PH (March 19, 1974), pp. 23–24 and tables II-8 and II-9. This may be an underestimate, however, since it is derived from preinvestment studies, which tend to minimize the size of fiscal savings for the investor. The ratio would certainly be higher if more projects were covered.

again since 1972; their scope has broadened, and investment has increased in capital-intensive and exporting sectors where the cumulative value of tax relief has been the greatest. In a large copper smelting and refining project now under consideration with BOI, for instance, the total investment cost has been estimated at US$239 million with incentives, and US$284 million without incentives; US$45 million worth of taxes forgiven represents a savings of 16 percent of the total project cost for the investor. For the government, this represents a clear-cut loss of revenue except that the project would probably not have been financed in the absence of incentives. The loss will presumably be partly offset by the increase in revenue after the expiration of incentives and by the secondary growth effects of the project. Whether there will be a net loss for the national economy depends on whether the amount saved (or foregone) will be invested in a preferred area.

The initial net revenue loss for the government probably amounts to 12 to 15 percent of the total cost of investments effected through government channels. In the Philippines 60 to 70 percent of the total cost of most large-scale projects relates to imports of equipment and other inputs. Since the minimum import duty is 10 percent and the compensating sales tax 7 percent of the c.i.f. value (cost, insurance, and freight) augmented by import duty, the tax relief on this account alone will amount to at least 10.5 to 12.5 percent of total project cost. Other tax exemptions make up the remainder. Owing to the long duration of postoperative incentives, an additional revenue loss builds up after a project has started to function.

Economic effects of investment incentives.   There is no doubt that favored investments (that is, of BOI-registered projects) make up a preponderant and growing share of total investment in the large-scale sector, although it would be difficult to document this for the years since 1972.[21] The implied investment requirements for all BOI projects (approved, registered, applied for, or planned, and as such included in the eighth IPP or sixth EPP) for 1976 would total ₱6,600 million at 1974 prices, perhaps four-fifths of total investment needs in organized industry in that year. From past experience, however, it can be safely assumed that actual BOI-spon-

---

21. Most BOI investment statistics relate to planned rather than actual investment. Moreover, the project coverage in the reporting system has usually been less than 50 percent.

sored investments will amount to much less than ₱6,600 million in 1976, though much more than the estimated annual levels of ₱1,500 million in the early 1970s (in 1974 prices).

The actual increment in investments that was or will be induced by the benefits associated with tax and other concessions is of course not known. Cursory evidence based on personal interviews with businessmen and on knowledge of prevailing profit rates in major investment areas seems to suggest that much of the investment would have been effected even without incentives. Equally important influences—though not actually fiscal benefits—seem to be factors such as preferred access to institutional finance and foreign exchange.

The way in which the incentives system influences the use of productive factors, employment creation, and industrial exports is also significant. The incentives are understandably geared to making investments more attractive by enhancing their profitability, but this is done primarily by cheapening the inputs, including imports and capital. Only general tax exemptions, the deduction of preoperational expenses, the additional deduction of incremental export sales, and the carry-over of net operating losses bear on profitability via output or sales levels. Except for labor, most inputs—especially capital equipment—are imported. The mere existence of input-oriented incentives thus produces a bias toward the use of capital and imported components. The relative net gain accruing to the investor enjoying tax forgiveness is directly proportional to the size and capital intensity of a project.

The following benefits are directly or indirectly related to the use of capital and, in fact, encourage it: exemption from customs duties and compensating taxes on imported machinery, equipment, and spare parts; tax credit for locally purchased machinery; accelerated depreciation; reinvestment allowance; reimbursement of infrastructure costs; double deduction of shipping costs; and tax credit for interest withheld on foreign loans. The share of these capital-biased benefits in all benefits provided by the incentives system is overwhelming, as can be seen from Table 13.9.

In 1970–72 capital-favoring incentives accounted for ₱229 million out of ₱285 million, or 80 percent of the total estimated amount of tax relief enjoyed by BOI projects. To counterbalance this capital bias somewhat the policymakers have devised certain labor-favoring incentives. Registered enterprises are entitled to deduct from their

Table 13.9 Estimate of Incentives Availed of by Projects Registered with the Board of Investments, 1970–72
(In millions of pesos)

Category	1970	1971	1972	Total
Capital-related incentives				
Transport duties on machinery	11.1	37.0	32.7	80.8
Compensating tax on imported machinery	7.3	23.2	10.8	41.3
Tax credit for locally produced machinery	1.0	0.3	...	1.3
Accelerated depreciation	1.4	11.5	3.7	16.6
Double deduction of shipping cost	3.8	6.2	4.0	14.0
Reinvestment allowance	38.3	29.8	6.6	74.7
Tax credit for tax on foreign loans interest	0.1	0.0	0.1	0.2
Total	63.0	108.0	57.9	228.9
Other incentives				
Preoperating expenses	3.0	0.5	0.1	3.6
Double deduction of promotional expenses	0.2	0.2	0.2	0.6
Net loss carry-over	2.6	2.4	0.2	5.2
Compensating tax on imported raw materials	1.6	13.1	7.6	22.3
Sales tax	12.3	2.1	4.5	18.9
Tax credit for exported finished products	0.9	4.1	0.1	5.1
Total	20.6	22.4	12.7	55.7
Total value of tax relief	83.6	130.4	70.6	284.6
Capital-related incentives as percent of total	75	83	82	80

Source: BOI, statistical appendixes to the fourth, fifth, and sixth Investment Priorities Plan. The number of reporting firms was 75 in 1970, 105 in 1971, and 70 in 1972.

taxable income half their labor-training expenses, up to 10 percent of the direct wage. In addition, they may deduct from taxable income the cost of direct labor and local raw materials used in the manufacture of export products as long as it does not exceed 25 percent of total export revenues for producers, 10 percent for traders, and 50 percent for service exporters. The first provision has been little used so far; and the second, introduced in 1973, will probably not have much impact on the use of labor for two reasons: (a) in many cases domestic raw materials alone are apt to approach the ceiling of 25 percent of total export value, leaving no allowance for the use of labor; and (b) the real weight of this measure is limited to a maximum of 8.75 percent of gross export sales (equivalent to the 25 percent income deduction), to which a tax rate of 35 percent is applied, and this maximum can be achieved only by firms with export profit margins of at least 25 percent of gross sales.

The relative importance of this measure is even smaller for enterprises producing for both domestic and export markets.

In another attempt to reduce the capital-favoring effect of incentives the BOI has imposed conditions on a relatively large number of industries. Unless a new project generates at least one job for every US$4,000 worth of imported equipment, it must earn through exports within five years the foreign exchange used in excess of US$4,000 per job created. The purpose of this condition is to make new projects in capital-intensive industries such as petrochemicals, pulp and paper, nickel and copper somewhat less advantageous, and at the same time give more weight to employment and export criteria in project selection. This provision is applied only to selected industries and is therefore unlikely to divert many resources from capital-intensive to labor-intensive sectors. Moreover it is difficult to understand the rationale for setting a uniform limit of US$4,000 worth of imported equipment per job in a variety of industries, each one of which has a different economic and technological profile. In addition, an industry should not be lead to undersell for export to be eligible for other benefits, and then seek to recover the profit loss through higher prices in the domestic market.

The need for revising the incentives system. The above analysis, together with the discussion of export incentives in Chapter 9, suggests that a thorough overhaul of the incentives system is needed. It will not be an easy undertaking, considering the complex interests involved. Any concrete proposals for a change in the system will have to be based on a comprehensive study, but a few comments can be offered on the principles of such a change.

It is easy to agree that investment incentives should be made less costly, more effective, and administratively more manageable. But what the system needs most is to focus on very specific goals. Employment creation and export expansion deserve the highest priority; a rapid expansion in labor-intensive exports is probably the single most important part of a future industrial strategy since the Philippines' comparative advantage lies here. The incentive system should be instrumental in pursuing these priorities.

Such an approach would imply a major restructuring of the present system. This could be done by changing either the selection of industries eligible for incentives or the incentives themselves.

A combination of both kinds of change is possible and perhaps preferable, particularly during the transitional period.

Under the first course, incentives would ultimately be confined to the industries complying with certain labor-intensity criteria and to exporting industries (other than extractive). Some improvements along this line could be made without much delay. The distinction between pioneer and nonpioneer project categories could be removed, since it is by no means clear why a certain product should enjoy benefits merely because it has not previously been manufactured in the Philippines, while another, perhaps more essential product should not. The list of overcrowded industries could be revised on the basis of recent changes in the rate of capacity utilization in individual manufacturing industries. More industries could be taken off the list of preferred activities on the basis of certain criteria (such as profit margins constantly above a certain level or above the average).

Restructuring the existing incentives through changing their composition and relative importance could also be effected gradually. In general the duration of tax holidays should be reduced. The National Internal Revenue Code currently grants an exemption from all taxes except the income tax at a 100 percent rate during the first five years and a diminishing rate for another ten years. Some of the incentives favoring the use of capital could be reduced or abolished, and new powerful incentives favoring the use of labor could be introduced. One example of a direct employment incentive would be an income tax deduction equivalent to perhaps 200 percent of the annual wage bill of production workers earning less than a certain amount per month; [22] another would be a direct employment subsidy. The revised system should also provide for a much more pronounced differential between export and other incentives in favor of the former. Under certain conditions a transfer of incentives should be allowed; for example, the main contractor should be entitled (or perhaps compelled) to pass on to his subcontractors a part of the benefits accorded him. Finally, the whole process of restructuring incentives could be made less painful by transforming some of the tax exemptions into tax deferrals.

22. This idea is proposed by Gerardo Sicat, *Economic Policy and Philippine Development* (Manila: University of the Philippines, 1972), pp. 46–51.

THE ROLE OF DIRECT FOREIGN INVESTMENT

In recent years the government has been attempting to attract a larger amount of direct foreign investment to the Philippines, and this drive appears to be succeeding. Since 1972 there has been a sharp increase in new commitments and in actual net inflows, reversing the pattern of net outflows that had prevailed for the previous fifteen years. Foreign companies are investing in such export ventures as component parts for automobiles, textiles, and other manufactured products. The sheer volume of investment required for the proposed projects in mineral ore processing, fertilizer production, and other major import-replacing projects will necessitate much larger inflows of direct foreign investment in the next decade.

Past pattern of direct foreign investment. Gross direct investment inflows totaled US$1,400 million during 1955–70, and related outflows were US$1,780 million, leaving a net outflow of about US$380 million.[23] Nearly half the firms surveyed had foreign equity participation, and its share was over 60 percent in about a quarter of them. Overall, foreign equity investment accounted for 40 percent of the total equity capital of all firms.[24] About four-fifths of the foreign investments were owned by U.S. nationals as a result of special postcolonial privileges granted U.S. investors. Nearly three-fourths of the total foreign investments were in mining and import-substituting manufacturing. Foreign firms made little attempt to take advantage of the relatively cheap labor and to produce manufactured goods for export, which is a development strategy widely followed in neighboring countries such as Korea and the Republic of China.

Incentives for foreign investors. The government has recently liberalized the rules for foreign investment to broaden the scope of incentives in desirable business activities. The BOI implements the general incentive system for foreign investments under three

23. See Government of the Philippines, *Inter-agency Study on Foreign Investments,* June 1972.

24. A similar study based on a survey of the nonfinancial corporate sector in 1964 and 1965 indicates foreign equity was about 32 percent of the total equity capital of the reporting firms. See Niceto S. Poblador, "Foreign Investment in the Major Nonfinancial Corporate Sector of the Philippines, 1964 and 1965" (Quezon City: University of the Philippines School of Economics, 1971; processed).

laws: the Investment Incentive Act, the Export Incentive Act, and the Foreign Business Regulation Law. Full foreign ownership is allowed for companies with a pioneer status, those that export 70 percent of their output, those in the Export Processing Zones, and those that are active in areas which are not "overcrowded" and that do not conflict with the nationality requirements of the Philippine constitution and nationalization laws. In the non-pioneer industries foreign ownership is limited to 40 percent. Foreign investors are entitled to certain basic rights and guarantees which include: repatriation of investment and remittance of profits, interest payments, and repayments of loans; guarantees against expropriation and requisition; protection from and action against foreign dumping; preferential treatment of registered enterprises by the government's financial institutions in extending loans; and provision for employment of foreign nationals for a period of five years.

Apart from these general incentives, there are various fiscal incentives to foreign investors which depend on the nature of the firm's activities. Under the National Internal Revenue Code pioneer firms are entitled to exemption from all taxes except income tax and postoperative tariff protection. Exporting firms enjoy additional privileges, including tax credits on taxes and duties paid on supplies, raw materials, and semimanufactured products; additional deductions from taxable income of the cost of direct labor and local raw materials (which cannot exceed 25 percent of total export earnings); and exemption from export taxes, imposts, or fees. Other fiscal incentives which are applicable to nonpioneer enterprises are summarized in Table 13.8.

Overall, the general as well as fiscal incentives for foreign investments in the Philippines appear competitive with those in other Southeast Asian countries.[25] Nevertheless the chief determinant of foreign investment flows, particularly direct investment, is apparently not fiscal inducements. According to a study of foreign investment in Singapore, investment decisions are generally made on the basis of the long-term outlook for political and economic

25. See the report of the Government of the Philippines, "Comparison of Laws and Regulations on Foreign Investment of Asian Countries," in *The Study of Private Foreign Investments in the Philippines* (Manila: BOI, 1972). The countries used for comparison are Hong Kong, Indonesia, Republic of Korea, Malaysia, Singapore, the Republic of China, and Thailand.

stability in the host country rather than on the basis of tax incentives.[26]

In the last few years foreign investments registered with the BOI have increased sharply; commitments jumped from US$30 million in 1972 to US$63 million in 1973 and almost quadrupled to US$234 million in 1974. More than half these investments were in mining, mineral processing, and chemical-based industries; there was also a trend toward agro-based enterprises. Data on foreign investments by country of origin reveal the increasing importance of Japanese and European investors in the Philippines. In 1974, 35 percent of the total direct investments were from Japan and about 18 percent each from the United States and Europe. The prospects for a continued increase in direct foreign investments appear promising in view of the current level of interest in the Philippines among potential investors and the opportunities for participation in the proposed major projects in industry and mining. These projects might involve a total investment of about US$4,600 million at 1974 prices in the next decade and require a considerable amount of foreign equity participation. If these projects materialize, the total of private foreign investments would provide a net inflow of about US$150 million a year during the decade.

The Role of the Construction Industry

If the proposed investment program for the Philippines is to be successfully implemented, the construction industry will have to expand by about 12 percent a year during 1975–85. This rapid growth would offer important opportunities for expanding productive employment in the economy. The sector could be creating close to 100,000 jobs a year in the 1980s, which would be a major contribution in both rural and urban areas. If this potential is to be realized, however, and if construction is not to become a bottleneck to implementing the investment program, government policies will need to encourage the orderly expansion of the sector.

26. Helen Hughes and You Poh Seng, eds., *Foreign Investment and Industrialization in Singapore* (Canberra: Australian National University Press, 1969), p. 183. See also Thomas W. Allen, *Direct Investment of U.S. Enterprises in Southeast Asia* (New York: Scott, 1973).

GENERAL CHARACTERISTICS OF THE INDUSTRY

The potential future contribution of the construction sector contrasts sharply with its actual performance in the past. One of the most striking features of the industry was its relatively small contribution to value added and employment during the 1960s, especially when compared with other countries in Southeast Asia. This was not always the case. In the postwar reconstruction period in the early 1950s, for example, the construction sector accounted for about 6 percent of GNP, and the share of construction in gross fixed capital formation was about 80 percent. But the industry stagnated during the 1950s with most of the new investment in the form of equipment. Its decline in relative importance continued in the 1960s, and by 1970 it accounted for little more than 2 percent of GNP, employed only about 3 percent of the labor force, and construction expenditures accounted for less than 30 percent of fixed investment. Since 1970 there has been an encouraging reversal of these trends. Value added by construction has grown by an average of about 8 percent a year in real terms, so that its share in GNP has begun to rise, and the share of fixed investment in the form of construction has increased to 40 percent. But the labor force in the sector has not yet shown a significant increase and remains at about the 1970 level of 400,000 workers.

An important characteristic of construction employment is the relatively low level of skill required. The proportion of manual workers and craftsmen to the total employed has been 90 percent or more, at least since the mid-1960s. Moreover, there is a high percentage of wage and salary employment in construction—consistently above 90 percent. By providing many jobs for unskilled workers, the sector has probably contributed to a more equal size distribution of income. But its contribution to a more equal regional distribution of income has probably been rather limited because of the concentration of investment activity in Manila and Central Luzon. The industry is also characterized by a large number of small contractors. Among a group of 1,109 contractors licensed in the Philippines in 1972, some 870 of them (almost 80 percent) had a net worth of less than ₱500,000 and 450 less than ₱50,000. Only one contractor had a net worth of more than ₱100 million.

Table 13.10. Projected Employment in the Construction Sector
(In thousands of persons)

Sector	1975	1980	1985
Public infrastructure	100	180	350
Housing	100	150	250
Other private construction	200	300	400
Total	400	630	1,000

Note: For public infrastructure and housing, the projection is based on the estimate in the ILO report, *Sharing in Development,* pp. 198-202, that, at 1967 prices, ₱1,000 expended on public infrastructure created approximately 25 man-days of employment. Dividing this ratio into actual expenditures on public infrastructure and housing in 1975 gave the base employment estimates of 100,000 in public infrastructure and 100,000 in housing. Because of the increase in the relative importance of power expenditures in future public investment—and hence an equipment component larger on average than the construction component—this man-day ratio was projected to drop to 20 by 1985 for public infrastructure. For housing it was assumed to remain at about 25 man-days per ₱1,000 expended.
Source: World Bank estimates.

THE POTENTIAL CONTRIBUTION OF CONSTRUCTION TO EMPLOYMENT

With an acceleration in the investment program along the lines proposed here, the construction sector could play a major role in employment creation in the decade ahead. Its precise impact will depend on the extent to which the productivity of construction labor rises, which in turn depends largely on the techniques used. According to World Bank estimates, the proposed investment program could result in an increase in construction employment of about 10 percent a year during 1975–85.

As Table 13.10 indicates, a substantial part of the increase could be expected to come from the proposed public infrastructure program and expanded investment in housing. It is estimated that ₱1,000 (at 1967 prices) spent on government infrastructure created between 40 and 50 man-days of work during 1967–72, although there was a downward trend over this period.[27] Because of the increasing relative importance of investments in power equipment, this decline may continue to about 20 man-days by 1985, but even so the proposed public investment program would account for an average of 25,000 new jobs a year during 1975–85. Employment on public works projects would rise to an estimated 350,000 by 1985, and in residential construction it could rise from the present level

27. ILO, *Sharing in Development;* see especially ch. 6.

of 100,000 to about 250,000 by 1985. If a somewhat slower growth in employment is assumed for private construction activity, total employment in construction could rise to about 1 million workers by 1985 compared with about 400,000 at present. By 1985 the sector could be absorbing 15 percent of new entrants into the labor force. Employment could be somewhat higher with the use of labor-intensive techniques, particularly for large earth-moving jobs on projects such as highways, irrigation, and flood control.

SCOPE FOR LABOR-INTENSIVE TECHNIQUES

The government has demonstrated considerable interest in labor-intensive techniques and in 1972 established a committee in the Department of Public Works, Transportation, and Communication to study their use in public works to help solve unemployment. The government supported extensive use of labor-intensive techniques on some projects, and its guidelines on the construction of feeder roads require that, as far as possible, these techniques be given preference. A presidential decree is being drafted which would propose the use of labor-intensive methods whenever it would not impair the structural integrity of the project, would not increase the financial cost by more than 10 percent over capital-intensive methods, and would not significantly divert manpower from the labor required for agricultural production.

Aside from this formal support, in 1972 the Bureau of Public Works, with the assistance of the ILO, undertook a relatively small pilot project that used labor-intensive methods to reconstruct about 750 meters of flood control levees which had been washed out. The project demonstrated that labor-intensive techniques could compete favorably with traditional capital-intensive methods, and as a result the committee studying the intensive use of labor endorsed a manual for constructing levees in this way.

More recently a pilot project was undertaken that involved field experiments with labor-intensive techniques on the Capas-Botolan road construction. The project was carried out in collaboration with the ILO and compared capital-intensive techniques with both traditional and modified labor-intensive techniques at both market and shadow prices.[28] A basic conclusion of the study was that the

---

28. The project and its results are discussed in detail in Lal, *Men or Machines*.

Table 13.11. Comparison of Employment Effect and Costs between Labor- and Capital-intensive Road-building Techniques

Item	Evaluated at market prices		Evaluated at shadow prices	
	Labor intensive	Capital intensive	Labor intensive	Capital intensive
Capas-Botolan road				
Man-days per kilometer	10,224	1,491	10,224	1,491
Total cost per kilometer (thousands of pesos)	176	209	—	—
With low wages, high rental	—	—	633	1,377
With high wages, low rental	—	—	813	1,082
Average Philippine gravel roads				
Man-days per kilometer	5,639	674	5,639	674
Total cost per kilometer (in thousands of pesos)	101	119	—	—
With low wages, high rental	—	—	62	131
With high wages, low rental	—	—	78	102

— Not applicable.

Source: Deepak Lal, *Men or Machines: A Philippine Case Study of Labour/Capital Substitution in Road Construction* (Geneva: International Labour Organisation; forthcoming).

modified labor-intensive methods had an overall lower cost (using market prices) and yet generated substantially more employment than did capital-intensive methods commonly used in the Philippines.[29] These results also held true when adjusted for an average gravel road in the Philippines. When shadow prices were applied to labor and equipment, the modified labor-intensive methods were again cheaper than the capital-intensive ones for both the Capas-Botolan road and the average gravel road. This was found for the two alternatives employed—high shadow wage/low equipment rental and low shadow wage/high equipment rental—although the superiority of modified labor-intensive techniques is more marked in the low-wage alternative. The results of these two studies are summarized in Table 13.11.

The study concluded that it is possible to devise technically efficient labor-intensive techniques (at least for certain tasks) for gravel road construction in the Philippines. The findings are encouraging, and the government should make use of them to ensure that labor is employed effectively. Some special problems should be kept

29. Based on an extrapolation of experimental productivity rates gathered from field observations on the project over a six-month period.

in mind, however. Experimental work often makes labor-intensive techniques appear more promising than they prove to be in actual production conditions for an extended period of time.[30] An important reason is that the management and supervision of large labor forces require skills, experience, and organization quite different from those needed in equipment-intensive operations. In a country where these methods have not been commonly practiced, large-scale implementation of civil works by labor-intensive methods without careful advance planning, organization, and training could render these techniques quite inefficient.[31]

Another possible problem is that there are frequently shortages of labor, even in labor-abundant countries, and that the social cost of labor fluctuates widely with season and location. Unless construction authorities are prepared to pay higher wages during peak periods (the harvest season, for example), projects may suffer costly interruptions.[32] In addition, although it has not been possible to quantify the costs, indications are that with larger labor-intensive projects the cost of management may increase more than proportionately with project size.[33] Thus, despite the encouraging results of the pilot studies undertaken in the Philippines, important questions remain as to their applicability on a large scale. Perhaps the most appropriate next step would be to apply these results to a large project under actual production conditions with careful attention to the organization of the construction units and the development of suitable supervision and management.[34]

The difficulties and unresolved problems of using labor-intensive

30. An observation made by the World Bank in its study on the substitution of labor and equipment in civil construction.

31. The World Bank found in studies in India and Indonesia, for instance, that good supervision was associated with productivities from 33 to 125 percent higher than those with fair supervision. See "Study of the Substitution of Labor and Equipment in Civil Construction: Phase II, Final Report," World Bank Staff Working Paper, no. 172 (January 1974).

32. In particular the World Bank study found that the supply price of labor increases when large projects must recruit workers from outside the local market. Even in labor-abundant economies, such labor can be obtained only by paying prices high enough to cover the additional costs of transportation and, in some cases, on-site housing.

33. The World Bank study concludes that labor-intensive methods suffer from diseconomies of scale as project size increases.

34. A possible model for such a project is the Kenyan Rural Access Roads Program, in which the ILO and World Bank are helping to implement labor-intensive techniques.

techniques should not be allowed to weaken efforts in this direction. The potential benefits require, if anything, an intensification of efforts to determine effective ways of employing more labor in public construction.[35]

MEASURES TO PROMOTE THE CONSTRUCTION INDUSTRY

If the proposed investment program were to be carried out, value added in the construction sector would grow by an average of about 12 percent a year during 1975–85. Such rapid growth may impose considerable strains on the sector, and measures may be needed from time to time to ensure adequate expansion of the industry so that program implementation is not held up.

At present few domestic firms are capable of undertaking large projects. The Upper Pampanga Dam and the Nonoc Island Nickel Project, for example, were built by consortia of relatively small local contractors. This formula may no longer work, however, with the growing number of large construction projects expected in both the public and private sectors. If the domestic industry is to compete successfully against large overseas firms, its adequate growth must be ensured.

---

35. The ILO estimated that use of labor-intensive techniques could add some 49 million man-days or 200,000 jobs during 1974–77, an amount equal to present employment in public construction. This estimate appears somewhat exaggerated, but even if employment creation is much less it could still be significant. See ILO, *Sharing in Development*, p. 210.

14

Domestic Resource Management

R AISING THE AGGREGATE LEVEL OF INVESTMENT from about 20 percent of GNP in the first half of the 1970s to about 25 percent by 1980 will require vigorous efforts to mobilize more domestic resources. The domestic savings rate will need to be about 22 to 23 percent, which will imply a marginal savings rate of 25 to 30 percent. As important as the level of savings, however, is the form that they take. Authorities should encourage saving in the form of financial savings with long-term maturities in order to meet the requirements of the planned investment program, which includes many new large projects with long gestation periods. Even after foreign financing has been taken into account, it is unlikely that the savings of either the government or the corporate sector will be sufficient for this program, which means that the household sector will have to generate larger surpluses.[1] The ratio of household savings to GDP, which has hovered around 5 percent in recent years, will probably have to increase to about 10 percent, the level that prevailed during the mid-1960s.

As more savings flow from households to government and the corporate sector through financial intermediaries, policies with respect to interest rates and credit will become increasingly important. The role of the government will be a critical one in ensuring that

---

1. This situation is in contrast to the economic expansion of the 1960s, which was financed primarily by the internal savings of the corporate sector.

the level and structure of interest rates are in line with the opportunity cost of capital in the economy and satisfy both savers and investors with rates that reflect varying maturities and risks. In addition, the institutional framework of the financial system will have to be strengthened if it is to be equal to its increasing responsibilities. The government, through the Central Bank, has started this process with a program to increase the capitalization of commercial banks. More needs to be done, however, to clarify the allocational function of each type of institution and to improve the quality and broaden the coverage of financial services. The growth of thrift banks, insurance institutions, and the rural banking system should therefore be stimulated, and the emergence and development of stronger securities markets should be encouraged.

Mobilization and Allocation of Savings

Aggregate domestic savings in the Philippines have generally been adequate for investment; the real constraint has been the availability of foreign exchange. Most of the domestic savings have been generated and used by the private sector for investment purposes. In the future there will be important changes in the flow of funds among the household, corporate, government, and financial sectors. To obtain a better perspective of the major issues involved and the measures that need joint action by the government and the private sector, it may be useful to review past trends of savings mobilization and allocation and the devleopment of financial institutions.

PERFORMANCE OF DOMESTIC SAVINGS

Savings performance in the Philippines during the 1960s improved moderately over that of the preceding decade, with gross domestic savings averaging about 20 percent of GDP, compared with an average of around 15 percent during the 1950s. Although savings rates have been comparable to those of other countries at a similar stage of economic development, the increase in the marginal savings ratio has not been exceptional (Table 14.1).[2] In the early 1970s

---

2. In 1972 the savings rate in the Philippines was 19.4 percent, in Colombia 19.5 percent, and in Korea 15.3 percent. The Republic of China, with a long history of financial reforms, exhibited a 30.9 percent domestic savings rate.

Table 14.1. Savings Performance, 1951–74

Year	Gross domestic savings[a] (millions of pesos)	Rate of growth of real GDP (percent)	As share of GDP (percent)	Annual marginal savings rate (percent)	Marginal savings rate[b] (percent)
1951	962	10.4	13.4	−3.4	38.6
1955	1,172	7.1	13.2	−13.4	−4.6
1960	2,130	1.9	16.3	−10.2	20.6
1961	2,367	5.4	16.6	20.7	9.0
1962	2,665	4.9	16.6	16.5	29.4
1963	3,971	6.8	21.4	51.2	27.5
1964	4,186	3.0	20.9	14.9	32.7
1965	4,789	5.3	21.9	32.0	24.6
1966	5,437	5.0	22.4	27.1	22.6
1967	5,697	6.1	20.9	8.8	9.8
1968	5,496	5.6	18.1	−6.6	2.2
1969	5,655	5.3	16.7	4.5	11.6
1970	8,408	6.0	20.4	37.0	19.8
1971	9,940	5.2	20.0	18.0	23.4
1972	10,994	4.5	19.4	14.9	14.8
1973	12,560	9.2	17.8	11.4	18.3
1974	20,487	5.1	20.9	28.4	—

— Not applicable.
a. Adjusted for statistical discrepancy and excluding net factor income from abroad.
b. Three-year-centered moving average.
Source: National Economic and Development Authority (NEDA), National Accounts Series, April 23, 1975.

the marginal gross domestic savings rate was 22 percent, close to the long-run marginal propensity to save of about 24 percent.

The primary determinant of domestic savings during 1951–74 was the growth of incomes. Other factors, such as changes in the price of foreign exchange, have also influenced the savings rate, but statistical analysis suggests that their effect was small in relation to that of income growth. The unavailability of data on incomes from wages and capital makes it impossible to analyze the effects of income distribution on savings performance or to identify and assess the relative importance of savings units in the country. The patterns of acquisition of financial assets, however, suggest that large savers dominate the market, although the extent to which they do so is unclear.

One aspect of domestic savings behavior that is not apparent from an analysis of average rates of saving is the cyclical movement of marginal rates of saving (Table 14.1). Instead of a secular upward trend in the postwar period, there has been a wide fluctuation of marginal rates of savings, primarily because of changes in real incomes.[3]

CHARACTERISTICS OF SAVINGS AND HOLDINGS OF FINANCIAL ASSETS

In addition to the general improvement in the aggregate savings performance between 1965 and 1975, there were also significant changes in the composition of savings and holdings of financial assets, especially in the early 1970s. There was an increase in gross government savings from 1 percent of GDP during the 1960s to about 4 percent in 1973,[4] a rise in the gross acquisition of financial assets by the private sector from about 7 percent of GDP in the 1960s to 12 percent in the early 1970s, and an increase in the share of short-term financial assets to total financial assets acquired by the private sector from an average of 17 percent in the 1960s to more than 40 percent by 1973–74. Most of these changes have taken place only during the last few years, and it is too early to determine whether these trends will continue for a longer period.

Recent increases in savings by the public sector, which had been quite low for a long time, illustrate the success of the recent fiscal

---

3. The troughs that occurred in 1955, 1961, and 1968 indicate that savings performance deteriorated almost in anticipation of foreign exchange crises. Although government spending was the immediate cause of the crises, the root cause was the slow growth of the export sector and the limited progress toward import substitution. One explanation that has been advanced is that the administration in power imported large amounts of rice before and during election years, depleting foreign reserves and precipitating foreign exchange crises in the process. See John H. Power and Gerardo P. Sicat, *The Philippines: Industrialization and Trade Policies* (London: Oxford University Press for the Organisation for Economic Co-operation and Development, 1971), pp. 50–53, and, especially, H. A. Averch and others, *Matrix of Policy in the Philippines*, Rand Corporation Research Study (Princeton: Princeton University Press, 1972), ch. 5.

4. These figures refer to gross public savings. Gross general government savings were calculated as the sum of net general government savings estimated from budget sources (see Chapter 15) and imputed general government capital consumption allowances. The latter were derived by applying the share of general government in total fixed capital formation in a particular year to the total capital consumption allowances in that year.

measures discussed in Chapter 15. The growth of financial assets held by the private sector also reflects a higher degree of financial intermediation and improvement in the financial mechanism. One reason for these important changes was the improvement in government savings owing largely to the major tax reforms undertaken after 1972. Government savings averaged more than 12 percent of gross domestic savings in the 1950s. As the growth of real income slowed down in the 1960s, the ratio of government tax receipts to GDP leveled off and the savings performance of the public sector deteriorated, with government savings accounting for less than 10 percent of the total. This situation persisted into the early 1970s. After the enactment of the tax reforms, however, government savings increased to about 25 percent of the largely unchanged total. The share of private savings declined correspondingly, particularly in 1973 when, apparently as a result of the large tax collections following the tax amnesty, there was a substantial transfer of savings to the government from households and from unincorporated enterprises. Private sector savings averaged around 19 percent of GDP in the 1960–72 period but only about 15 percent in 1973 and 1974 (Table 14.2).

Holdings of financial assets (unadjusted for liabilities) by the private sector increased significantly in the 1970s, especially after 1972. They rose from about 7 percent of GDP in the 1960s to about 12 percent in 1973–74 (Table 14.3). The immediate cause of this rapid growth was a substantial generation of income in the booming export sector, which created a large supply of liquid resources seeking quick investment with good returns. The preference for direct holdings of tangible assets by the private sector in the 1960s was due both to declining real yields on financial assets and to increasing opportunities for direct investments.[5] Corporate incomes, for example, were absorbed into fixed capital and transportation equipment as a result of liberal fiscal incentives; household incomes were used for residential construction, automotive equipment, and consumer durables. Attractive real investment op-

---

5. Tangible assets consist of earnings and depreciation reserves reinvested in fixed capital and inventories by corporations and unincorporated enterprises, residential construction, purchase of consumer durables, and nonmonetized agricultural improvements by households. Because existing accounts do not show a disaggregated flow of funds, the analysis is based on preliminary findings of the World Bank and may be considered indicative rather than definitive.

Table 14.2. Sectoral Composition of Gross Domestic Savings as a Percentage of GDP

Year	Gross domestic savings[a] (millions of pesos)	Gross domestic savings[a]	Gross general government savings	General government capital consumption[b]	Net general government savings[c]	Gross private savings	Private capital consumption	Corporate savings[d]	Household savings[e]
1960	2,130	16.4	2.0	0.8	1.2	14.1	5.1	3.6	5.4
1961	2,367	16.6	3.1	0.9	2.2	13.5	5.4	2.4	5.7
1962	2,655	16.7	2.1	1.0	1.1	14.6	5.8	3.3	5.5
1963	3,971	21.4	1.8	1.0	0.8	19.6	6.3	3.3	10.0
1964	4,186	20.8	0.3	0.7	-0.4	20.5	7.0	3.3	10.2
1965	4,789	21.8	0.3	0.9	-0.6	21.5	7.3	2.4	11.8
1966	5,467	22.3	-0.9	1.0	-1.9	23.2	7.3	3.6	12.3
1967	5,697	21.0	0.9	1.0	-0.1	20.1	7.3	4.0	8.8
1968	5,496	18.1	0.5	1.0	-0.5	17.6	7.6	4.7	5.3
1969	5,655	16.7	0.1	1.5	-1.4	16.6	7.6	3.5	5.5
1970	8,408	20.4	-0.4	0.8	-1.2	20.8	9.3	5.3	6.2
1971	9,940	20.1	1.5	1.1	0.4	18.6	9.8	3.6	5.2
1972	10,994	19.4	1.2	1.4	-0.2	18.2	9.8	3.1	5.3
1973	12,560	17.8	3.7	1.4	2.3	14.1	9.3	1.8	3.0
1974	20,487	20.9	5.3	1.9	3.4	15.6	8.9	0.8	5.9

a. Adjusted for statistical discrepancy and excluding net factor income payments from abroad.
b. Assumed proportional to the share of government in gross fixed capital formation during the current year.
c. Table 15.1.
d. Excluding net factor income payments from abroad.
e. Residual representing savings of households and unincorporated enterprises.
Source: NEDA, National Accounts Series, April 23, 1975.

Table 14.3. Changes in Gross Financial Assets, 1955–74

Year	Financial assets (millions of pesos)	Percentage of gross domestic product
1955	305	3.4
1961	1,078	7.5
1962	1,113	7.0
1963	1,559	8.3
1964	736	3.7
1965	1,404	6.5
1966	2,069	8.5
1967	2,584	9.4
1968	1,984	6.6
1969	2,936	8.7
1970	2,965	7.2
1971	3,811	7.7
1972	4,688	8.3
1973	8,653	12.3
1974	12,100	12.3

Sources: Tables 14.1 and 14.4.

portunities within the household and corporate sectors together with unattractive yields on financial assets meant that each sector absorbed the surpluses that it generated rather than channeling them to financial markets for investment.

This pattern apparently changed in the 1970s as attractive opportunities for direct intrasector tangible investments declined and as attractive yields on short-term financial instruments outside the traditional banking system became more readily available.[6] These instruments were free of the ceilings on deposit rates that governed the banking system and were therefore able to absorb the excess liquidity generated in the economy as a result of windfall incomes in the external sector. The rapid growth of these financial assets was further encouraged and facilitated by the emergence and growth of nonbank financial institutions such as investment houses, finance companies, and securities dealers and brokers, which rapidly began to offer a wider variety of instruments and savings features than

6. These instruments, generally referred to as "deposit substitutes," constitute the unregulated money market in the Philippines and include promissory notes, repurchase agreements, participation certificates, interbank loans, and commercial paper.

Table 14.4. Changes in Gross Financial Assets of the Private Sector, 1951–74
(In millions of pesos)

Year	Currency[a] (1)	Demand deposits[b] (2)	Deposit substitutes[c] (3)	Total short-term assets (4) = (1) + (2) + (3)	Savings, time, and other deposits[d] (5)	Life insurance[e] (6)	Government securities[f] (7)	Corporate bonds[g] (8)
1951	−30	−93	...	−123	−1	12	4	...
1955	−9	35	...	26	123	18	24	...
1961	97	95	...	192	336	175	27	...
1962	123	90	...	213	331	175	43	6
1963	190	207	...	397	457	214	49	6
1964	−38	−63	...	−101	221	120	40	6
1965	158	84	123	365	119	279	77	74
1966	60	203	12	275	835	283	37	52
1967	213	179	39	431	843	321	94	267
1968	22	80	154	256	342	379	104	151
1969	341	439	−14	766	584	393	236	226
1970	291	76	255	622	777	442	322	−42
1971	240	365	423	1,028	913	507	145	87
1972	785	457	308	1,550	302	573	1,117	38
1973	17	1,117	2,946	4,080	1,986	698	−129	444
1974	859	912	3,224	4,995	1,901	749	1,476	−138

... Zero or negligible.

a. Defined as currency in circulation—that is, currency issue minus inactive cash. *Source:* Table 2, *Central Bank Statistical Bulletin* (CBSB), various issues.

b. Demand deposits of private businesses and individuals. *Source:* Table 2, CBSB.

c. Figures for years earlier than 1971 were estimated by assuming that the importance of deposit substitutes increased gradually from 1965—the year when bills of the Bureau of Agricultural Economics were first issued—to 1971, when they accounted for 33.1 percent of total other net liabilities of the banking system. The step functions applied were 1965–67, 10 percent; 1968–69, 15 percent; 1970, 20 percent.

d. Consists of time and savings deposits in commercial banks which are viewed as elements of quasi money; time and savings deposits in rural banks, savings banks, postal savings banks, and savings and loan associations;

had been available earlier. These innovations appear to have effectively counterbalanced the substantially negative real yields on bank deposits in the 1970s. Consequently intersector flows increased, and more corporate investments were financed from sources outside the sector.

The shift in financial assets from longer to shorter maturities during the 1970s is a particularly noteworthy aspect of the increase in gross financial assets of the private sector. It represents an important policy issue for the second half of the 1970s in view of the long-term finance needs of the projects planned. The share of short-term financial assets (currency, demand deposits, and deposit substitutes issued by banks and quasi banks) rose consistently from 17 percent of gross financial assets acquired in the 1960–70 period to account for more than half of all financial assets acquired in

Corporate stocks[h] (9)	Investments in unincorporated enterprises (10)	Subtotal (11) = (5 + 6 + 7 + 8 + 9 + 10)	Total financial savings (12) = (4 + 11)	GNP deflator (13)	Real short-term savings (14)	Real long-term savings (15)	Real total financial savings (16)	Year
34	146	195	72	64.3	−191	303	112	1951
28	86	279	305	59.9	43	466	509	1955
241	107	886	1,078	70.7	272	1,253	1,525	1961
172	173	900	1,113	75.8	281	1,187	1,468	1962
239	197	1,162	1,559	82.3	482	1,412	1,894	1963
243	207	837	736	86.1	−117	972	855	1964
286	204	1,039	1,404	89.5	408	1,161	1,569	1965
353	234	1,794	2,069	94.5	291	1,898	2,189	1966
404	224	2,153	2,584	100.0	431	2,153	2,584	1967
498	254	1,728	1,984	105.3	243	1,641	1,884	1968
504	227	2,170	2,936	111.5	687	1,946	2,633	1969
616	228	2,343	2,965	127.7	487	1,835	2,322	1970
660	471	2,783	3,811	146.6	701	1,899	2,600	1971
779	329	3,138	4,688	159.9	969	1,963	2,932	1972
938	636	4,573	8,653	182.3	2,238	2,846	4,747	1973
2,321	796	7,105	12,100	243.3	2,952	2,921	4,973	1974

and capital accounts in mutual building and loan associations. *Sources:* Tables 5, 51–53, CBSB, and Central Bank of the Philippines.

e. Consists of legal reserves of private life insurance companies operating in the Philippines (domestic and foreign) and technical reserves of the SSS and the GSIS. *Source:* Office of the Insurance Commissioner.

f. Holdings of trust operations and the nonfinancial private sector. For years prior to 1957 it was assumed that the share of these two groups in the total was the same as in 1957. *Source:* Table 85, CBSB; for years earlier than 1957, Table 86, CBSB, but excluding issues of local governments, the Central Bank, and the Philippine National Bank.

g. Peso-denominated bonds only. *Source:* Securities and Exchange Commission.

h. Net holdings. *Sources:* Central Bank of the Philippines and NEDA.

1973–74 (Tables 14.4 and 14.5). In fact, the end of 1974 saw some reversal in gains that had begun in the 1960s in lengthening maturities of private holdings of financial assets. Long-term financial assets also grew during the 1970s, but at a much slower rate, and as a result their share in total financial assets actually fell.

The preponderance of short-term financial flows resulted in weaker corporate financial positions because the rollover of short-term debt could not be assured. Thus corporations financing projects with long gestation periods by means of short-term debt tended to be pressed for funds in periods of tight credit. More important, the private sector's preference shifted to assets with shorter maturities in recent years, thus impeding the further development of savings intermediaries and markets. With the supply and cost of short-term funds becoming volatile, the financial institutions—

Table 14.5. Changes in Percentage Composition of Gross Financial Assets of the Private Sector, 1955–74
(In percent)

Year	Currency[a] (1)	Demand deposits[b] (2)	Deposit substitutes[c] (3)	Total short-term assets (4) = (1) + (2) +(3)	Savings, time, and other deposits[d] (5)	Life insurance[e] (6)
1951	−41.7	−129.2	...	−170.9	−1.4	16.7
1955	−3.0	11.5	...	8.5	40.3	5.9
1961	9.0	8.8	...	17.8	31.2	16.2
1962	11.1	8.1	...	19.7	29.7	15.7
1963	12.2	13.3	...	25.5	29.3	13.7
1964	−5.2	−8.6	...	−13.8	30.0	16.3
1965	11.3	6.0	8.8	26.1	8.5	19.9
1966	2.9	9.8	0.6	13.3	40.4	13.7
1967	8.2	6.9	1.5	16.6	32.6	12.4
1968	1.1	4.0	7.8	12.9	17.2	19.1
1969	11.6	15.0	−0.5	26.1	19.9	13.4
1970	9.8	2.6	8.6	21.0	26.2	14.9
1971	6.3	9.6	11.1	27.0	24.0	13.3
1972	16.7	9.7	6.6	33.0	6.4	12.2
1973	0.2	12.9	34.0	47.1	23.0	8.1
1974	7.1	7.5	26.6	41.2	15.7	6.2

... Zero or negligible.

a. Defined as currency in circulation—that is, currency issue minus inactive cash. *Source:* Table 2, *Central Bank Statistical Bulletin* (CBSB), various issues.

b. Demand deposits of private businesses and individuals. *Source:* Table 2, CBSB.

c. Figures for years earlier than 1971 were estimated by assuming that the importance of deposit substitutes increased gradually from 1965—the year when bills of the Bureau of Agricultural Economics were first issued—to 1971, when they accounted for 33.1 percent of total other net liabilities of the banking system. The step functions applied were 1965–67, 10 percent; 1968–69, 15 percent; 1970, 20 percent.

d. Consists of time and savings deposits in commercial banks which are viewed as elements of quasi money; time and savings deposits in rural banks, savings banks, postal savings banks, and savings and loan associations;

especially commercial banks—found it difficult to extend longer-term credits, a practice already constrained by certain regulatory and administrative factors.

Sufficiently attractive long-term investment opportunities are lacking because excess capacity developed in several key import-substituting and export industries (particularly textiles, cement, sugar refining, and milling) in the 1960s and investment demand leveled off. Furthermore, the substantial devaluation of the peso in 1970 made imported capital goods more expensive in terms of pesos and reduced investment demand in the early 1970s. In 1974 and 1975 rapid inflation, fixed low rates on savings and time deposits, tax and institutional impediments to the placement and acquisition of longer-term securities, and the traditionally low rates

Government securities[f] (7)	Corporate bonds[g] (8)	Corporate stocks[h] (9)	Investments in unincorporated enterprises (10)	Subtotal (11) = (5 + 6 + 7 + 8 + 9 + 10)	Total financial savings (12) = (4 + 11)	Year
5.6	. . .	47.2	202.8	270.9	100.0	1951
7.9	. . .	9.2	28.2	91.5	100.0	1955
2.5	. . .	22.4	9.9	82.2	100.0	1961
3.9	0.5	15.5	15.5	80.3	100.0	1962
3.1	0.4	15.3	12.6	74.5	100.0	1963
5.4	0.8	33.0	28.1	113.8	100.0	1964
5.5	5.3	20.4	14.5	73.9	100.0	1965
1.8	2.5	17.1	11.3	86.7	100.0	1966
3.6	10.3	15.6	8.7	83.4	100.0	1967
5.2	7.6	25.1	12.8	87.1	100.0	1968
8.0	7.7	17.2	7.7	73.9	100.0	1969
10.9	−1.4	20.8	7.7	79.0	100.0	1970
3.8	2.3	17.3	12.4	73.0	100.0	1971
23.8	0.8	16.6	7.0	67.0	100.0	1972
−1.5	5.1	10.8	7.4	52.9	100.0	1973
12.2	−1.1	19.2	6.6	58.8	100.0	1974

and capital accounts in mutal building and loan associations. *Sources:* Tables 5, 51–53, CBSB, and Central Bank of the Philippines.

e. Consists of legal reserves of private life insurance companies operating in the Philippines (domestic and foreign) and technical reserves of the SSS and the GSIS. *Source:* Office of the Insurance Commissioner.

f. Holdings of trust operations and the nonfinancial private sector. For years prior to 1957 it was assumed that the share of these two groups in the total was the same as in 1957. *Source:* Table 85, CBSB; for years earlier than 1957, Table 86, CBSB, but excluding issues of local governments, Central Bank, and the Philippine National Bank.

g. Peso-denominated bonds only. *Source:* Securities and Exchange Commission.

h. Net holdings. *Sources:* Central Bank of the Philippines and NEDA.

of return on life insurance have all diminished demand for long-term instruments in relation to that for short-term assets.

The interest in short-term assets grew with the emergence of the money market as a significant mobilizer and allocator of short-term funds. Money-market rates were not subject to the controls applied to the banking system. As a result, funds were retained in the Philippines and within the formal financial system. Alternatives to the money market included the unorganized credit markets, over-seas deposits, and increased consumption, which in any case would have meant suboptimal utilization of funds. Even though the money market may have distorted savings patterns and institutional development, it has played a vital role in the last few years in mobilizing a larger share of incomes in the form of financial assets.

In 1974, in response to tight market conditions and in recognition of the high rates in the nonregulated money market, interest rates on savings and time deposits, which ranged from 5 to 9.5 percent, were increased by one to two percentage points to 6 and 11.5 percent; administrative ceilings were lifted on time deposits with maturities of over two years, and savings banks paid 14.5 percent on these deposits. Nevertheless high rates of inflation rendered real deposit yields more negative than they had been at any time during the 1956–74 period (Table 14.6), unregulated

Table 14.6. Annual Average Nominal and Real Interest Rates for Selected Assets, 1956–74
(In percent)

Year	Savings deposits Nominal	Real[b]	Time deposits Nominal	Real[b]	Government securities[a] Nominal	Real[b]	Deposit substitutes[c] Nominal	Real[b]
1956	2.00	0.60	2.25	0.80	4.69	3.25	n.a.	n.a.
1957	2.25	−1.70	2.75	−1.20	5.65	1.59	n.a.	n.a.
1958	2.25	0.10	3.25	1.00	4.83	2.57	n.a.	n.a.
1959	2.25	−0.20	3.25	0.80	6.06	3.58	n.a.	n.a.
1960	3.00	−2.10	3.50	−1.60	7.38	2.07	n.a.	n.a.
1961	3.00	−0.10	3.75	0.60	3.06	−0.40	n.a.	n.a.
1962	3.00	−3.90	2.75	−3.20	3.40	−3.54	n.a.	n.a.
1963	3.50	−4.70	4.25	−4.00	5.54	−2.82	n.a.	n.a.
1964	3.50	−1.10	4.50	−0.10	5.45	0.81	n.a.	n.a.
1965	4.50	0.60	6.25	2.30	8.89	4.80	n.a.	n.a.
1966	5.75	0.10	6.25	0.50	6.69	0.94	n.a.	n.a.
1967	5.75	0.10	6.25	0.50	8.25	2.41	n.a.	n.a.
1968	5.75	0.40	6.25	0.90	9.63	4.11	n.a.	n.a.
1969	5.85	−0.10	6.50	0.60	6.32	0.40	n.a.	n.a.
1970	6.00	−7.40	7.00	−6.60	12.17	−2.03	n.a.	n.a.
1971	6.00	−7.70	7.00	−6.80	12.03	−2.51	13.30	−1.31
1972	6.00	−2.80	7.00	−1.90	13.49	4.02	13.90	4.40
1973	6.00	−7.00	7.25	−5.90	15.05	0.92	9.40	4.03
1974	6.25	−20.40	10.00	17.60	16.54	−12.72	31.80	−1.27

n.a.: Not available.

a. Yields on government securities (which are tax free) have been recalculated on a before-tax basis (at a tax rate of 35 percent) to be comparable with the rest, which are fully taxable.

b. Deflated by the rate of increase of the GNP deflator (1967 = 100.0). Interest rates shown are the average rates on new issues.

c. Weighted average of all maturities.

Sources: CBSB and *Report of the Inter-Agency Committee on the Study of Interest Rates*, March 12, 1971.

money-market rates had risen in some instances to levels well above 30 percent on an annual basis in 1973 and 1974, and the growth of these latter instruments exceeded that of traditional deposits. Total short-term deposit substitutes outstanding, which had amounted to 24 percent of total medium- and long-term time and savings deposits in commercial banks and thrift institutions at the end of 1972, were equal to 82 percent at the end of 1974.

PATTERNS OF PAST CREDIT ALLOCATION

The trend of institutional credit allocation since the 1950s reveals two important characteristics: credit to the private sector averaged about 82 percent of the total; the share of credit to agriculture declined steadily from 40 percent in the early 1950s to 18 percent in the early 1960s and 7 percent in 1973, while the shares of credit to the manufacturing and trade sectors rose, partly because of the increased importance of industry in the economy. Sugar growers had been the main recipients of agricultural credit in the early 1950s, but their investments did not expand further after production reached the limits of the sugar import quota of the United States.

Most of the credit extended by all financial institutions except the Central Bank has gone to the private sector (Table 14.7). The patterns of allocation in the 1970s have been similar to those that prevailed in the 1950s and early 1960s. The private sector received an average of 82 percent of total institutional credit outstanding in the early 1970s, the rest going to the public sector (general government, including public enterprises). Commercial and development banks and government nonbank financial institutions—principally the Government Service Insurance System (GSIS) and the Social Security System (SSS)—were the most important sources of credit to the private sector in the early 1970s. Total institutional credit outstanding grew at an annual rate of 6 percent, while credit to the private and public sectors grew at 5 and 12 percent respectively. Growth of credit to the public sector was at a faster rate because in recent years financial institutions have made substantial purchases of government securities to meet the requirements for reserves and portfolio composition.

Table 14.7. Composition of Institutional Credit Outstanding by Sector, 1965-74
(In 1,000 millions of pesos)

Type of institution	1965	1966	1967	1968	1969	1970	1971	1972	1973	1974	Averages 1965-69	Averages 1970-74
Central Bank												
Private	6.0	6.5	9.4	9.7	9.0	6.6	5.7	5.8	3.7	7.3	8.1	5.7
Public	6.9	6.2	5.6	5.0	4.4	4.2	3.2	3.1	1.1	0.9	5.6	5.5
Subtotal	12.9	12.7	15.0	14.7	13.4	10.8	8.9	8.9	4.8	8.2	13.7	8.2
Commerical banks												
Private	50.9	47.6	45.0	41.2	39.6	42.0	42.8	43.7	49.0	48.8	44.9	45.3
Public	6.9	7.9	8.6	12.3	13.8	12.1	11.8	11.2	14.9	12.1	9.9	12.4
Subtotal	57.8	55.5	53.6	53.5	53.4	54.1	54.6	54.9	63.9	60.9	54.8	57.7
Savings banks												
Private	1.3	1.7	1.7	1.9	1.7	2.3	2.5	2.0	1.4	1.3	1.7	1.9
Public	0.2	0.3	0.4	0.2	0.7	0.7	0.6	0.5	1.0	0.9	0.4	0.7
Subtotal	1.5	2.0	2.1	2.1	2.4	3.0	3.1	2.5	2.4	2.2	2.1	2.6
Rural banks												
Private	2.4	2.6	2.7	2.7	2.7	2.8	3.0	3.0	3.1	4.1	2.6	3.2
Public	0.1	0.1	0.1	...	0.1	0.1	0.1	0.1	0.1	0.1	0.1	0.1
Subtotal	2.5	2.7	2.8	2.7	2.8	2.9	3.1	3.1	3.2	4.2	2.7	3.3
Development banks												
Private	12.6	12.0	12.4	12.9	13.8	15.0	15.3	14.4	13.1	11.0	12.7	13.8
Public	1.3	1.2	0.1	0.8	0.7	0.6	1.0	2.3	1.2	1.8	0.8	1.4
Subtotal	13.9	13.2	12.5	13.7	14.5	15.6	16.3	16.7	14.3	12.8	13.5	15.2
Nonbank fianancial institutions												
Private	0.2	1.2	1.2	1.2	1.2	1.2	1.5	1.6	0.5	1.5	1.0	1.3
Public	...	...	...	...	...	...	...	...	0.2	0.4	...	0.1
Subtotal	0.2	1.2	1.2	1.2	1.2	1.2	1.5	1.6	0.7	1.9	1.0	1.4
Government nonbank financial institutions												
Private	11.1	12.8	12.8	12.0	12.4	11.9	11.5	11.3	8.9	7.8	12.1	10.3
Public	...	...	...	0.1	0.1	0.6	1.1	1.2	1.7	2.1	0.1	1.3
Subtotal	11.1	12.9	12.8	12.1	12.5	12.5	12.6	12.5	10.6	9.9	12.2	11.6
Subtotal												
Private	84.5	84.4	85.2	81.6	80.4	81.8	82.3	81.8	79.7	81.8	83.1	81.5
Public	15.5	15.6	14.8	18.4	19.6	18.2	17.7	18.2	20.3	18.2	16.9	18.5
Total	100.0	100.0	100.0	100.0	100.0	100.0	100.0	100.0	100.0	100.0	100.0	100.0

. . . Zero or negligible.
Source: Central Bank of the Philippines.

Credit allocation by industry.[7] The composition of credit flows (loans and credits extended but not adjusted for repayments) among the four major sectors (agriculture, manufacturing, trade, and financial institutions) has undergone fundamental changes during the past two decades, reflecting the government's industrial policy and the evolving structure of the financial system (Table 14.8). The most striking feature of credit flows in the 1951–73 period was the consistent and substantial erosion of the share of agricultural credit, which declined from 40 percent in 1951 to 7 percent in 1973. Although part of the explanation lies within the agricultural sector itself,[8] the most important reason for this decline was the government's policy of encouraging the growth of import-substituting industries in various ways, including low long-term rates of interest and preferential access to substantial financial resources. As large-scale capital and import-intensive manufacturing industries became the focal point of the industrialization strategy, the flow of domestic institutional credit to the manufacturing sector increased.[9]

Credit to the manufacturing sector rose from ₱91 million in 1951 to ₱5,700 million in 1973 (in real terms), but the period of rapid growth was from 1955 to 1962 when real credit increased from ₱209 million to ₱2,500 million at an annual rate of more than 40 percent. The manufacturing sector's share of the total

7. Lack of comparable and consistent data on the direction of credit granted and credit outstanding of all the institutions included in Table 14.7 prevents a comprehensive discussion of credit flows during the 1951–74 period. The analysis that follows is therefore based on gross flows of credit (unadjusted for repayments) from commercial, savings, and development banks to the private sector. The term "institutional credit" will refer to credit from these three classes of institutions, which together account for about three-fourths of the total credit supply. The GSIS and SSS are also important sources of finance, but a large part of their industrial financing is channeled through the Development Bank of the Philippines (DBP); consequently omitting them from the discussion would not materially affect the conclusions and would preclude double counting.

8. See Chapter 7.

9. The true level of credit flows to manufacturing is understated to some extent in these figures, because since the mid-1960s part of the fixed capital formation in this sector has been financed by suppliers' credits from abroad guaranteed by the DBP. The World Bank estimates that DBP guarantees in calendar 1973 would have amounted to ₱1,517 million at prevailing rates of exchange. Adding this to credits granted to manufacturing raises the sector's share in the adjusted total from 23 to 25 percent.

Table 14.8. Amount and Composition of Loans and Credits by Commercial Banks, Savings Banks, and Development Banks to the Private Sector by Industry

Sector	1951	1955	1960[a]	1961[a]	1962	1963	1964
Millions of pesos							
1. Agriculture, fisheries, and forestry	168.7	200.4	502.7	660.4	844.2	1,115.9	1,200.1
2. Banks and other financial institutions	n.a.	n.a.	71.9	127.4	170.5	372.7	572.1
3. Construction	n.a.	n.a.	45.9	62.2	77.5	124.9	115.2
4. Consumption	14.5	35.2	98.0	109.3	105.3	150.2	157.4
5. Manufacturing	{58.5}	123.2	886.2	1,437.6	1,900.8	2,258.7	2,362.2
6. Mining and quarrying			36.7	51.2	59.9	60.3	85.6
7. Public utility[b]	3.5	11.7	65.1	112.8	158.8	195.9	164.3
8. Real estate	57.8	80.0	43.4	57.6	87.8	122.4	156.1
9. Services	24.4	73.8	41.2	48.9	63.9	88.7	96.5
10. Trade	98.9	307.7	1,077.5	1,478.5	1,708.9	2,546.4	2,275.7
11. Total	426.3	832.0	2,868.6	4,145.9	5,177.6	7,036.6	7,185.2
Percent							
1. Agriculture, fisheries, and forestry	39.6	24.1	17.5	15.9	16.3	15.9	16.6
2. Banks and other financial institutions	n.a.	n.a.	2.5	3.1	3.3	5.3	8.0
3. Construction	n.a.	n.a.	1.6	1.5	1.5	1.8	1.6
4. Consumption	3.4	4.2	3.4	2.6	2.0	2.2	2.2
5. Manufacturing	{13.7}	14.8	30.9	34.7	36.7	32.1	32.9
6. Mining and quarrying			1.3	1.2	1.2	0.9	1.2
7. Public utility	0.8	1.4	2.3	2.7	3.1	2.8	2.3
8. Real estate	13.6	9.6	1.5	1.4	1.7	1.7	2.2
9. Services	5.7	8.9	1.4	1.2	1.2	1.3	1.4
10. Trade	23.2	37.0	37.6	35.7	33.0	36.2	31.6
11. Total	100.0	100.0	100.0	100.0	100.0	100.0	100.0

n.a.: Not available.
a. Included in real estate for 1951 and 1955.
Note: Information on loans granted by development banks not available for 1960 and 1961.
Source: Department of Economic Research, Central Bank of the Philippines, *Twenty-Five Years of Economic and Financial Statistics in the Philippines,* vol. 1, 1974, tables 21, 32, and 41.

rose from 15 to 37 percent in this period. Following the devaluation of the peso in 1962, the flow of domestic credit to manufacturing declined, and by the end of the 1960s it was only 20 percent. It picked up again in 1970, contrary to what may have been expected, with another substantial devaluation of the peso as intermediate goods industries benefited from substantial imports of raw materials during the late 1960s and therefore required higher levels of working capital.

Another important change in allocations of institutional credit has been the sharp increase in credit to the domestic and external trade sector, whose share has more than doubled since 1955, reaching the exceptionally high level of about half of total credit outstanding in 1973. This growth reflects the importance of external trade for the Philippine economy, the country's dependence on

	1965	1966	1967	1968	1969	1970	1971	1972	1973
1.	1,210.3	1,356.7	1,699.7	1,813.2	1,888.8	2,260.9	2,575.4	2,653.0	2,988.6
2.	651.2	805.1	830.7	1,516.3	1,738.9	2,774.9	4,922.0	4,720.5	5,777.2
3.	143.5	133.2	151.9	192.3	223.8	187.3	227.6	364.6	368.8
4.	147.0	208.9	242.5	228.7	331.9	869.8	1,169.5	880.3	937.0
5.	2,322.2	2,721.0	3,122.3	3,767.8	4,039.7	4,102.2	5,985.4	7,431.2	10,447.5
6.	51.4	70.8	62.7	96.7	93.4	96.7	322.4	563.7	836.0
7.	157.1	256.0	226.3	281.1	211.8	314.9	470.7	821.8	871.3
8.	145.0	227.0	325.5	383.8	364.8	497.6	683.2	717.2	977.1
9.	88.1	167.4	170.9	251.8	265.5	368.5	496.5	552.0	595.1
10.	3,019.0	2,622.5	3,413.5	6,782.9	7,130.1	9,796.2	12,001.4	13,873.0	22,380.2
11.	7,934.8	8,568.6	10,246.0	15,314.6	16,288.7	21,269.0	28,854.1	32,577.3	46,178.8
1.	15.3	15.8	16.6	11.8	11.6	10.5	8.9	8.2	6.5
2.	8.2	9.3	8.1	9.9	10.7	13.2	17.0	14.5	12.5
3.	1.7	1.6	1.5	1.3	1.4	0.9	0.8	1.1	0.8
4.	1.9	2.4	2.4	1.5	2.0	4.1	4.1	2.7	2.0
5.	29.3	31.8	30.4	24.6	24.7	19.3	20.8	22.8	22.6
6.	0.7	0.8	0.6	0.6	0.6	0.5	1.1	1.7	1.8
7.	2.0	3.0	2.2	1.8	1.3	1.5	1.6	2.5	1.9
8.	1.8	2.7	3.2	2.5	2.2	2.3	2.4	2.2	2.1
9.	1.1	2.0	1.7	1.7	1.6	1.7	1.7	1.7	1.7
10.	38.0	30.6	33.3	44.3	43.8	46.1	41.6	42.6	48.5
11.	100.0	100.0	100.0	100.0	100.0	100.0	100.0	100.0	100.0

imports of capital goods, and the rapid expansion of domestic commercial activities in the 1951–73 period.

There has also been a significant rise in interfirm credits. Large urban-based firms have become net extenders of credit to smaller firms and households.[10] Another important change in the pattern of credit allocation has been the sharp rise of credit to banks and other financial institutions; constituting only a negligible share of the total in the early 1950s, credit to this sector rose to an average of about 15 percent in the early 1970s and has stood just behind that

10. Richard W. Hooley and Honorata A. Moreno, *A Study of Financial Flows in the Philippines*, Institute of Economic Development, Research Discussion Paper no. 74-16 (Quezon City: University of the Philippines School of Economics, 1974), pp. 134–35.

of the trade and manufacturing sectors in recent years. These developments reflect transactions within the finance sector and an increasing layering of the financial intermediation process in the early 1970s.[11]

Credit allocation according to maturity. The maturity structure of credits granted by the banking system shows that demand and short-term loans (that is, those extending for less than one year) accounted for around 95 percent of total credit since 1955. Although credit maturities have become shorter in recent years, as have most other financial flows, short-term credits generally revolve several times and are in fact long term. Statistics about the change in amounts outstanding, classified according to maturity, would be useful in this discussion, but they are not available. Similarly, although the practice of rolling over short-term credit is quite common in the Philippines, data on the actual extent of rollovers are not available. The extent to which corporations face the risk of a lack of liquidity and even default in the event of a credit squeeze and the attendant inability to roll over short-term obligations therefore cannot be assessed.

Structure of financial institutions. In the 1950s intermediation and the provision of financial services were performed primarily by the commercial and thrift banks and by the Development Bank of the Philippines (DBP, then known as the Rehabilitation Finance Corporation). The institutional base has since evolved into a widely diversified structure, which includes regional units (rural banks), insurance companies (both government and private), and nonbank investment institutions such as investment houses, finance and leasing companies, trust operations, and security dealers and brokers.

The importance of financial assets in the economy has also increased considerably. During 1960–74 total assets of financial institutions increased at an annual rate of more than 20 percent. Since this growth was consistently higher than the growth of GNP during the same period, assets of financial institutions as a percentage of GNP at current prices rose from 56 percent in 1960 to 96 percent in 1974 (Table 14.9). This achievement is comparable to that of Colombia and Venezuela, but it was exceeded by the Re-

---

11. See discussion in Chapters 7, 8, 9, and 15.

Table 14.9. Assets of Financial Institutions as Percentage of GNP

Year	Total assets of financial institutions (millions of pesos)	Assets of government institutions (millions of pesos)	Share of government institutions (percent)	Assets of financial institutions at current prices (percent of GNP)
1960	7,227	4,859	67	56
1961	9,311	6,305	68	66
1962	9,827	6,095	62	62
1963	11,671	6,742	58	63
1964	14,275	8,689	61	71
1965	15,598	10,957	70	73
1966	18,096	12,553	69	75
1967	22,315	12,465	56	83
1968	25,200	13,594	54	84
1969	28,855	15,508	54	86
1970	33,868	17,825	53	84
1971	38,537	19,392	50	78
1972	47,502	24,003	51	85
1973	66,549	33,344	50	95
1974	94,804	48,410	51	96

Note: Financial institutions include the Central Bank, the Philippine National Bank, Philippine Commercial and Industrial Bank, DBP, Land Bank, GSIS, SSS, and Agricultural Credit Administration.
Source: Central Bank of the Philippines.

public of China and Korea, both of which allowed higher interest rates and introduced special reforms to encourage the growth of financial institutions and markets.

The commercial banks constitute the most important class of financial institutions, and their growth reflects the patterns of acquisition of financial assets by the private sector discussed above (Table 14.10). The growth was fastest during the 1960–65 period because of the changes in interest rates and the improvement in financial services that were introduced in the late 1950s and early 1960s; acquisitions picked up again in the early 1970s as the money market became important. The experience of the commercial banking system was essentially similar to that of other banking institutions—except thrift banks, which suffered declines in growth rates in the 1970s because of their inability to attract deposits. Real yields on the deposit liabilities of commercial banks had become highly negative, and savers wanted to retain their flexibility by holding quick-maturing financial assets provided by other institutions.

Table 14.10. Structure of the Financial System, 1974
(In millions of pesos and percent)

Type of institution	Asset size		Real rates of growth[a]		
	Amount	Composition	1960–65	1965–70	1970–74
Central Bank	21,273.6	22.5	4.0	6.3	16.8
Banking system	54,457.9	57.4	16.4	8.8	10.9
Commercial banks	42,663.2	45.1	17.2	7.9	12.3
Private banks	30,114.3	31.8	17.0	8.8	14.0
Government banks	12,548.9	13.3	17.5	6.3	8.6
Thrift banks	1,743.6	1.8	28.2	15.0	-2.9
Savings banks	1,236.6	1.3	25.3	14.7	-5.5
Private development banks	296.3	0.3	46.5	9.2	-0.8
Savings and loan associations	210.7	0.2	. . .	. . .	17.3
Regional unit banks (rural banks)	2,110.7	2.2	23.0	10.5	14.0
Other banks	7,940.4	8.3	10.0	10.7	7.4
Development Bank of the Philippines	6,758.0	7.1	10.0	10.7	3.4
Land Bank	1,182.4	1.2	. . .	. . .	128.0
Nonbank financial intermediaries	19,072.2	20.1	11.5	8.5	2.7
Insurance companies	9,094.8	9.6	7.0	4.7	-4.5
Government[b]	6,537.4	6.9	4.8	4.1	-3.0
Private	2,557.4	2.7	13.3	6.2	-8.0
Investment institutions	6,835.0	7.2	. . .	16.6	11.2
Finance companies	2,306.1	2.4	. . .	9.3	-3.5
Investment companies (mutual funds)	n.a.	n.a.	. . .	. . .	. . .
Other	4,528.9	4.8	. . .	37.1	25.8
Trust operations	1,951.5	2.1	. . .	23.7	18.8
Other financial intermediaries	1,190.9	1.2	-8.4	22.3	13.9
Mutual building and loan associations	24.7	. . .	0.0	-2.0	-14.8
Credit unions	n.a.	n.a.	. . .	-1.9	. . .
Securities dealers and brokers	882.1	0.9	. . .	111.8	29.7
Nonstock savings and loan associations	71.2	. . .	. . .	. . .	-5.3
Agricultural Credit Administration	112.1	0.2	-23.3	12.0	-9.0
Pawnbrokers	100.8	0.1	. . .	. . .	. . .
Total	94,803.7	100.0	12.0	8.3	10.1

. . . Zero or negligible.
a. Deflated by GNP deflator (1967 = 100).
b. Includes GSIS and SSS.
Sources: Central Bank of the Philippines and Securities and Exchange Commission.

Among nonbank intermediaries, insurance companies grew slowly, with insurance coverage stagnating at about 4 percent of the population. This sluggish performance was largely due to the facts that insurance policies were not adjusted for rapid inflation and other changing situations and that the cost of insurance was relatively high owing to the widespread use of policy loans at low interest rates. Other investment institutions and securities dealers and brokers grew rapidly, however. Their growth is of course related to the importance of the money market in recent years, as well as to the expansion of stock brokerage facilities to handle increasing volumes of transactions on the three exchanges located in greater Manila.

In the early 1970s government-owned institutions controlled about half the total assets of the financial institutions. This was less than the 65 to 70 percent share that they had controlled in the 1960s, but it represented a higher proportion of total resources, since a much larger share of gross private savings was held in financial assets in the early 1970s than in the 1960s. Government-owned institutions are estimated to have directly controlled more than a third of total investable resources in the 1970–74 period. In reality government control over financial resources is even greater than these figures imply because it extends to the rural and private development banking systems, which were established and funded by the Central Bank and the DBP respectively. Moreover the government-owned financial institutions enjoy economies of scale and privileges not normally available to the private sector institutions. They have the advantage of repurchase facilities; government securities, which have relatively high tax-exempt yields are readily marketable; their bonds are acceptable as collateral for borrowing transactions, as banking reserves, and even as payment for the purchase of public lands (in the form of Land Bank bonds).

The private financial institutions have nevertheless thrived under these conditions, largely because the outlook of the government has been essentially favorable to private enterprise. In mobilization of savings, private institutions appear to have catered to urban savers who have invested in deposits, life insurance policies, deposit substitutes, high-yielding government securities, and corporate securities.[12] Government institutions, in contrast, have been more widely

---

12. The principal operations of private commercial banks, savings banks, investment houses, and finance companies are concentrated in or around Manila.

dispersed, with branches of the PNB and DBP in most urban centers outside Manila and the rural banking system operating in almost all rural provinces.

FUTURE ALLOCATION OF FINANCE

Allocation of resources has traditionally been very much influenced by direct import controls, overvalued exchange rates, heavy protective tariffs, sugar quotas, and liberal fiscal incentives, but there are likely to be significant changes in the future. One such change will probably be the increasing influence of financial policies in resource allocations. Increasing the level and improving the composition of domestic savings are of little value unless resources are allocated appropriately. Allocations for a suitable investment program will obviously determine the degree of the government's success in accelerating the real growth of the economy and in promoting the sectoral development outlined earlier.

The government's involvement in the allocation process will be critical. Capital will have to be priced correctly in relation to a level and structure of interest rates that appropriately match returns with risks and reflect the scarcity value of capital in the economy. In such an interest-rate structure, interest rates will have more to do with the allocational function than they have had earlier. Interest rates may have influenced the choice of technology and the build-up of productive capacity in the past, but their influence was circumscribed by the capital-intensive nature of the industries that were being encouraged and financed.[13]

The pattern of allocation of domestic resources in the future will be considerably influenced by the priority given to the proposed public investment program, which includes a domestically financed outlay of about ₱40,000 million (in 1974 prices) during FY76–85, over four times the actual outlays during the preceding ten years. Resources, including institutional credit, will have to be directed in large part to agriculture, agroindustries, small-scale industries, and the power sector—areas which are crucial to the government's development plans. The government's direct control over investable resources in the second half of the 1970s should remain adequate, because financial institutions in the public sector, such as

---

13. See Chapters 8 and 9.

the Central Bank, PNB, GSIS, SSS, DPB, and the Land Bank, are likely to continue to control almost half the total assets of all financial institutions.

This situation is likely to change in the future. Credit allocations by financial institutions will become more critical and involve larger shares of the total resources in the next decade. There will probably also be a considerable change in the pattern of financing. First, large amounts of financial savings will need to be transferred from the household sector to the government and the corporate sector. Second, an increasing share of these funds will flow to the public sector to finance the enlarged investment program of the government. Third, larger proportions of these funds will need to have longer maturities than in the past. Finally, the industrywide allocation of credit will need to reflect the objectives of industrial policy—that is, encouraging the domestic processing of primary products and developing export markets. The likely allocation and financing of investable resources by 1980 (at constant 1974 prices) is presented in Table 14.11; this allocation would be consistent with the government's development strategy.[14]

The public investment program in 1980 would amount to more than ₱7,000 million at constant 1974 prices, with 55 percent, or ₱4,000 million, financed from general government savings and the remainder by borrowings. As noted in Chapter 15, government borrowings from official and commercial sources abroad would be close to ₱2,000 million, leaving about ₱1,500 million to be borrowed from domestic sources. More than half these domestic borrowing requirements, or about ₱800 million, would be met from the monetary system—that is, from the Central Bank and commercial banks—and would be about 15 percent of the estimated liquidity expansion of ₱6,000 million in 1980.[15] This expansion would be consistent with price stability, since liquidity would increase at the same nominal rate as GNP and remain at a level equal to 30 percent

14. The rationale behind such an allocation and its implications is treated more comprehensively in the appropriate sections of Chapters 8, 9, 13, and 15. This chapter is concerned only with analyzing the financial requirements of the various investment programs in order to demonstrate their implications for savings performance and for the efficient use of capital to achieve stated national objectives.

15. See Chapter 13.

Table 14.11. Allocation and Financing of Investable Resources in 1980
(In millions of pesos at 1974 constant prices)

Category	Public sector	Private sector	Total
Fixed capital formation			
Agriculture	1,030	4,140	5,170
Mining and manufacturing	. . .	13,300	13,300
Power and other utilities	2,960	450	3,410
Transportation	2,510	4,430	6,940
Other	890	4,280	5,170
Subtotal	7,390	26,600	33,990
Increase in stocks	. . .	4,430	4,430
Total capital formation	7,390	31,030	38,420
Financing			
Direct investment of sector savings	4,070	12,000	16,070
Intrasector borrowings	. . .	13,190	13,190
Intersector borrowings	3,320	790	4,110
Foreign	1,840	2,270	4,110
Domestic	1,480	−1,480	. . .
Equities	. . .	5,050	5,050
Foreign	. . .	670	670
Domestic	. . .	4,380	4,380

. . . Zero or negligible.
Source: World Bank estimates.

of GNP in the 1976–80 period.[16] The rest of the government's domestic needs of about ₱700 million would have to come from nonmonetary financial institutions and the capital markets. Nonmonetary financial institutions will probably provide the bulk of these funds, since capital markets in the Philippines are still at an early stage of development.

Apart from these intersector transfers, private sector savings would have to allow for a large amount of intrasector transfers to finance large investment projects in mining, manufacturing, agriculture, and transport. A substantial amount of private sector savings will therefore have to be held in the form of financial assets.

16. The government's share in liquidity expansion, which is equivalent to the growth of domestic credit from monetary authorities, does not appear to be excessive and is equal to its historical share (Table 14.7); this would mean that the private sector would not be lacking domestic credits from the banking system.

The financial requirements of the private sector, about ₱19,000 million at 1974 prices, could be met primarily by domestic borrowings (about ₱13,000 million from financial intermediaries) and from direct sales of corporate debt instruments on the bond markets. About ₱2,000 million could be provided from foreign sources in the form of commercial credits and from foreign funds onlent by domestic financial institutions such as the DBP and the Private Development Corporation of the Philippines.

About ₱4,000 million could probably be met by equity funds, about ₱500 million of which are expected to be provided by foreign investors [17] and the rest by domestic savers (through the securities markets and private placements) and by corporate retained earnings and other reserves. The estimated equity needs would account for about 25 percent of total external finance requirements of the corporate sector.[18] While a major part of these equity needs would be met by private placements, a considerable amount—perhaps ₱2,000 million—would have to be mobilized through the primary market for equities. To date the organized equity markets have not been major sources of new funds, however, and for the securities markets to act as primary channels of funds in the amounts mentioned above would represent a significant development.

It is estimated that the monetary system would provide about ₱5,000 million of domestic credits to the private sector, or 85 percent of the estimated liquidity expansion of about ₱6,000 million. The balance of ₱6,000–7,000 million from financial intermediaries would be provided by nonmonetary financial institutions and by the bond market. Since the primary market for corporate bonds is at an even earlier stage of development than the primary market for equities, raising approximately ₱3,000 million from this source would be a considerable achievement.

17. Direct portfolio investments of about US$100 million at current prices, as discussed in Chapter 16.

18. The Board of Investments (BOI) recommends a 3:1 ratio for projects it endorses, a figure consistent with the historical aggregate ratio. The intra- and intersector financing patterns cited above would lower this ratio, however, because most of the direct investment of sector savings would be construed as equity. This welcome development would strengthen the financial position of Philippine enterprises by lowering the relatively high debt-equity ratios now prevailing.

Issues of Financial Policy

Future growth in aggregate savings will continue to depend primarily on the growth of incomes. If the economy were to grow at about 7 percent a year in real terms, given observed historical relations and no radical changes in savings behavior, gross domestic savings would rise from its present level of 20 percent of GDP to 22 to 23 percent by the early 1980s. The performance of public savings would depend primarily on the success with which the government mobilized resources through the fiscal measures discussed in Chapter 15. According to estimated increases in government revenues, government savings net of depreciation would not rise much beyond 3.5 percent of GDP by 1980. This would fall short of the total requirements of the public sector development program, which means that the balance would have to be financed by private savings.

With a higher rate of income growth there are likely to be more savings in the business sector and a recovery in the savings of households. This recovery, however, would be adversely affected by increasing mobilization of resources by the public sector. Given the continuing pressure for increasing government savings for financing development expenditures, the greater tax effort required might prolong the shift from private to public savings that has occurred in the last two or three years. Similarly, if inflationary pressures are not checked, the level of private savings and the form in which they are held could be affected adversely.

The primary concerns for the government in this area are to increase the share of financial savings and lengthen their maturities. The former is important for facilitating intersectoral transfers of resources, especially for major investment projects, while the latter is necessary to avoid short-term fluctuations in the credit markets and to strengthen financial institutions. Three aspects of financial policy have important implications for the levels and composition of savings and investments during the next decade. First, both the levels and structure of interest rates, which influence the mobilization and allocation of domestic resources, will need to be given a more important role. Second, the various instruments of credit policy which have so far been utilized by the government will have to be reexamined in the context of the proposed changes in interest rate policies and the development of financial institutions. Third, financial institutions and instruments will have to be developed if the financial system grows in the near future as envisaged.

MEASURES TO INCREASE DOMESTIC SAVINGS

An increasing amount of savings will have to be available in financial forms to facilitate the flow of funds required by the government and corporate sectors and also to sustain the investment pattern outlined in Chapter 13. In view of the characteristics that savings and holdings of financial assets displayed in the early 1970s, the success of the savings efforts in the second half of the 1970s will depend very much on the government's financial policies. Intrasectoral channeling of savings will probably grow at the same rate as investment requirements, and will account for 40 to 45 percent of the ₱35,000 million (at 1974 prices) required for the public and private investment programs. Consequently, whether the balance of about ₱20,000 million will be reached will depend on the amount of financial savings that the private sector can accumulate. This in turn will depend on the strength of the incentives to own financial assets.

Promoting financial savings. Yield is not the only factor in stimulating and sustaining the flow of private savings into financial assets. Nonyield considerations are equally important, as shown by the response of savers to innovations introduced in the early 1960s and 1970s, such as repurchase features, convenient terms with respect to withdrawals, and potential participation in capital gains. In the second half of the 1970s financial institutions should be able to attract a greater volume of savings by offering financial assets with differing characteristics of risk, maturity, and marketability or liquidity to suit a broad range of savers' preferences, while simultaneously improving the overall quality of financial services. Improvements could include making high-yielding assets accessible to savers in various income brackets, broadening the coverage of deposit insurance, providing full disclosure of all pertinent information, and protecting investors in other ways to sustain confidence in financial assets. Services should be made more convenient by the provision of more branch offices of banks and nonbank institutions.

In the recent past the existing financial institutions have rapidly widened the array of their financial instruments and as a result have mobilized a much larger proportion of savings. For example, commercial banks confronted with disintermediation adapted their operations to capture substantial savings through their money-market operations rather than through growth of deposits. In fact, despite the slow growth of deposits (which was even negative in late 1974 and early 1975), the assets of commercial banks have increased because of the large share of bills payable.[19] At the end of 1974 twelve of the thirty-six banks had bills payable representing at least 30 percent of their resources; the mode was 40 percent and the range was from 3 to 46 percent.

Other financial institutions can mobilize more savings by offering differentiated financial instruments or improved services. For example, savings banks have frequently adopted more attractive procedures for computation and payment of interest and opened branch offices to compete more aggressively for savings. The promulgation of a new and stronger insurance code in 1974 (Presidential Decree 612) has done much to increase the professionalism of life insurance companies, especially the private ones, and to improve their ability to market policies and thereby mobilize more resources. The potential strength of life insurance institutions in mobilizing funds is indicated further by the fact that new industrial insurance policies written in 1974 amounted to ₱102 million, and a substantial number of these were sold in rural areas.[20] As insurance coverage expands—which it has not in recent years—the contribution of life insurance to the mobilization of private savings in long-term maturities should increase correspondingly.

Lengthening maturities. To sustain the investment pattern outlined in Chapter 13 and to strengthen corporate financial positions, a substantial proportion of the private savings that will be mobilized in the second half of the 1970s should be in longer-term assets. Longer terms would ensure a reasonable blend of maturities in the total obligations of corporations and financial institutions and facilitate a sound intermediation process. Any measures to mobilize more domestic resources by increasing the financial assets

---

19. The bills payable, consisting of deposit substitutes and interbank borrowings, averaged 29 percent of commercial bank resources at the end of 1974, which is unusual by international standards.

20. Where premiums for individual life insurance policies with savings features are collected weekly.

of households should therefore also provide for lengthening the maturities of these assets and widening the array of financial instruments. Three kinds of measures would be needed: improvement of interest rates on long-term financial assets, reform of fiscal policy with respect to long-term financial instruments, and provision of incentives for investment-house placements in longer-term instruments.

In the past, low administrative ceilings on interest rates of longer-term deposit assets discouraged the use of these assets in favor of short-term money-market instruments. The impact of higher yields on portfolio composition has been seen since the July 1974 interest rate reform. Time deposits have grown at an annual rate of approximately 57 percent compared with 13 percent in the twelve months preceding the policy change. Although specific data are lacking, most of this incremental growth appears to be in deposits with maturities longer than two years, while savings deposits with lower yields have grown significantly but at slower rates.

A strong tax bias has been created in favor of money-market instruments because interest paid on a deposit or coupon is reportable for income tax purposes, whereas discounted interest earned on money-market instruments may easily escape reporting. The market for long-term financial instruments could benefit from tax policies that are more favorable to long-term maturities, such as a system of graduated withholding taxes. Other arguments favor neutrality of the tax system, however, to avoid interference with the mechanism of the market.

Finally, underwriting regulations and profit incentives greatly encourage the Philippine investment houses to deal in short-term instruments. Although a spread of three or four points may be realized on very short-term money-market transactions, the Securities Act establishes an effective ceiling of 5 percent on underwriting commissions. Thus, for example, the underwriting and placement of a three-year or a five-year bond, for which turnover may be small, would compete directly with the more profitable money-market operations of the investment houses.

The aim of measures taken with respect to interest rates, taxes, and investment houses should be the creation of an appropriate environment for the issue and purchase of longer-term instruments, which would undoubtedly bring a rapid response from savers. Government securities, high-grade corporate bonds, and mortgage-backed bonds issued by savings and mortgage banks should pave the way for greater confidence on the part of savers and greater demand for long-term financial assets. Given the attractive features of these securities, the establishment of secondary market liquidity, and the large financial needs outlined in this report, the securities market for long-term debts in the Philippines could be the major growth area in the country's financial system in the next ten years.

INTEREST RATE POLICY

The Anti-Usury Law, enacted in 1916, imposed statutory limits of 12 and 14 percent on secured and unsecured bank loans respectively and may have set an upper limit on deposit rates. This did not create a problem for the mobilization and intermediation of savings during the 1950s and 1960s when inflation rates were low and real deposit rates were still positive; but the situation changed dramatically in the early 1970s, and real rates on bank deposits, which were at a nominal level of 6 to 8 percent at the maximum, became negative. Money-market interest rates, however, were not subject to the limits set by the Anti-Usury Law, nor were the money-market institutions required to allocate certain portions of their lendings to sectors, such as agriculture, having high priorities. The annual rates of interest on interbank call loans and commercial paper sometimes exceeded 30 percent. Consequently money-market instruments rapidly began to capture a larger share of available savings, which they could allocate without any regulation. An urgent need for a responsive and regulated financial system was thus created.

Recognizing this need, the government issued a number of presidential decrees in 1972 and 1973 aimed at creating a well-regulated financial structure and making the financial system more responsive to the needs of economic development. The general thrust of these earlier reforms was to give the Central Bank authority over the entire credit system through regulatory powers over the nonbank financial intermediaries with respect to their obligations and uses of funds, reserve requirements against deposit substitutes, and interest rate ceilings. In July 1974 the Central Bank increased interest rates on bank deposits by 2 to 3 percent and removed the ceiling on interest rates on deposits of more than two years. Lending rates were not increased, but ceilings on charges other than interest rates were imposed at the rate of 2 percent for commercial banks and 3 percent for thrift banks.

These changes were steps in the right direction, but in real terms they did not change the situation greatly for depositors, and they merely confirmed existing practices of lenders. As a result, the government became increasingly concerned about the continued sharp growth of deposit substitutes and other money-market instruments at the expense of bank deposits, the fact that this excessive growth of money-market instruments would not provide finance for priority areas of national development, the continued high interest rates in the money market despite declining inflation in 1975, and the use of money-market operations for evasion of taxes.

At the beginning of 1976 the Central Bank enacted a series of changes in interest rates and reserve requirements affecting banks and nonbank financial institutions. Maximum deposit rates were increased further by 0.5 to 1 percent. For the first time a distinction between short-term and long-term lending rates was established. Ceilings on loans with maturities of more than two years were raised to 19 percent, whereas ceilings on loans with maturities of up to two years continued to be subject to the Usury Law ceilings of 12 percent on secured loans and 14 percent on unsecured loans. In the latter case, however, the regulations appear to permit other charges of up to 2 or 3 percent as before. Yields from the purchase of receivables and other obligations consisting of money-market instruments also became subject to regulation. The maximum yield, including all charges, is 17 percent a year on instruments with maturities of up to two years. There is no ceiling on yields in the case of instruments with remaining maturities of more than two years. The new structure of interest rates is presented in Table 14.12.

These recent reforms also raised the minimum denomination of deposit substitutes from the previous level of ₱50,000. After the increase took full effect on July 1, 1976, the minimum denomination of deposit substitutes of up to two years maturity became ₱200,000 and of those over two years maturity, ₱100,000. All banks now have to maintain a 20 percent reserve against deposit substitutes with maturities of up to two years, while nonbank financial intermediaries have to maintain a 20 percent reserve against all deposit substitutes.

These measures continue earlier efforts at reform, and the au-

Table 14.12. Maximum Interest Rates of the Banking System, January 1976
(In percent a year)

Type of instrument	Commercial banks	Thrift banks
Deposit rates		
Savings deposits	7.0	7.5
Time deposits		
3 months	8.5	9.0
6 months	9.0	9.5
1 year	10.0	10.5
1.5 years	11.0	11.5
2 years	12.0	12.5
Over 2 years	No ceiling	No ceiling
Lending rates		
Up to 2 years	12–14[a]	
Over 2 years	19[b]	
Yields from purchases of receivables and		
other obligations		
Up to 2 years	17[b]	
Over 2 years	No ceiling	

a. Excluding other charges of up to 2 percent for commercial banks and up to 3 percent for thrift banks.
b. Including all other charges.
Source: Central Bank of the Philippines.

thorities have stated their intention to follow them up with further corrective steps. In the meantime the rate of inflation has declined sharply from the annual average of 35 percent in 1974 to less than 10 percent in 1975, and consequently real deposit rates have again become positive. The revised rate structure fosters mobilization of long-term resources with no ceiling on rates for deposits of more than two years; at the same time the ceilings on yields for short-term deposit substitutes encourage savers to return to bank deposits.

Inasmuch as these measures have just been introduced, a full assessment of them would be premature. It is important to note, however, the extent to which these reforms represent a departure from past policies: There is a broad thrust toward increasing the mobilization and allocation of long-term resources instead of short-term funds; consequently efforts are being made to control short-term money-market operations and to strengthen the organized banking institutions. For the first time there is a distinction between short-term and long-term lending rates. The Monetary Board has been empowered to adjust ceilings on interest rates and to differentiate interest rates under these ceilings, and deposit rates have been raised for the second time in about eighteen months. The reforms therefore represent a positive attempt to rationalize the level and structure of deposit and lending rates.

CREDIT POLICY

Since the use of interest rates as an allocational tool was limited in the past, the government relied on a variety of instruments to channel credit into activities with high priorities. These instruments included an investment-priority plan administered by the Board of Investments, special programs to aid small- and medium-scale industry, the establishment of specialized institutions, preferential rediscounting by the Central Bank, tax exemptions, subsidies, and other administrative regulations.[21]

Reliance on collateral has most often been used to affect the rationing of funds among investments. It has made possible substantial flows of credit to large enterprises and has strengthened the bias for large, capital-intensive undertakings. This particular credit policy, however, has merely confirmed the directional bias of industrial policy. The pattern of investments and credit flows has been influenced most by the availability of foreign exchange, import licenses (which have allowed exemptions from customs duties for imported capital equipment), accelerated depreciation, and exemptions from income taxes. In addition, heavy protection of domestic markets has implied that even uneconomical enterprises could survive and generate adequate financial returns. These factors need to be kept in mind in the formulation of policies governing credit and interest rates.

The fundamental issues involved in allocating institutional credit in the future will probably be: ensuring that labor-intensive manufacturing enterprises in sectors such as food, textiles, wood processing, engineering, and other light industries obtain adequate financial resources; and improving the credit-delivery systems in general, and those in agriculture and industry in particular, to allow small- and medium-scale industries, as well as small agricultural borrowers, greater access to institutional credit.[22] Some steps have already been taken in this direction. The operations of the Industrial Guarantee

21. These have been discussed in Chapters 7, 8, 9, and 15.
22. See Chapters 7 and 9.

and Loan Fund, which assist the development of small and medium-size industries, have expanded considerably in the past two or three years. The flow of institutional credit to agriculture has also increased through the Masagana 99 program and through strengthening and expanding the rural banking system. The Development Bank of the Philippines is assuming a more active role in lending for rice production, fisheries, livestock development, and food processing. The government is also strengthening the Philippine National Bank by further expanding its network of branches to increase the availability of funds for agricultural and small- and medium-scale industrial development.

DEVELOPMENT OF FINANCIAL INSTITUTIONS

The issues for resource management that were discussed earlier in this chapter relate closely to the structure of the financial system. The development of financial institutions and instruments is an important element in raising the quality and extending the coverage of financial services. Because of its extensive influence over the financial system, the government will need to take the initiative by encouraging financial institutions to lengthen the maturities of their instruments and, as discussed in Chapters 7 and 9, by improving credit delivery, especially to agriculture and to small- and medium-scale industries. Improving the operating efficiency of financial institutions should lead to reduced spreads and lower costs. The growth of financial intermediaries in the Philippines has been quite extensive but uneven. Consequently, although there is no need to establish whole new classes of institutions, the less developed ones, such as savings and mortgage banks and the securities markets, should be given sufficient incentives to grow.

Issues in developing the financial system. The overwhelming need in the next few years will be to make the existing system work more effectively by encouraging certain new activities in both the mobilization and allocation of resources among the present institutions, by fostering competition, and by lowering the cost of intermediation. In the long run the government should aim at developing a strong securities market which can provide liquidity to holders of stocks and bonds and can thus be an effective mechanism for mobilizing and allocating funds directly from savers to government and corporate users. Various ways to strengthen the existing institutions and the future role of the money and securities markets are dealt with in broad terms in the following section.[23] Before the Central Bank's recent program to improve its equity position, many commercial banks weakened their financial structures by lending beyond normal limits and thus depleting excess and required reserves. The insolvency of the Continental Bank in June 1974 was only one symptom of more widespread difficulties. When, in the 1960s and early 1970s, the banks expanded their lending volume extensively, they had to operate with significantly reduced reserves. Entrepreneurs preferred financing through borrowing rather than through raising equity, since by borrowing loan capital they could maintain control over their enterprises. The authorities recognized the need to expand the equity base of banks, and in 1975 the Central Bank took a step in the right direction. It doubled the capital base of the whole commercial banking system to ₱3,000 million through increased capitalization, the merger or consolidation of commercial banks, and foreign equity participation.

The financial institutions best suited for dealing in long-term funds are development banks, thrift banks, insurance companies, and pension funds; they should grow in the next decade with the substantial increase in the demand for long-term funds to finance large investment programs. The development banks, especially the DBP, have been the main suppliers of long-term finance and are likely to continue to dominate in this field. The DBP will continue the important work of financing both capital-intensive industries, which require substantial amounts of foreign and domestic currency, and small- and medium-scale industries, which entail greater financial risks. Private development banks will perform a useful supporting function by focusing on local needs and absorbing the risks inherent in small-scale loans that do not receive the support of the DBP. In the long run, efforts of these institutions will be aided by an organized bond market and an invigorated stock market.

Thrift banks, such as savings and mortgage banks, should be the main vehicle for issuing long-term obligations. Mortgage and savings banks could be major issuers of consolidated mortgage bonds and could expand their operations in financing construction activity

---

23. The role of the rural banking system has been discussed specifically in Chapter 7.

and housing. To provide that service, however, mortgage and savings banks would have to extend their activities geographically beyond greater Manila and Southern Tagalog.

Life insurance companies are another institution with considerable potential for supplying long-term funds. These companies, both private and government owned, could provide long-term financing to agriculture and industry, either directly through purchases of corporate securities or indirectly through purchases of bonds of DBP, government, and other intermediaries. Life insurance companies also finance construction and residential mortgages. Insurance companies in general, and GSIS and SSS in particular, can act as catalysts in rationalizing and developing the mortgage market by moving away from direct mortgage lending and concentrating on their function as financial intermediaries through the purchase of consolidated mortgage bonds issues of savings and mortgage banks. Pension funds are similar to insurance companies in their ability to mobilize long-term funds, and they could be major factors in the development of securities markets.

The short-term money market. The money market will continue to perform a major intermediation function in the future. From the point of view of the management of liquidity, the money market is useful as the interbank market that allows banks and quasi banks to balance their day-end portfolios. But in the last few years, commercial banks have covered reserve deficiencies by direct borrowing from the nonfinancial private sector, thereby circumventing reserve requirements and interest rate limitations as savers moved out of currency and deposits and acquired higher yielding deposit substitutes.[24] It is equally important, however, to recognize that savings have been channeled to the money market partly because of tax advantages obtainable from deposit substitutes and partly because there have been few long-term instruments offered.

In the future the money market should emphasize the placement of large amounts of temporarily idle corporate funds and savings of large investors, since large amounts are normally required to permit

---

24. Before December 1974 it was not required that promissory notes and other dealer-issued paper be backed by liquid reserves. Central Bank authorities, however, recognized that these instruments were essentially banking liabilities and must be backed by reserves; they imposed a 5 percent reserve requirement on these instruments, which were issued by both banks and quasi banks.

economical and efficient money-market transactions; for this reason it is not a place for the small saver. But it is important to alter the conditions now prevailing in the market for savings, which allow large savers to obtain higher yields for shorter terms than do small savers for longer terms, and to offer better yields from longer term assets to all classes of savers.

In addition, it is important to segregate the interbank market from the rest of the money market to prevent the circumvention of reserve requirements permitted by present practices in the money market. One way of dealing with this problem would be to preclude commercial banks from originating issues in the form of promissory notes and repurchase agreements, and to encourage them instead to issue only long-term certificates of deposit subject to the same reserve requirement as time deposits. Since a market for overnight money is needed by all financial institutions, however, the Central Bank should perhaps consider allowing quasi banks to participate in the interbank market. But the Central Bank must ensure that these transactions are processed through its central clearing system to prevent insitutions from raising reserves by direct borrowing from the nonfinancial private sector.

The securities market. The Philippine financial system does not have an active and quantitatively important stocks and bonds market. In recent years only a small proportion of the capital expansion of Philippine corporations has been financed through issues sold in the three stock exchanges in Manila, Makati, and Quezon City. Only corporations such as San Miguel, Manila Electric Company, and the Private Development Corporation of the Philippines have been able to tap private savings directly. New firms—except for highly speculative mining ventures—have been unable or unwilling to sell equities as well as corporate bonds. No corporate bond offerings have been made to the public in recent years other than those issued by one finance company, which have already been redeemed. The peso-dominated corporate bonds included in the definition of gross private financial assets have been sold through private or direct placements rather than through the exchanges.

There are several reasons for the underdeveloped state of the securities market. The first is a supply constraint. Private owners are not disposed to share their control over the enterprises and have therefore avoided raising new equity through public issues. Moreover, there are no incentives for enterprises to go public, since the corporate income tax rate is the same for an open corporation as for one that is closed or privately held.[25] Second, high interest rates and tax advantages on short-term money-market instruments over those on long-term securities biased the preferences of savers toward short-term investments and constrained the demand for securities. Third, except for mining shares, the largest commercial and industrial issues, and a few that are speculative, shares are not investments of high liquidity because the market is limited. Fourth, the substantial swings in market activity reflect speculation that is inadequately controlled by the regulatory framework. Finally, there are deficiencies in the dissemination of information to the market and especially to smaller investors.

These structural problems can be resolved by a determined effort on the part of government authorities in cooperation with the private sector. The primary securities markets should mobilize more private savings by offering a greater variety of investment opportunities, and it should channel more of the mobilized funds into long-term assets. Direct financing through stock and bond markets would also represent the creation of an investment medium which is distinct from a money medium. It might be desirable to introduce long-term bonds gradually through the organized exchanges by starting with three- to five-year corporate debentures, followed by five- to ten-year mortgage bonds, stretching to twenty- to twenty-five-year maturities for government bonds. Under prevailing market conditions, issues could be sold to yield from 16 to 25 percent, depending on quality and maturity. These bonds should lead the way in creating a bond market and increasing the share of long-term assets in private financial savings.

Apart from their involvement in the money market, investment houses can play an important institutional role in broadening both the ownership base of private industry and its sources of finance. They were established to create a core of underwriters who could assist firms in raising capital in the securities market, but they have yet to fulfill this role. In taking steps to create a bond market and to strengthen the stock market, government authorities would not only pave the way for the issue of new long-term instruments

---

25. Twenty-five percent on taxable income of up to ₱100,000 and 35 percent on income above ₱100,000.

but would also enable investment houses to function as they were originally intended.

Measures to stimulate the supply of and demand for securities could also include fiscal incentives to induce privately held corporations above a certain size to go public. For example, a difference of ten percentage points in the rates at which open and closed corporations are taxed might be sufficient to promote the formation of open corporations. Better enforcement of tax laws, however, would make effective tax rates even more important than changes in the legal tax rate. As shown in Chapter 15, some of the corporations pay corporate income taxes of less than 5 percent. In addition, the confidence of investors in securities could be strengthened by improving stock exchange regulations. The Securities and Exchange Commission needs to be revitalized and to act more as a regulatory agency than as just a registry of corporations. The dissemination of information to the public, especially to the small investor, also needs considerable improvement.

Finally, the liquidity of the securities markets could be increased substantially by institutionalizing securities credit—that is, credit to purchase or hold stocks and bonds with the securities purchased as collateral. This would perhaps be the most important element in the effort to further the growth of Philippine securities markets, since investors could make larger purchases of securities with the available funds through appropriately structured margin accounts. The Central Bank would specify margin requirements to maintain its control over expansion of liquidity, and there would be sufficient regulation to prevent speculative excesses.[26] Brokers and underwriters could likewise broaden their operations by making more working capital available. In some countries where commercial

---

26. In a margin loan, an investor wishing to purchase an eligible security needs to put up a deposit representing only a fraction of the purchase price and to pledge the security to the broker. With a 60 percent margin requirement, for example, an investor purchasing ₱1,000 worth of stocks or bonds must put up only ₱600; the broker will extend him a loan of ₱400 with the security purchased pledged as collateral. Should the security value decline to ₱900, the investor must put up an additional ₱40 as deposit, because the loan value of the securities has declined to ₱360. Conversely, should prices rise and the security value increase to ₱1,100, the investor will have a credit balance of ₱40 in his account.

banks have been reluctant to lend to the securities markets—or do not have the expertise to do so, as seems to be the case in the Philippines—experience has shown that a specialized institution acting as a central source of securities finance could provide the required services.[27]

27. For instance, the Japan Securities Corporation and the Korea Securities Finance Corporation perform these functions for the Japanese and Korean markets respectively.

15

The Role of the Public Sector

UNTIL THE EARLY 1970s THE PHILIPPINE ECONOMY was controlled and dominated by the private sector. The public sector was small and played only a relatively minor role in economic development. By international standards, the Philippines had low levels of government revenues and expenditures. General government revenues hovered around 11 to 12 percent of GNP during the 1960s; general government expenditures were only marginally higher (Table 15.1).[1] Combined current and capital general government expenditures per capita (at current prices) increased by only 4.5 percent a year between 1950 and 1970.[2]

The country also suffered from inefficient fiscal administration and uncoordinated financial planning. The tax system had strong regressive features and tax enforcement was inadequate. The low level of effective tax rates which resulted from this situation necessarily reduced the potential of fiscal policies and incentives and discouraged the efficient use of the available economic and financial resources. The scarcity of financial resources and the constraints on

1. General government refers to national and local government combined.
2. General government current and capital expenditures rose from ₱30 per capita in 1951 to ₱60 and ₱83 in 1970. See Augustin Kintanar, "Financing the Public Sector," in *The Philippine Economy in the 1970s* (Manila: Institute of Economic Development and Research, University of the Philippines, and the Private Development Corporation of the Philippines, 1972), p. 164.

Table 15.1. Government Finances by Fiscal Year

Category	Millions of pesos					Percentage of GNP				
	FY59	FY64	FY69	FY72	FY74	FY59	FY64	FY69	FY72	FY74
General government										
Revenue	n.a.	2,434	3,603	6,388	12,800	n.a.	12.7	11.4	12.2	14.8
Expenditures	1,284	2,577	4,428	6,851	13,076	11.1	13.4	14.0	13.0	15.1
GNP (at current prices)	11,542	19,231	31,704	53,956	86,548	—	—	—	—	—
Public investment (including public corporations[a])	280[b]	405	681	877	1,760	2.4	2.1	2.1	1.6	2.0
Tax revenues										
National tax revenues	844	1,819	3,041	5,213	10,847	7.3	9.4	9.6	9.7	12.5
Local government tax revenues	150	210	334	424	560	1.3	1.1	1.0	0.8	0.7
Social security contributions	126	262	480	432	766	1.1	1.4	1.5	0.8	0.9
Total tax revenues	1,120	2,291	3,855	6,069	12,173	9.7	11.9	12.1	11.3	14.1

n.a.: Not available.

— Not applicable.

a. National Power Corporation, National Electrification Administration, Metropolitan Manila Waterworks and Sewerage System, Export Processing Zone Authority, Laguna Lake Development Authority, and the Philippine National Railways.

b. World Bank estimate.

Sources: World Bank Economic Reports, 1968 through 1972; R. M. Bird, O. Shimoni, and R. S. Smith, "Taxes and Reform in the Philippines" (Washington, D.C.: International Monetary Fund, 1974; restricted-circulation draft), tables 2, 3, and 4; National Economic and Development Authority (NEDA), *Statistical Yearbook of the Philippines, 1975.* National accounts as prepared by National Accounts Staff, Statistics Office (NEDA), revised as of December 1975.

administrative capacity resulted in inadequate levels of government investment in social and economic infrastructure and held back economic development severely. The accomplishments of the infrastructure programs, moreover, were uneven and in general unduly favored the major urban centers, especially greater Manila.

In addition, the potential of local governments was not tapped for generating grass-roots support of economic development or for furthering balanced regional development. Their administrative powers were not strengthened and their tax base was gradually eroded. Public authorities and corporations provided only a few basic services (power and railroads, for example), and, as indicated in Chapter 13, their investments were small and concentrated in urban areas. Finally, the lack of attention to management training in the public sector resulted in an overall deterioration of administrative capabilities at all levels.

The situation began to change in the early 1970s, when the Philippine government began to play a more active role in development. The government formulated a long-term strategy which called for substantial growth in public-sector investments, an expansion and improvement of government services at all levels, a reorganization and revitalization of local governments to involve them actively in development efforts, and increased economic activity on the part of publicly owned corporations, agencies, enterprises, and banks. The government began to expand public resources through a sharp increase in tax revenues. Although the Philippine government made considerable progress in all these areas, more difficult issues are expected to arise. Presenting new challenges will be the need for changes in the administrative structure of the public sector, the setting of new priorities for current and capital outlays, the implementation of tax reforms, the future organization of the public corporate sector, and sound debt management in the face of rapidly rising public corporate borrowings.

The economic activity of the public sector will have to expand significantly in the future if the development programs of the government are to be implemented. Large public investments in the economic and social sectors and substantially higher current outlays as public services improve will claim considerably more resources—both domestic and external—than they have in the past and will require concerted efforts to mobilize the required resources. An adequate mobilization of financial resources will depend largely on the results of the various tax reform measures now in progress or contemplated. The increased importance of the public sector will burden administrative capability even more and will require the government to step up administrative and organizational improvements, including training. The division of responsibilities among the various levels of government will also have to be redefined.

The Role of the National Government

Historically, the Philippines has had a centralized governmental structure. The delegation of authority by the national government to the provinces and other local governments has been more the exception than the rule. Under Philippine constitutional law, local governments have always been seen as entities formed by the national government, reflecting the centralized system of the Spanish colonizers. Consequently the national government and its agencies have dominated the public administrative system both politically and financially. The public sector has represented only a relatively small share of the economy as a whole, however, which has meant that the economic and financial authority of the national government was, until a few years ago, smaller than that in other countries with a similarly centralized structure.

The administration of the government was rather ineffective until the early 1970s. Functional responsibilities were ill defined, with a plethora of parallel departments and bureaus; budget preparation and implementation procedures, which were influenced by the budget system of the United States, were unusually complex; and, on the whole, fiscal policy lacked focus. The Department of Finance, which in other countries formulates policy and makes decisions in the fiscal field, had little authority in the Philippines. As a result of all these factors, the capacity of the government to identify, prepare, and implement development projects was inadequate. In addition, widespread corruption in public administration impaired the reputation of the civil service and contributed to the feeling that the government's role in development should be kept as small as possible. There was therefore little effort to increase the level of domestic resources for the public sector by higher and more effective taxation. Capital outlays by the government were small—between 1 and 2 percent of GNP—and current expenditures were around 7 to 8 percent of GNP—also low by international standards. The level of government services was inadequate, except for relatively large expenditures for public primary education. Because of a conservative budget policy and the low level of development expenditures, borrowing by the national government was, until a few years ago, insignificant.

In recent years the government has intensified its development efforts and changed its attitude in favor of an active role for the public sector. The government's capability for preparation and implementation of projects has improved, and overall measures have been undertaken to modernize budget procedures and to streamline the structure of the government. Government services have been expanded, especially for agriculture and rural development. Above all, infrastructure expenditures by the government have increased significantly, and large capital transfers have taken place from the government to its corporate sector. Local governments have been encouraged to participate actively in development by a more efficient and equitable distribution of financial assistance by the national government. In part, at least, these developments have been made possible by the increase in revenues, which was brought about by tax-reform measures and aided by the recent boom in exports. The government's desire to expand its role in the economy necessitates a larger base of resources, however, and continued efforts to expand revenues in relation to GNP will be required.

NATIONAL GOVERNMENT REVENUES

Tax revenues of the national government as a whole increased faster than GNP in the early 1960s; however, they remained fairly stable as a percentage of GNP from FY64 until FY72. Taxes of the national government (excluding contributions to the Social Security System) were between 9 and 10 percent of GNP during that time (Table 15.2), low in comparison with taxes of countries at similar stages of economic development.[3]

3. See Roy W. Bahl, "A Representative Tax System Approach to Measuring Tax Effort in Developing Countries," *IMF Staff Papers*, vol. 9, no. 1 (March 1972), pp. 87–124. The author examined the taxable capacity and tax effort of forty-nine developing countries during 1966–68. He concluded that the actual tax ratio of the Philippines in this period was about 36 percent below the expected tax ratio. He also shows that the tax effort in the Philippines was

Table 15.2. National Tax Revenue by Fiscal Year

Category	Millions of pesos							Percent[b]						
	FY59	FY64	FY69	FY72	FY73	FY74	FY75[a]	FY59	FY64	FY69	FY72	FY73	FY74	FY75
Taxes on income and wealth														
Corporate income tax	116	263	597	908	1,396	2,080	2,310	13.8	14.4	19.6	17.4	19.8	19.2	17.3
Personal income tax	66	158	204	443	562	641	858	7.8	8.7	8.0	8.5	8.0	5.9	6.4
Others	18	7	59	114	84	77	77	2.1	1.0	1.0	2.2	1.2	0.7	0.6
Tax amnesty	...	...	...	...	575	259	221	...	...	...	...	8.2	2.4	1.6
Total	200	428	860	1,465	2,617	3,057	3,466	23.7	29.1	28.6	28.1	37.2	28.2	25.9
Taxes on international trade														
Import duties	226	419	607	1,084	1,435	2,772	3,729	26.7 ⎰	23.0	20.0	20.8	20.4	25.6	27.9
Sales tax on imports	...	239	399	580	645	1,003	1,126	26.7 ⎱	13.1	13.1	11.1	9.2	9.2	8.4
Export duties	...	...	...	475	457	1,065	1,650	...	...	...	9.1	6.5	9.8	12.4
Total	226	658	1,006	2,139	2,537	4,840	6,505	26.7	36.1	33.1	41.0	36.1	44.6	48.7
Taxes on domestic goods and services														
Excise tax[c]	259	373	553	664	735	1,203	1,678	30.7	20.5	18.2	12.7	10.4	11.1	12.5
General sales tax	28	98	153	240	217	402	1,172 ⎰	3.3	5.4	5.0	4.6	3.1	3.7 ⎰	8.8
Other indirect taxes	77	133	245	357	438	668	⎱	9.1	7.3	8.1	6.8	6.2	6.2 ⎱	
Total	364	604	951	1,261	1,390	2,273	2,850	43.1	33.2	31.3	24.2	19.7	21.0	21.3
Other taxes														
Motor vehicle fees	30	49	85	118	137	156	164	3.6	2.7	2.8	2.3	1.9	1.4	2.2
Other	25	80	143	230	356	521	380	2.9	4.4	4.7	4.4	5.1	4.8	1.9
Total	55	129	228	348	493	677	544	6.5	7.1	7.5	6.7	7.0	6.2	4.1
Total national tax revenues	844	1,819	3,045	5,213	7,037	10,847	13,365	100.0	100.0	100.0	100.0	100.0	100.0	100.0
National tax revenues as a percentage of GNP	7.3	9.1	9.6	9.7	11.5	12.5	12.6							

... Zero or negligible.

a. Estimated in part.

b. Percentage totals do not always equal 100 because of rounding.

c. "Specific taxes" on tobacco products, petroleum products, and other.

Sources: Data for FY59, FY64, and FY69 are from Bird and others, "Taxes and Tax Reforms in the Philippines"; data for FY72, FY73, and FY74 are from National Tax Research Center, "Assessment of Tax Reforms in the Philippines," November 1975; data for FY75 are from the Budget Division of the Department of Finance.

Since the late 1960s the government has initiated various policies aimed at raising the level of tax revenues and reforming the tax system. Legislation has been enacted in the area of indirect taxes, especially those related to external trade. Partly as a result of these reforms national tax revenues increased by 35 percent in FY73 and by 55 percent in FY74 to reach 12.5 percent of GNP compared with 9 to 10 percent a few years earlier. About a quarter to a third of the revenue increments can be related to the new tax measures. Tax revenues were also boosted, of course, by the overall increase in economic activity and especially by the dramatic temporary improvement in export earnings. Despite the recent recession and falling export prices, the tax ratio in FY75 remained at the FY74 level.

The structure of national government taxes underwent some changes during the 1960s and the early 1970s. Although taxes on income and wealth increased in relative importance, the government continued to depend heavily on indirect taxation, which accounted for 70 to 75 percent of total tax revenues. Direct tax revenues increased largely because of the rise in the tax rate on top corporate incomes from 30 to 35 percent in 1969, but revenues from personal income taxes showed little responsiveness to growth of GNP and on the average were equivalent to less than one percent of GNP. Taxes on domestic goods and services declined as a share of total tax revenues, since selective excise taxes, which had been the major source of revenue in the 1950s, decreased sharply throughout the 1960s. Only revenues from the sales tax on imported goods showed significant gains during the period.

Apart from higher corporate income tax revenues, the entire increment in the national tax ratio in the early 1970s was the result of the increased importance of taxes on external trade—both imports and exports—particularly since the floating of the peso and the introduction of export taxes in 1970. With around 40 percent of total national tax revenue in FY72 derived from international trade, the internal revenue system of the Philippines became highly

---

generally low and was not attributable (as in other countries) to a very low intensity of use of one particular tax base. Of the shortfall of 36 percent, 15.6 percent was due to below-average intensity of use of the corporate income-export tax base, about 9.5 percent each to below-average use of the import base and the personal income–internal indirect tax base, and 1.3 percent to below-average use of property and personal taxes.

sensitive to the fluctuations of the country's international terms of trade.

A study for the International Monetary Fund on taxation and tax reforms in the Philippines calculated for FY60 through FY73 an elasticity of 1.1 for the tax system of the national government;[4] that is, tax revenues rose by 1.1 percent for each 1.0 percent growth in GNP. From an analysis of the varying actual elasticities of the individual tax categories, it was concluded that the built-in elasticities of the Philippine tax system as a whole (excluding the export tax) was 0.9 in FY73. Even with the export tax (which varies with the value of exports and not with GNP), the elasticity of the system was still only close to unity.[5]

The tax reforms of recent years have raised the level of revenues significantly, from around 9 percent of GNP in FY69 to an average of over 12 percent in FY73–FY75. This share will have to rise even higher, however, if the government's development goals are to be achieved. More improvements in tax enforcement and collection on the basis of the present tax laws would certainly produce some additional revenues but probably not enough to provide all the required funds. Major tax reforms will therefore be needed in the latter half of the 1970s. Moreover, apart from the need to generate sufficient revenues for financing the budget, the government may in the longer term want to correct the present social inequities of the tax system.

The main elements of reform that appear to be necessary are set out in Technical Note A at the end of this chapter. In brief, the main thrust of tax reform measures should be, first, to widen the domestic base of tax revenues and reduce the heavy dependence of those revenues on international trade, and second, to improve the social equity of the tax system by a sharp rise in direct taxation and higher indirect taxation of domestic goods and services consumed by the upper income groups of the population. In addition, the introduction of a national tax on land and on rural property war-

4. R. M. Bird, D. Shimoni, and R. S. Smith, "Taxes and Tax Reform in the Philippines" (Washington, D. C.: International Monetary Fund, 1974; restricted-circulation draft).

5. The methodology developed by Sheetal K. Chand and Bertram A. Wolfe in *The Elasticity and Buoyance of the Tax System of Peru, 1960–71: An Empirical Analysis* (Washington, D. C.: International Monetary Fund, July 1973) was used in this report.

rants careful consideration. If a series of reforms along these lines were implemented, it should be possible to raise national government taxes from around 12.6 percent of GNP in FY75 to at least 14.5 percent by FY80 and 17 percent by FY85 (Table 15.3).[6] Local tax revenues are likely to rise to 0.9 and 1.4 percent respectively in FY80 and FY85. Inasmuch as the coverage of social security benefits is being expanded, contributions to social security could reach 1.8 percent of GNP by FY85. The total aggregate tax effort would be more than 16.5 percent of GNP by FY80 and almost 20 percent by FY85. Such increases in revenues would require determined efforts on the part of the government to formulate concrete legislation and to take immediate action in enforcing existing tax laws fully.

In the short run the national government is confronted with recessionary conditions which make immediate increases in the tax rates difficult. Further increases in local government revenues will depend on the effective delegation of financial authority to the local governments and their capabilities to take over additional administrative functions. Policy decisions on tax measures will have to be made rather soon, however, if they are to produce results in the next few years, since more comprehensive reforms (for instance, those affecting income taxes) normally take a long time to be enacted and implemented.

The World Bank's projections of the tax revenues of the national government until FY85 (Table 15.3) are based on the information contained in Technical Note A. The base-year data are the cash budget revenue estimates of the government for FY76 (as of December 1975). In these projections the major policy objectives which are important for the reform of the Philippine revenue system are taken into consideration. For instance, it is assumed that the share of tax revenues from international trade as a percentage of total national government tax revenues will decline from 45 percent in FY76 to about 40 percent in FY80 and 30 percent in FY85.

The estimates regarding direct taxation are based on assumptions that are admittedly optimistic. It is assumed that personal and corporate income taxes will be better enforced in the short run as a result of the recently terminated tax amnesty program and determined government efforts to introduce a comprehensive income tax reform. An average annual increase of about 23 percent in revenues

---

6. The fiscal year will be identical with the calendar year beginning in 1977.

Table 15.3. Revenue Projections of National and Local Government Taxes and Social Security Contributions

Category	FY76[a]	FY80	FY85	Annual growth rate FY 76–85
Tax revenue (millions of pesos at current prices)				
National government	16,530	33,360	78,000	18.8
Local governments	1,050	2,300	6,620	22.6
Social security contributions	1,050	2,530	8,510	26.2
Total	18,080	8,190	93,130	19.6
Percentage of GNP				
National government	12.6	14.5	16.5	
Local governments	0.8	1.0	1.4	
Social security contributions	0.8	1.1	1.8	
Total	14.2	16.6	19.7	
GNP	131,080	230,055	472,765	15.3

a. Revenue figures for FY76 are budget estimates.
Source: World Bank estimates.

from taxes on income and wealth is therefore anticipated between FY76 and FY85. This would necessitate a sharp rise in tax elasticity from about unity in the last few years to more than 1.6 during the period as a result of better collections and higher rates. The estimates also assume a more rapid rise in the personal income tax, especially after FY78, and a time lag is included in the forecast to allow for the legislative work necessary for a tax reform in this field. Corporate tax revenues are expected to increase 22 percent a year as a result of higher effective tax rates and a rapidly expanding corporate sector.

A sharp rise in indirect taxes on domestic goods and services is also expected in the medium term, while the government compensates for some of the anticipated losses of revenue from taxes on international trade and while direct taxation is not yet providing all of the needed revenues. The share of these indirect taxes would rise from 20 percent in FY76 to 26 percent in FY80 and about 30 percent in FY85. In brief, the national government would in FY85 derive about 35 percent of its tax revenues from direct taxes (increased from only 26 percent in FY76), while about 30 percent each would come from indirect taxes on international trade and on domestic goods and services.

Administrative improvements are also needed in the Philippine revenue system, which lacks a strong, centralized authority in charge of revenue planning, legislation, and enforcement. The Bureau of Internal Revenue and the Bureau of Customs have worked as fairly independent agencies, collecting partly the same taxes though from different sectors of the economy. Decisions on tax policy toward various economic sectors have frequently been uncoordinated, thus contributing to the confusion in the incentive system mentioned earlier. Other government authorities also collect their own levies.

Even the simple monitoring of revenue trends has proved difficult, and detailed data have usually been available only after lengthy delays. Statistics issued by the various agencies have often conflicted and have contained extensive double-counting. A thorough evaluation of the results of the tax amnesty would be helpful in formulating additional tax reform legislation, but the relevant data cannot be provided on a consolidated basis by the various agencies until late 1976. A careful assessment of the tax amnesty in particular should aid in formulating the reform of the personal income tax and in improving the tools of tax enforcement to raise the very low effective rates of corporate taxes in various sectors.

All aspects of national government revenues—planning tax policy, drafting legislation, supervising and monitoring of collections, and strictly controlling tax administration—should probably be concentrated in the Department of Finance. The formulation of further tax reforms, particularly a comprehensive review of the tax incentives for all areas of the economy, should also rest with the Department of Finance.

NATIONAL GOVERNMENT EXPENDITURES

National government expenditures were about 9 to 10 percent of GNP for many years. A large portion of current expenditures was devoted to education and social services. Capital expenditures were constrained by the low level of public savings and by the limited capacity of the government to prepare and implement projects. Since 1972, however, both current and capital expenditures have been increasing in relation to GNP.

Current expenditures. Throughout the 1960s the overall level of current expenditures of the national government was low by international standards. Current outlays were equal to about 8 to 9 percent of GNP. Since the early 1970s, however, particularly since

Table 15.4. Percentage Allocation of National Government
Current Expenditures

Category	FY60	FY65	FY70	FY71	FY72	FY73	FY74	FY75
General adminis-tration								
General goverment	11.5	12.5	11.9	11.1	10.6	9.2	7.3	6.9
Justice and police	4.9	6.0	6.7	7.0	8.6	1.9	1.8	1.7
National defense (including trans-fer payments)	14.4	12.1	13.5	14.1	13.4	19.1	21.4	21.8
Total	30.8	30.6	32.1	32.3	32.6	30.2	30.5	30.4
Social services								
Education	28.1	32.5	32.0	32.1	31.1	24.6	23.4	19.6
Health	6.1	6.1	6.2	5.8	5.9	5.6	5.8	4.9
Labor and welfare	1.7	1.4	1.6	1.6	1.9	2.0	1.1	1.1
Total	35.9	40.0	39.8	39.5	38.9	32.2	30.3	25.6
Economic sectors								
Agriculture and natural resources	5.9	6.4	5.5	4.9	5.5	14.5	7.1	7.8
Transport and communications	11.8	9.4	7.2	8.8	8.2	7.5	9.3	7.1
Commerce and industry	0.8	1.5	1.2	1.4	1.4	1.0	2.9	1.0
Other economic development	2.3	2.0	4.5	2.5	2.1	2.5	4.4	3.2
Total	20.8	19.3	18.4	17.6	17.2	25.5	23.7	19.1
Subsidies and other transfer payments	5.1	3.6	2.4	1.1	3.8	3.8	8.3	17.0
Debt service								
Interest	3.0	3.0	4.5	5.7	5.2	5.0	4.4	5.0
Repayment[a]	4.4	3.5	2.8	3.8	2.3	2.3	2.8	2.9
Total	7.4	6.5	7.3	9.5	7.5	8.3	7.2	7.9
Total current expen-ditures[b]	100.0	100.0	100.0	100.0	100.0	100.0	100.0	100.0
Total (in millions of pesos)	1,050	1,843	3,328	3,758	4,371	5,901	7,915	11,620
Total (as percentage of GNP)	8.4	8.8	9.0	8.4	8.3	9.4	9.4	10.9

a. Loan repayments and sinking-fund contributions.
b. Totals do not always equal 100 because of rounding.
Note: Expenditures are on the basis of an obligational budget.
Source: Department of Finance, Budget Commission.

FY72, the overall level has risen significantly in relation to GNP, and there has been a noticeable shift in the sectoral pattern of allocation (Table 15.4). Current expenditures on an obligational basis increased about 3.5 times, reaching an amount equal to nearly 11 percent of GNP.[7] Much of the increase, especially in FY74 and FY75, was of course the result of severe inflationary pressures. Even at constant prices, however, the rise was around 65 percent, almost 11 percent a year, which is substantially higher than the average annual real GNP growth of over 6 percent and which reflects a large increase in government activities. Actual spending in the cash budget showed similar increases from FY72 through FY75.

Between the 1950s and the early 1970s the allocation pattern of current expenditures of the national government remained roughly the same. Approximately 40 percent was spent for social services, about 30 percent for general administration (including 12 to 13 percent for national defense), and 18 to 20 percent for economic services, especially for transport and communication and, to a lesser degree, agriculture and natural resources. Debt service (interest and repayments) was around 7 percent of the total. Subsidies and other nondefense transfers were very small. A special feature of current expenditures was the relatively high share (about a third) allocated to education. Expenditures for education in the context of the whole economy, however, were not excessive; they were the equivalent of somewhat less than 3 percent of GNP.

Since FY72 the sectoral distribution of current expenditures has been characterized by a substantial rise in expenditures for defense, a significant relative decline in expenditures for social services, and an increase in subsidy payments in FY74 and particularly in FY75. Defense outlays, largely as a result of the civil unrest in Mindanao, rose from 14 percent of the total before FY72 to about 20 percent during FY73–FY75. The relative share of expenditures for education

7. Data on an "obligational" basis are derived from budget documents in which receipts and expenditures are recorded on an accrual and obligational basis respectively. In contrast, data on cash budget expenditures are based on actual disbursements. The concept of the cash budget was introduced in the Philippines only in FY72 and a sectoral analysis is not yet available. For the discussion of the past, therefore, the World Bank used obligational data. For projections, the cash budget concept was used and roughly the same percentage analysis by sector was applied to the actual cash budget totals for FY73 through FY75.

declined to below 20 percent in FY75, and there was a decrease in the share of expenditures for health. In addition, the relative share of current expenditures for agriculture, transport, and other productive sectors declined in FY75 after a significant rise in FY73 and FY74. Current outlays for agriculture, which have been about 6 percent historically, were in fact around 7.5 percent in FY74 and FY75.

Another important aspect of the budget is the distribution of current expenditures according to income groups and geographical regions. Published financial statistics clearly show that most expenditure programs have benefited the large urban centers, especially greater Manila, and that government services have not been equitably distributed among income groups, but these problems have only recently been studied.[8] In general, the absolute value of benefits from government expenditures received by families appears to increase with the income level of the families. This is true even with government services designed to provide equal opportunities for the lower income groups, such as public education, medical care, and extension services in the rural areas. Low incomes, distance from the source of the services, and ignorance of the availability and cost-benefits of the services have probably prevented low-income families from availing themselves of these services. Although access to services is difficult even in the cities, it becomes a more severe problem in the outlying rural areas. It has been found that disparities in receiving government services increase sharply with the distance from greater Manila.[9] Most of the neglected provinces have received much less in services from the government than they have contributed to it through taxes, with the exception of primary education.

The government has become increasingly aware of the need for more equitable distribution of income in the Philippines. It has demonstrated its concern by major policy decisions, such as the agrarian reform, and by increases in government subsidies in the last

8. A national survey of households was undertaken between April and September 1974 to obtain allocators for the divisible and traceable services of the national government. The survey results were applied to the national government budget figures for FY71. The study was summarized with the assistance of the National Tax Research Center. See Edita A. Tan, *Taxation, Government Spending, and Income Distribution in the Philippines* (Quezon City: University of the Philippines Institute of Economics, 1975), pp. 37–42.

9. Tan, *Taxation, Government Spending, and Income Distribution,* pp. 37–42.

few years. Most of the subsidy payments for FY74 and FY75 were directed toward fertilizer, petroleum, and grains.[10] These subsidies reflected the desire on the part of the government to undertake some redistribution of income in favor of the poorer sections of both the rural and urban populations; the magnitude of the subsidies was the result of the sharp rise in international prices for food, oil, and other raw materials.

In the future the national government will be faced with an additional rise in current expenditures in relation to GNP if government services, especially those related to social and economic development, are to be expanded. In the absence of official projections of expenditures beyond FY76, the World Bank has made some forecasts of possible trends in current expenditures by the national government that would be needed to support the programs set out in the earlier chapters. The forecasts include substantially higher current outlays for economic and social services and increased national government financial support for local governments (see Table 15.5).

An increase in national government current expenditures to about 13 percent of the estimated GNP by FY80 is believed feasible. If tax revenues rise to 14 percent of GNP and nontax revenues to about one percent, current outlays would allow a current account surplus equal to 2 percent of GNP, which would be sufficient to finance an adequate share of the capital expenditures discussed below. On the basis of these assumptions, forecasts of national government current expenditures for FY80 are derived from the actual cash budget performance in FY75 and the estimated cash budget of the government for FY76.

In these forecasts it is assumed that real wages will rise 8 percent a year from FY77 through FY80. Another upward adjustment of 5 percent a year in wages and salaries is applied in FY77 and FY88 to compensate national government employees for losses of income suffered in earlier years on account of inflation. In addition, an inflation rate of 7.5 percent a year is assumed throughout the forecasting period. Wages and salaries would thus increase 20.5 percent

10. Subsidies in FY74 totaled ₱419 million, including ₱200 million for rice, corn, and sorghum; ₱132 million for petroleum; and ₱87 million for fertilizer. In FY75 subsidies amounted to ₱321 million, consisting of ₱150 million for fertilizer and ₱171 million for rice, corn, and sorghum (including ₱131 million for rice loan amortization payments). Other transfers in FY75 included a ₱1,300 million direct transfer to the Philippine Coconut Authority.

Table 15.5. Forecasts of National Government Current Expenditures
(At current prices)

	FY75			FY80		
Category	Millions of pesos	Percentage of total outlay	Percentage of GNP	Millions of pesos	Percentage of total outlay	Percentage of GNP
General administration						
Defense	2,690	21.8	2.2	4,585	16.2	2.0
Other	1,060	8.6	0.9	2,205	7.8	1.0
Total	3,750	30.4	3.1	6,790	24.0	3.0
Social services						
Education	2,410	19.6	2.3	6,540	23.1	2.8
Health	605	4.9	0.6	1,725	6.1	0.7
Other	135	1.1	0.1	650	2.3	0.3
Total	3,150	25.6	3.0	8,915	31.5	3.8
Economic sectors						
Agriculture and natural resources	960	7.8	0.9	3,255	11.5	1.4
Transport and communication	875	7.1	0.8	2,830	10.0	1.2
Commerce and industry	125	1.0	0.1	1,105	3.9	0.5
Other economic development	395	3.2	0.4	1,300	4.6	0.6
Total	2,355	19.1	2.2	8,490	30.0	3.7
Transfers	2,100	17.0	2.4	1,980	7.0	0.9
Debt service						
Interest	615	5.0	0.6	1,500	5.3	0.6
Repayment	360	2.9	0.3	625	2.2	0.3
Total	975	7.9	0.9	2,125	7.5	0.9
Total current expenditures	12,330	100.0	11.6	28,300	100.0	12.3
Allotments and other financial assistance to local governments	653	5.3	0.6	1,553	5.5	0.7

Source: World Bank projections.

each in FY77 and FY78 and 15.5 percent annually in subsequent years. The assumed annual increase of 8 percent in real wages should be used primarily to upgrade the quality of services of the national government; it should be used only to a lesser extent to hire additional employees. As for the generation of employment, the national government has been the fastest growing sector during the last ten years and should probably create additional jobs only as government services are extended into new fields and upgraded in the outlying regions.

A significant change in the pattern of allocation of current expenditures is forecast. Expenditures for general administration (including defense) are estimated to decline from 30 percent of total outlays in FY75 to about 24 percent in FY80, while the share of social and economic services is expected to rise sharply, each category reaching about 30 percent, reflecting a considerable expansion of government activity in these areas. Three sectors in particular—rural extension, primary education, health and family planning—need to upgrade the quality of their staffs. Although the public sector appears to be competitive with the private sector in the lower income brackets, an upgrading of positions in the public sector is probably necessary for middle- and upper-level skilled positions.

The fairly drastic decrease in allocations to education in the national budget since 1972 has caused concern, especially since such allocations in the past had not been very high by international standards. Although in absolute figures the obligational budget expenditures for public education rose from ₱1,360 million in FY72 to ₱2,230 million in FY75, they actually remained at the FY72 level (expressed in constant prices and applying the GNP deflator), and in real terms they declined by 15 percent per capita. Consequently, per capita expenditures for education in FY75 were only US$8 (at constant prices), about the same level as in Thailand.[11] Private expenditures for education are highly significant, however; the Roman Catholic Church, especially, plays an important role in secondary and tertiary education. Nevertheless it would be desirable for the share of expenditures for education to rise, probably to the equivalent of almost 3 percent of GNP by FY80, or about 23 percent

---

11. Per capita expenditures for education in Korea were US$11 and in Malaysia US$32 in 1974.

of current outlays, in order to support the expected expansion of public education. It is proposed that current expenditures for health services would rise to more than 6 percent of total outlays, or the equivalent of 0.7 percent of GNP. This would be in line with the proposed expansion of health services in rural areas and in urban areas outside Manila. The staff will have to be expanded in the health field proper, and the quality of the workers in family planning and in rural health services will have to be improved. The forecasts also allow for a relatively large increase in current expenditures for other social services, including social welfare, community development, and youth programs—areas in which the government plans to become much more active as part of its regional development program.

The forecast for economic services proposes a sharp rise in current outlays for agriculture and national resources, which would amount to almost 1.5 percent of GNP by FY80, or 11.5 percent of total current expenditures. As mentioned earlier, such an increase will probably be necessary to improve the extension services and other services for rural development. The forecasts also include outlays for additional maintenance associated with the various agricultural development projects in progress. The need for more emphasis on maintenance explains why the World Bank estimate provides for an increase in current outlays for transport from 0.8 percent of GNP in FY75 to 1.2 percent by FY80. Maintenance of the road system has been neglected in the past and will require significantly more financial resources in the next few years. Moreover, government transport services will have to be expanded to support more balanced regional development, which means that port services and air transport links will need upgrading. Telecommunication services will also need to be improved, especially in the outlying areas (the Visayas and Mindanao, for example).

Outlays for services for industry and commerce will also have to be increased in order to promote medium- and small-scale industries and to aid the industrialization process in the less developed regions. These outlays would amount to about 4 percent of total current expenditures, or 0.5 percent of GNP, by FY80. Current expenditures for supporting services such as electricity are also forecast to rise, including outlays for the National Electrification Administration (which is part of the national budget) in connection with the rural electrification program now in progress.

The World Bank projections also assume a reduction of national government subsidies and other nondefense transfers from around 17 percent of current outlays to about 4 percent by the end of the decade. The present large subsidy payments may have been necessary as an emergency measure, but they should probably not become a permanent feature of Philippine price policies. A reorganization of government services for the benefit of the lower income groups would allow direct price subsidies to be reduced. The thrust of such a policy would probably have to be different in urban and in rural areas, however. In urban areas, especially greater Manila where services are already at a considerably higher level than in the rest of the country, more emphasis should probably be given to reaching the lowest income groups rather than to expanding the quantity of services. In many rural areas, however, some of the basic services will have to be initiated or expanded from a very low level.

Capital expenditures. Until FY72 the volume of capital expenditures by the central government was very low, accounting for only 10 to 15 percent of total expenditures by the national government and averaging just over one percent of GNP.[12] Most of the capital expenditures were for public investment in infrastructure, although some outlays were transfers of capital for equity in public corporations and loans to the rest of the public sector. The sectoral composition of capital outlays shown in Table 15.6 reflects a heavy emphasis on transport, especially road construction, and on agriculture, owing to the construction of major irrigation projects.

Capital transfers to government agencies, development banks, public corporations, and government enterprises have become a major component of capital outlays by the government in recent years. This very significant change demonstrates the government's determination to provide public corporations and government-controlled development banks with an adequate financial base so that sufficient funds can be borrowed to finance their development programs without serious deterioration of their debt-equity ratios. For instance, increased capitalization of banks in the form of bonds

12. Serious statistical problems have impeded attempts to determine the amount of capital expenditures actually made. "Obligational authority" figures substantially overstate actual capital outlays of the national government; the cash-budget concept, introduced in FY72, probably gives the most accurate account, but it may understate somewhat the actual implementation of infrastructure construction, because cash disbursements to contractors take place some time after completion of a project.

Table 15.6. National Government Capital Expenditures
(Percentage of total capital expenditures)

Category	FY60	FY65	FY70	FY71	FY72	FY73	FY74	FY75
General administration								
Defense	1.4	0.8	1.1	1.6	1.5	3.5	1.7	1.6
Other	5.1	5.2	2.2	0.9	1.0	0.3	0.1	0.8
Total	6.5	6.0	3.3	2.5	2.5	3.8	1.8	2.4
Social services								
Education	12.5	2.6	9.1	5.8	3.6	4.6	2.0	4.6
Health	5.1	1.7	3.0	1.0	1.8	1.3	2.2	2.7
Labor and welfare	. . .	0.4	0.3	1.2	0.1	0.2	0.2	0.2
Total	17.6	4.7	12.4	8.0	5.5	6.1	4.4	7.5
Economic sectors								
Agriculture and natural resources	22.7	6.4	7.9	15.8	24.0	18.7	36.0	25.7
Transport and communication	41.7	76.8	61.3	46.5	35.5	37.2	24.0	41.4
Commerce and industry	0.5	0.8	2.3	9.4	1.8	0.8	4.7	3.4
Other economic development	11.0	5.7	12.8	17.7	30.5	33.3	29.2	19.5
Total	75.9	89.7	84.3	89.4	91.9	90.0	93.9	90.2
Total	100.0	100.0	100.0	100.0	100.0	100.0	100.0	100.0

Note: Data are on an obligational basis.
Source: Budget Commission.

reached ₱1,650 million in FY74 with the creation of financially
strong development banks that could assist in the implementation of
agricultural and rural development programs.[13] Direct capitalization
of government institutions and enterprises rose sharply in FY75 and
will probably be substantially larger in FY76. Such transfers
amounted to about ₱650 million in FY75; [14] as some of the transfer
outlays originally budgeted for FY75 will be spent in FY76, total
expenditures for the capitalization of government institutions and
enterprises in FY76 may rise to around ₱3,000 million.[15]

13. On a cash-disbursement basis. ₱290 million went to the Development
Bank of the Philippines, ₱530 million to the Land Bank, and ₱200 million to the
Philippine National Bank.
14. On a cash-disbursement basis.
15. Roughly ₱3,600 million was or will be spent for capital transfers in FY75
and FY76 combined; about ₱1,500 million of this amount has been earmarked
for the takeover of the Manila Electric Company, ₱450 million for the capitalization of the National Power Company, and another ₱270 million for the

Forecasts of capital expenditures by the national government are based on the projections of public sector investments discussed in Chapter 13 and on estimates of required loans from the central government and equity contributions to public entities as explained later in this chapter. National government infrastructure expenditures are projected to rise rapidly in order to implement the most important investment programs, particularly those for irrigation, flood control, and road construction. In addition, ambitious investment plans in the public corporate sector and expanded lending programs by government-supported development banks will require significant capital subsidies and equity contributions from the national government. Lending to local governments will also increase.

Under these assumptions, total capital outlays of the national government would need to reach a level of almost ₱12,000 million at current prices, or 5.2 percent of GNP, by FY80. Of this amount, ₱8,000 million, equivalent to 3.5 percent of GNP, would be for infrastructure investments by the central government, compared with only ₱1,100 million at current prices, or 1.0 percent of GNP, in FY75. Realizing this goal will require significant improvements in the preparation and implementation of projects, as well as a considerable acceleration of the government's ability to release appropriated funds for disbursement. Given the fact that cash releases for infrastructure investments in FY75 were already ₱1,540 million, while obligational authority was around ₱3,400 million a year in FY74 and FY75, it is reasonable to assume that the disbursement process can indeed be accelerated. The allocation of infrastructure expenditures to various sectors is summarized in Table 15.7.

Capital transfers to such entities as public corporations, government enterprises, and government banks are projected to rise to ₱3,900 million at current prices, or 1.7 percent of GNP, by FY80. A sectoral breakdown of transfers of equity during the next few years is difficult to predict because allocations will depend on

---

National Electrification Administration. Around ₱50 million is allocated to the Philippine National Oil Company for its oil and natural gas exploration program. Capital transfers of ₱200 million will go to the National Irrigation Administration, ₱100 million to the Land Bank, and ₱340 million to the Agricultural Credit Administration in order to broaden agricultural credit programs, especially those for rice and corn farmers and for the coconut revitalization program. Another ₱300 million is allocated for the equity of the Export Processing Zone Authority to expedite the establishment of the Mariveles Export Zone.

Table 15.7. Forecasts of National Government Capital Expenditures
(At current prices)

Category	FY75[a] Amount (millions of pesos)	FY75[a] Composition (percent)	FY75[a] Share in GNP (percent)	FY80 Amount (millions of pesos)	FY80 Composition (percent)	FY80 Share in GNP (percent)
General administration						
Defense	17	0.8	0.02	95	0.8	0.04
Other	8	0.4	0.0	50	0.4	0.02
Total	25	1.2	0.02	145	1.2	0.06
Social sectors						
Education	49	2.4	0.04	720	6.0	0.3
Health	29	1.4	0.03	240	2.0	0.1
Other	2	0.1	0.01	190	1.6	0.1
Total	80	3.9	0.08	1,150	9.6	0.5
Economic sectors						
Agriculture and natural resources	272	13.1	0.26	2,390	20.0	1.0
Transport and communications	440	21.3	0.41	3,830	32.0	1.7
Other	270	13.0	0.23	550	4.6	0.2
Total	980	47.4	0.90	6,770	56.6	2.9
Total infrastructure	1,085	52.5	1.0	8,065	67.4	3.5
Capital transfers to local governments	...	...	...	700	5.8	0.3
Other capital outlays	982	47.5	0.9	3,195	26.8	1.4
Total capital outlays	2,067	100.0	1.9	11,960	100.0	5.2

... Zero or negligible.

a. Total capital outlays are preliminary actual cash disbursements during FY75. They include "prior years accounts payable" which are assumed to comprise primarily appropriations for capital outlays made in earlier years but actually spent in FY75. The sectoral breakdown of infrastructure expenditure is analogous to the breakdown in the obligational budget.

Source: World Bank estimates.

individual investment programs. In addition, the extent to which government funds will be required to provide financial backing to large industries such as steel, petroleum, and fertilizer can be only roughly estimated. It was assumed that by FY80 about ₱700 million would be granted as loans to local governments to finance part of their investment programs, in accordance with increased government efforts to stimulate local participation in economic development.[16]

FINANCING NATIONAL GOVERNMENT EXPENDITURES

Throughout the 1960s tax performance was inadequate and non-tax receipts were low. As a result, national government savings on current account were insignificant—even negative in FY69 and FY70. The situation began to improve markedly after FY71 because of the export boom and the successful implementation of tax reform measures. As government revenues temporarily rose faster than current outlays, the current account surplus increased considerably, amounting in FY74 to ₱3,850 million, or 4.6 percent of GNP; but in FY75 it fell to ₱2,850 million when tax receipts were somewhat lower than the budget estimates. The high level of government savings on current account can be attributed in part to strict anti-inflationary fiscal management and in part to significant improvement in revenue performance.

In both FY74 and FY75 the current account surpluses far exceeded total capital expenditures, since cash disbursements for infrastructure and other capital outlays lagged considerably behind the rapidly rising appropriations. Because the government continued to borrow substantially from domestic and foreign sources, overall cash balances of the national government in FY74 and FY75 reached record surpluses of ₱3,200 million and ₱2,800 million respectively. In FY74 and FY75 combined, total net domestic borrowing was ₱4,000 million, 70 percent of which was derived from the issuance of bonds. Net borrowing from abroad, which was used exclusively for the support of investment programs, amounted to the equivalent of only US$25 million in FY74. In FY75, as the implementation of projects was accelerated, net borrowing from foreign sources on a

---

16. The government also plans to present for the first time a consolidated budget of the entire public sector by FY78. In addition, as mentioned earlier, the fiscal year is to be synchronized with the calendar year as of January 1, 1977.

cash disbursement basis rose to more than US$80 million, which financed more than 55 percent of the infrastructure expenditures of the national government in that year. World Bank forecasts of national government finances, given in Table 15.8, are based on the assumption that total current receipts of the national government will be equal to 16.0 percent of GNP by FY80. If the projections of current spending are realized, expenditures will not exceed 12.3 percent of GNP by that year, making possible national government savings of 3.7 percent of GNP, which would finance somewhat more than half the capital outlays of the government. The balance, roughly ₱3,500 million at current prices (US$460 million), or 1.5 percent of GNP, would have to be financed

Table 15.8. Summary of National Government Finances on a Cash Budget Basis
(In millions of pesos at current prices)

Category	FY75 Actual		FY80 Estimated	
	Amount	Percentage of GNP	Amount	Percentage of GNP
Receipts				
Taxes	13,365	12. 6	33,360	14.5
Nontax receipts	2,272	2.1	3,450	1.5
Total	15,637	14.7	36,810	16.0
Current expenditures	12,785[a]	12.0	28,300	12.3
Current surplus	2,852	2.7	8,510	3.7
Capital expenditures				
Infrastructure	1,085	1.0	8,050	3.5
Other capital outlays	982[b]	0.9	3,910	1.7
Total	2,067	1.9	11,960	5.2
Total cash deficit/surplus	785	0.7	3,450	1.5
Net borrowing				
Foreign	621	0.6	2,300	1.0
Domestic	1,420	1.3	1,150	0.5
Treasury bills and notes	881	0.8	550	0.25
Bonds	539	0.5	600	0.25
Total	2,041	1.9	3,450	1.5
Change in cash balance	2,826	2.6	—	—

— Not applicable.
   a. Includes Treasury Warrants from prior years outstanding and balances for guaranteed obligations minus collections of obligations of prior years as well as other so-called nonbudgetary operations on a net basis. These items are not included in current expenditures in the earlier tables.
   b. Includes ₱329 million of "Prior Years' Accounts Payable," which were assumed to comprise primarily appropriations for capital outlays in earlier years actually spent in FY75.
   Sources: Department of Finance and World Bank estimates.

by net borrowing from foreign and domestic sources in that year. This financing would not include direct borrowing from domestic and external sources by public corporations and government enterprises, such as the National Power Corporation or the National Steel Corporation, which would probably be guaranteed by the national government but which would not be channeled through its budget.[17]

The analysis in Chapter 13 indicates that about 30 percent of the infrastructure expenditures of the national government would be financed through foreign loans. This would result in net borrowing from abroad of ₱2.3 million (US$300 million at the present rate of exchange), which would be about one percent of the GNP estimated for FY80.

About ₱1,400 million, or 0.5 percent of GNP, would have to be financed from domestic borrowing in FY80—no more than in FY75 at current prices and in real terms a significant decrease. The underlying assumption is that claims on domestic savings from the private sector and from the briskly expanding public corporate sector will be very large.

As discussed in Chapter 9, the marginal domestic savings rate is expected to rise from about 21 percent of GDP in 1975 to 25 percent by 1980. This significant increase will not be easily achieved. Even with such a favorable rate of marginal savings, the national government may find it difficult to raise more than about ₱1,200 million (Table 15.8) without preempting funds that would otherwise be sources of financing for the private and corporate public sectors. In other words, the success of a development program of the size indicated here will depend to a large extent on the availability of as much external finance as is possible at reasonable terms, given the constraints of the balance of payments.

Public Corporations and Enterprises

Public corporations and government-owned or government-controlled enterprises have traditionally played a minor part in

17. The ₱3,500 million would include all borrowing for national government infrastructure programs (for irrigation, port construction, and education, for example), as well as for loans and transfers to local governments for infrastructure programs and for capital transfers to public corporations.

Philippine economic development. Their primary function has been to provide some basic services, including electricity, transport, water supply and sewerage, and gas. The government has operated a number of enterprises, but most of them have been quite small. A variety of self-governing boards, commissions, and agencies have also existed, but many have been included in the national budget, without budgets of their own. Several have had limited economic or legal responsibilities, although some, such as the Board of Investments (BOI), have held key positions in formulating development policies. The main exceptions to this pattern have been the government-owned banks, particularly the Philippine National Bank and the Development Bank of the Philippines, which have major roles in the field of finance.

By the end of FY73 government agencies included seven financial institutions, five public utility corporations, thirty-nine developmental and other corporations, and nineteen self-governing boards, commissions, and agencies with total assets of ₱38,300 million. The overall financial condition of these seventy government entities in 1972, 1973, and 1975 is summarized in Tables 15.9 and 15.10.

Investments by these corporations and enterprises were, on the average, probably equal to less than 0.3 percent of GNP throughout the 1960s. This situation began to change in the 1970s, however, as the government started to expand public investment; investments by the public utility corporations were probably equivalent to about 0.7 percent of GNP in the late 1970s. As discussed in Chapters 6 and 13, an even larger role for public corporations and enterprises

Table 15.9. Assets, Liabilities, and Net Income of Government-owned and Government-controlled Corporations
(In millions of pesos)

Item	June 30, 1972	June 30, 1973
Assets	28,506	38,265
Liabilities	22,828	29,951
As a percentage of assets	79	78
Net worth	5,678	8,314
Income	3,340	3,940
Expenses	2,870	3,377
Net income	470	563

Source: Philippine Commission on Audit, *1973 Annual Financial Report of Government-owned or Controlled Corporations* (Quezon City, 1973), p. 5.

Table 15.10. Assets and Liabilities of Selected Government Corporations, Enterprises, and Financial Institutions
(In millions of pesos)

Category	FY73 Actual		FY74 Estimated		FY75 Estimated	
	Assets	Liabilities	Assets	Liabilities	Assets	Liabilities
Government public utilities						
National Power Corporation	1,342.6	683.9	1,602.5	521.1	2,395.5	888.1
Philippine National Railways	547.1	48.3	593.8	46.5	618.7	40.1
Manila Gas Corporation	33.6	7.6	33.8	6.6	35.0	6.6
Manila Waterworks and Sewerage System	1,490.9	649.1	1,475.9	677.2	1,508.7	700.8
Total	3,414.2	1,388.9	3,706.0	1,251.4	4,557.9	1,635.6
Enterprises						
Manila Hotel Company	4.4	2.3	4.3	2.2	4.2	2.0
National Development Company	257.4	254.0	244.7	220.5	245.8	221.0
National Shipyards and Steel Corporation	138.7	137.8	109.8	111.0	107.6	110.2
People's Homesite and Housing Corporation	87.4	45.2	85.8	45.7	272.1	101.2
Home Financing Commission	6.3	1.0	7.5	0.4	9.0	0.5
Philippine Charity Sweepstakes Office	36.8	34.2	35.9	32.8	35.4	31.9
Philippine Coconut Administration	5.8	1.0	...	...	...	...
Philippine Sugar Institute	41.5	1.5	45.0	1.6	47.0	1.5
Philippine Tobacco Administration	45.3	7.7	49.6	4.2	59.3	4.2
Philippine Virginia Tobacco Administration	390.2	227.8	90.7	211.0	80.8	120.0
Total	1,013.8	712.5	673.3	629.4	861.2	592.5
Financial institutions						
Development Bank of the Philippines	4,702.9	2,843.6	5,279.4	3,304.1	7,475.9	7,324.4
Philippine National Bank	5,309.8	4,776.6				
Land Bank of the Philippines	129.2	54.8				
Government Services Insurance System	3,520.8	3,357.3	3,781.7	3,643.8	4,045.6	3,903.1
Social Security System	1,891.9	130.9				
National Investment and Development Corporation	348.7	88.8				
Central Bank of the Philippines (CBP)	14,433.3	14,433.3	21,273.6	20,947.4		
Total	30,336.6	25,685.3				
Total excluding CBP	15,903.3	11,252.0				

. . . Zero or negligible.
Sources: Department of Finance and annual reports of the various organizations.

is contemplated for the future. By 1980 investments by the public utility corporations could reach 2.2 percent of GNP, and investment by government-controlled enterprises in basic industries, including petroleum refining and the manufacture of fertilizer and steel, could also be quite significant.

The magnitude of these proposed investments represents a major change in the role of the government in the Philippine economy. Apart from the obvious issue of the manner in which these investments will be financed, a number of other questions need to be resolved. One is the degree of autonomy in decisionmaking with respect to investments that should be given to the corporations and enterprises. A closely related issue is the way in which operating surpluses are to be dealt with: Should the individual enterprise be allowed to reinvest earnings (either in its main line of business or in new and unrelated fields of production), or should at least some net earnings be transferred to the budget of the national government?

Since investments are being expanded rapidly, various corporations and enterprises may run deficits. The question of covering these deficits will depend on the amount that the national government is willing or able to finance through the budget and the extent to which public sector corporations and enterprises will have to borrow directly, either domestically or externally. The external borrowing of public sector corporations and enterprises could be very large and will have to be closely controlled to keep the amount of borrowing within the limitations set by the balance of payments and by external debt management. As for domestic borrowing, the competing claims of the public and private sectors will have to be resolved.

The expanding role of government corporations and enterprises also raises the issues of the way in which the administration of these institutions is to be organized and of which entity within the government will be responsible for their control. Obviously there are many possibilities with respect to administrative and financial control. Perhaps the most logical arrangement is for the National Economic and Development Authority (NEDA) to supervise the direction and economic consequences of the operations of the public corporate sector and for the Department of Finance to coordinate the financial and fiscal policies governing the public sector, including tax and pricing policies. Close cooperation with the Central Bank,

Table 15.11. Estimate of Investments by Public Utility Corporations
(At constant 1974 prices)

Public utility	Annual average 1970–74		FY80	
	Millions of pesos	Percentage of GNP	Millions of pesos	Percentage of GNP
Power	180	0.2	3,570[a]	2.5
Transport	265	0.3	150	0.1
Other utilities	180	0.2	450	0.3
Total	625	0.7	4,170	2.9

a. Includes purchase of existing facilities from the privately owned Manila Electric Company.
Source: World Bank estimates.

which will have to set priorities affecting the amounts and terms of borrowing, will also be required. All these issues are likely to become extremely important in the future, since the financial operations of the public entities are expected to increase significantly.

PUBLIC UTILITY CORPORATIONS

At present there are four primary public utility corporations in the Philippines: the National Power Corporation (NPC), the Philippine National Railways (PNR), the Metropolitan Waterworks and Sewerage System (MWSS), and the Manila Gas Corporation (MGC). In 1975 these corporations had combined assets of about ₱4,500 million, equivalent to about US$600 million at the present rate of exchange (Table 15.11). The NPC is by far the largest corporation in the Philippines, with assets totaling about ₱2,400 million (US$300 million).[18] The MWSS is also quite large by Philippine standards, with assets of about ₱1,500 million (US$200 million).

Investments by public utility corporations have been only about 0.7 percent of GNP in recent years, but by 1985 they may reach about 2.9 percent of GNP, or ₱4,200 million at 1974 prices. In real terms this would be more than six times the average amount spent annually by the public utility corporations during 1970–74. More than

18. For comparative purposes, the largest private corporations in 1970 were the Manila Electric Company and the Philippine Long Distance Telephone Company, with ₱900 million each. Other large corporations included Iligan Integrated Steel Corporation (₱800 million) and San Miguel Corporation (₱600 million).

80 percent of these expenditures would be in the power sector, the largest portion of which will be spent by NPC on its expansion program, which will require investment equivalent to almost 2.5 percent of GNP by 1980. Capital outlays are estimated to equal about 0.1 percent of GNP for the PNR and other transport corporations which may have been established by then. Another 0.3 percent of GNP would be invested in the expansion of other utilities, including large investments to upgrade services in some of the urban centers that are expected to grow significantly by 1985.

Investments of this magnitude raise two major questions: One concerns the manner in which the investments will be financed; the other, the need to continually improve the management capability of the corporations. On the matter of financing, the equity base of the corporations will need to be enlarged to a level commensurate with the investment program. Recently the amount of long-term debt (with a maturity of more than one year) in relation to equity—that is, the debt-equity ratio—varied significantly among the individual corporations.[19] Data for FY73 [20] show very little long-term debt incurred by the PNR, while the MGC had no long-term debt at all.[21] The MWSS showed a very unfavorable debt-equity ratio because most of the investment in water supply and sewerage has been financed by incurring long-term debts (of ₱425.6 million), while very little equity (₱6.2 million) has been built up. The debt-equity ratio of the NPC recovered in FY73.

The government has recently begun to raise the equity of the ailing corporations to acceptable levels by direct budgetary grants. In 1974 the authorized stock capital of the NPC was raised from ₱300 million to ₱2,000 million. In mid-1975 the authorized stock of the PNR was raised from ₱650 million to ₱1,500 million in order to widen the equity base of the corporation, enabling it to obtain loans for the further expansion of its network. Further increases in equity will probably be needed for all these corporations in the

---

19. This ratio is the one generally applied by the World Bank; it relates to assets in use.

20. See the Philippine Commission on Audit, *1973 Annual Financial Report of Government-owned or Controlled Corporations* (Quezon City, 1973).

21. The favorable debt-equity ratios actively reflect the discouragingly low level of investments rather than sound financial management. In other words, the corporations did not use their borrowing capacity to make investments which may have been very important from a developmental point of view.

future. These increases will be financed from internally generated funds or transfers from the budget of the national government. The amount of funds generated internally will of course depend on the future price policy of the government with regard to utilities. Because utility rates are highly political and have a considerable effect on the other sectors of the economy, the government has kept rates down in the past, with negative effects on the net earnings of the corporation. As a result, roughly ₱2,500 million of additional equity at current prices will be needed by 1980; this amount would be financed largely by grants from the budget of the national government. About ₱11,000 million (US$1,470 million), however, would have to be borrowed either externally or domestically. The largest portion would probably come from abroad; domestic borrowing would be primarily in the form of bonds. It is estimated that the foreign exchange component of the investments of the public utility corporations will be on the order of 65 percent, and it is assumed that virtually all these funds will come from external sources.

Table 15.12, which estimates the financing of investments by public corporations in FY80, shows that transfers of equity by the national government would amount to ₱850 million, or 0.4 percent of GNP, while around ₱1,100 million, or 0.5 percent of GNP, would have to be borrowed in the domestic market. Foreign borrowing would cover 64 percent of the investments, or US$550 million.

The large amounts involved in the investment program point to the need for substantial improvements in the organization and administration of the corporations; these improvements might

Table 15.12. Estimate of Financing Public Corporation Investments in FY80

Category	Amount (millions of pesos)		Composition (percent)	Share of GNP (percent)
	1974 prices	Current prices		
Foreign borrowing	2,710	4,170	64.0	1.9
National government equity contributions	550	850	13.2	0.4
Domestic borrowing	710	1,100	16.8	0.5
Other sources[a]	200	400	6.0	0.1
Total investment	4,170	6,520	100.0	2.9

a. Includes initial cash generation.
Source: World Bank estimates.

include intensive staff training, especially in the medium and highly skilled levels, as well as the hiring of new staff with sufficient training to deal with the issues that are forthcoming. In addition, the accounting systems of virtually all public utility corporations need revision. All utility corporations should collect the large accounts receivable, systematize their billing to preclude the accumulation of unbilled production, and conduct sustained studies of the advisability of transferring the control and operation of utilities in rural areas to local governments.

National Power Company (NPC). The assets of the NPC increased by almost 80 percent between FY73 and FY75, reflecting the sharp increase in the power investment program. Originally created as a nonstock public corporation in 1936, the NPC was converted into a stock corporation in 1960 with a government subscription of 100 percent. Although it has been competing with a number of privately owned utilities, particularly the Manila Electric Company (MECO), the NPC accounts for more than a quarter of the power generated in the Philippines.

With the promulgation of Presidential Decree 40 in November 1972, the NPC was made solely responsible for the construction of national grids and ultimately for the ownership and operation of all generating facilities in the Philippines. MECO, at that time the largest company generating as well as distributing power, will eventually become only a distribution utility. To meet the expected increase in the demand for power, the NPC has begun to expand its hydroelectric power facilities and to develop geothermal power plants. The total estimated construction program of the NPC for FY76–FY85 is ₱49,000 million, or US$6,500 million. At 1974 prices the proposed program would require outlays of about ₱24,000 million, or US$3,200 million, whereas actual NPC expenditures were only ₱1,100 million at 1974 prices between FY67 and FY75.

This large investment program will raise serious management problems for the NPC, which up to now has had a poor record of administrative and organizational performance with a much smaller investment program. The financial implications of the program are also significant; the proposed program dwarfs the existing fixed assets of the NPC. Because of the size of the program, its high foreign exchange component (64 percent), and the limited funds available domestically, the bulk of the financing will have to come from external borrowing. If a tariff level is assumed that would allow the

NPC to earn a return of 8 percent a year on fixed assets in operation, retained earnings are estimated to contribute about 14 percent of construction costs (including interest during construction). To obtain the required level of financing on favorable terms the equity base of the NPC will need to be greatly increased. A minimum contribution of ₱11,000 million in current prices (US$1,500 million), or about 25 percent of total investments, will be required from the national government to maintain an adequate debt-service coverage.

Philippine National Railways (PNR). The PNR has expanded its facilities very little in recent years. It suffered operational losses in the early 1970s, but these have been gradually reduced by administrative improvements. The government has decided to rehabilitate the PNR with a minimum expenditure in the hope that it will provide competitive low-cost passenger and freight service. The corporation, currently limited to central and northern Luzon, plans to expand its network to the south of the island with the help of the Asian Development Bank (ADB). It is also considering a modernization of its rolling stock.

As mentioned earlier, the government has increased the equity base of the corporation to ₱1,500 million to enable it to borrow on a larger scale, especially from abroad. Presidential Decree 741 of July 1975 explicitly empowers the PNR to contract loans from foreign governments and their agencies, from international organizations, or from firms extending suppliers' credits. It may also issue bonds in pesos or the equivalent in other currencies.

Investments of the PNR over the next ten years are assumed to be about ₱200 million (US$27 million) a year. About 60 percent of this amount will be raised by foreign borrowing to cover the estimated foreign exchange component of the program. The balance would come from domestic borrowing (about 10 percent) and from increases in equity. Assuming that the government will not allow a significant rise in tariffs, the World Bank has estimated an average annual transfer of ₱50 million to the corporation from the budget of the national government, which would be the equivalent of about 25 percent of the annual investment outlays. This share would be smaller if railway rates were raised to allow a higher rate of return.

Other utility corporations. The Metropolitan Waterworks and Sewerage System (MWSS) has undertaken substantial investments to enlarge its facilities in response to the pressures of urbanization in greater Manila. The Manila Gas Corporation (MGC), the smallest of the corporations discussed here, had total assets of only ₱35 million in FY73. Its main problems in the past have been the inadequacy of its bill collection and the enormous losses caused by gas leaks. The MGC has recently made some investments to modernize its distribution system and reduce gas losses from almost 25 percent of production to only 10 percent. Only a small allowance is made for transfers of capital to the corporation by the national government in the future, although the corporation continues to have current liabilities of more than twice its assets. Its weak debt-paying ability will probably require more capital transfers in the long term to finance necessary expansions of the system. Because of the FY75 boost in the equity of the MWSS by a ₱200 million transfer from the central government, however, other transfers of capital from the government will probably be small in the medium term.

GOVERNMENT-CONTROLLED INDUSTRIAL ENTERPRISES

During the first decade of Philippine independence the government created and operated a wide range of manufacturing and other industrial enterprises. According to Golay, the government was "directly producing coal, cement, steel, pulp and paper, and textiles and yarns and operating a shipyard and engineering shops." [22] In addition, the government had substantial investments in other manufacturing enterprises, in airlines, and in shipping. It was also indirectly involved in the production of a variety of manufactured goods through a government-owned holding company. In this early period there was a persistent faith in the capacity of the government to participate directly in industrialization, but the results of these activities led to an abrupt change in policy in 1954.

In the wake of widespread charges of mismanagement, the government initiated action in 1954 to sell many of its business enterprises to the private sector. Because of their poor financial conditions, however, it was difficult to dispose of the enterprises. During the 1960s and early 1970s the government confined its activities largely to public utilities or to special government functions, such as regulation of marketing and prices and the establishment of promotional boards for certain sectors of the economy.

22. Frank H. Golay, *The Philippines: Public Policy and National Economic Development* (Ithaca, N.Y.: Cornell University Press, 1961), pp. 242–43.

Table 15.13. Estimated Capital Requirements of Potential
Government-controlled Industries

Industry	Capital requirements (millions of pesos at 1974 prices)	Construction period planned by government
Philippine National Oil Company	5,000	1975–80
Urea fertilizer project	1,400	1976–78
Integrated steel project	7,700	1976–79
Total	14,100	

Sources: NEDA, BOI, and World Bank estimates.

After this period of quiescence the government now plans to forge ahead in certain industries such as petroleum, petrochemicals, fertilizer, and steel. The large investments expected during the next ten years raise the question of the extent to which domestic and external financing can be mobilized to fund these projects. Because some of these projects will be too large for domestic investors, the government will probably have to provide financial support. It could either guarantee equity up to a controlling 51 percent, or guarantee the borrowing of the corporations after having provided for an economically sound debt-service ratio. Contributions to equity could possibly also be provided by government-controlled financial intermediaries such as the DBP, the PNB, or the National Investment and Development Corporation (NIDC).

At this preliminary stage, when the size and timing of major projects have not yet been determined, it is difficult to make any precise estimates of the amount of government financing that will be required. To indicate some of the implications of such financial contributions for the government's budget, however, Table 15.13 lists a few major industries with large capital needs in which government intervention is most likely. They include the Philippine National Oil Company (PNOC), the planned urea fertilizer complex, and the integrated steel project. No government participation has been envisaged for the petrochemical complex in the medium term, since this project is still at a very early stage of preparation.[23]

Although the timing of these projects is not yet known, considerable delays in implementation have been assumed. A 70:30 debt-equity ratio was adopted as a desirable target for industrial

23. It is estimated to require ₱7.0 million.

enterprises. For the integrated steel and the urea fertilizer projects, it was assumed that the government would want to acquire a 51 percent share of equity. PNOC is already controlled by the government, but government equity will be increased further. A 51 percent share of equity by the national government in the former corporations would amount to about ₱1,400 million at 1974 prices. On the assumption that construction will be delayed and that equity will be paid as construction progresses, contributions to equity by the national government to the fertilizer and steel projects alone would be around ₱300 million a year by about FY80. Borrowing by the corporation is to be guaranteed by the government, with no immediate effect on the budgets. Apart from these contributions, the government is also expected to transfer equity funds of about ₱50–100 million to PNOC for its oil and natural gas explorations.

GOVERNMENT-CONTROLLED BANKS AND FINANCIAL INSTITUTIONS

During the 1960s and early 1970s, when the government withdrew from active participation in industry, government-controlled financial intermediaries continued to play an important part in the development of the Philippine economy. These institutions included (apart from the Central Bank of the Philippines) The Philippine National Bank (PNB), the Development Bank of the Philippines (DBP), the Land Bank of the Philippines, and the National Investment and Development Corporation (NIDC), a subsidy of the PNB. The two government social security funds, the Government Service Insurance System (GSIS) and the Social Security System (SSS), are also part of the government financial sector. Total combined assets of these institutions amounted to ₱28,900 million (US$3,850 million) at the end of FY73. The combined assets of government banks, including the Central Bank, were equivalent to 54 percent of the total assets of the banking system; excluding the Central Bank, they accounted for about 30 percent of total bank assets.

Since FY73 the government banks have greatly increased their activities in the implementation of major development programs. PNB, the largest commercial bank in the Philippines, accounted for a third of the total assets of the commercial banking system in March 1975.[24] As the intermediary of government funds and through

24. The commercial banking system more than doubled its assets in 1973 and 1974. The assets of the PNB had reached about ₱15,000 million by mid-1975.

its own borrowing abroad, the PNB has been providing more short- and medium-term financing for manufacturing (especially for small- and medium-size industries), commercial transport on land and at sea, and rural programs, particularly Masagana 99. The PNB's widespread network of branch offices in the provinces lends itself well to the implementation of rural programs, for which it also furnishes the services of its credit technicians. The government increased the equity of PNB from ₱500 million to ₱700 million in 1974 to support its further expansion. This increase in equity will also provide additional financing for NIDC, the long-term lending subsidiary of the PNB.

With the government focus on agricultural development, agrarian reform, and other rural development programs, the rural banking system has been expanded. In particular the Land Bank, which has existed since 1963, has been revitalized and awarded an important role in financing government development programs. In FY74 a government budget transfer raised the equity of the Land Bank from about ₱70 million to ₱600 million. Another ₱100 million transfer took place in FY75, and annual contributions to equity of ₱100 million are scheduled for the next eight years. Total equity should reach ₱1,500 million by FY83, which would make the Land Bank the major agricultural bank of the Philippines and enable it to be the main banking agency of the agrarian reform and the Masagana program.

The DBP is the most important provider of long-term financing in the Philippines. Its main private competitor, the Private Development Corporation of the Philippines (PDCP), holds the equivalent of only one-tenth of the total assets of ₱7,000 million of the DBP. The DBP finances projects in all sectors of the economy. In FY74 the government almost doubled the equity of the DBP, raising it above ₱1,700 million. Given the sheer size and diversity of its financing operations, the contribution of the DBP to the development of the Philippine economy is considerable.

An approximate evaluation of returns and partial economic indicators on a sample of DBP-financed industrial projects gives some impression of the economic benefits deriving from the operations of the DBP. In FY73 the DBP provided financial assistance to forty-five BOI-registered projects; its total contribution amounted to ₱592 million (US$84 million) out of a total investment of about ₱1,200 million. When completed, it is estimated that these projects will generate around 8,300 jobs directly, and net foreign exchange earnings or savings derived are projected to be US$50 million annually. The average financial rate of return of these projects in FY73 was estimated at 20 percent, and the average economic rate of return at 15 percent. The average cost of fixed investment per worker, although high—about US$14,000—was below the average for all BOI-registered projects.

With a sharp increase in lending volume, all government banks would have to improve their organizations considerably to ensure better preparation and supervision of projects. They would also have to enforce more systematic management of government debt and stricter observance of rules governing the relending of borrowed funds to their customers and the collection of outstanding credits. At present the DBP, the Land Bank, and the PNB have severe problems with collecting overdue amortizations, advances, and receivables of loan accounts.

Another important issue which may arise in the future is the extent of government intervention. As banks borrow more funds from international organizations or bilateral donors, the government, which will have to guarantee the loans, will want to supervise the lending activities of the banks more closely. Care will have to be taken, however, that government influence is not used to pressure these institutions into financially doubtful activities with little developmental significance.

The two government social security funds, the GSIS and SSS, had combined assets of ₱5,400 million at the end of FY73. The GSIS is for government employees and the larger of the two because contributions are obligatory. The SSS, created in 1954 to provide social security to nongovernment employees, had at that time only half the assets of the GSIS.[25] Its coverage has been expanded by various legislative measures, but so far only a small minority of nongovernment employees has joined. Social security contributions to both funds in the 1960s and early 1970s rose more slowly than GNP at current prices. In FY74 they amounted to ₱800 million, or about one percent of GNP, compared with ₱260 million, or 1.3 percent of GNP, in FY64.

The resources of both the GSIS and SSS have been used primarily to provide housing loans to their members at subsidized rates of

---

25. Social security includes disability, sickness, old age, and death insurance.

interest. Middle and upper income groups have apparently benefited the most from these loans.[26] Another matter of concern is the fact that the funds use contributions of their members to invest in short-term, money-market instruments to offset the subsidies on the loans to their members.

Contributions to the social security funds are likely to rise faster in the future because the government intends to expand coverage and increase rates and benefits. If contributions were to reach an amount equal to 1.1 percent of GNP by FY80 and 1.8 percent by FY85, the total would be approximately ₱2,530 million and ₱8,500 million respectively, a considerable increase in available funds. As in other developing countries, the social security systems could become an important source of government borrowing.

The resources of these institutions represent an important source of long-term public capital which has so far been underutilized. The SSS and GSIS, for example, are particularly well suited to finance the large-scale, low-cost housing program discussed in Chapter 4. Consequently, the present policy in these institutions of borrowing long and lending short should probably be terminated, and more resources should be channeled into long-term government infrastructure programs. Like similar institutions in other countries— Malaysia, for instance—the SSS and GSIS could be required to invest on a large scale in long-term government bonds.

Local Government Finance

The Philippine government has always been highly centralized with provinces, cities, municipalities, and barrios possessing only those powers delegated by the national government.[27] As a consequence, the system of local government has been weak in every

---

26. During 1962–72, 46,000 member borrowers used GSIS funds; the average loan was approximately ₱23,000. The borrowers—8 percent of total membership in 1970—had an average monthly family income of between ₱500 and ₱800, representing the highest 20 percent of the membership in income distribution. The GSIS is now making ten- to twenty-five-year housing loans at 6 percent a year on amounts less than ₱30,000 and at 12 percent a year on amounts from ₱30,000 to ₱70,000. See International Labour Office, *Sharing in Development* (Geneva: ILO, 1974), pp. 215–16.

27. A detailed review of local government administration in urban and rural areas is provided in Chapters 4 and 5 of this report.

respect, and local administration has been largely ineffective. Until recently local government finance was one of the most neglected areas of the development policies of the national government. Local governments had a limited revenue base and depended heavily on contributions from the central government. Early attempts to improve the situation, such as the Decentralization Act of 1967, actually did little to revitalize the administration and finances of local governments. In fact, local government revenues and expenditures continued to decline as a percentage of combined national and local government revenues and expenditures.

Since 1972 the national government has attempted to provide the local governments with more authority, better administration, and sounder finances. The four most important financial measures have been a revision of the system for allotting national revenues to local governments, the establishment of the Local Tax Code, increases in the real property taxes levied by local governments, and authorization for local governments to borrow from lending institutions in order to finance projects as well as to meet other budgetary needs. The national government, moreover, with the help of some of its agencies (for example, the National Tax Research Center) has begun to review the administrative and financial management of local governments in order to collect more information before further reforms are undertaken.

PAST REVENUE AND EXPENDITURE TRENDS

Local governments have derived their revenues from real property taxes, license taxes, and, in some cases, profits and receipts from the operation of public utilities and other business enterprises, including public markets. The revenues collected have never exceeded 1.3 percent of GNP, and in FY72 they amounted to only 0.9 percent. Since these revenues have usually fallen short of financing current expenditures, the local governments have received allotments from the national government consisting of a fixed percentage of all national collections of internal revenues. In addition, there have been national grants-in-aid and loans for some development projects. The amounts have varied from year to year depending on need, the availability of funds, and the attitude of the government toward granting financial assistance to local units.

Because their revenue base has been restricted as to the number of revenue sources available and the total amounts received, local governments have been unduly dependent on national financial aid even for minor projects, such as the construction of feeder roads. The inadequacy of their financial resources has largely kept them from assisting in the acceleration of economic development. The local governments have assumed only a few functions, while the national government, through the field offices of its various agencies, has administered most government services.[28] Contributions of the national government to local governments have also been subject to political pressures, so that the distribution of funds has often been dictated not by development needs but by regional and local influence at the national level.

The Decentralization Act of 1967 represented one attempt to revitalize local governments. It stated that "the policy of the State [is] to transform local governments gradually into effective instruments through which the people can in a most genuine fashion govern themselves and work out their own destinies." Although the act sought to provide local governments more functions and some additional financial resources, the results have been disappointing, and local dependency on national financial aid has in fact increased. Local government receipts and expenditures did rise noticeably in current prices after the act was passed, but there was hardly any per capita rise in real terms until FY74.

Since 1972 several other important legislative measures have attempted to strengthen the finances of local governments, increase the efficiency of local revenue collections, and improve the system of revenue sharing. One of these measures was the Local Tax Code (Presidential Decree 231), which put into a single code all the provisions related to the taxing and revenue-raising powers of different levels of local governments. In the past these local powers were stated in a variety of laws, such as the Local Autonomy Law, the Revised Administrative Code, and various barrio and city charters, which frequently led to overlapping impositions at different levels of government. The new code transfers the authority for collecting some national taxes to provinces and cities and redefines the extent and limitations of the taxing powers of each level of local government. Some of the new, although relatively minor, taxes transferred from the national government to the provinces, cities, and municipalities include taxes on the transfer of ownership of

28. Golay, *The Philippines*, p. 205.

real property, taxes on businesses engaged in printing and publishing, occupation taxes, and taxes on admission to amusements. The Local Tax Code also establishes nationwide maximum rates for a number of levies and fees.

Tax revenues. The single most important source of tax revenue for local governments has always been the real property tax, which is imposed by local governments as an annual ad valorem tax on real properties within their jurisdiction, including land, buildings, other improvements, and machinery.[29] Maximum tax rates, authorized by national legislation, have varied among provinces, municipalities, cities, and barrios. In many jurisdictions the rates imposed by the local councils have been significantly below the authorized levels. In addition, the assessment of real property averaged only 45 percent of actual market value in the 1950s and even less in the 1960s and early 1970s.[30] Most assessments are still outdated, and many taxable properties have not even been included in the assessment rolls because of the absence of tax maps and other basic assessment tools. A major cause for the ineffective identification of properties has been the absence of a nationwide cadastral survey; portions of many provinces and cities have not been surveyed, and jurisdictional boundaries are frequently defined inadequately. Finally, taxation of real property by local governments has been beset with the problem of undercollection. In the 1960s only half the real property taxes due were collected; often, unpaid or back taxes exceeded taxes currently due. In FY70 back taxes accounted for about a fourth of the total collections. Among the reasons cited for the failure to collect taxes are inadequate staffing with underpaid and consequently incompetent officials, and insufficiently coercive penalties for tax evaders.

Revenues from the property tax declined as a percentage of total receipts by local governments until FY73 (Table 15.14), when the national government initiated local tax reform. Measures to reform the real property tax dealt with the real valuations of properties, corrected assessment levels for different types of properties, and improved collection systems. Presidential Decree 76 (1973) made mandatory a new assessment of all properties, required owners to

29. Eduardo Z. Romualdez, Sr., Angel O. Yoingco, and Antonio O. Casem, Jr., *Philippine Public Finance* (Manila: GIC Enterprises, 1973), pp. 457–64.

30. Romualdez and others, *Philippine Public Finance*, pp. 463–64.

Table 15.14. Major Sources of Revenue of Local Governments
(In percent)

Fiscal year	Amount (millions of pesos)	Revenue from taxation		Assistance from national government			
		Property tax	Other[a]	Internal revenue allotment	National aid	All others	Total[b]
1955	227	19.9	30.8	23.5	6.9	18.9	100.0
1960	300	19.0	34.2	23.5	12.0	11.3	100.0
1965	567	15.7	26.8	38.0	8.2	11.3	100.0
1966	634	15.5	26.2	33.7	9.6	15.0	100.0
1967	674	16.5	27.1	36.9	6.4	13.5	100.0
1968	741	16.2	27.5	35.8	9.2	11.3	100.0
1969	849	13.2	26.1	40.7	8.9	11.1	100.0
1970	999	18.2	22.1	38.4	8.7	12.5	100.0
1971	1,144	12.8	21.2	42.7	6.0	17.3	100.0
1972	1,293	12.6	20.2	46.9	8.5	11.8	100.0
1973	1,465	14.0	22.2	42.9	7.5	13.4	100.0
1974	1,676	12.0	21.1	43.9	8.4	14.6	100.0
1975	1,814	18.6	21.0	31.1	n.a.	n.a.	100.0

n.a.: Not available.

a. Including taxes on licences to engage in any occupation or business or to exercise privileges; also fees charged for services rendered and for regulating certain activities.

b. Including profits and receipts from operations of public utilities and other business enterprises, including public markets.

Sources: Annual reports of the Commission on Audit on Local Governments (FY55 through FY73) and Department of Finance estimates (FY74 and FY75).

give sworn statements as to the true value of their properties, and threatened high penalties for evaders. The decree also introduced fixed levels of assessment for various types of properties, including progressive rates for residences, and required a reassesment of real property every five years.[31]

In more recent real property tax legislation, minimum tax rates of 0.25 percent for provinces and municipalities and 0.5 percent for cities have been imposed, with maximum rates of 0.5 percent

31. Assessment levels as a percentage of "current and fair market value" were 50 percent for commercial, industrial, and mineral lands; 40 percent for agricultural lands; 30 percent for residential lands; and 15 percent (market value of ₱30,000) to 80 percent (market value more than ₱500,000) for residential buildings. No increase in the current assessment level can exceed 10 percent of the prescribed levels or, in any case, exceed 80 percent of the current and fair market value of the real property, except upon prior approval of the Secretary of Finance.

and 2 percent respectively. To strengthen the finances of the barrios, 5 percent of the collections of the municipalities and 10 percent of the collections of the cities goes to the barrios in which the taxed property is located. Further, an annual tax of 1.0 percent on real property in a province or city (with an assessed value exceeding ₱3,000) accrues to the Special Education Fund of the national government for the support of local schools.

In addition to the real property tax, local governments collect a variety of license taxes and fees from businesses conducted within their jurisdictions. The most important of these has been the municipal license tax, which usually accounts for more than 10 percent of the total receipts of local governments. It is imposed upon persons engaged in any service occupation or small business, including manufacturers of drugs, proprietors of movie theaters, and vendors. The share of the municipal license tax, together with receipts from fees, declined sharply during the 1960s, however, and has only recently begun to rise again, as a result of tax reform measures.

National government allotments. National government financial assistance has been largely in the form of the internal revenue allotment, which consists of fixed portions of total collections of various taxes by the national government; the allotments are distributed among local governments from a central fund on the basis of prescribed formulas. In addition, there have been other national grants-in-aid and loans, the amounts of which have varied from year to year depending on the availability of funds. In the past, the formula for the distribution of the internal revenue allotment among the local governments frequently favored the rich and economically more active jurisdictions over the less developed areas.

The changes legislated in the last two years (especially Presidential Decree 144, which was later revised by Presidential Decree 559) have reduced the allotment as a whole and redistributed it. The new legislation decrees that the local governments are entitled to "20 percent of the national internal revenue tax collections of the third preceding fiscal year, not otherwise accruing to special funds and special accounts within the national government's general fund." [32] Out of this allocation of 20 percent to local govern-

---

32. For example, in FY77 the internal revenue allocation to the local governments will amount to 20 percent of the national tax revenues collected by the Bureau of Internal Revenue and not earmarked for special funds and accounts

ments, 25 percent will be earmarked for provinces, 40 percent for municipalities, 25 percent for cities, and 10 percent for barrios. Within each of these levels the horizontal distribution is determined by a formula which allocates 70 percent of the total according to population and 20 percent according to land area, with the remaining 10 percent distributed equally among the local units. For FY74 through FY76 transitional provisions ensured that local units would not gain more than 15 percent or lose more than 50 percent of the allotments they had received in FY71.

Other measures have made it mandatory that all local units set aside for development purposes 20 percent of their annual shares from the national allotments. Moreover, separate development funds established for the barrios are financed by the 10 percent share of the real property tax allotted to the barrios and by contributions from each province, city, and municipality to its barrios.[33] Another 5 percent of national internal revenue (not earmarked for special funds and accounts) has been set aside in a local government fund, to be released by the president as an aid to local governments whenever necessary.

Additional allotments are made by the national government to local governments for the maintenance and repair of existing roads and bridges, as well as for new constructions and improvement projects. These allotments are financed from the national government's excise taxes on gasoline and other petroleum products. Twenty percent of these special allotments goes to provinces, 30 percent to municipalities, and 50 percent to chartered cities. Within each level the sharing takes place according to the same 70–20–10 formula applied to the general allotments.

Expenditures. As pointed out earlier, local governments have played only a subordinate role in the activities of the public sector. Their total expenditures have been the equivalent of around 2 percent of GNP, and their capital outlays have been only about 0.2 to 0.4 percent of GNP. The structure of local government expenditures has remained almost unchanged since the late 1950s, with 45 to 50 percent of total outlays being spent for administration, about 20 percent for economic development (especially the con-

---

in FY74. An increase of the total allotment to 25 percent of total internal revenue is under consideration now.

33. The contributions are not to exceed ₱500 annually to each barrio.

struction and maintenance of roads and bridges), and around 15 percent for social services, particularly education (Table 15.15). Since borrowing by local governments has until recently been restricted by law, debt service has never exceeded 2 percent of total expenditures. About a fifth—lately even a fourth—of expenditures has' been for other outlays that are mainly statutory obligations on the part of local governments, that is, payments to agencies and corporations of the national government, as well as transfers to local government corporations. In the past the larger cities, especially greater Manila, which are the major source of revenue, have also benefited the most from the expenditures of local governments, but the government has stated that this unequal geographical distribution will be changed to give rural areas a larger share.

BORROWING BY LOCAL GOVERNMENTS

Another step in the direction of local financial autonomy was made in mid-1975 when the local governments were empowered to borrow from financial institutions under certain conditions (Presidential Decree 752). They may borrow to avoid a financial disruption that could affect vital public services or when local funds are

Table 15.15. Expenditures of Local Governments

Fiscal year	Expenditures (millions of pesos)			Composition of total expenditures (percent)				
	Current	Capital	Total	Admin-istration	Economic development	Social services	Debt service	Others
1960	279	22	301	48	19	17	2	14
1965	465	76	541	46	19	14	1	20
1966	531	107	638	45	18	14	2	21
1967	570	128	698	44	17	15	1	23
1968	652	104	756	45	19	15	1	20
1969	701	116	817	46	19	13	2	20
1970	808	125	933	45	19	15	2	19
1971	937	144	1,081	45	18	17	2	18
1972	1,098	165	1,263	48	19	13	1	19
1973	1,216	145	1,361	50	17	14	2	17
1974	1,471	194	1,665	41	18	13	2	26
1975[a]	1,532	281	1,813	41	19	12	2	26

a. Preliminary estimate.
Sources: Data for FY60–FY73 are from the Report of the Commission on Audit on Local Governments; data for FY74 and FY75 are from the Department of Finance.

insufficient to finance development projects. The Land Bank, the PNB, the DBP, and the GSIS are likely to be the main sources of financing for the construction, expansion, and improvement of development projects or for other capital expenditures. For the purchase of heavy equipment, the local governments may even seek short-term domestic suppliers' credits. The Central Bank may grant short-term advances to cover urgent cash needs of local governments, as long as they do not exceed 15 percent of the average income from regular sources of the borrowing local government. Provinces and cities are authorized to issue bonds, debentures, securities, collaterals, notes, and other obligations to finance self-liquidating or income-producing development projects if those projects are approved by the National Economic and Development Authority (NEDA). All local government bonds are tax exempt. Presidential Decree 752 also stipulates that the president may extend loans to a local government from foreign borrowing to finance development projects.

Strict rules have been established to discourage irresponsible borrowing by local governments. Failure of the borrowing local government to appropriate the annual debt service in its budget empowers the national government to declare the budget inoperative. The Secretary of Finance is then entitled to enforce payment of obligations by withholding corresponding amounts from the internal revenue allotments. Local officials can, to a certain extent, be held personally liable for unpaid debts. In the long run the new authorization to borrow can be interpreted as a first step toward replacing the internal revenue allotment from the national government with direct borrowing. In the short run it will allow richer jurisdictions, which will receive less in grants from the national government under the revised allotment formula, to make up for some of the lost aid.

Future role of local government finance

The recent reforms have been important first steps in improving the financial viability of local administration. The reforms reflect the concern of the government with promoting the regional balance of economic development and mobilizing grass-roots support for its "New Society" program. The government must still decide, however, which functions it is willing to delegate to or share with the local bodies and which administrative system is best suited to the implementation of those tasks.

Although recent reforms have broadened the revenue base of local governments and have reduced financial discriminations among jurisdictions, they have so far done little to enhance local administrative autonomy, with the possible exception of the recent authorization to borrow from lending institutions. It may be that the administrative structure of most local governments is still weak and probably unable to handle an increasing volume of funds and projects. In the long run, however, more administrative responsibilities should be delegated to local officials in both rural and urban areas, and this can be done only if effective spending and borrowing powers are also delegated.

Technical Note A. Tax Reform in the Philippines

As indicated in the previous analysis, taxes will have to be increased from the present level of around 12 percent of GNP if the government is to succeed in improving public services and expanding the public investment program. The government fully recognizes the need for a substantial increase in tax revenues for the financing of its long-term development program; it is studying various proposals for new tax legislation, as well as for improving collections and streamlining administration of taxes (see pp. 33–34). Some of the major issues that will be involved in future tax reform programs are discussed below.

TAXES ON INTERNATIONAL TRADE

The recent reform measures have heightened the already heavy dependence of revenues on the external sector, which rose to almost 50 percent in FY75 from around a third in FY69. Import duties and export taxes accounted for most of the improvements in the growth elasticity of the national tax system and contributed almost 55 percent of the increase in national tax revenues between FY72 and FY75. The financing of the budget is therefore made extremely vulnerable to the vagaries of foreign markets, as demonstrated by the shortfalls in export-tax receipts in the latter part of 1975, when export taxes on copper, cement, copra, and wood products had to be suspended. Substantial shortfalls are also likely in FY76 as a result of the lagging effect of the present low international prices for most Philippine export commodities. Obviously this dependence must be reduced if the public development program is to have a more stable internal revenue base in the long term.

Export taxes. Taxes on exports were introduced for the first time in 1970.[34] They were imposed mainly on traditional exports of raw material and agricultural products in order to capture some of the gains resulting from the 1970 currency devaluation. These taxes were originally intended as only a temporary measure and were to be phased out by the end of FY75. In 1972, however, the Stabilization Tax Law was repealed and the export taxes were made a permanent feature of the customs and tariff code, effective July 1, 1973. In addition, the government introduced a premium export duty, effective February 16, 1974, to capture some of the profits resulting from the commodity boom that began in 1973. Premium duties at rates of 20 to 30 percent were imposed on the difference between the current export price and a base price, which was initially set at 80 percent of the f.o.b. value of the exports established by the Bureau of Customs in February 1974.[35] The premium tax was no longer in effect after the commodity price boom ended in 1974 and some of the export industries began to feel the pinch of the recession in 1975. In the case of wood products, copper, and cement, the government temporarily suspended the export tax altogether.

Among the advantages of the export tax are its ready enforcement, its broad coverage, and its flexibility both in coverage and in the level and structure of rates.[36] The export tax and premium export duties were ideally suited to tax the high export profits of FY73–FY75 effectively. In the absence of a national land tax, moreover, and in view of the unsatisfactory system of personal and cor-

---

34. Under the Export Stabilization Tax Law of May 1, 1970 (Republic Act 6125), export taxes were imposed on two major groups of export products: 10 percent on logs, copra, sugar, and copper ore and concentrates; and 8 percent on molasses, coconut oil, desiccated coconut, copra meal and cake, iron ore and concentrates, chromium ore, abaca, tobacco, wood products, canned pineapples, and bunker oil. The taxes were subject to diminishing rates in subsequent years, falling to 4 percent and 2 percent respectively in FY74.

35. Should the current price of any export product be lower than the established base price, only the basic rate is applicable; that is, the premium tax is flexible only upward.

36. During FY70–FY73, 85 to 90 percent of Philippine exports, in terms of value, were subject to the tax.

porate income taxes, the export tax now represents the only significant tax on agricultural incomes and the only major levy on the exploitation of nonagricultural natural resources in the Philippines. By taxing hitherto untaxed or undertaxed sectors of the economy, the export tax has not only produced sizable additional revenues (₱2,700 million in FY74 and FY75 combined, equivalent to 1.4 percent of GNP) but, in the short run, has contributed to a more equitable application of the tax system.

In general, some form of permanent export tax with a premium-duty should be maintained because it provides the government with a means of siphoning off windfall profits when world market prices are temporarily high for certain products. It appears to have a firm place in the Philippine tax system for other reasons as well, at least until there are more effective ways of taxing the domestic incomes derived from these productive activities (whether for export or local sale).[37] For a closer examination of the question, exports of agricultural commodities such as sugar, coconut products, and bananas may be distinguished from exports of raw materials (or items manufactured from them), such as wood products and minerals.

The analysis in Chapters 6 and 16 indicates that the value of exports of agricultural products is not likely to grow very rapidly in the future, which means that taxes on these exports will not be a major source of growth in tax revenues. Export taxes are, however, one of the few means now available to the government for taxing noncorporate agricultural incomes, and there is a strong case for more effective taxation of such incomes on equity grounds alone. Apart from the export tax, which affects only a few agricultural products, agricultural activities in general contribute little to government revenue. In the early 1970s it was possible to attribute only about 5 percent of the income taxes to the agricultural sector (including forestry) despite the fact that this sector accounts for a third of GNP. Export taxes are not really suited for collecting revenue from the agricultural sector because their coverage, and hence their incidence, is very uneven. They do provide some form of taxation,

37. The question of whether export taxes can be used by the Philippines to restrict production for export, and hence influence international prices, is not taken up here. There has been some discussion of this issue with respect to taxing coconut products, since the Philippines provides about 40 percent of the world supply of coconut oil. See ILO, *Sharing in Development*, pp. 262–63.

however imperfect, and they have the advantage of being easy to collect and to administer. The real question is that of the possible alternatives, which include comprehensive land taxes, discussed below, and increased charges for government services.

Extractive industries present a somewhat different tax problem. There is a strong case to be made for taxing industries that deplete natural resources. As the analysis in Chapters 9 and 16 indicates, moreover, receipts from these exports are likely to increase rapidly through 1985 and are therefore a potentially important source of revenue for the public sector. But unlike agriculture, exploitation of the natural resources of the Philippines is dominated by the corporate sector, where a taxing mechanism already exists. The question is whether the level of taxation on the exploitation of re-sources in general is sufficient, regardless of whether the products are for local or export markets. It is recommended here that the export taxes on mineral resources, which are additional to the corporate tax, should be maintained, at least until the corporate tax system has been overhauled. There may even be some scope for expanding the export taxes in the interim if world market prices again become favorable. Taxes on copper, chromium, and more recently nickel may ensure the government a fair share in the exploitation of nonreplenishable natural resources by domestic and foreign private investors.

Differentiated rates of taxation could be used to encourage a higher degree of domestic processing, as has been done in the case of wood products by increasing rates for unprocessed logs. This raises the issue of the extent to which taxes should be levied on the value of forested land, as opposed to processed wood products. According to present investment plans, the wood-processing industry will be a major manufacturing subsector in the 1980s. It seems more appropriate, therefore, to tax this new industry by a more effective corporate tax system.

Import duties. Import duties are an extremely important part of the Philippine revenue system at present, accounting for between 25 and 28 percent of national tax receipts. Before 1973 the customs and tariff code was generally regarded as ill suited to the revenue and development needs of the Philippines; duty collections amounted on the average to only about 10 percent of imports. The main deficiencies of the code were the exorbitant rates on some items, which not only encouraged smuggling and false declarations but also undermined collection and protection; zero rates for a variety of goods declared "essential"; and the unsatisfactory structure of protection. The issue of protection is dealt with more fully in Chapter 8, but in brief the previous code encouraged local production of less desirable nonessential goods over essential goods, and it hampered industrialization by imposing heavier duties on machinery, equipment, and raw materials than on finished goods. A revised customs and tariff code was introduced in 1973. It simplified the rate structure considerably by reducing the number of specific rates from 271 to 2 and by fixing 6 ad valorem rates ranging from 10 to 100 percent for all other imports. The duty-free category was abolished. Following the introduction of the revised code, there was a doubling in revenues from import duties in FY74 and another rise of 35 percent in FY75 (which was, however, accounted for largely by the rapid increase in imports). In the same two years the ratio of duties to total imports rose moderately from 13 to 20 percent.

The World Bank does not recommend major changes in the level and structure of the import duty system purely for revenue generation. Consumer goods are the most highly taxed imports and, since their share is expected to decline steadily to less than 5 percent of total imports by the 1980s, it seems realistic to expect the elasticity of customs revenue to GNP to remain at slightly less than unity, where it has been since 1965. Consequently, the increase in revenue in real terms from this source during the next decade might be expected to approximate the growth in imports.

TAXES ON INCOME

Taxes on personal and corporate income now account for almost 25 percent of total collections by the national government. More than 70 percent of these collected taxes are derived from the corporate tax. Direct taxation in general, and personal income tax in particular, have been the most neglected areas of tax legislation. A comprehensive reform of the income tax system should be given high priority in the next few years, and is a prerequisite for making the tax system compatible with the goal of a more equitable society.

Taxation of personal incomes. The main features of the personal income tax in the Philippines have not changed since 1960. The tax is levied on a relatively small part of the population, and most

Table 15.16. Number of Income Tax Filers, 1960–73

Calendar year	Individuals			Corporations		
	Total filers	Taxable	Percent taxable	Total filers	Taxable	Percent taxable
1960	422,770	103,337	24.4	6,335	3,586	56.6
1964	636,775	166,734	26.2	8,056	4,446	55.2
1969	1,146,865	356,044	31.0	12,118	6,544	54.0
1970	1,295,415	399,350	28.0	12,807	6,766	52.8
1971	1,431,024	468,514	32.7	13,856	7,190	51.9
1972	1,439,077	n.a.	n.a.	n.a.	n.a.	n.a.
1973	4,540,303	440,581	9.7	15,352	10,063	65.5

n.a.: Not available.

Sources: Bird and others, "Taxes and Tax Reform in the Philippines," p. 49. Figures for 1973 are those reported by Bureau of Internal Revenue.

of it is paid by a tiny fraction of this already small group.[38] The rate of increase in returns filed has expanded steadily over the years, with a sharp boost in 1973 brought about by the amnesty granted to previous nonfilers (Table 15.16). As a percentage of the entire Philippines population, the number of tax filers rose from about 1.6 percent in 1960 to 3.5 percent in 1970 and 12.4 percent in 1973, which suggests that coverage of the personal income tax in the Philippines is considerably wider than in many developing countries. But the proportion of returns resulting in actual tax payments has continued to be very low, rising from 0.4 percent in 1960 to only 1.1 percent in 1970. Despite the sharp increase in the number of people filing returns, taxable filers have remained at around one percent of the total population.

The reform of the personal income tax needs to be given high priority. According to a recent study, tax rates on personal income in the Philippines are "reasonably progressive." [39] The beginning rates on personal income are among the lowest in Asia, however, and should probably be raised. The World Bank agrees with the recommendation of a recent report to the International Monetary Fund that the initial marginal rate should be increased to 10 per-

38. See Bird and others, "Taxes and Tax Reform in the Philippines," p. 27.
39. Gerardo Sicat, *Taxation and Progress* (Manila: National Economic Council, 1972).

cent from the present level of 3 percent.[40] Other elements of a reform would include broadening the base of the personal income tax, reducing the present system of personal deductions drastically, and revising and simplifying the tax structure. There is a low basic exemption for any single person, but this is offset by high exemptions for children. A case could be made for changing the pattern of deductions for children to support the efforts of the government in family planning.

A comprehensive reform will take some time to be formulated and implemented, but it would improve the elasticity of the system (the share of tax revenue that could be derived from the personal income tax could be increased from only 6 percent in FY75 to 10 percent by FY85), and if it were designed and administered in such a way as to capture an increasing share of increments in real and monetary incomes, it could contribute to a more equitable tax system in general.

Corporate income taxes. The present corporate income tax rates of 25 percent on taxable incomes of less than ₱100,000 a year and 35 percent on incomes exceeding ₱100,000 are not unduly low considering the need for investment incentives, although they are lower than those of such other countries in the region as Malaysia, Singapore, and the Republic of China. The main weakness of the corporate tax system seems to be its extensive and highly complex array of possible deductions. There are numerous loopholes, and tax incentives built into the system intentionally are practically inoperative because of the low effective rate of tax collection and the possibilities for tax evasion. High effective tax rates are important for other reasons besides the generation of revenues; the purpose of any tax-incentive system, whether it be development or some other objective, can be attained only if effective rates of taxation are reasonably high. The lower the effective rate, the weaker the effect of the incentive systems.

A recent report on income tax returns of corporations revealed that out of some 15,350 registered corporations that filed tax returns, about a third were exempt, with a recorded total gross income of ₱3,750 million.[41] Between 1959 and 1972, when there were fewer

40. Bird and others, "Taxes and Tax Reform in the Philippines."

41. Unpublished report submitted in April 1975 by Tomas C. Toledo, Director, Revenue Operations and Management Planning Division of the Bureau of Internal Revenue (BIR) to Misael P. Vera, Commissioner, BIR.

corporations registered, the percentage was between 50 and 60. The effective income tax rate of both taxable and exempt corporations decreased from an average 6.8 percent of gross income in 1973 to 4.0 percent in 1974. Taxable corporations derived deductions of from 65 to 85 percent of their 1973 gross income. Exempt corporations claimed deductions ranging between 105 and 155 percent of their gross incomes; in 1974 tax-paying and tax-exempt corporations combined claimed deductions ranging between 74 and 84 percent. A sectoral analysis showed that in 1973 the highest payers were agricultural and natural-resource industries, paying 9.7 percent of gross income, and manufacturing industries, paying 8.8 percent. The financial and real estate sectors paid only 4.9 percent of gross income, and other service industries paid 4.1 percent. The latter seem to have claimed abnormally high deductions or to have declared very low gross income.

Because of this situation, high priority should be given to a complete review of the present system of corporate tax incentives, with the aim of raising the effective tax rates. A consolidated and more easily administrable corporate income tax code will have to be established to close loopholes and apply tax privileges and deductions to those sectors and activities which the government actually wants to promote.[42] Since this review will have to be comprehensive, it would be convenient if it were centralized under the direction of the Department of Finance.

The implementation of a careful overall review will take time. In the interim, the government should raise the nominal corporate income tax rates, which, as mentioned earlier, are lower than those of comparable developing countries. An increase of the lower rate from 25 to 30 percent and of the higher rate from 35 to 40 percent could be enacted without economic difficulties. Also, tax treatment of partnerships and closely held corporations should be made uniform, and special rates for certain types of enterprises (building and loan associations, for example) should be reviewed. The government is now considering the imposition of an additional income tax of 5 percent on family corporations in order to induce these firms to go public. This would seem a welcome step in the direction of modernizing the corporate sector.

---

42. As indicated earlier, economic sectors that the government wanted to aid, such as agriculture and manufacturing, have paid taxes at higher effective rates than have the rest of the private corporate sectors in the past.

INDIRECT TAXATION ON DOMESTIC PRODUCTION OF
GOODS AND SERVICES

At present, taxes on domestic goods and services provide about
20 percent of the revenues of the national government, whereas
they provided more than 30 percent in the 1960s. This decline has
been one of the striking characteristics of the Philippine tax system.
The so-called selective excise taxes—the most important source of
revenues in FY54—declined sharply in relative importance throughout the decade, since rates remained very low.[43] The principal tax
on domestic production, the sales tax, proved even less responsive
to growth of GNP than did the personal income tax. This was attributable partly to its obsolete rate structure (basically unchanged
since 1939) and partly to the low priority given by the government
to its administration and collection.[44]

Luxury consumption should be subject to relatively heavier
taxation than it has been heretofore, but the government should
continue its present policy of abolishing or levying only low taxes
on basic necessities, especially those consumed by low-income groups.
There is ample scope for raising revenues from such indirect taxes
as sales taxes, excise duties, motor vehicle taxes, and taxes on services. Reforms in these areas would need to be focused on the
sales tax and on the motor vehicle tax, because these are the sources
of revenue that would contribute most effectively to a rise in the
elasticity of the tax system and also to an element of progressivity
in the system, although to a much lesser extent than would an income tax reform. While there is hope for increasing selected excise
duties on certain nonessentials, the excise taxes are the most regressive and inelastic components of the tax system and should be
raised only if revenues from other sources should prove to be inadequate.

With respect to the sales tax on domestic production, an increase
in the current basic rate of 7 percent on most domestically produced
goods appears to be justified. The World Bank concurs with the
proposals made by consultants reporting to the International Mon-

43. Those on such items as tobacco products, alcoholic beverages, oils and
fuels, and matches.
44. There is no separate sales tax administration in the Philippines. Taxes
levied at the import stage are collected by the Bureau of Customs, while sales
taxes are collected from domestic manufacturers by the Bureau of Internal
Revenue.

etary Fund that raising the basic tax rate to perhaps 15 percent would be a convenient means of increasing revenues.[45] The report suggests that the present luxury rates of 40 and 70 percent be consolidated to a uniform rate of 50 percent and that the special low sales tax rates on essentials, particularly on staple food products, should be maintained. The sales tax on domestic products is considered a particularly convenient vehicle for raising tax revenues rapidly, because rates can be quickly increased to bring in more revenue without the time lags required by income taxes or land taxes.

A reform of the present administration of the Philippine sales tax will be necessary in order to provide for the efficient collection of the tax. Such a reform should greatly improve the elasticity of the tax system and should also indirectly increase the progressivity of the tax system as a whole. A substantial portion of the poorer consumer groups will not be covered by the sales tax because they are either largely outside the market economy or consume mostly unprocessed—and therefore untaxed—food, which accounts for more than half of the household budgets in the Philippines.[46]

The taxation of motor vehicles and fuels would be another area with scope for considerable increases in revenue collection. Following the example of the United States, the level of motor vehicle taxation has in the past been tied to the perceived financial needs of road construction and maintenance. The potential of such taxation as a source of general revenue and as a means of improving distribution of income and allocation of resources has never been fully recognized or utilized. It was noted in the ILO report cited earlier that the present domestic sales tax on domestically assembled cars ranges from only 10 percent on cars selling for not more than ₱20,000 to only 20.5 percent on cars selling for ₱40,000. The recommendation was made that the beginning rate be raised to 40 percent.[47] The government is aware of this recommendation and recently raised the annual registration fee of private vehicles, partly as an energy conservation measure. The increased fee is not imposed on private vehicles being used for public transportation.

Gasoline taxes are low by international standards (29 centavos

45. Bird and others, "Taxes and Tax Reform in the Philippines."
46. Bird and others, "Taxes and Tax Reform in the Philippines," pp. 120, 120a.
47. ILO, *Sharing in Development,* p. 259.

a liter), and the diesel oil tax (10 centavos a liter) is even lower, for the benefit of those who use diesel oil other than for automobiles. The gasoline tax could be doubled and the diesel oil tax raised significantly, although the effect of these increases on urban mass transportation would have to be watched closely. The operating costs of jeepneys, in particular, might be seriously affected. The sales tax on private automobiles—between 10 and 20 percent at present—could probably also be raised.[48] In view of the high income elasticity of the purchase and use of automobiles, increases in sales taxes on fuel and motor vehicles should have a particularly desirable distributive effect and raise the progressivity and elasticity of the tax system. The administration of these forms of taxation, moreover, is relatively simple.

TAXATION OF LAND AND REAL PROPERTY

Another important aspect of tax reform in the Philippines is the improvement of taxation on land and real property. As land becomes scarcer, windfall profits and rents on land should be taxed more heavily. This is a complicated task, since such taxes should provide significant revenues and contribute to equalizing discrepancies in incomes, while at the same time they should be simple enough to be enforceable and administrable, in view of the relatively underdeveloped nature of the Philippine revenue administration. The issues affecting the rural sector, moreover, are different from those having to do with the urban sector. In any event, fast progress in this area of tax reform is unlikely to be achieved; consequently, projections in this report do not make any allowance for revenues derived from such taxes.

A system of effective taxation of agricultural land would fill an important gap in the tax system by incorporating the nonexporting, crop-growing farmers into the revenue system; it would therefore be applied in particular to the rice, corn, and livestock farmers who at present are virtually untaxed. Introducing land taxation is a formidable task in any country, and the legislation and administration of a land tax in the Philippines will take a great deal of time.

---

48. Bird and others, "Taxes and Tax Reforms in the Philippines," p. 20. It is estimated that an increase in the minimum sales tax on private automobiles from the present 10 percent to 50 percent would produce about the same yield as a 5 percent rise in the corporate income tax.

In the long run a comprehensive tax could produce significant revenues which would probably not be achieved by higher and better-enforced income taxation; it should be designed and administered as a national tax, with possible revenue-sharing for local governments.

In designing a system of land taxation, the government should focus not only on raising revenues but also on nonfiscal developmental objectives, such as distributing income better in the rural areas, using agricultural land more effectively, and bringing idle land into production. As the vast majority of the farmers have small farms and low levels of income, the land tax would have to be focused on higher income groups, with larger land holdings, through progressive taxation.[49] Small landowners should also be taxed effectively, however, whenever the productivity of their land increases as a result of rural development programs (for example, Masagana 99 and irrigation projects). The rate and collections will have to be as simple to administer as possible, and the effective rates of taxation should be high enough to realize the nonfiscal objectives of the tax. Assessment of the land tax will also have to take into account the charges to be paid by farmers for services rendered to them. If service charges, in addition to land taxation, become too high, fewer inputs may be utilized, with a resulting loss in productivity.

The issue of service charges in relation to the land tax is an important one. In a number of irrigation projects, for example, the collection of service charges has been significantly improved and some form of fair taxation has been established. To ensure that land users are charged for improvements on their land whenever services are available, the government should rely heavily on charges for the time being but gradually replace them by the land tax in the long term.

The most formidable preparatory administrative problem is the establishment of a uniform cadastral system. Registration of land titles in the Philippines is poorly administered and records are incomplete. Other countries have determined their tax base in two ways: agricultural income is estimated on the basis of assessed land value in Italy, and assessed by the physical yield of different

49. Ninety-four percent of all rice farmers have less than 4 hectares, and almost 70 percent have less than 2 hectares.

Table 15.17. Projections of National Government Tax Revenues
(In millions of pesos)

Source of revenue	FY76 Amount	Per-cent	FY77 Amount	Per-cent	FY78 Amount	Per-cent	FY79 Amount	Per-cent	FY80 Amount	Per-cent	FY85 Amount	Per-cent
Taxes on income and wealth												
Corporate tax	3,090	18.7	3,820	19.2	4,630	19.5	5,715	20.5	7,170	21.5	18,330	23.5
Personal income tax	975	5.9	1,170	5.9	1,540	6.5	1,950	7.0	2,440	7.3	7,800	10.0
Others	115	0.8	170	0.9	230	1.0	280	1.0	400	1.2	1,170	1.5
Amnesty	50	0.3	...	...	...	...	...	...	...	...	...	...
Total	4,230	25.6	5,160	26.0	6,400	27.0	7,945	28.5	10,010	30.0	27,300	35.0
Taxes on international trade												
Export tax	1,000	6.0	1,330	6.7	1,500	6.4	2,035	7.3	2,335	7.0	4,680	6.0
Import duty	4,600	27.8	5,550	28.0	6,600	27.8	6,550	23.5	7,505	22.5	12,480	16.0
Sales tax on imports	1,880	11.4	2,050	10.3	2,330	9.8	3,265	11.7	3,500	10.5	6,240	8.0
Total	7,480	45.3	8,930	45.0	10,430	44.0	11,850	42.5	13,340	40.0	23,400	30.0
Taxes on domestic goods and services												
Excise tax	2,720	16.4	3,130	15.8	3,320	14.0	4,045	14.5	5,005	15.0	13,260	17.0
General sales tax and others	920	5.6	1,370	6.9	2,370	10.0	2,925	10.5	3,670	11.0	11,310	14.5
Total	3,640	22.0	4,500	22.7	5,690	24.0	6,970	25.0	8,675	26.0	24,570	31.5
Other taxes	1,780	7.1	1,260	6.3	1,190	5.0	1,120	4.0	1,335	4.0	2,730	3.5
Total revenue	16,530	100	19,850	100	23,710	100	27,885	100	33,360	100	78,000	100
GNP (at current prices)	131,080		150,350		173,050		199,180		230,055		472,765	
Ratio of revenues to GNP	12.6		13.2		13.7		14.0		14.5		16.5	

... Zero or negligible.
Sources: Cash budget forecasts for FY76 (as of May 1975) and World Bank estimates.

farm products on "standard" land in France, a method that amounts to an income tax substitute. Given the lack of information on land values and ownership in the Philippines, the simplified Italian system may be better suited to Philippine conditions.

The taxation of urban land involves a different set of problems. There is no exclusively national tax on urban land at present. Provinces, cities, municipalities, and barrios are empowered to levy real property taxes on the assessed value of real property, as discussed earlier in this chapter. The real property tax constitutes the most important source of revenues for local governments and should remain under local authority to contribute to their financial strength. The maximum rates which individual local governments may impose could be raised significantly, especially in the large metropolitan areas, where the value of land has risen exorbitantly in recent years as a result of improvements in public services and increased economic development; the present 3 percent maximum rate of property tax in residential areas should become a minimum.[50]

In addition, the administration of the real property tax will have to be improved significantly. In the past it has been characterized by low levels of assessment and inadequate collections. In 1967 two-thirds of the provinces and half of the cities had no tax maps for identification of property. Assessment lagged about 15 years behind increases in the value of real property so that effective tax rates were low. Considerable efforts by the government will therefore be necessary to improve the enforcement of the real property tax on urban land.

Technical Note B. World Bank Projections of National Government Tax Revenues, FY76–FY85

Table 15.17 presents in some detail the projections of national government tax revenues based on the suggestions for tax reforms set out in Technical Note A. A significant increase in collections is assumed which would allow tax revenues of the national government to increase to 14.5 percent of GNP in FY80 and 16.5 percent in FY85. The structure of revenues indicates a shift away from taxes on international trade in favor of a long-term continuous rise in

50. ILO, *Sharing in Development*, p. 267.

the contribution of direct taxes and higher indirect taxes on domestic goods and services.

The base year for the projections is FY76, and the cash budget estimates of the Department of Finance for that year are used. For import duties, an average tariff rate of 20 percent was applied to 70 percent of the value of imports, as projected in Chapter 16 of this report. In the projections of export tax revenues the effective export tax rates of FY74 [51] of the various export commodities are applied to the export receipts from these commodities as projected in Chapter 16. Since the terms of trade are assumed to become less favorable than at present, only half the special export duty rates are applied to the projected export earnings in the future.

Regarding direct taxation, an average annual increase of 23 percent is assumed throughout the entire forecasting period. A slower increase is anticipated for both personal and corporate income tax revenues in the earlier years, because income tax reforms will take time. A sharp rise is expected in revenues from the general sales tax and other taxes, including those related to motor vehicles and gasoline, whose share in total national tax revenues would rise from only 6 percent in FY76 to reach 26 percent in FY80 and 31.5 percent in FY85.

51. Bird and others, "Taxes and Tax Reform in the Philippines," p. 175a.

16

External Trade and Finance

FOR MOST OF THE PERIOD FOLLOWING THE ACHIEVEMENT of independence, the Philippines suffered from a chronic shortage of foreign exchange that led periodically to major policy adjustments, including devaluations of the currency. The root cause of this problem was the slow growth of export receipts in relation to the demand for imports, resulting primarily from wide fluctuations and a long-term decline in the terms of trade. The Philippines depended in large part on the export of agricultural products for its foreign exchange needs; given the relatively inelastic world demand for these products, export receipts did not keep pace with the growth of demand for foreign exchange. As is indicated in the analysis in Chapters 8 and 9, the imbalance between the supply and the demand for foreign exchange continued even after the adoption of import-substitution policies in the 1950s and 1960s. Industrialization based on import substitution did not reduce dependence on imports in spite of substantial devaluations; it simply shifted the dependence from finished consumer goods to capital and intermediate goods. If the Philippines is to escape the constraint on growth that has been imposed by a lack of foreign exchange, a substantially better performance in the growth of exports will be needed in the future.

Exports must grow more rapidly than imports in order for the Philippines to reduce its present large resource gap. Whether the necessary growth can be achieved will depend on the country's ability to increase production for export, on the expansion of overseas markets, and on trade policies that will keep exports competitive. The current account deficit was equal to about 6 percent of GNP in 1975, largely because of the sharply increased prices for imported petroleum and related products. For the reasons given in Chapters 9 and 13, a reasonably smooth adjustment to the higher costs of imported fuel and petrochemicals should be made by accelerating the rate of growth of exports rather than by reducing imports, but it will be a number of years before the Philippine economy can reach the point at which these higher energy costs are fully absorbed. Increased investments will have to be made in the export sector, in import-replacing industries, and in alternative sources of energy. Some of these investments are necessarily capital intensive and have large foreign exchange requirements.

In order to sustain the investment program outlined in Chapter 13, the volume of imports will have to expand by about 7 percent a year between 1975 and 1985. If a rate of import inflation of about 7 to 8 percent a year is assumed, the import payments would increase by about 14 to 15 percent a year throughout this period. Any cutbacks in the level of imports would probably be concentrated on imports of capital goods and would have adverse effects on the growth of incomes and employment. Such import reductions at this time, when capital goods available locally are in short supply, would also hamper the adjustment to higher energy prices and have negative effects on programs aimed at expanding production. Similarly, reductions in imports of intermediate goods would have an immediate and unacceptable effect on production and employment, especially in the nontraditional manufacturing sector, where these imports are vital to growth. Since finshed consumer goods represent only a small proportion of total imports, reductions in this area would have less significance. Gains from the external terms of trade are expected to be modest during the next ten years; the volume of exports will therefore have to grow about 9 percent a year. A critical assumption underlying all these projections is that the countries of the Organisation for Economic Co-operation and Development (OECD) will recover during the next decade and enjoy rates of economic growth comparable to those of the 1960s. Sustained OECD growth will also be required to make the projected inflow of capital possible.

Even if the current account deficit can be reduced to about 4 percent of GNP by 1980 and 2 percent by 1985, the Philippines would need an average net inflow of foreign exchange of around US$1,000 million a year in the first half of the 1980s. The bulk of this amount will probably have to be in the form of medium- and long-term loans. External requirements of this magnitude do not appear excessive in relation to current levels of inflows nor to reasonable prospects for future inflows. The Consultative Group [1] and other official donors will have an important function in connection with this effort, since at least a third of the loans should be on concessional terms to ensure that the ratio of debt service payments to exports does not rise beyond its present level of about 17 percent.[2] For its part, the government will need to develop more sources of external capital. An inflow of the above magnitude would be sufficient to ensure that international reserves increase from the present level of about US$1,000 million to about US$4,000 million in 1985, a level equivalent to three months of imports. Considering the Philippines' chronic shortage of foreign exchange in the past, prudent management in the future should maintain reserves and the debt service ratio at the levels recommended here.

The outstanding amount of medium- and long-term debt would rise from about US$2,300 million at the end of 1975 to about US$11,000 million by the mid-1980s. The service of such a debt depends, of course, both on the future economic expansion of the Philippines and on the capital inflow that can reasonably be expected over the period. If the combination of loan maturities is along the lines suggested in this chapter, management of the debt and debt service should not present serious problems. Of course, the development program that the government has set for the country and for the people will not be accomplished without difficulties. The government appears to recognize the problems and un-

---

1. The Consultative Group for the Philippines was formed in 1970 following the postdevaluation stabilization program and rescheduling of some short- and medium-term external debt. It is a concerted international effort to help the Philippines deal with its long-term development problems after the government has taken steps to deal with the short-term financial difficulties. The primary objective of the group is to coordinate the provision of capital assistance by its members and channel it into high-priority development projects. For a list of the member countries and institutions, see Chapter 2, note 1.

2. Referred to as the debt service ratio, this is the ratio of amortization and interest payments on medium- and long-term debt to receipts from exports of goods and nonfactor services.

certainties of further development, however, and intends to modify and adjust policies and objectives as necessary to stay on an even and manageable course, both internally and externally.

External Trade and Foreign Exchange Needs

The Philippines cannot count on foreign inflows to finance the resource gap at its present level indefinitely and must reduce its dependence on such inflows to the equivalent of about 2 percent of GNP by 1985. Imports of capital and intermediate goods that are not manufactured domestically are, however, essential to sustain the investment program. The country will therefore have to expand its capacity to pay for these imports and aim for an average annual increase of about 19 percent in the value of exports during the next ten years. Since earnings from exports of traditional agricultural products will continue to expand slowly, the required growth in foreign exchange receipts will have to come from an aggressive program aimed at expanding exports of wood products, minerals, and so-called nontraditional industrial exports.

Even with this growth in export earnings, the requirements of net inflows of foreign borrowings would be substantial during 1975–84, with at least a third of the loans on concessional terms. If the expansion of GNP of 7 percent a year in real terms is to be sustained when the volume of exports is growing at a rate much lower than 9 percent a year, it is extremely unlikely that the present heavy dependence on foreign inflows can be reduced. The Philippines would then face the same constraints on the growth of foreign exchange that were characteristic of the 1950s and 1960s. In this case, rates of growth in output and employment would have to be adjusted downward.

IMPORT REQUIREMENTS FOR SUSTAINED GROWTH

The volume of imports is projected to increase at the rate of 7 percent a year during the next ten years, and, if the unit value of imports increased by about 7 to 8 percent a year, total payments for imports would rise from US$3,400 million in 1975 to US$6,900 million in 1980 and US$13,400 million in 1985 (Table 16.1). Import requirements would vary from year to year, however, depending on the short-term changes in domestic incomes and savings and on

Table 16.1. Import Payments in Current and Constant Values and Price Indexes

Item	Actual				Projected	
	1960	*1965*	*1970*	*1975*	*1980*	*1985*
Current value (millions of U.S. dollars)						
Cereals	25	95	33	143	105	159
Other consumer goods	75	90	98	357	502	718
Crude petroleum	21	59	103	752	1,516	2,875
Other raw materials	260	281	442	1,098	2,421	4,987
Capital goods	223	283	414	1,000	2,327	4,626
Total	604	808	1,090	3,350	6,871	13,364
Price indexes (1967–69 = 100)						
Cereals	62.5	68.2	72.0	214.2	245.5	354.1
Other consumer goods	100.7	112.1	91.6	244.0	354.2	496.8
Crude petroleum	115.2	102.2	99.9	832.8	1,198.4	1,680.8
Other raw materials	92.3	101.6	124.3	298.8	433.6	608.2
Capital goods	82.8	97.5	107.1	181.5	263.4	369.4
Total	89.4	95.8	108.8	274.1	392.0	549.5
Constant value (millions of U.S. dollars)						
Cereals	40	139	46	67	43	45
Other consumer goods	75	80	107	146	142	144
Crude petroleum	52	75	119	90	127	171
Other raw materials	239	258	344	368	558	820
Capital goods	269	290	387	551	883	1,252
Total	675	843	1,002	1,222	1,753	2,432

Sources: Data for 1960, 1965, 1970, and 1975 are from the Central Bank of the Philippines; those for 1980 and 1985 are World Bank projections.

the timing of individual investment projects. Import payments are particularly vulnerable to prices of petroleum products, which accounted for more than 22 percent of total import payments in 1975. Petroleum prices will probably rise in line with international prices through the next decade, and even a small change of, say, 10 percent in this price projection would affect the import bill significantly. Large investment projects in power, mining, steel, fertilizer, and other industries will also affect annual import requirements. The total investment cost of these projects is expected to exceed US$7,000 million during the next five years, with the individual cost of many of them exceeding US$200 million. As outlined in Chapter 8, government policy provides various incentives for import substitution and for increasing the use of domestic components. Several investment projects are likely to come up in this area in the next few years. If these plans materialize there will be considerable scope for import substitution in the 1980s.

Imports of consumer goods (including cereals) account for about 15 percent of total import payments. Because of the growing capacity of domestic industries to meet the needs of consumers, the share of finished consumer goods (other than cereals) in total payments for imports has declined steadily to about 11 percent at present. This trend is expected to continue, and by 1985 these items may account for about 5 percent of total payments. Given a reasonable degree of success in expanding agricultural production as discussed in Chapter 6, imports of rice and corn can be eliminated by 1980; imports of wheat will continue to grow, but by 1985 cereal imports will represent only about one percent of total imports, compared with about 4 percent at present.

As a result of the sharp increases in prices, payments for crude petroleum and products have jumped from about US$180 million in 1973 to about US$750 million in 1975, and their share in total payments for imports has doubled to 22 percent. Payments for imports of crude petroleum are now equivalent to about 5 percent of GNP. Since consumption of crude petroleum is projected to grow about 8 percent a year in the latter half of the 1970s, imports of about 100 million barrels are projected for 1980. During the 1980s a somewhat slower growth is expected, since the government program to develop alternative sources of energy should begin to have an effect on the demand for petroleum products by that time.[3] Although there are some prospects for discovering commercial quantities of petroleum in the Philippines, it has been assumed that all requirements will have to be met from imports, at least until 1985. Thus imports of crude petroleum are projected at about 140 million barrels for 1985.

The future course of petroleum prices is uncertain, but for the purposes of this analysis it has been assumed that the price of crude petroleum will rise in line with international prices generally, increasing by an average of 7 to 8 percent a year between 1976 and 1985. At this rate, with prices of US$15 a barrel in 1980 and

---

3. For a more complete discussion of the role of petroleum in the Philippine economy, see Appendix B.

US$21 a barrel in 1985, payments for crude petroleum would be about US$1,500 million in 1980 and US$2,900 million in 1985. In other words, imports of crude petroleum would still represent about 21 percent of total payments in 1985.

Other raw materials and intermediate goods now account for about 33 percent of total payments for imports; chemical products, iron, and steel account for more than half of the payments in this category. During the past decade imports of these items have grown an average of 6 to 7 percent a year in real terms, which is slightly higher than the growth rate of GNP and roughly in line with the growth of industrial output. In the expectation that this trend will continue for the remainder of the 1970s, imports are projected to increase about 8 percent a year in real terms (the same as the projected rate of growth of industrial output). Growth of imports of these items should slow down to an annual rate of about 6 percent in the 1980s, when output from the proposed major investments in steel, fertilizer, pulp and paper, and chemicals should begin to replace imports. After allowing for an average increase in prices of 7 to 8 percent a year, total payments for imports of raw materials and intermediate goods are projected to be about US$5,000 million by 1985, or about 37 percent of total payments for imports.

In the first half of the 1970s there was not much growth in imports of capital goods in real terms. Given the scarcity of domestically available capital goods, the projected expansion in industrial investment, and the program of investment in public infrastructure described in Chapter 13, imports of capital goods are projected to increase by about 8 to 9 percent a year during 1976–85. After allowing for an average increase of about 7 percent a year in prices, the payments for imports of capital goods should rise to perhaps US$4,600 million by 1985. The magnitude of this amount means that the Philippines will need access to significantly greater amounts of external capital to finance these purchases. As the subsequent analysis indicates, the Philippines will need a net inflow of medium- and long-term loans of around US$9,000 million during the next ten years. The country will be confronted with a scale of external borrowing that is much higher than in the past, and concerted efforts on the part of both the government and the international financial community will be required to ensure that these needs are met.

Expanding the Capacity to Import

If the Philippines is to sustain a real growth in imports of about 7 percent a year, exports will have to increase sharply and grow at least 9 percent a year in real terms between 1976 and 1985. This will mean a substantially greater volume of exports than in the past. According to statistics published by the Central Bank of the Philippines, the volume of exports grew at a relatively steady rate of 6 to 7 percent a year between 1950 and 1965. In the second half of the 1960s there was no significant increase in the volume of exports, but a somewhat better performance was recorded in the first half of the 1970s, when the trend rate of increase was about 7 percent a year.[4]

Prospects for exports. The expansion of exports will depend on the implementation of an aggressive program to stimulate export production, particularly of nontraditional manufactures, and diversify products as well as markets. Traditional agricultural exports are expected to grow slowly, and increasing emphasis must be placed on the processing of primary products, such as copra and logs, for export. Large investments in extractive industries are proposed to increase the value of mineral exports by the additional processing of ores and the development of new mineral products.

Exports of agroindustrial products—mainly copra, coconut oil, sugar, fruits, and vegetables—have traditionally provided the bulk of the foreign exchange earnings of the Philippines. In the early 1950s, for example, they accounted for about 85 percent of export earnings, but since receipts from these products increased less than 3 percent a year between 1950 and 1970, their share had dropped to about 43 percent by 1970 (Table 16.2). Primarily as a result of the boom in international prices of these commodities, earnings have risen sharply since 1972, and in 1975 this group of commodities accounted for about 59 percent of exports. From 1972 to 1975, however, the volume of these exports increased only moderately. As indicated in the analysis in Chapter 6, exports of these commodities are expected to grow about 4 percent a year in real terms during 1976–85, roughly in line with the projected growth of world demand. With an increase of about 6 percent a year in the unit value

---

4. Some caution is needed in interpreting the official trade statistics, however, since there is reason to believe that they understate actual earnings.

Table 16.2. Export Earnings in Current and Constant Values and Price Indexes, 1960–85

| | *Actual* | | | | *Projected* | |
Item	*1960*	*1965*	*1970*	*1975*	*1980*	*1985*
Current value (millions of U.S. dollars)						
Copra	139	170	80	161	238	188
Coconut oil	16	68	96	217	530	1,157
Sugar	133	132	188	697	895	1,506
Wood products[a]	102	195	295	226	793	1,423
Copper concentrate and copper	30	47	185	196	900	2,414
Other mineral products[b]	31	30	39	134	304	621
Other agricultural products[c]	96	104	107	288	668	1,275
Manufacturing and miscellaneous[d]	13	22	93	392	1,384	4,291
Total	560	768	1,083	2,311	5,712	12,875
Price indexes (1967–69 = 100)						
Copra	98.1	109.3	64.0	115.7	207.7	357.9
Coconut oil	98.2	106.0	104.3	132.9	227.7	383.6
Sugar	81.9	87.1	102.8	262.8	251.2	352.4
Wood products[a]	97.7	87.6	99.4	112.9	239.5	368.5
Copper concentrate and copper	56.7	70.9	123.2	121.3	259.8	416.5
Other mineral products[b]	150.3	111.9	162.1	242.9	390.9	596.0
Other agricultural products[c]	145.0	109.2	138.6	187.4	267.4	375.1
Manufacturing and miscellaneous[d]	30.8	40.0	189.8	378.3	549.1	770.1
Total	92.3	92.8	108.6	186.1	291.3	468.5
Constant value (millions of U.S. dollars)						
Copra	142	156	125	139	114	53
Coconut oil	16	64	92	163	233	302
Sugar	163	152	183	265	356	427
Wood products[a]	104	223	291	200	331	386
Copper concentrate and copper	53	66	150	162	346	580
Other mineral products[b]	21	27	24	55	78	104
Other agricultural products[c]	66	86	77	154	250	340
Manufacturing and miscellaneous[d]	42	55	49	104	252	557
Total	607	828	998	1,242	1,961	2,748

a. Includes plywood, veneer, lumber, pulp and paper.

b. Includes nickel ore, gold, chromium, iron ore, and other minerals.

c. Includes desiccated coconut, oil cakes, molasses, bananas, pineapples and other fruits, marine products, abaca, and tobacco.

d. Includes re-exports, artifacts, jewelry, and other minor products.

Sources: Data for 1960, 1965, 1970, and 1974 are from the Central Bank of the Philippines; those for 1980 and 1985 are World Bank projections.

of these items, earnings would rise from about US$1,400 million at present to about US$4,000 million by 1985.[5] Since earnings from these exports increase slowly, the required growth in export receipts will have to come from wood products, minerals, and nontraditional industrial products.

Exports of forest products were an increasingly important source of foreign exchange during the 1950s and 1960s. Starting from negligible amounts in the early 1950s, exports of logs and other forest products rose to about US$300 million by 1970 and accounted for 27 percent of export earnings. The growth in earnings in the first half of the 1970s was constrained by increasing difficulties in expanding log production and by the relatively slow growth of overseas demand, especially in 1974–75. Export earnings from wood products are projected to rise an average of about 20 percent a year and reach about US$1,400 million by 1985, however, as exports of logs are phased out and replaced by exports of processed wood products.

Minerals, particularly copper and nickel, are expected to be an increasingly important source of foreign exchange earnings for the Philippines. From small beginnings in the early 1950s, earnings from minerals have grown rapidly to the point where they now account for about 14 percent of export receipts. Production of minerals for export is expected to expand about 12 percent a year between 1976 and 1985; earnings are projected to grow about 25 percent a year, to a total of US$3,000 million by 1985.

It seems unlikely that substantially larger volumes of traditional agricultural products, wood products, and minerals will be exported during the next ten years, although actual earnings could be affected somewhat by price changes. But with the completion of projects concerned with the processing of primary products (copra and logs, for example) and the additional processing of minerals, earnings from these products would rise 16 percent a year to about $9,000 million in 1985. This would be substantially less than the minimum level of export earnings of about US$13,000 million that would be needed by 1985 to support the projected level of imports.

---

5. This 6 percent rate of increase is somewhat more rapid than that of the individual commodities, because the composition of the group would shift in favor of commodities, such as coconut oil (instead of copra), fruits, and vegetables, having higher unit values.

Earnings from nontraditional industrial exports and other miscellaneous items must therefore be expanded to about US$4,000 million in 1985 if there is to be sufficient foreign exchange for sustained growth of 7 percent a year in GNP. If the unit value of these nontraditional exports increases 7 to 8 percent a year, in line with assumptions about the behavior of international prices generally, an average growth in volume of about 18 percent a year would be required.

This growth can be achieved if the kinds of programs and policies set out in Chapter 9 are pursued. For most industries in which a large increase in export sales is projected, the main uncertainty with regard to supply appears to be the willingness of entrepreneurs to undertake the kinds of investments necessary for realization of the objectives. For a broad range of manufactures, the effective rate of foreign exchange apparently continues to favor investments in production intended primarily for the domestic market. The relative attractiveness of investments in production for export will therefore have to be increased by changes in the structure of incentives for export and import-substitution industries. This will probably require changes in the effective rates of foreign exchange for nontraditional industrial exports in relation to those for import-substitution industries.

External terms of trade. The other factor that will influence the capacity to import is the behavior of the external terms of trade. The instability in the international commodity markets in recent years has been a forceful reminder of the extent to which import capacities can be affected by changes in the terms of trade; it has also underscored the importance of having adequate foreign exchange reserves to minimize the disruptive effects of slumps in export earnings.

For the Philippines, the magnitude of the fluctuations in the external terms of trade in the past few years has been without parallel. In common with many other countries, the Philippines experienced a modest secular decline of about 2 percent a year in external terms of trade during the 1950s, but in the 1960s there was very little change. This situation changed dramatically in the 1970s. During 1970–72 the terms of trade declined about 20 percent, only to be followed by a recovery during 1973 and 1974, and a subsequent decline of about 25 percent in 1975 (Table 16.3). The Philippines is a relatively open economy (exports and imports are

Table 16.3. Actual and Projected External Terms of Trade
(1967–69 = 100)

Year	Export price index[a]	Import price index[a]	Net terms of trade
Actual			
1960	91.7	87.1	105.3
1965	93.6	96.0	97.5
1970	106.1	104.6	101.4
1971	105.3	112.9	93.2
1972	98.5	120.2	82.0
1973	140.0	142.9	97.9
1974	249.8	255.3	97.9
1975	203.0	274.5	74.0
Projected			
1980	310.2	393.8	78.8
1985	485.7	552.0	88.0

a. Goods and nonfactor services.
Sources: Data for 1960 to 1975 are from the Central Bank of the Philippines; data for 1980 and 1985 are World Bank projections.

equal to about 22 percent and 26 percent of GNP respectively), and, as indicated in Chapters 14 and 15, these wild swings in the terms of trade have posed major problems for management of the economy in the first half of the 1970s and profoundly affected the distribution of incomes.

In accordance with World Bank forecasts of international commodity prices, only a marginal recovery in the external terms of trade between 1976 and 1980 has been projected. There should be a further recovery in the 1980s because of the increasing importance of commodities of higher value in Philippine exports. But when set against the recent behavior of international prices, these statements about recovery in the terms of trade can be put forth only tentatively. The balance of payments is obviously quite sensitive to fluctuations in export prices that cannot be predicted. Fortunately, the Philippine government has in the past few years been quite adept at contending with large short-term fluctuations in prices. If efforts are made to maintain an adequate level of foreign exchange reserves, the Philippines should be able to ride out adverse short-term trade situations in the future.

EARNINGS FROM INVISIBLES AND TRANSFERS

The principal growth in receipts from services would come from tourism and from interest on foreign exchange reserves. Interna-

tional tourism in the Philippines is still at an early stage of development, but it has strong potential for sustained growth. The government has identified several areas for tourist development, and
substantial investments are already being made in hotels and industries related to tourism. Tourists are expected to be attracted to
the Philippines for short stopovers on round-the-world or Asian
tours, as well as longer visits from North America, Europe, Australia,
and Japan. An increase of about 17 percent a year is projected in
receipts from tourism, which are expected to reach US$500 million
by 1985.

During the next ten years significant increases in freight and
insurance payments should result from the projected expansion in
the merchandise trade of the Philippines. These payments are
likely to increase about 15 percent a year and reach US$1,400 million
by 1985. Dividend payments on growing foreign investments and
interest payments on a much higher level of external borrowings
should also expand rapidly; the total debt outstanding on a disbursement basis will probably more than double in the next five years,
and interest payments, for example, which amount to nearly US$200
million at present, should exceed US$900 million by about 1985.
Net transfers are expected to grow considerably during the next ten
years, however, largely offsetting the outflows on the services account.
A reduction in official transfers would be accompanied by a steady
growth in private transfers, primarily from the large and growing
number of Filipinos who work overseas and remit portions of their
earnings to relatives in the Philippines. Together, total net transfers
are expected to grow from US$280 million in 1975 to about US$500
million by 1985 (Table 16.4).

ISSUES IN TRADE POLICY

The extent to which the Philippines can successfully expand its
exports will depend not only on the ability to increase production
for export, but also on the expansion of overseas markets through
promotional activities and measures to keep exports competitive.
The long-established concentration of trade with the United States
has declined somewhat in the last two or three years, and Japan is
emerging as an important trading partner. Trade with other
countries has also grown gradually in recent years. As mentioned
in Chapter 13, the recent changes in policy to encourage foreign
investments have already increased participation of foreigners in

Table 16.4. Summary Balance of Payments
(In millions of U.S. dollars)

	Actual				Projected	
Item	1960	1965	1970	1975	1980	1985
Trade account (net)	−29	−24	−7	−1,039	−1,160	−490
Exports	575	784	1,083	2,311	5,710	12,870
Imports	604	808	1,090	3,350	6,870	13,360
Services (net)	−115	62	−141	−120	−460	−1,000
Transfers (net)	140	99	119	300	370	500
Current account balance	−4	137	−29	−859	−1,250	−990
Direct investment	29	−10	−29	100	150	200
Medium- and long-term loans	36	50	134	300	940	840
Short-term capital	−1	−117	76	40	270	400
Other capital[a]	−33	−113	−133	343	170	58
Change in reserves (− = increase)	27	−53	19	75	−280	−500

a. Includes net capital from the International Monetary Fund as well as errors and omissions.

Sources: Data for 1960, 1965, and 1970 are from the Central Bank of the Philippines; those for 1975, 1980, and 1985 are World Bank staff projections.

local enterprises. Through their contacts with the international market, these foreign investors can greatly assist in the diversification of trade sources and the exploration of new markets. The Philippines is also involved in several bilateral and multilateral trade relationships which might widen the scope of its international trade.

The Philippines has traditionally depended heavily on the United States both as a market for exports and as a source of imports. In the early 1950s, for example, the United States accounted for about three-quarters of the external trade of the Philippines. This dependence declined gradually during the 1950s and 1960s as trade with Japan expanded; by 1970 the United States and Japan each absorbed about 40 percent of the Philippines' exports, and they each provided about 30 percent of its imports (Table 16.5). By 1974 the United States and Japan together purchased more than three-quarters of the Philippines' exports, but because of the increase in the relative importance of petroleum in total import payments, these two countries supplied the Philippines with only about half its imports.

The only major trade agreement of the Philippines in the past was with the United States. The preferential treatment for exports from the Philippines in the United States market has now been

Table 16.5. Directions of External Trade
(In percent)

Trading partner	1960	1965	1970	1971	1972	1973	1974
Exports							
United States and Canada	50.7	45.7	41.8	40.8	41.0	36.5	42.9
Europe	19.5	20.6	9.3	14.1	16.6	16.2	14.2
Japan	21.9	28.4	39.7	35.1	33.8	35.8	34.8
Other Asian countries	3.4	3.8	7.7	8.4	6.8	9.1	5.2
Others	4.5	1.5	1.5	1.6	1.8	2.4	2.9
Total	100.0	100.0	100.0	100.0	100.0	100.0	100.0
Imports							
United States and Canada	45.5	36.6	30.5	27.2	27.4	29.4	24.5
Europe	13.2	16.7	18.4	19.4	15.6	14.9	15.2
Japan	26.5	24.3	31.7	30.3	31.8	32.4	27.5
Other Asian countries	9.0	12.7	8.1	11.0	9.0	6.9	7.1
Others	5.8	9.7	11.3	12.1	16.2	16.4	25.7
Total	100.0	100.0	100.0	100.0	100.0	100.0	100.0

Source: Central Bank of the Philippines.

phased out with the expiration of the Laurel-Langley trade agreement in July 1974 and of the United States Sugar Act in 1974. The governments of the United States and the Philippines are now considering a treaty to replace the Laurel-Langley agreement. In the meantime, the United States Congress has passed the Trade Reform Act, which provides some concessions to developing countries, including the Philippines. In the long term the Philippines should be able to maintain its share of the United States market as long as it can stay competitive in international prices.

The government has been active in attempting to reduce the dependence of Philippine exports on the markets of the United States and Japan, and the Japanese Generalized Scheme of Preferences is likely to benefit the Philippines and other exporters of agricultural and fishery products as well as of minerals and manufactured goods. Efforts have been made to eliminate legal obstacles and promote trade agreements with the Eastern European nations and the People's Republic of China. Some arrangements have already been made to exchange certain primary export commodities for Chinese products. These arrangements open a new source of imports of oil and rice in exchange for a potential export market for such items as sugar, wood, and coconut products. A trade agreement with Canada was also signed in 1972. The membership of the Philippines in the Association of South-East Asian Nations (ASEAN) might also lead to increasing trade with neighboring countries through the removal of trade restrictions and the promotion of preferential arrangements. In an effort to further multilateral trade relations, the Philippines became a member of the General Agreement on Tariffs and Trade (GATT) in 1973, thus obtaining most-favored-nation treatment from more of its trading partners.

The pattern of trade deficits may become increasingly important in the future. At present the trade deficit of about US$1,000 million consists of about US$700 million with the oil-producing states, primarily those of the Middle East, and US$300 million with other trading partners. Payments for oil are projected at about US$3,000 million in 1985, and, unless the Philippines can expand exports to these oil-producing countries by a substantial amount, it will have to run large trade surpluses with other trading partners. If exports to the oil-producing countries were increased to only about US$500 million in 1985, as projected, the trade surplus with the rest of the world would have to be about US$2,000 million.

Inflows of External Capital

If the projections of current account receipts and payments outlined in the preceding sections are realized, the cumulative deficit will be about US$5,000 million during 1976–80 and about US$6,000 million in the subsequent five-year period; that is, the projections imply an average current account deficit of more than US$1,000 million a year between 1976 and 1985. No provision is made in these figures for increases in external reserves, and prudent management of the balance of payments suggests that they should be kept at the equivalent of at least two and a half to three months of imports. This means that reserves should increase by about US$1,000 million during 1976–80 and then by a further US$2,000 million in 1981–85. Thus the Philippines will require a net inflow of foreign exchange of about US$15,000 million between 1976 and 1985, which will have to be met from inflows of direct private investment, short-term trade finance, and medium- and long-term loans (Table 16.6). Net inflows of direct private investment are expected to increase in the future and could provide a total of US$1,550 million between 1976 and 1985. Short-term finance will probably increase

**Table 16.6. Actual and Projected Requirements and Sources of
Foreign Exchange, 1966–85**
(In millions of U.S. dollars)

	Actual		Projected	
Item	1966–70	1971–75	1976–80	1981–85
Requirements				
Deficit on current account				
Trade deficit	770	1,373	5,640	4,830
Services and transfers	−395	−242	−160	1,640
Net deficit	375	1,131	5,480	6,470
Increases in reserves and other	201	395	1,040	2,030
Total requirements	576	1,526	6,520	8,500
Sources				
Medium and long-term loans				
Gross inflow	1,364	2,356	6,730	12,860
Amortization	823	1,392	3,000	7,490
Net	541	964	3,730	5,370
Direct investment	−50	105	650	900
Short-term trade finance	85	457	2,140	2,230
Total from all sources	576	1,526	6,520	8,500

Sources: Actual data for 1966–75 are from the Central Bank of the Philippines; data for
1976–85 are World Bank staff projections.

in line with the volume of trade to be financed. For the ten-year
period as a whole, it may be reasonable to expect a net inflow of
about US$4,400 million.

The balance of about US$9,000 million would have to come from
net inflows of medium- and long-term loans. The corresponding
gross inflow will depend on the proportions from commercial and
official sources. The need is large, and excessive reliance on commercial loans with relatively short maturities would almost certainly raise the debt service ratio to unacceptable levels. As a rough
guide for debt management, the government should aim at not allowing the debt service ratio to rise much beyond the present level of
about 17 percent. It should be possible to obtain some loans with
medium- and long-term maturities from private or quasi-official
sources. The bulk of the resources would have to be obtained from
official sources, however, including the members of the Consultative
Group. If it is assumed that about 40 percent of the medium- and
long-term loans will in fact have these longer maturities, gross disbursements of about US$19,000 million will be needed to support

Table 16.7. Actual and Projected Levels of Commitments and Disbursements of Medium- and Long-term Loans, 1971–85
(In millions of U.S. dollars)

Source	Commitments				Disbursements			
	Actual		Projected		Actual		Projected	
	1971	1975	1980	1985	1971	1975	1980	1985
Public loans	300	760	1,570	1,770	150	360	1,220	1,760
Official development assistance	140	510	780	760	50	280	590	780
Commercial sources	160	250	790	1,010	100	80	630	980
Commercial loans to private sector	280	300	620	960	100	300	600	960
Total loans	580	1,060	2,190	2,730	310	660	1,820	2,270

Sources: Data for 1971–75 are from the Cental Bank of the Philippines; those for 1980–85 are World Bank projections.

the required total net inflow of US$9,000 million (Tables 16.6 and 16.7).

FOREIGN AID AND THE CONSULTATIVE GROUP

For the reasons given above, the government should try to obtain about a third of the gross inflows of loans in the form of development assistance from official sources. This will ensure that the present good maturity structure of the external debt is maintained, and it would go a long way in helping to keep the debt service ratio from rising beyond the present level of 17 percent.

Thus the Philippines would need a gross inflow of about US$6,000 million from loans obtained from official sources. Disbursements would need to rise from an actual level of about US$280 million in 1975 to about US$600 million by 1980 and then to about US$780 million by the mid-1980s. To support this level of disbursements, commitments of new loans from official sources would need to be about US$7,000 million between 1976 and 1985. Although this would represent a major increase over the volume of aid extended to the Philippines in past years (see Table 16.8), it would not require a really major increase in the current level of commitments by members of the Consultative Group. New commitments of loans amounted to about US$500 million in 1975; they would need to be raised to about US$600 million in a year or so, after which a somewhat slower increase would be warranted.

Foreign aid has been important in the economic development of the Philippines since the 1950s and 1960s when it was provided mainly for rehabilitation and for institutional development. Most of the foreign assistance during the 1950s came from the United States, primarily in the form of grants and similar assistance; during the 1960s a significant proportion came from multilateral sources. In the span of both decades foreign aid provided about 10 percent of the foreign exchange requirements of the Philippines, and the total inflow was equal to about one percent of GNP.

The importance of foreign aid increased dramatically after the formulation of the Consultative Group for the Philippines in 1971. The total official development assistance committed in 1971–74 was larger than the total committed throughout the preceding twenty years. On the basis of disbursements, foreign aid, which had provided 7 percent of the foreign exchange requirements in 1965–69, provided about 14 percent in 1970–74. Since 1970 there has also

Table 16.8. Commitments of Official Development Assistance, 1952–74
(In millions of U.S. dollars)

Source and type of aid	1952–69	1970	1971	1972	1973	1974
Grants and similar assistance						
United States	439	38	44	55	57	23
Japan	7	1	1	5	3	3
Other	55	5	5	2	1	2
Total	501	44	50	62	61	28
Development loans						
Commodity loans						
United States	10	10	20	35	1	4
Japan	. . .	. . .	42	72	5	36
Other	. . .	. . .	. . .	. . .	. . .	4
Total	10	10	62	107	6	44
Bilateral project loans						
United States	. . .	. . .	1	34	32	78
Japan	10	. . .	. . .	. . .	. . .	72
Other	. . .	1	11	1	5	6
Total	10	1	12	35	37	156
Multilateral project loans						
World Bank	233	. . .	22	40	98	227
Asian Development Bank	. . .	26	29	43	54	83
Total	233	26	51	83	152	310
Total project loans	243	27	63	118	189	466
Total development loans	253	37	125	225	195	510
Total assistance	754	81	175	287	256	538
Total assistance at constant						
1967 prices	733	75	153	226	159	274

. . . Zero or negligible.

Sources: National Economic and Development Authority (NEDA); Mila Bulan, "A Study of Official Development Assistance to the Philippines, FY1952–72" (M.A. thesis, University of the Philippines, 1973).

been a considerable change in the composition of foreign aid. The proportion of grants and similar assistance fell from about 60 percent of the total during 1952–69 to about 18 percent in 1970–74.[6] Loans from multilateral sources, which accounted for only a third of the total assistance in the earlier period, provided about half the

6. Although it is convenient to discuss grants and similar types of assistance here, it should be noted that these are part of the current account transactions in the balance of payments of the Philippines. Since they are part of the item called "transfers," they are listed under "Requirements" in Table 16.6.

total in 1970–74. Another noteworthy feature is that the amount of aid provided by the Japanese government, though very small before 1971, has grown rapidly in the last three years. Assistance from the United States for commodity loans and project loans has also increased substantially during the same period.

There have also been major changes in the sectoral distribution of aid in recent years. As can be seen in Table 16.9, the share of development loans going to agriculture has remained relatively stable at about 20 percent, but there have been large decreases in the shares of industry and power, with corresponding increases in transportation and other sectors.

EXPANDING THE USE OF COMMERCIAL LOANS

Average gross disbursements of medium- and long-term commercial loans of about US$1,400 million a year between 1976 and 1985 would be consistent with prudent management of the balance of payments and debt. Disbursements of commercial loans would need to rise from the present level of about US$400 million to about US$1,200 million in 1980 and to about $1,900 million in 1985. To support these levels of disbursements, new commitments of commercial loans would need to rise from the present level of US$600 million to more than US$1,400 million a year by the early 1980s.

This increased use of commercial loans would occur in both the public and private sectors of the Philippines. In the past the public sector has used commercial loans mainly for financing imports of commodities; for example, lines of credit have been obtained from the Commodity Credit Corporation of the United States to finance imports of wheat, cotton, and tobacco, from the Canadian Wheat

Table 16.9. Sectoral Allocation of Official Development Loans, 1959–74

Sector	1952–69	1970–74
Agriculture	22.0	20.0
Industry	29.0	14.0
Power	36.0	15.0
Transportation	11.0	23.0
Other[a]	2.0	28.0
Total (percent)	100.0	100.0
Total (millions of U.S. dollars)	253	1,092

a. Includes water supply, education, and population loans.
Source: NEDA, Central Bank of the Philippines.

Board for imports of wheat, and from the governments of the Republic of China and Thailand for imports of rice. Between 1971 and 1975 a total of more than US$300 million was disbursed, primarily for these purposes. In the future there will almost certainly be a substantial increase in the use of commercial loans by the public sector. Aside from their continued use to finance imports of wheat and other commodities, they will also have to be used to finance a large portion of the power program. It is estimated that gross disbursements of foreign loans needed to finance imported equipment for the power program would be about US$2,700 million between 1976 and 1985. Other major investment projects that would require direct borrowing by the public sector or the issue of government guarantees include the fertilizer and steel projects and perhaps some petrochemical projects. In view of these various possibilities, new commitments of commercial loans to the public sector may account for more than half the total commitments of commercial loans between 1976 and 1985.

It is difficult to assess whether inflows of this size and reliability can be obtained in the next few years. If the prospect is realistic, it would be unfortunate for the Philippines to curb its potential for rapid development unnecessarily. Foreign donors could be of invaluable assistance to the government in obtaining suitable cofinancing arrangements for major projects both with bilateral partners and with the private sector. There is considerable scope for diversifying the sources of finance by tapping markets in Europe and the members of the Organization of Petroleum Exporting Countries (OPEC). The Philippines has already begun to do this and has obtained substantial amounts of capital from the Eurodollar market in recent years. Nevertheless it is apparent that sustained and vigorous efforts will be needed to ensure that the volume of funds available is sufficient for the needs of the Philippines.

Management of External Debt and Foreign Exchange Reserves

In the latter part of the 1960s imports grew faster than exports, and foreign commercial loans with relatively short maturities were widely used to finance the deficits. By 1970 about 60 percent of the debt outstanding had maturities of less than five years. This was one of the factors that precipitated the foreign exchange crisis in the early part of 1970, which in turn resulted in a major devaluation

of the currency, a rescheduling of some external debt, and the introduction of tighter controls over foreign borrowings. The Central
Bank established a system for approving, recording, and monitoring
all public and private external debt contracted in the Philippines
in 1970. As a result of subsequent policies of careful debt management, the maturity structure of the external debt has substantially
improved and the burden of debt service has been reduced. The
present careful control over external borrowings will undoubtedly
continue, and, provided that the composition of future inflows of
loans is along the lines already indicated, the projected increase in
external debt and debt service, though large, is not expected to
present serious difficulties.

Amount and composition of external debt

The outstanding amount of medium- and long-term debt (on a
disbursement basis) increased by about US$900 million between
1970 and 1975 [7] and at the end of 1975 stood at US$2,300 million.
Most of the increase was accounted for by loans from members of
the Consultative Group, and a large part of the medium-term debt
contracted in the late 1960s was retired. The maturity structure of
the debt thus improved significantly. For example, the share of
long-term maturities in the public debt increased from 38 percent
at the end of 1969 to 70 percent at the end of 1975, and the share
of public debt rose to more than half the total debt outstanding
(Table 16.10). This improvement has been the result of the careful
debt-management policies of the government and the generous
support of Consultative Group members whose loans have had
substantially better terms than loans from commercial sources.[8]

7. This includes US$200 million of short-term debt (that is, with maturities of
less than one year) that was rescheduled at the time of the 1970 policy reforms.
8. The average terms of loans from donors from 1952 to 1975 were as follows:

Donor	Average rate of interest (percent)	Average maturity (years)
U.S. government		
Public Law 480 loans	2.83	23.0
USAID development loans	3.05	35.9
Japanese government	3.45	23.6
Other governments	2.79	27.1
World Bank	6.18	22.0
Asian Development Bank	6.53	23.1

The amount of outstanding medium- and long-term external debt is projected to rise to about US$6,000 million in 1980 and to about US$11,000 million in 1985. By the mid-1980s the public sector might hold about three-quarters of the amount outstanding (Table 16.10). Because of the "softer" terms of repayment, the share of debt held by official sources is expected to rise steadily from the present level of about 40 percent to 50 percent by the mid-1980s, after which it should begin to decline.

Because of the heavy reliance in the late 1960s on commercial loans with relatively short maturities, the ratio of debt service payments to export receipts rose steadily. By 1971 the debt service ratio stood at 27 percent, but as a result of careful debt-management policies and the rapid increase in export receipts since 1972, the burden of debt service payments has eased substantially. Amortization and interest payments on medium- and long-term loans were about US$320 million in 1970, and, although they had risen to about US$500 million by 1975, these payments had declined to about 17 percent of export receipts. If the amount and composition of inflows of medium- and long-term loans that will be required between 1976 and 1985 are along the lines discussed earlier, and if the projection of export receipts is realized, debt service payments will not rise much beyond 17 percent of export receipts during the next ten years.

Table 16.10. Composition of Medium- and Long-term External Debt (Outstanding at End of Period)
(In percent)

	Actual			Projected	
Category	1964	1969	1975	1980	1985
Public debt					
Official development assistance	21.5	14.1	39.5	46.0	50.0
Other sources	26.3	15.2	14.3	24.0	22.0
Total	47.8	29.3	53.8	70.0	72.0
Private debt	52.2	70.7	46.2	30.0	28.0
Total	100.0	100.0	100.0	100.0	100.0
Total (millions of U.S. dollars)	390	1,360	2,320	6,000	11,000

Sources: Data for 1964, 1969, and 1975 are from the Central Bank of the Philippines; data for 1980 and 1985 are based on World Bank projections.

Table 16.11. Various Indicators of the External Reserve Position of the Philippines, 1964–75
(In millions of U.S. dollars)

Category	1964	1969	1974	1975
International reserves	38	119	1,166	1,090
Gross foreign exchange holdings of Central Bank	123	121	1,503	1,455
Net foreign exchange holdings of commercial banks	−85	−2	−337	−365
Net foreign assets of banking system	9	−78	602	100
International reserves as months of imports	. . .	. . .	3.5	3.0

. . . Zero or negligible.
Source: Central Bank of the Philippines.

MANAGEMENT OF EXTERNAL RESERVES

Because of the chronic shortage of foreign exchange, the external reserve position of the Philippines was inadequate until the commodity boom in 1973–74. This was true no matter how foreign exchange reserves are defined. (The various definitions of the external reserves of the Philippines are indicated in Table 16.1.) For the purposes of this report, the World Bank has relied on the definition of international reserves used by the Central Bank of the Philippines in its reserve-management policies.[9] International reserves stood at US$1,100 million at the end of 1975, in sharp contrast to earlier years when they were rarely more than US$200 million and were usually equal to less than two months of imports. The difference between international reserves and the net foreign assets of the banking system is that liabilities of the Central Bank are netted out of international reserves. The net foreign assets of the banking system were negative from the mid-1960s until 1972, but later they increased sharply, and at the end of 1974 they reached a level of US$600 million. Because of a sudden deterioration in the terms of trade in 1975, the net reserves again fell substantially, to about US$100 million at the end of 1975.

Despite the large trade deficits confronting the Philippines today, these reserves do provide the authorities with room to ma-

9. The gross foreign exchange holdings of the Central Bank plus the foreign exchange holdings of the commercial banks net of short-term liabilities.

neuver in managing balance of payments in the immediate future. For the longer term, import payments are expected to rise sharply, and as a consequence these reserves may not be judged adequate. The government is therefore likely to continue to make use of the facilities of the International Monetary Fund (IMF) in managing the balance of payments. There has been a standby agreement with the IMF each year since 1970, and purchases outstanding stood at US$80 million at the end of 1975.[10] In 1975 the Philippines also made use of the IMF Oil Facility, drawing a total of US$116 million.

In view of the large amounts of external capital that the Philippines will need to attract in the coming years, it is essential that external reserves continue to accumulate. International reserves should be maintained at the equivalent of about two and a half to three months of imports of goods and nonfactor services. The foregoing projections of capital inflows would provide for a buildup in reserves to these levels, and they should be sufficient to ensure that debt service payments on the one hand, and the flow of essential imports on the other, can be maintained if export earnings slump as a result of downturns in economic activity in overseas markets.

10. The Philippines currently has a quota of 155 million SDRs (special drawing rights) with the IMF.

Appendix A

Agrarian Reform

T HE PHILIPPINES HAS ONE of the highest farm tenancy rates in Asia. Tenants cultivate over 40 percent of all farms in the Philippines, compared with about 25 percent in Thailand and about 16 percent in the Republic of China. Higher rates of tenancy mark rice farming: 75 percent of the rice area is tenanted in Central Luzon, and 70 percent in Southern Tagalog. Existing data also suggest that as many as two-thirds of these tenant families earn incomes that fall in the bottom 40 percent of the national income distribution. In the Philippines as in other parts of Asia sharecropping often burdens the tenant with high rents, generally amounting to 50 percent of the harvest; unlawful ejections; and excessive interest rates, ranging anywhere from 50 to 400 percent.[1] The Philippines' history of peasant unrest, primarily in Central Luzon, is partly a result of these conditions. Consequently the government has had a long-standing commitment to a program of agrarian reform that would abolish sharecropping and provide greater security of tenure.

---

1. Joe R. Motheral writes: "Money lending is a source of revenue to many landowners that almost equals the rental share." See "Land Tenure in the Philippines," *Journal of Farm Economics,* vol. 38, no. 2 (May 1956), p. 467. In some cases, however, the landlord may not charge his tenant any interest for the loan. See the study by J. M. Manto and R. D. Torres, "Sources and Cost of Credit to Rice Farmers in Central Luzon" (National Food and Agriculture Council, Department of Agriculture, June 1974; processed), p. 11.

Land Reform before 1972

Measures to effect Philippine land reform date back to the early 1900s when the American colonial government purchased 160,000 hectares of tenanted land belonging to the Catholic church and attempted to promote homesteading and colonization. The colonial government's interest in promoting the rapid growth of exports and its political dependency on the landlords unfortunately deterred it from actively enforcing these land reforms.[2] A Rice Share Tenancy Act was passed in 1933, but the legislation was circumvented by landlord interests and was never implemented. Following World War II peasant unrest, supported by the armed Huk resistance, again made land reform a major issue. Republic Acts 1911 and 1400 in 1954 and 1955 established a formula for crop sharing, promoted the resettlement of public lands, and provided for the expropriation of landed estates to provide family-size farms for landless tenants. Due to a number of loopholes, including a ceiling of 300 contiguous hectares for individual landlords, only 19,155 hectares were purchased between 1955 and 1962.[3]

In 1963 the Agricultural Land Reform Code (Republic Act 3844) shifted the emphasis away from expropriation and resettlement to a two-stage conversion of sharecroppers into leaseholders and leaseholders into owner-operators. The code's objectives were to establish cultivation by owner and family-size farms as the basis for Philippine agriculture; to provide a dignified, more independent existence for small farmers; to increase productivity and farm incomes; and to apply labor laws equally to industry and agriculture. The code reduced the land ceiling from 300 to 75 hectares but provided no timetable for completion.[4]

Although significant as landmarks in the legislative history of Philippine agrarian reform, the 1954, 1955, and 1963 acts had little if any impact on agrarian relations. The acts suffered from a lack of administrative and financial support and strong political opposi-

2. Harold D. Koone and Lewis E. Gleeck, "Land Reform in the Philippines" (United States Agency for International Development [USAID] Country Paper, June 1970), p. 6.

3. Donald E. Douglas, "An Historical Survey of the Land Tenure Situation in the Philippines," *Solidarity*, vol. 5, no. 7 (July 1970), p. 76. The author also adds: "It is not exaggerating to state that some landowners made a proverbial 'killing' off the government through expropriation proceedings . . ." (p. 77).

4. In 1971 the land ceiling was lowered to 24 hectares.

tion. By 1971 only about 50,000 sharecroppers, or about 5 percent of the tenant farmers, had reached the leasehold stage; of these, less than a fourth had written contracts with fixed rents registered with the government.[5] The change in status from leaseholder to owner-operator had been attained by only 3,400 former tenants in 1971.

Agrarian Reform since 1972

In 1972 the government reaffirmed its commitment to agrarian reform and declared the entire country a land reform area. A number of decrees were issued to accelerate progress toward objectives set forth in the 1963 Agrarian Reform Code. The first phase of the reform emancipated tenants on rice and corn land; [6] but according to the 1963 code, which remains the basic law, farms producing sugar and tree crops such as coconuts were exempted, and their status under the 1972 reforms is thus unclear.

Ilocos and Central Luzon have the highest concentrations of rice and corn tenants and, together with Southern Mindanao—a major corn-growing area—they also have the largest tenanted areas. Ilocos has the largest number of landlords as well as the highest percentage of landlords with holdings less than 7 hectares. The largest percentage of landlords with holdings of between 7 and 49 hectares is in Southern Mindanao.

SCOPE OF THE PROGRAM

One of the first difficulties was in determining how many tenants and landlords on rice and corn farms would be affected and how

5. International Labour Office, *Sharing in Development* (Geneva: ILO 1974), pp. 474–75. L. C. Panganiban writes that between 1964 and 1971 there were about 47,000 conversions to a leasehold agreement and that almost 70 percent of these were oral agreements. See *Land Reform Administration Procedures in the Philippines: A Critical Analysis* (Madison: University of Wisconsin Land Tenure Center, 1971), p. 32.

6. Presidential Decree 27 outlined this first phase and established family-size farms of either 5 rain-fed hectares or 3 irrigated hectares for the former tenants; the retention of not more than 7 hectares by the landlord, provided he is cultivating the land; a fixed formula for the valuation of the land and for amortization; and the requirement that all former tenants become full-fledged members of a recognized farmers' cooperative.

Table A.1. Scope of Land Reform by Size of Tenanted Holding
(As of February 1975)

Size of tenanted holding (hectares)	Hectares	Tenants (thousands)	Landlords
100 and above	207.4	90.7	2.1
50–99.9	88.8	44.0	1.6
24–49.9	102.6	60.3	5.9
7–23.9	426.8	229.3	47.1
7 and below	693.3	531.9	374.4
Total	1,518.9	956.2	431.1

Source: Department of Agrarian Reform.

many hectares would be covered. When the reform was announced in October 1972 it was expected to cover about one million tenants and 350,000 landowners on about 1.8 million hectares of tenanted rice and corn land.[7] In 1973 the Department of Agrarian Reform (DAR) reported there were about 1.1 million tenants, 221,000 landlords, and about 1.3 million hectares. As of February 1975, however, the DAR indicated that the program would cover 956,000 tenants, 431,000 landlords, and about 1.5 million hectares (Table A1), which is the figure used in this book. The most significant change between 1973 and 1974 was a 119 percent increase in the total area for tenanted holdings of 7 hectares and below and a 40 percent decrease in the total area for holdings above 24 hectares. Many reasons could account for these shifts, including statistical error, the change in the DAR definition of size of holding from that of total farm size to that of tenanted rice and corn land, or illegal partitioning by some of the landlords.

TRANSFERRING LAND

Operation Land Transfer, being carried out under the overall direction of the DAR, consists of issuing and distributing certificates of land transfer and transferring titles to former tenants. The certificate is not a deed or title to the land but merely verifies that the tenant is the tiller of the land he claims to be cultivating. Although the intention in 1972 was to transfer titles for all 1.5

---

7. Corn land comprises about 10 percent of the area under the reform.

million hectares, in 1974 the government indicated that tenanted holdings of 7 or fewer hectares would be exempted from the land transfer. There are 374,000 landlords with tenanted holdings below 7 hectares, and the average tenanted holding of each landlord is less than 2 hectares.

Implementing the land transfer program proceeded at a fairly rapid pace during its first year but has since slowed considerably (Table A2). Administrative difficulties have arisen primarily as the result of the long delay in issuing rules and regulations for the DAR field teams. Although financing has become less of a problem than in the past, landlord opposition remains a major obstacle. The emphasis of the 1972 reforms on the transfer of ownership highlights the problem of incomplete records of land titles and land rights.

Table A.2. Progress of Philippine Land Reform

Item	December 1972	December 1973	December 1974	November 1975
Land transfer certificates issued				
Number of tenants	423	144,538	189,121	207,991
Number of certificates	423	207,417	268,541	293,994
Hectares covered	682	259,348	337,025	365,931
Number of provinces	4	54	64	64
Land valuations received by DAR				
Number of landowners	—	—	210	993
Number of tenants	—	—	13,554	37,194
Hectares covered	—	—	17,335	50,106
Number of provinces	—	—	27	39
Land valuations received by Land Bank				
Number of landowners	—	—	140	754
Number of tenants	—	—	6,381	27,860
Hectares covered	—	—	9,711	39,693
Estimated cost (thousands of pesos)	—	—	59,135	254,606
Number of provinces	—	—	19	34
Landowner compensation paid by Land Bank				
Number of landowners	—	—	88	593
Number of tenants	—	—	3,177	16,410
Hectares covered	—	—	5,799	31,325
Cost (thousands of pesos)	—	—	35,886	202,203
Number of provinces	—	—	12	31

— Not applicable.
Source: Department of Agrarian Reform (DAR).

Lacking sufficient cadastral data, the government has tried simultaneously to identify tenants and landlords, sketch and map individual farm parcels, and distribute transfer certificates. In the Republic of China—often cited as an example of a successful land reform program—registration of the land and information about its value, ownership, and cultivator were available in government records which had been updated in 1945, four years before the implementation of the land reform program.[8]

December 1977 was the original target date for completion of the land transfer, including the processing of landlord compensation and the beginning of amortization payments. In view of the many administrative problems that have been delaying implementation of the program this target now appears overly optimistic. If the government were to accelerate the pace significantly, a more realistic objective for December 1977 might be the completion of the first part of Operation Land Transfer: issuing and distributing transfer certificates and completing a national cadastral survey. Although tenant amortization and landlord compensation will take place simultaneously with the delivery of certificates, considerably more time will be needed to implement this phase. Most landlords and tenants, however, could possibly be covered by 1980.

Registration and enforcement of a leasehold system is a separate aspect of the reform that will cover over half the tenants and in the long term will probably prove to be the most difficult to enforce. It is not clear how many, if any, of these tenants have been registered by the DAR, but efforts should be made to implement the leasehold system as the availability of field staff permits.

Identifying tenants and landlords. The identification of tenants and landlords and a survey of the parcels is being carried out by field teams from the DAR and the Bureau of Land Acquisition, Distribution, and Development. As of July 1975 almost all tenants on holdings above 24 hectares had been identified and their parcels surveyed. Initially landlords and tenants were expected to cooperate

---

8. Beginning around 1900 under Japanese administration, cadastral surveys were conducted in the Republic of China every ten years. Consequently the transfer of land titles in 1953 (the third phase of the land reform program) could be carried out in one year. A. Y. C. Koo credits the cadastral system for enabling quick and effective implementation of the 1949 land reform legislation. See "Land Reform in Taiwan," (USAID Country Paper, June 1970), p. 4.

in verifying the boundaries of the parcels, but because of landlord opposition the DAR field teams have often had to proceed with only the tenant's description of the land. Discrepancies have been found between the Bureau of Land's maps and the land titles and many cases are delayed by resurveys.

When land parcels have been identified and mapped the tenant can fill out an application for farm ownership provided he does not already own 3 or more hectares of agricultural land. If the tenant's claim to the land is not disputed, or if and when the dispute is resolved by the Court of Agrarian Relations, the DAR issues a certificate of land transfer.

Although Presidential Decree 27 on land reform called for the establishment of family-size holdings of 3 irrigated hectares or 5 rain-fed hectares, this provision did not prove to be feasible. Consequently estates have been allocated among tenants on the basis of existing occupancy. Another aspect of the reform that has been altered is the condition that landlords cultivating their land could retain up to 7 hectares. For tenanted holdings above 24 hectares, no retention by the landlords has been allowed, but the practice is being modified for landlords with holdings below 24 hectares. Without authoritative guidelines some issues remain unclear, for example the definition of rice and corn tenants where mixed farming is practiced, and the status of home lots that are not contiguous to the cultivated land or that are rented from a different landlord.

It is not clear whether the government will exercise an option to exempt from transfer hectarage of landlords who are completely dependent on the land for their livelihood.[9] The DAR undertook a landlord identification survey to determine the number of absentee owners of 7 to 24 hectares and the financial dependence of these absentee owners on the land. The results indicate that about 96 percent of the landlords are absentee, 75 percent of these have never cultivated their land, and 70 percent are entirely or almost entirely dependent on the land for their income. The survey does not indicate, however, whether these absentee landlords are actually heads of households.

Land valuation. Using a method similar to that employed in the Republic of China, the 1972 reforms established that the valuation

9. Letter of Instruction 143, October 31, 1973.

of the land would be 2.5 times the average production for three normal crop years prior to October 1972, at the official price of ₱35 a cavan.[10] As of December 1, 1975, the land valuations received by the DAR covered about 37,000 tenants and 50,000 hectares. Initially valuation was to be undertaken voluntarily by the landlords and tenants through a Landlord-Tenant Production Agreement, but because many landlords have been boycotting the agreement responsibility for valuation has been given to the Barrio Committees on Land Production.

These committees are made up of the barrio captain and a DAR official, as well as elected representatives of the tenants, the owner-cultivators, the landlords, and the barrio association or Samahang Nayon. The barrio committees determine the average production for each holding based on data provided by the DAR field teams; interviews with farmers, landlords, rice thresher operators, rice millers, and others; and information gathered at public hearings. As of December 1, 1975, some 3,000 barrio committees had been organized out of a total of about 9,500 committees planned.

Delay in the valuation procedure raises the question of who is responsible for recording rental payments dating from October 1972, when Presidential Decree 27 was issued, until the time the tenant begins his amortization payments. In theory this rent should be credited toward the purchase of the land. The landlord is unlikely to cooperate by sharing his records, however, and the tenant may or may not be in a position to keep his own records.[11] While some tenants who have been issued certificates have stopped paying their rents, others are making payments without being able to credit them toward amortization.

10. The cavan is approximately equal to 75 liters, or about 2.13 bushels. In practice land valuations have been ranging from ₱6,000 to ₱12,000 for irrigated land and ₱4,000 to ₱6,000 for rain-fed land, which would mean the price being used is substantially higher than ₱35 a cavan. A negotiated price may be replacing the official price.

11. Hugh L. Cook, evaluating the effects of the 1954 and 1955 reforms, observed that: "Spot checks in which the author participated showed that only a small percentage of the tenants even know the law, that they keep no records of production or consumption credit received from the landlord, and that they merely turn over the crop at the end of the year according to the landlord's records and begin to borrow again." See "Land Reform and Development in the Philippines," in Walter Froehlich, ed., *Land Tenure, Industrialization and Social Stability* (Milwaukee: Marquette University Press, 1961), p. 173.

Certificates of land transfer. The rate at which certificates of land transfer were issued slowed considerably in 1974. By the end of 1973 certificates had been issued to about 144,000 tenants, but by December 1975 the number of tenants covered had grown only to about 208,000, or 50 percent of those on holdings above 7 hectares. This slowdown was caused by landlord resistance; difficulties created by inadequate records of ownership, yields, and tenancy; and administrative bottlenecks. There are indications, for example, that from 40 to 60 percent of the certificates issued have not been delivered to the respective tenants. Some 30 percent of these pending certificates are believed to be for holdings below 7 hectares, which as mentioned above are exempt from the land transfer, but other certificates have been delayed by incorrect land use classification, misspelled names, or legal disputes.

The DAR is attempting to correct the errors in the distribution of certificates and to streamline Operation Land Transfer by issuing the certificates simultaneously with the land valuations and the amortization schedules, and by instituting a receipt system to verify and document the delivery of certificates to tenants. Land titles are also being required before the Bureau of Land begins mapping in order to ensure greater accuracy of the maps. These measures should eventually improve administrative efficiency in handling individual cases, but in the short run they cause even greater delays in the implementation of the program.

Transferring land titles. Compensation and amortization payments have also been proceeding more slowly than originally expected. Although only a small percentage of landlords has received compensation, considerable progress was made during 1975. At the end of 1974 compensation covered only about 88 landlords, 3,000 tenants, and approximately 6,000 hectares—far below the government's target of 100,000 hectares. By the end of November 1975, however, nearly 600 landlords were covered, nearly 17,000 tenants, and about 31,000 hectares. This stage of the agrarian reform program is largely dependent on the progress of land valuation and the settlement of legal disputes over tenancy rights and ownership.

THE LEASEHOLD SYSTEM

The majority of the tenanted rice and corn holdings are less than 7 hectares in size. This category comprises about 56 percent of all tenants, 87 percent of the landlords, and 46 percent of the reform area. The government decision to exempt holdings of 7 or fewer hectares from the land transfer operation placed these farms under a leasehold system, which has the advantages over sharecropping of security of tenure and a legally fixed rent. The 1963 Agrarian Reform Code, the basic law for the leasehold system, sets the maximum rent at the equivalent of 25 percent of the average normal harvest, after deducting production costs, for the three crop years preceding the date of the contract.

Experience with other land reform programs indicates that rent reductions are not easily enforced.[12] Many tenants' inexperience with legal procedures, the structure of rural society, and problems with registration and the supervision of rents are factors that complicate implementation of a leasehold system. These difficulties would impose severe demands on the DAR administrative staff and the Court of Agrarian Relations, and dealing with them would require a relatively large and permanent field staff.

LANDLORD COMPENSATION

As described in Chapter 5, land reform could have a substantial and positive impact on tenant incomes. At the same time, landlords stand to suffer a considerable loss of rental income in relation to their incomes without the reform. The landlords were originally offered five different modes of payment under the 1972 reforms: (a) a cash payment of 10 percent and the balance in twenty-five-year, tax-free Land Bank bonds at 6 percent interest; (b) payment of 30 percent in preferred shares of stock issued by the Land Bank and the balance in twenty-five-year, tax-free Land Bank bonds at 6 percent interest; (c) full guarantee of the tenant's amortization payments in fifteen equal annual installments; (d) payment through annuities or pensions with insurance; and (e) exchange arrangements for goverment stocks in corporations that are owned or controlled by the government, or in private corporations where the government has holdings. Virtually all landlords have chosen the

---

12. Gunnar Myrdal has noted: "Because of all the avenues for evasion, tenancy laws are either showpieces full of loopholes or bulky and extremely complicated documents that would be incomprehensible to the tenants even if they were literate." See *Asian Drama: An Inquiry into the Poverty of Nations* (New York: Pantheon, 1968), vol. 2, p. 1324.

first option. Land Bank bonds are fully guaranteed by the government, are transferable, are acceptable payment for goods under Japanese government reparation payments, and are acceptable as collateral for loans in amounts up to 80 percent of their value. The loans carry an interest charge of 12 percent and are granted by public lending institutions specifically for the purchase of stock or assets of corporations owned or controlled by the government.

Landlords oppose the reform primarily because of dissatisfaction with the small cash payment and uncertainty about the value of Land Bank bonds over a twenty-five-year period. If a parcel of land were valued at ₱6,000 for example, with 10 percent cash payment and a discount rate of 10 percent, the present value of a ₱5,400 bond including interest payments would be ₱3,240, or 60 percent of its face value. At a discount rate of 15 percent the present value of the bond would be ₱2,106, or about 40 percent of its face value. In May 1975 the government attempted to mollify some of the landlords by amending the compensation package. Landlords with holdings between 7 and 24 hectares would receive 20 percent of the land value in cash and an additional cash payment of up to 10 percent for their children's education, insurance, or housing.

Comparing compensation packages to the rental payments landlords would receive without the reform shows that their loss of income could be substantial. The present value of the compensation payments over a twenty-five-year period would total about one-fourth the present value of the rental income (assumed to be 50 percent of the net harvest) without the reform.[13] For a landlord with a leasehold arrangement, the present value of rental income over twenty-five years would be about 60 percent of what it could be under a sharecropping arrangement. For the first five years, however, landlords holding 7 to 24 hectares would probably enjoy compensation payments about 50 percent higher than the present incomes of landlords with holdings below 7 hectares, who would retain their land under a leasehold system.

The form of compensation adopted in the Philippines differs from that in, for example, the Republic of China, where 70 percent of the compensation was made in commodity bonds at an interest rate of 4 percent and the remaining 30 percent was paid in stocks of government-owned industry. The stocks were invested in fixed

13. See the technical note to Chapter 5.

proportions in four public corporations. The result was that 40 percent of the total compensation was ultimately invested in industry and business. By contrast, the land reform in Japan became virtually confiscatory. Originally land valuation was based on 40 to 48 times the rental value in 1938, but from the time the land was valued until the tenants actually bought it from the government in 1950 rice prices in Japan increased 40 times. By 1950 inflation had made the yen worth only about 0.5 percent of its 1938 value. Consequently the tenants paid only about 2.5 percent of the estimated value of the land,[14] while the landlords received their total compensation in thirty-year bonds at 3.2 percent interest.

The Land Bank

Financing the transfer of land, including collecting amortization payments from the former tenants, is one of the main functions of the Land Bank of the Philippines. Created under the 1963 Agrarian Reform Code, the Land Bank has become the central financial institution for the land reform program. During the 1960s the bank lacked capital and organization; its bonds sold on the open market at a 20 to 40 percent discount. In July 1973 the government increased the bank's authorized capital to ₱3,000 million and expanded its powers.[15] As of December 31, 1974, the bank's paid-up capital was about ₱800 million, which was received from the government in the form of cash, government securities, real estate properties, and other assets.

Under the 1973 charter the main functions of the Land Bank were three: financing the transfer of ownership of farmland covered by the government's agrarian reform program; directing landlord investment into industry or other productive endeavors; and extending financial and technical assistance to the agricultural sector. The Land Bank is currently responsible for collecting amortization payments from about 425,000 tenants and financing compensation for some 57,000 landlords. As of December 1, 1975,

---

14. Chao Kang, *Economic Effects of Land Reform in Taiwan, Japan and Mainland China* (Madison: University of Wisconson Land Tenure Center, November 1972), p. 4.
15. Presidential Decree 251, July 21, 1973.

the bank had begun compensation payments in the amount of about ₱202 million to 593 landlords on behalf of some 16,400 former tenants. The most immediate problem facing the bank is the collection of amortization payments. Problems have arisen over the distribution of the "Farmers' Undertaking to Pay the Land Bank," a document containing the tenant's amortization schedule. This document is supposed to be issued by the bank at the same time payments are made to the landlords; the amortization payments begin one year later. In reality the distribution of the "Farmers' Undertakings" is being delayed, which puts the former tenants increasingly in arrears. As of February 10, 1975, only about 450 former tenants had received and returned "Farmers' Undertakings" out of about 4,400 tenants who should have received them.

The Land Bank may also have difficulties arranging for the collection of payments from the former tenants. To meet this problem, the bank has arranged for twenty-one private development banks and thirty-four rural banks to act as its agents. The payments are supposed to be guaranteed by the Samahang Nayons, but the number of tenants actually joining these barrio associations appears to be relatively small. Although the Land Bank itself provides the overall guarantee for the land transfer, a fall in the collection rate to much below 70 percent could create serious financial difficulties.

An important link with amortization collections will undoubtedly lie in the Land Bank's responsibility for guaranteeing financial support for reform beneficiaries to increase their productivity and incomes. Although the Masagana 99 and Masaganang Maisan programs to supply supervised production credit to rice and corn farmers have not been tied directly to the land reform, it is likely that in the future this form of government support will need to be assured for the reform beneficiaries. These programs are estimated to cover about 40 percent of the tenants, and they may need to be extended if the Land Bank is to maintain a reasonable collection rate.

In order to finance the transfer of holdings over 7 hectares, the Land Bank will be required to make initial cash payments of about ₱1,200 million.[16] Interest payments on its bonds will amount to

16. See technical note to this appendix.

about ₱277 million a year over most of the twenty-five-year period. The bank will be receiving ₱1,800 million in a capital subscription from the government as well as amortization payments of about ₱417 million each year. With earnings of 10 percent on its cash balance, deposits, and other forms of borrowing, the Land Bank should have no difficulty financing the land transfer.

The transfer of holdings over 7 hectares will amount to 826,000 hectares with a total asset value of about ₱5,800 million (US$773 million). For most of the medium- and small-scale landlords, their land has been their only earning asset and they have no experience with investments in productive activities unrelated to their land holdings. The government is anxious to see that as much as possible of the compensation paid to former landlords is channeled back into productive investments. To provide financial and technical assistance to the landlords, the Land Bank has undertaken a program of short-term lending and project identification for landlords to channel their resources into industry or other productive ventures. The Land Bank will grant loans in amounts up to 80 percent of the bond's face value for investment in an approved project. Assuming that even 25 percent of the landlords use their bonds as collateral for such loans, this would mean an additional cash requirement of about ₱921 million. Although the Land Bank has set up a program to identify acceptable projects for investment, at present it lacks the staff and network of regional offices required to carry out the program. Over a period of time it may be possible to expand the technical and administrative capacity of the bank to assist the landlords, but consideration should also be given to demands that the reform beneficiaries may place upon the institution, such as possible delays in amortization payments. In the short run the Land Bank might coordinate its efforts with the rural banks, the Development Bank of the Philippines, and other banking institutions that over the years have gained considerable experience in financing a wide range of projects.

Technical Note. Financing Land Reform

Estimates of the Land Bank's ability to finance the transfer of 826,000 hectares were based on six assumptions:

a. Holdings of 24 and more hectares (10 percent cash and 90 percent bonds) would be transferred over a four-year period:

Year	Hectares
1975	50,000
1976	100,000
1977	200,000
1978	49,000

Holdings of 7 to 24 hectares (30 percent cash and 70 percent bonds) would be transferred over a three-year period:

Year	Hectares
1978	151,000
1979	200,000
1980	76,000

b. The value of the land was set at ₱7,000 a hectare in 1974 prices.

c. The government's capital subscription to the Land Bank was assumed to be ₱800 million in 1974, and it was assumed that an additional ₱200 million would be paid by the government annually from 1975 to 1979.

d. It was assumed that earnings by the Land Bank on the current cash balance would be 10 percent.

e. The estimated collection rate of tenants' amortization payments would be 70 percent.

f. It was assumed that the bonds held by the landlords would be redeemed at the end of the twenty-five-year period.

Appendix B

The Role of Energy in the
Philippine Economy

IMPORTED PETROLEUM PROVIDES MORE than 90 percent of the total energy requirements of the Philippines. Because of this extreme dependence, the sharply increased costs of crude petroleum since 1973 have had a major impact on the Philippine economy. The most noticeable effect has been in the balance of payments. According to the trade statistics of the Central Bank of the Philippines, imports of crude petroleum and products amounted to about 69 million barrels in 1973, and the total amount paid for these imports was about US$180 million f.o.b., or 12 percent of the value of all imports. The volume leveled off in 1974 because of the restriction of supplies in the early part of the year and the substantially higher prices for oil and oil-intensive products. Nevertheless in 1974 the value of imported petroleum products rose to about US$650 million, the equivalent of 21 percent of total imports, and this rise of US$460 million accounted for 30 percent of the total increase in import payments. The increase in payments for petroleum was a major factor in the sharp deterioration of the external trade account of the Philippines (from a surplus of about US$270 million in 1973 to a deficit of about US$420 million in 1974), and it contributed indirectly to the deficit through its effects on the prices of imported petroleum-based chemical products. As a percentage of GNP, petroleum imports rose from 1.8 percent in 1973 to 4.5 percent in 1974.

The high cost of petroleum imports and the prospect of their rapid growth to meet the demand for energy has spurred the government to reassess its energy policies, and in 1974 a new energy plan was introduced. Although the search for indigenous deposits of petroleum is being stepped up, the plan is based on the assumption that commercial quantiites of oil will not be discovered in the Philippines. Thus the main objective is to reduce the country's dependence on imported petroleum to 76 percent of its total energy needs by 1985 and to 70 percent by the 1990s. These are ambitious goals, given the present dependence on petroleum products. The objective is to be accomplished by accelerating the development of nuclear, hydroelectric, and geothermal power and reducing the dependence on oil-fired thermal plants. Savings will be achieved in other sectors—particularly in transport and industry, which use 80 percent of all energy consumed—by conservation measures and improvements in energy efficiency. The question is the extent to which the Philippines can reduce its dependence on imported petroleum during the next decade or so.

According to the trends in energy use during the coming decade (see Table B1), total consumption of energy will probably grow

Table B1. Actual and Projected Domestic Consumption of Energy

Source	Energy consumption (millions of tons of oil equivalent)						Average annual increase (percent)	
	Actual				Projected			
	1960	*1965*	*1970*	*1973*	*1980*	*1985*	*1960–73*	*1973–85*
Petroleum products (net imports)	2.62	4.51	8.15	9.18	14.72	23.20	10.1	8.0
Hydroelectric	0.29	0.41	0.50	0.61	0.99	2.92	6.0	13.9
Coal	0.10	0.07	0.03	0.04	0.10	0.10	−6.8	7.9
Geothermal	. . .	. . .	. . .	. . .	0.19	0.81	—	—
Nuclear	. . .	. . .	. . .	. . .	. . .	0.64	—	—
Total	3.01	4.99	8.68	9.83	16.00	27.67	9.5	9.0

. . . Zero or negligible.
− Not applicable.
Note: The following conversion factors were used to compile this table.
   1 million tons of oil $\equiv$ 7.530 $\times$ 10^6 barrels of oil
   1 million tons of oil $\equiv$ 1.430 $\times$ 10^6 tons of coal
   1 million tons of oil $\equiv$ 0.400 $\times$ 10^4 gigawatt hours.
The last is the estimated conversion ratio of a modern power station.
Source: World Bank estimates based on information supplied by the Petroleum Institute of the Philippines, the National Power Corporation, and the Central Bank of the Philippines.

about 9 percent a year if GNP increases 7 percent a year in real terms between 1975 and 1985. By 1980, for example, consumption may have reached about 16 million metric tons of oil equivalents, and by 1985 about 28 million metric tons. Present consumption is about 10 million tons.

Given the limited natural energy base of the Philippines and the long periods required for the development of alternative sources of energy, this demand for energy will have to be met mainly with imported petroleum, at least until the mid-1980s, even if the program for developing alternatives is fully implemented. On the whole, the substitution possibilities are extremely limited in the short and medium term, or until about 1980. While greater efficiency and conservation in the use of energy may be feasible in some cases, this will be of little significance by itself, and the scope for saving energy by curtailing its luxury uses is limited. Significant changes in the use of petroleum products are likely to occur only through the incorporation of energy-saving technology in some sectoral investments. Such changes are unlikely to be effective earlier than 1980. Consumption of petroleum products is likely to increase 8.5 percent a year during 1974–80, and by 1980 imports will have reached about 110 million barrels (including petroleum products), or 93 percent of the total energy consumed in the Philippines. Thereafter, the government program to accelerate the development of hydroelectric, geothermal, and nuclear power should begin to show results. By 1985 consumption could approach 180 million barrels, or 89 percent of total energy consumption. Even if this noteworthy target is achieved, however, the substantial dependence of the Philippines on petroleum as a source of energy will continue for at least another decade.

Prospects for discovering oil in the Philippines are reasonably good, but even if commercial fields were found in the near future, the country would still have to meet the bulk of its needs with imported petroleum until the mid-1980s. Using World Bank projections for the price of petroleum crude, the value of petroleum imports would rise to about US$1,500 million f.o.b. in 1980, for example.[1] As is indicated in Chapters 13 and 16, it will require a number of years for the Philippine economy to complete a reason-

1. "Price Forecasts for Major Primary Commodities" (July 1975), restricted-circulation internal document no. 814.

ably smooth transition to a point at which these higher costs have been fully absorbed. Increased investments will be needed in the export sector, in import-replacing industries, and in alternate sources of energy.

Energy Sources and the Petroleum Sector

The Philippines has only limited known natural resources of energy. These include hydroelectric power, coal, natural gas, and geothermal energy. The hydroelectric potential is at present estimated in the range of about 4 to 7 gigawatts (GW), of which 582 megawatts (MW) are being utilized and 300 MW are under construction.[2] Coal reserves are estimated at 44 million metric tons, but the coal is geologically young, with a low heating value. Production has been declining and is now down to about 50,000 metric tons a year. This trend is likely to be reversed as a result of the increased cost of petroleum, but the contribution of coal to energy supplies is expected to continue to be quite small for the foreseeable future. Reserves of natural gas are now estimated at 250 million cubic feet. There is no commercial production at present, but plans are being made to develop this resource. Geothermal energy is estimated at about 1.3 GW, and strenuous efforts are being made to develop the Tiwi and Leyte geothermal fields.

Since 1960 the consumption of energy has increased at an average rate of almost 10 percent a year, and in 1973, 9.8 million metric tons of oil equivalents were consumed (Table B1). The use of energy in the Philippines during the past decade is characterized by, first, the extreme and growing dependence on petroleum, which accounted for 87 percent of energy consumed in 1960 and 93 percent by 1973; and second, by the rapid growth of energy consumption in relation to GNP. During the 1960s, when GNP was increasing at about 5 percent a year in real terms, the elasticity of energy consumption with respect to GNP was about 2.2. Since 1969 the growth of petroleum imports has slowed down appreciably because of the sluggish growth in the economy during 1970–72 and the effects since late 1973 of

---

2. The International Atomic Energy Agency in 1973 estimated the potential of hydropower on Luzon and Mindanao to be 3.7 GW, while M. Lechuga, "Actual and Potential Utilization of Hydroelectric Power in the Philippines" (Manila, n.d.), estimated the potential of hydropower to be 6.7 GW.

Table B2. Net Imports of Petroleum Products

Category	1960	1965	1970	1973	1974
Volume (millions of barrels)					
Exports	. . .	2.5	8.2	0.9	0.3
Imports	19.7	36.5	69.6	71.0	68.2
Crude	14.0	34.0	67.5	69.5	61.8
Other products	5.7	2.5	2.1	1.5	6.4
Net imports	19.7	34.0	61.4	69.1	67.9
Value (millions of U.S. dollars, c.i.f.[a])					
Exports	. . .	6	17	16	17
Imports	74	91	142	228	653
Crude	27	71	124	208	573
Other products	47	20	18	20	80
Net imports	74	85	125	212	636

. . . Zero or negligible.
a. Cost, insurance, and freight.
Sources: Petroleum Institute of the Philippines and the Central Bank of the Philippines.

higher oil prices. (The elasticity of energy consumption was only 0.7 during 1970–73, for example.[3]) In 1973 crude petroleum accounted for about 98 percent of petroleum imports, and oil producers in the Middle East provided 85 percent of the crude oil requirements of the Philippines (Table B2).

Only a small amount of oil exploration has been undertaken in the Philippines in the past. The Oil Exploration and Development Act, decreed in 1972, introduced a service-contract arrangement for local and foreign interests willing to engage in exploration. The new arrangements provide substantial incentives for investors that have helped to interest foreign companies in exploration in the Philippines. Twelve service contracts, covering an area of about 6.7 million hectares, have been awarded, mostly offshore in the Sulu Sea. In addition, the Philippine National Oil Company has itself been engaged in onshore exploration in the Cagayan Valley. The twelve service contracts signed by the Petroleum Board involved commitments to expenditures of around US$100 million. This exceeds the total amount spent on petroleum exploration in the previous twenty years. Only two wells have been drilled so far

3. The elasticity calculation is sensitive to short-term fluctuations in consumption of energy and growth of output, but the relatively high average elasticity of 1.7 for 1960–73 as a whole is typical of a range of lower income countries.

and both have been dry. At present only one offshore rig is active, but hydrocarbon tests have been encouraging. A few small rigs are also operating onshore in the Visayas.

The prospects for an oil discovery in the Philippines are believed to be good. Significant amounts of seepage have been observed in many onshore areas. The present offshore drilling activity ranges from an area near the coast of Borneo, along Palawan to the Calamian Group. Even if an oil discovery is made in the near future, however, production of crude petroleum in commercial quantities could not occur sooner than the mid-1980s.[4] In view of the probable future dominance of petroleum as a source of energy in the Philippines and the apparently good prospects for discovering oil, methods of accelerating the rate of exploration should be examined. There appears to be a shortage of drilling equipment at present, and a more concerted program of exploration would require enlarging the supply of technical skills and risk capital available in the Philippines.

Four refineries now produce almost all the refined petroleum products needed in the Philippines. The refining and marketing operations of the petroleum industry have been dominated by subsidiaries of the major international oil companies. In January 1974, however, the government, through the recently established Philippine National Oil Corporation, purchased Exxon's shares in the Bataan refinery (whose rated capacity is 116,00 barrels a day, or 41 percent of the national total), along with all of Exxon's marketing operations. This gives the government a substantial direct role in petroleum refining and distribution. The total rated capacity is about 284,000 barrels a day, but in 1973 actual production was about 175,000 barrels a day (excluding refinery losses and fuel). In view of the projected increase in the use of petroleum, the present refining capacity would meet demand only until about 1977. The government is therefore confronted with some major decisions about expanding the domestic refining industry. One possibility is to import a larger proportion of needed petroleum in the form of refined products and to rely less on the expansion of domestic refining capacity. Another is to depend on some relatively minor expansion in existing plants, which would provide refining capacity

---

4. In fact, oil was struck off Palawan's north shore in early 1976, reportedly in economic quantities.

sufficient to meet the needs of the country until about 1980. A third possibility is to bring about a major increase in refining capacity, perhaps coupled with large investments in the petrochemical industry.

Trends in Energy Consumption

No analysis of total energy use among the major consuming sectors is available, although there are data on the consumption of petroleum products. An analysis of these data provides a good guide to the overall pattern of energy consumption, in view of the dominant position of petroleum. As is indicated in Table B3, the main use of petroleum is for road transport, which accounted for 33 percent of refinery output in 1973. The other modes of transportation accounted for about 8 percent in that year (almost half of which was exported). The electric power and industrial sectors consumed about 19 percent and 29 percent respectively. By product, about 43 percent of output was fuel oil, primarily for power and industry, 25 percent was motor gasoline, and 20 percent was diesel oil for automotive and other uses.

The subsequent analysis of trends in the transport, power, industrial, and other sectors suggests that consumption of refined petroleum products could increase from about 65 million barrels in 1973 to about 150 or 160 million barrels a year by 1985. After refining losses are taken into account, this would imply imports of

Table B3. Consumption of Petroleum Products, 1973
(In millions of barrels)

Sector	Motor gasoline	Diesel oil	Fuel oil	Other	Total
Transport	16.3	6.9	1.9	2.0	27.1
Road	16.3	5.4	...	...	21.7
Other[a]	...	1.5	1.9	2.0	5.4
Electric power	...	0.4	11.4	...	11.8
Industry	...	4.0	13.7	1.4	19.1
Other	...	1.4	0.9	5.0	7.3
Total[b]	16.3	12.7	27.9	8.4	65.3

... Zero or negligible.
a. Includes sales to international carriers, bunkering, and U.S. military sales.
b. Excludes refinery fuel and losses during refining.
Source: Philippine National Oil Company.

about 170 to 180 million barrels of crude petroleum and products. As indicated above, the proportion that is imported as crude petroleum will depend on the forthcoming government decisions about the refining and petrochemicals industries in the Philippines; for the purposes of the balance-of-payments exercise in Chapter 16 it was assumed that about 140 million barrels of crude petroleum would be imported in 1985.

TRANSPORT SECTOR

The government recognizes that the future growth in the consumption of petroleum will depend heavily on the pattern of development in transportation. This in turn depends on pricing policies in the sector and future modal development, including urban mass transit systems.

There is little scope for energy substitution during the next decade within any mode of transportation, except for a continuing switch to smaller automobiles. The railway system, which is located on Luzon, is very small and accounts for less than 10 percent of freight and passenger traffic. The volume of traffic is not sufficient to warrant the heavy capital costs that would be involved in electrifying the railways. Because the bulk of passenger and freight traffic in the Philippines will continue to be carried by road, the consumption of petroleum products will be closely tied to growth in the volume of road traffic. Traffic will in turn be affected by changes in petroleum prices and gasoline taxes, and by the present policy of discouraging the importation of large automobiles. A plausible rate of growth for the number of vehicles may be 8 to 9 percent a year; if improvements in the efficiency of vehicles are offset by increased congestion in urban areas, consumption of automotive fuels will probably increase by about the same rate. This would mean consumption of about 45 million barrels in 1980 and 70 to 75 million barrels in 1985.

POWER SECTOR

The power sector now accounts for about a fifth of total consumption of petroleum in the Philippines, and it is the main focus of efforts by the government to reduce dependence on imported petroleum. As is indicated in the more detailed analysis of the power section in Appendix C, 80 percent of the present supply of electric power comes from oil-based thermal or diesel power plants; the rest is from hydropower plants.

Because of the large increases in the cost of production of oil-based power, the alternatives of using hydroelectric, coal, nuclear, and geothermal energy have become more attractive. The government has therefore reformulated its power-development program, putting more emphasis on local sources of energy and nuclear power. On the basis of the demand considerations set out in Appendix C, it is estimated that some 5,270 MW of additional capacity will be required during the next ten years. The extent to which the National Power Corporation (NPC) will be able to increase the nonthermal component while meeting this demand is not yet certain. It may be possible to reduce the oil-based power component to almost half by 1985, if the generating capacity projected in Table B4 is installed as planned. The projects include a 600 MW nuclear power plant, twelve geothermal units with a combined capacity of 745 MW, and sixteen hydroelectric power plants with a combined capacity of 2,070 MW.

If this program to generate nonthermal power is implemented, it would save 29 million barrels of oil annually by 1985 compared with the amount needed to supply an all-thermal program. This would represent a savings in foreign exchange of about US$620 million a year by 1985, or about 4 percent of the projected value of imports. If alternate sources of energy are thus made available, consumption of petroleum products would probably grow at the rate of about 10 percent a year until 1980, then decrease to 2 percent a year. The power sector would consume about 32 million

Table B4. Actual and Projected Capacity of Generating Facilities

Type of power	Amount (in megawatts)		Composition (percent)	
	1974	1985	1974	1985
Thermal diesel	2,517	4,372	80.6	52.1
Hydroelectric	607	2,677	19.4	31.9
Geothermal	. . .	745	. . .	8.9
Nuclear	. . .	600	. . .	7.1
Total	3,124	8,394	100.0	100.0

. . . Zero or negligible.

Sources: 1974 based on data supplied by the National Power Corporation; 1985 is the World Bank projection as described in Appendix C.

barrels in 1980 and perhaps 36 million by 1985, since most of the hydroelectric and geothermal plants and all the nuclear plants would be built after 1980.

INDUSTRIAL SECTOR

The industrial sector consumes directly about 29 percent of the output of the petroleum industry, but it also uses about 40 percent of the output of the power sector, so perhaps as much as 35 percent of petroleum imports are, in effect, used by industry. The production of light consumer goods, including food, beverages, and textiles, accounts for about 35 to 40 percent of the fuel and electricity consumed. Intermediate goods, particularly chemicals, cement, and other nonmetallic minerals, account for much of the remainder.

Possibilities for using petroleum substitutes in the industrial sector are far more rigidly constrained by technology than are those in the power sector, and the progress of technological adaption is difficult to foresee. Production methods offer little scope for saving energy apart from such measures as the use of the direct-reduction process in the proposed steel mill in place of the traditional blast-furnace process and the use of bagasse as a source of energy in sugar mills. Indirect substitution, through changes in the pattern of industrial demand and output and in the regional location of industry in areas such as Mindanao and the Visayas, where hydroelectric and geothermal energy is available, will perhaps be more significant responses to the energy crisis.

If, in fact, output in manufacturing and mining does grow at an average rate of 8 to 10 percent a year during the next decade, as projected in Chapter 9, direct consumption of petroleum products in the industrial sector could reach 30 million barrels by 1980 and perhaps 50 million barrels by 1985. The outcome could be affected by government decisions on the future development of the petrochemical industry. Major investments in petrochemicals in the 1980s, for example, could mean larger imports of petroleum in place of the petroleum-based chemical products imported before.

Appendix C

The Power Sector

T HE POWER SECTOR IN THE PHILIPPINES, unlike that in most other Asian countries, consists of more than 400 public and private utilities, most of which are very small. The National Power Corporation (NPC) is the largest public utility, supplying power in bulk to small utilities and large industries located primarily in rural areas. The Manila Electric Company (MECO), the dominant private utility, generates and distributes to retail consumers and some small utilities in the greater Manila area. In 1970 about half of the 335 privately owned and 121 municipally owned utilities purchased and distributed power from NPC or MECO. The other half, located in more isolated areas, generated their own and provided substandard yet very costly services. Private industry also generated a significant amount of power.

Development Policy

The National Electrification Administration (NEA), established in 1969, has initiated a vigorous program to provide electricity throughout the country by 1990. It set up electricity cooperatives to improve the supply in rural areas, integrate the small utilities, and extend services to remote areas. The Power Development Council (PDC), formed in 1970, was made responsible for coordinating the activities within the sector and promoting its systematic development.

In the early 1970s the fragmented ownership of generation and distribution facilities was becoming an increasingly important obstacle to power development on the main islands. Presidential Decree 40 of November 1972 declared the electrification of the entire country a national goal that would be achieved by establishing island grids, integrating generating systems, and consolidating the franchise systems for the distribution of electricity. NPC was made responsible for the construction of national grids, the development of all future generation supplying the grids, and ultimately for owning and operating all generating facilities. MECO, although it is currently the largest generating as well as distributing company, will eventually perform only a distributing function; negotiations began in August 1975 to transfer the bulk of MECO's generating and transmission plant to NPC.

Presidential Decree 40 also expanded PDC's role to make it more effective in planning and implementing the electrification program and in orienting the various sectors of the industry toward national development goals. Because of its limited budget and staff, however, PDC only sets basic guidelines and policies and does not play a direct role in coordinating the programs and operations of the major public utilities.

Presidential Decree 40 defined clearly the intrasectoral responsibilities, particularly those of NPC and NEA, and if properly implemented it should lead to better coordination in the development of the sector. It imposed tremendous managerial, financial, and technical burdens on NPC, however, which will have to develop the generation capacity to cover all future demand. The government amended NPC's charter in January 1974, raising NPC's authorized capital and the ceiling on its indebtedness and giving it more authority and independence. Continuing strong government support will be essential if NPC is to carry out its mandate.

In the early 1970s the government took steps to diversify its sources of energy for power generation. About 80 percent of the current generation capacity depends on imported oil. Because of the increased cost of petroleum and the uncertainty of supply in the future, the government accelerated the development of nuclear power and indigenous geothermal and hydroelectric energy. Geothermal explorations at Tiwi and Los Baños in southern Luzon have found high pressure steam sufficient to produce 40 megawatts of electric power. The capacity of the fields is estimated at several hundred megawatts, however, and NPC has contracted with Philippine Geothermal, Inc., a subsidiary of Union Oil of California, to supply up to 500 megawatts of steam. The exploration of another geothermal field recently began on the island of Leyte. A feasibility study of nuclear power was made by Electrowatt of Zurich for the International Atomic Energy Agency; the United States Export-Import Bank will finance the first unit of 600 megawatts, which NPC hopes to begin operating in 1982.

Demand and Supply of Electric Power

The capacities of NPC and MECO to generate and produce energy are known, but those of the small utilities and privately owned plants are not. In 1974 the World Bank estimated the capacity of the utilities and the consumption of electricity in each region (Table C1). The total installed capacity in the Philippines was

Table C1. Estimated Installed Electric Capacity and Consumption, 1974

Region and owner	Installed capacity (megawatts)	Energy consumption (gigawatt hours)
Luzon		
National Power Corporation	501	1,979
Manila Electric Company	1,517	5,969
Other[a]	228	900
Subtotal	2,246	8,848
Visayas		
National Power Corporation	2	5
Other[a]	385	1,400
Subtotal	387	1,405
Mindanao		
National Power Corporation	152	421
Other[a]	335	1,250
Subtotal	487	1,671
Philippines		
National Power Corporation	655	2,405
Manila Electric Company	1,517	5,969
Other	948	3,550
Total	3,120	11,924

a. Includes small utilities and private industrial generators. Utilities are estimated to represent about 30 percent and industries 70 percent.
Source: National Power Corporation (NPC) and World Bank estimates.

about 3,100 megawatts, of which 49 percent was owned by MECO, 21 percent by NPC, 20 percent by private industries, and the remaining 10 percent by NEA and small utilities. Total energy consumption was estimated at about 12,000 gigawatt hours.

THE LUZON GRID

In October 1975 the installed capacity in Luzon for NPC and MECO, which together supplied about 90 percent of the power in Luzon, was about 2,330 megawatts. The energy capability was about 10,600 gigawatt hours; there was an excess capacity of 2,000 gigawatt hours, and peaking capacity was slightly more than adequate with a reserve of 30 percent.

The power consumption in Luzon grew rapidly in the 1960s at an average rate of about 13 percent a year, but in the early 1970s growth slowed to about 8 percent. The International Engineering Company and MECO in 1973 forecast a growth rate of 9.5 percent a year until 1980 for the NPC-MECO grid. The oil crisis and the subsequent economic recession had a stagnating effect on electricity demand, however. Although NPC's demand in the provinces increased moderately in 1974, power consumption in the Manila area experienced an unprecedented decline. The latest demand forecast prepared by NPC and MECO predicted that consumption would increase at an average rate of 8.2 percent a year in 1974 and 1975, provincial demand would rise 14 percent a year, while demand in the Manila area would grow 6 percent annually. The forecasts were based on planned industrial development outside the metropolitan area, the historical growth rate, the economic outlook for the future, and the planned expansion of the transmission grids. The estimate appears to be reasonable although the forecast for the Manila area might be somewhat low.

To satisfy the estimated demand NPC has proposed a very ambitious program for the next ten years which, together with MECO's ongoing projects, would increase the installed capacity in Luzon threefold, from 2,246 megawatts in 1974 to 6,286 in 1985. The program reflects the government's policy of rapidly reducing the dependence on imported oil; it includes two 600 megawatt nuclear power projects (to be commissioned in 1982 and 1985) and ten geothermal units of 55 megawatts each (Table C2).

If implemented on schedule the program would provide more than sufficient capacity for the projected demand. The excess of

Table C2. Proposed Plant Additions

| | Luzon | | | | Mindanao (NPC program) | | Visayas (NPC program) | |
| | NPC program | | World Bank program | | | | | |
Year	Plant	Megawatts	Plant	Megawatts	Plant	Megawatts	Plant	Megawatts
1975	Malaya 1 (T)	310	Malaya 1 (T)	310	...	...	...	...
1976	...	...	Bataan 2 (T)	n.a.	...	...	...	...
1977	Bataan 2 (T)	150	Patabangan (H)	100	Agus VI, no. 5 (H)	50	Cebu II (D)	50
	Pantabangan (H)	100			Diesel 1-2	32	Bohol (D)	11
	Geothermal 1	55					Amlan (D)	11
							Panay (D)	30
1978	Malaya 2 (T)	380	Geothermal 1	55	Diesel 3-6	64	Cebu II (D)	90
	Geothermal 2	55					Sipalay (D)	108
							Panay (D)	7
1979	Geothermal 3-4	110	Malaya 2 (T)	330	Agus II (H)	180	Sipalay (D)	54
			Geothermal 2-3	110	Diesel 7-9	48		
					DLCPO[a]	62		

Year								
1980	Geothermal 5	55	Geothermal 4	55	Agus VII (H)	45	Panay (D)	7
							Cebu (T)	50
							Tongonan (G)	75
1981	Kalayaan 1 (H)	150	Kalayaan 1-2 (H)	300	Agus I (H)	100		
	Geothermal 6	55						
1982	Kalayaan 2 (H)	150	Geothermal 5-7	165	Thermal 1	150	Cebu (T)	50
	Geothermal 7-8	110					Tongonan (G)	75
	Nuclear I	600					Jalaur (H)	50
1983	Tabu (H)	400	Tabu (H)	400	Agus III (H)	150	Bago (H)	60
	Magat (H)	300	Geothermal 8	55			Wahig (H)	10
							Cebu (T)	75
							Ulot (H)	30
1984	Abulog I (H)	200	Nuclear I	600	Agus V (H)	150		
	Geothermal 9-10	110						
1985	Abulog I (H)	200	Abulog I (H)	200	Pulangui II (H)	200	Valencia (G)	100
	Nuclear II	600	Geothermal 9	55	Pulangui IV (H)	45		

. . . Zero or negligible.

a. Generation of 62 megawatts by Davao Light and Power Company will be connected to the grid in 1979.

Note: D = diesel; G = geothermal; T = thermal; H = hydroelectric.

Sources: NPC and World Bank estimates.

Table C3. Present Value of Alternative Development Programs for Luzon
(In 1,000 million pesos in 1975 constant prices)

Program	Discount rate (percent)		
	0	10	15
NPC program			
Capital	34.7	20.1	15.9
Fuel	15.8	9.9	8.2
Operation and maintenance	2.8	1.7	1.3
Total	53.3	31.7	25.4
World Bank program			
Capital	28.1	15.8	12.5
Fuel	16.5	10.2	8.4
Operation and maintenance	2.6	1.6	1.3
Total	47.2	27.6	22.2

Sources: NPC and World Bank estimates.

about 40 percent above an adequate reserve level would enable NPC to retire more than 1,300 megawatts of its oil-fired thermal plants by 1985. The NPC program is very costly, however, and its construction schedules, particularly those for geothermal and nuclear plants, are optimistic.

This report outlines a smaller and less expensive program which is believed to reflect more closely the demand projected by NPC; this program would require ₱6,600 million in 1975 prices, or 23 percent less than that of NPC during the 1975–85 period. Even if the higher fuel cost of ₱150 million a year included here continues to accrue until 1995, the smaller program would still cost ₱4,600 million less than that of NPC in 1975 prices,[1] including capital, fuel, and operating costs (Table C3). This is primarily because of the high capital cost of the nuclear projects and the larger number of plants proposed by NPC. The government will need to consider carefully the relative costs and benefits of pursuing the more expensive nuclear program.

The Mindanao grid

The existing generating capacity in Mindanao is relatively low; NPC has an installed capacity of only 152 megawatts. Information on

1. A present value of ₱3,700 million at a 10 percent discount rate.

the generating capacities of other utilities and private industry is incomplete, but the information that is available indicates that in 1974 there was an installed capacity of about 490 megawatts and that consumption of electric power from all sources was about 1,670 gigawatt hours (Table C1).

NPC predicts its own demand will increase by an average of 28 percent a year during the next ten years as a result of the expansion of its transmission grids to absorb the generating plants of small utilities and industries and the prospective industrial developments indicated by the Board of Investments (BOI) (Table C4). The proposed industrial development of an energy-intensive nature in Mindanao suggests that this forecast is reasonable.[2] NPC intends to meet the rapid growth in demand by installing diesel plants of 144 megawatts before 1980, completing a base-load thermal plant and major installations on the Agus River between 1979 and 1984, and later by developing the Pulangui River and potential geothermal fields. A large installation of diesel power is required to stabilize the supply of energy provided by the current generating system, which is exclusively hydroelectric, and to meet the rapid increase in demand that is expected to take place before other sources of power become available. NPC will increase its installed capacity in Mindanao from 152 megawatts in 1975 to 1,366 megawatts in 1985, or ninefold in ten years (Table C4).[3]

THE VISAYAS GRID

The power supply in the Visayas depends almost entirely on private utilities and on industrial generators; the total installed capacity is about 390 megawatts. Demand is constrained by an inadequate supply, however, and blackouts occur almost daily. This situation will continue for some time, and growth in energy consumption will be determined in large part by the rate of capacity increase. NPC has launched a major program of power generation

2. The proposed projects include the Kawasaki iron ore sintering plant (1977), a ferrosilicon plant (1977), an integrated steel mill at Cagayan de Oro (1979), the expansion of the Iligan steel mill, four activated carbon projects, a cement plant, a pulp and paper plant, a bauxite-processing plant, and expansion of the wood-processing industry.

3. The forecast of 1,366 megawatts for 1985 does not include the generation of 62 megawatts by the Davao Light and Power Company, which would bring the total installed capacity to 1,428 as shown in Table C4.

Table C4. Proposed Power Development in Luzon, Mindanao, and the Visayas

Region	1975	1976	1977	1978	1979	1980	1981	1982	1983	1984	1985
Luzon											
Peak demand (megawatts)	1,486	1,586	1,757	1,892	2,073	2,180	2,352	2,550	2,767	2,998	3,253
Energy (gigawatt hours)	8,609	9,236	10,394	11,202	12,322	13,001	14,078	15,266	16,564	17,957	19,659
NPC development program											
Dependable capacity (megawatts)	1,934	1,934	2,201	2,609	2,672	2,724	2,978	3,750	3,802	4,482	5,304
Available energy (gigawatt hours)	10,615	10,615	12,350	15,100	16,660	17,001	17,636	20,130	23,403	25,140	27,200
World Bank development program											
Dependable capacity (megawatts)	1,934	2,077	2,147	2,218	2,617	2,669	2,969	3,125	3,477	3,827	4,029
Available energy (gigawatt hours)	10,615	11,115	11,908	13,248	16,247	16,590	16,470	17,156	18,502	21,222	22,358
Mindanao											
Satisfiable demand (gigawatt hours)	570	1,057	1,090	1,545	2,070	2,874	3,318	4,350	5,321	6,081	6,570
NPC development program											
Installed capacity (megawatts)	152	152	234	298	588	633	733	883	1,033	1,183	1,428
Available energy (gigawatts)	1,077	1,077	1,164	1,545	3,093	3,309	3,775	4,825	5,768	6,713	7,969
Visayas											
Satisfiable demand (gigawatt hours)	7	7	379	1,123	1,936	2,293	2,798	3,527	3,890	4,325	4,819
NPC development program											
Installed capacity (megawatts)	2	2	104	309	363	420	495	670	740	845	945
Available energy (gigawatt hours)	8	8	590	1,758	2,065	2,412	2,905	3,771	3,955	4,494	5,020

Sources: NPC and World Bank estimates.

which will initially provide diesel plants and later thermal and geothermal plants; until 1980 almost 90 percent of the planned new capacity of 418 megawatts would be diesel power for the mining sector in Cebu and Negros. The program would add 943 megawatts during the next ten years (Table C4), a very ambitious goal since NPC has virtually no existing plant in the Visayas. Even if the program were successfully implemented, however, the result would be a growth in total capacity of only about 13 percent a year, including a moderate rate of 4 percent a year in the capacity of private utilities and industries.

THE TOTAL POWER PROGRAM

The inefficient plants presently owned by small utilities and industries will rapidly phase out as NPC's grids are expanded in accordance with Presidential Decree 40. NEA and some companies will continue to install their own generating facilities, however, in areas where power will not be available from NPC in the near future or where industries can utilize process heat to generate their own power. Generation by small utilities and industries is expected to decrease from the current level of 30 percent of the total to 15 percent in 1985, which will still be a sizable portion.

The overall growth of electricity consumption is expected to increase by 10.7 percent a year during 1974–85. Estimates of the projected growth in production and capacity by region and by utility are shown in Table C5. The high growth rates anticipated in Mindanao and the Visayas are due to their present low rates of electrification and to the government's policy of dispersing industries. The per capita consumption of electricity in 1985 would be 700 kilowatt hours in Luzon, 580 in Mindanao, and 560 in the Visayas.

If the overall growth rate of consumption were 10.7 percent the elasticity of power consumption to GNP would be about 1.5, which assumes a GNP growth rate of between 7.0 and 7.5 percent. Countries at a stage of development similar to that of the Philippines normally have elasticities of between 1.5 and 2.0. Korea, for example, uses an elasticity of 1.6 to project its demand. The projected growth rate of about 11 percent for the Philippines, although acceptable for planning purposes, may therefore be somewhat low.

Table C5. Actual and Projected Generating Capacity and Energy Production, 1974 and 1985

Region and utility	Actual 1974	Projected 1985	Average annual growth rate 1974–75
Energy production (gigawatt hours)			
Philippines (total)	11,924	36,527	10.7
Luzon	8,848	21,048	8.2
Visayas	1,405	6,980	15.7
Mindanao	1,671	8,499	13.3
Installed capacity (megawatts)			
By region			
Philippines (total)	3,120	8,516	9.5
Luzon[a]	2,246	5,097	7.7
Visayas	387	1,537	13.3
Mindanao	487	1,882	13.1
By utility			
Philippines (total)	3,120	8,516	9.5
NPC	655	6,632	23.4
MECO[b]	1,517	425	—
Other[c]	948	1,459	4.0

— Not applicable.

a. Projections for Luzon are based on the development program worked out by the World Bank and assume the retirement of 157 megawatts of old thermal plants.

b. The major generating plants of the Manila Electric Company (MECO) will be transferred to the National Power Corporation (NPC).

c. Generating capacity of small utilities and industries has been assumed to increase at a rate of 4.0 percent a year in each region.

Source: NPC and World Bank estimates.

Some Implications of the Program

The impact of the programs proposed in Luzon, Mindanao, and the Visayas are significant. Installed capacity would almost triple, amounting to about 8,500 megawatts in 1985, and the production of electricity would increase by about 11 percent a year. There would also be notable changes in the composition and sources of supply of electric power. If the program were implemented as proposed, the thermal-diesel component of installed capacity would fall from 81 percent of the total in 1974 to 53 percent by 1985 (Table C6); increases in hydroelectric, geothermal, and nuclear power would compensate for this reduction. There are financial and technical uncertainties in developing capital-intensive hydroelectric and nuclear sources, however, and in securing sufficient steam for planned

Table C6. Actual and Projected Sources of Electric Power, 1974 and 1985

Source	Installed capacity (megawatts)		Percentage of total	
	1974	*1985*	*1974*	*1985*
Thermal diesel	2,513	4,494	80.6	52.8
Hydroelectric	607	2,677	19.4	31.5
Geothermal	. . .	745	. . .	8.7
Nuclear	. . .	600	. . .	7.0
Total	3,120	8,516	100.0	100.0

. . . Zero or negligible.

Source: NPC and World Bank estimates.

geothermal installations in particular. If these uncertainties are not resolved, oil-fired thermal plants would have to account for the shortfall.

The proposed program would also dramatically change the distribution of electricity suppliers. In agreement with government policy, all major generating facilities would be constructed and owned by NPC except for the Malaya 2 project, which is currently being built by MECO but will be transferred to NPC after its completion. With only marginal increases in generating capacity by small utilities and industry, NPC's share of total installed capacity would increase from one-fifth in 1974 to over three-quarters by 1985 (Table C5).

IMPLEMENTATION CAPACITY

Since its inception in 1936 NPC has built only six power plants. To meet the above projections it will have to implement more than seventy power projects in the next ten years, including nuclear and geothermal ones. In the past NPC relied heavily on temporary staff for its infrequent construction activities, even for professional positions such as senior engineers. Although this policy prudently avoided high administrative costs during slack periods, it has ressulted in insufficient managerial and supervisory personnel.

Recognizing the technical and managerial burden that this much larger program will impose, NPC has taken a number of steps to improve its implementation capacity. It has established regional offices in Luzon, Mindanao, and the Visayas; improved salary scales and merit systems to make NPC more competitive with private industry; arranged to transfer engineers from other government agencies to NPC, particularly for the newly organized Nuclear and Geothermal Division; employed qualified engineering consultants to meet the immediate needs for priority projects; and provided some scholarship and training programs for NPC staff, although in an unorganized manner. These measures have proved effective in securing young engineers and skilled workers and should allow NPC to meet its immediate technical and managerial requirements from its own resources.

Much still remains to be done to transform NPC from an entity which executes projects to a well-organized operating utility. The present division of authority and responsibilities between the head office and regional offices emphasizes project execution, with little consideration given to planning and operation. NPC personnel, while experienced in construction work, lack experience in investment programming and in the managerial skills of financial and organizational matters that are crucial to the administration of a public utility. The World Bank and NPC have agreed that the organization of the head office should be reviewed, the responsibility of each work unit redefined, and a comprehensive training program established. Although educated and skilled manpower is available in the Philippines, there will be a shortage of qualified managerial staff in the short term.

FINANCIAL IMPLICATIONS

The World Bank estimates that the smaller program it recommends for the Philippines would require investment outlays of about US$6,100 million (₱48,900 million) in current prices for the construction of generating and transmission facilities and the acquisition of MECO plants (Table C7). In 1975 prices about US$4,200 million (₱31,600 million) would be required compared with actual expenditures by NPC of about ₱1,500 million in 1975 prices during 1967–75.

NPC currently has the largest corporate asset base in the Philippines with ₱2,700 million in current prices at the end of 1975; by the end of 1985 the asset base will be ₱53,900 million in current prices, or ₱24,900 million in 1975 prices (Table C8). Because of the program's size, its high foreign exchange component, and the

**Table C7. Investment Requirements of the National Power
Corporation, FY76–FY85**
(Millions of pesos)

Region	Current prices[a]			1975 prices		
	Generation[b]	Transmission[b]	Total	Generation	Transmission	Total
Luzon	31,302	3,267	34,569	19,651	2,192	21,843
Mindanao	7,831	981	8,812	4,998	917	5,915
Visayas	4,223	1,338	561	2,946	914	3,860
Total	43,356	5,586	48,942	27,595	4,023	31,618

a. Assumed inflation rate of 8 percent a year.
b. Including transmission lines associated with generating plants.
Note: Investment requirements include interest during construction.
Sources: NPC and World Bank estimates.

limited funds available domestically, the major portion of the funds
required (64 percent, corresponding roughly to the estimated foreign
cost) will have to be borrowed abroad. To obtain such financing,
NPC will require an equity contribution from the government of
about ₱11,500 million in current prices (including ₱2,300 million
to finance the acquisition of MECO's plants), or about a fourth of
the total cost of the program during the period (Table C9). NPC's
debt-equity ratio would then be about 58:42 (excluding the reserves
that would be necessary in the event of a revaluation). Funds to
cover the debt service would be adequate if the financing for the
second and subsequent nuclear plants could be obtained on better
terms than those for the first.

   If tariffs are set at levels that would earn NPC an 8 percent rate
of return on the current value of net fixed assets in operation, net
cash generation would probably contribute about 14 percent of the
construction costs, including the interest during construction. The
financing plan is shown in Table C10.

   It is estimated that NEA will require ₱1,200 million (US$160
million) from the government through 1980, excluding subsidies
that may be required to operate the cooperatives until they break
even. If the revenue projections shown in Chapter 15 are realized,
an equity contribution of this magnitude would be possible, although it would place a significant financial burden on the government. Changes in tariffs and tariff structures could provide some
of the funds. An increase in the rate of return on net fixed assets

Table C8. Balance Sheets of the National Power Corporation
(In millions of pesos)

Category	1976	1977	1978
Assets			
Fixed assets			
Plant in service	4,839	6,809	8,255
Less: Depreciation	1,283	1,580	1,934
Operating plant	3,556	5,229	6,321
Work in progress	2,602	3,839	6,386
Investments	42	42	42
Current assets			
Cash	66	179	179
Inventories	121	171	207
Receivables	411	544	697
Subtotal	598	894	1,083
Other	64	64	64
Total assets	6,862	10,068	13,896
Equity and liabilities			
Equity			
Paid-in capital	3,115	3,865	4,557
Retained earnings	443	757	1,164
Revaluation reserve	1,065	1,368	1,807
Total equity	4,623	5,990	7,528
Long-term debt			
Debt due	1,892	3,743	5,928
Total debt	1,892	3,743	5,928
Current liabilities			
Payables	317	305	411
Bank overdraft	. . .	. . .	. . .
Total	317	305	411
Other liabilities	7	7	6
Contributions	23	23	23
Total equity and liabilities	6,862	10,068	13,896
Memorandum items			
Average gross plant/gigawatt hours (thousands)	481	564	1,633
Increase in gross plant (percent)	77.6	40.7	21.2
Debt/net plant (percent)	53.2	71.6	93.8
Debt/debt + equity (percent)	29.0	19.2	44.0
Current ratio	1.9	2.9	2.6
Debt as a percentage of debt + equity, excluding revaluation.	34.7	44.7	50.9

. . . Zero or negligible.
Source: NPC.

1979	*1980*	*1981*	*1982*	*1983*	*1984*	*1985*
12,042	15,251	19,050	24,450	28,766	45,000	53,903
2,411	3,049	3,860	4,923	6,318	8,271	10,661
9,631	12,202	15,190	19,527	22,448	36,729	43,242
8,278	11,479	15,483	17,452	21,200	12,694	12,378
42	42	42	42	42	42	42
126	111	125	177	200	221	637
301	381	476	612	720	1,126	1,348
862	1,003	1,159	1,379	1,555	1,787	2,056
1,289	1,495	1,760	2,168	2,475	3,134	4,041
64	64	64	64	64	64	64
19,304	25,282	32,539	39,253	46,229	52,663	59,767
5,999	6,667	8,595	9,624	11,485	12,377	12,466
1,650	2,257	2,868	3,697	4,646	5,618	7,330
2,332	3,123	4,118	5,352	6,932	8,747	11,605
9,981	12,047	15,591	18,673	23,063	26,742	31,401
8,666	12,544	16,124	19,698	22,225	24,928	27,305
8,666	12,544	16,124	19,698	22,225	24,928	27,305
623	653	795	853	912	964	1,032
5	9	...	...	...	...	...
628	662	795	853	912	964	1,032
6	6	6	6	6	6	6
23	23	23	23	23	23	23
19,304	25,282	32,539	39,253	46,229	52,663	59,767
680	834	916	1,019	1,141	1,542	1,426
45.9	26.6	24.9	28.3	17.6	56.4	19.8
90.0	102.8	106.1	100.8	99.0	67.9	63.1
46.5	51.0	50.8	51.3	49.1	48.2	46.5
2.1	2.3	2.2	2.5	2.7	3.3	3.9
53.1	58.4	58.4	59.6	57.9	58.1	58.0

Table C9. Funds Flow Statement of the National Power Corporation, FY76–FY85

(In millions of pesos)

Category	1976	1977	1978	1979	1980	1981	1982	1983	1984	1985	Total
Internal sources of funds											
Operating income	207	352	462	638	873	1,095	1,387	1,678	2,370	3,202	12,264
Depreciation	154	194	228	322	446	567	754	1,000	1,448	1,729	6,842
Total	361	546	690	960	1,319	1,662	2,141	2,678	3,818	4,931	19,106
Operational requirements											
Increase or decrease in working capital	−9	195	83	47	191	109	298	225	586	423	2,148
Interest charged	13	38	55	152	266	474	568	729	1,398	1,490	5,183
Debt repayments	44	56	155	594	619	723	658	622	746	861	5,078
Total	48	289	293	793	1,076	1,306	1,524	1,576	2,730	2,774	12,409
Internal funds available for investment	313	257	397	167	243	356	617	1,102	1,088	2,157	6,697
Capital investment											
Proposed project					247				...	...	954
Other construction	3,187[a]	2,419	2,827	4,174[a]	4,496	5,743	4,791	4,923	4,690	4,231	41,481
Interest during construction	145	222	368	511	684	821	1,035	1,166	718	837	6,507
Total	3,332	2,801	3,428	4,999	5,427	6,564	5,826	6,089	5,408	5,068	48,942
Balance to be financed	3,019	2,544	3,031	4,832	5,184	6,208	5,209	4,987	4,320	2,911	42,245
Sources of financing											
Loans	891	1,907	2,339	3,332	4,497	4,303	4,232	3,149	3,449	3,238	31,337
Equity	2,156	750	692	1,442	668	1,928	1,029	1,861	892	89	11,507
Total	3,047	2,657	3,031	4,774	5,165	6,231	5,261	5,010	4,341	3,327	42,844
Cash increase or decrease	28	113	0	−58	−19	23	52	23	21	416	599
Cash at beginning of year	38	66	179	179	121	102	125	177	200	221	221
Cash at year's end	66	179	179	121	102	125	177	200	221	637	637
Debt service coverage	1.8	1.7	1.2	0.8	0.8	0.8	0.9	1.1	1.3	1.5	1.1
Internal cash ratio	6.5	3.8	4.8	1.4	1.6	1.9	2.5	3.8	2.4	4.0	12.4
Annual contribution to construction	9.4	9.2	11.6	3.3	4.5	5.4	10.6	18.1	20.1	42.6	13.7

. . . Zero or negligible.

a. Includes ₱1,516 million in 1976 and ₱804 million in 1979 for acquisition of MECO power plants, assumed to be financed by equity in both years.

Source: NPC.

Table C10.   Financing Plan of the National Power Corporation, FY76–FY85

Category	Millions of pesos	Millions of U.S.dollars	Percentage of total
Internal cash generation	19,100	2,500	39.0
Less: Debt service and working capital requirements	13,000	1,700	26.6
Internal funds available for investment	6,100	800	12.4
Borrowings	31,300	4,200	64.1
Equity	11,500	1,500	23.5
Construction expenditure	48,900	6,500	100.0

Note: Table C9 shows a detailed funds flow statement for NPC, and C8 and C11 show forecasts of income and balance sheets.

in operation from 8 to 10 percent, for example, would yield an additional ₱3,000 million but would require an increase of about 6 percent in the tariffs that are forecast (Table C11). Another ₱2.8 million could be generated if the tariff levels in Mindanao were made equal to those in Luzon throughout the ten-year forecast period. Better control of receivables could yield about ₱1,000 million during the same period.

About ₱31,000 million in current prices (US$4,200 million) would have to be borrowed, primarily from foreign sources. By December 1975 NPC had arranged about ₱800 million (US$1,100 million) of foreign financing, including ₱5,000 million (US$690 million) from the United States to finance the first nuclear project.

Power Pricing Policy

A comprehensive tariff study of the power sector in the Philippines has never been made because of the large disparities in the tariff levels among regions and suppliers. NPC has different tariffs in Luzon, Mindanao, and the Visayas; tariffs in Mindanao in 1975 were much lower than those in Luzon—3.08 centavos (4.1 U.S. mills) a kilowatt hour compared with 9.5 centavos (12.6 U.S. mills). Small utilities providing electricity to final users also have a wide range of operating costs depending on their size, load density, and source of energy. A residential consumer of a utility purchasing cheap power from NPC's hydroelectric system in Mindanao, for example, would have to pay only ₱0.12 a kilowatt hour while a similar con-

Table C11. Income Statement of the National Power Corporation, FY76–FY85

	1976	1977	1978	1979	1980	1981	1982	1983	1984	1985
Revenues										
Sales increase (percent)	—	31.3	19.1	21.3	9.6	14.5	13.9	9.2	2.6	8.1
Energy sales (gigawatt hours)	7,862	10,325	12,298	14,922	16,357	18,727	21,339	23,309	23,911	25,857
Average price per kilowatt hour (centavos)	16.11	19.72	22.23	23.99	26.50	27.96	30.28	31.80	36.34	40.20
Energy revenue	1,267	2,036	2,734	3,580	4,335	5,236	6,461	7,412	8,690	10,394
Other revenue	...	...	...	...	...	...	...	...	...	...
Total	1,267	2,036	2,734	3,580	4,335	5,236	6,461	7,412	8,690	10,394
Operating expenses										
Fuel	852	1,410	1,932	2,473	2,831	3,353	4,035	4,411	4,472	4,996
Operation	54	80	112	147	185	221	285	323	400	467
Depreciation	154	194	228	322	446	567	754	1,000	1,448	1,729
Total	1,060	1,684	2,272	2,942	3,462	4,141	5,074	5,734	6,320	7,192
Operating income	207	352	462	638	873	1,095	1,387	1,678	2,370	3,202
Net income before interest	207	352	462	638	873	1,095	1,387	1,678	2,370	3,202
Interest	158	260	423	663	950	1,295	1,603	1,895	2,116	2,327
Charged to construction	145	222	368	511	684	821	1,035	1,166	718	837
Charged to operations	13	38	55	152	266	474	568	729	1,398	1,490
Net income	194	314	407	486	607	621	819	949	972	1,712
Retained earnings	194	314	407	486	607	621	819	949	972	1,712
Financial indicators										
Net fixed assets in operation (millions of pesos)	2,607	4,393	5,776	7,977	10,918	13,697	17,359	20,988	29,589	39,986
Rate of return (percent)	7.9	8.0	8.0	8.0	8.0	8.0	8.0	8.0	8.0	8.0
Operating ratio (percent)	83.7	82.7	83.1	82.2	79.9	79.1	78.5	77.4	72.7	69.2
Average gross revenue/average plant in operation (percent)	33.5	35.0	36.3	35.3	31.8	30.5	29.7	27.9	23.6	21.0

— Not applicable.
... Zero or negligible.
Source: NPC.

sumer of a small utility generating its own power might have to pay ₱0.50 a kilowatt hour. There are no direct cross-subsidies among different categories of consumers although indirect cross-subsidies occur because NPC and NEA benefit from tax and duty exemptions and the lower financing costs of official aid available to them. The World Bank has suggested that a comprehensive study be made of the power sector's costs and tariffs on a marginal cost basis to enable the government to make more informed decisions on its pricing policy.

Statistical Appendix

Table SA1. Total Population, 1877–1974

Year	Census population [a]	Estimated midyear population [b]	Annual intercensal growth rate
1877	5,567,685		
1887	5,984,727		
1896	6,261,339		
1903	7,635,426		2.9
1918	10,314,310		1.9
1936	16,000,303		2.2
1948	19,234,182		1.9
1960	27,087,685	27,372,420	3.1
1961		28,174,753	
1962		29,001,656	
1963		29,858,498	
1964		30,749,682	
1965		31,673,693	
1966		32,633,087	
1967		33,629,509	
1968		34,664,683	
1969		35,740,434	
1970	36,684,468	36,851,954	3.0
1971		37,919,096	
1972		39,040,439	
1973		40,218,819	
1974		41,432,623	

a. Data to 1896 excludes non-Christian population.

b. The 1960–69 estimates are interpolated from census populations. The 1970–72 estimates are from L. Baal, C. Que, and P. Yunkin, "New Population Projections by Age and Sex for the Philippines and Each Province, 1970–2000," Bureau of the Census and Statistics (BCS), Population Research Division (Manila, n.d.).

Sources: BCS, *Yearbook of Philippine Statistics, 1966,* and *Monthly Bulletin of Statistics* (March 1972).

Table SA2. Population and Demographic Rates, 1960–85

Year	Population (millions)	Birth rate (per thousand)	Death rate (per thousand)	Population growth rate (percent)	Total fertility rate	Life expectancy[a]	Dependency ratio
1960	27.1	n.a.	n.a.	3.0	n.a.	n.a.	.94
1965	31.4	42	12	3.0	6.3	n.a.	.94
1970	36.7	41	11	3.0	6.0	57.1	.94
1975	42.5	38	10	2.8	5.4	60.0	.86
1980	48.5	35	9	2.6	4.7	62.0	.78
1985	55.3	32	8	2.4	4.1	63.6	.74

n.a.: Not available.
a. Average of life expectancies for males and females.
Note: Assumptions underlying estimates for 1975 projections for 1980 and 1985 are discussed in the technical note of Chapter 10.
Source: National Census and Statistics Office (NCSO), *Age and Sex Population Projections for the Philippines by Province, 1970–2000* (Manila, 1974).

Table SA3. Population Projections and Implicit Growth Rates to the Year 2000

Year	Population projections (millions)			Implicit growth rates[a] (percent)		
	Medium projection	Medium-low projection	Low projection	Medium projection	Medium-low projection	Low projection
1970	36.9	36.9	36.9			
1975	42.5	42.4	42.2	2.9	2.8	2.7
1980	49.1	48.5	47.9	2.9	2.7	2.5
1985	56.7	55.3	53.8	2.9	2.6	2.3
1990	65.0	52.3	59.6	2.8	2.4	2.1
1995	73.9	69.4	64.9	2.6	2.2	1.8
2000	83.4	76.7	70.0	2.4	2.0	1.6

a. Growth rates are for the five-year period preceding the year at which they are listed; thus the medium projection of 2.9 shown for 1975 applies to the 1970–74 period.

Source: Medium and low projections are from NCSO, *Age and Sex Population Projections for the Philippines by Province: 1970–2000.* Medium-low projection is the average of these two.

Table SA4. Labor Force, Employment, and Unemployment, 1956–74
(In thousands)

Year	Working-age population[a]	Participation rate[b] (percent)	Labor force	Employed	Unemployed	Unemployment rate (percent)
1956	16,206	56.8	9,205	8,285	921	10.0
1957	16,719	56.6	9,463	8,791	672	7.1
1958	17,247	56.1	9,676	8,979	697	7.2
1959	17,971	55.1	9,803	8,225	578	5.9
1960	18,354	54.9	10,076	9,441	635	6.3
1961	18,934	55.5	10,508	9,835	673	6.4
1962	19,532	56.0	10,938	10,227	711	6.5
1963	20,149	56.4	11,364	10,841	523	4.6
1964	20,786	55.1	11,453	10,720	733	6.4
1965	21,443	55.0	11,794	11,063	731	6.2
1966	22,121	54.3	12,012	11,171	841	7.0
1967	22,820	53.1	12,117	11,184	933	7.7
1968	23,541	51.1	12,029	11,079	950	7.9
1969	24,285	49.2	11,948	11,147	801	6.7
1970	25,057	49.4	12,378	11,437	941	7.6
1971	25,901	49.2	12,743	12,068	675	5.3
1972	26,782	49.8	13,337	12,617	720	5.4
1973	27,700	49.4	13,683	13,026	657	4.8
1974	28,656	49.4	14,156	13,576	580	4.1

a. Ten years of age or older.

b. Labor force participation rate is defined as the proportion of the working-age population holding or seeking employment.

Source: World Bank estimates based on BCS labor force surveys.

Table SA5. Employment by Sector, 1956–74

Year	Employment (thousands)	Commerce		Electricity, gas, and water		Government services		Personal services	
		Percent	Thousands	Percent	Thousands	Percent	Thousands	Percent	Thousands
1956	8,285	10.4	861	0.3	24	5.1	422	6.1	505
1957	8,791	9.6	843	0.2	17	4.8	421	6.0	527
1958	8,979	8.9	799	0.3	26	5.4	484	5.5	493
1959	9,225	9.5	876	0.2	18	5.2	479	5.5	551
1960	9,441	8.8	830	0.2	18	5.0	472	6.0	566
1961	9,835	9.6	944	0.2	19	5.9	580	6.0	590
1962	10,227	9.5	971	0.3	30	5.9	603	5.8	593
1963	10,841	10.5	1,138	0.2	21	6.0	630	5.9	639
1964	10,720	11.3	1,211	0.2	21	5.4	578	5.9	632
1965	11,063	11.0	1,216	0.2	22	7.0	774	7.2	796
1966	11,171	10.3	1,150	0.3	33	7.2	804	6.8	759
1967	11,184	9.9	1,107	0.3	33	7.1	794	6.7	749
1968	11,079	10.8	1,196	0.3	33	8.6	952	7.2	797
1969	11,147	9.9	1,103	0.3	33	7.9	880	7.3	813
1970	11,437	9.8	1,121	0.3	34	7.7	880	7.1	812
1971	12,068	12.4	1,496	0.4	48	7.5	905	7.5	759
1972	12,617	11.8	1,488	0.4	50	8.5	1,072	6.9	870
1973	13,026	11.1	1,445	0.3	39	8.6	1,120	7.2	937
1974	13,576	11.2	1,521	0.3	41	8.6	1,167	7.0	950

Table SA5. (Continued)

Year	Agriculture		Mining and quarrying		Manufacturing		Construction		Transport, communication, and storage	
	Percent	Thousands	Percent	Thousands	Percent	Thousands	Percent	Thousands	Percent	Thousands
1956	59.0	4,938	0.4	33	12.5	1,035	2.6	215	3.0	248
1957	60.9	5,353	0.3	26	12.3	1,081	2.8	246	2.7	237
1958	63.4	5,692	0.3	26	11.1	996	1.9	170	2.7	242
1959	61.8	5,701	0.4	36	11.6	1,070	2.4	221	2.9	267
1960	61.2	5,777	0.3	28	12.1	1,142	2.7	254	3.2	302
1961	60.6	5,960	0.3	29	11.3	1,111	2.5	245	3.1	304
1962	61.4	6,279	0.4	40	11.0	1,124	2.5	255	3.0	306
1963	59.2	6,417	0.3	32	11.7	1,268	2.8	303	3.3	357
1964	58.6	6,282	0.4	43	11.8	1,265	3.0	321	3.3	353
1965	56.7	6,272	0.2	22	10.9	1,205	2.9	320	3.4	376
1966	57.5	6,423	0.2	22	11.2	1,251	2.6	290	3.5	390
1967	58.3	6,520	0.4	44	11.3	1,263	2.5	279	3.4	380
1968	53.8	5,960	0.4	44	11.8	1,307	3.3	365	3.5	387
1969	58.3	6,498	0.5	55	11.5	1,282	3.1	345	3.4	379
1970	54.7	6,256	0.5	57	12.1	1,383	3.4	389	4.4	503
1971	50.4	6,404	0.5	60	11.5	1,387	3.4	410	4.2	506
1972	54.5	6,876	0.3	37	10.5	1,324	3.4	428	3.7	466
1973	56.0	7,294	0.4	52	10.1	1,315	2.5	325	3.6	494
1974	55.6	7,548	0.3	40	10.4	1,412	2.9	394	3.7	502

Source: Labor force surveys of BCS, as published in various issues of *Survey of Households Bulletin* and National Economic and Development Authority (NEDA), *Statistical Yearbook*, adjusted to reflect growth of working-age population as implied by 1970 census.

Table SA6. Expenditures on Gross National Product at Current Prices
(In millions of pesos)

Item	1960	1965	1968	1969	1970	1971	1972	1973	1974
Private consumption	10,444	17,514	22,626	24,369	28,729	36,343	40,642	48,699	71,580
General government consumption	1,087	2,104	2,833	3,287	3,521	4,344	5,186	5,989	7,221
Fixed capital formation	1,999	4,342	6,091	6,333	7,599	9,258	10,197	12,670	21,307
Increase in stocks	231	486	555	591	1,005	1,022	1,236	1,800	3,389
Exports (goods and nonfactor services)	1,408	3,858	4,465	4,315	7,797	8,790	9,675	15,623	21,575
Less: Imports (goods and nonfactor services)	1,508	3,897	5,615	5,584	7,993	9,130	10,114	13,716	25,872
Gross domestic product	13,661	24,407	30,995	33,311	40,658	50,627	56,822	71,065	99,200
Net factor income from abroad	−203	−123	−406	−299	−779	−588	−865	−450	553
Statistical discrepancy	−575	−2,491	−646	493	583	−867	−95	−590	−809
Gross national product	12,883	21,793	29,903	33,505	40,462	49,172	55,862	70,025	98,944

Source: NEDA, National Accounts Staff, Statistical Office.

Table SA7. Expenditures on Gross National Product at 1967 Constant Prices
(In millions of pesos)

Item	1960	1965	1968	1969	1970	1971	1972	1973	1974
Private consumption	15,057	19,319	22,146	23,178	23,872	24,897	25,735	27,545	29,214
General government consumption	1,911	2,436	2,648	9,902	2,683	2,905	3,135	3,356	3,658
Fixed capital formation	3,000	4,643	5,933	5,942	5,622	5,921	6,031	6,690	8,217
Increase in stocks	308	537	543	557	775	723	785	986	1,252
Exports (goods and nonfactor services)	2,518	4,340	4,221	4,018	4,548	4,591	5,945	6,155	4,673
Less: Imports (goods and nonfactor services)	3,255	4,072	5,643	5,479	5,041	4,832	4,794	5,995	7,218
Gross domestic product	19,539	27,203	29,848	31,118	32,459	34,205	36,837	38,737	39,796
Net factor income from abroad	−331	−127	−411	−296	−480	−305	−383	−200	86
Statistical discrepancy	−418	−2,723	−1,046	−786	−297	−364	−1,508	−122	773
Gross national product	18,790	24,353	28,391	30,036	31,682	33,536	34,946	38,415	40,655

Source: NEDA, National Accounts Staff, Statistical Office.

Table SA8. Industrial Origin of Net Domestic Product: Factor Cost at Current Prices
(In millions of pesos)

Sector	1960	1965	1968	1969	1970	1971	1972	1973	1974
Agriculture, fishery, and forestry	3,579	5,970	8,592	10,091	11,951	14,624	16,531	20,004	28,477
Commerce	1,865	2,914	3,842	4,075	4,889	5,863	6,823	8,266	11,124
Construction	395	758	815	930	813	927	1,262	1,411	1,891
Manufacturing	2,141	3,400	4,692	5,073	6,476	7,808	8,979	12,260	19,564
Mining and quarrying	128	232	419	530	847	928	1,051	1,693	2,154
Services	2,647	4,571	6,106	6,645	7,497	8,515	9,731	11,124	13,229
Transport, communications, storage, and utilities	560	781	1,004	1,070	1,255	1,443	1,651	1,955	2,574
Net domestic product	11,315	18,626	25,470	28,414	33,728	40,108	46,028	56,713	79,013
Rest of the world	−203	−123	−406	−299	−779	−588	−865	−450	553
Net national product	11,112	18,503	25,064	28,115	32,949	39,520	45,163	56,263	79,566

Source: NEDA, National Accounts Staff, Statistical Office.

Table SA9. Industrial Origin of Net Domestic Product: Factor Cost at 1967 Constant Prices
(In millions of pesos)

Sector	1960	1965	1968	1969	1970	1971	1972	1973	1974
Agriculture, fishery, and forestry	5,638	6,954	7,893	8,375	8,549	8,556	8,642	9,306	9,626
Commerce	2,496	3,193	3,791	3,935	4,149	4,357	4,643	4,972	5,197
Construction	536	854	757	826	657	678	884	925	1,064
Manufacturing	2,945	3,672	4,570	4,811	5,108	5,497	5,828	6,527	6,755
Mining and quarrying	256	281	408	468	559	653	686	730	734
Services	4,135	5,158	5,760	5,955	6,196	6,424	6,732	7,145	7,653
Transport, communications, storage, and utilities	680	847	972	1,015	1,082	1,148	1,210	1,298	1,384
Net domestic product	16,686	20,959	24,151	25,385	26,300	27,313	28,625	30,903	32,413
Rest of the world	−331	−127	−411	−296	−480	−305	−383	−200	86
Net national product	16,355	20,832	23,740	25,089	25,820	27,008	28,242	30,703	32,499

Source: NEDA, National Accounts Staff, Statistical Office.

Table SA10. Gross Domestic Incomes and Resource Gap
(In millions of U.S. dollars at constant 1967 prices)

Item	1960	1965	1970	1971	1972	1973	1974
Gross domestic product	6,513	6,957	5,577	5,353	5,529	5,722	5,768
Gains from terms of trade	31	13	134	−60	−270	18	5,874
Gross domestic income	6,544	6,970	5,711	5,293	5,259	5,740	5,874
Imports (goods and nonfactor services)	831	1,044	1,286	1,242	1,205	1,381	1,492
Exports (goods and nonfactor services)[a]	749	1,115	1,269	1,220	1,162	1,702	1,353
Resource gap	82	−71	17	22	43	−321	139

a. Import capacity.
Sources: NEDA, National Accounts Staff, Statistical Office, and World Book estimates.

Table SA11. Balance of Payments: Goods and Services Account
(In millions of U.S. dollars)

Item	1960	1965	1968	1969	1970	1971	1972	1973	1974
Receipts									
Merchandise (f.o.b.)	560	769	858	855	1,062	1,130	1,079	1,768	2,620
Nonmonetary gold	14	15	19	20	21	19	29	103	74
Freight and insurance	4	14	17	18	29	20	14	20	24
Other transportation	...	...	8	6	8	24	21	30	47
Travel	3	21	48	49	95	66	122	74	58
Investment income	6	19	15	7	10	15	23	65	171
Government (n.i.e.[a])	22	68	126	89	68	83	116	200	126
Military services	11	42	96	59	31	36	41	42	44
Other	11	26	30	30	37	46	75	158	82
Other services	34	174	76	80	48	56	51	250	408
Total	643	1,092	1,166	1,123	1,341	1,413	1,455	2,510	3,528

Payments

Merchandise (f.o.b.)	604	808	1,150	1,132	1,090	1,186	1,230	1,597	3,143
Freight and insurance	56	66	104	96	107	102	109	167	324
Other transportation	...	6	1	22	21	19	13	11	17
Travel	14	53	68	60	27	28	24	15	17
Investment income	81	50	112	85	140	115	148	178	226
On direct investment	73	17	65	35	25	24	33	60	80
Other interest	8	33	47	50	115	91	115	118	146
Government (n.i.e.[a])	7	8	16	15	16	24	32	47	62
Other services	26	63	100	103	88	64	76	221	219
Total	788	1,054	1,551	1,512	1,489	1,538	1,632	2,236	4,008
Goods and services account surplus or deficit	−145	38	−385	−389	−148	−125	−177	−274	−480

... Zero or negligible.
a. Not included elsewhere.
Source: International Monetary Fund (IMF), *Balance of Payments Yearbooks*, as revised by Central Bank of the Philippines.

Table SA12. Balance of Payments: Consolidated Account
(In millions of U.S. dollars)

Item	1960	1965	1968	1969	1970	1971	1972	1973	1974
Trade account (net)	-29	-24	-274	-257	-7	-37	-122	274	-449
Exports	575	784	876	875	1,083	1,149	1,108	1,871	2,694
Imports	604	808	1,150	1,132	1,090	1,186	1,230	1,579	3,143
Services (net)	-115	62	-110	-132	-141	-88	-55	...	-32
Transfers (net)	140	99	134	155	119	134	188	246	271
Current account	-4	137	-250	-234	-29	9	11	520	-210
Direct investment (net)	29	-10	-3	6	-29	-4	-22	54	54
Medium- and long-term loans (net)	36	50	222	150	134	36	140	82	59
Short-term capital (net)	-1	-117	178	67	76	92	56	75	199
Nonmonetary capital (net)	64	-77	397	223	181	124	174	211	312
Errors and omissions (net)	-33	-75	-196	-125	-147	-144	-107	-66	-8
Allocation of special drawing rights	...	...	...	...	18	17	16	...	...
Overall balance	27	-15	-49	-136	23	6	95	665	110

... Zero or negligible.
Source: Central Bank of the Philippines.

Table SA13. Foreign Exchange Reserves of the Central Bank and Commercial Banks at Year's End, 1960–74

(In millions of U.S. dollars)

	Gross reserves			Foreign exchange liabilities			Net reserves			International reserves[c]
	Central Bank[a]	Commercial banks	Total	Central Bank[b]	Commercial banks	Total	Central Bank	Commercial banks	Total	
1960	120.0	76.0	196.0	5.0	4.0	9.0	115.0	72.0	187.5	192.0
1961	44.1	63.7	107.8	61.0	4.6	65.5	16.9	59.2	42.3	103.3
1962	75.0	76.3	151.3	43.0	10.5	53.5	32.0	65.8	97.8	140.8
1963	109.5	88.3	197.8	10.7	50.3	61.0	98.8	38.0	136.3	147.5
1964[d]	123.3	74.3	197.6	29.8	159.1	188.9	93.5	84.8	8.7	38.5
1965[d]	188.5	91.7	280.2	109.5	188.6	298.1	79.0	96.9	17.9	91.6
1966	166.1	114.2	280.3	128.1	135.4	263.5	38.0	21.3	16.7	144.8
1967	179.8	139.6	319.4	234.6	105.4	340.0	-54.8	34.2	20.6	214.0
1968	161.4	145.7	307.1	120.1	119.5	239.6	41.3	26.2	67.5	187.6
1969	120.7	129.0	249.7	196.4	131.2	327.6	-75.7	-2.3	-78.0	118.4
1970	251.0	125.3	376.3	259.6	163.0	422.6	-8.6	-37.7	-46.3	213.3
1971	375.5	148.5	524.0	174.1	279.8	453.9	201.4	-131.3	70.1	244.2
1972	548.8	185.9	734.7	144.4	452.8	597.2	404.4	-266.9	137.5	281.9
1973	1,037.1	378.6	1,415.7	83.2	539.7	622.9	953.9	-161.1	792.8	876.0
1974	1,502.5	475.4	1,977.9	231.2	812.5	1,043.7	1,271.3	-337.1	934.2	1,165.4

a. Includes IMF gold tranche position and excludes foreign balances of the Money Order Fund and the Fiscal Agency Fund.
b. Consists of short-term loans from U.S. commercial banks, the Export-Import Bank, and the Federal Reserve Bank of New York.
c. As defined by the Philippine authorities: gross reserves of the Central Bank plus net reserves of commercial banks.
d. Revised as of November 22, 1966, to include deferred payments and liabilities previously unreported by commercial banks. These revisions supersede those previously made on end of 1964 data.
Source: Central Bank of the Philippines.

Table SA14. Exports by Major Commodity Groups
(F.o.b. value in millions of U.S. dollars at current prices)

Commodity group	1960	1965	1968	1969	1970	1971	1972	1973	1974
Coconut products									
Coconut, desiccated	19	20	25	16	19	21	18	32	60
Coconut oil	16	68	77	51	96	103	84	151	381
Copra	139	170	123	87	80	114	110	166	140
Copra meal or cake	5	12	11	9	14	16	16	23	28
Subtotal	179	270	236	163	209	254	228	372	609
Forest products									
Logs	85	155	208	215	237	215	164	304	216
Lumber	7	8	9	11	13	11	10	35	30
Plywood	6	18	21	19	20	24	34	58	27
Other	4	14	24	14	25	14	27	47	60
Subtotal	102	195	262	259	295	264	235	444	333
Fruits and vegetables									
Bananas	..	..	..	1	5	15	24	28	45
Pineapple products	8	12	20	18	22	20	21	23	35
Other	2	3	2	1	7	6	7	7	11
Subtotal	10	15	22	20	34	41	52	58	91

Mineral products									
Chromite ore	17	11	3	5	9	6	5	9	13
Copper concentrates	30	47	89	133	185	185	191	275	397
Gold	...	...	...	...	...	7	27	103	74
Iron concentrates	...	2	10	9	10	11	8	17	12
Iron ore	9	7	2	2	3	2	1	1	...
Other	5	10	10	11	17	12	7	17	21
Subtotal	61	77	114	160	224	223	239	422	519
Sugar and products									
Centrifugal and refined	133	132	144	149	188	212	211	275	737
Molasses	5	10	7	7	8	8	6	19	28
Other	5	5	...	2	...	...	1	1	1
Subtotal	143	147	151	158	196	220	218	295	766
Abaca and products	45	26	13	16	17	15	16	23	35
Chemicals	2	2	4	8	5	6	6	10	15
Mineral fuels and lubricants	...	6	15	13	17	24	19	16	17
Textiles and clothing	3	6	4	6	5	8	11	26	20
Tobacco and products	7	16	16	17	15	15	18	27	30
Miscellaneous manufactures and others	8	7	20	33	41	52	90	176	256
Re-exports	1	2	1	3	5	8	4	2	3
Total	560	769	858	856	1,062	1,130	1,136	1,871	2,694

... Zero or negligible.
Source: Central Bank of the Philippines.

537

Table SA15. Volume and Unit Value of Principal Exports

Category	1960	1965	1968	1969	1970	1971	1972	1973	1974[a]
Volume (thousands of metric tons)									
Abaca, unmanufactured	101	89	57	62	55	49	50	54	43
Coconut products									
Coconut, desiccated	59	68	62	54	67	73	76	78	64
Coconut oil	60	236	256	202	339	398	446	427	416
Copra	804	883	640	509	445	692	926	734	522
Copra meal or cake	81	182	189	177	231	288	352	263	271
Logs[b]	1,455	2,963	3,517	3,586	3,926	3,578	3,021	3,291	1,993
Lumber[b]	60	50	62	78	93	67	77	181	120
Minerals									
Iron and ore and concentrates	1,008	838	234	199	363	186	163	136	121
Chromite ore	746	592	174	279	442	275	238	478	534
Copper concentrates	227	279	412	470	632	815	824	764	861
Pineapple, canned	45	44	111	109	100	101	108	91	125
Pineapple, juice[c]	12	17	10	12	14	12	11	11	13
Unit value (U.S. dollars per metric ton)									
Abaca, unmanufactured	416	271	197	232	273	265	263	362	461
Coconut products									
Coconut, desiccated	322	302	397	298	284	288	231	416	938
Coconut oil	267	289	302	250	283	259	181	354	916
Copra	173	192	192	172	180	165	119	226	268
Copra meal or cake	62	65	59	51	61	56	46	87	103
Logs[d]	58	52	59	60	59	60	54	92	108
Lumber[d]	117	143	139	141	140	164	136	194	250
Minerals									
Iron ore	9	8	8	9	8	8	8	9	10
Chromite ore	23	19	19	18	20	22	23	19	24
Copper concentrates	130	167	216	283	293	227	232	360	461
Pineapple, canned	165	197	170	174	210	198	181	217	244
Pineapple, juice[e]	500	432	355	409	359	312	337	783	1,085

a. Preliminary.
b. In millions of liters
c. Per thousand liters

Table SA16. Quantum, Price, and Value Indexes and Net Terms of Trade
(1965 = 100.0)

Year	Quantum index		Price index		Value index		Net terms of trade
	Imports	Exports	Imports	Exports	Imports	Exports	
1960	82.4	72.2	88.4	101.2	72.8	73.0	114.5
1961	84.5	69.8	89.7	93.1	75.8	65.0	103.8
1962	80.0	76.5	91.4	94.1	73.1	72.1	103.0
1963	78.6	94.1	97.5	99.1	76.7	94.2	101.6
1964	97.3	97.4	98.3	98.3	95.6	95.8	100.0
1965	100.0	100.0	100.0	100.0	100.0	100.0	100.0
1966	106.4	106.0	101.6	100.9	108.1	107.2	99.3
1967	126.7	102.3	103.9	102.7	131.6	105.1	98.8
1968	138.3	103.8	103.3	107.9	142.9	112.0	104.4
1969	132.4	100.4	105.9	109.8	140.2	110.2	103.7
1970	123.8	114.5	109.0	120.5	134.9	138.0	110.6
1971	124.8	131.2	119.1	112.1	148.6	147.1	94.1
1972	124.6	143.7	128.0	100.0	151.9	143.7	78.1
1973	132.8	163.3	149.1	149.0	198.0	243.3	99.9
1974	146.3	124.8	260.2	278.9	380.7	348.0	107.2
1974 January–June	n.a.	n.a.	244.0	263.8	n.a.	n.a.	108.1
July–December	n.a.	n.a.	275.4	294.0	n.a.	n.a.	106.8
1975 January–June	n.a.	n.a.	284.5	241.8	n.a.	n.a.	85.0

n.a.: Not available.
Note: Unit value of imports is based on c.i.f. value; of exports, on f.o.b. value.
Source: Central Bank of the Philippines.

Table SA17. Imports by Commodity Group
(F.o.b., millions of U.S. dollars)

SITC[a]	Commodity group	1960	1965	1968
0	Food and food preparation	85	155	133
02	Dairy products	24	26	35
03	Fish and fish preparations	22	14	23
041	Wheat	8	24	27
042	Rice	2	61	. . .
	Others	29	30	48
1	Beverages and Tobacco	1	2	9
2	Crude materials, inedible	33	36	68
263	Cotton	17	14	28
266	Synthetic and artificial fibres	. . .	5	18
	Others	16	17	22
3	Mineral fuels and lubricants	60	77	106
312	Petroleum crude	21	59	92
	Others	39	18	14
4	Animal and vegetable oils and fats	3	4	5
5	Chemicals	55	73	109
51	Chemical compounds	14	20	34
54	Medicinal and pharmaceutical chemicals	10	7	15
	Others	31	46	60
6	Manufactures	131	151	233
64	Paper and paper products	17	22	27
65	Textile yarn, fabrics, and made-up articles	31	17	44
681	Iron and steel	47	61	84
69	Metal products	14	18	33
	Others	22	33	45
7	Machinery and transport equipment	217	276	443
71	Nonelectrical machinery	87	141	239
72	Electrical machinery	21	48	61
73	Transport equipment	110	87	144
8	Miscellaneous manufactures	17	21	32
9	Miscellaneous	3	14	13
	Total imports (rounded)	604	808	1,150

. . . Zero or negligible.
a. Standard International Trade Classification.
Source: Central Bank of the Philippines.

1969	*1970*	*1971*	*1972*	*1973*	*1974*	SITC[a]
125	104	146	175	202	310	0
37	33	39	46	45	74	02
18	17	21	20	20	32	03
28	26	27	34	49	39	041
. . .	. . .	28	34	45	79	042
42	28	31	41	43	86	
11	9	6	9	10	17	1
59	60	67	70	90	145	2
19	19	20	19	30	34	263
22	21	29	27	29	53	266
18	20	18	24	31	58	
107	119	141	149	188	653	3
94	103	127	134	166	573	312
13	16	14	15	22	80	
5	6	6	4	7	12	4
114	126	144	148	218	491	5
35	37	40	48	75	216	51
16	17	18	16	21	36	54
63	72	86	84	122	239	
231	236	195	214	306	530	6
29	29	34	35	34	57	64
34	24	23	25	47	69	65
90	114	65	87	115	228	681
34	22	26	23	48	60	69
44	47	47	44	62	116	
444	401	444	418	469	795	7
259	235	255	240	296	424	71
60	59	66	54	71	106	72
125	106	122	124	102	265	73
31	27	31	34	45	61	8
7	5	6	9	62	129	9
1,132	1,090	1,186	1,230	1,597	3,143	

Table SA18. External Public Debt Outstanding as of December 31, 1974
(In thousands of U.S. dollars)

Type of creditor	Disbursed	Undisbursed	Total
Suppliers			
Belgium	2,132	. . .	2,132
France	460	. . .	460
Germany (Federal Republic)	8,174	1,630	9,804
India	. . .	3,070	3,070
Italy	3,358	1,403	4,761
Japan	11,362	40,360	51,722
United Kingdom	1,240	6,930	8,170
United States	3,051	. . .	3,051
Subtotal	29,777	53,393	83,170
Private banks			
Australia	. . .	6,574	6,574
Bahamas	16,145	. . .	16,145
Belgium	950	5,924	6,674
France	. . .	48,256	48,256
Germany (Federal Republic)	4,142	. . .	4,142
Italy	. . .	46,194	46,194
Japan	34,313	. . .	34,313
Netherlands	4,198	. . .	4,198
United Kingdom	22,488	7,046	29,534
United States	198,816	1,281	198,097
Subtotal	279,052	115,275	394,327
Publicly issued U.S. bonds	7,323	. . .	7,323
Privately placed Kuwaiti bonds	16,979	262	17,241
Other private financial institutions			
Hong Kong	. . .	11,000	11,000
United States	11,267	1,652	12,919
Subtotal	11,267	12,652	23,919
International organizations			
Asian Development Bank	41,965	198,527	240,492
World Bank	164,107	339,809	503,916
International Development Association	8,314	23,902	32,216
Subtotal	214,386	562,238	776,624

Type of creditor	Disbursed	Undisbursed	Total
Governments			
Belgium	1,539	3,303	4,642
Canada	14,894	5,102	19,996
China, Republic of	6,538	. . .	6,538
Denmark	4,862	5,758	10,620
Germany (Federal Republic)	8,111	13,308	21,419
Japan	192,759	70,585	263,344
Spain	1,465	8,535	10,000
Thailand	25,170	. . .	25,170
United States	217,144	114,355	331,499
Subtotal	472,482	220,946	643,428
Total external public debt	1,031,266	964,766	1,996,032

. . . Zero or negligible.

Note: Excludes uncommitted parts of frame agreements (Japan: $17,252,000) and private debt guaranteed by the Development Bank of the Philippines and the Philippine National Bank/National Investment and Development Corp. amounting to approximately $582.3 million as of December 31, 1974.

Source: External Debt Division of the World Bank, based on data supplied by the Central Bank of the Philippines.

Table SA19. External Medium- and Long-term Debt Transactions, 1965-74, by Type of Borrower
(In millions of U.S. dollars)

	New loans		Debt service			Debt outstanding at end of period		Adjustments
Year	Committed	Disbursed	Amortization	Interest	Total	Committed	Disbursed	
Public[a]								
1965	n.a.	135.4	35.9	8.4	44.3	n.a.	285.5	
1966	n.a.	41.9	50.4	14.7	73.1	353.3	269.0	
1967	104.0	92.1	80.6	13.6	94.2	376.7	280.5	
1968	213.2	219.2	67.0	17.4	84.4	522.9	432.5	
1969	124.3	90.1	42.9	15.8	58.7	604.3	479.7	
1970	149.3	173.7	80.0	26.6	106.6	838.6	738.4	+164.8
1971	295.9	146.9	117.1	39.4	156.5	1,008.1	768.2	-9.3
1972	455.4	263.7	124.7	37.4	162.1	1,334.0	907.2	-4.8
1973	369.1	90.8	198.2	60.6	258.8	1,552.0	963.9	+27.1
1974	738.5	181.6	186.0	58.0	244.0	2,130.6	1,174.1	+80.7
Private								
1965	n.a.	40.8	54.6	n.a.	n.a.	n.a.	189.5	
1966	n.a.	65.5	46.1	n.a.	n.a.	293.0	208.9	
1967	362.1	285.4	49.8	n.a.	n.a.	605.3	444.5	
1968	425.3	326.6	73.3	n.a.	n.a.	957.3	697.8	
1969	439.2	400.3	138.9	n.a.	n.a.	1,257.6	959.2	
1970	231.0	275.7	185.8	n.a.	n.a.	1,302.8	1,049.1	
1971	281.2	163.5	198.7	33.3	232.0	1,351.1	979.7	-34.2
1972	129.5	180.2	154.5	45.6	200.1	1,303.9	983.2	-22.2
1973	128.1	n.a.	199.7	55.6	255.3	1,298.6	1,041.0	+66.3
1974	306.2	194.5	178.1	53.6	231.7	1,455.6	1,213.1	+74.4

Total

Year								
1965	n.a.	176.2	90.5	n.a.	n.a.	n.a.	475.0	
1966	n.a.	107.4	104.5	n.a.	n.a.	646.3	477.9	
1967	466.1	377.5	130.4	n.a.	n.a.	982.0	725.0	
1968	638.5	545.6	140.3	n.a.	n.a.	1,480.2	1,130.3	
1969	563.5	490.4	181.8	n.a.	n.a.	1,861.9	1,438.9	
1970	380.5	449.4	265.8	n.a.	n.a.	2,141.4	1,787.5	+164.8
1971	577.1	310.4	315.8	72.7	−388.5	2,359.2	1,747.9	−43.5
1972	504.9	443.9	279.2	83.0	362.2	2,637.9	1,890.4	−27.0
1973	477.2	n.a.	397.9	116.2	514.1	2,850.6	2,024.9	+93.4
1974	1,044.7	376.1	364.1	111.6	475.7	3,586.2	2,393.1	+155.1

n.a.: Not available.

a. Includes transactions with IMF under the standby agreement.

Note: Excludes revolving credits and credits with maturities under one year.

Source: External Debt Management Office, Central Bank of the Philippines.

Table SA20. National and Local Government Tax Revenues
(In millions of pesos at current prices)

Revenue source	FY65	FY68	FY69	FY70	FY71	FY72	FY73	FY74	FY75 [a]
National government taxes									
On income and wealth									
Corporate income	284	445	597	679	873	908	1,396	2,080	2,310
Personal income	198	220	204	267	350	443	562	641	858
Others	12	17	59	60	89	114	84	77	77
Tax amnesty	—	—	—	—	—	—	575	259	221
Subtotal	1,900	2,653	3,045	3,442	4,750	5,213	7,037	10,847	13,365
On international trade									
Import duties	380	546	607	612	861	1,084	1,435	2,772	3,729
Export duties	—	—	—	108	577	475	457	1,065	1,650
Sales tax on imports	236	340	399	398	503	580	645	1,003	1,126
Subtotal	616	886	1,006	1,118	1,941	2,139	2,537	4,840	6,505
On domestic goods and services									
Excess tax	394	519	553	562	607	664	735	1,203	1,678
General sales tax and others	252	355	398	487	572	597	655	1,070	1,172
Subtotal	646	874	951	1,049	1,179	1,261	1,390	2,273	2,850
Other taxes	144	211	228	269	318	348	493	677	544
Total national tax revenues	1,900	2,653	3,045	3,442	4,750	5,213	7,037	10,847	13,365
Local government tax revenues	241	324	334	403	389	424	530	560	719
Total tax receipts	2,060	2,872	3,379	3,845	5,139	5,637	7,567	11,407	14,084
Share in GNP (percent)									
National government	9.1	9.3	9.6	9.3	10.4	9.7	11.5	12.5	12.6
Local government	0.8	0.8	1.1	1.1	0.9	0.8	0.6	0.7	0.7
Total	9.9	10.1	10.7	10.4	11.3	10.5	12.1	13.1	13.3

— Not applicable.
a. Preliminary actual figures; components of subtotals partly estimated.
Sources: Bureau of Internal Revenue, Bureau of Customs, Auditor-General on Local Government, and Department of Finance.

Table SA21. Current Expenditures of the National Government
(In millions of pesos at current prices)

Expenditure	FY65	FY68	FY69	FY70	FY71	FY72	FY73	FY74	FY75
Administration									
General government	231	264	292	395	421	462	541	580	802
Justice and police	110	161	197	223	263	378	111	140	198
National defense (including transfers)	223	329	367	450	530	584	1,130	1,690	2,533
Subtotal	564	754	856	1,068	1,214	1,424	1,782	2,410	3,533
Economic services									
Agriculture and natural resources	118	138	186	184	184	238	857	558	906
Commerce and industry	27	29	68	41	53	62	60	232	116
Transport and communications	124	259	282	241	330	360	443	737	825
Other economic development	37	61	61	149	95	91	143	348	372
Subtotal	356	487	596	614	662	751	1,503	1,875	2,219
Social services									
Education	598	819	939	1,066	1,205	1,360	1,451	1,855	2,272
Health	113	135	167	204	219	260	329	457	570
Labor and welfare	26	31	21	53	61	80	122	89	133
Subtotal	738	985	1,127	1,323	1,485	1,700	1,902	2,401	2,975
Debt service									
Capital transfers[a]	64	85	183	95	145	99	194	227	340
Interest payments	55	92	103	149	213	228	295	345	578
Subtotal	119	177	286	244	358	327	489	572	918
Subsidies and other transfer payments (including defense)	66	71	191	100	39	168	225	657	1,975
Total current expenditures[b]	1,843	2,474	3,056	3,328	3,758	4,371	5,901	7,915	11,620

a. Loan repayments and sinking fund contributions.
b. See Table SA22 for total of capital and current expenditures.
Source: Budget Commission. Data are derived from budgetary documents where receipts and expenditures are recorded on an accrual and obligational basis respectively.

Table SA22. Capital Expenditures and Total Expenditures of the National Government
(In millions of pesos at current prices)

Expenditure	FY65	FY68	FY69	FY70	FY71	FY72	FY73	FY74	FY75
Administration									
General government	11	20	11	14	...	8	7	6	41
Justice and police	1	7	7	2	6	5	...	...	...
National defense	2	16	16	8	11	18	81	93	93
Subtotal	14	42	35	24	17	31	88	99	134
Economic Services									
Agriculture and natural resources	15	68	99	57	106	292	429	2,025	1,461
Transport and communications	179	262	271	445	312	432	850	1,352	2,350
Commerce and industry	2	6	9	17	63	23	19	264	195
Other economic development	12	40	78	93	119	372	762	1,640	1,113
Subtotal	209	376	457	612	600	1,119	2,060	5,281	5,119
Social Services									
Education	6	43	50	66	39	44	105	115	260
Health	4	7	15	22	7	22	29	122	152
Labor and welfare	1	1	...	2	8	1	6	9	11
Subtotal	11	51	65	90	54	67	140	246	423
Capital expenditures	233	469	555	726	671	1,217	2,288	5,626	5,676
Current expenditures (Table SA21)	1,843	2,474	3,056	3,328	3,758	4,371	5,901	7,915	11,620
Total expenditures	2,076	2,943	3,611	4,054	4,429	5,588	8,189	13,541	17,296

... Zero or negligible.
Source: Same as Table SA21.

Table SA23. Consolidated Statement of Local Government Revenues and Expenditures
(In millions of pesos at current prices)

Item	FY65	FY68	FY69	FY70	FY71	FY72	FY73	FY74[a]	FY75[b]
Revenues									
Internal revenue	229	266	346	384	488	607	628	569	565
Real property tax	89	120	112	182	147	163	205	330	337
Municipal licenses	71	99	105	103	116	125	157	201	382
Fees and charges	81	105	110	116	127	136	168	220	} 530
National aid	47	68	75	87	68	110	110	140	
All other	64	83	101	127	198	152	197	216	
Total	581	741	849	999	1,144	1,293	1,465	1,676	1,814
Expenditures									
General administration	250	340	377	417	489	604	685	682	745
Economic development	102	142	153	180	192	241	232	306	343
Social improvement	75	112	110	144	191	168	192	220	226
Debt service	7	11	15	14	17	15	23	26	30
Other (including statutory obligations)	107	151	162	178	192	235	229	431	469
Current outlays	465	652	701	808	937	1,098	1,216	1,471	1,532
Capital outlays	76	104	116	125	144	165	145	194	281
Total local government	541	756	817	933	1,081	1,263	1,361	1,665	1,813
Surplus or deficit	40	−15	32	66	63	30	104	11	1

a. Preliminary actual.
b. Estimate.
Source: Data for FY65–73 from reports of the Commission on Audit of Local Governments; estimates for FY74 and FY75 from the Department of Finance.

Table SA24. Infrastructure Expenditures from Domestic Sources
(In millions of pesos at current prices)

Sector	FY67	FY68	FY69	FY70	FY71	FY72	FY73	FY74	FY75
Power and electrification									
Power	46.8	50.1	28.3	37.8	49.5	58.9	38.3	49.2	125.0
Rural electric	...	...	...	0.3	8.5	14.9	37.4	60.1	64.3
Subtotal	46.8	50.1	28.3	38.1	58.0	73.8	75.7	109.3	189.3
Social infrastructure									
National buildings and hospitals	5.0	9.0	13.2	22.2	11.4	23.3	25.9	12.1	2.8
Schools	27.2	70.2	36.3	21.0	13.6	17.6	41.5	48.5	87.8
Subtotal	32.2	79.2	49.5	43.1	25.0	40.9	67.4	60.6	91.4
Telecommunications	8.5	7.4	9.8	8.8	0.5	8.2	14.6	0.8	0.3
Transport									
Airports	7.3	10.2	32.1	33.3	16.6	41.0	56.5	21.1	28.3
Highways	170.9	217.5	226.5	252.0	227.7	307.4	590.2	546.1	1,294.4
Port works	15.4	27.0	22.3	18.7	35.7	15.9	41.4	12.2	98.7
Railways	...	...	...	6.9	...	13.1	27.6	36.7	36.5
Subtotal	193.6	254.7	280.9	310.9	280.0	377.4	715.7	672.1	1,457.9
Water resources									
Flood control and drainage	0.8	2.9	11.2	6.5	8.3	5.6	60.7	117.7	261.1
Irrigation	25.0	25.0	37.9	36.1	71.2	70.6	157.3	197.2	350.4
Water supply and sewerage	51.1	43.2	61.8	40.9	33.9	18.3	13.1	49.9	23.1
Subtotal	76.9	71.1	110.9	83.5	113.4	94.5	231.1	364.8	634.6
Miscellaneous[a]	6.0	10.0	7.9	45.2	50.1	29.1	25.8	20.0	129.5
Total	364.0	472.5	487.3	529.6	527.0	623.9	1,130.3	1,231.6	2,502.2

... Zero or negligible.

a. Includes expenditures on shore protection, preliminary engineering studies, export-processing zone at Mariveles, and miscellaneous public works.

Sources: FY67–73, based on cash releases as reported by Infrastructure Operations Center, "Implementation of the Infrastructure Program," for relevant years. FY70 (domestic sources), revised estimates provided by NEDA. FY74, actual cash disbursement estimated by NEDA. FY75, World Bank estimates of actual cash disbursement based on estimates of first three quarters provided by NEDA; it is assumed that the first three quarters were underestimated by 5 percent because of late reporting and that the fourth quarter equals the average of the first three quarters.

Table SA25. Infrastructure Expenditures from Foreign Sources
(In millions of U.S. dollars)

Sector	FY67	FY68	FY69	FY70	FY71	FY72	FY73	FY74	FY75
Power and Electrification									
Power	3.2	2.5	2.1	3.8	5.7	...	0.9	5.1	7.8
Rural electric	...	...	...	...	...	...	...	6.7	11.1
Subtotal	3.2	2.5	2.1	3.8	5.7	...	0.9	11.8	18.9
Social Infrastructure									
National buildings and hospitals	...	...	...	...	...	...	...	...	...
Schools	...	2.1	13.6	2.2	2.2	3.0	6.0	...	...
Subtotal	...	2.1	13.6	2.2	2.2	3.0	6.0	...	...
Telecommunications	1.8	2.6	3.0	9.2	...	...	...	...	...
Transport									
Airports	0.6	0.4	0.3	3.8	2.8	3.7	...	9.8	...
Highways	2.0	10.7	0.8	16.9	2.6	7.8	8.6	9.3	23.0
Port works	3.5	1.9	...	...	...	...	0.2	2.4	6.9
Railways	...	...	...	...	...	...	...	...	...
Subtotal	6.1	13.0	1.1	20.7	5.4	11.5	8.8	21.5	29.9
Water Resources									
Flood control and drainage	...	...	...	...	...	...	...	3.0	2.8
Irrigation	...	2.0	2.0	0.2	7.5	5.6	6.0	8.3	13.6
Water supply and sewerage	3.0	5.0	5.6	3.3	0.2	...	...	...	0.1
Subtotal	3.0	7.0	7.6	3.5	7.9	5.6	6.0	11.3	16.5
Miscellaneous[a]	...	...	...	...	...	...	...	...	...
Total	14.1	27.2	27.4	39.4	21.0	20.1	21.7	44.6	65.3

... Zero or negligible.
a. Includes expenditures on shore protection, preliminary engineering studies, export-processing zone at Mariveles, and miscellaneous public works.
Source: Same as Table SA24.

Table SA26. Total Foreign and Domestic Sources of Infrastructure Expenditures
(In millions of pesos)

Sector	FY67	FY68	FY69	FY70	FY71	FY72	FY73	FY74	FY75
Power and Electrification									
Power	59.6	60.1	36.7	53.0	83.9	58.9	44.3	83.7	178.8
Rural electric	...	...	...	0.3	8.5	14.9	37.4	105.4	140.9
Subtotal	59.6	60.1	36.7	53.3	92.4	73.8	8.7	189.1	319.7
Social Infrastructure									
National buildings and hospitals	5.0	9.0	13.2	22.2	11.4	23.3	29.9	12.1	2.8
Schools	27.2	78.6	90.7	29.8	26.8	37.7	81.7	48.5	87.8
Subtotal	32.2	87.6	103.9	52.0	38.2	61.0	107.6	60.6	90.6
Telecommunications	15.7	17.8	21.8	45.6	0.5	8.2	14.6	0.8	0.3
Transport									
Airports	9.7	11.4	33.3	48.5	33.4	65.8	56.5	87.3	28.3
Highways	178.9	260.3	229.7	319.6	243.2	359.7	647.8	609.0	1,453.1
Port works	29.4	34.6	22.3	18.7	35.7	15.9	42.7	88.4	146.3
Railways	...	...	...	6.9	...	13.1	27.6	36.7	36.5
Subtotal	218.0	306.3	285.3	393.7	312.3	454.5	774.6	821.4	1,664.2
Water Resources									
Flood control and drainage	0.8	2.9	11.2	6.5	8.3	5.6	60.7	138.0	280.4
Irrigation	24.0	32.8	45.4	36.9	116.2	108.1	197.5	253.3	444.2
Water supply and sewerage	63.1	63.2	84.2	54.1	35.1	18.3	13.1	49.9	23.8
Subtotal	87.9	98.9	140.8	97.5	159.6	132.0	271.3	441.2	748.4
Miscellaneous[a]	6.0	10.0	7.9	45.2	50.1	29.1	25.8	20.0	129.5
Total	420.2	580.7	596.4	687.3	653.1	758.6	1,275.6	1,533.1	2,952.7

... Zero or negligible.

a. Includes expenditures on shore protection, preliminary engineering studies, export-processing zone at Mariveles, and miscellaneous public works.

Source: Same as Table SA24; foreign sources from Table SA25 converted to pesos at the following exchange rates to US$1: FY67–70, ₱6.0; FY71, ₱4.0; FY72–73, ₱6.7; FY74, ₱6.76; FY75, ₱6.9.

Table SA27. The Monetary System at Year's End, 1965–74
(In millions of pesos)

Item	1965	1968	1969	1970	1971	1972	1973	1974
Domestic credit								
Net claims on national government	525	1,163	1,967	1,799	1,795	1,754	1,223	−84
Claims on other public sector	1,075	1,602	1,973	2,081	1,912	1,819	1,352	1,974
Claims on private sector	4,684	7,008	7,456	8,764	10,358	12,602	16,204	24,179
Total	6,284	9,773	11,396	12,644	14,065	16,175	18,779	26,069
Net foreign assets	−162	−399	−897	−450	−354	−408	3,966	5,929
Monetary resources								
Money	2,688	3,463	4,279	4,660	5,399	6,797	8,152	10,220
Quasi money	2,448	4,532	4,680	5,480	6,321	6,446	8,685	9,546
Total	5,136	7,995	8,959	10,140	11,720	13,243	16,837	19,766
Other items (net liabilities)	986	1,379	1,540	2,054	1,991	2,524	5,908	12,232

Source: Central Bank of the Philippines.

Table SA28. Total Loans and Investment Outstanding by Institution

Institution	1965	1968	1969	1970	1971	1972	1973	1974
Amounts in millions of pesos								
Commercial banks	5,547.7	8,530.8	9,463.7	10,968.0	12,497.6	14,983.1	21,595.9	31,709.0
Development banks	1,288.9	2,025.7	2,416.7	2,935.3	3,567.6	4,389.9	4,845.0	5,329.6
Rural banks	234.6	402.8	463.1	547.7	663.2	808.4	1,103.3	1,748.3
Savings banks	141.2	310.4	382.7	564.0	678.1	692.3	819.3	965.5
Private nonbank financial institutions	15.6	1,182.0	197.8	233.1	319.8	427.2	610.2	676.9
Government nonbank financial institutions	1,023.5	1,800.3	2,075.1	2,360.3	2,761.4	3,722.5	4,831.2	5,637.2
Total	8,251.5	14,252.0	14,999.1	17,608.4	20,487.7	2,502.3	33,804.9	46,066.5
Composition (percent)								
Commercial banks	67.3	64.4	63.1	62.3	61.0	59.7	67.2	68.8
Development banks	15.6	15.3	16.1	16.7	17.4	17.5	14.9	11.6
Rural banks	2.8	3.0	3.1	3.1	3.2	3.2	3.4	3.8
Savings banks	1.7	2.3	2.6	3.2	3.3	2.8	2.5	2.1
Private nonbank financial institutions	0.2	1.4	1.3	1.3	1.6	1.7	0.6	1.5
Government nonbank financial institutions	12.4	13.6	13.8	13.4	13.5	14.9	11.4	12.2
Total	100.0	100.0	100.0	100.0	100.0	100.0	100.0	100.0

Note: Figures for commercial banks and savings banks are adjusted to include investments.
Source: Central Bank of the Philippines.

Table SA29. Credits Outstanding of Commercial and Savings Banks to the Private Sector
(In millions of pesos)

Sector	1965	1968	1969	1970	1971	1972	1973	1974[a]
Agriculture, forestry, and fishery[b]	1,035.7	1,478.1	1,617.0	1,720.7	1,784.6	1,777.3	2,247.6	2,708.7
Mining and quarrying	33.0	37.1	40.0	45.7	92.7	194.5	235.5	460.4
Manufacturing	1,268.4	1,518.9	1,500.6	1,820.0	2,196.1	3,323.5	5,111.8	7,052.8
Construction[c]	89.3	114.6	120.4	135.7	148.6	210.7	353.3	345.5
Transportation, storage, and communication[d]	116.3	149.2	130.2	141.5	172.5	273.3	251.8	241.6
Electricity, gas, and water	10.2	21.3	14.4	31.3	38.3	70.7	99.7	141.3
Trade	1,656.4	1,940.0	2,063.6	2,490.5	3,061.1	3,580.5	5,823.1	6,952.3
Banking and other financial institutions	192.0	183.9	275.6	587.0	422.9	774.9	660.5	708.0
Real estate	201.4	471.1	581.4	624.3	902.2	847.9	987.6	1,023.7
Services[e]	82.4	182.7	181.4	249.9	302.1	398.7	392.8	508.3
Consumption	114.9	225.0	295.5	313.1	759.1	463.7	203.3	712.5

a. As of June 30, 1974.
b. Commercial bank component for 1965–67 excludes fishery and forest services.
c. Data for 1965–67 represent contract construction.
d. Including operation of wharves, drydocks, warehouses, water supply system, and others.
e. Commercial bank component for 1965–67 includes fishery and forest services.
Note: No breakdown of outstanding credit of the development banks is available by industry. Commercial banks' data from 1962–67 include credits to semi-government entities but do not distinguish among them.
Source: Central Bank of the Philippines.

Table SA30. Distribution of Credits Outstanding to the Private Sector by Commercial and Savings Banks
(In percent)

Sector	1965	1968	1969	1970	1971	1972	1973	1974
Agriculture, forestry, and fishery	21.6	23.4	23.7	21.1	18.1	14.9	13.3	13.0
Mining and quarrying	0.7	0.6	0.6	0.6	0.9	1.6	1.4	2.2
Manufacturing	26.4	24.0	22.0	22.3	22.2	27.9	30.3	33.8
Construction	1.9	1.8	1.8	1.7	1.5	1.8	2.1	1.7
Transportation, storage, and communication	2.4	2.4	1.9	1.7	1.7	2.3	1.5	1.2
Electricity, gas, and water	0.2	0.3	0.2	0.4	0.4	0.6	0.6	0.7
Trade	34.5	30.7	30.3	30.5	31.0	30.0	34.5	33.3
Banking and other financial institutions	4.0	7.4	8.5	7.6	9.1	7.2	3.9	3.9
Real estate	4.2	7.4	8.5	7.6	9.1	7.2	5.9	4.9
Services	1.7	2.9	2.7	3.1	3.1	3.3	2.3	2.4
Consumption	2.4	3.6	4.3	3.8	7.7	3.9	4.2	3.4
Total	100.0	100.0	100.0	100.0	100.0	100.0	100.0	100.0

Sources: Table SA29 and Central Bank of the Philippines.

Table SA31. Total Assets of the Financial System: Banking Institutions
(In millions of pesos)

Banking institution	1965	1968	1969	1970	1971	1972	1973	1974
Central Bank	3,096.6	4,516.5	5,111.3	6,003.2	6,912.6	9,414.3	14,744.7	21,273.6
Banking system								
Commercial banks								
Private	4,228.6	7,222.0	7,971.0	9,340.2	11,776.4	15,309.3	22,360.8	30,114.3
Government	2,442.2	3,688.6	4,078.7	4,725.9	4,277.6	4,688.5	7,398.9	12,548.9
Subtotal	6,731.0	10,910.6	12,049.7	14,066.1	16,054.0	19,997.8	29,759.7	42,663.2
Thrift banks								
Savings banks	287.1	583.3	667.4	812.2	943.7	950.8	1,087.1	1,236.6
Private development banks	72.1	130.1	144.0	161.0	184.1	199.8	236.9	296.3
Stock savings and loan associations	. . .	26.1	36.9	59.1	83.5	102.9	114.2	210.7
Subtotal	359.2	739.5	848.3	1,032.3	1,211.3	1,253.5	1,438.2	1,743.6
Regional unit banks (rural banks)	279.0	466.7	562.9	655.0	783.6	982.3	1,382.6	2,110.7
Other								
Development Bank of the Philippines	1,308.4	2,231.5	2,738.5	3,106.8	3,796.3	4,607.8	5,086.4	6,758.0
Land Bank	. . .	8.6	17.1	23.2	66.1	126.2	670.3	1,182.4
Subtotal	1,308.4	2,240.1	2,755.6	3,130.0	3,763.4	4,734.0	5,756.7	7,940.4
Total banking system	8,677.6	14,358.9	16,216.5	18,883.4	21,812.3	26,967.6	38,337.2	54,457.9

. . . Zero or negligible.
Source: Central Bank of the Philippines.

Table SA32. Total Assets of The Financial System: Nonbank Financial Intermediaries
(In millions of pesos)

Financial intermediary	1965	1968	1969	1970	1971	1972	1973	1974
Insurance companies	3,173.7	4,501.8	5,089.0	5,743.8	6,524.4	7,635.6	8,000.1	9,094.8
Government[a]	2,229.3	3,106.3	3,503.0	3,879.9	4,346.3	5,078.3	5,356.5	6,537.4
Private	944.4	1,395.5	1,586.0	1,863.9	2,178.1	2,557.3	2,643.6	2,557.4
Investment institutions	762.2	1,297.6	1,611.0	2,347.4	1,291.5	2,479.8	3,218.2	6,835.0
Finance companies	625.2	960.1	1,041.0	1,394.2	n.a.	984.3	1,434.1	2,306.1
Investment companies (mutual funds)	...	...	5.3	5.4	n.a.	n.a.	7.4	n.a.
Others	137.0	337.5	564.7	947.8	1,291.5	1,495.5	1,776.7	4,528.9
Trust operations	124.8	326.4	383.6	514.5	n.a.	529.7	1,099.1	1,951.5
Other financial intermediaries	96.0	193.7	438.6	370.4	203.9	475.3	969.5	1,190.9
Agricultural credit administration	34.1	42.2	59.5	86.1	92.4	88.0	112.2	112.1
Credit unions	39.6	42.8	42.5	50.7	38.6	56.5	n.a.	n.a.
Mutual building and loan associations	19.2	23.5	25.3	24.8	23.7	24.2	24.4	24.7
Nonbank savings and loan associations	n.a.	32.0	36.4	45.7	49.2	55.3	61.1	71.2
Security dealers and brokers	3.1	53.2	274.9	163.1	n.a.	159.2	680.5	882.1
Pawnbrokers	n.a.	n.a.	n.a.	n.a.	n.a.	92.1	91.3	100.8
Total	4,156.7	6,319.5	7,522.2	8,976.1	8,019.8	11,120.4	13,286.9	19,072.2

... Zero or negligible.
n.a.: Not available.
a. Includes Government Service Insurance System (GSIS) and Social Security System (SSS).
Source: Central Bank of the Philippines.

Table SA33. Consumer Price Indexes
(1965 = 100)

Item	1968	1969	1970	1971	1972	1973	1974
Consumer price index for the Philippines							
All items	113.0	114.5	131.5	160.2	173.4	194.5	271.9
Food	115.5	116.8	134.0	173.2	189.1	213.7	305.5
Clothing	115.8	118.7	140.9	165.6	189.0	227.6	328.2
Rent and repairs	108.4	109.7	116.0	121.7	126.9	133.5	146.2
Fuel, light, and water	103.1	104.3	127.7	152.8	156.5	173.2	312.8
Miscellaneous	109.9	111.7	129.3	143.1	150.9	164.2	214.2
Consumer price index for Manila							
All items	114.6	116.9	133.7	153.2	168.9	187.5	251.9
Food	119.1	121.0	139.5	167.5	190.0	215.4	299.1
Clothing	108.5	109.8	142.1	168.5	185.8	218.4	318.2
Rent and repairs	114.3	116.9	127.5	137.0	146.1	155.5	169.6
Fuel, light, and water	104.1	103.9	128.7	144.7	168.9	180.0	356.9
Miscellaneous	110.4	113.5	128.1	140.9	148.8	162.2	211.5
Rate of change for the Philippines (percent)							
All items	2.2	1.3	14.8	21.8	8.2	12.2	39.8
Food	1.6	1.1	14.7	29.3	9.1	13.0	43.0
Clothing	3.5	2.5	18.7	17.5	14.1	20.4	44.2
Rent and repairs	3.7	1.2	5.7	4.9	4.2	5.2	9.5
Fuel, light, and water	−0.5	1.2	22.4	19.7	2.4	10.7	80.6
Miscellaneous	3.5	1.6	15.8	10.7	5.4	8.8	30.5
Rate of change for Manila (percent)							
All items	2.3	2.0	14.4	14.6	10.2	11.0	34.3
Food	0.1	1.6	15.3	20.1	13.4	13.4	38.9
Clothing	2.6	1.2	29.4	18.6	10.3	17.5	45.7
Rent and repairs	6.2	2.3	9.1	7.5	6.6	6.4	9.1
Fuel, light, and water	1.1	−0.2	23.9	12.4	16.7	6.6	98.3
Miscellaneous	4.2	2.8	12.9	10.0	5.6	9.0	30.4

Source: Central Bank of the Philippines.

Table SA34. Manila Wholesale Price Index
(1965 = 100)

Item	1968	1969	1970	1971	1972	1973	1974
Index							
General index	109.9	111.4	137.7	159.3	175.4	218.4	337.5
Domestic products	111.6	112.8	137.9	160.2	177.0	219.4	344.4
Export products	120.4	118.3	146.9	157.5	161.2	248.1	437.8
Import products	100.5	103.7	136.3	155.0	166.4	212.9	300.4
Rate of change (percent)							
General index	2.7	1.4	23.6	15.7	10.1	24.5	54.5
Domestic products	3.1	1.1	22.3	16.2	10.5	24.0	57.0
Export products	12.0	−1.7	24.2	7.2	2.3	53.9	76.5
Import products	−0.3	3.2	31.4	13.7	7.4	27.9	41.1

Source: Central Bank of the Philippines.

Table SA35. Wage Indexes
(1965 = 100)

Item	1968	1969	1970	1971	1972	1973	1974 [a]
National wages [b]							
Skilled labor	118.7	125.0	132.8	139.7	146.6	154.4	168.6
Unskilled labor	125.0	130.9	145.2	155.0	164.3	168.7	182.1
Real wages [c]							
Skilled labor	103.6	106.9	99.3	91.3	86.8	82.8	67.2
Unskilled labor	109.1	112.0	108.5	101.3	97.4	90.4	72.5
Real wages [d]							
Skilled labor	108.9	112.2	96.4	87.7	83.6	70.7	50.0
Unskilled labor	114.7	117.5	105.4	97.3	93.7	77.2	54.0

a. Preliminary.
b. This is the 1955=100 series shifted to 1965=100 series.
c. Money wage rate index deflated by the consumer price index (1965=100) in Manila.
d. Money wage rate index deflated by the wholesale price index (1965=100) in Manila.
Note: Applies to laborers in industrial establishments in Manila and suburbs.
Source: Central Bank of the Philippines.

Index